POLICY STUDIES REVIEW ANNUAL
Volume 5

EDITORIAL ADVISORY BOARD

POLICY STUDIES REVIEW ANNUAL

1981   Volume 5

Edited by
Irving Louis Horowitz

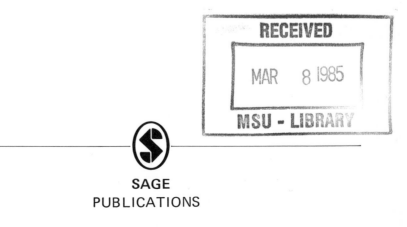
SAGE
PUBLICATIONS

Beverly Hills   London

For information address:

SAGE PUBLICATIONS, INC.
275 South Beverly Drive
Beverly Hills, California 90212

SAGE PUBLICATIONS LTD
28 Banner Street
London EC1Y 8QE, England

Printed in the United States of America

International Standard Book Number 0-8039-1315-X

Library of Congress Catalog Card No. 77-72938

International Standard Series Number 0163-108X

FIRST PRINTING

CONTENTS

INTRODUCTION

Irving Louis Horowitz

In its short history, the *Policy Studies Review Annual* series has served to highlight some of the best work in the area of policy research. It has justifiably earned the attention of the academic community and the policy-making sector. For the editor, this fifth volume faces a series of challenges: First, it must at least equal the performance of the previous editors and rival the contents of the earlier volumes. Second, it must develop a unique angle of vision that demarcates it from the others. Third, it must distinguish continuity and discontinuity in the policy process and, by so doing, reveal the current state of affairs.

My decision was essentially to establish continuity with past volumes in the indicators and topics selected. Hence, with some modification, the work is divided into two main sections: "General Perspectives and Approaches" features major articles on theoretical foundations; facts, values, and biases; policy research; and applications and alternatives. "Policy Issues," the larger of the two sections, is divided into a series of subsections along the lines of social indicators. These include Government Support and Regulation, The Electoral Process, Defense and Military Policy, Urban Affairs, Crime and Criminal Justice, Civil Liberties and Equal Rights, Health and Welfare, Education, and State Power and Public Policy. Like previous volumes, *PSRA 5* contains approximately 60 selections chosen from a body of literature at least ten times larger. In the task of selection, I have had the benefit both of the advisory board members as well as colleagues who were kind enough to offer their opinions and suggestions concerning the best available writings of the past several years in the policy area.

The discontinuity with previous volumes derives from my selection of articles which, whenever possible, were developed in response to policy experiences overseas and not solely from a U.S. context. This does not mean mechanically emphasizing policy dilemmas and problems in Third World areas, but rather considering issues within the West European democratic and East European socialist blocs as well. It is becoming increasingly clear that policy experiences in a wide variety of areas from hospital management to inner-city transportation are not unique to the United States but exist in many parts of the developed world. As other peoples and nations determine their outcomes and plan their futures based on their specific social systems, comparative policy study becomes a matter not simply of sentiment or goodwill toward others but an essential learning mechanism, a way to avoid duplication of effort, drawing upon the best policy orientations and plans on a worldwide basis.

Indeed, by editing this volume in this fashion I have been able to combine two of my central social science interests: international development and social policy. Both ultimately have to do with the political foundations of decision-making. Development is more than a given series of strategies aimed at achieving preeminence over or parity with others, and policy is more than an articulation of goals. Development and policy involve implementation, organization, and evaluation of choices. Most articles in *PSRA 5* exhibit these dimensions.

There are times when such a development of overseas emphasis is not possible. It would have been a mistake to choose an article simply because it had an overseas emphasis over another that had only a national framework but was superior on other intellectual counts. Given the choice between two essays *of equal merit,* one with and one without this overseas emphasis, the nod went to the overseas-oriented essay. But when this was not the case, the choice was the best article with a national orientation. In the absence of an international context, I selected articles with a clear comparative analytic framework; approaches to policy that stressed alternatives rather than unilinear policy recommendations. By "comparative" I also mean articles and essays written on a relatively high level of macro-analysis rather than case study analysis.

For the most part, the articles selected were derived from the work performed by social scientists. I have also included essays written by social historians whose work shows a strong policy orientation, such as the history of penal institutions or the history of welfare programs. But aside from such exceptions, the volume features mainly those efforts of the social scientific community. There is a good reason for this. The task of such a volume is to describe and highlight the best scholarship published on the policy level, not necessarily the kindest proposals implemented or those with the highest moral qualifications.

There is a wide gap between the analysis of policy and the advocacy of a policy—not unlike the gap between political scientists and politicians. Once in a rare while a good political scientist becomes a good politician; sometimes vice versa. Similarly, once in a while a good policy analyst becomes a good policy maker, but this is also a rare event, an ideal more frequently pledged than practiced. Since the volume is to be read by a wide variety of people with widely differing political ideologies, I thought it best to emphasize those essays and articles that would be of use to people whatever their specific biases.

A particular challenge in preparing *PSRA 5* was the necessity to review the mushrooming number of specialized journals publishing within a policy-making context. There are at least ten journals (and perhaps a good deal more) that are directly related to social policy inputs. To fully register the work in these journals alone, without ignoring the standard journals or those journals with specialized substantive concerns of which policy may be one of several, becomes a challenge that can best be described as monumental.

I sincerely hope that this approach to *PSRA 5,* premised as it is on including (a) innovative research, (b) an overseas dimension, and (c) a comparative rather than case study framework, is a perspective that can easily be continued in years ahead by other editors with other political biases. I believe that comparative research as a method no less than as a theory will preserve from error the policy-making practitioner working in local as well as global contexts.

One value in doing large systems research is that the kinds of problems that plague Nairobi also exist in Los Angeles, and other available solutions may be in an even more advanced planning stage in Berlin or Paris than they are in Chicago or New York. Just as the oneness of humanity is expressed in a variety of ways, so is the oneness of the policy situation expressed in a variety of forms. The challenge of doing social science in a policy-relevant context is precisely the dilemma of stating universal concerns in concrete settings affecting specific lives. This statement expresses no simple-minded plea for one-worldism or abstract appeal to humanity, but the most practical awareness that policy-making has become a near universal tool and hence a finer instrument for all.

What unites the policy enterprise is an appreciation that people make a difference. What distinguishes one policy system from the other is that these differences are expressed in a variety of contexts. Each of the 14 sections will carry brief descriptions of the subject and the essays themselves. I will eschew the usual practice of summarizing each individual essay, indicating instead the significance of the particular topics to the policy-relevant audiences addressed. It is my hope that *PSRA 5* will be useful to all concerned. Moreover, it is my intention that the volume reflects well upon the best work being done at this time in the comparative and contextual world of policy-making.

PART I

GENERAL PERSPECTIVES AND APPROACHES

In past decades, the policy field was characterized by much soul-searching and debate as to its scientific status. In fact, there was more questioning of the legitimacy and autonomy of the policy arena than effort to tease out what was new and innovative about the field. Curiously, as the debate on whether policy-making is a separate "science" or an integral part of other social and behavioral sciences quieted, innovative work began to emerge, giving sharper focus to the policy arena. The mushrooming of the field led to a healthy consciousness of how powerful an analytic tool policy studies can be in understanding the everyday life of societies. What resulted was not so much an abstract solution to the dilemma of whether policy-making is science or handmaiden to science as the modest realization that social and behavioral science research itself is laced with policy implications that help to shape and reshape general perspectives and approaches to policy-making.

The first part of this volume underscores the degree to which policy, in its theoretical thrust, has become identified with the social research process as a whole. Policy studies are caught up in the same kinds of facts and value dichotomies that have long dominated the social science literature. This indicates that the emergence of policy-making in new and innovative institutional and networking arrangements has taken place as part of ongoing efforts to integrate theory and applied research in concrete decision-making contexts. In all real scientific advances need precedes elegance. The pieces still may not be in place, but the need to know—not to mention the capacity to solve—has its own inexorable logic.

In his pathbreaking paper on "Policies as Theories," Majone shows how the philosophy of science has helped to illuminate the policy-making process. For if advocacy is sometimes a basic framework for settling issues in a problem-solving context, then policies can be viewed as nascent theories of society. Both craftwork evaluation of research programs and policy evaluation as such involve certain methodological prescriptions based on a theory of persuasion. The question thus becomes what forms of persuasion are usable rather than whether persuasion has a legitimate role in the discovery process. The point is not the scientific status of policy-making, but that key features of the policy process are linked to scientific method. Steinberger's paper may be considered an extension of this new vision of the relationship between science and policy. Since most policies can be coherently understood and defined and are not simply pro or con statements, a meaningful typology can be developed to assist in the formation of a useful theory of the policy process. Steinberger, in suggesting how each typology reflects one of several ways in which policies can be conceptualized, moves toward a wider discussion of the scientific status of policy-making.

The Glazer essay notes that the current state of disillusionment with impacting the policy process among some social scientists has less to do with the relevance of such efforts than with the false premises under which researchers have often operated. The lack of scientific understanding of society, the inability to sense that there are levels of heterogenetic approaches, the absence of any vision of the place of authority leads to a clash of values, not a resolution of problems. Estes' paper can be viewed as an illustration of the Glazer thesis. Estes bluntly states that social policies for the aged are a failure. Although the essay focuses on policies for the aged, its general import is revealed in its assertion of the need to address questions of politics, economics, and social structure by supplying jobs, housing, and health care rather than by targeting policies for a group that accepts as a given their stigmatized, dependent, and depersonalized status.

The paper by van de Vall and Bolas is important in a variety of ways: first, in its revealing look at the low correlation between public utilization and sophisticated methods of research, but more important in its observation that value-oriented rather than value-free types of research tend to be highly utilized and prized; further, that the professional paradigm emerging in sociology—and in all likelihood throughout the social sciences—tends toward a social policy research model rather than a traditional normative framework. Rein reviews the spate of new literature which assumes a high correlation of knowing to acting. He views the present challenge as establishing linkages of research to policy, showing the latent policies that organize empirical research or the study of those theories used by practitioners. Rein's essay captures the intent of most articles in this section: to show which forms of knowledge are embedded in which forms of action and, further, to identify and isolate the nature of the knowledge implicit in the policies undertaken.

1

POLICIES AS THEORIES

Giandomenico Majone

The received view of the scientific method, as represented for instance by logical positivism, has only historical interest for the specialists, but it is still widely, if implicitly, held by decision and policy analysts. On the other hand, recent developments in philosophy and the history of science, which stress the fallibility of theories and the social and historical character of scientific knowledge and criteria, have not yet been assimilated by analysts. This paper argues that these recent methodological developments offer important insights into many theoretical and professional problems facing students of policy-making. Thus, an appreciation of the craft aspects of scientific inquiry not only clarifies the subtle relationship between theory and practice in any type of systematic analysis, but also suggests a conceptual model of the analyst's task that is quite different from the conventional decision-making paradigm. Again, Popperian and post-Popperian views of the evolution of knowledge are shown to be relevant to the evaluation of policies and to the study of their development. Particularly important in this respect is the notion, due to Lakatos, of problem shifts in competing research programmes. Even the role of advocacy in policy arguments appears in a new light after we realize the importance of persuasion and propaganda in the history of scientific development. There are reasonably well-defined situations in which the use of persuasion, far from violating the analyst's code of professional behavior, is not only unavoidable but also rationally justifiable.

1. INTRODUCTION

IF SCIENTIFIC knowledge is in fact, in Popper's phrase, "common sense knowledge writ large," what can we learn, as systems or policy analysts, from recent developments in the philosophy and history of science? Methodological debates cast long shadows over the most pragmatic domains, though the images are often fuzzy, and sometimes reflect patterns of thinking that are already obsolete.

The received view on scientific method, which in one form or another has dominated the philosophy of science from the 1920s to the 1950s, has by now only historical interest for the specialists; but it is still accepted by many researchers as a general scientific ideology. In particular, the influence of logical positivism—a key component of the received view—has been felt throughout the social and behavioral sciences, and nowhere more strongly than in the study of decision-making.

Appeals to the scientific method (rather glibly equated with problem-solving-through-mathematical-modeling) preface textbooks on operational research and systems analysis, and figure prominently in the programmatic statements of the professional societies. For many of its advocates, systems analysis is nothing more than the scientific method extended to problems outside the realm of pure science. Cost–benefit analysts stress the scientific virtues of their methods: quantification, formalization, explicitness, objectivity. Evaluation researchers are supposedly engaged in the scientific assessment of public programs. Even the rational–deductive ideal for ranking policy alternatives according to a strictly defined hierarchical system of values is said to represent an ideal of science transferred to the field of values.

In reality, these references to science and the scientific method are not so much methodological commitments as they are ideological props. They do not direct attention to any deep affinities, but are attempts to increase the collective confidence of a group of new disciplines striving for academic and social recognition. It could not be otherwise, for the conception of

Reprinted with permission from *Omega: The International Journal of Management Science,* Vol. 8, No. 2, Giandomenico Majone, "Policies as Theories," Copyright 1980, Pergamon Press, Ltd.

science implicit in such proclamations of method lacks historical reality and epistemological substance. Few scientists and philosophers of science still believe that scientific knowledge is, or can be, proven knowledge. Many would, in fact, agree with Toulmin that "if we wish to understand how actual sciences operate... we must abandon the assumption that the intellectual contents of natural sciences actively in debate have 'logical' or 'systematic' structures: we must instead consider how such sciences can succeed in fulfilling their actual explanatory missions, despite the fact that, at any chosen moment in time, their intellectual contents are marked by logical gaps, incoherences, and contradictions" [17, p. 605].

To repeat the initial question: what can students of policy-making learn, not from the idealized textbook image of science that in the past has been foisted on them, but from the 'unsystematic', 'illogical', and all too human activity which is the daily experience of the working scientist? This is a very broad question, and no more than a partial and tentative answer will be given in this paper. The selection of themes necessarily reflects my personal interests, and specific results in the philosophy or history of science are presented in capsule form. I hope not to have misrepresented the views of the scholars whose works I have used. At any rate, the reader is urged to check the correctness of my interpretations through the references given in the text.

In section 2, I consider the craft aspects of scientific inquiry and argue that this perspective, derived mainly from the works of Polanyi, Kuhn and Ravetz, throws new light on some important, but generally overlooked, characteristics of policies and of policy analysis.

Section 3 is concerned with the implications for policy evaluation of Popperian and post-Popperian views on scientific knowledge and its evolution. Of particular importance, here and in the next section, is Lakatos' notion of 'research programmes'.

Section 4 makes use of Popper's 'World 3' to introduce the idea of an autonomous policy space (an idea which can be found, in more or less explicit form, in the writings of a number of students of policy). Strictly related to the notion of an autonomous policy space is that of problem-shifts (Lakatos). I argue that explanations of policy development in terms of

policy-space constructs are more satisfying, and potentially more powerful, than other types of explanations.

Finally, in section 5, I discuss the role of persuasion and propaganda in science (taking my clue from Feyerabend's discussion of Galileo's advocacy of Copernicanism). Policy advocacy and 'rationalizations'—far from being, under all circumstances, capital sins against the analyst's professional integrity and intellectual honesty—are not only unavoidable but also rationally justifiable.

2. THE ART OF INQUIRY

Fallibilism and its consequences

Logic shows the inconclusiveness of the basic patterns of argument used in science; history testifies to the possibility of genuine scientific knowledge. This apparent paradox cannot be resolved within the traditional epistemological concerns of the older philosophy of science. Since individual endeavors are fallible, the emergence of a (provisionally) accepted body of knowledge must be explained in terms of social mechanisms. "Nature," writes Ravetz, "is not so obliging as ever to give marks of True or False for scientific work, and so a scientific community sets its standards for itself" [15, p. 82].

Some form of conventionalism is the inescapable logical consequence of fallibilism. If there is no demonstrative certainty for the conclusions of science, their 'truth' or, at any rate, their acceptability as scientific results, must be established by convention: through a consensus of experts in the field, and the fulfilment of certain methodological and professional canons—the rules of the scientific game.

The problem of testing the correctness of a policy or decision is analogous to that of determining the truth of a scientific theory. According to the received view of policy analysis—in which policy-making is equated to decision-making, and the latter is formalized as a means–end relationship—a decision is correct "if it can be shown to attain some specific objective, where the objective can be specified without describing the decision itself" [12, p. 49]. Such a proof requires that three conditions be simultaneously satisfied: (a) it must be possible to detect the specific effects of the decision against a noisy background of concomitant decisions, measurement errors, and random fluctuations of the system; (b) a well-tested theory connecting means and ends is available; and (c) there is agreement on goals.

If even one of these conditions is violated, no objective test of correctness is possible. It has been argued that in such a case agreement on policy is the only practicable test of 'good' policy: policy-makers may agree on policy itself, even if they do not agree on goals or theory. But even more important than such direct agreement on policy as a test of correctness, is agreement on procedures, on the rules of the policy game. In the law, in public administration and, to an increasing extent, also in business administration, decisions are accepted not because they can be shown to produce desired outcomes, but because of a generalized agreement on decision-making procedures. Reliance on detailed procedures, whether in environmental regulations, in the licensing of nuclear power plants, or in industrial quality control, greatly increases the costs of decision-making, but it is also an unavoidable consequence of the cognitive and social complexity of today's problems. As long as the correctness or fairness of the outcome can be determined unambiguously, the manner in which the decision is taken is largely immaterial: only results count. But when the factual or value premises are moot, when no objective criterion of truth exists, procedural aspects acquire special significance.

Belief in the possibility of discovering correct solutions for a wide variety of problems has probably served a useful ideological function in the early stages of development of systems and policy analysis. Today, the traditional preoccupation with analytic methods stressing outcome rather than process must give way to a broader approach, in which procedural design (alternative methods of structuring the decision process) assumes primary importance. Naturally, the criteria for choosing among decision-making procedures are not the same as those used in choosing among alternatives for a particular decision. While in the latter case effectiveness and efficiency are the dominant criteria of choice, the metacriterion for evaluating procedures is legitimacy—the capacity of a procedure to elicit generalized acceptance for the decisions it produces, regardless of their substantive consequences. One hopes, of course, that good procedures will increase the probability of good decisions, but, as Popper has often remarked, it is impossible to justify the rules of a game (including the rules of the scientific game) only in terms of success.

Science as craft work

The work of the scientist requires knowledge that is acquired only through practice and precept and which therefore is not scientific in character. Earlier traditions in the philosophy of science, being mainly concerned with the epistemological problem of truth, have ignored the craft aspects of scientific knowledge. Yet, without an appreciation of these aspects "there is no possibility of resolving the paradox of the radical difference between the subjective, intensely personal activity of creative science, and the objective, impersonal knowledge which results from it" [15, p. 75].

Craft knowledge is a repertoire of procedures and judgments that are partly personal, partly social. Thus, when a scientist decides whether a batch of data is of acceptable quality, he applies standards that derive from his own experience, but also reflect the professional norms of his teachers and colleagues, as well as culturally determined criteria of adequacy. Personal and social judgments are also involved in data manipulation, in the choice of tools and models, in the selection of evidence, and in the construction of an argument.

The importance of craft knowledge and experience is even greater in policy analysis. Because the conclusions of a policy study cannot be proved in the sense in which a theorem is proved, or even in the manner of the propositions of natural science, they must satisfy generally accepted criteria of adequacy. Such criteria are derived not from abstract logical canons but from craft experience, depending as they do on the special features of the problem, on the quality of data and limitations of available tools, on the time constraints imposed on the analysts, and on the requirements of the client.

Craft knowledge—less explicit than formalized theoretical knowledge, but more objective than pure intuition—is essential in any kind of professional work. Aristotle's analysis of traditional craft work (in terms of the four constituents or 'causes' of the task: material, efficient, formal and final) has been applied by Ravetz to the task of scientific inquiry. He identifies the material constituent with the intellectually constructed things and events in whose terms the problem is formulated. The researcher, with his tools and methods, is the efficient constituent of the task. The formal constituent is the argument that supports the conclusion of the inquiry, the latter corresponding to the Aristotelian 'final cause'.

The same scheme can be applied to the work of the policy analyst. The material component of the analyst's task is represented by the data, information and other conceptual inputs used in formulating a problem. The technical tools and methods of analysis represent the efficient component, while the formal component is an argument in which evidence is cited and from which a conclusion is drawn. The 'final cause' is the conclusion itself, together with the related activities of communication and implementation.

This way of describing the fine structure of the analyst's task enjoys one considerable advantage over the more conventional decision-making paradigm. The categories suggested by this paradigm (goals, alternatives, constraints, and so on) focus attention on a rather narrow and specialized use of analysis as an applied 'logic of choice'. The craft analogy, on the other hand, suggests categories (data, information, tools, evidence, argument, conclusion) that are applicable to any type and style of analysis, and can be shown to be particularly useful for assessing the technical adequacy of analytic work [13].

Problem solving on artificial objects

For all its usefulness, the craft analogy conceals an important difference between the work of the traditional artisan and that of the intellectual craftsman. The artisan works with physical tools and materials to produce tangible objects having a certain form and capable of performing given functions. The intellectual craftsman works with conceptual tools and inputs; his end product is an argument leading to certain conclusions about the properties of the intellectual constructs that form the object of his inquiry. This leads to Ravetz's characterization of scientific inquiry as problem solving on artificial objects. The objects of scientific knowledge are not directly apprehended natural phenomena, as asserted by an influen-

tial tradition going back to Bacon and Galileo, but classes of intellectually constructed things and events: elementary particle, force, field, chemical element, and also the phyla and genera of 'natural' taxonomy.

Similarly, the objects of policy analysis and policy arguments are not directly perceived social events, but theory-laden constructs resulting from definition, convention, and abstraction. Terms like 'price', 'cost', 'inflation', 'GNP', 'standard of living', 'intelligence'. 'crime', are used so often that we tend to forget their abstract and conventional nature. Even the most basic social and economic statistics— for instance, the unemployment and balance-of-payment data that make headlines and are discussed at length on radio and television— are extremely abstract things. In no way do they resemble "the measurements which arise from a direct apprehension of something, as when we measure a length. One cannot, even with good eyesight, go out onto the Treasury steps and observe the domestic level of economic activity" [4, p. 823].

The abstract character of the language of policy and of policy analysis can evoke two different, but equally mistaken, reactions. On the one hand, there is the ever-present tendency to mistake for concrete things what are in fact theories and abstractions—Whitehead's fallacy of misplaced concreteness. On the other hand, one finds the equally widespread suspicion of a general conspiracy of politicians, bureaucrats, managers, and experts to prevent citizens from seeing the true essence of social problems by some kind of verbal magic. But while sympathizing with the desire for a more direct and transparent official language, the philosopher of science cannot fail to notice the similarity between the necessary artificiality of a developed legal or administrative system and that of a developed science. Like the natural world, the social world is just too complex to be comprehended in terms of the concepts we build up in our ordinary experience [15, p. 114]. Naturally, the more elaborate policy constructs are ultimately derived from common-sense experience, but in concrete applications formal requirements of procedure and internal consistency assume greater importance than any desire for immediate intelligibility.

Since analysts with a technical or scientific background are often impatient of legal and administrative formalities, it will be instructive to give an actual example of the unexpected difficulties that may arise in the attempt to simplify a formalized language. In the early days of the Communist regime in Poland a sustained effort was made to draft the laws so clearly that they would be intelligible to the worker and peasant.

"It was soon discovered, however, that this kind of clarity could be attained only at the cost of those systematic elements in a legal system that shape its rules into a coherent whole and render them capable of consistent application by the courts. It was discovered, in other words, that making the laws readily understandable to the citizen carried a hidden cost in that it rendered their application by the courts more capricious and less predictable" [8, p. 45].

3. EVALUATION

Traditional scientific methodologies

The different philosophies of science can be viewed as alternative methodologies for evaluating scientific theories. In this section of the paper, I intend to examine some implications of different forms of scientific appraisals for the evaluation of policies. More specifically, I shall argue that while the approach prevailing in policy evaluation (particularly in the United States) has been severely handicapped by outdated philosophical premises, recent work by Lakatos and other philosophers of science suggests a basic reformulation of the goals and methods of evaluation analysis.

Following Lakatos, three traditional methodologies for the evaluation of scientific theories may be identified: Justificationism; Dogmatic Falsificationism; Naïve Falsificationism.

Justificationism or inductivism—the doctrine that the only scientific propositions are those that either describe hard facts or are correct inductive generalizations from them—is logically untenable. As Hume argued more than two centuries ago, theories cannot be derived from facts.

Dogmatic falsificationism—science cannot prove, but it can disprove—must also be rejected since no conclusive disproof of a theory can ever be produced. Theories always involve hidden background knowledge, *ceteris paribus* conditions, and auxiliary hypotheses: it is not clear which part of a theory would be refuted by a negative result. There are no crucial experiments, except with hindsight:

"nature may shout 'no' but human ingenuity...may always be able to shout louder. With sufficient resourcefulness and some luck any theory may be defended 'progressively' for some time, even if it is false" [11, p. 100].

According to naïve falsificationism, a highly corroborated scientific theory refutes a less corroborated theory which is inconsistent with it. But the history of science offers many examples of 'refuted' theories being resuscitated. This shows that refutation should not be confused with elimination. If most theories are born refuted, mere refutations can play no dramatic role in science: "if any and every failure to fit were grounds for theory rejection, all theories ought to be rejected at all times" [10, p. 145]. Naïve falsificationism uses a monotheoretical model of criticism; one single theory is confronted by potential falsifiers supplied by authoritative experimental scientists. This amounts to introducing an arbitrary dichotomy into the corpus of scientific knowledge between what is treated as problematic and what is regarded as unproblematic. But experiments, instruments, and observations are theory-laden, and such theories are often no more corroborated than the theory to be tested (as in the case of the physiological and optical theories involved in Galileo's reports of telescopic observations of Jupiter's planets [7]).

Lakatos' methodology of research programmes

If theories are falsified all the time, the important epistemological issue is not when an unrefuted theory is better than a refuted rival one, but when a theory is better than a rival one if both are known to be refuted. Moreover, since problems are not solved but only shifted, the basic unit of appraisal is not an isolated theory but a whole 'research programme'. A research programme is characterized by a *hard core* (conventionally accepted and made provisionally irrefutable by a methodological decision of its adherents), a *positive heuristic*, which defines problems and outlines the construction of a belt of auxiliary hypotheses, and a *negative heuristic* indicating the paths of research to be avoided. Thus, the Cartesian research programme (the universe is a huge clockwork with push as the only cause of motion) tells us to look behind all natural phenomena, including life, for mechanistic explanations, and rules out Newtonian action at a distance.

Examples of competing research programmes in the social sciences are neoclassical and Marxian economics. The core of neoclassical economics is the notion that the economy is composed of free agents who perform different functions but are united by the common goal of maximizing individual utility. The idea that society is divided into competing social classes is rejected, being considered neither correct nor analytically useful. On the positive side, the object of economics is conceived of as the study of rational allocation of scarce resources among competing uses. This study can be carried out at an abstract level, regardless of specific historical conditions, since the goal of maximizing individual utility has universal validity. The core idea of Marxian economics, on the other hand, is that society is divided into classes pursuing different, and conflicting, goals. According to the negative heuristics of the Marxian research programme, economic phenomena cannot be explained in terms of individual behavior, and it is impossible to define a criterion of economic efficiency valid for an entire society. The positive heuristics of the programme direct attention to class struggle, exploitation, and a labor-theory of value as the basic categories of analysis. And because class struggle characterizes one particular type of society, an economic theory of capitalism can be valid only for this particular phase in the history of humanity.

Rival research programmes can be evaluated in terms of the problem-shifts they induce. A problem-shift is progressive if is has greater explanatory and predictive power than previous formulations. A research programme is progressing if it generates progressive problem-shifts, otherwise it is stagnating. Thus, the methodology of research programmes offers not only a rational reconstruction of scientific continuity as well as scientific change, but also a set of normative concepts to evaluate theoretical developments.

Policy evaluation

Evaluators of administrative programmes are justificationists at heart—their working hypothesis is that the programme is accomplishing what it set out to do—but falsificationists by necessity. To get on with their work they must assume that their measuring techniques are unproblematic, or at least less problematic

than the hypotheses incorporated in the programme they evaluate; they accept a mono-theoretical model of criticism. Like good behaviorists, evaluators think of themselves as objective experimental scientists supplying the policy-maker with hard facts, the 'potential falsifiers' of the programme. In reality, they formulate goals, assign them relative weights, identify actors, define system boundaries and choose yardsticks. Paraphrasing Lakatos, we can say that the target of the arrow of evaluation is shaped while the arrow is already in the air. Evaluation does not assume a fully-articulated policy or programme; it creates it.

Traditionally (and quite understandably, given the expectations of their clients), evaluators have been concerned with goal achievement. But the hope of being able to justify or falsify an action programme by comparing results with goals has been dashed by the discovery of the ubiquitous phenomenon of 'little effect'. As Carol Weiss writes, one of the major obstacles to putting evaluation results to use is precisely their dismaying tendency to show that the program has had little effect [18]. For example, many careful evaluation studies have revealed that the effects of variation in school policies on students' performance are not significantly different, once the students' socioeconomic characteristics are held constant. Interestingly, organizations do not fare better: "Measured against the Olympic heights of the goal, most organizations score the same—very low effectiveness. The differences among organizations are of little significance" [6, p. 258]. Thus policies and organizations, like scientific theories, seem to be 'born refuted' and evaluation, as usually conceived and practiced, can play no crucial role in their development.

The phenomenon of 'little effect' becomes less surprising once we recognize that policy evaluation exclusively in terms of results is bound to be inconclusive at best, and must be supplemented by a careful consideration of process. This raises the question of the appropriate unit of evaluation. If policy problems are never solved but only shifted (and, hopefully, ameliorated), the objects of evaluation cannot be discrete decisions or actions, but related sequences of decisions and actions, together with their behavioral, cognitive and ideological supports. A set of dispositions, theories, proposals, decisions and acts will form a recognizable policy if they are held together by a central core of value commitments. In such a case, following Hylton Boothroyd [3], we speak of *action programmes*, the policy equivalent of Lakatos' scientific research programmes. The limitations of evaluation by results now become clear. If a programme is not to be abandoned at the first signs of difficulty, the core must be made (temporarily) immune to criticism by a common decision of the participants in the policy process. The core may eventually be overthrown, but this will signify a major change in policy—a revolution in some sense. Debate, controversy, and corrections are redirected on to the decisions and administrative arrangements that form the protective belt of the core. The effort to adapt the particular institutional embodiments of the programme to ever-changing economic, political, and technical conditions keeps the protective belt in constant flux, but such changes hardly affect the policy core.

The methodology of action programmes puts evaluation in a new perspective by explaining the apparent paradox of the surprising stability and continuous flux that characterize the life cycle of all major policies. The prescriptions of policy evaluators often appear irrelevant because they are directed at the wrong target. This point is well illustrated by the comments of Mark Blaug on some recurring criticicms of the British National Health Service. Blaug writes:

"Whether we like it or not, the British National Health Service effectively replaced individual choice in the distribution of health services by collective choice. Thus, arguments about 'market failure' in justifying either government ownership or government finance are totally irrelevant in Britain, unless of course the thesis is that they ought to be made relevant by returning health to the market mechanism. It would seem that there is now a consensus among all segments of British society and among all shades of public opinion that health should be distributed in accordance with need rather than ability to pay, in other words, 'communism in health'" [2, p. 324].

Neither Blaug nor any other competent analyst would deny that there are serious problems of allocation. But as long as the consensus about the use of collective-choice mechanisms survives, solutions have to be found at the level of specific administrative measures (e.g. by selective charges within the National Health Services), without compromising the integrity of the policy core.

4. POLICY DEVELOPMENT

Policies versus decisions

In order to understand policy development it is necessary to draw a distinction between policies and decisions. A decision, in the sense of decision theory, is a choice or judgment made on the basis of available data among well-defined courses of action whose consequences under alternative 'states of the world' are reasonably well understood. The decision-theoretic paradigm does not recognize any essential difference between decision and action: if the decision does not lead to the corresponding act, it was because something occurred to prevent it, and a new decision problem arises. Nor does it differentiate between policies and decisions; policies are simply bigger, high-level decisions, or perhaps, sequences of such decisions. Consequently, good policy-making, rational decision-making, scientific problem-solving are, in this view, largely synonymous expressions. The same analytic categories are used indifferently as an idealized description of good policy-making or as prescriptions for conducting policy analysis.

Now, public and private managers must often make choices in situations which closely approximate the decision-theory model: where to build a school or a hospital; which curriculum to adopt for the next school year; whether to expand an existing plant or build a new one. But policies do not live by decisions alone. The basic constituents of policies viewed as action programmes—dispositions to act, core commitments, theories, plans and their institutional embodiments—remain largely outside the pure logic of choice. In taking a decision, one simply tries to do one's best in the present circumstances, to choose wisely among the available gambles. Policies are characterized by a certain deliberate quality, a relative permanence, and the possibility of further development; they tend to become doctrines, directing future action and giving coherence to past actions. This gives policies an objective character which decisions do not possess.

The decision-maker of decision theory, like the consumer of economic theory, is the sole judge and executor of his own choices. But even in the most tightly centralized organization, few decisions are made and carried out by only one person. Hence the problem of communicating and legitimizing decisions in inter-subjective terms. Subjective choices must be related to a plan, a doctrine, a strategic viewpoint, in other words, to an articulate action programme. It should be noticed that, while such post-decision developments are irrelevant to the logic of choice, they are an essential element of organizational policy-making.

As long as policies are identified with decisions, development can only be interpreted as decisionmakers changing their minds. This is a rather simplistic view of policy and does not explain many important events (such as the emergence of unanticipated consequences, and various forms of interaction and feedback in the policy space) that are neither planned nor intended.

The policy space

Lakatos and the later Popper concentrate on the growth and development of theories rather than on their refutation. Theories develop and grow in a quasi-autonomous space of objective intellectual constructs, of thoughts-in-themselves. Popper distinguishes three 'worlds' or levels of reality: first, the world of physical objects and physical states; second, the world of mental states, of subjective preferences and beliefs; and third, a world of objective structures that are produced by human minds but which, once produced, exist independently of them (theories, artistic creations and styles, norms, institutions, problem situations, critical arguments). This 'World 3' is autonomous from the other two levels of reality, though it is related to them by a number of links and feedbacks. Developments in World 3 occur largely as the result of unanticipated consequences of previous theories, and of the problem situations they generate. Lakatos' methodology of research programmes represents a fine-structure explanation of the process of theory development, and adds normative criteria to distinguish between positive and negative developments.

I will now introduce the notion of a policy space consisting of (actual and potential) policy problems, policy arguments, norms, constraints, tentative solutions and their institutional embodiments. The policy space is a subset of Popper's World 3 and, as such, it is largely autonomous though still interacting with the psychological second world of subjec-tive preferences, beliefs, goals, and decisions. In fact, some of the most interesting phenomena appearing in the policy space arise as the unplanned consequences of men's decisions. They are, in Hume's words, the results of human action but not of human design (think of phenomena like traffic congestion, pollution, or inflation). Historian AJP Taylor expresses tersely the objective character of the policy space when he writes that statesmen take one step, and the next follows from it.

In policy-space terms, policy development is a sequence of partly overlapping action pro-grammes. The focus of the analysis is not on individuals and groups as change agents, but on objective features like policy content, evolving doctrines and problem situations, changing constraints, and interactions among different policies. Ideally, one attempts to explain policy development by showing how some overall pattern, which one would have thought had to be produced by an individual's or group's successful attempt to realize the pattern, instead was generated and maintained by a process that in no way had the overall pattern 'in mind' [14]. Perhaps this approach is not as intuitively appealing as a 'second world' approach which, by focusing attention on the actors and the moves leading to specific decisions, seems to offer a more direct causal explanation of the dynamics of policy change. But numerous case studies provide evidence that the influence of particular decision makers and special interest groups on actual (as opposed to anticipated) developments is often over-estimated. At any rate, policy-space explanations have the methodological advantage of minimizing the use of notions constituting the phenomena to be explained; they do not explain complicated patterns by including the end-result as the object of people's preferences or beliefs.

As was mentioned above, Lakatos proposes some normative criteria for evaluating the development of research programmes: a research programme is progressing as long as it keeps predicting novel facts with some success; it is stagnating if it gives only *post-hoc* explanations either of chance discoveries or of facts anticipated by a rival programme. It is, however, very difficult to decide when a research programme has degenerated hopelessly, or when one of two rival programmes has achieved a decisive advantage over the other;

one must not demand progress at each single step.

Criteria for evaluating policy development are even more difficult to discover and to apply. Here I can only suggest some possible adaptations of Lakatos' criteria. First, an action programme may be said to be progressing as long as it succeeds in disposing of issues, i.e. in moving them from the stage of contention to a class of issues which the actors in the policy process judge to be in a state of satisfactory, if temporary, resolution. In comparing two action programmes, *A* and *B*, *A* is progressing if it succeeds in solving or ameliorating problems which proved intractable for *B* (the comparison between the Keynesian programmes of the New Deal and the laissez-faire approach of President Hoover comes to mind). Such criteria of progress may be further refined by distinguishing programme shifts that represent faithful developments of the policy core from those that do not. For example, since the core principle of a national health service is that health care should be distributed according to 'need', a return to the principle of ability-to-pay (e.g. through generalized user charges) would be a regressive move by this criterion, whatever its merits in terms of allocative efficiency. One could, of course, argue that an apparently regressive move (such as Lenin's New Economic Policy) may in fact be the best strategy for blocking serious threats to the integrity of the policy core, for gaining time, and for attracting new support. But this only proves Lakatos' point that, whatever criterion one adopts, one must not demand progress at each single step. Nor should we forget the role that persuasion can play in modifying the standards by which progress is assessed.

5. PERSUASION

Scientific advocacy

New ideas are even harder to sell than new products. Time is needed until favorable evidence accumulates and auxiliary ideas come to the rescue. The very criteria of evaluation have been patterned after the prevailing conceptions, and moulded by existing institutions; and what is counted as relevant evidence is determined by methodological rules distilled from past practice. Because established scientific · paradigms tend to become parochial in their range

of interests and intolerant of inconsistencies, ideas in agreement with accepted doctrines enjoy a considerable comparative advantage over unconventional proposals.

The Copernican heliocentric theory is probably the best-known example of an epoch-making idea gaining recognition only gradually and indirectly. Significant supporting evidence (stellar parallax and effect on falling bodies of the earth's rotation) could not be produced until about 300 years after the first announcement of the theory. According to Ravetz, "up to the early seventeenth century, a judicious astronomer who had no metaphysical bias in his assessment would return the opinion 'not proven' on the Copernican system, and treat it as an hypothesis" [15, p. 127].

Alexandre Koyré, and other historians of science after him, have likened to propaganda the work of Galileo in support of the Copernican hypothesis.

"But propaganda of this kind is not a marginal affair that may or may not be added to allegedly more substantial means of defence, and that should perhaps be avoided by the 'professionally honest scientist'. In the circumstances we are considering now, *propaganda is of the essence*. It is of the essence because interest must be created at a time when the usual methodological prescriptions have no point of attack; and because this interest must be maintained, perhaps for centuries, until new reasons arrive" [7, p. 52].

As one would expect, the role of persuasion is even more significant in the social sciences. Thus, in discussing Adam Smith's principles of division of labor and free exchange, the authors of a well-known textbook write: "It is interesting that Smith's book did not contain a logically correct exposition; instead it contained a masterfully persuasive statement of the results of free exchange. It was Robert Torreus, who some forty years after the idea had been 'sold', demonstrated its logical validity. Possibly, had Smith tried to give a logically air-tight demonstration, instead of suggestive plausible interpretation, he would never have made his 'point' popular" [1, p. 211]. George Stigler adds Jevons and Böhm-Bawerk to the list of outstanding economists who "have employed the techniques of the huckster". According to Stigler, techniques of persuasion "have preceded and accompanied the adoption on a large scale of almost every new idea in economic theory" [16, p. 5].

If persuasion plays such an important function in the development of scientific ideas, can policy analysts afford to slight it in the name of an historically mistaken view of scientific method? The moral of our examples is clear: the question is not whether analysts should use persuasion in proposing new policy ideas, but which forms of persuasion may be used effectively and without violating basic principles of professional ethics.

Legitimate uses of persuasion

Analysts attempt to influence policy by modifying the attitudes of policy-makers. When they produce relevant information, check for feasibility, develop models, and compare profits and costs, they seek to change attitudes through cognitive means. But since attitudes do not depend exclusively on rational factors, cognitive means must often be reinforced by noncognitive modes of persuasion. Thus, style, elegance of expression, tension of plot and narrative may be needed to strengthen the effect of descriptive statements which, by themselves, would be incapable of altering prevailing attitudes. Indeed, in our culture maximum effectiveness in communication is achieved neither by purely rational, nor by purely persuasive means, but by a subtle blend of these two means of redirecting attitudes.

Philosophers like Charles L. Stevenson have called attention to the phenomenon of 'persuasive definitions'. Even specialized languages contain many terms that have both a descriptive meaning (sometimes made precise by a technical definition), and an emotive (laudatory or derogatory) meaning. The purport of a persuasive definition is to alter the descriptive meaning of a term by giving it greater analytical precision; but the definition does not make any substantial change in the term's emotive meaning. In the context of policy analysis, one needs only to think of terms like efficiency, optimality, rationality, scientific method, risk, pollution, and needs (as in 'medical needs'). The emotive meaning of such expressions cannot be obliterated by any technical definition, however precise. What is even more important, the definition is actually used, often unconsciously, in an effort to modify attitudes by the interplay of emotive and descriptive meanings. Even the term 'analysis' profits from the laudatory connotation derived from triumphs of the analytic method in mechanics. Thus, we continue to speak of systems or policy *analysis*,

though most people agree that synthesis and design are actually more important.

Since persuasion is such a pervasive linguistic phenomenon, the practical question is not whether to reject it, but which forms of persuasion to reject. The history of science can help us in identifying situations in which persuasion can be used legitimately in support of, but not in place of, rational analysis. Consider first a situation in which the psychological effect of purely rational arguments is not strong enough to overcome the inertia of long-established patterns of thinking—even after the need for a change has become clear. For example, it is unlikely that Copernicans could have survived the long march through the social and scientific institutions of their time had they accepted battle on the grounds chosen by their adversaries (mostly entrenched in the universities). Their propagandist appeals to "a new secular class with a new outlook and considerable contempt for the science of the schools, for its methods, its results, even for its language" [7, p. 182] appear justifiable in this context.

Again, the impact of rational arguments on human minds may operate too slowly to bring about timely decisions. For instance, it is doubtful that sorely needed energy policies, requiring profound changes in values and attitudes, can be made acceptable by purely technical arguments. Not surprisingly, some recent proposals (such as Amory B Lovins' soft energy paths) owe their strong popular impact to an extremely sophisticated use of persuasive techniques—backed by some hard analysis.

As a third example, consider the case in which the persuasive support of a new idea is in advance of the rational support. It may be that full evidence is hard to obtain (as in Galileo's case); or that the technical tools for an adequate treatment of the problem do not exist; and it may be that experts disagree and science gives only ambiguous answers, as in many controversies over nuclear safety. In such cases, persuasive arguments (bolstered by whatever empirical and theoretical knowledge is available), may succeed in stimulating interest in the issue and keeping it alive until more adequate methods of analysis have been developed. More generally, since policy analysis cannot produce logically binding proofs but only more or less reasonable arguments, it is

clear that persuasion can always play a significant role in increasing the credibility of the
conclusions.

One particular form of persuasion is 'rationalization', which psychologists define as the
attempt to explain *a posteriori* one's actions by
means of rational motives rather than by the
'real' (unconscious) motives. One of the recurrent criticisms of policy analysis is that it provides 'pseudoscientific rationalizations' for
politically or bureaucratically determined positions. Thus, former US Secretary of Defense,
McNamara, has been criticized for using cost-
effectiveness studies as ammunition against
congressmen who opposed antiballistic missiles
(ABM), even though his own opposition to
ABM was based on other factors. Whether or
not this particular allegation is true, it is important to understand that it is not necessarily
dishonest to use justificatory arguments based
on considerations different from those that lead
us to the adoption of a given policy position.
Policy arguments are always directed to particular audiences, and there is nothing intrinsically reprehensible in selecting the combination
of facts, values, and analytic methods which
seems to be most appropriate for a given
audience. Indeed, there is no unique way to
construct an argument: data and evidence can
be selected in many ways from the available
information, and there are several alternative
methods for analysis and ways of ordering
values. A policy, like a theory [9], is a cluster
of conclusions in search of a premise; not the
least important task of analysis is discovering
the premises that make a set of conclusions
internally consistent, and convincing to the
widest possible audience.

In this paper I have discussed a number of
methodological issues suggested to the student
of decision- and policy-making by the recent
literature on the history and philosophy of
science. Some interesting analogies between the
policy process and its cognitive supports on
the one side, and the process of scientific
inquiry, on the other, have emerged. Of course,
it is not so much the analogies that are important (however striking and heuristically useful
they may be), as the methodological
approaches they suggest. While these remain
still largely untested, it seems possible to assert
that the ideas discussed here clearly point in
the direction of professional attitudes and intellectual orientations that differ significantly
from those associated with older views of scientific method.

One question that has not been explicitly
discussed is, how scientific is policy analysis?
For, as Professor Eilon has pointed out, one
cannot debate such a question in the abstract,
but only with reference to a particular conception of science [5]. With respect to Popperian
hypothetico-deductive methodology, Eilon
concluded that operational research is a scientific activity, but not in every respect. An analogous conclusion may be stated for policy
analysis. In this paper I have stressed the similarities with the process of scientific inquiry,
but the differences are also important and perhaps deserve a separate investigation.

REFERENCES

1. ALCHIAN AA & ALLEN WR (1974) *University Economics*. Prentice–Hall International, London, UK.
2. BLAUG M (1970) *An Introduction to the Economics of
Education*. Penguin, Harmondsworth, UK.
3. BOOTHROYD H (1974) *On the Theory of Operational
Research*. Report No **51**, Centre for Industrial Economic and Business Research, University of Warwick.
Coventry, UK.
4. CODDINGTON A (1969) Are statistics vital? *The Listener*,
11 December 1969, 822–823.
5. EILON S (1975) How scientific is OR? *Omega* 3(1), 1–8.
6. ETZIONI A (1960) Two approaches to organizational
analysis: a critique and a suggestion. *Admin. Sci. Q.*
5(2), 257–278.
7. FEYERABEND P (1975) *Against Method*. NLB, London,
UK.
8. FULLER LL (1969) *The Morality of Law*. Yale University Press, New Haven, Connecticut, USA.
9. HANSON NR (1958) *Patterns of Discovery*. Cambridge
University Press, Cambridge, UK.
10. KUHN TS (1962) *The Structure of Scientific Revolutions*.
The University of Chicago Press, Chicago, Illinois,
USA.
11. LAKATOS I (1971) History of science and its rational
reconstruction. In *Boston Studies in the Philosophy of
Science*, **8**, 92–122 (Eds BUCK R & COHEN R). Reidel,
Dordrecht, Holland.
12. LINDBLOM CE (1959) The science of "muddling
through". *Pub. Admin. Rev.* **19**, 79–88.
13. MAJONE G (1977) *Pitfalls of Analysis and the Analysis of
Pitfalls*. Research Memorandum 77–1, International
Institute for Applied Systems Analysis, Laxenburg,
Austria.
14. NOZICK R (1974) *Anarchy, State and Utopia*. Basic
Books, New York, USA.
15. RAVETZ JR (1973) *Scientific Knowledge and Its Social
Problems*. Penguin, Harmondsworth, UK.
16. STIGLER G (1965) The nature and role of originality in
scientific progress. In *Essays in the History of Economics*, 1–15. University of Chicago Press, Chicago, Illinois, USA.
17. TOULMIN S (1974) The structure of scientific theories.
In *The Structure of Scientific Theories* (Ed. SUPPE F).
University of Illinois Press, Urbana, Illinois, USA.

18. WEISS C (1975) Evaluation research in the political context. In *Handbook of Evaluation Research* (Eds STRUENING EL & GUTTENTAG M), Vol. 1, pp. 13–25. Sage Publications, London, UK.

ADDRESS FOR CORRESPONDENCE: *Professor Giandomenico Majone, International Institute for Applied Systems Analysis, 2361 Laxenburg, Austria.*

2

TYPOLOGIES OF PUBLIC POLICY
Meaning Construction and the Policy Process

Peter J. Steinberger

THE BURGEONING FIELD OF PUBLIC POLICY ANALYSIS SEEMS FINALLY to have acquired a fairly well-articulated research agenda. While many ambiguities and disputes inevitably remain, most scholars can agree on the need to investigate (among other things) the environmental correlates of public policy, the various processes of implementation and the complex nature of policy impact (for a convenient summary, see Hofferbert, 1974). In pursuing these kinds of tasks, moreover, scholars have produced a good deal of important research, frequently building upon—and improving upon—one another's work. Indeed, the development of research on the environmental and systemic correlates of policy is almost a model of how a cumulative and rigorous social science should proceed (see, for example, the literature described by Godwin and Sheperd, 1977).

Although most of this work is certainly of great interest, we might also suggest that the most intriguing aspect of the field has been the effort to *classify* public policies, or, more specifically, the attempt to categorize policies in such a way that the relationship between substance and process can be more clearly understood. Especially relevant is the "typological" tradition of policy analysis. Dating back to Lowi's (1964) now classic review article, the typological tradition has produced a variety of conceptions that have proven to be immensely appealing and influential. Nearly all summarizations of the policy field make reference to the typological literature, and usually do so in a favorable light, emphasizing the conceptual and theoretical insights it provides. And, indeed, there appears to be good reason for this. There can be no doubt, for example, that Lowi's typology of distributive, redistributive and regulatory policies seems to zero in on some useful and very fundamental distinctions. There is a certain plausibility in the formulation, and a fortuitous clarifying of common sense understandings, that has led numerous scholars to accept its accuracy and relevance virtually on the face of it. Even more importantly, Lowi's typology does indeed suggest a powerful and useful *theory* of the policy process. By arguing that different kinds of policies

[1] I am grateful to Maureen Farnan Steinberger, Sheldon Edner and Noel Reynolds for their valuable comments and suggestions.

From Peter J. Steinberger, "Typologies of Public Policy: Meaning Construction and the Policy Process," 61(2) *Social Science Quarterly* 185-197 (September 1980). Copyright © 1980 by the University of Texas Press. Reprinted by permission.

have different kinds of politics associated with them, Lowi provides an attractive explanatory scheme, one in which linkages between substance and process would appear to be concrete, testable and entirely credible.

Much the same can be said for several of the other typologies that have been influential in the field. Particularly notable, of course, is the "public goods/non-public goods" distinction from economics which has been enthusiastically adopted by contemporary policy analysts (see Olson, 1965). But one must also mention several other important classificatory schemes, especially Froman's (1967) "areal/segmental" distinction, Eulau and Eyestone's (1968) taxonomy of "adaptive" and "control" policies, and Edelman's (1974) emphasis on the "symbolic" dimension of politics. Each of these typologies seems to focus on a particularly salient aspect of public policy and to provide a basis for sound theorizing. It makes sense that redistributive policies will engender more conflict; or that public goods will produce the kinds of problems described by Olson; or that homogeneous cities are more likely to pursue areal policies than heterogeneous cities. As Lowi indicates, it is only through such efforts to conceptualize—to typify—that policy analysts can overcome the limitations inherent in the case-study method.

Unfortunately, this most promising of approaches has also proven to be most frustrating. What originally looked like a useful set of theories has, in fact, turned out to have serious practical limitations. There have been at least two reasons for this.

First, the various typologies may each be understood as an attempt to identify what is most fundamental, most distinctive, in public policy. Thus, in an important sense they have developed as rivals. One typology is offered, at least tacitly, as an improvement over another and, yet, there seems to be little to choose between them. The result is that policy analysis has retained at least some of its noncumulative character. An analyst interested in this approach must select one of the typologies, but the criteria for selection are by no means clear. Moreover, any particular study will be truly comparable only with other studies using the same typology. Thus, the effort to establish a general conceptual scheme has not been successful.

The second and more important difficulty has to do with the classification of actual cases. In brief, it has proved nearly impossible to confidently indentify a particular policy as being of this type or that (Lineberry and Sharkansky, 1971). Most actual policies tend, upon analysis, to overlap categories. For example, in examining the "areal-segmental" distinction, Froman (1967) classifies urban renewal policy as segmental (i.e., affecting only a section of the city) and annexation policy as areal (affecting the entire city). Yet there are numerous reasons for finding this a dubious, indeed misleading, classification. It can hardly be denied that annexation has a certain segmental quality; the area annexed, as well as adjacent areas, will likely be affected in special ways. Similarly, while urban renewal certainly is segmental in one sense, there can also be no doubt that it is likely to have a profound impact on the entire urban area. Thus, an objective classification appears to be impossible (Greenberg et al., 1977; Dornan, 1977). This problem has proved to be a general one. Few policies can be easily pigeonholed in terms of any of the typologies. Lowi himself notes, for example, that virtually every policy has a redistributive aspect of some kind.

The upshot of this has been well outlined by Hofferbert (1964): "To date, little empirical work has been fruitfully conducted with any of these typologies. . . The evidence is as yet incomplete regarding the typologies discussed here. It is disturbing, however, at least with respect to the Lowi scheme, that the bait has not been taken by other researchers. Lowi's insightful review is often noted in critical essays, but there is no instance in the literature I have read where his classification scheme has been examined with specific data and tested propositions" (Cf. Greenberg et al., 1977; Wilson, 1973).

This is disturbing indeed. The seemingly fruitful and enlightening conceptualizations outlined above have thus far been barren, and for very good reasons as we have seen. We appear to have a set of theories that are clearly insightful and perceptive but which seem to be, in practical terms, useless.

The purpose of this article is to offer, if only provisionally, a way out of this situation. Specifically, it suggests an approach to policy analysis which would fully utilize the insights of typological theory while recognizing, and indeed taking advantage of, the very limitations described above. As will be shown, such an effort must involve a significant reorientation of the typologies, and a considerable change in perspective. But, hopefully, the result will be an approach to policy analysis that vindicates our interest in, and demonstrates the usefulness of, the typological tradition.

A PHENOMENOLOGICAL APPROACH TO POLICY ANALYSIS

Appropriately enough, our starting point is the complex and ambiguous nature of public policy. As indicated above, this frustrating complexity has made it difficult to classify policies with confidence. Such a consistent lack of success must, at some point, raise the possibility that the enterprise is not merely difficult but, in a fundamental way, impossible.

Indeed, the premise of this paper is that we should regard ambiguity not as a defect in understanding but, rather, as a salient and ineluctable characteristic of public policy. The elusiveness of policy should not be considered a nuisance, an obstacle in the way of sound analysis. Rather, it should be regarded as a fundamental, defining element. By and large, policies are not self-explanatory. Once we accept this, the way may be open for a methodological approach to typological analysis that is both feasible and fruitful.

The central hypothesis is that most particular policies can be, and are, coherently understood and defined in a wide variety of ways. Indeed, policy-related controversies rarely involve simple questions of pro and con, or good versus bad. Rather, they generally involve two (or more) entirely different and competing understandings or definitions of the very same policy, of its purpose, its substance and its potential impact. That is, for one group a particular proposal or initiative may be fundamentally a matter of (say) regulatory policy, while for another it may be a question of distribution or redistribution. The implications are that each policy is likely to have different *meanings* for different participants; that the exact meaning of a policy, then, is by no means self-evident but, rather, is ambiguous and manipulable; and that the policy process is— at least in part—a struggle to get one or another meaning established as the accepted one.

Indeed, we must go a bit further than this and suggest—again provisionally—that a particular policy has virtually *no* relevant meaning *until* one is attached to it by some kind of participant. Normally, of course, policy is initially formulated by a participant who has an explicit meaning in mind. But this meaning is by no means final or definitive. The import and significance of any particular policy is, in the most general sense, indeterminate and open to interpretation and dispute.

As indicated above, Lowi himself appears to recognize something like this when he admits, for example, that in the long run virtually all government policies have redistributive impacts, and regulatory ones as well. But he seems to think that this is the case only in a trivial sense, and that most policies are clearly more of one type than another. The present argument, on the other hand, suggests that we regard ambiguity as fundamental and unavoidable. Few policies are obviously or "objectively" distributive rather than redistributive or regulatory; few are clearly more "adaptive" than "control," or "segmental" rather than "areal." In general, we should at least consider the possibility that the meaning of a particular policy must therefore be constituted by the various participants in the policy process.

The idea of reality and meaning as a social construct is an old one in epistemology, traceable, without doubt, to Kant and to his philosophical heirs. However, it has also had a profound impact on the social sciences. Berger and Luckmann's classic work on the social construction of reality is merely a recent example of an important, if controversial, social science tradition that dates back to Dilthey, Weber, Mead and especially Schutz. According to this general view, the social world— and its institutions, roles, ideas, etc.—is essentially a series of socially constructed meanings. In the words of Berger and Luckmann (1966):

> Men *together* produce a human environment, with the totality of its socio-cultural and psychological formations . . . (S)ocial order is a human product, or more precisely, an ongoing human production. It is produced by man in the course of his ongoing externalization. . . Social order exists *only* as a product of human activity.

Clearly this perspective is intended to apply to all of social reality, including (we must presume) the realm of policy meanings. It is precisely here, then, that the typological tradition can be especially useful. The interpretive approach to social science relies heavily on the concept of "type." Indeed, Berger and Luckmann, following the lead of both Weber and Schutz, indicate that socially constructed meanings generally appear as "typifications." That is, meanings tend to take on a variety of basic, more-or-less agreed-upon, typical forms. Such typifications, taken together, describe not merely social meanings but also social reality, since that reality can be nothing more than structures of meaning. Thus, the central function of the social scientist is to discover and analyze these forms. In this sense, and most importantly, we can suggest that the achievement and insight of the typological tradition is not in its analysis of "objective" policy characteristics. Rather, the best of the typologies are plausible and useful in that they describe (or, rather, can be used to describe) *typifications* that are generally and commonly employed by participants in the political process to define public policies. In other words, they are insightful in elucidating and in specifying socially constructed meanings.

Thus, when we talk about distributive, redistributive and regulatory policies, for example, we are not talking about objectively different kinds of policy. Rather, we are conceptualizing some of the ways in which participants tend to define policies. The participants inevitably engage in typification, in meaning construction, and the typological tradition is useful in specifying, categorizing and conceptualizing those various typifications. It is thus that we can explain the appeal of the typological approach and can begin to show its research potential.

Most emphatically, the argument is *not* that policies have no concrete, objective characteristics. Obviously, any policy proposal specifies courses of action, allocations of resources, methods of implementation, etc. These characteristics are salient, real and, indeed, crucial. They work to shape and constrain and mold the policy's meaning (though they do so in ways we can only hypothesize about). But they are not identical with that meaning. By the *meaning* of a policy (and, hence, of its objective characteristics) we refer essentially to the understandings that participants have regarding the policy's purpose, its potential impact and its relationship to other policies. Even when these things are somehow "spelled out" in the policy, there can—indeed must—be interpretation and reinterpretation. Thus, the meaning of a policy can only be something which has been attached to it by the various participants in the policy process (Edner, 1976).

MEANING CONSTRUCTION AND THE POLICY PROCESS

Interestingly, Lowi (1964:707) has suggested something rather like the approach here outlined. In his own words:

> . . . it is not the actual outcomes but the expectations as to what the outcomes *can be* that shape the issues and determine their politics. One of the most important strategies in any controversial issue is to attempt to define it in redistributive terms in order to broaden the base of opposition or support.

But unfortunately, and revealingly, Lowi relegates this comment to a footnote and does not pursue it. Nor do the other writers in the typological tradition. Thus, the perspective described above has been largely overlooked in favor of what has proven to be a less promising approach. This is particularly surprising in light of the influential literature on the *strategy* of the policy process, most notably the work of Schattschneider. Indeed, the method suggested in the present paper is largely useful in bringing together, and thereby broadening, the insights of Schattschneider (among others) and those of the typological writers. Schattschneider (1960) has taught us much about the way in which participants attempt to manipulate the scope of conflict in order to further their policy preferences. His formulation provides a good perspective on the policy process, and has been valuable as a research tool. But in at least a couple of ways, the approach here suggested can extend and improve upon Schattschneider's theory.

First, by emphasizing the social construction of reality, the present perspective helps to clarify the nature of the processes involved. For what we are concerned with is not just questions of good and bad, nor simple efforts to control the scope of conflict. Rather, we are interested in broad questions of social meaning. This emphasis tends to locate the policy process more squarely within the social world generally, helps to specify the mechanisms by which contexts are manipulated, and suggests a particular research agenda, viz., the empirical examination of typifications. Further, the present approach does away with certain pejorative connotations by demonstrating the very necessity of meaning construction. Efforts to define and redefine policies are not, as Schattschneider would have it, simply matters of strategy or distortion; they are in fact unavoidable if policies are to be at all relevant and meaningful. This, of course, implies also that various participants will define a single policy in various ways not simply out of tactical or prudential considerations but, rather, because of contrasting perspectives or worldviews. In this sense, the sociology of knowledge is obviously relevant; different groups are likely to see things differently. Conflict can therefore be a result of genuine definitional disagreements about the meaning of a policy.

Moreover, the typological tradition broadens Schattschneider's insight by demonstrating the wide variety of possible policy meanings. The typologies show that conflict or disagreement is not limited to the issue of scope, of public versus private, but may also include an entire range of other questions dealing with political impact, economic impact, motive, relationships to basic values, etc. The possibilities are numerous.

And as indicated below, this greater complexity can, in turn, significantly broaden our theoretical and research opportunities.

Even a casual reexamination of the case study literature in public policy would turn up a good deal of support for the perspective outlined in this essay. The literature on the War on Poverty presents an interesting example. A reading of the numerous relevant case studies suggests tnat this set of policies was initially defined as "adaptive," in the sense outlined by Eulau and Eyestone. That is, proponents of the War on Poverty understood it as an attempt by government to adapt its practices to meet the special political needs of the poor (see, for example, Kramer, 1969). Thus, the establishment of community action agencies would considerably change the decision-making process so as to include representatives of the poor and give them real power over the allocation of resources. But the same literature indicates that certain key opponents thought the War on Poverty had a rather different meaning (see especially Piven and Cloward, 1971). They defined it as, perhaps, a series of "control" policies. According to this view, the government wasn't actually adapting itself in any real sense. Rather, the purpose was to control the environment, to co-opt the poor and take the sting out of social protest. No real change in the distribution of power resources was involved.

Of course, space limitations forbid even a cursory examination of the case study literature along these lines. But among the many other cases that could be reinterpreted in this way are Bailey's (1950) analysis of the Full Employment Bill of 1946, Banfield's (1961) description of a transit subsidy dispute in Chicago, Altshuler's (1965) study of an inter-city freeway controversy, Art's (1968) research on the TFX decision, Halperin's (1972) history of the ABM decision, Pressman and Wildavsky's (1973) discussion of an EDA job program in Oakland, and Greenstone and Peterson's (1973) research on citizen participation and the War on Poverty. In each case, a dispute over policy meaning appeared to be crucial in shaping the nature of political controversy and in influencing the nature of ultimate policy settlements.

Before considering more specifically the research consequences of this perspective, one additional question presents itself immediately. This concerns the *evaluation* of meaning and definition. Even assuming the variability of meanings that can be attached to a single policy, one may still wonder if some meanings are more correct, or more appropriate, than others. If so, then surely one of the primary tasks of the policy analyst would be to determine the truest meaning of a particular policy.

There are a number of feasibility problems here, especially relating to the vagaries of the implementation process. But, more importantly, we may wonder if such an evaluation effort, even if possible, would be at all appropriate. To evaluate a particular meaning as more or less "correct" would surely be to violate one of the basic premises of the approach here suggested. The emphasis on social construction implies that, for practical purposes, there is no objective "right" and "wrong," at least in an a priori sense. The objective elements of a policy (e.g., specific conferrals of power, allocations of resources, proscriptions, etc.) do, in all likelihood, tend to shape the kinds of meanings attached to it. But those meanings, rather than being judged according to some objective standard of truth, in fact create the truth of the policy. They give it its definition. Hence, for the researcher to impose his own standards on the definitional process would be for him to become, in effect, a part of the political process itself, just another participant with biases and predispositions of his own.

However, we may still be able to identify a useful and legitimate "political" role for the policy analyst, one that he can adopt without compromising his scholarly status. Insofar as policies can be defined in numerous ways, we have said that their potential socially relevant impacts are also numerous. Any policy is likely to have distributive, redistributive and regulatory consequences, as well as various other kinds. However, the political process is likely to focus on only a limited number of such consequences. Actors are apt to seize upon one or two dimensions and to frame their definitions accordingly. In this way, many potential implications of a policy are almost certain to be ignored.

Thus, the policy analyst can perform a useful function in trying to unearth and specify possible consequences. And it is here, again, that the typological tradition can be of help. By identifying a number of socially generated dimensions along which policy meanings can be formulated, the various typologies point to the kinds of impacts which, when made manifest, are likely to be considered socially relevant. They can serve, then, as a guide or a checklist for the politically oriented researcher. And he can play a valuable public role by pointing out potential consequences which the political process has, for whatever reason, failed to uncover.

RESEARCH CONSEQUENCES

While this kind of evaluative procedure might have a good deal of merit, the primary value of the typological tradition would seem to involve analysis of the policy process itself. More specifically, it promises to provide the basis for a sound theoretical approach to the relationship between substance and process. This, of course, was Lowi's central concern in initiating typological analysis. He hypothesized that different types of policy would have different kinds of politics associated with them. Once again, little progress has been made in actually examining this thesis. But the transformation that has been suggested here can, in my view, significantly facilitate research in this regard.

In order to fully utilize the typological tradition, some coherence, some semblance of order, must be made out of the various existing schemes. The major typologies have generally been formulated in isolation from one another and, moreover, have never been adequately integrated. However, once we accept each of the major typologies as presenting a useful and enlightening perspective on public policy, then a unified approach is both possible and desirable. It would seem, most importantly, that none of the typologies are antipathetical to any of the others. Thus, we may suggest that each typology simply reflects one of the several ways in which policies can be conceptualized. Taken together, they indicate the various salient dimensions of public policy. This is illustrated in Table 1.

TABLE 1

Typologies of Public Policy

Dimensions of Public Policy		Categories of Public Policy	
Substantive impact:	Distributive	Redistributive	Regulatory
Political impact:	Adaptive	Control	
Scope of impact:	Areal	Segmental	
Exhaustibility:	Public Goods	Private goods	
Tangibility:	Symbolic	Tangible	

There is, of course, no pretense that the list outlined here is definitive or final. But the implications of the table are numerous. For example, it suggests that participants in the policy process do not merely select certain meanings; they also select, or emphasize, thereby certain *dimensions* of meaning. Thus, it is entirely conceivable that two sides of any particular controversy will choose not only different meanings but also different dimensions. Further, the table suggests that the potential socially-revelant impacts of a policy are—in theoretical terms—much more numerous than previously expected. Rather than three possibilities, as Lowi has suggested, the table indicates a much more complex conceptual scheme. Indeed, if combinations of multiple meanings are considered (e.g., "distributive-areal" or "control-symbolic"), the range of possibilities is obviously enormous.

At least three different sets of substantive issues may be addressed in terms of this table, issues which, taken together, would seem to comprise a stimulating research agenda. One such group of issues concerns the *definitional process* itself. This would especially refer to the way in which particular policy meanings are developed and disseminated. Among the more specific questions that could be raised here are the following:

—Do certain policies (that is, policies having certain objective characteristics) tend to be defined in characteristic ways? For example, it
seems likely that tax policies will usually be defined in terms of "substantive impact" (see, for example, Friedman, 1962). But this may not
be generally true. In some circumstances, tax policies might be defined
as primarily "control," or "symbolic," or even "segmental" policies.
Moreover, there is the further question of (what might be called)
historical paradigms. It may well be that certain policies are defined
one way in a particular era and rather differently in another. The
recent history of environmental politics in America, for example, might
be understandable in these terms.

—Do certain actors and groups tend to see all policies in terms of one
or two specific dimensions? Rather than the policy itself being the decisive factor, here we raise the possibility that the participants' particular
perspectives are crucial. For example, it seems plausible that business
groups, labor organizations, environmental groups, professional associations, etc., will each have a distinctive and particular set of concepts
with which to make sense out of the political world. These concepts
might be usefully analyzed in terms of the typological tradition. Thus,
it could be hypothesized that business groups see everything in terms
of "substantive impact," environmental groups in terms of "exhaust-
ibility," and so on.

—How are definitions actually formulated and disseminated? There is
a good deal of research on interest group behavior, but little of it focuses
on the question of meaning selection. It is important to understand the
ways in which meanings are thought up, ratified and propagated by
organized political forces. This, indeed, might well get to the crux of
the entire group process.

A second set of substantive questions concerns the *decision-making
process*. Here the focus would be on "politics" as Lowi understands it,
that is, on the process by which policy initiatives are approved or rejected. Again, several specific questions arise:

—Are there characteristic juxtapositions of meaning? That is, does the
adoption of one particular meaning by Group A tend to lead Group B
to adopt a logically alternative meaning? If so, one might then be able
to formulate a taxonomy of oppositions and, ultimately, of decision-
making processes in general.

—Does the nature of political conflict, for example, its intensity, correlate with the juxtaposition of definitions? It may well be that certain
kinds of meaning disputes are particularly conducive to rancor. In this
regard, we would ask if it makes a difference whether opposed meanings
are intra- or interdimensional. Controversies involving interdimensional
juxtaposition might be more diffuse, less focused, hence less rancorous.
Indeed, conflict may actually be most intense if opposing groups *agree*
on definition but disagree on evaluation. For example, opponents on
certain welfare proposals might well agree that the proposals are

essentially "redistributive" but disagree violently as to whether or not redistribution is a good thing. In such a case, the controversy would perhaps be especially pointed, the issues clear, and the interest obvious.

—Are meanings likely to multiply during the course of the decision process or are they likely to become fewer? This is roughly the same as asking if things are likely to grow more complex or more simple. Since both phenomena undoubtedly do occur at various times, we would also want to know under what circumstances these changes take place.

A third and final set of substantive questions concerns the process of *implementation*. In this regard, one could ask, among other things:

—To what extent are implementors conscious of, and interested in, policy meanings? The discretion of many administrative institutions may well include leeway in terms of which particular policy meaning to adopt. This, in turn, may have a profound effect on the way a particular policy is implemented. From a research point of view, the problem is a particularly complex one, but it may be crucial in formulating a comprehensive theory of the policy process.

—A related question would be the following: to what extent do implementors ignore the meanings generated by the "political" process and redefine policies to suit themselves? Again, this is a complex problem, but it seems to put the issue of administrative discretion in a particularly interesting light.

—Does meaning ambiguity, i.e., the lack of clear-cut definitions, make implementation especially difficult? An example of this might again be the community action provision of the War on Poverty in which such crucial but vague phrases as "maximum feasible participation" made it nearly impossible for planners to decide how to proceed.

This has been an exploratory and provisional discussion. Indeed, the purpose has been merely to suggest an alternative approach to policy analysis in the hopes of generating some dialogue. Clearly, the essential question is whether or not the research agenda outlined above can amount to a feasible and valuable approach to the study of public policy.

In their intelligent and provocative article on policy analysis, Greenberg et al. (1977) offer some stimulating suggestions relating to the policy field in general and include a discussion of the typological tradition. But though they point to the usual criticisms of typological analysis, they too fail to free themselves from the limitations inherent in the older approach. Thus, for example, they show that "there is *no* a priori way for the researcher to determine which . . . impacts are to be considered 'areal' or 'segmental'" (p. 1538); but they offer nothing very tangible in the way of an alternative strategy. Similarly, they demonstrate several problems inherent in the inevitable existence of a multiplicity of "perceptions" (or meanings), but all they can tell us is that we must somehow decide whose perceptions are most important (p. 1543).

The present discussion can be usefully considered supplemental to the analysis provided by Greenberg et al. It is, in effect, an attempt to meet their challenge by placing certain conceptual insights from the existing literature on a firmer theoretical foundation. Thus, the tentative list of hypotheses outlined above can provide a starting point for policy analysts interested in pursuing more fully the insights of the typological tradition.

REFERENCES

Altshuler, Alan. 1965. *Locating the Intercity Freeway*. (New York: Bobbs Merrill).

Art, Robert. 1968. *The TFX Decision: McNamara and the Military*. (Boston: Little, Brown).

Bailey, Stephen K. 1950. *Congress Makes a Law*. (New York: Columbia University Press).

Banfield, Edward. 1961. *Political Influence*. (New York: Free Press).

Berger, Peter and Thomas Luckmann. 1966. *The Social Construction of Reality* (Garden City: Doubleday).

Dornan, Paul. 1977. "Whither Urban Policy Analysis: A Review Essay," *Polity*, 9 (Summer): 503–27.

Edelman, Murray. 1974. *The Symbolic Uses of Politics*. (Urbana: University of Illinois Press).

Edner, Sheldon. 1976. "Intergovernmental Policy Development: The Importance of Problem Definition," pp. 149–68 in Charles O. Jones and Robert D. Thomas, eds., *Public Policy Making in a Federal System* (Beverly Hills, Calif.: Sage Publications).

Eulau, Heinz and Robert Eyestone. 1968. "Policy Maps of City Councils and Policy Outcomes," *American Political Science Review*, 62 (March): 124–43.

Friedman, Milton. 1962. *Capitalism and Freedom*. (Chicago: University of Chicago Press).

Froman, Lewis. 1967. "An Analysis of Public Policy in Cities," *Journal of Politics*, 29 (February): 94–108.

Godwin, R. Kenneth and W. Bruce Shepard. 1976. "Political Processes and Public Expenditures: A Re-Examination Based on Theories of Representative Government," *American Political Science Review*, 70 (December): 1127–35.

Greenberg, George et al. 1977. "Developing Public Policy Theory: Perspectives from Empirical Research," *American Political Science Review*, 71 (December): 1532–44.

Greenstone, J. David and Paul Petersen. 1973. *Race and Authority in Urban Politics*. (New York: Russell Sage).

Halperin, Morton. 1972. "The Decision to Deploy the ABM," *World Politics*, 25 (October): 62–95.

Hofferbert, Richard. 1974. *The Study of Public Policy*. (New York: Bobbs Merrill).

Kramer, Ralph. 1969. *Participation of the Poor*. (Englewood Cliffs, N.J.: Prentice-Hall).

Lineberry, Robert and Ira Sharkansky. 1971. *Urban Politics and Public Policy*. (New York: Harper & Row).

Lowi, Theodore. 1964. "American Business, Public Policy, Case Studies, and Political Theory," *World Politics*, 16 (July): 677–715.

Olson, Mancur. 1965. *The Logic of Collective Action*. (Cambridge, Mass.: Harvard University Press).

Piven, Frances Fox and Richard Cloward. 1971. *Regulating the Poor*. (New York: Vintage).

Pressman, Jeffrey and Aaron Wildavsky. 1973. *Implementation*. (Berkeley: University of California Press).

Schattschneider, E. E. 1960. *The Semi-Sovereign People*. (New York: Holt, Rinehart & Winston).

Wilson, James Q. 1973. *Political Organizations*. (New York: Basic Books).

3

"SUPERSTITION" and SOCIAL POLICY

N. Glazer

GLAZER N. (1978) 'Superstition' and social policy, *Reg. Studies* **12**, 619–628.
Sociologists have become highly concerned with guiding public policy.
With some exceptions, there is disillusionment as to this role. This failure of
social science has three main causes: ignorance of how society works: the
heterogeneity of many societies: and (most importantly) the insistence that
traditional inequalities and differences must be eliminated. So long as radical
and egalitarian individualism wins over traditional authority, social policy
will not create more harmonious social relations.

Sociology   Social policy   Family
Neighbourhood   Traditional roles

Editor's note
This is the first John Madge Memorial Lecture, named by the Regional
Studies Association in memory of one of its most distinguished founders.
The lecture was delivered in London on September 22, 1977. Though its
subject matter does not fall within the narrow remit of *Regional Studies*, the
Editor and Executive Committee agreed that it should be published as an
outstanding contribution in the field of urban social studies.

THE SOCIOLOGIST who engages himself with
social policy—as John Madge did—plays
many roles. In his humblest capacity, he can
conduct research on what people want, what
they like and don't like, their numbers and
family status and the like, and certainly this is
an essential base for any informed and decent
social policy. John Madge and other sociologists have had greater ambitions than
simply providing the data for social policy,
valuable and necessary as this is. Sociology has
always been more than numbers, though
admittedly when it got past numbers it
became, in the eyes of many, vague, diffuse
and imprecise. The large ambition of sociology in its relations with social policy has
been to guide it: Using its insights into what
we may call the fine structure of society—
family, community, informal association—
sociologists have hoped to assist in creating a
more humane, and by that token, a more
effective social policy. Sociologists have
hoped that they could help create designs for
housing, neighborhoods and towns that made
the lives of communities and families and
individuals more satisfying, or at the very
least, did not damage them; they have hoped
they could provide schemes for welfare and
the support of the poor that contributed to
overcoming dependency and helped develop

poor children into more effective adults, or at
the very least, did not contribute to family
breakup and poor relations between parents
and children, husbands and wives. And
similarly they have hoped that they could
contribute to policies for health, to policies
for the treatment of delinquent and wayward
children, and to other branches of social
policy insights arising from their studies of
communities, families, and individuals in
different stages of life.

Their contribution has characteristically
taken a very specific form. Sociologists have
studied how communities work, and how
families work. They have emphasized the role
of informal associations and social networks
based on residence in a single neighbourhood
in giving people a sense of security, a base of
values, a location from which they emerge to
do their business with the more formal
institutions of society, school, workplace,
government office, and to which they return
to find support. They see family, nuclear and
extended, playing the same role. Basically
sociologists have studied the informal structure of society; not government as such; not
the economy; not public administration; but
social bonds. And as such, their role has been
very much one of 'viewing with alarm' as
they have seen these bonds weaken. Students

of the family have described how its traditional functions have been taken over by
school and social institutions, and how the
focusing of energies within the family has
been weakened by work and its demands
outside the family, by mass amusements and
by the values spread by the mass media.
Students of community have described how
its bonds have been weakened as work and
residence are separated, as the church and
other locally-based institutions decline before
the competition of the mass media, and as the
new values spread by school, science, and
mass media make the values and satisfactions
of the community appear narrow, mean, and
stultifying.

If all of modern society and what underlies
it—science, economic development, rapid
transportation and communication, and the
new values they permit—conspired to undermine the social bonds of community and
family, there was, one could sadly conclude,
little one could do about it. Men would not
give up the undoubted truths of science, and
the conveniences it made possible; they
would not give up modern economic development, and its necessary separation of
work from community and family; they
would not give up the pleasures, specious
though they may be, of rapid transportation
and communication. Nothing could be done
about all that—or, in any case, in modern
democratic societies, very little—but something undoubtedly could be done, using the
insights and research of sociologists and other
social scientists, to design social policies to
enhance community and family values rather
than undermine them. And in particular, one
would think this task would be all the easier
since the social policies in question were
devised to strengthen community and family.
This was the purpose of better housing for the
poor, better planning of residential communities, welfare assistance for those in
distress, improved health policies, and the
other branches of social policy. And thus it
was with a certain enthusiasm and self-
confidence that sociologists in the postwar
world, like John Madge, began to get
involved with the study of these policies, with
high hopes that they could contribute to there
design and improvement.

It is too much to say flatly that these hopes
have been disappointed. There are as many
sociologists—indeed more—working in
areas of public policy today as ever before,
and one can see the effects in public policy of
various critiques that sociologists and other
social science-oriented analysts have launched

against particularly egregious faults in public
policy. In the United States and in Britain,
too, massive clearance of deteriorated urban
properties and the building for low-income
tenants of tall residential blocks, are now in
bad odor. Certainly the kind of work that
Herbert Gans, Marc Fried, Michael Young
and Peter Wilmott did in describing and, in a
restrained way, approving the tight network
of social connections that existed in what
planners considered slum neighborhoods
contributed to the present distaste for massive
clearance and massive residential structures to
replace them. Of course other things contributed too, and very likely were more
influential. For example, local political resistance to such mega-schemes of urban
renewal and the experience of families with
children in high residential towers, undoubtedly played a role, as did more sophisticated studies of relative cost which did not
give an encouraging picture of the total costs
of large schemes and large structures.
Undoubtedly the work of sociologists and
anthropologists has led to much greater
sensitivity, on the part of many social service
workers and administrators, to the possible
harm—or ineffectiveness—of policies applied
across the board without sufficient regard for
social networks.

Nevertheless, it remains true, in Britain as
well as America, that the optimistic vision of
social science guiding policy, and in particular, by the use of its knowledge of the fine
structure of society, improving policy affecting family, neighborhood, community, has
faded considerably. One hears more and
more voices raised against the impersonal
administrator, the blind effects of large
policies. The startling thing is that these
policies were designed *precisely* to respond to
human needs, to shore up families, to
strengthen neighborhoods, ensure better care
for damaged children, better rehabilitation
for juvenile delinquents. The work of the
modern state is increasingly a work for social
ends—for better housing, health, education,
treatment of the handicapped, for the overcoming of poverty and distress. Yet the
modern state reminds one—in the description
of its critics—of a friendly but clumsy giant,
who, in his efforts to help, tramples over
delicate and sensitive growths.

In the United States, housing and neighborhood policies are revised, sometimes
radically, every few years, and with considerable input from social scientists. And yet the
cry goes up ever louder, that neighborhoods
are ignored, are made incapable of maintain-

ing their distinctive values and integrity, very often just because of government policies, which make it difficult to maintain old buildings, or to keep out undesirable individuals and uses. Our welfare system also undergoes continual expansion and correction, again with input from social scientists. From support of children alone, we have gone on to support those who take care of them. Originally limited to broken families without resident fathers and husbands capable of work, welfare has gone on to support intact families. Earnings of welfare recipients may now be in large measure retained without affecting the benefit. Regulations that imposed residence requirements have been abandoned. It is no longer possible to lose welfare benefits simply because a mother of children cohabits with a male. Nor is it possible in many jurisdictions to require that a working male contribute to the support of the children of the mother with whom he lives. The numbers supported on welfare have increased greatly; food stamps have become an enormous program, and medicaid, by paying for all health care, has also helped alleviate the strain on the poor family. Many of these changes have come about administratively, some through law, some through court decision—the three great sources of change in social policy in the United States. Despite all these changes and improvements, the new administration of President Carter took as its major task in the field of social policy reforming the welfare system, which everyone agreed was a mess. And one reason was the ever-rising cry that it is damaging the family, encouraging family break-up, encouraging fathers to abandon children, even though many of the changes welfare has undergone in the past ten years were designed just to overcome these untoward efforts.

No one disputes that the welfare state is here to stay. The alarm of which I speak is by no means an alarm simply from the right, from conservative nostalgia for a time when the state stood apart at least consciously from any concern for social ills and devoted itself to war and roads. In the United States, and in Britain too, the defence of the neighborhood attracts a confusing mixture of people on the right and the left. Milton Kotler, clearly a man of the left, and a socialist, was one of its first advocates, and has been joined by Michael Novak and Peter Berger and many others who even if we abandon the unsatisfying distinction of right and left are certainly of a very different political persuasion. The defence of the family was once reserved to

Catholic Bishops and conservative Republicans critical of the possible impact on the family of large-scale government programs designed to help it. But it became a leading theme of President Carter's campaign and has now lost its conservative ideological coloring. And so we have the paradox that a state increasingly concerned with social ends, with family, neighborhood, individual growth and development, and which now devotes far more of its resources to such ends than to war, and traditional state functions, finds itself increasingly under attack for blindness, ineffectiveness, damage, insensitivity.

Indeed, in the present atmosphere it is not surprising to find a distinguished French social scientist, Claude Lévi-Strauss, echoing, in the suspicion of the state and his enthusiastic support for small structures based on irrational custom, Edmund Burke. In a fascinating essay that was published in *New Society*, Lévi-Strauss comes out squarely for English irrationality against French reason as a support for liberty and defence against state despotism. He surprisingly finds a French predecessor for such a position. He informs us that the first anthropological textbook to appear in French, by Jean Nicholas Démeunier, in 1776, already made the distinction. Démeunier, after pointing out that the ancients avoided flouting popular beliefs, whatever their absurdity, went on to write:

'The same could be said of the English. The proud islanders look with pity on writers who combat religious prejudice: they laugh at their efforts; and convinced as they are that the human race is born to fall into error, they do not strive to destroy superstitions which would soon be replaced by others. But the freedom of the press and the constitution of their government allow them to attack their administrators, and they are forever sounding the alarm against despotism ...' (LEVI-STRAUSS, 1976).

Continuing in his own voice, Lévi-Strauss writes:

'Almost 100 years later, in 1971, Renan in *La Réforme Intellectuelle en France* was to make similar observations: "England has attained the most liberal condition that the world has so far seen by developing her mediaeval institutions...Freedom in England ... stems from the country's entire history and from the respect equally accorded to the rights of the King, the rights of the Lords and those of the Commons and corporations of every kind.". . . Across the Channel, Sir Henry Sumner Maine had written ten years earlier in his famous book, *Ancient Law*: "The philosophers of France, in their eagerness to escape from what they deemed a superstition of the priests, flung themselves headlong into a superstition of the lawyers."

Of these three parallel observations, Démeunier's goes the farthest, by unhesitatingly locating superstition as the surest antidote to despotism. His opinion is relevant today, for despotism is still with us; if anyone wonders where, I would reply by borrowing another expression from Renan, even more apposite today than it was in his own time: it is to be found in the arrogant impertinence of the administration which exerts an intolerable dictatorship over every citizen.' (LEVI-STRAUSS 1977).

In making these remarks, of course, Lévi-Strauss is not referring to the same contrast between France and England that Démeunier, Renan and Maine referred to: Britain, alas, is no longer devoted to its ancient superstitions, and vigorously engages in modifying daily its laws, the ancient boundaries of its communities, the rights of old corporations and bodies. Thus, in its respect for superstition, it is no longer very different from France. Rather Lévi-Strauss is pointing to the paradoxical fact that old, traditional, and unexamined institutions and customs—he does not hesitate to call them 'superstitions', but we have given them milder and more acceptable names—serve as a barrier to, as he puts it, quoting Renan, 'the arrogant impertinence of the administration', which is to be found in Britain today as well as in France, in our backward welfare state of the United States as well as in the most advanced welfare states, such as Sweden.

And why does he defend superstition, or as I have put, traditions and customs and institutions whose roots are obscure? Because in them we find

'that infinite number of everyday allegiances, the web of private solidarities which save the individual from being crushed by society as a whole, while preserving society from being pulverized into a mass of interchangeable and anonymous atoms; the threads that bind every individual to a certain locality, way of life and form of belief or unbelief; all of which do not merely balance each other, like Montesquieu's separated powers, but also constitute a set of counter-forces capable of resisting abuses of public power'.

'By placing freedom on what is claimed to be a rational basis, one is condemning it to forgo this rich content and thus to undermine its own foundations. For the attachment to freedom is all the stronger when the rights it is asked to protect are based in part on the irrational: they consist of those minute privileges, perhaps negligible inequalities which while they do not interfere with a general equality nevertheless provide the individual with some firm footholds in his immediate surroundings. . . .'(LEVI-STRAUSS, 1977).

A distinguished American sociologist, Peter Berger, has been recently emphasizing the same theme. He speaks of family, neighborhood, church and informal associations as mediating structures they mediate between the individual and the state and he emphasizes, as Lévi-Strauss and those he quotes do, the significance of mediating structures in preserving liberty. And he also summons a body of great social thinkers to the support of mediating structures:

'This understanding of mediating structures is sympathetic to Edmund Burke's claim; "To be attached to the subdivision, to love the little platoon we belong to in society, is the first principle (the germ as it were) of public affections." And it is sympathetic to Alexis de Tocqueville's conclusions drawn from his observation of Americans: "In democratic societies the science of association is the mother of science; the progress of all the rest depends on the progress it has made." Marx, too, was concerned about the destruction of community, and the glimpse he gives us of post-revolutionary society is strongly reminiscent of Burke's "little platoons".'

To Berger, just as to Lévi-Strauss, an excessive rationality is suspect:

'Liberalism's blindness can be traced to its Enlightenment roots. Enlightenment thought is abstract, universalistic, addicted to what Burke called "geometry" in social policy. The concrete particularities of mediating structures find an inhospitable soil in the liberal garden. There the great concern is for the individual ("the rights of man") and for a just public order, but anything "in between" is viewed as irrelevant, as even an obstacle, to the rational ordering of society. What lies in between is dismissed, to the extent it can be, as superstition, bigotry, or (more recently) cultural lag.' (BERGER and NEUHAUS, 1977).

And so Lévi-Strauss and Berger, from very different traditions, are willing to band together, in the defence of the fine structure, the mediating structure, family community and association, of 'superstition', and are willing to risk what is today lèse-majesté in criticizing an over-exact attachment to equality, rationality, and the rights of the individual.

Thus they give a grand role to superstition—custom, tradition, irrational allegiances—in the defence of liberty, one to which Tocqueville and Burke also pointed, as well as Démeunier, Renan and Maine, and I would not deny for a moment they play this role. But I would emphasize another role they play, not unrelated to this grander one: custom, tradition, irrational allegiance, give people a footing, an identity, a sense of modest security, all of which are of greater importance than ever in a society in which mega-institutions, private and public, dominate, and spread a sense of helplessness among ordinary people. And yet it is just this—custom, tradition, irrational allegiance, 'superstition'—that modern social policy cannot accommodate itself to, despite all the shouting and advice from the sidelines by journalists and sociologists, anthropologists and architectural critics, socialists and free enterprisers. Despite every effort to adapt social policy to the needs of the fine structure of society, one senses, with some gloom, that it is not going to be an easy task, even when undertaken by new and enthusiastic administrations such as that of President Carter. It is easier to recognize these needs symbolically than do something about them in concrete policy. A leading defender of the ethnic neighborhoods is appointed an assistant secretary of H.U.D., and sociologists are consulted on what social policy is doing to the family. But what more will be done we will have to see.

The social scientist, because he is rooted in an intellectual tradition that has emphasized mediating structures and their significance, comes to social policy with his little kit of suggestions—take into account the way the family and small informal groups use the community, note that families are linked together in self-defense and policy should not divide them, leave space for informal associations whether devoted to religion, politics, culture or just gossip, and to all this the administrator nods in approval. But if the voices we have quoted are correct, and we could have added many more from many political orientations, we still face, and more oppressively than ever, the 'arrogant impertinence of the administration.' The insights of the social scientist still seem incapable of incorporation—at least to the extent many of us would wish and many of us have believed possible—into the work of the administrator.

Why? I would like to elaborate on three contemporary sources of this inability to adapt. They are as serious, I believe, as the first consideration that generally comes to mind, the simple imperviousness of bureaucracies, their arrogance because they have power and cannot easily be disciplined, and their insistence—an insistence which in many ways we can justify—on fixed rules and regulations which they apply to all. All this is true. Bureaucracy is inevitably with us if the state tries to undertake a great deal for a great many people, as it does, and as we wish it to. There are, however, some other reasons for the frustration of social scientists to which I would like to point.

The first is that we are still in large measure ignorant of how the fine structure of society works, and often we simply give the wrong advice, which if taken may only advance the sickness we are trying to arrest. A few examples will make the point.

The American poverty programme, which began in 1964, and which in any recognizable form was drawing to an end in 1973, owed much to the advice of social scientists. Poverty, they pointed out, was not only a matter of money. It was also a matter of the spirit, and could only be overcome, in all the senses which we consider important, by the involvement of the poor themselves in the programs that were to assist them. There was much in this insight that was correct, and that we must continue to cling to. But 'maximum feasible participation', the programmatic thrust that encapsulated these insights, seemed in the end to do not very much to involve the poor significantly in the programs that were to assist them. There has been much discussion of what went wrong, but it is agreed generally that one result was the creation of a new 'povertocracy', a bureaucracy of the poor, drawn admittedly in part from among those who originally qualified as poor, but which was rapidly involved in the infighting for salaries, positions, and prestige that afflict bureaucracies that are not drawn from the poor. Further, since local government already had a democratic base, these new poverty bureaucracies were drawn into futile conflict with more legitimately based institutions. In time one heard the same disdain for the poverty politicians from the social scientists who had assisted them in coming to their modest power as they had originally felt for the elected officials whom they had tried to circumvent with the new poverty establishment. What went wrong? I have some ideas and others have, too but the point is the advice was taken, and then the results were not those expected. And I would say that our analysis was incomplete, based on ignorance and insufficient knowledge of how municipal government and local communities worked.

Another example: in 1967, the Supreme Court of the United States issued one of its most important decisions in social policy in a case titled *in re Gault,* dealing with the rights of juveniles brought before family courts. This laid down rules as to how these courts were to operate, which reduced their informal aspect and made them more like proceedings for criminal offenses before regularly constituted courts. These rules called for written notice, the right to counsel, and the privilege against self-incrimination. The family courts had originally been set up to deal with wayward juveniles in a way that would encourage sympathetic consideration of their problems based on wide-ranging consultation, without adherence to strict rules of procedure or evidence, with parents and teachers and others who might not have, in strict legal terms, standing to participate. But since these informal proceedings could result in serious punishment, such as confinement of juveniles in training schools, the Court decided to extend to juveniles the protection given to adults charged with offenses.

Up to now, we deal only with the familiar extension of rights under the Constitution through interpretations of the Supreme Court, and social scientists play no role. But the court also took notice of social scientific investigations into the operation of juvenile courts, and, as Donald Horowitz tells the story in his fascinating recent book, *The Courts and Social Policy,* used these findings to buttress its decision. The Court quoted a government commission report, which asserted:

> 'There is increasing evidence that the informal procedures, contrary to original expectations, may themselves constitute a further obstacle to effective treatment of the delinquent to the extent they engender in the child a sense of injustice provoked by seemingly all-powerful and challengeless exercise of authority by judges and probation officers.'

Underlying this quotation, as Horowitz shows, were speculations by social scientists, not evidence, for there was as yet no research on this question. In this case, evidence did accumulate later that these speculations, reasonable as they might appear, were simply unfounded: juveniles consider both informal and formal procedures, it turns out, fair (HOROWITZ, 1977). This support for the new dispensation was wrong. But the replacement of the informal with the formal procedures has had serious effects: to my mind, it contributes to that undermining of confidence in, and acceptance of, informal social controls which is one evil of social policy we are trying to address.

And yet a third example: in 1972, an important case was brought before a Federal judge in New York charging that a large state institution for mentally retarded children deprived them of their constitutional rights because of their poor custodial treatment and the inadequacy of efforts to rehabilitate them. The judge agreed, and on the basis of expert advice, decreed that this institution, then containing 5000 children, and reflecting a period in treatment when large institutions were considered efficient (and perhaps effective), treated children unconstitutionally, and treatment must be given in institutions containing no more than 250 children. He set

up a panel of experts to oversee the state's efforts in meeting the judgement. In the meantime, New York State, apparently deciding on its own and on the basis of the best knowledge in the field that institutions for retarded children should be much smaller, commissioned a distinguished American architect, Richard Meier, to design what would be the finest institution of its type, for 384 retarded children (they are now called development centers in the United States). The institution is completed, is visited regularly by architects who consider it a wonder, but it contains no children. For in the meantime, experts have concluded that institutions of even 250, one which they had advised the judge to consider as an upper limit, are also too large, for such children should be treated in small home-like settings. The state has been forbidden to transfer children to the new center (NEW YORK TIMES, 1977). I have no doubt the experts are right, but if they are right now, they were wrong when they were advising the judge a mere five years ago, and since any public action requires time for planning, bids, construction and the like, one conclusion a judge may come to the next time is, don't trust the experts the first time around, for they may change their minds by the time your decree is ready to come into effect.

So then, one reason why the efforts of social scientists to get social policy to take account of the fine structure of society and the mediating structures fails, is that they may simply be wrong, and suggest something that will not have the effect they hope, even if incorporated into policy.

There is a second problem. Those of us who consider the workings of social policy in different societies have the suspicion that policy will work better in taking account of fine structure when a society is homogeneous than when it is heterogeneous. Thus things work better in Sweden, we tend to think, than in Britain; better in Britain than in the United States. Increasing heterogeneity, ethnic, racial, regional, should have something to do with it, as well as other things one can think of, such as size and political traditions. And when we consider the role of 'superstitions', customs and traditions and mediating institutions, we can see why. Administrators and administered are likelier to be bound by the same superstitions in a homogeneous country; what the administrator proposes or insists upon in social policy is less likely to be seen as wrong, immoral or amoral, or incomprehensible, since it is based on the common understanding of what is the proper way to raise children, or how the family should be constituted, or what is proper behavior in the community, or in seeking work. In a mixed society, one will run into clashes of superstitions, of the unexamined grounds on which people act.

One can point to many examples. In the case of Britain, the admirable police worked wonderfully well as long as they were dealing with British people. They had more trouble with the Irish. They now have, one reads in the newspapers, a great deal of trouble with the West Indians. Our police who have been of Irish background worked better when the cities were in larger measure Irish. They did not do quite as well with Italians and Jews, and have done worst of all with blacks and Puerto Ricans.

The theme can, of course, be explored through other social services too. Alvin Schorr a few years ago studied the French social assistant, who undertakes the role of child-care officer, giving advice, distributing necessary funds and ensuring their proper use. They have a wide range of authority, and act with a certain authoritativeness (SCHORR, 1968). My impression is that an American welfare worker would be much more inhibited in doing so. She would limit herself to the regulations. There are many reasons for the confidence and authoritativeness of the French social assistant compared to her American parallel, but one perhaps is the lesser range of cultural style of 'superstitions' of child-care, if you will, that the French worker would meet. In the French case, there would be a less-challenged national cultural norm, which the social assistant would think was perfectly proper to propose or even forcefully to insist upon.

There are other examples on the continent of close supervision of families with problems and troubles: special housing projects in the Netherlands and Germany, for example, in which problem families are concentrated for what we can call social training. We do not have anything of the sort in the United States. Once again, the question of how intrusive state authorities should dare to be with family styles would come up. The American housing administrator would be limited to either expulsion or simply allowing the problem family to stay and make life increasingly unbearable for its neighbors. Of course both in the case of the welfare worker and the housing administrator, there is another and perhaps more important reason for caution and restraint in the United States, and that is

the explosive development of legal rights—including rights to privacy and to services without *quid pro quo* obligations—that limits administrators and that requires separate discussion. But certainly one reason for this restraint and caution, whose other side is dependence on administrative and legal rule and bureaucratic distance, is cultural diversity.

But now what is the effect of withdrawal and distance from family and personal problems of social workers and administrators because of ignorance of customs and their meanings, and fear of arousing anger and distrust? (I have left out the case, probably still more common, of unwarranted self-confidence and authoritativeness of social service providers in dealing with those of other cultures, but I do believe the tendency—because of developments in professional education and law—is in the direction I have emphasized, certainly in the United States.) One effect is that teaching to a common norm of behavior is radically neglected. We fail to instill the customs and habits, the 'superstitions', that a complex society needs to work well and smoothly. And so we have in my judgement such incredible aberrations as the looting and burning, by middle- as well as lower-class people, that accompanied the blackout in New York City and gravely damaged the important beginnings of independent business development in the black and Puerto Rican communities. The social-service provider loses authority because he is now seen as fulfilling only formal legal regulations, rather than operating on the basis of a common morality, a role he has now eschewed.

Admittedly, there is a positive side to this development. Distinctive customs and habits can continue unconstrained, and have many virtues, like all old customs and traditions. But if our large objective is concern by the administrator for the fine structure of society, not only what exists in the past, but what is continually being recreated, the results can only be negative, because the administrator and service provider withdraws from playing any role in this field, whether censure or approval, sanction or reward. A cold neutral eye ranging indifferently over the range of custom replaces an involved one, whether warm or authoritative, because diversity and the legal doctrines which defend it has made this appear intrusive, unwarranted, impertinent.

Yet must we not expect that England and the continent, as they become more diverse ethnically and racially, will follow the United States in this withdrawal of the social services from concern with the fine structure of society? The degree to which this diversity has developed is startling. The debate over the proportion of new Commonwealth colored in the United Kingdom continues, but a recent authoritative estimate puts this population at 3%, rising to 6% by the end of the century. This is substantial, and I would think already has effects, worth analysing, on British social policy and its effectiveness. A similar diversity, but with a different legal status for the newcomers, may be found in France and Germany, Belgium and Holland, with similar effects. Even Sweden, until recently, the most homogeneous of countries, ethnically, religiously, culturally, now has large minorities and a rising concern about them.

This diversity is not only ethnic and racial and religious; it is also a diversity of values and customs in a society in which old superstitions have weakened gravely and new ones have not become binding. In every developed society, I imagine, the social services scratch their heads over the family-like commune, the homosexual couple, and other new family-like forms which their rules and regulations fit poorly.

Clearly sociologists have a role to play in the development of social policy for diverse and heterogeneous societies. But the record of the United States is not encouraging. The problems are difficult, and the social scientist is hampered first by his strong concern for the superstitions that exist, which makes the development of a new binding norm, a new superstition, difficult, and second by his ignorance of how, without gravely interfering with human rights and dignity, a new norm is to be created and imposed.

And this brings me to the third, and to me the most important reason why social policy finds it difficult to accept and incorporate the insights of social sciences on the fine structure of society. This is because the doctrines of equality and human rights, the ruling doctrines of our age, make it impossible to leave superstitions, customs and traditions in darkness, playing their role with the conscious or unconscious connivance of government. All dark places must now be illuminated by the doctrine of equality and rights. Everything must be made straight and plain and clear and equal. And this is a contradiction limiting the effectiveness of social policy that I do not see any way to overcome. Perhaps—hopefully— our knowledge will expand so we can give good advice; perhaps—hopefully—we will find ways to accommodate cultural diversity while still maintaining the authority and effectiveness of social services and social service providers. But I wonder how a doctrine that demands the most exact and severe examination of inequalities and differences in rights can be reconciled with the need to accommodate, to take into account, and for decent social functioning, indeed to maintain social relations which have always taken for granted inequalities and differences in rights. The type case is the family, where children of different ages, mothers and fathers, have different roles, roles which cannot be easily reconciled with our societies'—all our societies'—thrust to perfect equality.

Let me give some examples. All I imagine would arouse dispute. They will be drawn from the United States, which has pushed the development of legal equality and rights furthest. In taking a society in which lawyers are more numerous than in any other, courts more powerful, and the processes for the establishment of rights against the authority of traditional or government agents of any kind most completely developed, I choose an extreme case, but one by no means irrelevant to other developed societies. If America is backward in social policy, it is forward in rights, and other societies, equally committed to the extension of equality and development of rights, look to the United States as a leader in this respect. If we have—as we do— lawyers and associations and movements devoted to children's rights and women's rights and minority rights, it is not because, I would argue, we are most backward in these respects, but because our constitutional and legal system makes it easier to claim and establish rights, and if I interpret some discussions in Britain correctly, this is considered one aspect of American practice and experience to be followed rather than to be avoided. Let me give some of the examples which prevent me from feeling complete satisfaction as we achieve ever more equality and protection for individual rights.

The first is that of a girl, below the age of 18, who established in court the right to have an abortion without the permission of her parents. I assume this will not be too common an experience. One wonders how, in the most practical fashion, such a case was carried to court. Presumably the girl made contact with a lawyer, who was willing to be her confidential counsellor and act for her against her parents. One can argue that this is only a further step in the freeing of children from parental tyranny. Children have rights to privacy and the control of their own fate, and the state will protect these against the family. The child has been made more equal, more rights have been guaranteed to her. But one considers the other side of it. The authority of the parents has been reduced. If—as I believe—the education of children, their rearing, the establishment of moral attitudes and values in them is still primarily the role of the family, then this role has been further undermined, and it is already terribly weakened.

Another example. The Supreme Court's rulings on obscenity and pornography made it difficult, on the grounds of the right to free speech, for communities to control the increasingly rapidly growing business of pornography—pornographic movies and live displays, adult bookstores, massage parlors, and the like. Now in many communities these are looked upon as disgusting and disgraceful, and they would like to ban such displays. They have found it very difficult. Just as a family is prevented from being the family it would like to be (and when I say this, I of course already take for granted that that must be the decision of the parents), communities, through the expansion of rights, are prevented from being the communities they would like to be. Let me point out, by the way, that the most recent authoritative Supreme Court ruling gives some rights to community attitudes in determining whether local ordinances may limit pornography, and some techniques have now been developed for control.

Another example: the Supreme Court has recently ruled 5–4, that a zoning ordinance, which limited those who could occupy a house to a nuclear family, and which was used to prevent grandchildren from living regularly with grandparents, is unconstitutional. I personally agree with this ruling. It had been applied blindly and bureaucratically, and as the majority of the Court wrote, 'The tradition of uncles, aunts, cousins and grandparents sharing a household has roots equally venerable and equally deserving of constitutional recognition' as local autonomy. Different kinds of family and family structure are equally legitimate and have equal rights. I agree. But the community has been further constrained in what kind of community it creates. And when it is constrained, a cynicism and indifference develops as to the possibility of informal or formal social control, the cynicism and indifference that makes large American cities harder places in which to live and raise children than suburbs.

Not all court rulings and administrative rulings, which I have not discussed, move toward the establishment of equality and rights against traditional patterns and superstitions but most do. Sometimes the right of a community as such is maintained against individuals and groups who want to change its patterns. Thus, the Supreme Court has been cautious in requiring communities to zone for poorer families or multiple dwelling units, if their plans do not call for them, though these have been challenged on grounds of discrimination against the poor and blacks. Some State Courts have, on the other hand, required such plans. In another and important case, the Supreme Court ruled that the Amish community need not send their children to school until 16, as the state of Wisconsin required, an age which the conservative Amish believe provides more education, secular and worldly, than is good for their children if they are to maintain the pattern of god-fearing living in closely-knit agricultural communities that they have maintained for centuries. Here the 'right' of the child to an advanced education, required by the state, was balanced by the 'right' of the community to maintain its old patterns— 'superstitions'—and the community won out.

I would not underestimate the difficulties of making such rulings, but their general direction has been to further equality, establish the same rights for persons in different roles. It is distinctive roles that we are talking about when we consider the fine structure of society. And there is no question that rights undermine roles. And so we have Lévi-Strauss pleading for rights based on the irrational, the unequal: 'they consist of those minute privileges, perhaps negligible inequalities, which, while they do not interfere with a general equality, nevertheless provide the individual with some firm footholds in his immediate surroundings.' (LEVI-STRAUSS, 1977). The family, the community, the Amish. But what is a negligible inequality to one will be a formidable one to others, one which is infamous and must be banned by law or administrative or judicial decree.

I have suggested three reasons why the good advice of sociologists, reminding people of the fine structure of society, of mediating structures, of custom, traditions, irrational allegiance and superstition, even when accepted, seems not to have improved social policy.

Or not as much as we expected 30 years ago. Is there anything to be done? If the problem is ignorance, we can try to improve social science; and while progress is not marked, I think we understand many things today better than we did 10 or 20 years ago: at least we understand how much we didn't understand. If the problem is cultural and ethnic and values diversity, the matter is more serious, but once again this is one area in which social science has not been helpless: it has been able to teach administrators and social workers the virtues of a variety of informal institutions, and it has been able to show that common functions and common roles link the institutions and customs and irrationalities of very different cultures. But when it comes to the rising passion for equality and secured human rights, secured against all authority, whatever its sources, one sees no particular role for social science. For there we come to a real clash of values, one which will have to be fought out. And as in all serious conflicts, there is much to be said for both sides, for the insistence on a radical and egalitarian individualism, and the defence of complex institutions and social bonds, incorporating authority and, if you will, 'superstition', as an unexamined but accepted element. But if the first wins out, as it is doing, the hope that social policy will assist in creating more harmonious social relations, better-working social institutions, broadly accepted as the decent and right way to order society, cannot be realized.

REFERENCES

BERGER P. L. and NEUHAUS R. J. (1977) *To Empower People: The Role of Mediating Structures in Public Policy*, American Enterprise Institute for Policy Research, Washington D.C.

HOROWITZ D. L. (1977) *The Courts and Social Policy*, The Brookings Institute, Washington D.C.

LEVI-STRAUSS C. (1977) *New Society* **40**, 385–8.

SCHORR A. (1968) *Explorations in Social Policy*. Basic Books, New York.

4

SOCIAL POLICY ALTERNATIVES
A Redefinition of Problems, Goals, and Strategies

Carroll L. Estes

A man's aging and his decline always takes place inside some given society: it is ultimately related to that society and to the place that the individual occupies within it [de Beauvoir, 1972, p. 39].

Social policies for the aged in the United States are a failure. This failure is socially constructed and is based on our attitudes toward the aged, as well as our political, economic, and social structures. The dominant view of the aged, which many of the elderly share, is that they are unproductive and dependent persons whose lives are steadily deteriorating. To the extent that this view reflects reality, that reality is determined largely by society. The problem was described poignantly and forcefully by Simone de Beauvoir (1972) when she observed that people enter old age "with empty hands." Society's role in this, she added, is "morally atrocious."

Politics, economics, and social structure have far more to do with the role and the status of the aged than does the aging process and its effects on the individual. Most important are economic policies, particularly those relating to employment and retirement.

But also of great importance are the role of special interests in the policy-making process and the extreme fragmentation of policy-making responsibility, which is scattered among federal, state, county, city, regional, and special district jurisdictions and authorities. The price of this fragmentation is high, as McConnell has observed: "The structuring of much of the political system about the array of private associations and other small political units has selected from the values which Americans cherish and has emphasized and given particular effect to narrow and material values. The cost is larger than we normally confess—in limitations on liberty, equality, and . . . public values" (1969, p. 160).

Coupled with this structural diversity is the American ethos that supports a limited role for government, as exemplified by the adage: "That government is best which governs least." More recently, this ethos has been described as the "American reluctance to seek public solutions . . . if there is any possibility of private solutions" (Heidenheimer, Heclo, and Adams, 1975, p. 226). It has been argued that European political structures and culture are more conducive to social change and public planning; certainly they provide less opportunity for special interests to sway policy decisions.

The pluralism that characterizes the American political system, considered by many to be one of its strengths, leads to the belief that the best public policies are those that result from the clash of various special interests; this belief is predicated on the false assumption that the public interest is represented by the congerie of special interests competing for policy control. Pluralism allows interest groups' preferences to replace citizen-based preferences. Interest group pressures and the fragmentation of policy-making responsibilities inhibit broad social change—instead channeling policies in incremental directions. Once a policy is established, organized and resourceful special interests, rather than the largely unrepresented general public, have the advantage in terms of structural power and influence. By contrast, "In less fragmented political systems, policy makers, without disregarding the issues of special interest to particular groups . . . deal from positions of greater strength with the broad policy guidelines which affect everyone in general and no one in particular" (Heidenheimer, Heclo, and Adams, 1975, p. 185). But in the United States, policy inertia is the rule, particularly when it is a question of altering income distribution or tax burdens and benefits. Once a policy is established, change is extremely difficult to effect because "so much is invested in building the consensus [that] the mechanism exhibits little capacity for moving that consensus [and] overcoming the extreme disaggregation in policy" (p. 262).

Historically, state and local governments have been more conservative than the federal government in the initiation of social reforms. States and localities are highly subject to localized interest-group pressure since political choices are made close to home and the cost of such decisions is often immediately experienced through direct taxation. Thus, it has been federal politics and the financial inducement of federal policies that have pulled state and local governments in new directions. Regrettably, new federalism has diluted this source of political vigor and national vision precisely at a time when fiscal crises and taxpayer revolts are creating a demand for cutbacks in social programs at state and local levels. The consequences are likely to be a retreat from policies that included some benefits for the most disadvantaged.

But what has been the overall effect of these social and ideological forces on policies for the aged in the United States? What are the common threads in Social Security, Medicare, Medicaid, food stamps, housing policies, Title XX (social services) and the Older Americans Act? The most important conclusion to be drawn about these policies and the many others designed to benefit the aged directly or indirectly is that they are not meeting the needs of the aged. The policies are largely symbolic and reflect dominant perspectives about the aged. They tend to segregate the aged, often with the poor, as a special class within society. Based on the concept that the aged are in need of services, these policies are often of more benefit to providers of service (physicians, hospitals, banks, mortgage insurance companies) than they are to the aged.

The Older Americans Act reflects many of the problems that characterize other social policies for the aged. This mid-1960s version of national policy for the aged was largely a symbolic gesture that provided limited social and recreational opportunities, "needed" most by middle-income older Americans. The Older

Americans Act reflected the growing visibility of interest groups for the elderly and the awakening of academic, recreational, and social work professionals to a new field of work. The states were originally assigned the major role in determining the needs of the aged and developing plans to meet these needs. The 1973 amendments of the Older Americans Act incorporated a planning and coordination strategy that reflected the growing emphasis on decentralization and local control. Federal revenue sharing and local resources were to provide the needed funds for programs. Thus, as the economic crisis worsened in the 1970s, funding responsibility for services for the aged was shifted from the federal level to the decentralized network of state units and area agencies on aging. By assigning these agencies responsibility to garner local resources in anticipation of continued federal fiscal strain, it was hoped that the growth of federal level economic commitments could be minimized. In the late 1970s, Older Americans Act policies have begun to shift again, abandoning even a limited conception of the social foundations of the problems of the aged and adopting theories that view the problem of old age as one of individual capacity and functioning. In its darkest interpretation, the emerging concern with the functional capacity of the old could preface the time when the aged will be stigmatized even further and forced to be even more dependent on professional certifiers, planners, and providers to obtain needed services—or else will be required to continue working long past current retirement age due to fiscal pressures of the economy. Many assume that Social Security will continue in its present form—a pay-as-you-go system financed by wage earners who may refuse to accept continually escalating Social Security withholding taxes. Such a tax revolt could necessitate the extension of working years well beyond current retirement ages.

The Older Americans Act, like many of the other social policies designed to meet the needs of the aged, receives support and legitimation from theoretical perspectives that have long dominated gerontological research and training in the United States. These perspectives include the disengagement, activity, and developmental theories, all of which contain strong social-psychological components. Another social-psychological theory, lodged within the symbolic interactionist school, is emerging, as are behavioral-exchange, ecological, and environmental theories. However, none of these derives from, or is based upon, macrolevel political economy approaches to old age—approaches that might give theoretical and empirical attention to the social creation of dependency through forced retirement and its functions for the economy (for example, as a contribution to surplus labor), or to the production of senility and the economic, political, and social control functions of such processes. Instead, the individual aspects of aging have been made a primary focus of research, and this emphasis has spawned a research tradition concerned with the social integration of the old, their morale, and adjustment. Underlying many such approaches has been an implicit value bias toward social policies and programs that would enhance the social activity and life satisfaction of the aged, with far less attention being given to the economic, political, and social conditions that largely determine the quality of their lives.

A brief review of these theories of aging and their policy implications will suffice. Disengagement theory prescribes either no policy intervention or interventions that aid the withdrawal of the individual and society from each other. Under such a framework, retirement policies receive legitimation, as do other separatist approaches. Disengagement theory provides the rationalization for a purely symbolic policy because both society and the individual are seen as better off as a consequence of the exclusion of the aged. In contrast, activity theory, which is essentially a (classless and universal) prescription for continued activity in old age, supports policies that assist in the social integration of the aged. Policies focusing on recreational and social activities, that is, life-enhancing rather than life-sustaining activities, are preferred under the tenets of activity theory. In a somewhat similar way, developmental theories, which are based on the "live and let live" principle, emphasize policies that would enable people to maintain their social status throughout the life cycle. This theory calls for highly individualized social policies to meet each individual's needs. Interactionist approaches accord a crucial role to interactional opportunities that build, sustain, or, if necessary, reconstruct the self-esteem of the old, including environmental interventions that foster positive self-images in old age and "aging group consciousness" (Rose and Peterson, 1965). Economic policy is seen as relevant only insofar as it affects socially constructed images of the elderly. None of these approaches, for that matter, begins with the aggregate economic or social condition of the aged; nor does any analyze the economy, legal or political institutions, or the social structure in ways that might lead directly to questions of equity and distributive justice (Estes, 1978). Thus American gerontological perspectives lend little support to social policies that might dramatically alter the distribution of resources in favor of the aged, for such policies are irrelevant to their theories!

Overall, social scientists in the United States have effectively legitimized incrementalist and individualistic approaches, demonstrating Harvey's observation that "social science formulates concepts, categories, relationships, and methods which are not independent of existing social relationships" (Harvey, 1973, p. 125). These social relationships link the social scientist with the social structure (Gouldner, 1970). The most important implication of this is that "the concepts are the product of the very phenomena they are designed to describe" (Harvey, 1973, p. 125).

The conservative role of social science has been a sore point for the Gray Panthers, as illustrated by their public and somewhat bitter criticism of the profession of gerontology: "Gerontology has assumed the deterioration of the aged, and has attempted to describe it in terms which ignore the social and economic factors which in large measure precipitate that deterioration. By reifying the attribute 'old,' gerontology reinforces societal attitudes which view older people as stuck in an inevitable chronological destiny of decay and deterioration. . . . When persons who are old, poor, and stigmatized by society become objects of gerontological research, they are seen as problems to society, rather than as persons experiencing problems created by the society. The natural result of such research is to suggest ways in which older people may adjust to society, rather than how society might be changed to adjust to the needs of older people" (Gray Panthers, 1977). The efforts of the Gray Panthers and other aging-based organizations to confront and redirect societal processing and treatment of the aged are critical to the very necessary construction of a new reality about old age. The central contention of this book, at least, is that aging is something that is done to the chronologically old; that is to say, aging "is not a biological transformation . . . it is a political transformation" (Comfort, 1976b, p. 28).

Additional social aspects of aging posited early in this book were that the experience of old age depends largely upon how others react to the aged; that social context and cultural meanings are crucial influences on this experience; and that older persons individually are powerless to alter their social status and condition because their problems and the appropriate remedies are for the most part defined by the dominant members (the structural interests) of society. Since the labels and definitions applied to any group in society result from reciprocal relationships in which the relative power, class, and social status of interactants play a part, the aged cannot unilaterally alter their relationship to the rest of the society. Nevertheless, the active resistance of the elderly to labels applied to them may contribute to altering the unjust treatment so often accorded them. And as noted by Geiger, current attitudes toward the aged, far from appearing by accident, are "a product of a social structure and a political economy that disposes of people as if there were not enough economically productive work to go around" (1976, p. 5).

Strategies for Failure

What then can we say about the requisite construction of a new reality about old age? It calls for a new perception of old age and a clear understanding of the social, economic, political, and cultural factors that create the very problems now being assiduously discovered by social scientists and policy makers. It calls for a new research agenda as well. Without knowledge about those facets of old age that are socially produced and more knowledge about economic contributions and consequences of aging in the United States, policies for and attitudes toward the aged are likely to continue as symbolic gestures aiding the structural interests that dominate the political scene. It calls for an appreciation which a true "sociology of knowledge" in gerontology might provide in understanding the scholar's and policy maker's contribution to the transformation of objective conditions into public problems and policies (Gusfield, 1976). Further, and even more important, it calls for a true "sociology of knowledge" in gerontology that would make it possible to understand how the scholar and policy maker transform objective conditions into public problems and policies.

America's social policies for the aged are structurally segregated, particularistic policies that tend to separate the old from others in the society. One issue here is whether the "insistence on the special programs just for [older persons creates] tension between [them] and the rest of society" (Etzioni, 1976, p. 29). But the main problem with such an approach is that its rationale has often been predicated upon demeaning images of the aged, and it explicitly invokes negative stereotypes in order to secure resources for the elderly. The deleterious consequences of any process that encourages the portrayal of a social group as impotent, frail, disabled, demented, or dependent cannot be overestimated. As previously noted, the labeling of social groups conditions the way others react to them. Thus, the negative imagery associated with the aged may not only damage the psychological self-esteem of the aged themselves but severely impair their capacity as a group to engage in interest-group politics and thereby gain their just share of resources.

Other consequences of the separatist ideology are that, by setting the aged apart from the rest of society, it makes them accessible as targets for blame, as well as stigmatization. Age-based approaches that rely on adverse labeling of those sixty years of age and older may increase resentment toward the aged. Society easily comes to look upon the elderly population as an economic and social albatross. Such perceptions exemplify a case of blaming the victim—that is, blaming the aged for economic hardships that are actually a consequence of larger economic and structural factors in the United States and the world economy—among them, involuntary retirement and an economy plagued by inflation and recession. Separatist policies, therefore, have the potential effect of increasing the backlash against the aged.

Conceptions of older persons as unproductive stem from the American belief that only those who work for pay are productive. But older persons are forcibly made "unproductive" by mandatory retirement policies. (It should be noted that all the legislative fanfare about abolishing mandatory retirement has succeeded in delaying this occurrence only from age sixty-five to seventy—and this extension does not apply to all categories of workers.) Such socially created unproductiveness in turn makes the old dependent on society. What is not recognized is that involuntary retirement is a kind of coercive unemployment that aids the economy by reducing unemployment among younger workers. To blame the aged for their forced dependency is to misunderstand the social causation of their condition.

Other examples of "blaming" the aged are found in current controversies over Social Security and health care costs (Samuelson, 1978a). Recent legislation to assure the financial soundness of the Social Security System has resulted in significant increases in the Social Security taxes levied on both employee and employer. What is important about Social Security financing is that it derives solely from taxation related to wage-earning employment. Revenues from corporate taxes, capital gains, dividends, or other benefits of corporate investment are excluded from Social Security taxes. The Congress of the United States, in contrast to a number of other countries, has rejected the principle of supplementing Social Security taxes from general revenues.

As a result, the average wage earner in the United States experiences Social Security as a form of regressive taxation, and the young or middle-aged worker may blame the elderly for the burdens created by its financing mechanism. The fact that inflation and the continuing refusal of Americans to draw on general revenues to stabilize Social Security are major sources of the wage earner's financial hardship is easily overlooked in the face of much simpler explanations. Again, under a separatist ideology it is easier to blame the aged than to try to comprehend the complex and oblique processes by which social expenses are generated.

Such blaming of the aged justifies limiting expenditures and benefits for them to lower-than-subsistence levels. Workers at the same time are encouraged not to believe that an adequate retirement income can be provided through Social Security withholding taxes. Thus, current Social Security financing methods serve as a way of using members of society as agents for controlling the potential expansion of income supports for the aged.

In the same way, discussions of escalating health costs almost invariably lead to accusations that Medicare—and hence, by implication, the elderly population—is the culprit. It is simply ignored that increases in hospital bills and physician fees account for more than 50 percent of the increase in costs over the past fifteen years, and more than 70 percent of the spiraling increases of the last few years. It is also overlooked that third-party payment mechanisms contain built-in incentives to expand the scope and number of services provided (and costs incurred) and that fraud and abuse by providers have cost billions in the Medicare and Medicaid programs (U.S. Senate, 1976b). Older persons have little control over the services they are provided. It is the physician, after all, who orders the tests, prescribes the drugs, orders the hospitalization, and performs the surgery. It is likely that over 70 percent of medical care costs are physician generated. Rather than attributing rising health costs to the demands of the aged, society should place the blame squarely at the door of the incentive structures—reimbursement mechanisms, for example—and a system that makes the provision of health services increasingly profitable to a growing segment of the private economic sector (Ehrenreich and Ehrenreich, 1970).

The crucial dilemma surrounding the politics of old age, however, is whether any disadvantaged group in society can gain access to the resource system without itself becoming a special interest, given the fact that American social policies are determined by bartering among the most vigorous and powerful interest groups. Part of the answer may lie in collective efforts by disadvantaged groups and members of the general population, pressing for universalistic approaches to such shared social problems as poverty (Binstock, 1977; Etzioni, 1976). Examples might be income maintenance policies that would define and, where necessary, provide a given level of income to Americans of all ages and social groups and health security policies that would provide a floor of basic medical coverage regardless of age or other special attributes. Social policies that are not age based would minimize the adverse labeling—often officially legitimated—of those over sixty years of age.

*Social policies for the aged in the United States are characterized
by policy segmentation and organizational constraint.* The potential success of the Older Americans Act and other federal programs for
the aged has been jeopardized by the creation of separate departments and government agencies to deal with different facets of the
problems of a single population group. The situation in which the
Administration on Aging finds itself offers a good example of this
problem. As a separate agency within the Department of Health,
Education, and Welfare, it operates independently of the Health
Care Financing Administration (which administers both the Medicare and Medicaid programs), and it is also distinct from the Social
Security Administration, which administers the Old Age and Sur-
vivors Insurance Program, along with the Supplementary Security
Income program. It is of course separate from the departments of
Housing and Urban Development, Transportation, Labor, and
Agriculture, all of which administer major programs directly affecting the elderly, as well as from the Veterans Administration,
which provides long-term care for many elderly veterans and han-
dles various veteran benefit programs.

In addition, Congress failed to grant sufficient authority to
the very organization—the Administration on Aging—that it established to carry out the objectives of the Older Americans Act.
Its objectives relate to health, housing, employment, recreation,
retirement, community, and social services, which are dealt with by
at least a dozen federal departments and independent agencies. It
was not until the 1978 reauthorization of the Older Americans Act
that language was inserted to require the Administration on Aging
to coordinate with these various governmental agencies on the federal level, with the exception of those administering general revenue sharing and Title XX social services. The problem is equally
serious in Congress, where dozens of committees and subcommit-
tees deal with the problems of the aged in a piecemeal, fragmented
fashion.

This policy segmentation results in an inability to treat any
major problem coherently and holistically, and what then occurs
is growing public skepticism about the ability of government programs to solve social problems—a skepticism that not only justifies

reductions in resource allocations but also gives support to the various solutions that interest groups, providers, and professionals bring forward. In fact, the more complex the problem appears, the more willing the public is to permit discretion to policy makers and experts who claim to have answers—and the more willing the public is to accept the continual failure of those policies because it comes to assume that the problem is so complex as to defy solution anyway. Perhaps most important, policy segmentation causes the public elderly to experience the political world as a series of distinct events and to look upon the environment as basically unpredictable. Not surprisingly, as the public experiences a complex and difficult social problem, such as aging, it becomes increasingly vulnerable to the actions of politicians and interest groups (Douglas, 1971).

Another aspect of policy segmentation is that organizations frequently do not have jurisdiction over areas that are vital to their assigned responsibilities. Welfare agencies, for example, have little authority over the employment resources essential to getting their clients off welfare rolls. Organizational effectiveness is largely determined by organizational jurisdiction. As Edelman has described it: "The names for jurisdictional allocations constitute one of the most potent devices for divorcing organizational accomplishments from their symbolic evocations" (1977, p. 90). The Administration on Aging provides a classic illustration of this problem.

A related problem is that services strategies encourage the breaking down of policy interventions into specialized categorical services to meet individual needs, thereby increasing fragmentation of service provision and preventing an integrated attack on the multifaceted and complex problems of the old person. This specialization itself produces ever-growing classes of service-provider specialists, leads to continual conflicts between public and private agencies, and creates a requirement for adminstrative mechanisms to rationalize and coordinate the many different services and levels of care for which new needs are discovered or manufactured. Again, while the goal of the Older Americans Act was to coordinate services for the aged, the act instead fostered fragmentation of services, and this in two ways—by segregating the aged from younger persons in many, if not most, of the services

provided and by establishing separate and, until 1978, uncoordi-
nated titles within the act that frequently have been in competition
with one another (for example, between the area planning and
nutrition program).

*America's social policies for the aged predominantly fall into a ser-
vices strategy that aids in the maintenance of social harmony and the preservation of existing social-class distinctions.* Human services strategies
reflect different classes of "deservingness" and entitlements among
the aged that in turn correspond to different socioeconomic sta-
tuses. Nelson (1978) cites government policies for (1) the "marginal
aged" (the "undeserving poor"); (2) the downwardly mobile aged,
belonging to the middle and lower-middle classes and newly poor
in old age (the "deserving poor"); and (3) the integrated aged, belonging to the middle and upper classes (the nonpoor).

Most services policies tend to favor the downwardly mobile
aged, in large part because they are thought of as both deserving
and deprived; in addition they have become increasingly organized
and are able to press their demands on legislators. The integrated
aged have the resources to permit their relatively "unrestricted
access to public and private resources" (Nelson, 1978, p. 3) without
the necessity of government intervention. The "undeserving" marginal aged are assisted largely through income maintenance policies such as Supplementary Security Income (which does not provide income even at the prevailing poverty level established by the
federal government) and health policies that, while highly variable
from state to state, consistently encourage removal of the elderly
poor from society—first through impoverishment because of inadequate income maintenance policies and then through institutionalization. Medicaid, for example, automatically covers nursing home care, but coverage for home health care is a state option.

The access of the most needy and marginal aged to extant
services is restricted by lack of income, transportation, and education, as well as by insufficient knowledge of how to manipulate
the system. In contrast, the downwardly mobile elderly, who are
more knowledgeable and have more education than the marginal
aged, are better able to manage and to take advantage of available
benefits. In fact, the services strategy has been designed to meet
the needs of the recently deprived aged, since it provides exactly

the kinds of services that enable them to maintain their middle-class life-styles. These are "life-enhancing services" that are aimed at enlarging social opportunities (Nelson, 1978, p. 22) rather than life-support services needed by the aged poor. The congregate meals program (which is mainly lauded because of the opportunities it provides for socialization) and senior center programs under the Older Americans Act are examples of life-enhancing services, as are the services that provide access to other needed services under the area planning strategy. Thus, a major consequence of America's services policies is the perpetuation of existing social-class differences; they sustain stratification in that they do not alter the distribution of prestige, income, or other critical resources among or to the aged.

Service strategies are increasingly characterized by the new federalism philosophy that fosters universal eligiblity instead of targeting resources to particular subpopulations of the elderly. Because universal eligibility works to the advantage of those who have the most knowledge about and access to services, it "inherently favors those who . . . are not necessarily in greatest need" (Nelson, 1978, p. 19). Thus, the remedial effects of the already limited services for the most needy are diluted at the outset.

The Older Americans Act reflects this trend toward universal entitlement by granting automatic eligibility at age sixty. Similarly, the 1975 reform of Title XX of the Social Security Act broadened entitlement criteria so that consumers from all classes now have an increasing stake in these services (Gilbert, 1977, p. 624). As Gilbert points out, the percent of Title XX service recipients who are not on welfare has increased significantly relative to those who are on welfare because of the broadened eligibility permitted under Title XX. Given the initial 2.5 (now 2.9) billion dollar national ceiling on Title XX appropriations and the expanded entitlement, the poor must compete for services with other classes of potential recipients. And, "for the aged this means that more nonpoor will compete with, and will receive more services relative to, the poor aged" (Nelson, 1978, p. 24).

The services strategy has serious implications for America's aged because it fosters unequal power relationships between recipients and providers of service. In addition, it creates dependency on two levels: first, for the aged themselves and second, for the society as a whole.

First, the aged who are economically prohibited from creating their own choices and options and who must depend on service providers for minimal assistance quickly learn that they must be cooperative (perhaps even submissive) to receive services. Publicly funded social services are more than systems for distributing services; they are systems of *social relationships* that reflect and bolster power inequities between experts and lay persons, as well as between providers and recipients of service. An increased emphasis on the services solution also means a greater degree of bureaucratization. This is likely to increase the alienation and isolation of the elderly client population, since they must negotiate their way through complex organizations in order to receive services. Further, services that might contribute to the independence of the old (for example, home health care) are given low priority.

Second, policies that provide for the jurisdictional expansion of service providers and middle-level bureaucrats are likely to increase the general public's dependency on services. Thus, social services previously rendered by other institutions (for example, family or church) now come to be performed by paid providers. This leads to further atrophy of traditional support systems, and a vicious circle is thus created that allows the expansionary tendencies of human services professions and industries free rein.

Services strategies in general, and those for the aged in particular, tend to stigmatize their clients as recipients in need, creating the impression that they have somehow failed to assume responsibility for their lives. The needs of older persons are reconceptualized as deficiencies by the professionals charged with treating them, regardless of whether the origins of these needs lie in social conditions over which the individual has little or no control, in the failings of the individual, or in some policy-maker's decision that a need exists.

In addition, services strategies may inadvertently exacerbate the problems for which they are the policy-prescribed solution. The adverse effects that medical treatment can produce (physician-created disease) have long been recognized, and some critics believe that the ill effects of medical care exceed its benefits (Illich, 1977). Similar questions have been raised about the efficacy of social services (Edelman, 1977; McKnight, 1977; Blenker, 1969). Has the growing number of social workers been associated with an increase in family breakups? Why are we spending more and more on education while our children learn less and less? "The question is not whether we get less service for more resources. Rather, it is . . . whether we get the reverse of what the service system is supposed to produce" (McKnight, 1977, p. 112). Yet, the longer the services conception of the problems and solution persists—and particularly in a market economy where profits can be made in human service delivery—the greater the incentives for providers to expand the net of individual needs for which they can provide services.

Finally, services approaches are likely to inhibit thinking about the problems of the aged as related to (or concomitant with) larger social or economic conditions. This occurs because service policies individualize problems. And when the needs of an individual are converted into deficiencies requiring the manufacture and provision of services, his or her problems become isolated from their social context. McKnight notes the strong effect of this individualization of the problem "upon [a] citizen's capacities to deal with cause and effect. If I cannot understand the question or the answer—the need or the remedy—I exist at the sufferance of expert systems . . . I am the object rather than the actor. My being is as a client rather than [as a] citizen" (1977, pp. 110–111).

Social policies under consideration for the 1980s will continue the trend toward indirect services. Government-financed service strategies for the aged are largely based upon the theory that direct services are not as necessary as the more indirect services that link and provide access for the client to the (theoretically) already available services. The new emphasis of the 1978 Older Americans Act Amendments on long-term care reinforces the services strategy as the best policy solution, while also strengthening the notion that aging is a decremental process that requires interventions focusing on the biological and not the social aspects of old age. The return to the biological metaphor as a means of describing the problems of the elderly (Freeman, 1978) is consonant with the growing national concern over economic scarcity that has made it increasingly imperative to find intervention strategies that will not add to either the costs or the expectations of the public. There is also an emerging consensus among policy makers, professionals, and government agencies that Older Americans Act agencies should provide an alternative to the institutional-care bias of current federal health policies—Medicare, for example, provides coverage for hospitalization but virtually none for outpatient home health services unless preceded by a hospitalization period, and Medicaid provides much more coverage for hospital and nursing home care than for home health care.

Enlightened as policies for community-based and long-term care may appear, early and growing indications of the Administration on Aging's role in this policy arena do not suggest that the aged themselves will receive many direct benefits. As introduced in the 1978 reauthorization bill, long-term care is being developed as another "indirect" service; the key "services" would be geriatric screening, assessment, and case management. Demonstration programs are being instituted to develop these screening, assessment, and management aspects of long-term care. Often referred to as "personal advocacy," this strategy is likely to foster the development of yet another class of professional troubleshooters who will siphon off a large proportion of the appropriated funds. The costs of such services are likely to be abridged not only by salaries for professionals and paraprofessionals to certify eligibility and manage the aged, but also by the cost of developing yet another set of bureaucracies to house these workers and develop the technology to detect the eligible degree of disability to qualify for services.

Other prospects are that the current long-term care strategy will lead to: (1) the "medicalization" of the problems of the aged, which engenders a perception of their problems as largely physiological, biological, and inevitably decremental; (2) a growing emphasis on individual and case-by-case remedies, an emphasis that will divert attention from the broader economic and social problems of the elderly; (3) a new form of stigmatization of the aged because application of the "vulnerability," "disability," and "frailty" labels in current usage may become a requirement for service eligibility under such a strategy; (4) the increasing isolation of the aged from the rest of society, as their problems come to be processed, screened, and managed through special age-segregated diagnostic agencies; (5) an expansion of the network of social control mechanisms affecting the aged, for the aged who seek assistance may be required to accept such damaging labels as "frail" or "disabled" in order to receive services (Estes and others, 1978)— the threat of which might reduce service demand by entitled age, while also encouraging the dependency of those who receive services; and (6) the potential infringement of the civil liberties of the aged who may be precipitously labeled mentally or physically unfit (possibly without due process) in the rush of program enthusiasm and altruism (Cohen, 1978).

From an economic perspective, the outcomes of indirect service policies will be no more positive. If left in the hands of certifiers and case management officials, these policies will simply produce burgeoning demands for personnel to certify the eligibility of more and more elderly people. Further, there is a serious potential cost boomerang in discovering (or creating by certification) increased numbers of disabled in the population, for this of course could result in more, not less, institutionalization. The bleak truth is that, without a clear federal commitment to direct services that include structural incentives for rehabilitation of the elderly and for supporting their maintenance in their communities, no amount of diagnostic screening or follow-up is likely to help.

The social needs of the aged, then, are defined in ways compatible with the organization of the American economy. The effect of a services strategy is to transform these needs into government-funded and industry-developed commodities for specific economic markets, commodities that are then consumed by the elderly and their "servants." As categories of need are selected for service intervention, these needs are seen as distinct from the system of the production and distribution of wealth that is largely responsible for the needs in the first place. As the focus of attention is shifted from system inequities to individual problems, the blame for the inadequacies of the economic system is displaced onto the aged and the poor (Kincaid, 1973).

Thus a services policy treats the problems of the aged, their illness, and needs independent of their social causes, while positing solutions in the consumption of services. Also, the legitimation of experts to treat only those aspects of the problem to which services are aimed results in a fragmented divisibility of problem-conception and the inadequacy of problem-solving efforts. Such policies

serve the multiple functions of obscuring the social and environmental origins of social problems and facilitating the economic
growth and expansion of human services technologies, industries,
and professions, while isolating problem individuals through categorical and separatist policies that ultimately "pit" disadvantaged
groups against one another.

Also disturbing is the trend toward policies (for instance,
coordination and functional assessment) that institutionalize indirect services, for their major purpose appears to be the economic
functions they provide in the employment of largely white middle-
class human service and professional-managerial workers. The
"indirectedness" of social services is one key to understanding why
there is growing frustration among the aged, the public, and
policy-makers; precisely as programs for the aged appear on the
ascendancy, there appears to be little tangible result.

But then, services policies are instituted not so much to produce results as to provide a substitute for adequate income maintenance policies. Regrettably, analyses that might expose the conditions of the aged in America remain subordinate to the untested
but unshakeable confidence of policy makers that services will solve
all problems. Such approaches will probably result in the development of human service monopolies (O'Connor, 1973) that will
challenge and eventually control the resources and power structures of the relatively competitive market of small private agencies
now supported under the Older Americans Act.

None of these developments will alter the status or condition
of the aged. In fact, if the development of "services" continues
along current lines, they will remain frustratingly marginal in their
capacity to touch the aged. The "services" of planning and coordination (now major emphases of the Older Americans Act) have
only indirect effects on the lives and experiences of the aged—and
the same will be true of the screening, assessment, and case management services being developed as a consequence of the 1978
amendments to the Older Americans Act. Thus the likelihood is
that pressures to expand services will continue to be channeled into
"broker" services that effectively augment the resources of providers and the power of professionals (planners, case managers, eligibility certifiers) but that ultimately only place new bureaucratic

barriers between the aged and the government-financed services that they are supposed to receive.

As the government provides more and more service-related resources and as the dependency ratio among the elderly increases, coupled with continuing inflation and recession at all levels of government, politicized demand is likely to escalate service demand— further expanding the resources, power, and profits of service agencies and industries and legitimating the professions that provide the indirect social planning, assessment, screening, and case management services. Thus there will be pressures on the federal government to develop and expand policies for the aged from the structural interests that have the most to gain from these policies, and the continued and very legitimate dissatisfaction of the aged, whose condition the government policies do not seem to touch. In light of these demands and the predictable failure of current policies for the aged, several outcomes are possible. A backlash against the elderly may weaken support for future intervention efforts on their behalf, given what appears to be their unending demands; and/or the notion may arise that a crisis exists, that this "crisis" must be worse than formerly imagined, and that what is needed is more resources for the same policy strategy. In the latter case the inability of social policies to ameliorate the problems of the aged will provide the rationale for ever-increasing demands by growth industries of providers and professions that stand to benefit from servicing the needs of the aged—whether or not they alleviate their suffering. Thus, the belief that a crisis exists calls forth new solutions, which generate further crises. Crises of this kind do not necessarily reflect actual demands or needs, but may indicate successful shaping of popular "demand" for symbolic and political purposes (Edelman, 1977).

A New Vision of Aging

What can be concluded from my examination of the aging enterprise? Will it be possible to develop effective policies without a new perception of old age? Will it be possible to radically alter our vision of aging and the aged in America? I believe that policy changes are essential on three levels. At the first and most impor-

tant level would be major shifts in perceptions and structural alignments, altering both the objective condition of the aged and the
social processes by which policies are made and implemented. At
the second or middle level would be shifts in current major policies
and programs to more effectively meet the needs of the aged—
income maintenance (Social Security, Supplemental Security Income, food stamps), health care (Medicare, Medicaid), and housing
(low-income housing assistance, rent supplements, housing for the
elderly, property tax relief). At the third level would be incremental changes and fine tuning of the eighty or more federal programs
of potential benefit to the aged. My preference is for change on
all three levels, but with primary emphasis on the first.

Policies to facilitate intergenerational bonding and support,
as well as the genuine economic independence and raised social
status of the aged, are imperative, and these would require changes
at the *first level*—namely, an adoption of universalist policies and
principles that would not place the aged in a separate (and potentially unequal) status but would instead eradicate the structural segregation of aging policies from those for other groups in the society. In this sense, my policy recommendations are similar to those
of the Carnegie Council on Children with respect to universal entitlement. After reviewing the constitutional guarantees of freedom of speech, religion, and assembly and the gradual development of such universal entitlements as free public education in the
nineteenth century and unemployment insurance, workers compensation, and Social Security in the twentieth century, the council
observed:

> This concept—sometimes known as universal en-
> titlement—contrasts with another principle of public policy
> which we have repeatedly found unsound—the concept of
> special programs for special people. (One observer has
> called them poor programs for the poor people.) They are
> targeted at specific groups implicitly or explicitly defined
> as inadequate, who deserve help not by right but only
> because of the humanitarian kindness of the donors and
> only as long as the recipients demonstrate their worthiness,
> gratitude, and compliance. These programs—of which wel-
> fare is the classic example—stigmatize their recipients and

commonly subject them to special investigations, tests, requirements, and restrictions. In the short run, special programs for the poor may remain necessary, but the long-range goal of family policy should be to include their recipients in programs that are universal [Keniston and the Carnegie Council on Children, 1977, p. 77].

This book subscribes to the principle of equity that would provide benefits corresponding to relative differences in need (Nelson, 1978), and it also subscribes to Rawls' (1971) conception of social justice, which argues that differences in life prospects are just if the greater expectations of the more advantaged improve the expectations of the least advantaged and that the basic structure of society is just throughout provided that the advantages of the more fortunate further the well-being of the least fortunate. Society's structure is perfectly just provided that the prospects of the least fortunate are as great as they can be.

To achieve equity for the aged it is essential to work jointly on the structural and process levels wherein the social construction of reality emerges. Since current social policies for the aged construct reality in ways that help to maintain existing social-class arrangements, structural changes must begin with income, retirement, and employment policies that at present accentuate class differences among the elderly. Income guarantees are required as a matter of right for every American citizen. Full employment is a national imperative as well, because present levels of unemployment cut the flow of money into Social Security, reduce the income of millions of potential wage earners, and in general contribute to human misery. As a result of forced retirement, the elderly have to rely on publicly financed state benefits and through this reliance are "trapped into poverty" (Walker, 1978, p. 5). Reflecting the "supreme value" that industrial societies place on work, a person's status as independent or dependent is determined largely by his or her participation in the labor market: "The implicit assumption of income maintenance policies [is] that the rewards from work should, in general, be higher than social [that is, governmental] benefits" (p. 9). That work is possible for many, if not most, elderly persons is evident in the continuing activity of physicians, lawyers, farmers, and self-employed businessmen well past the conventional retirement age of sixty-five.

The work ethic in America essentially determines how resources will be apportioned for the elderly, reinforcing class differences forged by a person's lifelong location in the class structure and his or her accompanying employment status. Ignored is the fact that the aged are not at fault for their retirement; in fact, retirement policies aid economic development and have been a requirement of industrialized nations. The aged are not personally at fault for their longevity or for the inflation that has eradicated their savings. Regrettably, as Ackley has pointed out, "There is no recognized constitutional right to the basic necessities of life . . . [and this] failure to recognize a right to subsistence stems directly from a refusal to acknowledge the part played by government in creating the conditions of poverty" (1978, pp. 4, 6).

Employment policies must treat seriously the right of all Americans to work at any age past minority. Similarly, definitions of "deservingness" and productiveness in old age must not be based on the employment status of the elderly. Federal employment policies for the aged have been described as virtually non-existent (Batten and Kastenbaum, 1976). For example, the few references of the National Commission for Manpower Policy to older workers have usually been to the small employment and volunteer programs for the elderly under the Older Americans Act. As Batten and Kastenbaum show, the de facto federal policy "goes something like this":

> Social Security and Supplementary Security Income are viewed as the major income support sources for most Americans once they retire. Other supports such as Medicare, Medicaid, food stamps, and social services are thought to provide adequately for our older population.
>
> Older workers are presumed to retire at age sixty-five or earlier.
>
> Americans between the ages of forty and sixty-four are presumed to be gainfully employed. Their unemployment rates tend to be low. Whatever vicissitudes they encounter in the labor force are by and large left up to them to cope with.
>
> Employment and training programs are considered to be for youth.
>
> Small categorical programs such as the Senior Aide program provide income supplements for the elderly poor which are regarded as adequate [1976, p. 32].

Current employment and retirement policies must be revised in such a way as to lessen the vulnerability of older workers to unemployment and to abolish forced retirement—without augmenting the surplus labor market so that wage labor is underpaid and there is a general reduction in the standard of living of American workers. This shift will require commitment to a full employment economy and an adequate floor on universal income maintenance.

Middle-level policy changes would include restoring to the Social Security Act those provisions for general-revenue financing that had been in force between 1944 and 1950; establishing a "floor" of Social Security benefits at least at the level of the Bureau of Labor Statistics intermediate budget (which provides a meager $6,738 per year for an elderly couple); obtaining cash grants in place of food stamps to provide additional income for food stamp beneficiaries; elevating Supplementary Security Income payments above the present federal base, which still does not provide income at the prevailing poverty level (California Congress of Seniors, 1977); and raising income levels for the determination of the poor and the near poor so that a realistic appraisal of the extent of poverty in America can be made and social policies based on poverty indexes will not guarantee impoverishment. For, even with the extremely low poverty level currently utilized, "the proportion of persons unable to afford a minimum adequate diet has not changed" over the last ten years; it "remains at about 25 percent of the elderly population" (Binstock, 1977, p. 14).

Middle-level health security measures would require national health insurance for all ages, under provisions that would provide disincentives rather than incentives for increasing profits (replacing the current incentive structure with one that gives special attention to the humane care of Medicare as well as to the health outcomes of such care). Emphasis should be on chronic illness, disability, and rehabilitation rather than on acute care. Because of the present malfunctioning medical care system with its incentives for overuse and profit, these changes will not be easy. But certain interim measures would help. For example, costly deductibles and coinsurance could be eliminated from Medicare and an adequate prescription drug benefit added. The federalization of Medicaid could make available an adequate scope of benefits to all the poor. Finally, a long-term care policy that emphasizes support for the family and the aged (and that is based in the community and limits institutional care to only that which is essential) could be developed.

A national housing policy to meet the needs of the aged is also clearly needed. Various national organizations have emphasized three general principles as essential in this area: (1) housing needs for older Americans cannot be divorced from the needs of the population as a whole, even though the housing needs of the elderly constitute a special and significant component of a national housing goal; (2) a national program focused on meeting the housing needs of the elderly must be flexible, both in the types of housing that are made available and in the income eligibility requirements; and, (3) the special living environment needs of elderly people (for example, medical and social services) must be taken into consideration to prevent their premature institutionalization, and attention must be given to the qualitative aspects of federal housing programs so that communities rather than housing ghettos are constructed (Crowley in U.S. House, Committee on Banking, Finance, and Urban Affairs, 1978). Adoption of these broad principles and their implementation with adequate appropriations is urgently needed to deal with the very serious housing problems facing the elderly today. Equally important is the need for continued housing subsidies until the aged are able to have a decent income in retirement.

Legal services, transportation, homemaker-chores, home health, and advocacy services are clearly needed. In too many communities even the elderly with adequate income are unable to obtain these needed but sometimes absent services; information about them is often not available to the elderly or the services are not responsive to the needs of the aged.

Who controls the services for the individual is critical to the delivery of social services. Services such as Medicare, although inadequate for all needs, provide the individual with more choice and the possibility of obtaining a more adequate range of services than is usually the case when decisions about service availability and access are made by the provider of service. For example, a small cash grant to an individual for the purchase of social services might produce a more effective result than the allocation of funds directly to social agencies providing homecare or transportation services, one means to restore a partial balance of power in the hands of the elderly. The dilemma in such approaches (and the shortcomings) lies in the assumption that the market will naturally respond—that it will hear the perhaps silent and unorganized "demand" for certain types of services and provide them—and in the potential abandonment of institutional change approaches. But my argument here is that there is little to be expected in the way of institutional changes by simply allocating resources to service providers directly. Institutional changes necessitate major structural changes, such as reorganizing the reward system around health care so that decisions about its availability, quality, and financing are not made based on its being a commodity to be sold at a profit. In the short run, as long as the current structural interests hold (and market decisions, profits, and losses weigh most heavily in the calculus of policy making), the structuring of social service provision in the United States will be basically unchanged. My preference would be for allocating the few remaining choices concerning services to the individual, within limits.

Where does this leave the Older Americans Act? Because it does not deal with the fundamental problems facing the aged, changes in the Older Americans Act belong under the category of *third-level* policy changes. Incremental by definition, they are fine-tuning adjustments of existing policies and processes. In the case of the elderly, third-level changes assume continuation of present decentralization and new federalism policies; they assume that the Older Americans Act, Social Security, Supplementary Security Income, food stamps, housing subsidies, and Medicare/Medicaid will remain the framework for national policy for the aged. With regard to the Older Americans Act, Congress, the Department of Health, Education, and Welfare, and the Administration on Aging must give greater attention to the ambiguities in legislative intent and program implementation. The broad and ill-defined objectives of the Act must be replaced with more specific definitions of objectives, target populations, types and costs of services (direct or indirect), and administrative structures. The lack of clarity, for example, in the roles of the Office of Human Development and the Administration on Aging must be eliminated. Another important change would be the abandonment of strategies that support "indirect services," such as coordination and geriatric screening, at the expense of more direct services—for example, legal and income assistance. Greater incentives are needed to foster cooperation in achieving national goals and to lessen duplication of state and local program goals. Finally, the development of a sound data base for a system of performance monitoring and accountability is also essential. Additional third level policy changes include the need to assure that Social Security and Supplementary Security Income payments do not fall below the poverty level for any recipient. Medicaid benefits must be improved to assure greater equity in access to care for the poor. Medicaid eligibility standards should be federalized in order to cover the medically indigent, as well as those receiving public assistance payments. Federal funds and housing subsidies should be modified to reflect more directly the impact of rising food and housing costs for the elderly.

Although policy and program changes are needed at the second and third levels in the short run, the long-range goal must be policies that provide for an adequate income, a job, decent housing, and health care; that alter the objective condition of the aged; and that change the social processes by which social policies are made and implemented in such a way that the public interests, rather than private special interests, are served. To accomplish these objectives requires the development of a comprehensive national policy on aging that does not segregate the elderly, stigmatize them or place them in a dependent and depersonalized status. To achieve such a national policy will require basic changes in our values, in our attitudes, in our behavior, and in our actions toward the elderly.

The choices are clear. It is time that America became dedicated to the task of transforming old age itself and, in the process, to dismantling the aging enterprise.

5

APPLIED SOCIAL DISCIPLINE RESEARCH OR SOCIAL POLICY RESEARCH
The Emergence of a Professional Paradigm in Sociological Research

Mark van de Vall and Cheryl Bolas

Modern sociology is showing signs of professionalization. In professionalization, a predominantly decision-oriented "Practice" is undergoing theoretical, methodological, and normative developments which are partly independent from a related but predominantly conclusion-oriented "Discipline." The following results are based upon an analysis of 120 projects of social policy research, or applied social research, in The Netherlands, in the areas of industrial and labor relations (40), regional and urban planning (40), and social welfare and public health (40). Theory: While in the sociological discipline high priority is given to constructing nomothetic, or formal, theories, the authors found that reports of social policy research containing such theories scored lower on utilization than reports lacking formal theory or concepts. By the same token, reports using ideographic, or grounded, concepts scored higher on utilization than reports containing either formal theory or no theory at all. Methods: Although in the discipline of sociology priority is given to a number of methodological standards, the degree of methodological perfection of the projects was found to correlate negatively (external researchers) or not at all (internal researchers) with degree of utilization. Values: While in the sociological discipline lip service is paid to the premise of value free investigation, research projects neutrally diagnosing a problem were found to score lower on utilization than reports also providing suggestions for designing and/or developing policy measures. Together, the data indicate the latent operation in sociology of a professional paradigm of social policy research.

PROFESSIONALIZATION IN SOCIAL RESEARCH

In a number of sciences, "discipline" and "practice" have developed into distinct methodological, theoretical, and normative paradigms. The practice of medicine, for instance, covers considerably more than merely applying the disciplines of physiology and biochemics to health problems, just as engineering encompasses more than applying the laws of physics to construction problems. Even in psychology, theory oriented experimental researchers work with a paradigm that in many respects differs from the one used by most therapy oriented clinical practitioners.

Sociologists call this gradual emancipation of a practice from a discipline "professionalization" (Foote, 1974). In their own area of knowledge, however, sociologists have experienced relatively little professionalization. In the social sciences, client oriented social policy re-

* Revised paper read at the 85th Annual Convention of the American Psychological Association, San Francisco, 1977, Section "Toward a Reconceptualization of Research," Bernard Bass, Coordinator, Frank Friedlander, Chair. The research project was funded by the Netherlands Government Ministries of Economic Affairs, Social Affairs and Public Health, Education and Welfare, Public Housing and Urban Planning. The senior author received a special research fellowship #F03 HS 44,982 for 1969–1970 and 1970–1971 from the National Center of Health Services Research and Development. Completion of the paper was funded by Grant #1 R01 MH 26687 01 SP of the National Institute of Mental Health. Requests for reprints should be addressed to: Mark van de Vall, Department of Sociology, University of Leyden, 242 Stationsplein, Leyden, The Netherlands.

search still is generally referred to as "applied social science discipline research" (Gouldner, 1965; Gelfand, 1975; Lazarsfeld and Reitz, 1975; Dunn and Swierzeck, 1977).

Although this identification of social policy research with applied discipline research recently has come under attack (Etzioni, 1971; Coleman, 1972; 1975), we have relatively little hard information about the epistemological differences between these two branches of sociological research. Even Coleman's six principles of social policy research, valuable as they are, are based upon this researcher's experience with one case—one of the least reliable methods in social research (Isaac and Michael, 1976).

While academic sociologists, for instance, generally conform to the epistemological standards of validity, reliability, representativeness, and exactness, the question of whether or not social policy researchers cope with the same or additional standards has not yet been answered systematically. Put in operational terms, the problem has not been solved of whether or not in social research the traditional academic requirement of scholarly publication is identical with the professional requirement of research utilization.

In an effort to provide a systematic answer to these and other questions, the authors have investigated three separate samples of projects of client oriented social policy research conducted in The Netherlands. Using data from 120 projects of client oriented research in three areas of social policy making, several theoretical and methodological characteristics of the reports of social policy research were related to the projects' impact upon organizational policy decisions.

METHOD OF RESEARCH AND EVALUATION

Samples of 40 projects of client oriented social research were drawn from the following sectors of social policy making in The Netherlands: (1) industrial and labor relations, (2) regional and urban planning, and (3) social welfare and public health. For analyzing each of the 120 research projects a triangulated design was used (Webb et al., 1969; Smith, 1975; Denzin, 1978) combining data from the following sources: (1) a theoretical and methodological analysis of the report of social policy research, (2) a semistructured interview with the social researcher who conducted the project, and (3) a similar interview with the policymaker responsible for translating the research results into policy measures.[1]

In our analysis data are used from all of these sources. In Tables 1 through 5, the independent variables stem from the analysis of the research reports. The dependent variable, used for evaluating the degree of utilization or impact, is based upon four questions in the interviews with the social researchers (SR) and the policymakers (PM). Policy impact was operationally defined as "specific organizational decisions or measures which, according to the researcher and the policymaker, can be traced to the investigated project of social policy research."[2] Summating the four indicators resulted in Overall Policy Impact scores or (OPI/4) scores for the social researcher (SR/OPI-4) and the policymaker (PM/OPI-4). Averaging these two scales resulted in a more comprehensive indicator, the Mean overall Policy Impact score or ($\overline{X}$/OPI-4), that was used in our analysis.[3]

---

[1] For a description of the sampling procedures and method of data collecting, see Appendix A. For a more complete description, see Appendix (A) in van de Vall and Bolas (1977).

[2] With few exceptions, we found the impact scores rated by the policymakers (PM/OPI-4) to exceed the corresponding impact scores rated by the social researchers (SR/OPI-4). To explain this trend, we compared the frequencies of DK (Don't Know) between these two groups of respondents in all 16 tables underlying this analysis (5 of which are published in this article). In 14 tables we found the number of DKs among the researchers to exceed that among the policymakers, indicating that the latter are better informed about the utilization of social policy research in organizational decisions (sign test: n = 16, x = 3, p ≤ .05). Thus, when evaluating the impact or utilization of social policy research, it is imperative to include the policymakers' assessment of utilization in the ratings.

[3] For a description of the construction, validity, and reliability of the (X/OPI-4) score, see Appendix B. For a more complete description, see Appendix (B) in van de Vall and Bolas (1977).

THEORETICAL CHARACTERISTICS OF THE PROFESSIONAL PARADIGM

Nomothetic vs. Ideographic Theory

When approaching a concrete social problem, social researchers will choose between operationalizing nomothetic theory consisting of formal concepts or generating ideographic theory, consisting of so-called sensitizing or grounded concepts. When deciding for the nomothetic approach, the researcher will scan the literature for abstract concepts that have been validated in his own or related subject areas, with the purpose of creating a more or less coherent sub-system of verified generalizations.[4] When using the ideographic approach, the researcher will generate concepts of low abstraction directly from his data, with the primary aim of understanding the social problem in a specific, i.e., local manifestation. Because traditionally abstract generalizations are highly valued in social science, contributing to nomothetic theory is from a discipline point of view considered preferable to generating ideographic concepts.

Keeping this priority in mind, we will first evaluate the impact of research projects using nomothetic theory and concepts for diagnosing a concrete social problem, followed by an evaluation of research projects using ideographic or grounded concepts for the same purpose.

Evaluating the Impact of Nomothetic Theory

According to such policy oriented scholars as Etzioni (1971) and Argyris (1972), nomothetic sociological theory has relatively low applicability, i.e., is of little use in research aimed at solving a concrete social or organizational problem. In an attempt to systematically verify this impression, we have, for all three policy sectors, compared the impact of research projects analyzing a problem in terms of formal theoretical concepts, with the impact of projects which, unintentionally or on purpose, have abstained from using abstract sociological concepts.[5] The results of this comparison are presented in Table 1.

Although significance at the .05 level is obtained only in the combined samples (n = 120), the parallel trends in the three sectors of social policy making suggest that the use of formal sociological theory and concepts operates as a *deterrent* in the utilization of client oriented social policy research.[6] When controlling for research projects conducted by external consultants or in-house staff employees, this result is upheld for the two categories of research projects (F = 4.60, P ≤ .03). Thus, in projects of social policy research there is a negative relationship between conforming to the traditional disciplinary standard of using nomothetic theory and concepts, and the policy standard of research utilization.

Evaluating the Impact of Ideographic Theory

Discussing the low applicability of sociological theory, Lazarsfeld et al. (1967) have reintroduced Blumer's "sensitizing concepts" as a worthwhile diagnostic alternative. Sensitizing concepts, defined by Blumer (1954) as "grounded on sense," are expected to "facilitate the intellectual and practical (!) handling of social reality" (Lazarsfeld et al., 1967). In a simultaneous but unrelated statement, Glaser and Strauss (1967) advocate the use of "grounded concepts" in social policy research. Grounded concepts are directly generated from collected data, belonging to what Homans (1951) calls "the first order of abstraction."

---

[4] This is an ideal type construct, i.e., representing a partly rational course of action, and not exhausting the full empirical reality of constructing formal theory in sociological research. The model does have an empirical base, however, in the various ways social research is conducted and taught. This is illustrated, for instance, by the fact that in one of the most widely used readers in social research (Golden, 1977), about 70 percent of the research contributions conform to one or more parts of the model.

[5] For the purpose of our analysis "formal sociological theory" is operationally defined as: "quoted from a published sociological source or sociological author."

[6] Using the related but different (PM/OPI-5) score, an identical trend (T = 2.52, p ≤ .02, df = 1, n = 40) was established in the sector of industrial and labor relations (van de Vall et al., 1976).

TABLE 1. Use Versus Non-Use of Formal Sociological Concepts in Social Policy Research, and Degree of Policy Impact ($\overline{X}$/OPI-4)*

Use of Nomothetic (Formal) Theoretical Concepts	Industrial and Labor Relations	Regional and Urban Planning	Social Welfare and Public Health	Combined 3 Samples (n=120)
Formal Concepts ARE Used	11.96 (17)	12.32 (16)	9.16 (16)	11.47 (49)
Formal Concepts Are NOT Used	15.58 (23)	16.25 (24)	12.44 (24)	14.31 (71)

* Industrial and labor relations: F=1.29, P≤.09. Regional and urban planning: F=2.37, P≤.13. Social welfare and public health: F=3.14, P≤.08. The combined samples: F=4.60, P≤.03. The independent variable is based on an analysis of the research reports; the dependent variable on averaged scores by social researchers and policymakers.

TABLE 2. Use Versus Non-Use of Grounded Sociological Concepts in Social Policy Research, and Degree of Policy Impact ($\overline{X}$/OPI-4)*

Use of Ideographic (Grounded) Theoretical Concepts	Projects of Social Policy Research Conducted by:	
	External Researchers	Internal Researchers
Grounded Concepts ARE Used	12.93 (14)	19.44 (8)
Grounded Concepts Are NOT Used	10.09 (52)	13.66 (40)

* All 120 projects. External vs. internal researchers: F=7.48; P≤.007. Grounded concepts used vs. not used: F=10.89, P≤.002. The independent variable is based on an anaysis of the research reports; the dependent variable on averaged scores by social researchers and policy makers.

Because none of the above statements are supported by systematic verification, we have compared the impact scores of projects of social policy research using grounded (sensitizing) concepts with research projects not using such ideographic concepts. Controlling for research conducted by external consultants *versus* projects conducted by in-house researchers, the results are presented in Table 2.

According to the data in Table 2, the hypothesis of the applicability of ideographic concepts, based upon Lazarsfeld et al. (1967) and Glaser and Strauss (1967), is confirmed. Projects of client oriented social policy research that use sensitizing or grounded concepts score higher on utilization in decision making than research projects not generating ideographic concepts.[7]

When comparing the data used in Tables 1 and 2, we find that in regional and urban planning (n = 40) and the combined samples (n = 120) projects of social policy research using ideographic (grounded) concepts score higher on impact than projects which either use formal concepts or use no theoretical concepts at all.[8] In fact, the impact of projects using ideographic concepts ($\overline{X}$/OPI-4 = 19.44) is highest of all impact scores in our Tables, indicating that none of the independent variables reaches a higher level of utilization.

The conclusion is that for enhancing the applicability of social research the, according to scientific standards, relatively low ranking procedure of generating ideographic (grounded, sensitizing) concepts will be more effective than the traditionally more highly valued procedure of operationalizing nomothetic (formal) concepts. Thus, the professional paradigm of social policy research is, in terms of theory, found to differ fundamentally from the academic paradigm of social science discipline research.

METHODOLOGICAL CHARACTERISTICS OF THE PROFESSIONAL PARADIGM

Epistemological vs. Implemental Validity

Underlying a scientific discipline are epistemological values which, in the research process, manifest themselves as methodological requirements. In social

---

[7] Using the related but different (PM/OPI-5) score, and identical trend (T = 2.08, p ≤ .05, df = 1, n = 40) was established in the sector of industrial and labor relations (van de Vall et al., 1976).

[8] Projects using ideographic concepts: ($\overline{X}$/OPI-4) = 15.89 (n = 22). Projects using either formal concepts or no concepts: ($\overline{X}$/OPI-4) = 11.56 (n = 98), F = 6.04, P ≤ .025, r = −.19, P = .018, (r2) partial correlation external *vs.* internal researchers: −.22. Regional and urban planning: F = 3.18, n.s., r = −.28, p ≤ .04. Industrial and labor relations and social welfare and public health: n.s.

science discipline research as opposed to social policy research, for instance, high priority is given to the requirement of epistemological validity, which requires that the collected data provide a true and undistorted basis for theoretical verification. Social policy researchers seek in addition "implemental validity," which requires that the collected data provide a relevant basis for formulating policy decisions (van de Vall, 1975).

This dual standard raises the question whether the requirement of epistemological validity in social discipline research is fully compatible with the requirement of implemental validity, which in addition is used in social policy research. Or, in terms of our investigation of 120 research projects: does aiming at methodological perfection correlate positively or negatively, or not at all, with the degree of research utilization?

Methodological Perfection and Policy Impact

With the aim of comparing the 120 projects of social policy research along the independent variable "methodological perfection," we have selected 11 criteria which together constitute a fairly comprehensive methodological model of social science discipline research (Boalt, 1969; McTavish et al., 1977). The 11 requirements are: (1) formulating the problem in terms of independent and dependent variables, (2) explicitly presenting *a priori* hypotheses, (3) using representative sample designs, (4) applying controls against sample distortion, (5) adhering to reliability standards and controls, (6) testing for significance using acknowledged significance levels, (7) using external and internal standards of validity, (8) unbiased and verifiable procedures of data analysis, (9) presenting conclusions only drawn from empirical information, (10) disclosure of data for and against the conclusions, and (11) miscellaneous requirements pertaining to a particular method used in the project.

By attaching weights of (x = 1) to each of these criteria, a methodology score was constructed ranging from 0 through 11, and, subsequently, correlated with the impact scores ($\overline{X}$/OPI-4) of the 120 projects of social policy research. Contrary to our hopes and expectations, this procedure resulted in a *negative* correlation between the methodology scores and the impact scores in the three sectors of social policy making (significant in two) and the combined samples: industrial and labor relations $r = -.34$, $P \leq .01$; regional and urban planning $r = -.13$, n.s.; social welfare and public health, $r = -.24$, $P \leq .001$; and, the combined samples (n = 120), $r = -.24$, $P \leq .05$.

This leads to the rather unsettling conclusion that in social policy research, rigorous adherence to the methodological requirements of social science discipline research is not instrumental in enhancing research projects' utilization in organizational policy decisions.

Naturally, this negative result raises additional questions about the relationship between research methodology and utilization. For instance: are these negative correlations due to an *inherent* incongruity between the epistemological and the implemental requirements, or are they due to the operation of an intervening variable?

Is the Incongruity Inherent?

If we hypothesize that in social research the dual requirements of epistemological and implemental validity are inherently in conflict, the implication is that this will be the case in 100 percent of the investigated projects. The negative correlation between methodology and utilization should not be affected, for instance, by conditions such as whether the research has been conducted by external consultants or by internal staff employees. If the negative correlation were found in only *one* of these two categories of projects, however, the hypothesis of inherent incongruity between the two requirements should be rejected.

To investigate this problem in detail we have, for each of the eleven methodological standards, compared the impact scores of the conforming projects with those of the projects deviating from the standard, while at the same time controlling for research conducted by external *versus*

TABLE 3. Projects of Social Policy Research Conducted by External or Internal Researchers Which Differ From or Conform To a Specific Methodological Standard, and Degree of Policy Impact ($\overline{X}$/OPI-4)*

Methodological Standard	External Researcher Differ ($\overline{X}$/OPI-4)	Internal Researcher Differ ($\overline{X}$/OPI-4)	External Researcher Conform ($\overline{X}$/OPI-4) %		Internal Researcher Conform ($\overline{X}$/OPI-4) %	
Formulating problem	12.11	14.50	10.12	(65)	14.37	(58)
A priori hypotheses	11.06	14.18	9.30	(40)	14.32	(37)
Representative sample	10.52	13.50	9.99	(59)	14.17	(58)
Controlled sampling	11.36	14.90	10.01	(65)	13.05	(63)
Reliability of data	10.62	12.79	10.75	(71)	14.78	(70)
Significance testing	12.50	15.71	9.55**	(57)	12.80**	(42)
Controls for validity	13.25	14.64	9.98	(57)	14.42	(40)
Objective analysis	15.62	13.28	9.71	(79)	13.87	(63)
Empirical conclusions	11.87	15.33	9.86	(79)	13.64	(54)
Presentation pro & con	13.67	15.00	9.69***	(59)	13.90***	(58)
Miscellaneous standards	12.50	14.95	9.62	(59)	14.08	(46)

* All 120 research projects. External researchers: n=68. Internal researchers: n=52. Total > 100% due to multiple response. Except where noted P>.05.
** F=4.16, P≤.04.
*** F=3.98, P≤.05.

internal researchers. The results are presented in Table 3.

While in Table 3 the projects conducted by external researchers reach a higher rate of impact when deviating from, rather than conforming with, methodological standards (sign test: n = 11, x = 1, P ≤ .012), this is not the case with the projects conducted by internal researchers. In more exact terms, while among the external consultants the average impact of the methodologically deviating projects exceeds the average impact of the conforming projects with 2.32, this disparity is, with a mean difference of .48, not only lower (F = 6.85, P ≤ .02) but almost negligible among internal researchers.

Although in neither of the two categories of projects is methodological conformation found to actually contribute to research utilization, the data in Table 3 refute the hypothesis of an inherent incongruity between the epistemological and the implemental requirements in social policy research.

Instead, the data suggest the operation of an intervening variable, namely that external researchers have difficulty combining the discipline's goal of creating new knowledge through diagnosing a problem with the nondisciplinary goals of designing policy measures and developing policy action for solving the problem. In comparison, the internal (in-house) researchers encounter fewer difficulties

combining epistomological and implemental requirements in social policy research.[9]

THE PROFESSIONAL PARADIGM OF SOCIAL POLICY RESEARCH

It is evident by now that the traditional view of social policy research as applied social science discipline research is not supported by data from our three independent samples of research projects. On the contrary, the major theoretical and methodological features of social science discipline research were found to have negative applicability: projects of social policy research that conformed to traditional academic standards—theoretical as well as methodological—scored lower on utilization than projects deviating from these standards.

This conclusion triggers a new question, namely, whether there are any values social policy researchers should adhere to in order to secure or enhance the utilization of their research output.

---

[9] This may be related to the fact that among the methodologically conforming projects in Table 3 those conducted by the external researchers consistently outnumber the projects conducted by internal staffers (sign test: n = 11, x = 0, P ≤ .001). This finding suggests that external researchers more often have a predominantly scholarly orientation than internal staffers and, consequently, are more often inclined to neglect the non-scholarly requirements of policy utilization.

To answer this question, we have divided the process of organizational policy making into three subsequent stages: (1) *diagnosis*, i.e., investigating the social problem; (2) *design*, i.e., drafting suggested policy measures; and (3) *development*, i.e., transforming one measure into policy action (van de Vall, 1975). For operational purposes, the three stages were combined in terms of the independent variable "implemental span." The implemental span of a research project is determined by the relative number of the three policy stages covered in the research report, which leads to the following hypothesis: The greater the implemental span of a project of social policy research, in terms of the number of stages covered in the research reports, the higher the project's impact upon organizational policy decisions. This hypothesis is verified in Table 4.

TABLE 4. The Variable "Implemental Span" in Reports of Social Policy Research, and Degree of Policy Impact ($\overline{X}$/OPI-4)*

Implemental Span in the Research Report	Policy Impact	n
1. Diagnosing the policy problem	10.72	(20)
2. Designing policy measure(s)	12.09	(22)
3. Developing policy action	11.91	(11)
4. Diagnosing the policy problem and designing policy measure(s)	14.58	(13)
5. Designing policy measure(s) and developing policy action	17.04	(14)
6. Diagnosing the problem, designing measure(s), and developing policy action	16.92	(6)

* Excluding 11 projects not fitting in this framework. Total: F=2.60, p≤.02, rho=.89, p≤.05. Industrial and labor relations: F=4.70, p≤.002. Regional and urban planning and social welfare and public health: n.s. The independent variable is based on an analysis of the research reports; the dependent variable on averaged scores by social researchers and policy makers.

The trend manifest in Table 4 is evident in all three policy sectors, although significant only in industrial and labor relations (P ≤ .002) and in the combined sectors (n = 120, P ≤ .02), which is taken as an indication that our hypothesis is confirmed. Thus, extending the implemental span of social policy research, in terms of the number of policy stages covered in the report, has the effect of enhancing the

project's utilization in policy decisions. Additional analysis supports this conclusion. Reports merely diagnosing the problem, for instance, score lower on impact than projects also covering the stages of design and development (F = 2.34, P ≤ .05).

These conclusions are corroborated by another one, about the role of projects in the third stage of the policy process, i.e., developing a course of policy action. In Table 5, the research reports are categorized according to the degree of manifest attention (explicit, implicit, ab-

TABLE 5. Degree of Explicating the Development of Policy Action in Reports of Social Policy Research, and Degree of Policy Impact ($\overline{X}$/OPI-4)*

Degree of Explication the Development of Policy Action in the Research Report	Policy Impact	n
Development of policy action *explicit* in the research report	14.20	(42)
Development of policy action *implicit* in the research report	13.40	(15)
Development of policy action *absent* in the research report	7.80	(14)

* Only reports including policy problem and policy goal. F=4.44, p≤.01, r=−.21, p≤.04. The independent variable is based on an analysis of the research reports; the dependent variable on averaged scores by social researchers and policy makers.

sent) devoted to developing a specific course of policy action.

The data in Table 5 show a positive correlation between the degree of explicit attention in the reports to developing a specific policy measure and the projects' impact upon organizational decisions.[10] This result is upheld when controlling for projects conducted either by external consultants or internal staff employees (F = 7.02, P ≤ .002).

---

[10] The question can be raised whether, to enhance their impact, social policy researchers should be familiar with the various aspects of the complicated process of organizational policy formation. Several data support this suggestion. For instance, internal researchers devoting more than one-third of their average working load to policy tasks (i.e., nonresearch tasks) are found to score higher on impact than those among their colleagues devoting less than 33 percent of their average working time to policy related activities (P ≤ .05). See also: van de Vall (1979).

Thus, the conclusion is that the more effective social policy researchers are in (1) combining epistemological and implemental requirements in their projects, and (2) extending the implemental span of their research projects, the more easily the research results will be co-aligned with the other streams of throughput constituting the process of organizational policy making (Thompson and Tuden, 1959).

CONCLUSION

Analyzing projects of social policy research conducted in three sectors of social policy making in The Netherlands, we found several indicators regarding the emergence of a professional paradigm of social policy research. Projects that generate ideographic concepts have higher impact than research projects which either operationalize the traditionally more highly valued nomothetic concepts or use or produce no sociological theory at all. Strictly conforming to 11 methodological standards of social science discipline research does not substantially contribute to research utilization. Exploring this rather unsettling result, internal researchers are found to be more successful in combining epistemological and implemental requirements in social policy research than external researchers. The latter's greater attention to methodological requirements indicates a latent conflict between the values of discipline oriented social researchers, who prefer explanatory power to policy impact, and the values of policy oriented researchers, who favor utilization over explanation.[11] Extending the implemental span of social policy research, in terms of the number of policy stages covered in the report and explicit involvement in developing a course of policy action, intensifies the utilization of research results in organizational policy making. Together, the findings suggest a number of theoretical, methodological, and normative differences between the traditional academic paradigm of social

[11] For additional research information about this distinction between the two paradigms, see van de Vall and Bolas (1977).

science discipline research, and an emerging professional paradigm of social policy research.

Appendix A: Sampling Procedures and Data Collecting

Sampling of the (3 × 40) projects of client oriented social policy research in The Netherlands took place in three stages:

(1) All projects of social policy research conducted in The Netherlands between 1960 and 1971 were registered in the three areas of social policy making: industrial and labor relations, regional and urban planning, and social welfare and public health. A questionnaire was mailed for this purpose to the membership of The Netherlands Association of Social Researchers (VSWO).

(2) From each of the resulting populations a sub-population was drawn, which, according to the researcher *and* the policy maker, had resulted in a certain degree of utilization (impact).

(3) From each of the sub-populations a representative sample of 40 projects was drawn with the following characteristics: (a) use of social research methods, (b) conducted by a professional (i.e., graduated) social scientist, and (c) research results presented in a written report.

Data about the projects of social policy research were obtained through a methodological and theoretical analysis of the research report, followed by independent semi-structured interviews with the social researcher and the policy maker.

Appendix B: Construction, Validity, and Reliability of the Dependent Variable

I. The Construction of ($\overline{X}$/OPI-4)

To measure the effect of the projects of social policy research on organizational policy making (utilization), four indicators of policy impact were selected, each consisting of a sub-score based on the following questions with social researchers and policy makers:

A. Manifest Impact: "Identify spinoffs in decisions or measures (describe in full) from the research project at the following stages of policy formation:

		Weight
1. initiating a policy	(a) advising	3
	(b) deciding	6
2. preparing a policy	(a) advising	2
	(b) deciding	4
3. executing a policy	(a) advising	1
	(b) deciding"	2

B. Stage Impact: "Identify spinoffs in decisions or measures (describe in full) from the research project at the following stages of the investigation: 1. formulating the problem, 2. operationalizing the problem in research terms, 3. sampling and data collecting, 4. analyzing the data, 5. (in-)formal SR-PM discussions, 6. (in-)formal interim reporting, 7. submitting the final research report, 8. translating the research results into policy measures, 9. follow-up on policy recommendations, 10. correcting and/or adjusting the policy recommendations, 11. otherwise." Summed weights ranging from 0 through 11.

C. Certainty Impact: "Identify spinoffs in decisions or measures (describe in full) in: 1. better perceiving the problem, 2. better understanding the problem, 3. better assessing the problem, 4. better solving the problem." Specification required. Summed weights ranging from 0 through 4.

D. Latent Impact: "Identify the following spinoffs in decisions or measures (describe in full): 1. postponing a decision, 2. enhancing rank and file participation in decisions, 3. enhancing awareness of the problem, 4. improving the policy maker's status, 5. establishing an information monopoly, 6. preventing (a) policy error(s)." Summed weights ranging from 0 through 6.

II. The Validity of (X̄/OPI-4)

A. Content Validity: to ensure content validity, open interviews were conducted with researchers and policy makers outside the samples, and used for constructing the schedules of the semi-structured interviews. The mean correlation coefficient of the four scale items is .405 (P ≤ .01).

B. Pragmatic Validity: this requirement involves prediction with respect to an outside criterion (Kerlinger, 1964). (X̄/OPI-4)'s pragmatic validity is indicated by the fact that although the three samples of research projects were drawn from independent populations, basic trends in one sample were also found in the other two. For a specific example, we refer to van de Vall (1975).

C. Convergent Validity: this implies that when combining ratings from two groups of respondents, i.e., researchers and policy makers, the two scores will measure the same concept, in our case policy impact or utilization. Using Bohrnstedt's (1969) method for measuring convergent discriminant validity of a set of scores, the following correlations between (SR/OPI-4) and (PM/OPI-4) were established: industrial and labor relations, r = .49; regional and urban planning, r = .69; social welfare and public health, r = .52. The mean correlation of the three combined samples (n = 120): r = .57.

D. Item-to-Total Validity: lacking hard indicators required for criterion related construct validity, the total score was used as a substitute criterion (Bohrnstedt, 1969). Item analysis of the (2 × 4) items within the three samples resulted in a mean item-to-total correlation of .41.

III. The Reliability of (X̄/OPI-4)

Using Cronbach's alpha for establishing internal consistent reliability (Bohrnstedt, 1969), the results are: industrial and labor relations = .71; regional and urban planning = .75; social welfare and public health = .95; the three samples combined = .74.

REFERENCES

Argyris, C.
1972   The Applicability of Organizational Sociology. Cambridge: Cambridge University Press.

Blumer, Herbert
1954   "What is wrong with social theory?" American Sociological Review 19:3–10.

Boalt, Gunnar
1969   The Sociology of Research. Carbondale: Southern Illinois University Press.

Bohrnstedt, George W.
1969   "A quick method for determining the reliability and validity of multiple-item scales." American Sociological Review 34:542–548.
1971   "Reliability and validity assessment in attitude measurement." Pp. 80–99 in Gene Sommers (ed.), Attitude Measurement. Chicago: Rand-McNally.

Coleman, James S.
1972   Policy Research in the Social Sciences. Morristown, N.J.: General Learning Press.
1975   "Problems of conceptualization and measurement in studying policy impacts." Pp. 19–40 in K. M. Dolbaere (ed.), Public Policy Evaluation. Beverly Hills, CA: Sage Yearbooks in Politics and Public Policy.

Denzin, Norman K.
1978   The Research Act: A Theoretical Introduction to Sociological Methods. New York: McGraw-Hill.

Dunn, William N. and F. W. Swierzeck.
1977   "Planned organizational change: Toward grounded theory." The Journal of Applied Behavioral Science 13:135–157.

Etzioni, Amitai
1971   "Policy research." The American Sociologist 6:8–12.

Foote, Nelson N.
1974   "Putting sociologists to work." The American Sociologist 9:125–134.

Galtung, Johan
1970   Theory and Methods of Social Research. London: Allen and Unwin.

Gelfand, Donald E.
1975   "The challenge of applied sociology." The American Sociologist 10:13–18.

Glaser, Barney G., and Anselm L. Strauss
1967   The Discovery of Grounded Theory. Chicago: Aldine.

Golden, M. Patricia (ed.)
1977   The Research Experience. Itasca, IL: Peacock.

Gouldner, Alvin W.
1965   "Explorations in applied social science." Pp. 5–22 in A. W. Gouldner and S. M. Miller, Applied Sociology: Opportunities and Problems. New York: The Free Press.

Homans, George
1951   The Human Group. London: Routledge and Kegan Paul.

Isaac, Stephen and W. B. Michael
1976   Handbook in Research and Evaluation. San Diego: Edits.

Kerlinger, Fred N.
  1964 Foundations of Behavioral Research. New
        York: Holt, Rinehart and Winston.
Lazarsfeld, Paul F. and J. G. Reitz
  1975 An Introduction to Applied Sociology. New
        York: Elsevier.
Lazarsfeld, Paul F., W. H. Sewell, and H. L.
  Wilensky
  1967 The Uses of Sociology. New York: Basic
        Books.
McTavish, Donald G., J. D. Clearly, E. E. Brent, L.
  Perman, and K. R. Knudsen
  1977 "Assessing research methodology: The
        structure of professional assessments of
        methodology." Sociological Methods and
        Research 6:3–44.
Smith, H. W.
  1975 Strategies of Social Research: The Method-
        ological Imagination. Englewood Cliffs, NJ:
        Prentice Hall.
Thompson, James D. and A. Tuden
  1959 "Strategies, structures and processes of or-
        ganizational decision." Pp. 195–216 in J. D.
        Thompson (ed.), Comparative Studies in
        Administration. Pittsburgh: Pittsburgh
        University Press.

van de Vall, Mark
  1975 "Methodology and utilization in applied so-
        cial research: Four complementary
        models." The Journal of Applied Behav-
        ioral Research 11:14–38.
  1979 "Functions and structure of applied be-
        havioral research in organizational decision
        making: A theoretical framework." In F.
        Baker and M. Schulberg (eds.), Program
        Evaluation in the Health Fields, Vol. II.
        New York: Behavioral Publications.
van de Vall, Mark and Cheryl Bolas
  1977 "Policy research as an agent of planned
        social intervention: An empirical analysis of
        methods, standards, data collecting and
        analysis." Sociological Practice 2:77–95.
van de Vall, Mark, C. Bolas, and T. S. Kang
  1976 Applied social research in industrial organ-
        izations: An evaluation of functions, theory
        and methods:" The Journal of Applied Be-
        havioral Science 12:158–177.
Webb, Eugene J., Donald T. Campbell, Richard D.
  Schwartz, and Lee Sechrest
  1969 Unobtrusive Measures: Nonreactive Re-
        search in the Social Sciences. Chicago:
        Rand McNally.

6

METHODOLOGY FOR THE STUDY OF THE INTERPLAY BETWEEN SOCIAL SCIENCE AND SOCIAL POLICY

Martin Rein

The study of the interplay between science and policy has grown enormously in recent years. Witness the impressive number of new empirical studies that have emerged, and several new journals, amongst them *Knowledge: Creation, Diffusion, Utilization*, created by Sage Publications further to promote the subject. There are several reasons for this heightened interest: the dramatic increase in expenditures for social science; the United States Congressional mandate for programme evaluation for new social legislation; and the possible development of 'sunset' legislation, which requires the periodic reassessment of a large portion of national legislation. A similar interest in the contribution of social science to policy-making is evident in the reports of international organizations such as the OECD (the earlier Brooks Report and the recent *Development and Utilization of the Social Sciences*) and Unesco's conferences on social science policy and the utilization of research findings.

This enormous burst of activity, not surprisingly, has led many scholars to approach the subject from several different perspectives. I have chosen the term 'interplay' to describe the relationship between social science and policy rather than the more customary word 'use'. This is because the concept of utilization and the empirical attempts to study it are so heterogeneous that we need a more general term to describe the subject. In addition, because the term 'use' implies a one-way process, it is not the appropriate framework to interpret an essentially interactive process. 'Interplay' is a neutral term to encompass the many different meanings of how social science and social policy influence each other, allowing for competition as well as co-operation.

While it is not the purpose of this essay to explore substantively the many different theories about the conceptualization of the research policy interplay, a brief review of some of these theories will help set the stage for our discussion of methods.

Roos's study of welfare and social policy provides a subtle analysis of the substantive issues involved in an analysis of the nature of the research policy alliance. His work essentially criticizes a narrow conception of policy-making, which, he believes, runs the risk of undermining the democratic model of decision-making as a political process by focusing exclusively on a model of a single decision-maker as the user of social science knowledge.[1]

Roos is concerned with the decision-maker bias in studies of utilization. I can also call attention to a strong empirical bias of much of the writing on the subject. A great many analyses of underutilization have implicitly been concerned with social science research. One of these is an influential book edited by Carol Weiss, entitled *Using Social Research in Public Policy Making*. This emphasis on empirical inquiry, i.e. research, rather than on the more general subject 'social science', obscures the question of the critical role of theory in gathering and analysing the world of facts. Increasingly, we have come to recognize that there are no facts independent of the theory that organizes them. Hence, to talk about research must also, even if only implicitly, presume a theoretical conception which organizes the study. Theory in social science is shaped by academic disciplines, by political ideologies, and by ideas in good currency (jobs), each providing a view of

* Professor of Social Policy, Department of Urban Studies and Planning, Massachusetts Institute of Technology, Cambridge, Mass., United States.

From Martin Rein, "Methodology for the Study of the Interplay between Social Science and Social Policy," XXXII (2) *International Social Science Journal* 361-368 (1980). Copyright 1980 by UNESCO. Reprinted by permission.

the world from very different perspectives. Theory calls attention to the importance of the intellectual framework for the interpretation of evidence and the discovery of meaning in fact.

A third analytical approach addresses the implicit assumption of a unilateral direction where knowledge essentially is thought to influence action, but not the other way round. To correct the weakness of this position, a number of writers such as David Donnison and Carol Weiss have tried to suggest either interactive models of mutual influence or a model that highlights the way in which policy shapes the research agenda.

Yet another line of theorizing is directed at the hidden normative assumption involved in the concept of use. There are often unspecified standards by which a research utilization is judged, and these standards imply the concept of 'good' and 'bad' use. For example, the political use of information to postpone decisive action and the use of knowledge to justify positions reached on other grounds are regarded as disreputable uses of 'knowledge' by politics. In fact, any disinterested review of the alliance between social science and policy-making would discover many political uses of knowledge, many of which are regarded as disreputable because they violate the norms of science rather than the norms of politics.

This clearly shows that a substantive analysis of the science-policy alliance raises fundamental issues about the nature of policy and of social science. The questions are deeply philosophical and sociological in that they raise questions about the nature of knowing and acting. They are philosophical in that they pose critical epistemological problems about the nature of knowledge. They are sociological in that they question the forum in which various social groups try to establish their legitimacy, because knowing is a form of acting. This latter point needs to be made clear. Knowing and acting are linked when people's livelihood and social position depend on the social importance of theory. That theory precedes and should influence action is an idea which supports a socially defined group in society and, in this sense, is a class interest. Ideas are set forth as the stock in trade of various occupational groups, including both academics and policy-makers.

The papers of Robert Redfield contain a clear statement of the values grounded in the academic tradition. Redfield argues that scientific knowledge requires a commitment to 'objectivity, honesty, accuracy and humility before the facts'.[2] But these values reflect a social position in society, the position of the institutionally supported scholar, who does not need to gain support from any particular interest at a point in time. Hence the scholar is privileged to be able to think in an individual way. Of course when the scholar turns to mission-oriented agencies and to contract research for financial support he becomes caught in a bind between autonomy and responsiveness.

Any discussion of methods for the study of the science-policy alliance encounters unresolved conceptual issues because the analytic conception of the phenomenon, the interplay between knowledge and action, and the methods of studying it cannot be separated. I shall start, then, by reviewing the assumptions under which we study the knowledge-action alliance. That knowledge in the social sciences exists independent of policy is the first assumption. It carries a secondary assumption that politics in action are not a form of knowing but only of doing. Thus, the process of thinking and acting is split. Following from this is the second assumption: that there is a divorce between the knowing and the acting person. One of the corollaries of this separation and the idealization of science as a way of knowing is the third assumption that an ideal knowledge should precede action, i.e. we should think before we act. Fourth assumption: optimistically many believe that there is more 'knowledge' embedded in the structuring than is presently used for policy and practice and that this 'under-use' of knowledge is largely a result of the arcane nature of knowledge and the rigidity of politics. Therefore, according to the fifth assumption, a programme of interpreting and simplifying social science and the need for intermediaries to interpret the knowledge for the politician is essential. In brief, then, a process designed to 'educate' the politician can increase the utilization of knowledge.

It is these assumptions that inform many studies of social science research utilization and are the methods for studying the interplay between knowledge and action. At the end of this essay I shall re-examine these assumptions and propose an alternative approach. I shall next review three of the most interesting methodological approaches for the study of the research policy interplay—usability, use, and diffusion.

Studying usability

Usability studies are an attempt to answer questions about the usefulness of particular types of information for the policy process. Usability studies deal either with information that actors in the policy-making process believe to be inherently or potentially useful, or information that analysts consider potentially useful, depending upon their interpretation of the nature of the policy process. The two approaches call for somewhat different methodologies.

Carol Weiss's essay illustrates the study of usability from the actors' perspective. It is an attempt to define which characteristics of social research can be most useful for decision-making. Weiss explains why she and her colleagues avoided the concept of 'use':

We decided to finesse the collection of data on actual use of social research for a variety of reasons. First, it is exceedingly unclear what constitutes use. Is 'use' the adaptation of research recommendation intact, the nudging of a decision in the direction suggested by research findings, the reinforcement of a likely decision by research, the consideration of research findings (even if these are overwhelmed by other considerations in the situation), rethinking the nature of the policy issue, redefining informational needs? What kind of use is 'real' use?[3]

In order to avoid these difficulties Weiss attempts a study of usability which she defines as research that makes a substantive contribution and/or is likely to be considered by policy actors. She and her colleagues selected fifty empirical studies of research as a basis for reviewing usability defined by these criteria. The research reports were in the fields of mental health, alcoholism, and drug abuse. The studies varied in terms of research quality, conformity to user expectations, action orientation, and challenge to the status quo. They conducted a series of 250 intensive interviews of policy-makers who occupied five different positions in the administrative hierarchy of the mental-health field. Abstracts of the major findings of the fifty studies were given to policy-makers who were asked to comment on their intrinsic merit and potential usefulness in their work.

One of the major findings from the study has to do with the idea that usable knowledge reinforces already established beliefs. According to the authors, in the mental-health field a further distinction should be drawn between personal beliefs and the beliefs underlying professional practice. Research that challenges personal belief systems, they say, is interpreted as counter-intuitive and rejected, but research that challenges agency practices is seen as usable. It may be surprising that studies challenging agency practices are just as likely to conform with user expectations as they are to conflict with them. This happens because decision-makers are themselves likely to question existing agency practices. They accept the studies because they reinforce their own beliefs.

A quite different approach to the study of usability is found in the work of Charles Lindblum and David Cohen.[4] Their approach is more synthetic. Instead of interviewing policy-makers they reviewed the literature on the subject and, drawing on their personal experiences, proposed a critical framework for examining the field as they understood it. Their approach to usability rests on a number of assumptions. Most important is that there are many ways of knowing: ordinary knowledge, social learning and interactive problem-solving, and knowledge from science. Second, there is a mistaken pursuit in social science of authoritativeness. Man has only a limited cognitive capacity to grasp the complexity inherent in the social world, and social science research is inherently inconclusive. Thirdly, social science is most usable when it serves as a supplement to other ways of knowing. Fourth, the search for authoritative and definitive knowledge is illusory, and most positivist social scientists work within a framework that overestimates the contribution of their work for policy.

The Lindblum and Cohen approach to usability is essentially based on an attempt to grasp as a whole the nature of the research policy interplay and to deduce from that conception a set of propositions about potential usability. Theirs is a critical study of usability, which tries to challenge the axioms on which policy studies rest. They feel that to interview policy-makers and to accept their definition of usability would be a mistake, because policy-makers share a common assumption about the authoritativeness of social science knowledge.

The direct study of use

There are several different approaches to the direct empirical study of use. First is the case-study method. Robert Rich's study of unemployment insurance provides a good example.[5] Rich identified a single policy arena, and within it he selected a single substantive policy issue, the duration of benefits.

Rich defines bureaucrats as experts whose behaviour depends upon the acquisition, processing, and utilization of knowledge. He sees a latent conflict between the bureaucrat's imperative maximizing of organizational interest and his technical imperative as an expert to acquire scientific allegiance that informs this particular study of use and dictates the types of issues examined. Briefly, Rich studied in depth the following issues: the channels used to communicate information to officials; the level of use of information; the extent to which information is shared and/or kept secret by officials working in a common problem area; the extent to which officials within the same department communicate with each other and/or share information; and the extent to which officials from different departments communicate with each other and work on the particular issue of the duration of benefits.

The study interviewed twenty-eight federal officials who were responsible for decision-making or who devoted at least 10 per cent of their working time to dealing with the problem of the duration of benefits in unemployment insurance. Rich's basic methodology was to conduct direct interviews of informants on the specific subjects mentioned above. Such an in-depth case study rests on the assumption that the issue and the arena in which the issue is worked out significantly influence the findings. However, a comparative analysis of use across arenas and issues is premature because, as yet, we lack a clear conceptual framework of what the units of comparison are and where use is most or least likely to occur.

In contrast to the case-study method, the survey-research approach takes a random sample of decision-makers and directly asks them to cite examples, where research has influenced decisions they have taken. Karen Knorr's study of policy-makers in Vienna, and Caplan's study of federal decision-making in the United States are examples of this method.[6] These studies permit the investigators to examine the stage of the policy-processing at which research enters, the kind of information used, and the quality of the study cited. A major conclusion is that knowledge is used in a variety of ways—instrumentally, as a means toward solving a problem, or more broadly, as a source of insight for understanding or interpreting problems. Thus, they help clarify the interpretive and instrumental uses of knowledge.

A third type of study examines research utilization as only incidental to a broader case-study of the development of policy. The National Academy of Science, for example, carried out a study of the policy-formation process.[7] The Academy identified five components in the policy-formation process: contextual conditions (socio-economic, political, and cultural conditions in society); principles and ideas as they are represented or promoted by various individual leaders; politics (including legislative, bureaucratic, and interest-group politics); research and analysis; and the media as they represent public information and understanding. This kind of study permits the exploration of the relative importance of research and analysis as a component of a broader decision-making process. It also allows comparisons of the ways in which knowledge is used for decision-making by assuming that pragmatic areas shape the policy process.

A fourth approach to the direct empirical study of use identifies different types of knowledge and examines their individual contributions in a field of action. This approach attempts to examine knowledge in a decision-making context, but the critical variable is neither the decision-maker, the policy process, nor the comparison across arenas but the nature of the knowledge itself. A two-year collaborative research programme between the Massachusetts Institute of Technology (MIT) and the Centre de la Recherche Scientifique (CNRS), in Paris, on science and decision-making provides an example of this approach.[8] The case-study, carried out in the field of health, focused on the problem of tobacco-smoking, its effects on health, and the issues surrounding the introduction of policies designed to alter the behaviour of smokers and the toxicity of tobacco by the tobacco industry. The research examined three types of information: medical evidence, economic evidence, and anthropological or sociological evidence. Medical evidence came from retrospective aeteological studies of smokers with control groups of non-smokers designed to determine the link between cancer and smoking. Economic evidence came from information on the costs of smoking to society and to the individuals in terms of sickness and mortality. The economic analysis had to address the question of the balance between the cost of sickness and death and the benefits of the income generated by the manufacture and sale of tobacco. The sociological evidence addressed the reasons why people smoke, on the assumption that understanding the causes of behaviour can contribute to the development of effective policies for changing it.

This kind of study permits a much more subtle answer to the question of the role of social science knowledge because the different types of knowledge raised different questions about the authoritativeness of the knowledge and an ethical issue surrounding the control of individual behaviour. The MIT–CNRS tobacco case-study revealed that the medical evidence was incontrovertible, the economic data inconclusive, and the sociological and cultural evidence ultimately decisive but presented questions of ethics and moral anguish. Because the ethical issues are so important it is worth quoting Lisle's analysis of the policy issue posed by sociological research.

The ultimate effectiveness of policy will turn on the public's response and whether or not deeply ingrained social and cultural behavior patterns and the pleasures associated with them will alter significantly once the risks attached thereto are made much more fully perceived. But this in turn rests on individuals' attitudes to life and death, hedonism or pleasure versus asceticism, and more prosaically to their 'time preference', to their relative appreciation of the future (their life expectancy) as against the present, an appreciation which itself tends to change with age but which is nevertheless largely the product of the education received at home and at school and thus with the ethical values embodied in the educational process.

Another case-study approach tries to differentiate types of knowledge and stages of the policy-development process. The study of the Negative Income Tax in the United States, carried out by Hugh Heclo and myself, examines three types of knowledge—economic, administrative and sociological—and tries to show how different types of knowledge entered at different stages of policy-

making. Thus, economic knowledge dominated the initiation phase of policy, but administrative and sociological knowledge entered at the legislative stage. The different types of knowledge, however, by entering at different stages in the policy-making process created paralysis and inaction because each type of knowledge addressed different questions and had different insights into the nature of the process under review. Like the MIT–CNRS study of tobacco, the study of the Negative Income Tax showed how different types of knowledge must be differentiated because each makes a somewhat different contribution to the policy-formation process.

The diffusion of knowledge

Studies of knowledge diffusion are similar to the other studies of the use of knowledge, but they tend to use a very different time frame in examining the research/policy interplay. Diffusion studies tend to be historical studies of the evolution and the transmission of knowledge over time and across space. This broad time frame permits an assessment of a much more subtle process of diffusion.

Two studies of diffusion can be cited: the attempt of M. T. Manning and R. Rappoport to perform a retrospective analysis of the diffusion of knowledge about milieu therapy in mental health and Robert Cole's study of the diffusion of knowledge about worker participation in business enterprise.[9]

Manning and Rappoport examined the processes affecting the utilization and reception of new ideas in mental health, by tracing, over a twenty-five-year period, the reception of a book they had written entitled *Community as Doctor: New Perspectives on a Therapeutic Community*. Their study of diffusion examines the development of the initial research project in its social context to the publication of the book, the initial reactions of the community to the book, and the broader reaction of the academic and professional community at a later point. As the title of the study suggests, its main conclusion is that the reception of ideas depends upon a process through which ideas are first rejected before they are ultimately accepted.

Cole's study of inventive work structures

at the plant level examines the processes of the diffusion of social science knowledge across space and time. Methodologically he presents a rich and detailed account of actors, events, and processes. He does not operate within a hypothetical-deductive framework. Instead his task is interpretative. The story he tells in the preliminary report is not fixed or rigid, but evolves with insight. It can be summarized as follows. Drawing on the literature, Cole frames his narrative as a theory of diffusion stages, moving from motivation, to search, to discovery, to transmission, to decision, to implementation. Of course, staging events that occur simultaneously as well as sequentially poses awkward analytic problems, but it still provides insights about the processes of rejection or incorporation, which are often missed in survey studies of use and usability.

His analysis of these stages also poses troublesome questions about the reputable and disreputable uses of social science theory. For example, Cole observes that ideas are 'sanitized', or purged of their radical content at an early stage before they are incorporated into practice. Sanitization is a means of transforming ideas so that they are administratively acceptable in the new setting in which they are to develop.

Before sanitizing can take place, a prior stage must be passed through, that is, a consensus about the direction policy should take. In Japan, a managerial consensus and, in Sweden, a broad national consensus emerged that accepted worker participation in some aspects of decision-making at the plant level as an acceptable remedy for such problems as absenteeism and turnover. In addition the decision-makers created an institutional infrastructure to promote these innovative ideas.

Given a consensus in this context research evaluating the results of such innovations tends to be carried out by technical personnel in the firm that views the evaluation more like a demonstration project than a social experiment. A demonstration project selects examples of administrative, social and technically feasible aspects of the innovation to be circulated as examples of good practice. Unlike an experiment it is less concerned with measuring impacts in a controlled setting.

By contrast, no consensus prevailed in the United States. Only a modest and unstable infrastructure developed and research was carried by

outsiders with a strong emphasis on objectivism and measurement. For every dollar spent on the innovation, three dollars were spent on evaluation. But the search for the disinterested truth as to whether the innovations worked or failed seemed to threaten the very consensus it hoped to inspire. Paradoxically this attention to science in quest of truth was accompanied with proprietary knowledge used by consultants entrepreneurially to promote the 'sale' of the innovation for profit. By calling attention to the way theory is purged and redefined, by focusing of the consensus as precondition to diffusion and measurement as a threat to consensus, Cole provides us with subtle, reflective analysis of the interplay between inquiry and action.

The two diffusion studies differ methodologically as well as in the insights they offer. The first study relies largely on the reception of ideas as they appear in academic journals and the reception as experienced by the authors. The second study relies on detailed, in-depth interviews, which are informed by an historical and cross-national perspective.

A challenge to the study
of utilization

All these various studies of usability, use, and diffusion share the assumptions reviewed in the beginning of this essay, which in varying degrees accept a dichotomy between the knowing and the acting person and take as a premise that knowledge informs action. In the concluding section of this essay I want to review a study of the interplay between research and policy which proceeds under a very different assumption about the nature of the interplay between knowing and acting. The critical assumption in this approach is that concepts, ideas, and knowledge have no meaning independent of their use. Hence the task of research is to uncover the uses and interests that are served by knowledge rather than the other way around. This approach can be studied methodologically from two perspectives: the overt uses of knowledge and action and their latent uses. Each will be reviewed in turn.

Gunnar Myrdal is perhaps the most articulate spokesman for the general argument I have been developing. In a detailed review of the concept of the utilization of labour he demonstrates the close connection between ideas and their practical implication. Myrdal argues that

> the study of the functional relationship between policy and the utilization of the labor force . . . cannot be assisted by the use of the concept of 'underemployment' in general allowed to be 'objectively' established in relation merely to the facts and perhaps even measured in advance of any consideration of policy.[10]

Myrdal is essentially arguing that one cannot study the facts of underemployment without having a clear understanding of the policy implications to which the concept leads. In other words, there are no facts about underemployment and unemployment that are independent of the policy considerations that inform them. Hence, all studies that use these analytic concepts and attempt empirically to measure the extent to which they take place have an implicit policy reference because the meaning of the concept is derived from the practical policy significance. To put it another way, the analytic concepts are themselves policy concepts and are derived from a coherent conception of the policies behind them.

Perhaps the clearest example of Myrdal's point is the study by Joan Robinson in 1936 on disguised unemployment.[11] Essentially, she argued that workers who lost their jobs were forced to accept inferior employment. These workers were pushed down to less productive and less remunerative jobs in order to support their families. Disguised unemployment was essentially a mismatch between the level of skill and the occupational position that workers held during the Depression. In the framework of Robinson's argument, personal misery and economic inefficiency went hand in hand. The policy solution lay in policy analysis. The way to reduce personal economic misery was by making the economic system more productive. The analytic concept was wedded to the policy reference.

However, in the modern welfare state the elaborate system of compensatory claims against government makes it possible to replace income when there is a loss of work. We can no longer easily translate personal misery into economic inefficiency. Modern industrial societies can operate efficiently because they have a stock of low-paid workers (e.g., blacks, women, migrants) who will accept low wages and job insecurity. This secondary labour market enables the economy to adapt to economic fluctuations and to provide high wages and job security to most workers. Some theorists have argued that it is the structure of the labour market rather than its productivity that determines the pattern of underemployment and personal hardship. According to this argument two new measures are needed if we are to preserve the natural link between evidence and action. One is a measure of economic hardship that points to the policy implications relieving distress by income support programmes; the second is a direct measure of market inefficiency. The failure to recognize the close link among theory, evidence and policy produces only intellectual confusion.

This approach to the study of the research policy interplay requires an altogether different methodology because it proceeds from a different starting assumption than the earlier studies. The studies we have reviewed focused primarily on the gathering of empirical evidence for later utilization by policy. This is, of course, consistent with the first position proposition that positive knowledge is grounded in empirical evidence about the world of facts. A now generally accepted proposition is that factual knowledge is based on definitions, rules of logic, and theory. Thus the analytic and the theoretical cannot be divorced from the empirical.[12] The methodology for the study of use we are now reviewing is based on the position that theory itself cannot be divorced from practice or policy and is simply another expression of it. The study of utilization seeks to elucidate the interplay between theory and policy because they provide the framework in which facts are gathered. The challenge is not linking research to policy but uncovering the latent policies which organize the empirical research carried out by social science. Or, to put the matter in other terms, we need to discover a method for the 'doing of understanding'. This may require not only the translation of theory into practice, but also the study of theory by the practitioner.

Research on study of utilization seen from this perspective is not plentiful. Lisa Peattie and I have written an essay that tries to explicate this interplay in the study of poverty research in the United States.[13] That review shows how a policy commitment to income distribution rather than the redistribution of jobs served as the starting premise of the work of the Poverty Research Institute at the University of Wisconsin, and influenced their analysis. In beginning with a policy decision, the designers of a programme face problems. In this case, the critical design question facing government was how to create a system of redistributing income to relieve poverty without allowing it to conflict with other values held by society, in particular, the incentive to work. The Poverty Research Institute launched a ten-year programme of research to solve the design problem for which the policy conclusion was already established. It was only when the policy position was challenged by advocates who believed in an alternative policy framework, namely job creation,

that the normative perspective of the research carried out by the Poverty Research Institute became evident.

In summary, then, this essay has reviewed the various methods for the study of the research/policy interplay: usability, use, and diffusion. I argued that these studies have developed a methodology based on an assumption that knowledge precedes action. I am proposing an alternative approach based on the assumption that every form of knowledge is embedded in a latent or implicit form of action and the task of inquiry is to identify and isolate and criticize the nature of the knowledge implicit in the action we take.

Notes

[1] J. P. Roos, 'Welfare State and Social Policy: A Study in Policy Science', *Commentationes Scientiarum Socialium*, Helsinki, The Finnish Scientific Society, 1973, p. 212–25.

[2] *Papers of Robert Redfield*, Vol. 11, Chicago, Ill., The University of Chicago Press, p. 193.

[3] Carol H. Weiss, 'The Challenge of Social Research to Decision Making', in Carol H. Weiss (ed.), *Using Social Research in Public Policy Making*, p. 213, Lexington, Mass., Lexington Books, 1977.

[4] Charles A. Lindblum and David K. Cohen, *Usable Knowledge: Social Science and Social Problem Solving*, New Haven, Yale University Press, 1979.

[5] Robert S. Rich, 'Translating Research into Policy: Can Evaluation be Used for Policy Action?' Paper presented at the American-German Workshop on Evaluation Research; the Free University of Berlin, Federal Republic of Germany, June 1979, p. 23. (Mimeo.)

[6] Karen D. Knorr, 'Policymakers' Use of Social Science Knowledge: Symbolic or Instrumental', in Carol H. Weiss, op. cit.; Nathan Caplan, A. Morrison, and R. J. Stambugh, *The Use of Social Science Knowledge in Policy Decisions at the National Level*, Ann Arbor, Mich., Institute for Social Research, University of Michigan, 1975.

[7] *Evaluating Federal Support for Policy Research: The Committee on Evaluation of Policy Research, Assembly of Behavioral and Social Science, National Research Council*, Washington, D.C., The National Academy of Science, 1979.

[8] Edmund Lisle, 'Politics, Science and Science Policy: The Case of the Social Sciences'. Lecture given at the London School of Economics and Political Science, February 1979. (Mimeo.)

[9] M. T. Manning and R. Rappoport, 'Rejection and Reincorporation: Case Study in Social Research Utilization', *Social Science and Medicine*, Vol. 10, 1976, p. 459–68; Robert Cole, 'The Diffusion of New Work Structures in Japan, Sweden and the United States', n.d. (Mimeo.)

[10] Gunnar Myrdal, *Asia Drama*, Vol. 3, p. 2060, New York, Pantheon, 1968.

[11] Joan Robinson, 'Disguised Unemployment', *Economic Journal*, Vol. 46, No. 182, June 1936, p. 225–37.

[12] The recognition of this link has given rise to what has been described as the theory/fact dilemma: Choice among competing theories must depend upon fact, but facts derive their meaning from the prior choice of a theory that organizes and selects facts.

[13] Martin Rein and Lisa Peattie, 'Action Frames and Policy Research', 1979. (Mimeo.)

PART II

POLICY ISSUES AND SOCIAL INDICATORS

The maturation of the policy sciences in the 1960s led to new forms of disaggregating the mass of material generated in policy studies. In earlier decades the effort seemed to be on treating the area as a whole, without differentiation. The series of conflicts between federal and university policy perspectives in the 1960s made it painfully clear that it was no longer possible to treat the policy pie as a whole. The social indicators movement, along with rather ambitious and as yet unfulfilled plans for a Council of Social Advisors, eased the problem of disaggregation considerably, even if it did not entirely resolve it. This volume's division of policy issues into 12 segments is organically linked to the way in which the government itself, through its organizational and budgetary formations, has come to treat the policy arena. In certain cases, as with the LEAA, concentration on a specific area such as crime permitted a direct correlation between agency and policy. In other cases, such as foreign affairs, there remain a multiplicity of agencies, from the DoD to the DoS, that are responsible for policy-making. In addition, constitutional requirements dictate centralization of policy-making even if a plethora of agencies still exists and seems ever-expanding.

What is increasingly clear is that the areas mapped out in this volume represent a solid structure in which to place policy output. This disaggregation has its problems: For example, it is evident that overlaps still exist, not only among policy-making agencies but among specific policies recommended. This encourages problems of cross-cutting and cross-purpose decision-making. While *inter*agency and *intra*agency rivalries hardly began in the 1980s, they have become so cumbersome that they require a policy-making approach of their own. As a result, the Senate maintains a standing committee on governmental organization and reorganization. We seem to require policy commissions on how to make policy; a series of decisions are required to enable government at all levels to adjudicate claims between agencies charged with policy-making responsibilities.

But even if a higher level of esoteric behavior is invited by the multiplication of agencies and organizations involved in regulating, monitoring, and evaluating policy decisions, the rise of the social indicators movement has permitted a more rational intellectual environment in which the policy sciences can go forward. We have moved from the realm of the philosophic to the concrete, from speculative accounts of the broad purposes of policy to the practical integration of policy-making into the everyday needs of an advanced citizenry. By so doing, policy-making has managed to keep pace with the rise of interest group politics, a politics that is responsible for specific and measured efforts to obtain key changes through legislative relief, judicial review, and executive order.

Ultimately, the social indicators approach to policy issues has opened up the possibility of a more humanistic social science; it has done this by its keen appreciation of the need to move beyond raw statistics into refined quantitative *and* qualitative measures of success and failure. In a country nearly totally wired for television viewing, the number of sets in operation is of far lesser consequence than the character of viewing: the structure of station ownership, network allegiances and alliances, public information services, specialized broadcasting, ratings techniques, supplemental issues such as television games and education, and so on. In other words, disaggregation allows for more refined and sophisticated measures, and hence more refined and sophisticated forms of policy analysis and policy review. The task of this section is both to show the consequences of segmented policy-making and how to bring about a new—and more realistic—sense of the whole.

GOVERNMENT SUPPORT AND REGULATION

Policy-making has reached such an impressive level of importance in the federal decision-making process that policy itself has become disaggregated from other forms of governmental activity. The relationships among policy-making, regulatory mechanisms, evaluation procedures, monitoring devices, and their overall effectiveness has moved to front and center on the policy stage. We have reached a level of sophistication in which organizational forms not only embrace specific policy recommendations but are themselves largely determined by the policy context. In this sense, policy is less an abstract need to know than a series of specific guidelines informing all and sundry of the capacities and limits of agencies to guide human destinies.

With the enormously expanded role of federal agencies and administrations has come demand for monitoring and evaluation of programs. Nathan outlines the main tools of social science in this area: statistical and mathematical techniques, survey research, and case studies. Despite the complementarity which exists, it is Nathan's view that not enough social scientific studies deal with the obstacles to evaluating the effect of governmental grant-in-aid programs. He feels that too often self-interested agencies are in the best position to hire the necessary evaluation teams needed for the promulgation of further agency life. He suggests as an antidote an increased role for agencies such as the National Science Foundation in order to function as an arms-length agency in the monitoring and evaluation of programs, one that can insulate evaluator from evaluatee. The Katz paper on the Office of Science and Technology Policy shows how difficult such a policy proposal would be, since if the adviser serves as too rigid a policy analyst, instead of a servant of the agency, agencies will simply stop using such a person. He will be perceived not as an evaluator but one more budgeteer, an opponent. But if the adviser is too close to the agency, his effectiveness will also be diminished by the overextended advocate role. Policy-making in such governmental contexts are thus laden with tension-filled relations that can more easily be managed than truly overcome. A failure to do so means a failure to carve out a niche within the flow of forces in the political system itself. The study by Attewell and Gerstein on methadone treatment for heroin addicts led the authors to the conclusion that, far from government policy being relatively impotent in local settings, government domination is enormous. In fact, part of the reason for program failure is precisely the absence of decision-making latitude at the local level. Specifically, the struggle for funding, and the fear of losing funds, has the effect of a loss in autonomous decision-making and adoption of policies to local conditions, which in turn helps to explain policy failure more profoundly than the older notion of the local being cut adrift from the national in the policy process.

7

EVALUATING BROAD-GAUGED, MULTIPURPOSE GRANTS
Policy Issues

Richard P. Nathan

For the past eight years, a group of policy analysts at the Brookings Institution and the Woodrow Wilson School of Princeton University have been conducting field network evaluation studies of three major federal grant programs—general revenue sharing, community development block grants, and the public service employment component of CETA. All three are broad-gauged, multipurpose grants which distribute large amounts of money to hundreds, in some cases thousands, of states and local governmental jurisdictions. In the dynamic, pluralistic setting of contemporary American federalism, the job of obtaining systematic information about the uses and effects of these fiscal subventions is both important to policy makers and challenging to policy researchers. In addition to these three major studies of individual programs, we are also preparing a set of twelve uniformly organized case studies showing how all types of federal grants have affected major cities included in the Brookings-Princeton field network.

Many publications are available on the methods and findings of this research.[1] For each of the three field network studies, we have issued two books or reports, plus articles, and congressional testimony. The findings from these studies have contributed to the policy discussion of federal grant-in-aid issues and programs. This paper discusses some of the lessons learned from and implications of this research.

AUTHOR'S NOTE: This is a revised version of a paper prepared for the Committee on Taxation, Resources, and Economic Development, September 26, 1980, Cambridge, Massachusetts. The views expressed here are the sole responsibility of the author.

EVALUATING THE NEW FEDERALISM

American domestic policy is made in spurts. The spigot is opened widest in the early years of a new administration. A classic case is the outpouring of new social legislation following Lyndon Johnson's election in 1964. A similar spurt of new domestic laws came in the first term of the Nixon administration.

It is now commonplace for observers of the Great Society period to say that these programs failed to deal with the nation's social ills. Indeed, I believe—but can't document—that the role of social scientists in the Great Society period focused too much on policy formulation and not enough on the evaluation of programs once adopted.

I was a participant in the spurt of domestic policy-making in President Nixon's first term. When I returned to the Brookings Institution in 1974, I decided to work on the evaluation of these New Federalism programs. My attitude was that if they fell apart or worked badly, at least these conclusions would be reached with systematic information from social scientists as input.

How can this be? How can a participant in the policy process (presumably a person committed to what came out) evaluate the results? I would answer in several ways. One response is that social scientists should be serious about the second word of the name—science—and should exercise objectivity and rigor in conducting evaluation research. Second, I would point out that our studies, as it turned out, involved many participants (approximately 30 economists and political scientists from around the country for each study). Even the most extraordinary research manager would have been hard put deliberately to insert a bias into the findings of the social scientists who were part of these field networks.

The third reason I felt comfortable with the role of evaluator of programs I had helped design has to do with the way the evaluation research industry operates. Many flowers bloom. Other studies would give users an opportunity to compare and cross-check results. The existence of multiple studies, while sometimes overdone, helps to keep the evaluation industry honest and above-board.

Having decided to conduct evaluation studies of the New Federalism programs, I faced a difficult question: How do you do this? The New Federalism programs, as is true of many federal grants which existed prior to the New Federalism, have qualities that make them exceedingly difficult to evaluate.

The purposes of these programs are not always clear, a characteristic typical of American intergovernmental subventions. On the whole, the New Federalism involved broader and less conditional grants than the "categorical" grants of prior periods. This approach was designed to increase the recipient government's flexibility and opportunity for discretionary action. This was the *decentralization* aim of the New Federalism.

But other goals entered the picture. The more goals there are, the more difficult it is to say what a given program is supposed to do and to evaluate whether it actually did what it was supposed to do. Was general revenue-sharing supposed to enable recipient governments to cut taxes? Was it supposed to equalize aid among jurisdictions? Was it supposed to spur innovation?

The problem of competing goals is even more pronounced with the block grant components of the New Federalism. The community development block grant program is an example. Was decentralization its principal purpose? Was it supposed to aid the poor, the downtowns, the uptowns, the suburbs, the construction industry? Was it, as the law stated, supposed to give priority to achieving "spatial deconcentration?"

These goals are not only broad but frequently shifting. Such qualities present both problems and opportunities. The problem is deciding what to evaluate. The opportunity is that in such a setting evaluators can evaluate whatever they want. Hence, there is always the opportunity, often subtle and not recognized as such, for the evaluator—or worse yet, for the government agency paying his or her bills—to set up the design in a way that biases the research.

This is by no means the only obstacle to the evaluation of broad-gauged, multipurpose subventions. There is also the problem of "universality." Every jurisdiction that has certain specified statistical characteristics receives a grant under these programs. There is no opportunity to select a comparison group of similar jurisdictions to determine the difference a grant made.

The very nature of our intergovernmental system causes further difficulties. So many different jurisdictions receive revenue sharing and block grants that the "treatment" (that is, what recipients do with the money) is highly varied.

Another barrier to evaluation research on federal grants warrants mention. The grants themselves are often relatively small—that is, small in relation to what state and local governments spend in the aided functional area. We are often looking at a thin margin of federal aid. This, too, complicates our task.

There is, finally, the issue of "contamination," applying in this case to the individual recipients of services under grant-in-aid programs. Here, the problem is the possibility that a supposedly unaided control or comparison group of individual recipients under a given program was aided under a different but similar program. Let me illustrate with the CETA programs. Efforts have been made—for example, using Current Population Survey data—to construct a comparison group of persons eligible for various CETA-funded employment and training services. But how do we know that the persons in these groups were not aided under another program just like, or very similar to, the CETA program? There are a number of such programs that help low-income persons through local job creation, training, and special school programs.

We have, then, five problems. First, the grant-in-aid programs have multiple and sometimes conflicting objectives, and it is not easy to decide what to evaluate. Second, we cannot study control jurisdictions because under formula systems all similarly situated jurisdictions receive funds. Third is the problem of pluralism; different governments use federal aid in very different ways. Fourth is the problem of marginality; federal grants often are small relative to what is spent for the aided functional area or program. Fifth is the contamination problem, which makes it difficult, even with ingenuity, to obtain or construct an unaided comparison group of individual program recipients.

There are other complications, too, but I think this list is long enough to get us started. In this diverse and constantly changing political and administrative environment, how does the social scientist get a handle on whether "grant A" brings about different results than "grant B" or no grant at all?

Since getting into this area of research, I have been approached by various certified experts on research design with patented remedies to overcome these and other problems. Consider one example: What you can do, I am told, is to recognize all of this messiness and instead of evaluating "programs" evaluate "projects." That is, go out and find jurisdictions that do the same things under a particular grant and compare them with jurisdictions that do other things. I'm not sure why anyone would want to do this, but one thing I do know is that, while it may sound nice in a textbook, it would be exceedingly difficult to execute in the field.

Words are just that—words. Recipient jurisdictions draw up elaborate plans to satisfy federal officials. But what goes on in a program can be very different from what is on paper. Even if a jurisdiction tells you it is going to do A, it may in fact do B, or it may shift to B midway in the program. What looks even semiorderly from Washington or the regional office, we have learned from hard experience, frequently is a very different animal out in the corral.

Despite these problems, if social science is to be "relevant," we have to go after the hard questions that are important to policy makers. Does it make a difference that we now have revenue sharing, that the grant system was changed to provide block grants for community development or employment and training services, or whatever?

It is not easy, furthermore, to define "making a difference." Are we interested in whether grant A changed the way the recipient governmental jurisdictions do their business or changed the business they do? Or should we focus on whether grant A made a difference to the man or woman who got a public service job, or to the homeowner who got a housing rehab loan under CDBG, or to the taxpayer who felt better because the general revenue-sharing program cut his property tax bill?

THE TOOLS OF SOCIAL SCIENCE

Social scientists have three major types of tools for evaluating grant programs. First are statistical and mathematical techniques. With these we can construct models of how the world would look without grant A. We can then say something about how the real world—the world with grant A—compares with the model. But the statistics are weak and limited. They are collected infrequently. Often they are not available for the units of analysis we want to work with. And the regression techniques applied involve many definitions that require assumptions that, to say the least, are very difficult to make and often are not sufficiently well understood or accepted by the users of a program evaluation study.

The second tool is survey instruments. We can go out and ask people: "Did grant A make a difference?" But who do we ask and how do we ask them? Suppose we ask officials of the recipient governments. Shouldn't we expect the respondents to give us back chapter and verse of what the law says, or what they think we want to hear, or what they want to tell us (whether true or not)? What if we go out and ask the final recipients: "What do you think of CDBG or CETA?" No matter how we spell it, the man in the rehab house or the woman in a CETA job is often unlikely to have the foggiest idea of what we are talking about.

The third instrument available is the case study approach. We can have smart people look closely at specific cases. But no matter how smart a person is, he or she can study only so many cases. And if different people study different cases, they are likely to do so in different ways. So you don't have comparability.

To recapitulate, we have now looked at problems in evaluating multi-purpose formula grants-in-aid that distribute funds widely. We have looked briefly at the instruments that can be used to evaluate these grants and the kinds of problems involved in using three types of instruments. It has also been asserted that the game is worth the candle—that policy makers want to have, and need to have, answers to the question of whether a given program made a difference, and, if so, what kind of difference.

FIELD NETWORK EVALUATION RESEARCH

The emphasis of our research has been on *the intergovernmental effects* of New Federalism and other broad-gauged grants—that is, their effects on the recipient governmental jurisdictions. Our orientation is both *analytical* and *descriptive.* We are interested in the effects of large and important grant programs in three main areas: (1) on the finances of the recipient jurisdictions, (2) on the program mix and program content of the aided activities, and (3) on the political processes and system for determining their allocation and specific program use.

Our view from the outset has been that formal survey research is not a good instrument for evaluating these types of effects of grant programs. It is our view, furthermore, that the other two approaches mentioned—econometric and case studies—work best if they are used together. This is the essence of the approach urged in this paper. It is the idea of the *complementarity* of the econometric and case study research methods. We have used such a tandem approach in one of our studies, the general revenue-sharing study.[2] We are currently in the process of using this dual approach in another, the study of the CETA public service jobs program. I know of several other cases where parallel studies, using both the econometric and field network approach, are underway.

Note that in the last sentence I changed the reference from "case studies" to "field network approach." There is a difference.

The way we have adapted the case study approach at Brookings and Princeton is not unique, but it is noteworthy because we have used this approach on an extensive scale. What we have done is to build networks of indigenous field researchers, along with a central management group to work with the researchers so that they use a common approach to a common set of questions. The field researchers (called "associates") *do* the analysis. They make *their* assessments of the effects of a given grant. The central group then compiles these assessments—with the close involvement of the field associates—into a report that cuts across a representative sample of recipient jurisdictions.

Two points in the above paragraph need to be elaborated. First, I used the word *"effects"* in referring to what is studied. The term is important. Because the objectives of grant programs, especially broad-gauged programs, are diverse, frequently shifting, and sometimes inconsistent, we cannot precisely define the aims of a particular program. Instead, we have concentrated on studying their effects. The second point introduced in the paragraph above has to do with the samples used for these studies. We have chosen *"representative"* samples. These samples of 40 to 60 recipient jurisdictions are much larger than can be included using the comparative case study approach. They are not random samples.

The main reasons for using representative samples have to do with cost and logistics. To have a manageable research group, in many cases we need to ask an associate to report on more than one field site. In addition, in order to make sure that the associates are familiar with the field sites and have access to the best sources of data about them, we have often organized the field sites in clusters. Such a cluster might, for example, include three or four rural jurisdictions close to a university research center, a central city and one or two of its suburban jurisdictions, or a state capital and a nearby small city. It would not be possible to do this with a random sample.

If the research design for one of the field network evaluation studies had focused on a dominant governmental type, we might have been able to use a random sample. Our experience suggests that locating competent field researchers on this basis would be possible if such a study focused on large governmental jurisdictions—for example, cities above 50,000 population. The tradeoff here is between a random sample focused on one jurisdictional type and a larger stratified sample that permits researchers to compare various types and groups of recipient jurisdictions—central cities and suburbs, large cities and small ones, cities and counties, rich and poor communities.

Yet, even a random sample of the larger units—for example, a sample of the 1072 cities and counties above 50,000 population—would fail to take into account adequately the layering of some of these units (cities within counties) and the functions of state governments and various special districts, township governments, and small municipal governments. In the combined field and statistical study of the general revenue-sharing program cited earlier, Charles F. Adams, Jr. and Dan Crippen conducted an econometric analysis of the fiscal impact of revenue-sharing using a sample of 1424 local units. They compared these findings with those from the field network research and found a close fit between the results of the two studies. The size of their statistical sample was determined by the availability of time-series data from the Bureau of the Census. We could have used a smaller random sample of local units, but it still would have been too large in relation to the resources available for a monitoring study.

Not everyone will agree, but I believe that local governmental units in America are too diverse and too numerous to warrant using a random sample in a field network evaluation study of the intergovernmental effects of major federal grant programs.

Field network research is longitudinal. We have made three rounds of field observations on revenue sharing. There will be four each for the CDBG and CETA job studies. Although the basic research design has not changed, we have changed the emphasis of our reports on these programs to reflect current issues and the specific stage of a particular program—just starting, changing, or resulting in actual expenditures. For example, in the CDBG study, the first report concentrated on what was being planned and how it was being planned; the second report concentrated on whether the program had a decentralization effect; the third report concentrated on whether CDBG funds were being "targeted" on the poor within jurisdictions; and the fourth report will emphasize how CDBG money actually has been spent (program implementation).

Associates in a field network study submit a completed field research "Reporting Format" for each round of field research. These reports include extensive specific data which associates use to reach and justify their analytical findings.[3]

IMPACT ISSUES

From a methodological point of view, the most interesting issues we have dealt with in the field network evaluation studies are *impact* issues: Did jurisdictions that received revenue-sharing money spend more, or did they substitute these funds for locally raised money they would have spent anyway and cut back their own revenue? Did the CETA jobs program result in the creation of new jobs, or did it result in displacement—that is, the substitution of CETA funds for funds that would have been paid to workers who would have been hired anyway?

These are tough, yet very important, questions. They have been studied with both the field network and econometric approaches. In our research, these issues are being studied with the two approaches married to each other. May they live happily together.

SYNTHESIS

Think of it this way. In evaluating a program that is operating everywhere, we must find a way to study the counterfactual state. We need to determine what the world would be like if the program were not operating. There are two ways to do this: the econometric approach and the field network approach. Both build a model of what would have happened if the program did not exist and then compare that model to the real world in which the program does exist. The econometric approach does this modeling in a computer with a system of equations. In constructing these equations, the researcher must make judgements about economic conditions, program conditions, administrative structures, and the like. The field research associate in a field network study does this modeling in his head, also making many assumptions. The field researcher can use more variables and can define and manipulate them in more ways. The human brain is a powerful instrument. But there is a catch. The computer model can be replicated. The process (no matter how bad it is) can be specified for other researchers to review. Although I believe that the human equations can deal more effectively with the tremendous diversity and complexity of American federalism, they cannot be specified in replicable form. So, what should we do? *We should do both.*

We should do field network evaluation studies, for one thing, because they can be conducted while a new program gets underway. Field researchers can begin when a new program gets started, whereas the statistics needed for econometric modeling often lag years behind the starting date of a new program.

But there is a more important reason for doing both. We should do both because they can *reinforce* each other. Information and insights gained from a field network evaluation study can be used to develop and refine the equations for manipulating the program and census data that go into an econometric evaluation of the impact of a particular grant-in-aid program. With the aid of field network research, it can produce better and more refined answers than econometric research by itself.

WHY DO EVALUATION RESEARCH?

There are two more issues I want to deal with in this paper. Why should we do grant-in-aid evaluations? If we do them, how should they be organized and funded?

On the first issue, useful lessons can be learned by comparing practices in different countries. In a study recently initiated by the Woodrow Wilson School on comparative policy research, we have found that evaluation research is much less common and much less public in Europe than in the United States. When such studies are done in European countries, they are often done for the internal use of agency officials who hold the results closely.

By contrast, the combined effect of the existence of privately funded evaluations in the United States with the Freedom of Information Act applying to publicly funded studies produces a veritable cacophony of commentary on the merits and demerits of public programs. Some observers believe we have too much evaluation research in the United States and that in some situations this impairs our ability to get things done in the domestic public sector.

My view as a practitioner of the art and science of program evaluation is the one you would expect. I do not think there are enough thoughtful studies by social scientists who do their best to deal with the kinds of obstacles described in this paper that must be overcome in sensibly evaluating the effects of intergovernmental grant-in-aid programs in the fluid environment of American federalism. It may not be orderly or beautiful to behold, but the pluralism of our political system is a fact to be reckoned with. If everybody can play government and there are lots of levels and players, then we had better do as much as we can to provide systematic, well-developed information about the effects of intergovernmental programs and actions.

A PROPOSAL FOR THE JOINT SPONSORSHIP
OF SOME EVALUATION STUDIES

This brings me to the final subject of this paper: Who should do evaluation studies? One of our field network studies (the general revenue-sharing study) was funded by the Ford Foundation. The other two, plus the 12-city case study research, have been funded by U.S. government agencies. We have had good relations with the government agencies that have funded our studies. This has happened in no small part because, in keeping with Brookings policy, we have insisted on explicit language in our contracts that gives us independence in designing and executing these studies and in presenting and interpreting our findings.

Despite our good experience with these contract provisions, and taking into account the experience of other evaluation researchers, I believe that consideration should be given to alternate ways to organize and conduct some government-funded evaluation studies.

The evaluation of multi-billion-dollar government programs is expensive. The result often is that the only funding source big enough and interested enough to pay for an evaluation study is the government agency responsible for administering the program to be evaluated. And, to phrase a point badly, their interest is not always disinterest. No matter how scholarly the research managers in a given agency may be (and some have very high standards), bias can enter, or be thought to have entered, the relationship between agencies that sponsor and fund research on their own programs and the evaluation researchers who conduct such studies. This can happen in many ways that are not easily recognized or dealt with.

These difficulties are made more serious by the fact that in recent years we have seen the growth of large contract-research houses. They have to think about the future—a future in which they continue to get contracts.

If we add back into this picture the problems and issues discussed earlier that have to be dealt with in doing evaluation research on broad-gauged, multipurpose grant programs, what we have is a situation in which problems relating to the design and execution of evaluation studies may arise, even with the best of intentions.

There are, I believe, relatively simple administrative devices that could be adopted to avoid these problems. I can envision a system in which a government agency in a neutral position would play an intermediary role in contracting for certain evaluation studies. A good candidate for this role would be the National Science Foundation. The NSF, or some similar organization, might be given a charter to cosponsor evaluation studies, along with an appropriate amount of funding to do this. An agency that administers a program would specify the type of evaluation that is needed and provide a share of the money to conduct such a study. The NSF, or whatever intermediary agency is chosen, would then work with the program agency in preparing a "Request for Proposals" and would provide the rest of the funds required. Either on its own or through a special panel, the NSF (or another chosen agency) would then oversee the research. Along with officials of the program agency, it would receive and review the reports on all studies conducted on this basis.

The essential aim of this proposal is to create a mechanism which, under certain circumstances, can be used to insulate the evalua*tor* from the evalua*tee*. Not all evaluation studies would need to be undertaken through such a joint sponsorship. Such a mechanism might, for example, be limited to impact studies or very large studies. It could be made optional to the program administering agency.

Regardless of the specifications, a system of this general character would serve a number of major purposes. It would (1) help to advance the art and science of evaluation, (2) stimulate efforts to develop new and better evaluation research designs and techniques, (3) help to identify the most talented evaluation researchers, and (4) give the public greater confidence in the results of evaluation studies.

NOTES

1. See the Appendix for a list of some of these publications.

2. See Charles F. Adams, Jr. and Dan Crippen, "The Fiscal Impact of Revenue Sharing on Local Governments," Office of Revenue Sharing, U.S. Department of the Treasury, May 1978.

3. Analytical findings and the supporting data are reviewed with the central staff; however, as noted earlier, a field associate's analytical findings are not changed without the associate's involvement and concurrence.

APPENDIX:
SELECTED BOOKS AND PAPERS

Books and Reports

Nathan, Richard P., Allen D. Manvel, Susannah E. Calkins, and Associates, *Monitoring Revenue Sharing.* Washington, DC: Brookings Institution, 1975.
_____ Charles F. Adams, Jr., and Associates *Revenue Sharing: The Second Round.* Washington, DC: Brookings Institution, 1977.
_____ Paul R. Dommel, Sarah F. Liebschutz, and Milton D. Morris, *Block Grants for Community Development.* (Prepared under contract with the Department of Housing and Urban Development, Office of Policy Development and Research.) Washington, DC: Government Printing Office, 1977.
Dommel, Paul R., Richard P. Nathan, Sarah F. Liebschutz, and Margaret T. Wrightson, *Decentralizing Community Development.* (Prepared under contract with the Department of Housing and Urban Development, Office of Policy Development and Research.) Washington, DC: Government Printing Office, June 1978.
Dommel, Paul R., and Jacob M. Jaffe, *Report on the Allocation of Community Development Funds to Small Cities.* (Prepared under contract with the Department of Housing and Urban Development, Office of Policy Development and Research.) Washington, DC: Government Printing Office, November 1978.
Nathan, Richard P., Robert F. Cook, Richard Long, and Janet Galchick, Job Creation Through Public Service Employment, Volume 2. *Monitoring the Public Service Employment Program,* An Interim Report to the Congress. Washington, DC: National Commission for Manpower Policy, March 1978.

_____ Robert F. Cook, V. Lane Rawlins, Janet M. Galchick, and Associates, *Monitoring the Public Service Employment Program: The Second Round.* Washington, DC: National Commission for Manpower Policy, Special Report No. 32, March 1979.

Articles and Papers

Manvel, Allen D., "The Fiscal Impact of Revenue Sharing." *The Annals,* Vol. 419 (May 1975).

Nathan, Richard P., Paul R. Dommel, Sarah F. Liebschutz, and Milton D. Morris, "Monitoring the Block Grant Program for Community Development." *Political Science Quarterly,* Vol. 92, No. 2 (Summer 1977).

_____ and Paul R. Dommel, "Federal-Local Relations Under Block Grants." *Political Science Quarterly,* Vol. 93, No. 3 (Fall 1978).

Adams, Charles F., Jr. and Dan Crippen, "The Fiscal Impact of Revenue Sharing on Local Governments." Office of Revenue Sharing, U.S. Department of the Treasury, May 1978.

Cook, Robert F., V. Lane Rawlins, "Job Displacement under CETA Public Service Employment." American Statistical Assoc., *Business and Economic Statistic Section Proceedings,* 1978.

Cook, Robert F. and V. Lane Rawlins, "Local and National Objectives in Public Service Employment." Industrial Relations Research Association, *Proceedings of the Thirty-Second Annual Meeting,* December 1979, Atlanta.

Nathan, Richard P., "Public-Service Employment," in Employing the Unemployed, Eli Ginzberg (ed). New York: Basic Books, 1980.

Federal Aid Case Studies

Hall, John Stuart, *The Impact of Federal Aid on the City of Phoenix.* Case Studies of the Impact of Federal Aid on Major Cities, No. 3. Washington, DC: U.S. Department of Labor, 1980.

Liebschutz, Sarah F., *The Impact of Federal Aid on the City of Rochester.* Case Studies of the Impact of Federal Aid on Major Cities, No. 5. Washington, DC: U.S. Department of Labor, 1980.

MacManus, Susan A., *The Impact of Federal Aid on the City of Houston.* Case Studies of the Impact of Federal Aid on Major Cities, No. 2. Washington, DC: U.S. Department of Labor, 1980.

Orlebeke, Charles J., *The Impact of Federal Grants on the City of Chicago.* Case Studies of the Impact of Federal Aid on Major Cities, No. 6. Washington, DC: U.S. Department of Labor, 1980.

Schmandt, Henry J., George D. Wendel, and E. Allan Tomey, *The Impact of Federal Aid on the City of St. Louis.* Case Studies of the Impact of Federal Aid on Major Cities, No. 1. Washington, DC: U.S. Department of Labor, 1979.

Steib, Steve B. and R. Lynn Rittenoure, *The Impact of Federal Aid on the City of Tulsa.* Case Studies of the Impact of Federal Aid on Major Cities, No. 4. Washington, DC: U.S. Department of Labor, 1980.

8

ORGANIZATIONAL STRUCTURE AND
ADVISORY EFFECTIVENESS
The Office of Science and Technology Policy

James Everett Katz

The increasingly complex, technological and interrelated nature of our society, as well as of the problems confronting it, has resulted in an ever-growing emphasis on science and technology as instruments for problem analysis and resolution.[1] This is reflected by the proliferating scientific advisory staffs at the local, state, national, and international levels.

Because of this important role assigned to scientific and technological advice at most levels of government, one important aspect to consider is the structural aspect of advisory mechanisms with an eye to the conditions which enhance the effectiveness of scientific advice. This paper considers the structural aspects of one major advisory group, the United States' highest science policy office, the Office of Science and Technology Policy (OSTP), a part of the Executive Office of the President (EOP). The major objectives of the OSTP are (1) to advise the President, the National Security Council, the Domestic Policy Staff (DPS), and other EOP units on matters concerning science and technology; (2) to assist the Office of Management and Budget (OMB) with reviews of proposed budgets for Federal R&D programs; (3) to provide general leadership and coordination of the Federal R&D programs; (4) to promote a stronger partnership between Federal research funders, State and local governments and the scientific community; and (5) to provide Executive branch perspectives regarding science and technology policy to the Congress.[2]

The Presidential offices for science and technology had been reestablished and strengthened under the Ford Administration, which also lobbied for the passage of the National Science and Technology Policy, Organization and Priorities Act of

James Everett Katz (b. 1948), author of Presidential Politics and Science Policy *(1978), is Research Associate Professor in the Department of Social Sciences, Clarkson College, Potsdam, New York. He previously held research fellowships at the Center for Science and International Affairs, Kennedy School of Government, Harvard, and at the Center for Policy Alternatives, Massachusetts Institute of Technology; and has taught at Indiana University and William Paterson College. The author thanks W. O. Baker, Harvey Brooks, Donald Hornig, Jürgen Schmandt, Eugene Skolnikoff, and Richard Garwin for their helpful comments.*

Reprinted with permission from *Technology in Society,* Vol. 2, James Everett Katz, "Organizational Structure and Advisory Effectiveness: The Office of Science and Technology Policy," copyright © 1980, Pergamon Press, Ltd.

1976 (P.L. 94-282). Presidential Science and Technology Adviser H. Guyford Stever made organizational and substantive contributions to the effectiveness of the Office of Science and Technology Policy (OSTP). Thus far in the Carter administration, Presidential Science Adviser Frank Press has acquired the confidence of the President and restored to the position some of the prestige lost during earlier administrations.

The OSTP itself has fared less well under the Carter Administration. The OSTP "has almost been completely destroyed," said one former science adviser. The Carter re-organization team had recommended the abolition of the science advisory mechanism in early 1977, but Carter and his staff were prevailed upon to save at least the OSTP's organizational essence, provided the OSTP's role was rigidly circumscribed. The President's Committee on Science and Technology was disbanded, however. While the OSTP did survive, it was in a greatly diminished role and subject to several limitations. The staff had to be very small (which would, it was anticipated, hamper its effectiveness) and was proscribed from undertaking policy initiatives without the express permission of the political staff. The OSTP was blocked from a pro-active role in defense, natural resources, and especially energy. The vision of a vigorous, politically significant science policy office was snuffed-out, largely because the President's top advisers recognized that many areas of science and technology were politically sensitive and hence should be handled at the political level. They wished to see no competing centers of influence arise in the White House that would dilute their control over these issues.

Congress and some leading elements of the scientific community have tried to have OSTP's role expanded in line with the original authorizing legislation; much criticism has been directed at the White House's handling of the OSTP and coordination of science policy.[3] However, few challenge directly the concept that since the OSTP is part of the President's staff, he has the right to arrange his staff however he wishes. Press has aligned himself solidly behind the President's position. Press said recently that the Science Adviser "must recognize that he is not in the White House as a lobbyist, or as a representative of a constituency. He is there as an assistant to the President, serving the President."[4]

Experience indicates that the science adviser must be one of the "President's men." Yet, having limited authority, resources and power to confront the vast Federal science and technology enterprise has created a series of operational and organizational quandaries for the Presidential Science Adviser and his staff.

A Major Dilemma

A major ongoing dilemma concerns the way to best use slender staff and resources to work on the highly-complex, diffuse and intractable problems the staff is called upon to analyze. The size of the White House staff was an early campaign target of Carter and he pledged to pare the White House staffs by 30%. (He only accomplished a 12% over-all reduction from the highest number during the Ford Administration.) This meant that the Congress's original plan for a large OSTP staff of about 40 did not materialize. Under administration pressure to demonstrate good faith, Press reduced his staff by 30%.

Many maintain that the OSTP full-time staff of 24 (which includes support and secretarial assistance) and the 16 people detailed from other government agencies is too small. The OSTP must prepare reports, participate in committee work and proffer science advice, and oversee the breadth and depth of Federal science and technology. Press himself has said, "If we had a larger staff, we probably could do things better," and that Carter "prefers to have small staffs. . .He's my boss. I have to do things his way."[5] While not questioning the ability of the specific OSTP detailed staff, it is a truism in government that when staff are detailed, whether to another agency, or for committee work, the people selected are not necessarily the best but are instead those available.

To conveniently cover the amorphous subject of science and technology, the OSTP is broken into three divisions. These areas are (with representative illustrations of work): (1) National Security, International and Space Affairs, dealing with such topics as the test ban treaty, East-West technology transfer, the MX and cruise missiles, UNCSTD, Antarctica policy, and space arms control; (2) Natural Resources and Commercial Services involved in evaluating earthquake and dam hazards, radioactive waste management, climate research as well as oceans, energy, mineral and mining policies; and (3) Human Resources, Social and Economic Services concerned with research policies for nutrition, bio-medicines, social science, and agriculture. It has also studied drug legislation and radiation standards. Combinations of OSTP staff members have also prepared special reports on issues in response to presidential requests (such as the construction of a sea-level canal in Central America) or in anticipation of future problems that will be confronting the President.

In addition to these activities, the OSTP director chairs the Federal Coordinating Council for Science, Engineering, and Technology (FCCSET) and the Intergovernmental Science, Engineering and Technology Advisory Panel (ISETAP). FCCSET operates as a sub-cabinet group addressing the Executive Branch in R&D-related affairs. ISETAP, while originally given wider functions, now, after 1978 Reorganization Plan No. 1, has the narrower role of advising the OMB on ways to have Federal technology better meet State and local government needs. Some flexibility is maintained since the OSTP director has a free hand in selecting the members of these groups. As worthwhile as these groups' activities are, they do take Press's time and absorb OSTP staff resources and effort.

All these Herculean labors could not possibly be accomplished by the small OSTP staff itself. On many issues the OSTP serves as the lead agency, taking responsibility for pulling together and chairing interagency panels to address the issue. In addition, the OSTP has attempted to develop a network of panels, advisers, and support staff to supplement its own meager staff. The OSTP has tapped outside resources to do much of the work instead of trying to develop staff resources in-house. Often the OSTP relies on the NSF as well as other governmental agencies for manpower, money, and administrative support. Frequently organizations completely outside the government are utilized to do the actual inquiries. The National Academy of Sciences (NAS), the National Research Council (NRC), the Committee for Scholarly Education, the American Physical Society, and several for-profit contractors are among the organizations tapped by the OSTP. In the future the OSTP hopes to expand the list of those undertaking OSTP work to include organizations such as the American Association for the Advancement of Science and the American Chemical Society.

Reliance on Outside Support

Relying on outside support to do the OSTP's work creates problems both for the contractor and the OSTP. The conflict over assigning public responsibilities to private organizations has periodically plagued the government. At times Congress and the Executive have expressed disapproval of this practice; at other times its advantages have been applauded. Thus, in 1962 the Bell report[6] pointed to a pernicious cycle through which the Federal government became increasingly dependent on non-governmental laboratories to conduct its own research. This was because the government itself was underwriting the raiding of manpower and ennervation of work in its own labs. At the same time it is generally recognized that Federal research organizations tend to become debilitated through bureaucratization and because the Federal researchers become isolated from the cutting edge of the research community.

An illustration of the farming-out process is the preparation of the five-year forecast and plan for science and technology as mandated by the law re-establishing the White House science offices. The preparation of this plan was detailed to the NSF, who, in turn, used the NAS to provide major inputs into the study. However, the acceptance of this assignment caused some problems for the NAS, both in terms of its standard operating procedure and its position of autonomy from governmental politics. (The NAS is a private organization established by an act of Congress during the Civil War to provide advice to the government.)

The first major problem revolved around the fact that the NAS was being requested to produce a confidential report for the government's own use. It was feared that the White House could be highly selective about the parts of the report it chose for inclusion in its own plan and that regardless of what was omitted the resulting work would have the quasi-NAS legitimacy. Thus the NAS might be lending its name to something it actually opposed. The NAS sought to avoid this dilemma by agreeing to publish and publicly release its own report. From this report the President and his staff assistants could accept or reject whatever they wanted in preparing the government position. This attempt to safeguard NAS autonomy has drawbacks and dangers of its own. The second problem is that the NAS could arrive at a plan different from that which the administration wanted. Contradictions between the two approaches could be seized upon by the media, Congress, or other watchdog groups and in turn cause political furor.

Of all the non-governmental organizations the NAS and the NRC have taken up the largest share of the work. Their assignments from OSTP have included an evaluation of the scientific exchange program with the Soviets and the drafting of an issue paper for the development of the national position paper to be submitted to UNCSTD. Professional societies representing specific disciplines have also been drawn upon. For example, the American Physical Society has received a contract to explore the future costs and likelihood of success of solar photovoltaic energy.

One OSTP strategy to defuse the problem of relying so heavily on private organizations is to diversify the sources of advice. By expanding the inputs to include the ACS, AAAS, and other organizations, the NAS and OSTP should be able to avoid much of the potential for criticism. To some extent, however, this conflict seems irresolvable given the present strictures on OSTP. Yet OSTP is outstanding among Presidential-level offices because it is the only one of the few offices with a regular outreach program to draw in experts from the private community.

The resources of OSTP have been spread even thinner as a result of its involvement with a growing user group—state (as part of its outreach and public involvement program, mandated by Congress) and local governments. The OSTP supports the Intergovernmental Science, Engineering and Technology Advisory Panel (ISETAP) composed of 19 state and local government officials, and the National Science Foundation and the OSTP directors. Meeting at least 10 times a year, ISETAP works with Federal, state and local governments to identify high priority problems at the state and local levels which science and technology can help resolve and to determine research issues associated with these problems that the Federal government needs to address. ISETAP is also developing recommendations for enhancing the utilization of research funding by state and local governments. There is some criticism that the OSTP is not wholehearted in its ISETAP role—that it is simply acting in response to Congressional pressure. The massive workloads combined with this high rate of dispersal of the tasks to various agencies and organizations has led to problems of coordination for the OSTP. It is difficult for the director and the second-rung assistant directors to know what is going on in each division and the information problem is magnified for those lower down in the hierarchy. In the past the lack of communication has led to inefficiency and overlapping responsibilities within OSTP.

Problems of Coordination

There are also problems with coordination between the OSTP and the other Executive Office of the President (EOP) staff, such as the Office of Management and Budget (OMB), the National Security Council (NSC), and the Domestic Policy Staff (DPS).

Coordination, obviously, is not a problem that can be solved once and then forgotten, but rather is a continuing process that needs constant adaptation to the developing situation. The need for flexibility in policy supervision is even more pronounced in a rapidly changing field such as R&D. There are a host of ways R&D can be divided among agencies—for example, basic research is concentrated in the NSF while applied research is largely conducted through the line agencies such as NASA, DOD, and HEW. Programs and disciplines, such as oceanography, energy, social science, biochemistry, and atmospherics, cross cut numerous agencies as well.

As part of their centralized responsibility for science policy, the OSTP and FCCSET must coordinate four different types of R&D management activities:

- Budgeting for R&D, including planning and analyses. Here there is a special need to review resource allocations in relationship to national goals and priorities. The advisers should be able to recognize opportunities and anticipate future needs in a timely manner.

- Comprehensiveness of R&D programs. This is necessary to reduce duplication and assure that there are no gaps between programs. It should be noted that in crucial areas, duplication tends to be encouraged in order to have several paths to the same problem. This is the case for fusion research.

- Cross functional policy-setting. These are issues which affect several agencies but are not within the bailiwick of any particular agency. Here, for example, are issues of patent policy and laboratory utilization.

- Implementation. Here OSTP coordination involves assuring that R&D performers are coupled to the ultimate users, and facilitating the delivery and utilization of federally created technology. Both the pull of users in the private or public sector and the push of the technology need to be considered.[7]

These four areas of coordination are characterized by two approaches to coordinating science and technology—horizontal and vertical.[8] Horizontal approaches use coordination among individuals of equal standing within their own agencies. This type of research coordination, usually not very dramatic in its activity or results constitutes the bulk of Federal science and technology coordination. A forum is provided to develop personal linkages and exchange information. Minor issues are resolved and low-level questions discussed, often on an informal basis. However, once larger issues are introduced, the games of bureaucratic politics and strategic maneuvering take place. Horizontal coordination is relatively easy where the stakes do not involve vital organizational interests, but when they do, this type of coordination is especially difficult to accomplish, since there is no hierarchical structure immediately available to which committee leaders can appeal against their peers. Horizontal coordination presents a sharp challenge to both committee leadership and the larger managerial organization in numerous ways. First, since the committees operate by consensus, any decisions tend to be at the lowest common denominator. The committee members may agree to particular outcomes or recommendations, but these are not necessarily meaningful results. Each member represents an agency which has its own vested interests and goals and hence avoids confronting issues or making decisions that will adversely affect the prerogatives of the represented agencies. One result is that only general or vague recommendations or decisions are arrived at. As a consequence, national programs involving interagency cooperation fail to develop in one lead agency through interagency coordination. Instead, agencies use the forum to legitimate what they are already doing.

A necessary condition for the effectiveness of these interagency committees is that policy-level personnel participate in them. These people tend to be the most important members, hence, the busiest, and consequently tend to progressively deputize attendance. These high-level policymakers delegate attendance to their subordinates who in turn send their subordinates until (regardless of the individual's specialization in the area in question) the representative will not have the authority to speak on policy changes or compromises his or her agency would be willing to make.

A horizontal coordinating body has no authority to implement its decisions. Only the operating agencies have implementation resources and powers. As a result interagency committees can decide, but not execute. If any agency or section of that agency disagrees with a policy decision, the committee cannot coerce the agency into the agreed-upon action. Similarly, when studies are performed there may be no recipient or specifically intended audience for the committee recommendations. Studies are produced, decoupled from anyone who would or could exercise authority to implement actions recommended.

A vicious cycle takes place in which the usefulness of the interagency committees is downgraded, which in turn leads to frequent absenteeism and delegation of alternates to attend meetings. This reduces the importance of the committee and so on. In sum, horizontal coordination is used most often, but tends to be effective only on issues that matter least. For the most vital issues, vertical coordination is necessary.

The Vertical Approach

The vertical approach to coordination means that the power and prestige of the President is directly or indirectly involved to secure the desired results. Here the most significant vertical coordinators are the OMB and the OSTP. The major vertical activities take place in the EOP, and often involve Presidential budget-making. Less frequent, but also influential, is intervention on the part of Presidential staff offices in bureaucratic operations. Effectiveness here is largely a function of association of the science staffs with either the budget process or with the President and his top operatives. The perceived lack of proximity with the President weakened the OST (Office of Science and Technology, OSTP's predecessor) during the Nixon administration; this reduced OST's ability to vertically coordinate agency operations.

This general situation is in marked contrast to agency reaction to the New Technological Opportunities Programs (NTOP). Unlike the usual lackadaisical reaction to OST initiated proposals, the direct request from the President to move on NTOP conveyed through the OST (prior to its replacement by a subsequent organized group) spurred the agencies to great action.[9] The main source of power for these staffs is not so much persuasiveness, or rationality as much as association with the President. This association can be either direct, as through personal contact with the President and Presidential directives, or derived from association with the budget process.

The American system relies heavily on the budget process to review the activities of the departments and this budget analysis enables issues of effectiveness in actual performance to be raised periodically for Presidential decision. While the creation of a Federal budget in no way assures that science and technology will be coordinated, it does give an opportunity to discuss and integrate R&D issues which crosscut the Federal agencies. The budget has the additional advantage of being an institutionalized tool to coordinate activity annually and routinely.

In this regard the OSTP's relationship with the OMB is extremely important, for the statutory authority of the OSTP in budget matters is sharply delimited. The OMB is the powerful budget agency of the President, and Science Adviser Press and his staff have gone to great lengths to keep an open and helpful relationship between the two agencies. Thus far the relationship seems to be mutually beneficial; laudatory remarks have been made by each group about the other. An example of this fruitful cooperation was a joint study in which the President commissioned Press and the Deputy Director of the OMB to do an in-depth cross-functional study of Federal research. The study panel included Cabinet officers and the Vice President. The end result of this study was a Presidential budget increase for basic research of about 11% across the government.

In addition to substantive budget review and analysis, the OSTP can serve other roles in conjunction with the vertical coordination with the OMB. For example, the OSTP can assume a brokerage or expediting role, as when it facilitated the transfer of unneeded labs from one agency to another that could use them. The OSTP can also play an advocate's role, encouraging agencies to assume programs that fall between agencies or have been overlooked. This is a role that needs to be handled very gingerly since in the past this activity has caused problems for the OST when it became identified as a lobby for science. Great lengths must be taken in order to insure that the advocated programs are truly programs desired by the President and not just something the OSTP itself would like to see accomplished.

Vertical coordination, especially in terms of intervention into operational programs of the agencies, must be pursued to avoid ennervating over-commitment. There are an infinite number of issues the OSTP could address, so very sharp limitations must be levied in order to prevent too much effort being devoted to fire-fighting and managerial intervention, in practical terms trying to fill a bottomless pit. Effort should be given to setting and periodically reviewing priorities in this effort and assessing the potential benefits and the likelihood of their being achieved.

Centralized Coordination

Centralized coordination, both horizontal and vertical, tends to be resisted by the Federal agencies. Interagency groups tend to be seen as having a practical use; agencies have little to gain through participation in interagency coordination bodies and something to lose, especially if their representative is not an astute negotiator. Centralized coordination can yield increased efficiency in governmental operations if handled properly. But the entire concept of coordination, both horizontal and vertical, implies accountability—that the Federal agencies must hold up their practices and policies for review and examination by higher authorities, and that the agencies are also subject to change or discipline as a result of this examination.

In effect a more vigorous OSTP and FCCSET means a greater degree of centralization of policy oversight responsibility and accountability for R&D in the Federal system. One of the most notable characteristics of the US R&D science policy is its pluralism, a marked contrast with other systems such as Japan, France, and to a lesser extent, West Germany. There are dangers in overplanning and inflexibility, yet there is no reason why centralization of some responsibility and the maintenance of flexibility are mutually exclusive. There are costs to centralization but there are likewise costs to decentralization. In an era of scarce resources and sharp foreign competition, R&D must be marshalled as efficiently and effectively as possible.

Here some lessons might be learned from the centralized, but flexible, Japanese science policy. The Japanese have succeeded not in becoming pre-eminent in the production of new scientific knowledge, but in the production of manufactured items. This is in part due to the fact that their science policies are designed to facilitate harnessing the research of other countries rather than the creation of new findings in and of themselves. While certainly the US would not want to forego its leadership in national security related research, a re-direction of R&D towards industrial, social, and commercial applications could be of great benefit. A more closely integrated program of interaction between researchers and industry could be of benefit in ameliorating trade, productivity, regulatory, safety, environmental, and a host of other problems. Some criticism has been directed at the OSTP for by-passing industrial innovation and engineering aspects of science and technology policy in favor of pure research. For example, a GAO report faulted a Federal Council's Coordinating Committee for Materials R&D for its "strong basic science orientation with little or no engineering or other input."[10] A minor point, perhaps, but indicative of the mindset that was operating was the resistance by some of the scientists associated with the re-structuring of the White House science offices to the addition of "Engineering" in FCCSET and ISETAP titles. Hyperbolizing, science was to remain unsullied by "profane" applied engineering. This situation is gradually becoming rectified, as is exemplified by recent efforts to establish programs to stimulate private sector innovation, but much remains to be accomplished.

Centralized coordination bodies require skillful leaders, careful supervision, and clear objectives in order to succeed. Implementation of recommendations, for example, has been a key issue in the operational success of science offices, both past and present. In the past especially, the OST and Federal Council would issue reports, but would address no particular recipient who would or could exercise authority to implement the actions recommended. This weak coupling between policy recommendations and the R&D management was a source of frustration for both the Science Advisers and policy-makers and of course reduced a report's impact and the adviser's influence.

Likewise, inadequate leadership permits the potential drawbacks of committees to come to the surface. David Beckler, the long-time former executive officer of PSAC and later acting OST director, argues that the science coordinating mechanism operated "on the basis of self-interest, consensus and compromise, and its proposals have been implemented only to the extent the agencies wished to take advantage of its conclusions."[11] In many cases log-rolling took place when representatives would agree to support favored projects of others in return for a similar endorsement.

While personalities are important, some of the organizationally-based problems could be reduced through the limited centralization of authority over R&D programs in the hands of the Science Adviser and through delegation to the OSTP. This centralization would mean greater power for the Science Adviser and his staff. Such enhanced authority would improve the Science Adviser's ability to have recommended policies implemented. In the past, even though the appropriate official in an agency might agree that a particular program should be implemented, no action would be forthcoming because of agency resistance. Money can even be put in the budget, but still, because of bureaucratic resistance, the program may not be properly implemented. While being far less than a "science czar," increased authority for the Science Adviser could permit him to be more effective in identifying areas where more work or a changed emphasis would be helpful and to have the wherewithall to see that his recommendations are carried out.

Centralization also means that the OSTP could more effectively aim at harmonizing the various aspects of "high policy" and assuring that the Federal R&D management environment is structured in a way that will motivate the most efficacious allocation of resources and programs. A primary goal of OSTP centralized coordination should be oriented towards strengthening science and technology programs of mission agencies in the civilian and domestic spheres. The management of these programs has lagged in contrast to weapons and space research. Unlike national security and related areas, civilian issues such as urban transportation, welfare and health tend to be "moving targets," rather than "stationary" ones. The result is that flexibility needs to be a hallmark of the centralized structure, and this flexibility is as much a result of good leadership as it is of good program policy design.

In the past the OST was not noted for its flexibility or its ability to respond to changing situations, either in the political atmosphere of the White House or to the larger necessity of including political, economic and social factors in the construction of the reports and recommendations. In part this lack of flexibility was due to a "bureaucratization" of the OST. As staffs grew larger, the utility of their output diminished. Despite the disadvantages mentioned earlier, the strict proscription of large staffs in the current White House will reduce the likelihood of bureaucratic ossification taking place on the staff level.

Curbing Task Forces

The constituency nature of government, which includes not only agencies, Congress, and the concerned public, but various factions within the scientific community as well, means that science policy will have a tendency to become pluralistic, decentralized, and fractionated. It also means that there will be constant pressure for the creation of specialized committees in FCCSET and on lower interagency levels to represent those interests. In recognition of this danger and despite the increased use of outside resources, the OSTP has attempted to curb the use of interagency task forces. The task forces were especially characteristic of the Johnson Administration. These task forces and the OST committee system tended to proliferate in number and missions, creating new goals as they accomplished their initial objectives. These committees were like hydras; an attempt to kill a committee would induce it to resurge and diversify.

Under the present system, the number of committees working with OSTP has been severely restricted. Precise aims and specific termination dates are assigned. At any given time there are usually five or six committees in operation with an average lifespan of 12 to 18 months.

Trimming committees also have been used with some success in FCCSET, the chief formal government-wide coordinating mechanism for science and technology issues. FCCSET operates as a sub-cabinet group under Press's chairmanship and is composed of chief officials for R&D in the various government bureaucracies. After an OSTP review, a number of committees were pared down or eliminated—in the latter case, the committee's responsibilities were reassigned to a lead agency. The lead agency coordinates activity on the issue with occasional reports back to OSTP. This decentralization concept conforms with Carter's emphasis on program management by agencies where possible. Special problems are dealt with by an ad hoc FCCSET committee when necessary.

Although hampered by limited resources, Press has sought the opinions of outside experts in reviewing the working of these committees. An example of this took place with the Interagency Review Group on Nuclear Waste Management (IRG). The task force report has been reviewed by the National Research Council's committee on radioactive waste management, by other experts such as Harvey Brooks and David Deese and public comments have been invited. The IRG also exemplifies greater attempts to attain public participation and win broad support for the resultant policy.[12]

Quality assurance is problematical in any organization and no less so in the OSTP. Outside semi-public review is a current attempt to accomplish this objective. Before the White House science office's disbandment by Nixon, this function was served by the President's Science Advisory Committee (PSAC) which was a small body of some of the most talented "policy-oriented" scientists in the nation. PSAC was able to insure the report quality of its own panels and of the OST and its panels, and was also able to inject something of a general public policy orientation to the more parochial special interest reports. At times the PSAC impact on the reports was substantial, especially in areas of technical quality or delineation of options. Today Press is operating almost exclusively through panels without utilizing any central review groups, relying instead on a piecemeal approach to review and evaluation.

Under contemporary conditions it would be almost impossible to have a group similar to PSAC that could operate effectively. In large part this is due to the Freedom of Information Act, which allows citizen access to governmental meetings and documents under certain conditions. PSAC was only willing and able to fulfill its role because it was an anonymous one. The critical procedure of review and criticism cannot function in the public eye because of the reprisals that would be levied against the reviewers. Clearly people are willing to say things in private that they would not say for the public record.

Problems in Critical Reviews

The problems inherent in critical reviews of politically sensitive projects or reports are illustrated by an incident that occurred during the Kennedy administration. PSAC studied Project Rover, a nuclear powered rocket, strongly supported by the Congress's Joint Committee on Atomic Energy. Several industry people were on the panel reviewing Rover and these individuals concluded that the project was nonsensical and said as much in their report. This report enraged a powerful committee member, Clinton Anderson, who attempted to discover who had been on the panel. He wanted this information in order to carry out reprisals against the firms employing these members. The reprisals were to take the form of a "bill of attainder" in the defense and space appropriations measures saying that these particular companies would receive no contracts. Whether or not Anderson could have carried out his threat remains moot, but the threat alone is enough to demonstrate that political considerations can easily erode objectivity unless there are appropriate safeguards.

The loss of a group to perform a PSAC-like role is a major weakness which transcends the quality assurance and review function. It was generally believed that PSAC served as a lobby for basic research. But, in areas not involving its own interests, PSAC earnestly sought to represent the President's interests in line with the technological realities of the situation. PSAC did give advice that was contrary to the prevailing conventional wisdom within an administration, and took positions contrary to the expressed desires of a President. This was true in the case of the Skybolt missile, the antiballistic missile, and the supersonic transport plane. (In each of these cases the administration in office would probably have done better to heed instead of ignore PSAC's advice.) Yet in these situations it was clear that PSAC was representing the President's interests as opposed to any parochial interests. This continued to be true even though the membership of PSAC became more and more diverse as the years went by.[13]

Under the current arrangement of relying on specialized groups, this unity of Presidential focus is much more difficult to insure. And even if Presidential interests remain the paramount orientation, it will be more difficult for people to believe that this is in fact the case. This in turn means that the impact and credibility of OSTP reports will be diminished since the primary audience for the reports is the President and his staff. In that rarified atmosphere there is no tolerance for special interests that try to assume the mantle of Presidential legitimacy. The value of the Science Advisers had to be proven again and again with each new administration or operative. Initially, in each administration they were perceived as useless, or worse as representing special interests.

The political staff of the President has always been competitive with the science advisory staff. The only products any of these advisers have to sell are information, opinion, and advice (these are usually indistinguishable), and the only market is "the President's ear." Being highly political both in nature and job description, the Presidential advisers have an inside track over the Science Advisers. In the exercise of sheer power over policy, the Science Adviser is at a great disadvantage, although he may carry the day on the strength of the technical merits to his case.

In this situation, an appropriate analogy is that the scientific advice office is like a transplanted organ: the body's defense mechanisms are always present, waiting until they are no longer suppressed to reject the foreign body (science advisory apparatus). A President, of course, can either encourage or discourage those rejection mechanisms. President Nixon quite obviously encouraged those mechanisms which ultimately led to the office's reorganization out of existence.[14] The chronic resistance of White House staff to Science Advisers and staffs is motivated by more than considerations involving power politics. The scientists are seen as being overspecialized and their advice as too esoteric and narrow for the Presidential level. They are also perceived as indulging in special interest pleading and ax grinding, and as unwilling to respect the sensitive and privileged nature of White House matters.[15]

Overcoming the Doubts

Press has sought to overcome these doubts about scientists in the White House, and has met with significant success. OSTP staff has been able to work closely with the OMB on science budgets and has been able to share in some national security discussions. An approach to enhancing cross-agency communication has been tried: an OSTP assistant director, Ben Huberman, has a joint appointment to the National Security Council staff. This move symbolizes the efforts to integrate the OSTP more closely with the mainstream of presidential concerns.[16]

A particular dilemma for the science advisers is that unlike the other Presidential advisers they always appear to have a constituency, whether or not they are actually representing that constituency. This problem became most obvoius during the Vietnam war. The scientific and academic communities were centers of protest over the war, and the nearest face of this community was the White House scientists. To many advisers, dealing with these scientists became the "moral equivalent of trading with the enemy."

There are certain advantages to the Science Adviser's position vis-a-vis other Presidential advisers. To some staff members, the Science Advisers can be seen as "neutral," since they are not competing for influence in their areas. Of the coterie of advisers, it is almost invariably only the Science Advisers that know anything about technical matters, and are able to give sound advice on these subjects. Because of the seeming neutrality in this situation, the adviser's position might actually be enhanced. This was certainly the case when Press was chosen to select an advisory panel to overhaul the White House information system. Given the aphorism in Washington that information is power, it is notable that Press was selected to carry out this sensitive assignment. This assignment fortuitously coincided with Press's attempt to gain more office space for his staff.

The contradiction between thorough study and analysis and the policymaker's need for immediate information and recommendations has accompanied every science policy office. It is neither new nor resolvable in the foreseeable future. But the contemporary arrangement of the OSTP seems to intensify this contradiction. Many of the reports must be produced quickly in order to be of a value to the policymaker. This is difficult first of all because the resources for the study exist outside the staff, and must be drawn together and organized in order to be utilized. Secondly, the short time frame for the study is incompatible with the proper functioning of review mechanisms. This is particularly true of the NRC which has an institutional review mechanism in place to review any reports and recommendations generated by that organization. Thus, by the time policy requests are passed down to staff, time compression is even more severe.

To a limited extent, this issue has been circumvented by Press. He anticipates what the likely issues are going to be, and then thoroughly prepares himself and his staff on a small number of issues. On selected issues the OSTP has become highly expert, but this narrow focus consequently means that Press's and OSTP's overall impact is reduced. Press simply does not, and cannot, become engaged in the broad array of issues confronting the President. The narrow focus is nonetheless a source of great strength on the issues which he does become involved in. His superior substantive knowledge on a particular issue helps him prevail even against Cabinet level officials. This has occurred in a number of cases, for instance in defense policy (weapons systems) and space policy (satellite programs). Obviously, when Press has been able to get the support of the rest of the governmental officials on an issue, his job of selling a program to the President is eased considerably.

The Institutional Factors

There are institutional factors that work to reduce the Science Adviser's effectiveness. Specialized White House advisory agencies, both scientific and non-scientific, tend to wane quickly; in fact, it is often counterproductive for narrowly-focused groups to have functionaries closely linked to the President. Long-term observation demonstrates that the Presidents grow hostile to special-topic advisory staffs, despite the usually warm initial reception. This characterizes the fate not only of the previous OST, space, and marine councils, but also the Office of Drug Abuse Policy, the Office of Telecommunication Policy, the Council on Environmental Quality, and the consumer-affairs advisers. There are both institutional and psychological reasons why this takes place.

The special-topic adviser represents an imbalance that automatically discounts his advice; the scientist, for example, is concerned with particular issues and even more so with particular solutions to those issues (i.e., techni-scientific answers). While this might be acceptable in critical periods such as World War II and Sputnik, it does not seen to serve the President well in ordinary times. Balanced and objective advice is important to the President, his staff, and the OMB. The belief that the special topic group's advice will have to be counterbalanced adds an additional burden to the advice they receive, hence the advice (and its source) is downgraded.

A Tension-Charged Relationship

The more focused and specific the specialist's domain is, the more tension-charged will be his relationship with the President. Consequently, the "half-life" of his impact on Presidential decisions will be foreshortened or lengthened depending on the specificity or diffuseness of the perspective he is representing. This has been the key to the viability and power of the OMB and also to the long-term impact of the Council of Economic Advisers. The OMB is useful because its views cut across the whole spectrum of governmental activities; it represents no single perspective or interest. Likewise, the economy is the linchpin of the nation. Hence the Science Adviser and his staff must be certain to assure that no taint of special interest appears in their recommendation and that all conflict of interest is eschewed. Conventional wisdom dictates that the Science Adviser's usefulness is predicated entirely on his personal rapport with the President, the "sine qua non." Although this perception does contain an element of truth, it mistakes effects for causes. The personal relationship grows out of the President's appraisal of the Science Adviser; more specifically, the relationship hinges on what the President feels the Science Adviser can do for him politically, or to keep him out of trouble politically. While compatibility of style is important, the President still has to feel that he needs the Science Adviser. If he does, the personal relationship will flourish. Obviously some advisers are able to demonstrate their utility more easily than others and, while this is partially a result of personal characteristics, it also depends on the particular period and events which structure the political needs of the President and the ability of the Science Adviser to respond to those needs. By extending this point it becomes discernible that when R&D budgets are growing, the Science Adviser will be more useful to the President than when they are shrinking (at which time he is likely to be a liability to the President).

All the former Presidential Science Advisers have echoed George Kistiakowsky's sentiment that "the Science Adviser to the President first and foremost is a servant of the President."[17] In órder to securely maintain his rapport with the President, the Science Adviser must repeatedly demonstrate that he is indeed "first and foremost" a servant. But in order to be effective there are a number of fine lines the adviser must read; servitude itself is only a necessary, not a sufficient, cause of effectiveness.

The Science Adviser must deal with conflicting roles of representing agency programs and being a neutral and disinterested analyst of those programs. On the one hand, if the Science Adviser too rigidly serves as a policy analyst, the agencies will stop using him and sharing their programs with him; he will be perceived as just one more budgeteer, an opponent—and probably a highly knowledgeable and influential one. On the other hand, if he encourages and supports agency programs, his credibility with the OMB and White House staff will be diminished. Either choice results in diminished effectiveness. Similarly, the Science Adviser must be able to foster the feeling among the scientific community that he is representing their interest in order to be able to communicate freely with that community. Without this, he will be hampered in service to the President. Should the Science Adviser be perceived as the exponent of the scientific community, however, his usefulness would be terminated: "It would be a complete political disaster" to be "the spokesman of the scientific community in the White House," said Kistiakowsky.[18] The need for balance and diplomacy means that there is no simple recipe for a Science Adviser's effectiveness. Each Science Adviser must carve out his own niche within the flow of the dynamic and powerful forces surrounding the central position in the US political system, or be swept away by them.

References

1. In this paper, science policy is used generally to include "high technology" and scientific research and development. Science advice includes both science for policy and policy for science. See H. Brooks *The Government of Science* (Cambridge, Mass.: MIT Press, 1968).
2. US Congress, House Committee on Appropriations, "Department of Housing and Urban Development—Independent Agencies Appropriations for 1980," Part 6, Office of Science and Technology Policy (1979), p. 60.
3. Critical assessments are contained in the US Congress, Senate Committee on Commerce, Science and Transportation, "Oversight on OSTP" (1979), in *Chemical and Engineering News*, July 16, 1979, p. 16 ff., in a Congressional Research Service report on the Office of Science and Technology prepared by Dorothy Bates, and an American Society for Public Administrators report prepared by Edward Wenk, Jr.
4. *Ibid.*, p. 54.
5. US Congress, House Committee on Appropriations, "Department of Housing and Urban Development—Independent Agencies Appropriations for 1979," Part 5, Office of Science and Technology Policy (1978), p. 22.
6. US Bureau of the Budget, "Report to the President on Government Contracting for Research and Development," 1962.
7. US Congress, House Committee on Science and Technology, "Interagency Coordination of Federal Scientific Research and Development: Special Oversight Hearings," 1976. p. 31.
8. *Ibid.*, p. 44-49. Harold Seidman, *Politics, Position and Power.* London: Oxford University Press, 1970.
9. J. E. Katz, *Presidential Politics and Science Policy*, New York: Praeger Press, 1978, pp. 205-208. An almost identical series of events occurred when a Presidential Review Memorandum was prepared by the Department of Commerce entitled "Domestic Policy Review of Industrial or Technological Innovation" (The White House, 1979).
10. US Government Accounting Office, "Federal Materials Research and Development: Modernizing Institutions and Management" (OSP-76-9, December 2, 1975), p. 7.
11. *Op. cit.*, House Committee on Science and Technology, p. 107.
12. US Congress, House Committee on Science and Technology, "National Science and Technology Policy Issues, 1979." Part I, 1979, p. 12.
13. *Op. cit.*, Katz.
14. D. Beckler, "The Precarious Life of Science in the White House." *Daedalus* 103, Summer 1974, pp. 115-34.
15. J. R. Killian, Jr., *Sputnik, Scientists and Eisenhower.* Cambridge, Mass.: MIT Press, 1977), p. 65.
16. Huberman is not the first person with a joint appointment between OST(P) and NSC. Spurgeon Keeny held a similar position during the Kennedy and Johnson Administrations.
17. Franklin Institute, *Science Policies for the Decade Ahead* (Philadelphia: Franklin Institute Press, 1976), p. 61.
18. *Ibid.*, p. 62.

9

GOVERNMENT POLICY AND LOCAL PRACTICE

Paul Attewell and Dean R. Gerstein

Pressman and Wildavsky's (1973) popular view that government policy becomes ineffectual in the face of local exigencies is questioned. In contrast, using a case study of government policy on methadone treatment for heroin addiction, we show that federal decision making has profound impact even at microsociological levels of clinic life. A model drawn from organizations theory is developed to explain the efficacy of federal action. Policy is seen often to embody conflicting or contradictory demands due to governmental agencies' attempts to coopt or placate interests hostile to new policy directions. Governmental monopsony ensures that competing local agencies acquiesce to the details of federal intentions. But internal contradictions in policies limit or undermine local agencies' resources for gaining compliance from their clientele. Thus compromised policies, effectively translated by federal regulation into local practice, result in dysfunctional adaptations by clients, and the policies "fail."

Introduction

A position currently popular among policy scientists views government policy as relatively impotent in local settings because, it is argued, original policy intentions become diluted in the face of daily exigencies at the local level (Pressman and Wildavsky, 1973). It follows from the Pressman-Wildavsky approach that the apparent failure of many government policies stems not from the faults of the policies themselves, but rather from the complexities of implementation at the local level and especially from the diffusion of power among multiple local decision makers. Such a perspective therefore implies broad discontinuity between governmental policy making and local program outcomes, as a result of essentially particularistic aspects of local circumstances.

Based on our research on government policy and its implementation in the area of drug abuse, we present a different conceptualization of government policy, which has implications opposite to those of the Pressman-Wildavsky approach. Drawing on organizations theory we demonstrate that under certain specifiable conditions, federal policy can be seen to directly determine local program behavior even down to the microsociological level. The "failure" of local efforts is seen to flow *systematically from the structure of policy making,* especially insofar as contradictory interests, embodied in policy, undermine crucial resources which local agencies require to gain the compliance of their clientele on a day-to-day basis.

Using a case study approach, we attempt to link the macrosociology of federal policy on opiate addiction to the microsociology of methadone treatment, in order to show how the sociopolitical forces which shape government policy subsequently determine the practical realm of daily clinic life. The link between public policy and the clinical Lebenswelt is structured by the managerial responses of treatment agencies to the institutionalization of government regulation.

Our model is developed in the sections below. The material is presented in five stages. The first is an historical overview

* Address all communications to: Paul Attewell; Institute for the Study of Social Change; University of California; Berkeley, CA 94720.

This research was supported in part by NIMH training grant #5T32 14640-03, and by USPHS grant #MH 14 583. We would like to thank Mark Baldassare, Phil Bonacich, Oscar Grusky, Eugenia Miller, Katherine Newman, and four anonymous reviewers for advice received during the preparation of this manuscript. We also wish to thank Lewis L. Judd and Audrey Holliday for their administrative support during one part of this project. Finally, we are grateful to the many individuals who, over the five-year course of our research, gave of their time, trust, and intimate knowledge of these problems. The views expressed in the paper are, however, the responsibility of the authors alone.

of U.S. heroin policy. Secondly there follows a more detailed analysis of the policy towards methadone maintenance implemented in the late 1960s. The purpose here is to examine why policy took the form it did, and what this implied for treatment outcomes. A third section goes into the response of treatment agencies to federal regulations and local pressures. The fourth section analyzes the impact of this process upon the clinic milieu, especially upon the actions of addicts and staff. The final section summarizes the practical dilemmas of gaining compliance in the clinical setting as the ultimate result of the policies involved, and generalizes from the specific case-study findings to a more widely applicable model of governmental regulation and its likely outcome.

We have utilized two kinds of data in this research. First, in characterizing clinic and addict life, we draw upon our own work in several methadone clinics (from 30 to 160 clients in size) in one California city. This included ten months of intensive participant-observation research in three clinics (Gerstein, 1975; 1976), detailed, transcribed interviews with a representative sample (N = 100) of present and past clients of the clinics (Judd and Gerstein, 1975; Attewell et al., 1976), and statistical analyses of program records for five clinics over a four-year period. We obtained comparative data on clinics elsewhere from published ethnographies of treatment settings (Gould et al., 1974; Nelkin, 1973; Soloway, 1974), materials published by program administrators (Dole and Nyswander, 1976; Mandell, 1971); and from our own discussions with treatment managers and personnel in several other cities.

Second, in characterizing government policy, we have drawn upon government publications and upon historical materials including those published by principal figures (Lindesmith, 1965; Musto, 1973; Chambers and Brill, 1973; Finney, 1975; Dole and Nyswander, 1976).

Evolution of U.S. Opiate Policy

Prior to this century, opium and all of its derivatives were available virtually free of legal restriction throughout the United States. Their use for recreational and a broad range of medicinal and quasi-medicinal purposes was widespread. However under pressure from social reformers, and for supplementary reasons stemming from international politics, a series of federal actions between 1906 and 1920 made distribution and use of many opiates illegal (Musto, 1973). Even physicians were constrained to use opiates strictly for analgesic purposes. By 1938, some 25,000 medical doctors had been arraigned and 3,000 imprisoned because they attempted to prescribe narcotics to addicts (Brill, 1973:11).

Thus with the exception of a few short-lived clinics (1912–1924), addiction effectively was taken out of the jurisdiction of private physicians and became defined as a law enforcement rather than a medical problem (Brecher et al., 1972:116). Thereafter, medical involvement was limited to the Public Health Service, especially its Lexington prison-hospital.

Throughout the 1950s criticism grew over a purely law enforcement approach to addiction, culminating in a 1963 recommendation by a Presidential Commission on Drug Abuse that medical treatments be reconsidered. A technique was developed in 1964, by Vincent Dole and Marie Nyswander at Rockefeller University, based on earlier work by Isbell and Vogel (1949), which involved weaning an addict off heroin and substituting a daily oral dose of the synthetic opiate methadone. The addict entered an inpatient (later ambulatory) facility, received progressively larger doses of methadone until no heroin withdrawal symptoms were evident, and then was expected to take this dose of daily methadone *indefinitely*. Intensive supportive therapy to reestablish ego integration and normal social functioning—especially a steady paying job—ensued, and patients were put on an ambulatory (outpatient) basis, with renewable prescriptions for methadone, once such normal functioning had been established.

The major achievement of Dole and Nyswander in the mid-1960s was not simply their perfection of this clinical technique. Rather it was their gaining legitimation for the medical approach to addiction as a treatable disease. This legitimation involved a postulated analogy between addiction and chronic diseases such as diabetes. Addicts, it was argued, suffer a permanent metabollic deficiency. Just as diabetics require insulin medication for an indefinite period of time, so addicts require ongoing methadone, for an indefinite period, in order to "cure" their disease (Chambers and Brill, 1973:350). In addition, it was claimed that methadone (a) blocked the addict's craving for heroin, and (b) blocked the addict's pleasure from taking heroin (Dole and Nyswander, 1965; 1966; 1967).

Government Policy and Early Institutional Regulation

Dole and Nyswander not only were faced with the task of legitimating methadone maintenance treatment in the eyes of the general public and fellow doctors. They also faced a variety of institutional actors: the Food and Drug Administration (FDA), the Bureau of Narcotics and Dangerous Drugs (BNDD), and local political officeholders. The early clinical trials with methadone treatment carried out by Dole and Nyswander took place in a context in which legality was unclear, and early researchers took the risk of prosecution and of censure for practicing unethical medicine. In 1962, the Medical Society of the County of New York partially legitimated the treatment of addicts, including prescribing narcotics to them, by ruling that such treatment in a strict clinical research setting was ethical medicine (Nelkin, 1973:41). Such clinical programs later were specifically authorized by a 1965 law passed by the New York state legislature. Nevertheless the legal situation remained ambiguous (Brill, 1973:21–2), and both the FDA and the BNDD attempted to secure their jurisdiction in the area, as we shall explain below.

Critics of Dole and Nyswander attacked methadone maintenance on two bases. The first was that it was morally wrong to give narcotics to addicts. One medical critic argued that methadone researchers were "openly giving addicts narcotics to gratify and perpetuate their addiction" (Ausubel, 1966). The second objection in-

volved the possible diversion or misuse of methadone by addicts. This issue was particularly salient to the BNDD, the federal police agency responsible for controlling illegal drugs. In spite of the New York law, the BNDD maintained that methadone programs were illegal under the 1914 Federal Harrison Act (Nelkin, 1973:48). Although the BNDD went so far as to approach certain clinics and make its views known, it did not take the step of prosecuting the clinics (Brecher et al., 1972: 164). Hence its jurisdiction remained ambiguous until a later period.

The FDA has no legal power to control the practice of medicine. However, it does have certain powers to control new drugs, especially to monitor their production, quality, availability, etc. As methadone clinics began opening in various hospitals, the FDA asserted its jurisdiction by categorizing methadone as an "Investigational New Drug," this despite methadone's use in the U.S. and abroad since 1943. This special status of methadone continued well into the 1970s, even after tens of thousands of cases had shown methadone maintenance to be quite safe under clinical management. However, the invocation and protraction of investigational status gave the FDA a continuing mandate to license and inspect clinics prescribing the drug. The latter police function it delegated to the BNDD in 1970.

Initially the FDA simply required physicians wishing to treat addicts with methadone to obtain permission to use this "Investigational New Drug." However, in 1970/1971 the FDA promulgated a "model protocol" which specified in considerable detail various constraints on, and procedures to be carried out in, methadone programs. As we shall see this protocol had a dual function. Firstly it acted to consolidate the practical control of the FDA over physicians wishing to provide methadone treatment, by detailing program regulations and behavior. More importantly, however, it sought to coopt or placate significant critics of methadone treatment by casting their objections in the form of FDA regulations. For example, the BNDD was given direct control over medication security, and had veto power over licensing. Similarly the FDA bowed to the interests of medical critics such as Ausubel (1966), and included in the contents of the model protocol a variety of measures (to be detailed momentarily) designed to reassure critics that their specific fears concerning methadone would not be realized.

This response of the federal government, to *insist on its jurisdiction* over a new area, and to embody *in policy itself* the views of a variety of interested and often critical parties, was to have crucial consequences for implementation at the local level. This phenomenon is an important element in our general model of government action. We shall return to this in our discussion below.

Substantive features of the FDA model protocol included the following stipulations:

(1) Minors (under 18) were excluded. This was later modified to allow special exceptions.

(2) Documentation had to be provided of prior and present addiction, and a confirmed history of one or more prior failures of treatment, before an addict could obtain methadone.

(3) Consideration had to be given to eventually discontinuing the drug for patients who had adjusted well to maintenance.

(4) Termination from treatment was required for patients who continued to use narcotics or other drugs, or who exhibited alcoholism or continued criminal activity after entering treatment. Drug use was to be checked by at least weekly collection of urine specimens for laboratory testing.

(5) Prior BNDD approval of any methadone program was required. (See U.S. Food and Drug Administration 1970.)

It is central to our argument that these and other provisions in the FDA model protocol strongly determined the future course of methadone maintenance. To demonstrate this, we shall first make four points concerning these particulars of the protocol, and then we shall consider why the protocol in general had such an impact on program behavior.

A. The protocol resulted in the virtual exclusion from methadone maintenance of the primary vector of heroin "contagion": adolescents who have themselves only started heroin use comparatively recently, and who rapidly introduce their friends to the drug (Hunt and Chambers, 1976). FDA item #1 above excluded many of these from treatment on age grounds alone. Moreover item #2 above, documentation of prior failures at abstinence, requires considerable addiction history. Long-term addicts who have served jail sentences (which constitute "forced abstinence") are easily able to furnish documentary proofs of prior failure. However younger or recently-addicted individuals are unlikely to have accumulated such documentation. Consequently this FDA protocol stipulation precluded maintenance programs from treating the recently addicted individuals who keep the heroin system supplied with recruits, and instead limited methadone maintenance to a "treatment of last resort." This bowed to the views of those critics who claimed methadone simply addicted heroin users to a new drug. By allowing only long-term, "hard-core" addicts access to methadone, the FDA staved off the argument that it was turning young drug users into permanent methadone addicts.

B. The diabetes analogy of Dole and Nyswander was effectively struck down. Although item #3 above did not require methadone patients to be terminated after a time, it set up the ideal that a successful patient be weaned from methadone and end up drug free. This was in direct contrast to the Dole-Nyswander view of methadone as a lifelong medication like insulin, and instead made the drug-free "graduate" the standard of success. This shift in the criterion of successful treatment of a methadone patient was to have strong implications for the future behavior of clinics.

C. The BNDD's institutional interest was to prevent methadone from reaching the illegal market (Dole and Nyswander, 1976). It had no responsibility for treatment. Yet in order to obtain and maintain BNDD approval, methadone programs were obliged to institute rigorous control, security, and accounting procedures.

Thus security preempted therapy in the design of dispensing procedures.

D. The FDA protocols stipulated a maximum daily dose of 160 mg. Despite assurances that local programs could argue for a higher figure, the FDA succeeded, via this "suggestion," in controlling dosages and making lower doses a measure of better programs. As we shall see below, mean dosage levels were to decrease steadily in subsequent years, eroding yet more of the Dole-Nyswander method. However this FDA protocol item countered charges made by critics of maintenance programs to the effect that methadone would be prescribed in high dosages which would allow addicts to get "high," and hence abet their "moral decay."

At this point we have to raise the issue of why the provisions of the FDA protocol had such a profound and long-lasting effect, even though they were not enforceable as law. The FDA itself was obliged to state that the protocol was "intended only as a guide to the profession," while "modification of the protocol and completely different protocols will be accepted, provided they can be justified by the sponsor" (U.S. Food and Drug Administration, 1970). In more general terms we are raising the issue of why governmental agencies' policies often acquire considerable force even though they are not embodied in law.

First, in the short term, program applicants who were faced with a lengthy and difficult FDA licensing procedure tended to stick closely to the model protocol, rather than risk delay or rejections by diverging from the guide. In the longer term, the FDA guide gained its force because it was adopted by most of the crucial organizational actors who constituted the external environment of the methadone programs. The FDA protocol provided potential criteria for evaluating a program: numbers of drug-free graduates, changes in arrest records, etc. State and local agencies therefore took these as standards by which to assess a program's requests for licensing and refunding.

In addition the FDA protocol became a model for permanent state legislation. (The states *do* have jurisdiction over medical practice.) State laws were usually more restrictive elaborations of the FDA protocol. For example, in California, state regulations required *two* or more documented treatment failures, and proof of *two* years addiction prior to entry into a methadone program, compared with one failure and one year in the FDA protocol.

We see here a process not uncommon in situations where federal agencies set technically-complex safety standards: less-expert political bodies show their concern by toughening up the standards. This often occurs at the behest of state regulatory agencies which increase their areas of jurisdiction and autonomy by arguing for controls which go beyond those already covered at the federal level. Similar phenomena have been discussed in other settings by Becker (1963:147–63). In his analysis of the impact of institutionalization and enforcement upon "moral entrepreneurship," he notes both a tendency for legislators to insert their own interests at the rule-making stage, and the fact that enforcement personnel feel the need to justify their existence, and the goal displacement which often results from this (Becker, 1963:152, 156–62). One can see both of these processes operating in the case of methadone maintenance.

Thus the FDA protocol, many of whose elements were ideals or suggestions, become elaborated into state law. The protocol and the laws then became the bases upon which authorized inspectors judged programs during site visits. In some cases these inspectors were empowered to revoke program licenses. In other cases, which we will discuss below, they simply could discredit programs by feeding negative evaluative findings to the local news media.

In sum, the FDA protocol molded the external environment within which programs operated by providing a standard against which programs could be judged. The ways in which programs responded to this process are the subject of the next section.

Managerial Response at the Program Level

The rapid appropriation of millions of dollars for drug treatment, and the relative paucity of organizations already in the field, led to a proliferation of programs, as universities, hospitals, community groups, and private corporations responded to the existence of funding (Mandell, 1971; Finney, 1975:20–30; Diaz and David, 1972). Because the FDA invoked an investigational status for methadone, which required that a potential program show evidence of medical and administrative expertise, community-based groups were hindered considerably in acquiring methadone licenses. This frequently led community groups to develop drug-free addiction treatment modalities. In contrast, university and hospital-affiliated groups, and private organizations with medical and bureaucratic expertise, did well in gaining FDA authorization and government funding for methadone. Since community-based drug-free treatment agencies and methadone maintenance programs provided alternative approaches to treatment, and often competed for funding and addict clientele, community agencies frequently became pitted against the more medical-establishment methadone agencies for such resources. In cities where community groups were able to wield political influence, this acted to make local government especially cautious over methadone treatment (cf. Nelkin, 1973:90–2).

Even among methadone programs "range wars" erupted, and a process of monopolization or oligopolization later occurred in many cities (cf. Finney, 1975:25). In the early years, however, there was something of a funding bonanza, and many agencies sought to enter the field. Typically programs were set up as pilot projects, subject to continuation only if acceptable performance was demonstrated.

Programs responded to this situation by developing what we shall term a *reality construction* or *presentation of self* capability in order to convince·funding and regulatory agencies that they were doing a good job (Goffman, 1959). Waiting lists were adopted as one indicator of the need for a program, its success in the eyes of the addict community, and, of course, the need for more money. Characteristics of

addicts in treatment, e.g., time in treatment, positive changes in employment status, reduction in criminal activity, also became widely publicized as indicators of success. A program's statistics were compared with others' in order to show its efficiency (Proceedings of the National Conference on Methadone Treatment, 1971; 1972; cf. Thompson, 1967). It took several years to realize that time series data of the type collected by programs were particularly susceptible to statistical "sleight of hand." By 1973, Brill and Chambers (1973:362–3) were complaining: "Unfortunately, not everyone counts everyone when compiling 'retention' or 'attrition' statistics to share with their professional peers, with funding sources, or with the less-than-informed public." Even indices of reduced criminal activity and increased employment proved subject to manipulation or misinterpretation (Holzman and Lukoff, 1976:6ff).

In addition to these positive presentational activities, methadone programs also had to manipulate their public image in order to stave off external criticism. This became progressively more important over the years as state and federal laws gave regulatory control to a variety of watchdog agencies. For example, a California Board of Pharmacy inspector complained in the local press of one program: "It is a failure to the agencies monitoring it, to the agencies administering it, to the patients using it, and to the taxpayers." His major complaint was that program administrators would not define "just what constitutes a successful *completion* of the program" (emphasis added).

We see here the impact of the FDA protocol in ignoring Dole and Nyswander's rationale for indefinite methadone treatment (like insulin). Instead of regarding the fact that addicts were in treatment as itself a success, regulators invoked the FDA ideal of a drug-free addict (weaned from methadone) as measure of success. The newspaper which reported this inspector's complaints subsequently divided the total methadone program budget by the small number of drug-free graduates and headlined their article: "Each 'Cure' Costs Taxpayers $53,000."

Thus Dole and Nyswander's original conception of methadone treatment was forgotten.

This perilous external environment (cf. Nelkin, 1973:138) and the desire to look good to funding and regulatory agencies increased the importance of manipulating the public image of methadone programs. These presentational needs were reflected in three particular contexts: (A) aggregate movement of methadone dosage levels; (B) numbers of clients admitted and discharged; and (C) staff composition. In each case it will be seen that the programs studied showed increasing sensitivity toward outside regulatory agencies and other potential threats, and hence reorganized or toughened up clinical practices to avoid any possible external criticism.

A. Methadone dosage levels. From the earliest days of methadone maintenance, critics had accused programs of helping addicts get high. Thus one physician attacked Dole and Nyswander: ". . . they are simply substituting the euphoric action of methadone for the euphoric action of heroin by administering massive dosages of the former" (Ausubel, 1966:949). Equally the BNDD pushed for lower dosages in the belief that dispensing higher ones meant a higher likelihood of illegal diversion. In such an environment, programs' mean dosage levels became strategic symbols of their toughness and desire to wean addicts from methadone. High doses came under public criticism from surveillance agencies, and programs responded by further lowering their dispensing averages.

Consequently, methadone dosage became a pawn in an organizational struggle, its individual impact on each particular addict lost in presentational politics. In response to external agencies there was pressure on clinicians from program administrators to deny addict requests for increases, and to lower stable doses. The result was a steady decline in average dose over the years.

An additional matter, manipulated for similar reasons, involved "take home" methadone. The requirement to attend the clinic seven days a week in order to ingest methadone was first seen as a temporary measure during a client's initial stabilization. Thereafter, in order to encourage more normalized lives, including employment, clients periodically were allowed to take home and self-administer one, two or more days worth of methadone. However this was a security risk, since take home methadone could potentially be sold illegally. In line with the increasing sensitivity to possible sources of criticism, the clinics studied, progressively reducing take home privilege over the years, made it available to fewer and fewer individuals and hedged its use with greater restrictions.

B. Admissions and discharges. In the early days of the clinics studied, waiting lists existed and program success could be demonstrated by burgeoning numbers of clients in treatment. Some clients continued using illegal drugs, but this was not seen as prima facie failure, since the figures showed considerable reductions in drug use relative to untreated addicts (Chambers and Taylor, 1971). However, as regulation intensified, as community media became more critical, and as federal and local funding sources grew more begrudging, program administrators pushed harder for stringent enforcement of rules, backed by detoxification (discharge from the program following stepwise reduction of methadone dose). In 1973 a policy shift was undertaken to toughen up clinical behavior, which resulted in a rapid *doubling* of the rate of termination of clients, as those with records of continuing heroin abuse were expelled from treatment. The new policy caused a precipitous (30%) decrease in total caseloads over the year.

The point here is that administrative fiat, oriented toward external regulatory and surveillance agencies, succeeded in rapidly changing program census. There was no indication based on a study of clinical records that these actions resulted from changed patient behavior during that period.

C. Staffing. In the early days of methadone maintenance many programs utilized exaddicts (i.e., persons currently presumed abstinent) as front-line staff in the clinics. This pattern of exaddict staffing was quite common nationwide, as exaddict peer counselling provided role models for clients, job prospects for exaddicts, and inexpensive labor for programs, all at one sweep (Mandell, 1971). In the clinics studied, physicians, as expensive resources, primarily were involved in signing prescriptions and in performing periodic physical examinations. Doctors did wield considerable power by regulating dosages; however they were seldom involved in therapy, this being the task of the paraprofessional exaddict counsellors.

While some commentators on methadone maintenance have stressed that the impact of government regulation was to limit the role of physicians in treatment (Dole and Nyswander, 1976:2119), our data indicate that the most profound change in staffing policy was a movement away from hiring exaddicts as staff. This has been commented upon at the national level (Espada, 1977), and is borne out in the clinics which we studied, where a steady turnover of exaddict staff in early years turned into a full-scale rout in later years. As we shall describe below, this again took place in response to the program's increasing concerns with rigid adherence to mandated rules, and its need to present an efficient, tough image to the external environment.

In summary, what we see in these several program responses to government regulation is a progressive displacement of organizational goals, away from therapeutic aims per se and toward an increasing concern with manipulation of clinic practices in order to look good to outside agencies, particularly to powerful surveillance and funding agencies. At a more general level we would suggest that this kind of organizational goal displacement is typical of programs heavily dependent on government money or licensing for their continued existence. Since the goal of maintaining the continued existence of an organization is logically prior to that of the instrumental task at hand, there is a constant tendency to become preoccupied with the former at the cost of the latter. In the case of detailed governmental regulation and surveillance this implies the rise of bureaucratic interests in the organization and the subordination of other inter-

ests to the primary one of adapting to one's external environment in order to keep the organization safe (cf. Thompson, 1967; Dole and Nyswander, 1976:2119).

We now shall consider the cumulative effect of these organizational responses upon the experiential realm of daily clinic life.

Clinic Life for Clients and Staff

Once the initial disorientation of entering a new setting has been dispelled, the experience of a patient within a methadone clinic is fundamentally one of regulation, of rules, of specified procedures which have to be carried out: in short, of grown adults in a high school setting. Everyone knows the rules, virtually everyone present dislikes the rules, but everyone's behavior is rule-governed, even if only in grudging ritualistic compliance.

The fundamental business at hand is the distribution of methadone. There is no casualness here. Fixed hours are set—a couple of hours each in the morning and afternoon. Anyone who is late misses his/her methadone. Persons are called singly to a nurse at an enclosed dispensing station. Although client and nurse see one another daily, the client must always produce a special I.D. card, in the ritualistic fashion of military security, here mandated by BNDD. Methadone is prepackaged in coded bottles of fruit drink, of fixed volume to disguise the dosage, which is meant to be a secret to clients and even counselors. Each client must drink in full view of the nurse, and then respond to questions, to assure that the drink has been swallowed; all this also is mandated by BNDD. Methadone dispensing, the basic ritual, occurs seven days a week, 365 days per year.

Other practices are equally mandatory but less regular: especially the "urine drop." Once a week (he/she never knows quite when) each client is approached by a counselor for a urine specimen. The purpose of obtaining this specimen is for detection of illegal drug use. The urine donation (like the dispensing ritual) is a regular reminder of distrust. It bears no relation to the euphemistic privacy of a urologist's office. The addict enters a bathroom, followed by a counselor. The rules specify that he/she must be watched while urinating into the bottle. Mirrors are even installed to facilitate this surveillance. Some counselors look away, act indifferently, or dissemble a lack of attention, but the underlying rule is strengthened by such interactional camouflage work.

An important activity occurs when a urine sample has shown ''dirty''— evidence of residues of heroin, barbiturates, etc. The client, confronted with the report, often denies all knowledge: ''. . . [I]t's a mistake. The test screwed up. . . . The counselor messed up the bottles;'' protests of injured innocence to save face. The counselor must act peeved: warnings that the next time may be the last, threats of future retribution, occasional real retribution, notice of a (21-day) ''punitive detoxification.'' Since urinalysis only detects a heroin injection from the prior day or two—and then only if the heroin was relatively pure and the urine not too dilute—injecting heroin becomes Russian Roulette. In the context of ''probably they won't ask for a drop today,'' or ''I fixed [injected] two days ago, probably it'll turn up negative,'' being caught is a nasty surprise, an unlucky event, a good reason to be angry.

Another weekly ritual is an interview with the counselor. Again, a degree of interpersonal concern and interest often exists, although counselors have on the average ten minutes per client per week for face-to-face counselling. Occasionally therapeutic relationships blossom. But in each interview a formal mandated agenda of information must be obtained: ''Did you work this week?'' Engage in illegal activities? Were you arrested, convicted, etc.?''

To these repetitive activities are added an occasional group therapy session, extended personal counseling, a doctor appointment for some physical complaint, and so on. But such activities are only leaven. The essential routines consist of waiting for methadone, giving urine, and checking in with the counselor. Many patients totally ignore voluntary therapeutic offerings. The senior administrator of one program felt obliged to point out to

the press in the fifth year of the program's operation: ''We put in a rule eighteen months ago that anybody on the program was to participate in counselling. That rule is still in effect for patients until they and their counselors decide sessions are not needed.''

While the clinical experience of the typical client is a one-dimensional exchange of weekly urine for daily methadone, the clinical reality of the staff is necessarily more complex. The backstage operation of a methadone clinic can be seen as involving an interpenetration of three different realities, each with its own rationale and interests. The first involves self-definition, particularly for the counselors and clinic directors, who were at first (1970–1972) virtually all exaddicts, though individuals without heroin experience were later hired. The exaddicts' job credentials were principally their firsthand knowledge of addict behavior, presumed (since Synanon's publicity) to give them special efficacy in drug treatment. Exaddict counselors had to put this folk knowledge in service of a clinical perspective, while shifting their own self-image from down-and-out to upwardly mobile. They had, on the one hand, to convince addict clients of their savoir faire, that they could not be ''conned,'' and, on the other, to establish themselves as paraprofessional clinicians. This was accomplished in part by language and style. Counselors and clinic directors dressed and spoke with a streetwise style, but also with a facile psychiatric terminology: ''subconscious motivation,'' ''defense and coping mechanisms,'' ''denial'' and ''confrontation,'' etc. This combination set them off from the clientele, without sacrificing their claim to an insider's knowledge of addiction.

A second reality, which all staff shared, was a bureaucratic-administrative one. Each clinic director was sandwiched between the top program administrators far from the clinic, and the day-to-day problems of staff and clients. Through the clinic director came administrative directives, the majority involved with getting paperwork done, new government edicts and inspections, and making sure security was kept tight. Since rules were constantly breached or bent in the day-to-day life of the clinic, and were, in any case, so complex and frequently changed that often it was unclear what rule applied, there was always room for criticism (and grounds for firings) by the administration. Getting the paperwork done, and avoiding or patching up administrative upsets, were constant concerns for the staff.

The third reality involved the day-to-day management of addicts as nonmedical, nonbureaucratic, nonpassive people. A typical day of staff concerns would be as follows (using their own terminology): Client X is being a pain about needing more methadone, is kicking up a fuss about being screwed over, loudly telling anyone who will listen. Client Y is a slick S.O.B. whom the staff would like to get rid of, but whom no one can catch making heroin deals in the clinic, or using heroin. Client Z keeps coming up dirty, but her old man has just gotten out of jail, lives with her, and is shooting up all the time. The staff knows she has two kids, cares desperately about staying in the program, and would go back to dope and hooking if kicked off the program.

The experiential immediacy of concerns like these enables them to compete in the minds of staff with bureaucratic and other demands.

Staff Responses to the Clinical Milieu

It is clear that the staff members' *normal* situation, particularly for exaddicts, was one of profound role conflict. This was exacerbated as bureaucratization progressed, although it was partially "solved" by the steady elimination of exaddicts. The role conflict drew its power from all of the interests working at cross purposes in the clinic. First and foremost, counselors—particularly exaddict ones—sympathized and even identified with clients. Some knew at firsthand that success in the program meant new life chances: keeping a job, gaining status and self-respect, regaining hope. They also knew what involuntary expulsion from the clinic could mean: the extraordinary mental and physical pressures of hustling, seeking dope, pain, finding dope, shoot-

ing, near or actual overdoses. Often superimposed upon this is constant harassment by police and narcotic agents, and emotional and sometimes physiological blackmail as police lock addicts up until withdrawl prompts them to "cooperate." Exaddict or nonaddict counselors were too close to this reality not to be influenced by it. The cold administrative calculus of punishment broke down when the client was known as an individual and the situation into which he/she would be thrust was viewed as abominable.

The first level of conflict, then, derived from the counselor's proximity to the client world, crossed with demands to enforce punitive sanctions. This conflict was not simply a matter of counselor's social background, but was *genuinely organizational in its origins*. Counselors qua therapists were expected to establish supportive relationships with clients. The establishment of therapeutic thrust was and always is predicated upon notions of care and respect for the individual client. A lack of such particularistic solidarity empties a therapeutic relationship of its meaning and force. Nevertheless, due to the increasing concern with the external environment the counselors were increasingly required to be disciplinarians, enforcers of universalistic rules, organizational moralists. The conflict arose from contradictory demands to be particularistic while universalistic, and trusting while punitive.

While counselor conflict derived at one level from opposition between therapeutic and rule maintenance interests, a second conflict involved self-image. Counselors wished to see themselves as persons of status, individuals with skills, and more specifically, professionals able to help others. Perhaps the term *altruistic orientation* overstates the real professionalism involved, but counselors were undoubtedly caught in this imagery. Administrative policies increasingly undermined such bases of self-definition. A subordinate force which thought it knew what was best for addicts could not be tolerated, especially as the watchdog and punitive functions of counselors began to overshadow therapeutic concerns. Thus in addition to having to integrate contradictory pressure in their *duties*, counselors had to stave off contradictory definitions of their status. Their role as counselor had positive cultural value, while the role of policeman was particularly abhorrent in addict society, in which police and snitches were loathed. The administration, far from euphemizing the punitive, watchdog functions of counselors, left increasingly little doubt that they were there primarily for that purpose. The most cogent testimony to the assault upon counselors' self-images was the terminology used by a senior program administrator, who began referring to counselors as "urine monitors."

Staff response to these cross pressures in the clinics studied varied between demoralization, acquiescence, and hostility. The importance of these jobs for the exaddicts gave the process extra poignancy. Counselling paid comparatively little, but it was generally the first white-collar work exaddicts had had, their first experience of a respectable niche in which they could keep working successfully. Under these cross pressures some exaddicts left early for other programs. Others dropped out, were kicked out, or acquiesced to demands which redefined their role. For those who did leave, the blow often propelled them directly towards their only other social identity: dope fiend. Completing the circle, some later reappeared as clients in the program.

The Client Point of View

In the sections above, we have given our (sociological) view of several changes which took place in methadone maintenance, e.g., shifts in dosages, staff changes, sudden changes in program expulsions, etc., and have tried to explain these changes in terms of program response to its external environment and mandated policies. It is important to realize however that our analytic perspective on these matters is not that of the addicts themselves. While these same topics were constantly addressed in the course of our interviews with addicts, their folk perceptions of these phenomena clustered instead around the apparent arbitrariness of clinic life, especially as

regards disciplinary actions against addicts.

We wish to make two points concerning this addict world view: first, that the addict perspective was a rational response to real phenomena, i.e., that a high degree of arbitrariness did, in fact, exist. Secondly, we wish to show that the addict's world view was readily rendered irrational and indeed seen as one aspect of addict personality pathologies, by staff members who viewed addict responses through a psychiatric framework. The mutual unintelligibility of addict and staff world views is best illustrated in terms of urinalysis requirements and punitive detoxification (i.e., incremental reduction of methadone dose to zero and expulsion from the clinic).

Examining the issue of urinalysis, we find that a high degree of arbitrariness (or luck) is involved in the process. On the one hand, addicts were faced with uncertainty as to what day they would be called to give a urine sample. Thus, being caught with a "dirty urine" was not simply a matter of scientifically catching those clients who were illegally continuing heroin use. Rather it was a matter of being the unlucky one who happened to be caught on a certain day for a urine sample. This arbitrariness was intensified by problems in the technique of urinalysis itself, having to do with variations in personal metabolism and laboratory procedure. Residues of heroin used two days previously might be identified in the urine of one individual, while heroin shot hours before testing might not be detected in another addict. Drinking beer prior to giving a urine sample would often dilute the sample so that no heroin was detectable. False positives were also not unknown in urinalysis: even when urines were split into two portions for separate urinalysis, the results rarely agreed (C. Lidz, personal communication). Thus addicts did not experience urinalysis as an objective system of surveillance in which if one had cheated program rules one was caught. Rather, they experienced urinalysis as a form of unpredictable Russian Roulette. Staff, however, noting the BNDD licensing of laboratories and the high prices for urinalysis, had to take the official line that urinalysis results were accurate, and a fair method of catching those individuals who broke program rules.

Given the addict experience of the arbitrariness of urinalysis, there was a widespread belief by addicts that staff members switched urine samples, either to protect friends, earn bribes, or hurt enemies. This was often interpreted by psychiatric staff as a magical or paranoid belief system. Similarly a widespread addict response to urinalysis results was to claim that the outcomes were simply wrong. This was seen by staff as denial in the psychiatric sense. Finally addicts tended to respond to being caught with a dirty urine by becoming angry. Indeed, anger is a rational response to a situation where a series of low-probability outcomes (day urine requested, metabolism, accuracy of urinalysis, etc.) all coincide causing the addict to be caught. Yet anger was seen by staff as addicts' refusal to take personal responsibility for their actions.

A similar mutual unintelligibility underlay staff and client views of involuntary or punitive detoxification, where again addicts viewed the punitive process as arbitrary and ill-intentioned. Program rules were fairly specific: if a client continued using illegal drugs for long after entering the program, the client would first be verbally warned, and then obliged to sign a contract agreement that more "dirties" would result in detoxification and termination from the program. This organizational rule reflects federal and state regulations.

As indicated, the timing and results of urinalysis exhibit a degree of randomness. But in addition, an examination of program records revealed that the number of dirty urines permitted before one received a contract varied according to counselor, concurrent level of administrative strictness, frequency or imminence of audit, etc. Even after a contract was written, the actual number of dirty urines tolerated could vary.

Yet even after the contract was deemed violated and detoxification begun, a further mystification occurred. Clients saw the *process* of the 21-day "detox" as *itself* the punishment, rather than seeing their subsequent *termination* from the program as the *real* punishment, with detoxification merely a technical means of withdrawing methadone prior to termination (Attewell et al., 1976). Although federal regulations set the minimum time for detoxification at 14 days, addicts felt that even 21 days was so abrupt that one suffered severe withdrawal pains. Forty-five percent of the clients interviewed in our interview sample (Judd and Gerstein, 1975; Attewell et al., 1976) objected specifically to the length of detoxification. Allied to this was the knowledge that expulsion from the program—ostensibly the *real* punishment—was manipulable. Addicts could, and did, return to the program very shortly after being punitively detoxified. Detoxified patients were sometimes on the rolls again within two weeks. Thus, addicts saw the punitive response of the program as centering on the physical pains of detoxification, rather than the moral censure of expulsion or exclusion from treatment.

What then was the consequence of this contradiction between staff and addict world views? Given this context of unpredictability concerning detection of illegal drug use, unpredictability of program response, and addict redefinition of the termination process, a significant proportion of clients denied the fairness or validity of the system of punitive governance upon which the clinics operated. Combined with the various humiliating rules, e.g., viewing one urinating etc., this led to many addicts taking an alienated and instrumental view of the program. Many began a cyclical revolving-door pattern of program involvement: repeated entries to clinics, detoxifications due to continued drug use, and subsequent reentries to treatment after weeks or months on the street hooked on heroin. This was abetted by federal documentation rules which enabled expatients to rapidly reenter, while new addicts, who never previously had been treated, would often have to hang on for weeks or months, awaiting documentation. The program, meanwhile, was able to keep up its case census by admitting "retreads," some up to six times in a four-year period.

This type of career virtually coopted methadone maintenance as a complementary adaptation to preexistent street life. Typical street heroin use involves a period of sporadic shooting (injecting) which escalates to a daily fixed-interval schedule, reinforced by the onset or threat of withdrawal. But the body learns to tolerate a given mean level of heroin, and addicts often respond by taking larger doses. This procedure has finite limits, because money and heroin become relatively hard to get in ever-larger quantities. Addicts responded to this, prior to the existence of methadone maintenance, by experiencing withdrawal pains frequently and eventually going cold turkey (withdrawing from heroin), often in jail. Later, the pattern of injecting would start over.

This stereotypical picture of periods of addiction interspersed with periods of abstinence, has become modified by the revolving-door methadone maintenance career. (Some 37.5% of addicts in one program studied showed this career type by late 1974; Judd and Gerstein, 1975.) These addicts entered the maintenance program, reduced their heroin use considerably, and ultimately were detoxified and expelled for not quitting completely. They resumed full-time street use of heroin until their tolerance got too high, legal or personal problems grew unmanageable, or their heroin connection dried up. Then they reentered the program. Methadone maintenance provided a cushion for such people, by helping them control their heroin needs, and keeping them out of prison.

This creative cooptation of methadone maintenance did interfere with those addicts in treatment who were motivated to avoid heroin entirely, and was not exactly beloved by revolving-door addicts, since it involved continual harassment and degradation by a plethora of treatment practices. But as a "rational" response to an institutional pattern which preached treatment and practiced control, this career pattern, of using treatment to buffer the more unmanageable aspects of addiction, is strikingly symbiotic. The encumbered institutional attempt at treating a social problem produced its antithesis in addicts' use of treatment to solve their own problems.

The Dilemmas of Compliance

We have indicated above that the addict's experience in treatment involved on the one hand a routine of repetitively demeaning rituals, and on the other a series of uncertain and/or irregular surveillance and punitive measures. This combination, we have argued, is demoralizing for addicts, leads to an alienated and instrumental perspective, and does little to encourage respect for the program. One possible explanation for this could be that these negative consequences result from a lack of adequate bureaucratization, rather than a surfeit (cf. Perrow, 1972). In other words, residual particularistic attitudes (constant bending of rules regarding detoxification, etc.) rendered unpredictable an otherwise rational system of treatment as defined by the FDA.

In countering this "underbureaucratization" thesis we have to demonstrate two things. First we shall show that particularism was not some peculiar aberration of the clinics studied but on the contrary was a necessary consequence of the organizational structure imposed on methadone maintenance. Secondly, we shall argue that clinical practices were not hindered by particularism per se, but rather by the undermining of such particularism resulting from increased attention to FDA and state regulations. In explaining these processes we shall use Etzioni's (1961) work on compliance in which he distinguishes between three types of organizations (coercive, remunerative and normative), each of which employs a specific set of tactics in gaining the compliance of its participants.

From our preceding review of methadone treatment, it becomes apparent that programs have difficulties in using *any* of the typical organizational constraints or compliance mechanisms to control addict-clients. For example, coercive compliance depends above all upon physically restraining an individual from leaving an institution. Even though addicted to methadone, the addict in treatment does have the option of quitting the program and returning to street narcotics. Thus, methadone programs cannot effectively operate as coercive organizations.

Remunerative compliance requires a set of variable rewards which may be adjusted to match a subordinate's behavior, and hence entice the subordinate to follow organizational rules. Unfortunately, methadone programs' abilities to marshall such rewards were very limited. Therapeutic offerings such as counselling were not perceived as rewards: indeed, we saw earlier that addicts had to be forced to attend counselling sessions. One possible reward structure—allowing methadone dosage to slide up and down according to good behavior—was ruled out by physicians' ethical objections to utilizing medication as a variable reward. The only other meaningful reward, take-home privileges, had been curtailed and made inflexible due to BNDD and other external pressure. Thus there was a paucity of remunerative compliance in methadone clinics.

The third type, normative compliance, was similarly hamstrung. As Etzioni argued, normative mechanisms (e.g., rituals of solidarity, prestige and status rewards, exclusion, moral stigmatization, etc.) only work in a situation where participants have a high degree of commitment to organizational goals. The various degrading and status-deflating aspects of methadone maintenance, e.g., I.D. cards, urine monitoring, punitive rules, all acted to destroy any possibility of status or prestige rewards and hence undermined the basis for normative compliance.

Normative control was similarly encumbered in terms of its major negative sanction: explusion and moral stigmatization. There was a contradiction between the use of exclusion or explusion as a compliance/control device, and culturally dominant notions of medical treatment. Having successfully defined themselves as providers of medical treatment, programs could not exclude on a long-term basis those expelled exclients who had returned to the street and become readdicted. To do so would be to deny a sick person medical treatment, which bites too deeply into social mores and taboos. Thus, because of the medical definition, programs could neither effectively exclude rule breakers, nor, after readmission, deny them any of the treatment provisions of the program. Methadone programs therefore had to live with their own treatment failures. Consequently, programs totally lacked any effective negative sanctions for normative control of erring subordinates.

In sum, most of the major mechanisms which complex organizations typically utilize for controlling subordinate participants were absent or unavailable in the case of methadone maintenance programs. Programs were therefore unable to mold effectively the behavior of their addict-clients.

In such a situation the only remaining lever for obtaining compliance involved the use of personal loyalties between staff and clients generated in the day-to-day life of the clinic and in counseling sessions. These friendships produced respect and trust, feelings of mutual understanding and personal obligation. To be kicked out of a clinic involved loss of face to some addicts, not because they felt commited to the program per se, but because they had betrayed the personal trust of a specific staff member to whom they felt obligated. To the extent that a counselor believed and acted as though a client was an individual worthy of being trusted—by imbuing the relationship with importance and solidarity—a counselor could impose such a personal commitment upon the client, which might be reciprocated.

The major method of imposing such a commitment and establishing mutual respect involved treating a person individually rather than as a typical case among many. Particularistic behavior thus meant special treatment, making exceptions to rules, doing more than the standard minimum. By being flexible with rules, a counselor could show that he/she cared, understood the client as a particular individual with special problems, and had enough trust to go out on a limb. In a situation where few other bases for gaining compliance existed, for the reasons outlined above, the particularism of program staff became a crucial organizational resource for compliance.

How then does this fit into our wider framework? We have shown that particularistic decisions by counselors were made on the basis of, in Weber's term, substantive justice. The historical intensification of bureaucratic routinization in the clinics, in response to external pressure towards strict enforcement of government regulations, favored formal justice—enforcing rules universalistically, without regard to particular circumstances. But the insistence on increasing formal rationality fatally undermined the particularistic basis of clinical compliance. As the counselors were denied discretionary powers, they became simple enforcers of rules, urine monitors, while the clients, treated more and more as cogs in a metered dispensing machine, increasingly were removed from sources of commitment to treatment.

Thus the mounting pressure to comply with the externally mandated rules intensified the contradiction between strict universalistic application of program rules (designed to prevent abuse of methadone), and a particularistic therapeutic outlook designed to change addicts' behavior. As programs attempted to respond to outside agencies by strictly enforcing federal and state regulations they simultaneously became the agents of their own therapeutic demise.

Summary and Conclusion

In this paper we have tried to give a developmental perspective on methadone maintenance and to link macrosociological levels to the experiences of participants. Methadone maintenance was an attempt to reintroduce a medical treatment model for heroin addiction after 50-year history of punitive prohibition. Government agencies, principally the FDA, succeeded in gaining an early jurisdictional mandate to control these medical interventions. Its model protocol redefined the parameters of methadone maintenance away from the original intentions of Dole and Nyswander, and incorporated the ob-

jections of the BNDD and medical critics into its protocol stipulations. Programs had little choice but to accept this redefined model of methadone maintenance. They were in a situation of lopsided dependency upon federal and state licensing, surveillance, and funding agencies, and upon the goodwill of local media and local government. Since all these institutional actors took the FDA protocol as the template against which to evaluate local programs, such programs had to appear to succeed according to the FDA model. Programs made elaborate efforts at manipulating their public image in order to maintain the support of those external agencies. As surveillance intensified, this involved an increasing attempt at strict compliance with federal and state regulations. These efforts in turn led to intense role conflicts within clinic staff, and alienation and mystification among addict clients. The already limited bases of organizational compliance in the clinics became further undermined, and an adaptational client role—the revolving-door syndrome—grew increasingly prevalent.

Generalizing from the particular case of methadone, we can derive certain insights into the workings of government policy in general, and return to the debate with the Pressman-Wildavsky position described earlier. The first thing to note is that the strength of government policy in this area (in contrast to their notion of federal impotence) derived primarily from the monopsonic position of government as buyer of certain services, such as methadone maintenance. In such monopsonic situations where government is faced with a myriad of competing sellers, and where a non-governmental market for the services barely exists, one is likely to find a much greater degree of "potency" to government policy than elsewhere.

Secondly we see that government policy is frequently contradictory in the sense that it embodies conflicting principles of action. In the case of methadone maintenance this involved the multiple goals of limiting methadone to specific subpopulations, and of strictly policing its distribution, while simultaneously attempting to set up a successful clinical milieu. Such conflicted policies are likely to emerge, we would suggest, in many instances of policy making precisely because of the political context of federal agencies. In our case the FDA, attempting to appease or coopt both friends and foes of methadone maintenance, allayed the criticism of foes via a hedge of restrictive regulations. This attempt by government policy regulations to appease all interested parties is quite general, especially in contentious areas. It is frequently a prerequisite for obtaining the necessarily broad political support required for the passage of enabling legislation, and also stems from the policy bureaucracy's desire to minimize conflict and opposition to its plans. In most cases this kind of policy-making behavior leads mainly to an excess of regulation and lack of flexibility. At its worst, it results in quite incompatible demands being included in policy and placed upon local implementing agencies.

The impact of such compromised policies is particularly severe in contexts of monopsony or lopsided dependence of local agencies on national government. Agencies then have to involve themselves in institutional presentation-of-self, which involves actively selling their ability to perform contradictory tasks, in order to obtain central financing. Any attempt to fight the irrationalities in policy would simply result in some other competing organization receiving funding.

Finally the manner by which these policy demands have their impact at the program level involves a displacement of program goals towards sustaining funding via strict adherence to government regulations and active presentational work. But compromised policies also impact upon programs by restricting their organizational resources for gaining the motivated compliance of subordinates. Many organizations under the best of circumstances find it difficult to develop an effective reward structure and an appropriate form of normative, remunerative, or coercive compliance mechanisms. But under the burden of detailed government regulations such resources may be severely limited, leading to organizational failure due to paucity of rewards. Alternatively, as in

the case of methadone maintenance, government policy may mandate the use of quite incompatible compliance mechanisms, e.g., normative alongside coercive control, in which case the programs begin to unravel from within as they cannot hold the loyalty or commitment of their members. In either case government policy unwittingly forces programs into presiding over their own demise: the closer the programs attempt to obey the dictates of government, the worse become their problems of organizational control.

Thus far from conceptualizing government policy as impotent on the local level and regarding outcome as detached from policy, we recommend, at least in the context of governmental monopsony, a model which emphasizes the power of policy and of its consequences, both intended and unintended, upon local practice.

REFERENCES

Attewell, Paul A., Lewis L. Judd and Dean R. Gerstein
1976 ''A client evaluation of involuntary detoxification from methadone.'' Proceedings of the National Conference on Drug Abuse.
Ausubel, David P.
1966 ''The Dole-Nyswander treatment of heroin addiction.''Journal of the American Medical Association 195:949–50.
Becker, Howard S.
1963 Outsiders: Studies in the Sociology of Deviance. New York: Free Press.
Brecher, Edward M. and the Editors of Consumer Reports
1972 Licit and Illicit Drugs. Boston: Little, Brown.
Brill, Leon
1973 ''Introductory overview: historic background.'' Pp. 5–40 in C.D. Chambers and Leon Brill (eds.), Methadone: Experiences and Issues. New York: Behavioral Publications.
Brill, Leon and Carl D. Chambers
1973 ''Summary and conclusions.'' Pp. 347–65 in C.D. Chambers and Leon Brill (eds.), Methadone: Experiences and Issues. New York: Behavioral Publications.
Chambers, Carl D. and Leon Brill (eds.)
1973 Methadone: Experiences and Issues. New York: Behavioral Publications.
Chambers, Carl D. and W. J. Russell Taylor
1971 ''The incidence and patterns of drug abuse during maintenance therapy.'' Paper presented to the annual meeting of the Committee on Problems of Drug Dependence, National Research Council, National Academy of Sciences, Division of Medical Sciences, Toronto.

Diaz, William A. and Stephen M. David
1972 The New York City Addiction Services Agency 1971–1972. New York: Fordham University Institute for Social Research.

Dole, Vincent P. and Marie E. Nyswander
1965 "A medical treatment for diacetylmorphine (heroin) addiction: a clinical trial with methadone hydrochloride." Journal of the American Medical Association 193:646–50.
1966 "Narcotic blockade: a medical technique for stopping heroin use by addicts." Archives of General Medicine 118:304.
1967 "Heroin addiction: a metabolic disease." Archives of General Medicine 120:19.
1976 "Methadone maintenance treatment: a ten-year perspective." Journal of the American Medical Association 235: 2117–9.

Espada, Frank
1977 "Contemporary government policy: response." Proceedings of the National Conference on Drug Abuse.

Etzioni, Amatai
1961 A Comparative Analysis of Complex Organizations: On Power, Involvement, and Their Correlates. New York: Free Press.

Finney, Graham S.
1975 Drugs: Administering Catastrophe. Washington, D.C.: Drug Abuse Council.

Gerstein, Dean
1975 Heroin in Motion: A Working Paper in the Theory of Action. Ph.D. dissertation, Department of Sociology, Harvard University.
1976 "The structure of heroin communities (in relation to methadone maintenance). American Journal of Drug and Alcohol Abuse 3:571–87.

Goffman, Erving
1959 The Presentation of Self in Everyday Life. Garden City: Doubleday.

Gould, Leroy, Andrew L. Walker, Lansing E. Crane and Charles W. Lidz
1974 Connections: Notes from the Heroin World. New Haven: Yale University Press.

Holzman, Paula and Irving E. Lukoff
1976 "A plea for the long route: an evaluation of methadone maintenance and other short cuts to the cure of heroin addiction." Unpublished paper.

Hunt, Leon and Carl D. Chambers
1976 The Heroin Epidemics: A Study of Heroin Use in the United States, 1965–1975. New York: Spectrum.

Isbell, Harris and Victor H. Vogel
1949 "The addiction liability of methadone (amidone, dolophine, 10820) and its use in the treatment of the morphine abstinence syndrome." American Journal of Psychiatry 105:909–14.

Judd, Lewis L. and Dean R. Gerstein
1975 Follow-Up and Evaluation Study of the UCSD-San Diego County Narcotic Treatment Program, 1970–1974. Department of Substance Abuse, San Diego.

Lindesmith, Alfred
1965 The Addict and the Law. Bloomington: Indiana University Press.

Mandell, Arnold J.
1971 "The sociology of a multimodality strategy in the treatment of narcotics addicts." Journal of Psychedelic Drugs 4:132–7.

Musto, David
1973 The American Disease: Origins of Narcotic Control. New Haven: Yale University Press.

Nelkin, Dorothy
1973 Methadone Maintenance: A Technological Fix. New York: Braziller.

Perrow, Charles
1972 Complex Organizations: A Critical Essay. Glenview: Scott-Foresman.

Pressman, Jeffrey L. and Aaron B. Wildavsky
1973 Implementation. Berkeley: University of California Press.

Proceedings of the National Conference on Methadone Treatment
1971 Proceedings, Third National Conference on Methadone Treatment, November 14–16, 1970. Public Health Service Publication No. 2172. Washington, D.C.: U.S. Government Printing Office.
1972 Proceedings, Fourth National Conference on Methadone Treatment, January 8–10, 1972. New York: National Association for the Prevention of Addiction to Narcotics.

Soloway, Irving H.
1974 "Methadone and the culture of addiction." Journal of Psychedelic Drugs 6:91–9.

Thompson, James D.
1967 Organizations in Action. New York: McGraw-Hill.

U.S. Food and Drug Administration
1970 "Conditions for the investigational use of methadone for narcotics addicts." Reprinted as pp. 23–40 in Carl D. Chambers and Leon Brill (eds.), Methadone: Experiences and Issues. New York: Behavioral Publications.

THE ELECTORAL PROCESS

At an earlier stage in analytic time, the political process was thought to represent the voice of the people, juxtaposed over and against the policy process, or the presumed voice of an elite. Electoral procedures were viewed by bureaucrats as episodic, discontinuous, and even capricious; whereas the policy apparatus was seen as tied into an administrative process that was immutable with respect to political currents and impervious to politicians' blandishments. We have now come to the sharper realization that older antinomic formulations are intellectually naive, having failed to realize the linkages between political parties and socioeconomic policies. It is now axiomatic that different constituencies represented in the electoral process have real, if not immediate, impact on policy decisions. Changing leaders does have the consequence of changing policies. How this interaction occurs, the time frame over which policies alter, and the varieties of options available all become central to serious contemporary analysis of the policy process.

The three studies by Ginsberg, Hibbs, and Pomper well illustrate how intimate the connection between politics and policy has become. Ginsberg rightly sees as a central question of democratic politics the relationship between popular choice and public policy; in a longitudinal analysis covering a wide array of fundamental issues he is drawn to conclude that American public policy is significantly shaped by the behavior of voters. Hibbs' seminal paper shows that political parties tend to map out either a configuration of low unemployment and high inflation or high unemployment and low inflation, with the Democratic party tending toward the former choice and Republican party impulses moving toward the latter. Macroeconomic outcomes are thus a function not simply of economic necessity but of political priorities as well. The essay by Pomper with Lederman goes one step further, noting that party platforms are serious, and that, despite the cynical expectations, platforms are not forgotten in the postelection climate. Although they are not uniformly fulfilled, in a wide array of matters, such as social security measures, political parties have distinctive policies which do not duplicate those of the other; in fact, campaign pledges are often redeemed. The best writing in this area thus lays to rest the myth that politics and policies have little or no connection. And echoing Pomper's conclusion, "academic research thus underlines political practice."

10

ELECTIONS AND PUBLIC POLICY

Benjamin Ginsberg

The central questions of democratic politics concern the relationships between popular choices and public policy. With the advent of survey research, these relationships have been the objects of intensive scrutiny. Although the techniques of survey analysis are essential for dealing with many important questions about the linkages between voting and policy, it is not true that all major problems in this area require survey data for an adequate solution. Moreover, to the extent that survey analysis is of relatively recent vintage a capacity to examine voting and policy linkages without such data would add considerably to our understanding of historical periods for which opinion surveys are unavailable.

Though much of this analysis must be considered exploratory and tentative, my aim is to examine the links between public policy and popular voting between 1789 and 1968. To this end, criteria are established for citizen policy choice that permit drawing meaningful conclusions without interview data. Then, data from party platforms, United States statutes, and aggregate voting statistics, are used to determine to what extent electoral choices are translated into policy decisions over time.

Voting and Public Policy

The absence of historical survey data precludes inferences about the reasons behind an individual's electoral decisions. Our lack of information, however, does not make this decision any less of a choice. Whatever the preferences of voters, votes are, in effect, choices among alternatives. In the same sense that the behavior of consumers vitally affects the national economy whether or not consumers are completely aware of the differences among products, the decisions made by voters can have major policy consequences whether or not voters are fully aware of the implications of their actions.

* The author wishes to thank E. W. Kelley, Duncan MacRae, Jr., and Robert Weissberg for their many ideas, corrections and suggestions. David Greenstone, Theodore Lowi, and T. J. Pempel read and carefully criticized earlier versions of the manuscript. Sandra Ginsberg, Richard Joslyn, and Richard Klein provided valuable assistance in the collection and analysis of data.

If we concentrate on the effects of voting behavior, two factors become particularly important. First, the effects of voting behavior are conditioned by the alternative policy positions represented by opposing candidates and parties. Given the presence of alternatives, the electorate makes at least implicit choices. If opposition candidates offer policy alternatives substantially different from those defended by incumbents, electoral choices can result in changes in national policy. In European political history, for example, the presence of radical alternatives offered the potential for change even when voters did not take advantage of these possibilities. Second, voting behavior can directly affect public policy to the extent that winning candidates and parties implement policies based on their preelection positions. If winners behave randomly in relation to their preelection positions, the electorate's choice is irrelevant. If sets of winning candidates, in fact, implement policies based on their preelection positions, the electorate's implicit choices are translated into national policy.

The effects of voting behavior are, thus, a function of both the magnitude of the choices available to voters and the extent to which electoral choices are implemented. Given these criteria, we can ask to what extent, over time, popular majorities govern.

Public Choice and Electoral Realignment

Our principal clues about the historical relationships between voting behavior and public policy are provided by the theory of critical elections. Seminal studies of American voting behavior conducted by V. O. Key and others suggest that during critical periods in American political history, major reorientations have occurred in the partisan attachments of large portions of the electorate.[1] The voter alignments established during these critical periods, 1798–1800, 1826–36, 1852–60,

[1] V. O. Key, "A Theory of Critical Elections," *Journal of Politics*, 17 (February, 1955), 3–18. Walter Dean Burnham, *Critical Elections and the Mainsprings of American Electoral Politics* (New York: Norton, 1970), p. 10. Also, Walter Dean Burnham, "Party Systems and the Political Process," in *The American Party Systems*, ed. William N. Chambers and Walter Dean Burnham (New York: Oxford University Press, 1967), p. 289.

From Benjamin Ginsberg, "Elections and Public Policy," LXX(1) *The American Political Science Review* 41-49 (March 1976). Copyright 1976 by The American Political Science Association. Reprinted by permission.

1874–80, 1892–96 and 1928–36, support, over relatively long periods of time, the dominance in government of the victorious party.

Schattschneider, Burnham and others have suggested that voter realignments involved choices about national policy.[2] During realigning periods discontented elements penetrated or replaced one or the other of the two major parties, altered the terms of partisan conflict and substantially increased the magnitude of choice available to the electorate. Alteration of the substance of electoral alternatives, "redefinition of conflict," in Schattschneider's terms, forced voters to make new decisions and thus had the effect of altering the voting behavior of some segments of the electorate. The emergence of the Republican party in the 1850s, for example, resulted in redefinitions of partisan conflict to emphasize competing sectional rights. Populist control of the Democratic party in the 1890s presented the electorate with the opportunity to vote in favor of redistributions of economic rights in favor of small-scale agrarian entrepreneurs. Our first problem is to determine empirically whether the suggestions made by Schattschneider and Burnham are correct. We want to discover whether voter realignment was associated with increases in the magnitude of choice available to voters. We shall, then, examine the policy consequences of voter choices.

The content of all Democratic and Republican national party platforms (1844–1968) has been analyzed employing seven broad categories of issues.[3] Some results of this research are reported elsewhere, but for the sake of clarity the essentials of the analysis are repeated here.[4]

Platforms were analyzed in terms of the following categories:

(1) *Capitalism:* the aggregation of wealth and control over the distribution of wealth by business, financial and mercantile elites.
(2) *Internal Sovereignty:* exercise of the power and increase of the sphere of action of the central government *vis-à-vis* states, localities, and individuals.
(3) *Redistribution:* reallocation of wealth in favor of the economically disadvantaged.
(4) *International Cooperation:* open-ended cooperation with and friendship toward foreign objects.
(5) *Universalism:* equality of rights and privileges for domestic minorities.
(6) *Labor:* labor and labor organizations.
(7) *Ruralism:* farms, farmers and the rural way of life.

These categories were selected, in part, because of their inclusion of policy areas which have been important throughout American history. The categories were defined in such a manner as to permit the scoring of positive and negative advocacy statements. The unit of measure is the paragraph. A score indicates that within a given paragraph there occurred a statement or symbol of positive or negative advocacy of the category as defined above. Thus, the statement, "We oppose federal interference in local affairs," would be considered a negative advocacy of Internal Sovereignty, i.e., opposition to "the exercise of the power and increase of the sphere of action of the central government." A paragraph containing this statement would, if the symbol "federal interference" were found in the set of dictionary entries under Internal Sovereignty, be scored as a negative mention of the category for the appropriate party and year.

Any given paragraph may receive a maximum of fourteen scores—one positive and one negative for each of the seven categories. In practice, because the platforms tend to be divided into relatively short, thematic paragraphs, the range tends to be zero to three scores per paragraph. To compare platforms, absolute scores were converted into percentages based on N, the number of paragraphs. The rescoring of a sample of one-third of the platforms by a second coder resulted in a .94 overall level of agreement as determined by a standard intercoder reliability equation. The scores reported by the first coder were employed throughout.

To determine whether the degree of choice available to voters increases during critical eras requires examination of the scope of the alternatives presented to voters by the Democratic and Republican parties over time. The degree of difference between the two parties on any issue involves at least two elements. First is the relative polarity of the parties' positions on the issue dimension in question. Liberalism and conservatism, for example, define differential polarities of position along some issue dimensions. The second element defining the degree of difference between the two parties is the relative weight or importance assigned by the parties to the policy area in question. In those instances, for example, when the parties present differential polarities of position on some particular policy, given the expectation of relatively fixed budgets of money and time, they may also differ on the issue's salience or priority on the agenda of public policy. The total degree of difference between the two parties on any issue is a function of the interaction between differences of polarity and salience. The issue alternatives presented by opposing parties are conventionally said to be radically different, for example, when differences of polarity on issues are exacerbated by differences on the salience or priority of the issues.

In a hypothetical case, the Democratic and Re-

[2] E. E. Schattschneider, *The Semi-Sovereign People* (New York: Holt, Rinehart and Winston, 1960).

[3] We are aware that few voters read platforms. Platforms are employed as indicators of the general preelection positions of the two parties. Although some historical problems are raised, Democratic and Whig platforms were compared in 1844, 1848 and 1852. Source of party platforms: *National Party Platforms*, ed. Kirk H. Porter and Donald B. Johnson (Urbana: University of Illinois Press, 1966), and 1968 supplement.

[4] Benjamin Ginsberg, "Critical Elections and the Substance of Party Conflict: 1844 to 1968," *Midwest Journal of Political Science*, 16, No. 4 (November, 1972), 603–625.

publican parties might offer voters a choice both of differential issue polarities and of the importance to be assigned to social welfare policy. The distance between the positions of the two parties, and thus the degree of choice available to voters on the issue is a function of both the differential polarities and the weights assigned to the issue by the two parties. This total distance between the positions of the parties can be defined as the product of the two differences, or $P_D S_D$, where P_D equals the difference in polarity and S_D is equal to the difference in salience assigned the issue by the two parties.[5]

In any given year, the two parties may differ on a number of individual issues. The total degree of difference between the "bundles" of issue polarities and weights presented by the two parties defines the overall degree of choice available to voters. This total difference is defined as the sum of the products of the differing polarities and weights of the parties on each individual issue or $\sum_{i=1}^{N} P_D S_D$. The larger this overall difference, the greater the total distance between the bundles of issue positions presented voters by the two parties.

For any issue, the difference in polarities between the two parties is given by the percentage difference between the positive percentages of references to that issue by each party weighed by the total salience of the issue.[6]

Set : A = the proportion of positive references in the Democratic platform
B = Democratic, negative
C = the proportion of positive references in the Republican platform
D = Republican, negative

Then for any issue the difference in polarity, P_D, is equal to

$$\left[\frac{AD - BC}{(A + B)(C + D)}\right][A + B + C + D]$$

The differential salience between the two parties on any issue, S_D, is given by

$$(A + B) - (C + D)$$

Then, the total distance between the positions of

the two parties on any individual issue is given by $P_D S_D$. The overall distance between the positions of the two parties across issues is $\sum_{i=1}^{N} P_D S_D$.

Table 1 reports the overall distance between the issue positions of the two parties during each national election year from 1844 to 1968. Differences on each individual issue are reported by Table 2. For convenience, signs appearing on Table 2 always indicate the relative direction of Democratic polarity.[7]

Table 1. Overall Differences of Issue Position Between the National Parties Over Time

Year	Degree of Difference
1844	.016
1848	.177
1852	.292
1856	.228
1860	.111
1864	.118
1868	.132
1872	.029
1876	.017
1880	.075
1884	.008
1888	.016
1892	.063
1896	.094
1900	.080
1904	.063
1908	.018
1912	.054
1916	.028
1920	.009
1924	.031
1928	.007
1932	.069
1936	.017
1940	.026
1944	.014
1948	.008
1952	.019
1956	.009
1960	.007
1964	.041
1968	.013

The data reported by Table 1 indicate that the overall degree of difference between the issue positions of the two parties has varied considerably over time, with the greatest degrees of difference occurring during periods of voter realignment.

Extremely large issue differences occur throughout the Civil War and pre–Civil War periods, centering particularly around 1852 and 1856. Indi-

---

[5] Every unit of difference in polarity is acted upon by a unit of difference in salience. We are, therefore, interested in the product of the two differences. Intensity and polarity cannot be summed in either a scalar or vector sense. The vector sum or Euclidean solution might be appropriate if the two independent variables were comparably measured and addable. Not only is this not the case, but our assumption is that the effects on the dependent variable are the results of a multiplicative interaction. Whether this assumption is correct depends upon whether our results are consistent with the hypothetical results.

[6] We assume that the magnitudes of differences in polarity are, in part, related to the total importance of the issue.

[7] Signs indicate the polarity of the Democrats relative to the Republicans not the absolute polarity of the Democratic position.

Table 2. Degrees of Difference Between the National Parties Over Time

Year	Capitalism	Internal Sovereignty	Redistribution	International Cooperation	Universalism	Labor	Ruralism
1844	− .009	0	0	+ .007	0	0	0
1848	− .046	− .100	0	− .031	0	0	0
1852	− .050	− .239	0	− .001	− .002	0	0
1856	− .030	− .144	0	+ .054	0	0	0
1860	0	− .023	0	− .059	− .029	0	0
1864	0	− .118	0	0	0	0	0
1868	− .018	− .084	0	− .027	− .003	0	0
1872	0	− .011	0	+ .018	0	0	0
1876	+ .012	− .005	0	0	0	0	0
1880	− .021	− .023	0	0	− .031	0	0
1884	0	− .005	0	− .003	0	0	0
1888	− .011	0	0	+ .005	0	0	0
1892	− .051	− .008	0	+ .004	0	0	0
1896	− .086	0	0	+ .008	0	0	0
1900	− .045	0	0	+ .035	0	0	0
1904	− .006	− .005	0	+ .052	0	0	0
1908	− .015	0	0	+ .003	0	0	0
1912	− .049	− .003	0	− .002	0	0	0
1916	− .015	0	0	+ .013	0	0	0
1920	+ .001	0	− .001	+ .007	0	0	0
1924	− .029	0	0	.001	0	.001	0
1928	− .004	0	0	+ .003	0	0	0
1932	− .064	0	0	− .005	0	0	0
1936	− .007	+ .005	+ .005	0	0	0	0
1940	− .015	+ .004	+ .004	+ .003	0	0	0
1944	+ .002	0	0	− .010	0	.002	0
1948	− .006	0	0	+ .002	0	0	0
1952	− .005	+ .004	+ .004	− .005	0	.001	0
1956	− .005	0	0	+ .004	0	0	0
1960	− .001	+ .002	− .002	+ .002	0	0	0
1964	− .002	+ .002	+ .009	+ .020	+ .001	0	0
1968	0	+ .006	+ .006	+ .001	0	0	0

* The absence of a sign indicates that polarities were virtually identical.

vidual issue differences, reported in Table 2, indicate that differences on "Internal Sovereignty" issues account for the bulk of the differences between the two parties during this period.[8] Issue differences between the parties during the Populist period, centering at 1896, rank second in order of magnitude. These differences occur primarily in the "Capitalism" category. Relatively large issue differences are exhibited in 1880, at the close of Reconstruction, primarily in the "Capitalism," "Internal Sovereignty," and "Universalism" categories. The 1932 platforms rank fourth in terms of degree of issue difference between the two parties. The bulk of this difference occurs in the "Capital-

ism" category. All these findings indicate that during each realigning period, the overall degree of difference between the two parties and thus the relative degree of choice available to voters was considerably greater than usual.[9]

While data on the attitudes of voters during these periods do not exist, electoral realignment appears to have been associated with increases in the scope of choice available to voters. During these critical periods, the insurgent party exhibited considerably more than usual policy disagreement with the incumbent party. Whatever the attitudes of voters, these increases in the scope of voter

[8] This finding is very much in accord with Stokes's assertion that the period just prior to the Civil War was *the* era in American political history when political conflict was most nearly focused on a single issue dimension. Donald E. Stokes, "Spatial Models of Party Competition," Angus Campbell, Philip E. Converse, Warren E. Miller and Donald E. Stokes, *Elections and the Political Order* (New York: Wiley, 1966), p. 177.

[9] It is interesting to note that 1912 and 1964, years often associated with substantial amounts of partisan conflict and changes in voting behavior, rank fifth and sixth, respectively, in terms of the magnitude of the difference between the two parties. It is also interesting that the level of conflict between the two parties appears to have diminished considerably over time. Analysis of the causes and consequences of this diminution of conflict is, unfortunately, beyond the scope of this paper.

alternatives meant that votes in favor of the insurgent party during each of these periods were also implicit choices favoring policy changs. During two realigning eras, 1828–36 and 1892–96, voters defeated insurgent parties, while during the four remaining periods, 1798–1800, 1852–60, 1874–80, and 1928–36, voter realignment resulted in victory for insurgents and changes in party control of the government. The data suggest that during these four periods the electorate's behavior represented, in effect, a majority choice in favor of policy changes.[10] Now, let us see whether the electorate's implicit choices were translated into national policy.

Changes in Public Policy Over Time

To determine whether major changes in public policy occur in 1801, 1861, 1881 and 1933, the dates immediately following insurgent victory during critical eras, all United States statutes between 1789 and 1968 were analyzed.[11] Each statute was scored as nominally favoring or opposing policy objectives within the same seven broad categories used in the analysis of national party platforms. For example, a statute which granted privileges or property to a railroad corporation received a +Capitalism score as nominally promoting "the aggregation of wealth by business, financial and mercantile elites." Because a single statute might be aimed at more than one object, multiple scores were permitted. Each statute could, therefore, receive a maximum of seven scores, one positive or one negative in each category. The object, in the case of each statute, was the nominal intention of policy makers rather than the law's impact or effect. The focus of concern is whether policy makers nominally attempt to implement policies consistent with their preelection positions. Obviously, policies often fail to achieve their objectives, but the reasons for failure are numerous and

not necessarily related to the aims of policy makers.

These procedures required reading and analysis of each of the more than 60,000 public laws issued in the United States over a 180 year period. Fortunately, American public laws in the 18th and 19th centuries, at least, tended to be short and to the point. The precise intent of most statutes is obviously subject to varying interpretations. In every instance we attempted to make as general and straightforward an interpretation of the stated intent of the law as the statute's wording would permit. With the aid of historical materials and congressional hearings and records, it proved relatively easy to determine the place of a statute in the broad domains defined by our policy categories. The recording of samples of statutes by additional coders resulted in an overall level of intercoder agreement of .86.

In spite of the many months of labor required, analysis of statutes rather than some other form of policy output (governmental expenditures, for example) appeared to represent the method best suited to the purposes of this study. Since the aim was to determine whether the preelection positions of policy makers were implemented in public policies, it appeared to us to be necessary to look directly at the substance of the relevant public policies. Governmental expenditures offer another reasonable type of indicator and are extremely useful for some purposes. But, expenditures are based, at least in part, on the actual cost of effecting policy aims. Differential costs of implementing various aims make comparisons across types of policy difficult.

Clearly, some statutes are more important than others, and statutes vary considerably in the magnitude of the policy objectives they attempt to achieve. This analysis, which weighs each statute equally, ignores important qualitative differences among statutes. It is, however, difficult to conceive of any procedure which would permit systematic qualitative comparisons of the importance of laws. The aims of policy makers in any policy area can best be characterized in terms of their overall behavior. The behavior of policy makers in the case of a relatively minor piece of legislation is not necessarily a less important indicator of their general aims than is their behavior in the case of a major piece of legislation. This assumption is also implicit in most studies of roll call voting, for example. In addition, during the course of the analysis an impressive consistency became evident, during each year, between the nominal aims of minor and major pieces of legislation in each individual policy area. It is very probable that many statutes which are generally thought important are so considered because, and only if, they set the tone for other pieces of legislation, i.e.,

---

[10] Because of the temporal limitations of our data we can, of course, only make inferences about the 1798–1800 period. The 1874–80 period, in many respects, respresents an anomalous case. Voter realignment during this period primarily, but not exclusively, involves the return of the Southern Democratic vote. Party competition during this period includes the Conservative Republican and Southern Democratic alliance which led to Hayes's disputed election in 1876. Changes in Radical Republican policy, though of different types, were espoused by both parties during this period. In some respects, the election of 1880 represented the electorate's implicit ratification of the results of the elite compromise reached in 1876, i.e., to proceed with rapid industrial expansion while permitting the formal return of the South to national political participation. This compromise meant that the South would be an economically and, for a time, politically subordinate region but, would be autonomous in the area of race relations.

[11] *United States Statutes at Large* (Washington, D.C.: U.S. Government Printing Office, 1789–1968), Vols. I to LXXXII.

are trend breaking or trend setting. For these reasons, to determine the extent to which policy makers attempted to effect policies consistent, on the aggregate, with the implicit choices made by voters, each U.S. statute was analyzed and each was weighed equally.

To search for changes in public policy over time, a variant of a procedure suggested by Ezekiel and Fox[12] and used by Burnham in his analysis of electoral data was employed.[13] The time series provided by each category of policy has been separately regressed on time, the linear trend removed, and a residual series obtained for each category.

[12] Mordecai Ezekial and Karl A. Fox, *Methods of Correlation and Regression Analysis* (New York: Wiley, 1959), p. 343.
[13] Burnham, *Critical Elections*, p. 13.

A *T*-test for difference of means was then applied to successive sets of five residuals within each category—years 1 through 5 compared with years 7 through 11, and so on. It should be noted that *T* is not used here as a conventional statistical test. Since we are dealing with a population rather than a sample, there is no question of statistical significance. Therefore *T* is simply a convenient aggregative device: the numerator compares true population means, the pooled deviation in the denominator smoothes out the effects of isolated deviant years.

This search procedure permits comparison of the magnitudes of the differences between all successive five year periods in each policy category. These magnitudes are reported by Table 3. The data reported in Table 3 do not directly permit us

Table 3. Changes in Public Policy Over Time

Year	Con-gress	Capitalism	Internal Sovereignty	Redistri-bution	International Cooperation	Universalism	Labor	Ruralism
1799	1	2.404	.4627	2.080	.6059	− 1.258		− 2.034
1801	2	3.242	− .5872	1.628	.3531	.3558		− 3.126
1803	3	2.442	− .2490	1.809	.8696	1.540		−.5.157
1805	4	2.754	.2646	3.389	2.008	1.044		− 5.453
1807	5	2.725	− .4130	1.595	1.188	2.566		− 3.765
1809	6	.6497	− .9051	− .0809	.8588	1.372		− 3.185
1811	7	.1249	− 1.303	.0947	.8176	.0197		− 1.375
1813	8	.0644	− 1.199	− .7543	− .7217	− .5746		− .9991
1815	9	− .3686	− 2.062	− 1.576	− 3.645	− .5741		− 1.133
1817	10	.0463	− .7611	− 1.287	− 2.753	− 1.378		− 0.4637
1819	11	− 1.249	.6290	− .6445	− 1.948	− .2224		− .8654
1821	12	1.250	2.632	− 1.818	− 2.251	.7890		− 2.309
1823	13	.8284	2.219	− 1.762	− 1.545	.7883		− 1.843
1825	14	1.931	1.335	− 2.170	− 1.948	.7874		− 1.057
1827	15	.9497	.4042	− 1.850	− .3269	.7867		− .4348
1829	16	1.646	− .3936	− 1.391	− .4465	1.469		.0851
1831	17	1.535	− 2.002	− 2.016	+ .3362	.0452		1.552
1833	18	.5960	− 1.086	− 1.929	.0218	.4525		2.983
1835	19	.2163	− .2727	− 1.827	.8070	.4529		2.798
1837	20	.1433	+ .6916	− .0513	1.285	.4533		1.406
1839	21	.0422	+ 1.448	− .6049	1.444	.4593		1.017
1841	22	− 1.083	+ 1.820	1.047	.3105	2.318		1.230
1843	23	− .0304	+ .7740	1.245	.2865	.9749		.2161
1845	24	− .7008	+ .2114	1.836	− .0261	.9792		− 1.029
1847	25	− 1.012	− .7630	1.394	− 2.047	.9834		− .6953
1849	26	− 1.023	− 1.521	3.398	− 2.376	.5208		− 1.721
1851	27	.0485	− 1.468	2.831	− 2.410	− .9617		− 2.645
1853	.28	− .4774	− 1.974	1.267	− 1.626	− 1.060		− 1.001
1855	29	− .5709	− 1.723	2.710	− 1.746	− 1.520		.1227
1857	30	.4708	− 1.741	.8729	− 2.137	− 2.102		.8435
1859	31	− .4557	− 2.247	.4010	− 1.157	− 3.737		3.459
1861	32	− 1.680	− 1.836	.2166	− .5131	− 5.404		4.219
1863	33	− 2.172	.3797	− 1.432	− 1.893	− 1.405		2.022
1865	34	− 1.802	.4246	− .5248	− .6049	− .5779		1.233
1867	35	− .7695	.7320	1.067	− .2604	.6924		.0331
1869	36	.3661	1.651	− .0884	.0701	2.014		− 2.057
1871	37	1.463	2.057	− .2197	.2371	3.920		− 3.766
1873	38	1.860	3.822	.5447	1.745	1.814		− .7491
1875	39	1.300	4.214	− .3133	2.156	1.904		.5416

Table 3. Continued

Year	Con-gress	Capitalism	Internal Sovereignty	Redistri-bution	International Cooperation	Universalism	Labor	Ruralism
1877	40	− .4939	2.629	.4837	2.669	1.961		2.044
1879	41	−1.838	3.669	1.594	2.355	3.079		2.108
1881	42	−3.329	2.935	1.813	1.873	6.095		4.303
1883	43	−4.532	.9464	.8442	2.841	2.892	−3.610	2.333
1885	44	−6.494	.8770	1.729	1.900	1.859	−2.722	.8434
1887	45	−3.352	.3538	.8962	.3324	.5711	− .3363	.3344
1889	46	−1.273	− .4317	.5892	−1.122	.1783	+1.096	.8014
1891	47	−1.070	− .1263	.8852	− .5680	.0543	1.325	1.368
1893	48	− .7090	.8583	1.206	− .8249	1.264	2.544	.6042
1895	49	− .4614	.3872	.7299	− .5897	1.584	3.428	.3561
1897	50	− .2047	.4540	.4078	− .2153	1.658	1.898	.3211
1899	51	−1.309	− .0323	.0796	1.542	1.111	1.417	−1.299
1901	52	− .3272	− .1618	.1809	.6232	.0492	.3198	−4.712
1903	53	.8196	−1.009	.0726	.8418	−1.111	− .1174	−3.285
1905	54	1.527	−2.230	.4442	.4496	−1.809	−1.800	−1.945
1907	55	1.997	−2.494	− .5348	.5268	− .8971	−2.420	−2.224
1909	56	1.998	−3.837	.4979	1.018	−1.141	−1.863	−1.899
1911	57	2.117	−3.959	.0376	1.224	−1.183	.2429	−2.389
1913	58	1.962	−3.012	.4169	1.146	−1.285	.7035	−2.963
1915	59	1.503	−2.467	.5045	1.192	−1.287	2.064	−2.231
1917	60	2.109	−1.197	.5630	.9470	−2.524	3.510	.8564
1919	61	1.806	+ .6090	− .0605	−1.109	− .2001	6.087	.1816
1921	62	3.838	1.581	.9064	−1.414	.6271	3.160	1.827
1923	63	3.569	.9089	.9591	−1.306	1.257	1.463	3.012
1925	64	2.464	1.424	− .2818	−1.293	1.312	− .1819	1.010
1927	65	2.227	.7017	−1.097	−1.080	1.578	−1.100	−1.161
1929	66	3.743	.4354	−1.977	− .3414	1.236	−2.483	−1.471
1931	67	3.882	.7295	−3.152	1.704	1.565	−2.975	−3.111
1933	68	3.777	'0949	−3.499	1.285	.6000	−5.261	−4.427
1935	69	4.868	.4640	−2.445	1.863	1.960	−4.938	−2.113
1937	70	3.644	.4185	− .7498	2.219	1.983	−5.706	− .3685
1939	71	3.384	.3852	− .5285	2.390	− .1929	−2.863	1.056
1941	72	2.352	− .2912	− .3880	1.827	− .1921	−1.234	1.883
1943	73	.8203	−1.064	− .9960	− .0030	− .4547	− .7014	2.436
1945	74	− .5583	−3.444	− .5833	−1.055	−1.425	1.106	2.088
1947	75	.0693	−3.718	−1.036	−1.371	−2.625	1.786	.5297
1949	76	.3789	−3.820	−.0473	−1.427	− .9545	1.218	− .5189
1951	77	.6324	−2.596	.0698	−1.217	−2.408	1.736	− .4934
1953	78	1.375	−1.078	1.405	−1.006	−2.928	3.587	−1.226
1955	79	1.465	.3420	.2967	.4166	−1.709	1.833	− .5184
1957	80	.4668	.9128	− .6556	.3896	− .9949	.9864	.9305
1959	81	.9521	2.071	−1.921	.7790	−1.356	1.590	1.536

Positive Score = *Decrease*
Negative Score = *Increase*

to determine whether insurgent victory during realigning periods is associated with major policy changes; discrete changes in national policy may result from any number of factors unrelated to realignment—international events, economic changes, and so on. To determine whether the policy changes occurring at 1801, 1861, 1881, and 1933 are of a greater magnitude than changes occurring during other years, the means of the absolute values of the T scores in each policy category for each year were obtained. The resulting summary scores, reported in Table 4, indicate the overall magnitude of the difference between

public policies before and after each year. The highest summary value occurs in 1881, followed in order of magnitude by 1933, 1805, and 1861. Each peak value summarizes a set of policy changes occurring around that year. 1805, 1861, 1881, and 1933 appear, indeed, to mark center points of transition for national policy.[14]

[14] We should note that minority party victory is, on the average, associated with greater than usual degrees of policy change:

Mean change following critical years: 2.52(.124).
Mean change following other minority victories: 1.66(.064).

Table 4. Total Change in Policy Over Time

1799	1.475	1881	3.391
1801	1.549	1883	2.571
1803	2.011	1885	2.346
1805	2.486	1887	.882
1807	2.042	1889	.784
1809	1.175	1891	.771
1811	.624	1893	1.144
1813	.810	1895	1.077
1815	1.560	1897	.737
1817	1.115	1899	.970
1819	.926	1901	.911
1821	1.842	1903	1.037
1823	1.498	1905	1.458
1825	1.538	1907	1.584
1827	.792	1909	1.751
1829	.905	1911	1.593
1831	1.248	1913	1.641
1833	1.178	1915	1.607
1835	1.062	1917	1.672
1837	.672	1919	1.436
1839	.837	1921	1.915
1841	1.310	1923	1.782
1843	.588	1925	1.138
1845	.797	1927	1.278
1847	1.149	1929	1.669
1849	1.760	1931	2.446
1851	1.728	1933	2.706
1853	1.734	1935	2.664
1855	1.399	1937	2.156
1857	1.361	1939	1.543
1859	1.910	1941	1.167
1861	2.312	1943	.925
1863	1.551	1945	1.466
1865	.861	1947	1.591
1867	.592	1949	1.195
1869	1.043	1951	1.307
1871	1.944	1953	1.872
1873	1.756	1955	1.012
1875	1.738	1957	.763
1877	1.714	1959	1.458
1879	2.441		

Reexamination of Table 3 to determine the elements that account for each summary value indicates that the 1805 peak is composed primarily of negative changes in the Capitalism, Redistribution and International Cooperation categories, and positive changes in the Ruralism category, all occurring in the period from 1801 to 1805 following the Jeffersonian victory. The primary components of the 1861 peak are positive changes in the Internal Sovereignty and Universalism cate-

Mean change, all other years: 1.32.

The mean degree of choice available to voters prior to both critical changes and other minority party victories is given in parenthesis. The number of cases is too small to permit the use of measures of association. The 1848 election is included as a minority victory although the Whigs captured only the presidency.

gories and negative changes in the Ruralism category, from 1860 to 1863. The 1881 peak is accounted for primarily by positive changes in the Capitalism category and negative changes in the Internal Sovereignty, Universalism and Ruralism categories from 1875–1885. The major components of the 1933 peak appear to be negative changes in the Capitalism category and positive changes in the Redistribution, Labor and Universalism categories from 1933–1935.

In each case, while the issue categories suggested by our analysis of platform content are among the principal elements of policy change, large changes also occur in other categories. Although random association cannot be excluded, historical analyses of party ideologies in many instances suggest relationships between these additional changes in policy and the set of issues on which we expected to find policy change. While issues related to "Capitalism" were emphasized by the two parties during the 1928–36 period, for example, belief systems during this period associated negative positions on Capitalism with positive positions on "Labor" and "Redistribution," so that the coincidence of changes in these three categories is not surprising.[15]

Given such historical associations, the clusters of policy change we have identified seem to be consistent with the Schattschneider-Burnham thesis and our analysis of platform content data. Thus, the policy changes associated with Jefferson's victory in the election of 1800 are consistent with an electoral choice in opposition to a pro-British foreign policy and neomercantilist economic policy.[16] Republican victory in 1860 is associated with changes in national policy consistent with an electoral choice in favor of national sovereignty and opposing the expansion of slavery.[17] The policy changes centering around 1881 are consistent with an implicit electoral choice favoring the termination of Reconstruction and the expansion of industrial and commercial activity.[18]

[15] William E. Leuchtenburg, *The Perils of Prosperity* (Chicago: University of Chicago Press, 1958), Samuel Lubell, *The Future of American Politics* (Garden City: Doubleday, 1955), and Arthur M. Schlesinger, Jr., *The Age of Roosevelt* (Boston: Houghton-Mifflin, 1957), vol. I, remain excellent sources.

[16] Two excellent sources are William N. Chambers, *Political Parties in a New Nation* (New York: Oxford University Press, 1963) and Noble E. Cunningham, *The Jeffersonian Republicans* (Chapel Hill: University of North Carolina Press, 1963).

[17] Among the best historical accounts are William W. Freehling, *Prelude to Civil War* (New York: Harper, 1966) and Eric Foner, *Free Soil, Free Labor, Free Men: The Ideology of the Republican Party Before the Civil War* (New York: Oxford University Press, 1970).

[18] Stanley Cobben, "Northeastern Business and Radical Reconstruction: A Reexamination," in *The Economic Impact of the American Civil War*, ed. Ralph Andreano

Changes in policy after 1933 are in keeping with voter choices favoring alterations in the economic system and redistributions of opportunities in favor of urban working class elements.

It appears to be the case that the choices made by the electorate during these critical periods are translated into major changes in national policy.

Electoral Choices and Voter Alignments

Approximately once in a generation, voters are given the opportunity to alter national policy significantly. The decisions made by voters during these critical periods define the termini of broad epochs in American political history.

Between critical periods, the degree of issue difference between opposing parties and the opportunity for voter choice are diminished. In the case of two issue areas, "Internal Sovereignty" and "Universalism," the implicit choices made by the electorate at the termination of radical reconstruction—in effect to leave the South politically subordinate but autonomous in the area of race relations, and to affirm the changed status of blacks while making no further changes in race relations —were not offered again until the 1960s. In these policy areas, the electorate's role ended when it made its choices in 1876 and 1880.

In every other instance, however, choices continue to be available to the electorate following realignment. While the magnitude of the difference between the two parties and thus the opportunity for voter choice generally diminishes fol-

lowing the critical era, in each case, the general terms of choice established by the two parties prior to voter realignment persist following realignment. Some opportunity for choice thus continues beyond critical periods. Stable voter alignments, in effect, represent continuing policy choices on the part of the electorate. Our findings suggest that voter alignments are, in effect, organized around substantive issues of policy and support the continued dominance in government of a party committed to the principal elements of the choice made by voters during critical eras. Stable partisan alignments are, in effect, the electorate's choice in favor of the continuation of a particular set of policies. Partisan alignments form the constituent bases for governments committed to the translation of the choices made by the electorate during critical periods into public policy over a relatively long period of time. The absence of major policy changes between realigning periods suggests that these implicit voter choices in favor of continuity are also translated into national policy. The policy-making role of the electorate is, in effect, a continuing one.

A perennial question of American politics involves the extent to which national policy represents the choice of the people. This question necessarily has a temporal dimension. While some particular policy may or may not be in accord with the wishes of a majority at any particular point in time, the more general and perhaps more significant question is whether, on the whole, national policy is related to electoral choice most of the time.

Our longitudinal analysis indicates that American public policy is shaped to a significant degree by the behavior of voters. Whether or not voters are completely aware of all of the implications of their actions, popular majorities appear, over time, to govern.

(Cambridge: Schenkman, 1962), pp. 144–164. Also Louis Hartz, "Government-Business Relations," in *Economic Change in the Civil War Era, Proceedings of a Conference on American Economic Institutional Change, 1850–1873,* ed. David T. Gilchrist and W. Donald Lewis (Greenville, Delaware: Eleutherian Mills-Hagley Foundation, 1965).

11

POLITICAL PARTIES AND
MACROECONOMIC POLICY

Douglas A. Hibbs, Jr.

This study examines postwar patterns in macroeconomic policies and outcomes associated with left-and right-wing governments in capitalist democracies. It argues that the objective economic interests as well as the subjective preferences of lower income and occupational status groups are best served by a relatively low unemployment-high inflation macroeconomic configuration, whereas a comparatively high unemployment-low inflation configuration is compatible with the interests and preferences of upper income and occupational status groups. Highly aggregated data on unemployment and inflation outcomes in relation to the political orientation of governments in 12 West European and North American nations are analyzed revealing a low unemployment-high inflation configuration in nations regularly governed by the Left and a high unemployment-low inflation pattern in political systems dominated by center and rightist parties. Finally, time-series analyses of quarterly postwar unemployment data for the United States and Great Britain suggests that the unemployment rate has been driven downward by Democratic and Labour administrations and upward by Republican and Conservative governments. The general conclusion is that governments pursue macroeconomic policies broadly in accordance with the objective economic interests and subjective preferences of their class-defined core political constituencies.

In so far as stable prices are regarded as desirable for their own sake, as contributing to social justice, it must be recognized that justice to the rentier can be achieved only by means of the injustice to the rest of the community of maintaining a lower level of effective demand than might otherwise be achieved. We are here presented with a conflict of interests ... and actual policies are largely governed by the rival influences of the interests involved. (Joan Robinson, *Essays in the Theory of Employment* (New York: Macmillan, 1937), p. 35.)

From one important point of view, indeed, the avoidance of inflation and the maintenance of full employment can be most usefully regarded as conflicting class interests of the bourgeoisie and the proletariat, respectively, the conflict being resolvable only by the test of relative political power in the society. (Harry G. Johnson, "Problems of Efficiency in Monetary Management," *Journal of Political Economy,* 76 (September/October 1968), p. 986.)

We tend to get our recessions during Republican administrations. ... The difference between the Democrats and the Republicans is the difference in their constituencies. It's a class difference ... the Democrats constitute the people, by and large, who are around median incomes or below. These are the ones whom the Republicans want to pay the price and burden of fighting inflation. The Democrats [are] willing to run with some inflation [to increase employment]; the Republicans are not. (Paul A. Samuelson, "Some Dilemmas of Economic Policy," *Challenge,* 20 (March/April 1977), pp. 30–31.)

*This article is taken from my longer monograph *Economic Interest and the Politics of Macroeconomic Policy.* Earlier versions of the paper were delivered to the Econometric Society World Congress, Toronto, Canada, August 1975, and the Annual Meeting of the American Political Science Association, San Francisco, August 1975. The research has been supported by National Science Foundation Grants GS 33121 and SOC75–03773. The Computer Research Center of the National Bureau of Economic Research provided computational support. I am indebted to Hayward Alker, Suzanne Berger, Bob Brito, Randy Forsberg, J. David Greenstone, David Held, Mike Intriligator, Robert Jackman, Peter Lemieux, Frank Lerman, Andrew Martin, Benjamin Page, Adam Przeworski, Martin Rein, William Schneider, Robert Solow, and Paolo Sylos-Labini for comments on an earlier draft. The research assistance of Warren Fishbein, Marilyn Shapleigh and especially Nick Vasilatos is gratefully acknowledged. I retain the usual responsibility for errors of fact and judgment.

The most important problem of macroeconomic policy facing public authorities in industrial societies during the postwar period has been the unfavorable trade-off that exists between unemployment and inflation—the so-called "Phillips curve." Although the unemployment/inflation trade-off has not exhibited great stability in recent years—for example, the U.S. economy is undoubtedly more vulnerable to inflation at low levels of unemployment now than it was a few years ago—there is widespread agreement among economists that in capitalist economies wage and price stability requires relatively high levels of unemployment, and, conversely, that low rates of unemployment

From Douglas A. Hibbs, Jr., "Political Parties and Macroeconomic Policy," LXXI(4) *The American Political Science Review* 1467-1487 (December 1977). Copyright 1977 by The American Political Science Association. Reprinted by permission.

yield relatively high rates of inflation.[1] Put another way, price stability and full employment are incompatible goals in the sense that conventional macroeconomic policy has not been able to achieve both simultaneously. Since political authorities can (and do) influence the rate of unemployment and inflation by manipulation of monetary and fiscal policy instruments, macroeconomic policy has been the focus of intense controversy and conflict between key political actors and interest groups.

This article examines postwar patterns in macroeconomic policies and outcomes associated with left- and right-wing governments in capitalist democracies. The main body of the article has three parts. The first section briefly reviews evidence, which is documented in great detail elsewhere,[2] indicating that different unemployment/inflation outcomes have important, class-linked effects on the distribution of national income. It is argued that the economic interests at stake in various macroeconomic configurations are (implicitly) reflected in public opinion data on the relative aversion of different income and occupational groups to unemployment and inflation. The second part of the article presents a general scheme rank-ordering the preferences of political parties, arrayed along the traditional left to right spectrum, toward various economic goals, and analyzes highly aggregated data on unemployment and inflation outcomes in relation to the political orientation of regimes in 12 West European and North American nations. These international comparisons suggest that the "revealed preference" of leftist governments has been for relatively low unemployment at the expense of high rates of inflation, whereas, comparatively low inflation and high unemployment characterize political systems dominated by center and right-wing parties. The third and longest section of the article presents time-series analyses of quarterly postwar data on unemployment in the United States and Great Britain. The estimation results from the time-series models support the conclusion that unemployment has been driven downward during the tenure of Democratic and Labour administrations and has moved upward during periods of Republican and Conservative

rule in the United States and Great Britain, respectively.

The general conclusion of the study is that the macroeconomic policies pursued by left- and right-wing governments are broadly in accordance with the objective economic interests and subjective preferences of their class-defined core political constituencies.

Unemployment and Inflation: Objective Economic Interests and Subjective Preferences

A common rationalization for deflationary macroeconomic policies is that inflation adversely affects the economic position of wage and salary earners and, in particular, erodes the economic well-being of the poor. Empirical studies, however, give little support to this argument. The work of Blinder and Esaki, Hollister and Palmer, Metcalf, Thurow, Schultz, and others strongly indicates that a relatively low unemployment-high inflation macroeconomic configuration is associated with substantial relative and absolute improvements in the economic well-bring of the poor and, more generally, exerts powerful equalizing effects on the distribution of personal income.[3]

Although these studies suggest that inflationary periods with tight labor markets are associated with a general equalization of the income distribution—the poor and certain middle income groups gaining at the expense of the rich—it nevertheless has been argued that the economic position of a substantial fraction of the labor force suffers a net decline during periods of vigorous economic expansion. The usual observation is that price rises tend to outstrip money wage increases during cyclical upswings and real wage rates therefore fall. Moreover, business expansions bring a general inflation of profits which yields increases in the

---

[1] A detailed review of the theoretical and empirical literature on Phillips-curve inflation models is given in my *Economic Interest and the Politics of Macroeconomic Policy*, No. C/75–14, Center for International Studies, M.I.T., Cambridge, Mass., January 1976. Copies of this monograph are available at cost from the C.I.S. Publications officer.

[2] Ibid.

[3] See, for example, A. Blinder and H. Esaki, "Macroeconomic Activity and Income Distribution in the Postwar U.S." (mimeo., November 1976); Robinson G. Hollister and John L. Palmer, "The Impact of Inflation on the Poor," in *Redistribution to the Rich and the Poor*, ed. K. E. Boulding and M. Pfaff (Belmont, Calif.: Wadsworth, 1972), pp. 240–70; Charles E. Metcalf, *An Econometric Model of the Income Distribution* (Chicago: Markham, 1972); Lester C. Thurow, "Analyzing the American Income Distribution," *American Economic Review: Papers and Proceedings*, 60 (May 1970), 261–69; and T. Schultz, "Secular Trends and Cyclical Behavior of Income Distribution in the United States: 1944–1964," in *Six Papers on the Size Distribution of Wealth and Income*, ed. L. Soltow (New York: National Bureau of Economic Research, 1969), pp. 75–100.

share of the national income going to capital.[4] If the profit-inflation and wage-lag hypotheses are accurate, it is possible in principle that the relative and absolute gains enjoyed by lower income groups during economic booms come at the expense of other wage earning groups and conceal substantial declines in the national income share of labor as a whole.

However, contemporary empirical work provides little or no evidence in favor of either the profit-inflation or wage-lag hypothesis. Long's examination of historical relationships in the United States (1860 to 1958) found that real wage movements were not countercyclical, as Keynes and others argued, but on the whole corresponded quite closely to business fluctuations.[5] Bodkin's analysis of postwar quarterly and longer-run annual data on trend-corrected real wage changes in Canada and the United States detected no systematic association one way or the other between real wage movements and unemployment in Canada, whereas inverse associations prevailed in the United States.[6] Finally, studies by Bach and Stephenson, Boddy and Crotty, Burger, Hibbs, Kuh, Hultgren, and the Organization for Economic Cooperation and Development on the cyclical behavior of factor shares, i.e., shares of the national income going to capital and labor over the business cycle, show that in general the ratio of profits to wages increases steadily after a trough in business activity, reaches its highest point about midway through an expansion, and thereafter drops off markedly.[7] Thus the latter

halves of business upswings, during which unemployment typically falls and the rate of inflation rises, are associated with a pronounced squeeze on profits and are more accurately described as periods of *wage-lead* and *profit-deflation*. Although it is difficult to say whether these patterns in the cyclical behavior of wages and profits would persist in prolonged expansions, the evidence does demonstrate that the economic position of wage and salary earners as a group improves substantially, both in relative and absolute terms, during periods of relatively low unemployment and high rates of inflation.

If sustained economic expansions confer such obvious benefits on wage and salary earners generally and on low and middle income groups in particular, why have macroeconomic policy makers exhibited such keen sensitivity to the inflationary consequences of full employment? One explanation of why political authorities have been willing to accept less than full employment is that the mass of wage and salary earners have an "irrational" aversion to inflation, perhaps because people tend to view rising prices as an arbitrary "tax."[8] Deflationary macroeconomic policies may therefore represent the political response to widespread anti-inflation sentiment in the mass public.[9] Sample survey evidence for the United States and Great Britain squarely contradicts this argument. For more than 20 years George Katona and has associates at the Survey Research Center of the University of Michigan

---

[4]These hypotheses have a distinguished pedigree. They have appeared, among other places, in Earl J. Hamilton, "Prices and Progress," *Journal of Economic History*, 12 (Fall 1952), 325–49; Alvin Hansen, "Factors Affecting the Trend of Real Wages," *American Economic Review*, 15 (March 1925), 27–42; John Maynard Keynes, *The General Theory of Employment, Interest and Money* (New York: Harcourt, 1936); Jacques Rueff, "Nouvelle discussion sur le chomage, les salaires et les pris," *Revue d'Economie Politique* (1951), 761–91; and Sidney Weintraub, *An Approach to the Theory of Income Distribution* (Westport, Conn.: Greenwood Press Inc., 1958). Weintraub, for example, has flatly asserted that ". . . only entrepreneurs and the actual unemployed have an unequivocal stake in maximum employment, while rentiers and the employed find their interests better served at lower levels of activity," p. 60.

[5]Clarence D. Long, "The Illusion of Wage Rigidity: Long and Short Cycles in Wages and Labor," *Review of Economics and Statistics*, 42 (May 1960), 140–51.

[6]Ronald G. Bodkin, "Real Wages and Cyclical Variations in Employment: A Re-Examination of the Evidence," *Canadian Journal of Economics*, 2 (February to November 1969), 353–74.

[7]G. L. Bach and James B. Stephenson, "Inflation and the Redistribution of Wealth," *Review of Eco-*

nomics and Statistics, 61 (February 1974), 1–13; Raford Boddy and James Crotty, "Class Conflict and Macro-Policy: The Political Business Cycle," *Review of Radical Political Economics*, 7 (Spring 1975), 1–19; Albert Burger, "Relative Movements in Wages and Profits," *Federal Reserve Bank of St. Louis Review*, 55 (February 1973), 8–16; Hibbs, "Economic Interest"; Edwin Kuh, "Income Distribution and Employment over the Business Cycle," in *Brookings Quarterly Econometric Model of the United States*, ed. J. Dusenberry et al. (Chicago: Rand McNally, 1965), pp. 227–78; Thor Hultgren, *Costs, Prices, and Profits: Their Cyclical Relations* (New York: National Bureau of Economic Research, 1965); and OECD, *Inflation, The Present Problem* (Paris: OECD Publications, 1970).

[8]This has been proposed, for example, in William D. Nordhaus, "The Political Business Cycle," *Review of Economic Studies*, 42 (April 1975), 169–90.

[9]As one White House economist reportedly put it in April of 1975 "One hundred percent of the people have been hit by inflation. Only 10 percent really worry about unemployment." Quoted by S. Golden, "High Joblessness Expected to Persist as a Condition of U.S. through Decade," *New York Times* (April 21, 1975), p. 46.

have polled national samples of American households about their expectations and attitudes toward inflation, unemployment, and other socioeconomic issues. Katona writes that until 1973 more people felt that unemployment was a greater evil than inflation. Moreover, a majority of the respondents in the SRC surveys repeatedly indicated that they were hurt "little" or "not at all" by inflation and that they would not be willing to accept substantial increases in unemployment in order to halt increasing prices.[10]

My own analyses of survey data from Great Britain and the United States on public aversion to unemployment and inflation supports the inferences of Katona and his associates. Space permits me to report only the general conclusions of these analyses here.[11] First, the British and American public opinion data clearly show that in the period through 1972 (which is the relevant period for the purposes of this study) solid majorities of the mass public(s) typically expressed greater aversion to unemployment than inflation. Second, popular concern about unemployment and inflation is class-related. Low and middle income and occupational status groups are more averse to unemployment than inflation, whereas, upper income and occupational status groups are more concerned about inflation than unemployment. Although the available survey evidence is by no means definitive, it does appear that the subjective preferences of class or status groups are at least roughly in accordance with their objective economic interests, insofar as these are reflected by the behavior of wages, profits, and the distribution of personal income under various unemployment/inflation macroeconomic configurations.[12]

Having outlined the group or class cleavages surrounding the unemployment/inflation trade-off, we now turn to the main task of this article and consider to what extent these cleavages are reflected in the economic policies pursued by governments of different political orientations.

Macroeconomic Policies and Outcomes: International Comparisons

The evidence reviewed in the previous section suggests that the objective economic interests and subjective preferences of lower income, blue-collar groups differ markedly vis-à-vis the unemployment/inflation trade-off from those of higher income, white-collar groups. Although the importance of socioeconomic status as a basis of electoral cleavage varies substantially across party systems, the mass constituencies of political parties in most advanced industrial societies are distinguished to a significant extent by class, income, and related socioeconomic characteristics. Even a casual examination of the historical record makes it clear that differences in the economic interests and preferences of income and occupational groups are reflected in the contrasting positions toward various economic goals associated with left- and right-wing political parties. (This is not to suggest, incidentally, that the influence linkages between mass constituencies and party elites are unidirectional.) Hence, labor-oriented, working-class-based Socialist and Labor parties typically attach far greater importance to full employment than to inflation, whereas business-oriented, upper middle-class-based Conservative parties generally assign higher priority to price stability than to unemployment. The implied preferences or issue positions of political parties (or *tendances*), arrayed along the traditional left-right spectrum, are outlined more systematically in Table 1. The table is adapted from a study by Kirschen et al. and is based on questionnaires administered to experts in eight industrial societies.[13] The most important thing to notice

---

[10]George Katona, "Disputing Galbraith," *New York Times* (December 22, 1974), and George Katona et al., *Aspirations and Affluence* (New York: McGraw-Hill, 1971). Many of the results from these surveys appear in annual volumes of the *Survey of Consumer Finances* (Ann Arbor: Survey Research Center, 1960–72). Results of surveys taken before 1960 are available as mimeo reports from the SRC.

[11]The analyses are presented fully in the section "Public Opinion Toward Inflation and Unemployment" in Hibbs, "Economic Interest," pp. 24–40.

[12]The class interests at stake in unemployment/inflation outcomes and policies show up in the policy positions taken by organized labor and capital as well as in the distribution of mass opinion. Throughout the postwar period, trade union spokesmen have invariably placed primary emphasis on the objective of full employment, while business elites have attached far more importance to price stability. A clear statement of labor's position is given by Nat Goldfinger, "Full Employment: The Neglected Poli-

cy?" *The American Federationist*, 79 (November 1972). Data on corporate thinking on the inflation and unemployment issues is presented in L. Silk and D. Vogel, *Profits and Principles: The Social and Political Thinking of American Businessmen* (New York: Simon and Schuster, 1977).

[13]E. S. Kirschen et al., *Economic Policy In Our Time*, Vol. I (Amsterdam: North-Holland, 1964). With the exception of the balance of payments issue (the importance of which depends critically on the inter-

in the table is the reversal in the relative preferences of the parties regarding various economic goals as one moves from left to right across the political spectrum. In particular, notice that the party preferences concerning unemployment and inflation are consistent with the class-related cleavages surrounding these issues that were identified previously.

Since political authorities in the post-Keynesian age have considerable influence on macroeconomic outcomes, we would expect to observe (*ceteris paribus*, of course) a relatively low unemployment-high inflation macroeconomic configuration under leftist regimes and conversely under rightist regimes. Highly aggregated, cross-national evidence supporting this proposition appears in Figure 1, which shows a Phillips curve-like scatterplot of the average rates of unemployment and inflation over the 1960 to 1969 period in 12 industrial societies. The vertical and horizontal axes in this Figure identify the median average rates of unemployment and inflation, respectively. Five of the six nations enjoying an average level of unemployment below the West European-North Ameri-

can median (i.e., the nations to the left of the vertical axis) are countries with large Socialist or Social Democratic parties (closely linked to organized labor) that have governed for much or most of the time since World War II. Looking at the postwar period as a whole, Socialist parties have been in power (or have shared power as members of coalition governments) for the entire period in Sweden, for the bulk of the period in Denmark, Finland, and Norway, and for about two-thirds of the period in the Netherlands. As one would anticipate from the Phillips curve (inverse association of unemployment and inflation), the majority of the nations᾽ lying below the unemployment median have on the average experienced above-median rates of inflation. The principal exception to these generalizations is West Germany, which has been governed for most of the postwar period by the conservative CDU party and has experienced both low unemployment and low rates of inflation.

With the exception of Belgium and to a lesser extent the United Kingdom, the governments of all nations in Figure 1 falling above (i.e., to the right of) the average unemployment median have been dominated by center or right-wing political parties. In the United States and Canada, where problems of deficient aggregate demand are chronic, unemployment rates have consistently been the highest in the Western industrial world. Neither of these countries has politically important Socialist or

national economic position of a given nation), the positions attributed to the various *tendances* were homogeneous across countries. For a similar scheme, see Bruno Frey and Lawrence J. Lau, "Towards a Mathematical Model of Government Behaviour," *Zeitschrift für Nationalökonomie*, 28 (1968), 355–80.

Table 1. Preferences of Political Parties in Advanced Industrial Societies
Regarding Various Economic Goals[a]

	Socialist-Labor	Center	Conservatives
Decreasing Importance of Goals	Full Employment		Price Stability
	Equalization of Income Distribution		
		Price Stability	
	Economic Expansion		
		Economic Expansion	Balance of Payments Equilibrium
		Full Employment	
		Equalization of Income Distribution	
	Price Stability		Economic Expansion
		Balance of Payments Equilibrium	Full Employment
	Balance of Payments Equilibrium		
			Equalization of Income Distribution

[a]Based on Kirschen et al., 1964.

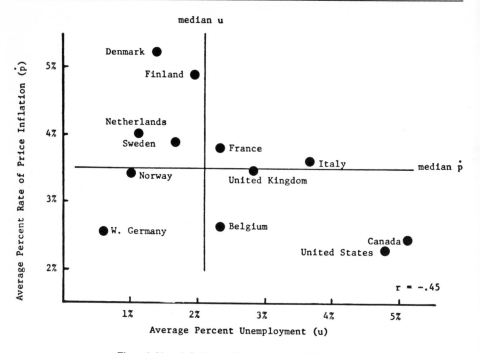

Figure 1. Mean Inflation and Unemployment, 1960–1969,
in 12 West European and North American Nations

Source: Unemployment data for Canada, France, Italy, Sweden, U.K., and W. Germany are adjusted to the U.S. definition and are from Constance Sorrentino, "Unemployment in the United States and Seven Foreign Countries," *Monthly Labor Review*, 93 (September 1970), 12–23. All other data are from I.L.O., *Yearbook of Labor Statistics*, various volumes.

Labor parties,[14] and centrist or rightist governments have ruled throughout the postwar era.

The Communist and Socialist political blocs in France and Italy have commanded a sizable share of the vote in all postwar elections, but aside from the governments of national unity in the immediate postwar period and the marginal representation of the French and Italian socialists in various Center coalition governments, they have been largely frozen out of positions of executive power.[15] Belgium deviates from

[14]Canada's New Democratic Party, a genuinely socialist party with close connections to organized labor, has exhibited increasing political vitality in recent years (capturing several provincial governments) but remains at this writing a "minor" party with little influence on national policy.

[15]Actually there was one brief period of Socialist-led rule in France after 1951: Guy Mollet's government of February 1956 to May 1957. Analysis of

annual data shows that unemployment was lower and inflation higher during Mollet's government (as well as during the subsequent Center-Left government of Bourgès-Maunoury) than during the right-wing Gaullist governments of the late 1950s and 1960s. The Center-Left governments of the middle 1950s clearly assigned higher priority to full employment and expansion than the Gaullist regime, which pursued policies geared to disinflation and economic "stabilization." As a result, France's location on the "international Phillips curve" has changed dramatically. (Contrast the data shown in Figure 1 to a similar display of average rates of inflation and unemployment reported by D. Smyth, "Unemployment and Inflation: A Cross-Country Analysis of the Phillips Curve," *American Economic Review*, 61 (June 1971), 426–29, for the period 1950–1960.) Of course France's entry into the EEC in 1958 increased the importance of the external balance-of-payments constraint during the Fifth Republic. However, the deflationary policies of the Gaullist governments must be attributed to some extent to the priorities of the regime. See M Maclennan et al., *Economic Planning and Policies in Britain, France and Germany* (New York: Praeger, 1968).

the general pattern in that the Socialists have ruled (in coalition with other parties) for just over half of the postwar years, and the average rate of unemployment stands just above the West European-North American median. However, unemployment has on the average been lower (and the rate of inflation on the average higher) during the tenure of Socialist coalition governments than during periods of Center-Right rule. Great Britain also constitutes something of an exception. The Labour and Conservative parties have alternated in power (although the Conservatives ruled continuously from 1951 to 1964) and the average unemployment rate is above the median. The mean British unemployment rate, however, is substantially less than the average rates prevailing in the United States, Canada, and Italy.

Taken as a whole, the evidence in Figure 1 indicates that the "revealed preference" of governments of the nations in the northwest quadrant of the figure has been for relatively low unemployment at the expense of high inflation, whereas the opposite appears to be true for governments of the countries in the southeast quadrant of the figure. This is rein-forced by Figures 2 and 3, which show simple scatterplots of the average rates of inflation and unemployment in relation to average government participation (percentage of postwar years in the executive branch) of Socialist and Labor parties. These plots merely provide a slightly different illustration of the earlier argument. Nations in which Social Democratic and Labor parties have governed for most or much of the postwar period have generally experienced high rates of inflation. Conversely, low rates of inflation have prevailed in countries where center and right-wing parties have dominated the policy-making process (Figure 2). The reverse is true of the association between average unemployment and average Socialist-Labor executive participation. Comparatively low rates of unemployment characterize systems in which left-wing parties have regularly controlled the executive, and high unemployment rates have been typical in systems governed primarily by center and right-wing parties.[16]

[16]Since the macroeconomic policies (and outcomes) of the 1960s were to a significant extent

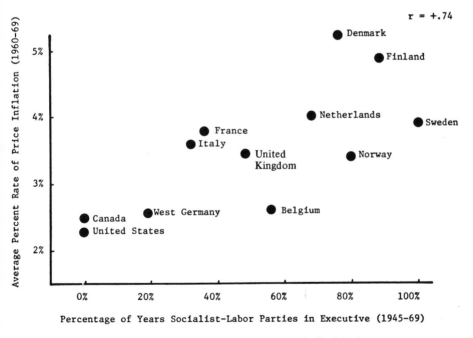

Figure 2. Mean Inflation and Socialist-Labor Executive Participation in 12 West European and North American Nations

If a common unemployment/inflation trade-off (or "menu of policy choices") confronted each of the nations appearing in Figures 1 through 3, the cross-national variation in unemployment/inflation configurations might be attributed primarily to systematic differences in the short-run monetary and fiscal policies pursued by political authorities.[17] The

modest but inverse relationship between the average rates of inflation and unemployment (the correlation is −.45) suggests that there is some merit in this interpretation. Rates of unemployment even approaching those typical of Canada and the United States are simply not politically feasible or acceptable in countries with large Socialist-Labor parties that are frequently governed by the Left. Prior economic performance and continued emphasis on low unemployment in political discourse has gen-

---

influenced by the performance record of the late 1940s and 1950s (especially in countries in which Social Democratic-led governments managed to maintain full employment after the war), the Socialist-Labor participation rate has been calculated over the entire postwar period (1945–69) rather than for the years 1960 to 1969 alone.

[17]This has been suggested, for example, in reference to the difference in unemployment rates between

North America and Western Europe, by Albert Rees, "The Phillips Curve as a Menu for Policy Choice," *Economica,* 37 (August 1970), 227–38. Monetary policy instruments include interest rates and the supply of credit and money. Fiscal policy instruments include taxation and public spending.

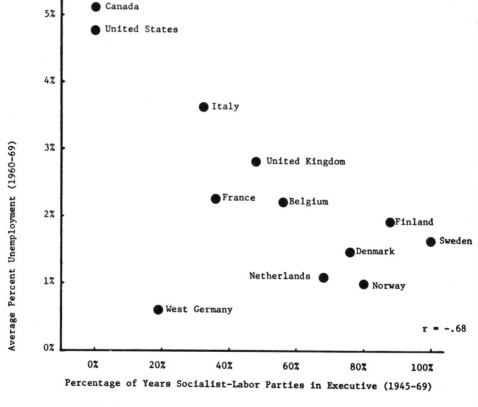

Figure 3. Mean Unemployment and Socialist-Labor Executive Participation in 12 West European and North American Nations

erated widespread public expectations of sustained full employment, which insures that short-run macroeconomic policy is geared to preserving the low unemployment, continuous inflation pattern observed in the northwest quadrant of Figure 1.

However, empirical time-series studies have established that unemployment/inflation trade-offs exhibit considerable cross-national diversity. A comparative investigation by Flanagan, for example, has shown that over the 1951 to 1968 period the Phillips curve trade-off available to political authorities in the United States was less favorable than the trade-off curves for Great Britain and Sweden.[18] Evidence of this sort indicates that international differences in institutional and structural arrangements underlie, at least to some extent, the cross-national variation in aggregate, equilibrium outcomes, depicted in Figures 1 through 3. In particular, the enormous emphasis placed on full employment in nations with large Socialist-Labor parties has led to the introduction of centralized economic planning and coordination, extensive public sector investment, and, perhaps most important, a wide range of labor market and manpower policies that are designed to minimize the incidence and duration of unemployment.[19] Hence, the critical historical role of the Left in shaping longer-run policies and institutional arrangements must also be considered in order to account adequately for cross-national variation in unemployment/inflation configurations.

Macroeconomic Policies and Outcomes: Time-Series Analyses

Thus far only static, aggregated evidence has been presented in support of the hypothesis that macroeconomic outcomes systematically covary with the political orientation of governments. A dynamic country-by-country analysis of postwar time-series data might provide a more convincing test of this general proposition except for the major constraint that many advanced industrial societies have simply not experienced very much partisan variation (defined in the traditional left-right sense) in their governments.

Time-series analyses of unemployment rates have been undertaken for Great Britain and the United States. Great Britain is an ideal candidate for dynamic analysis in that national political power has oscillated between the working class-based Labour party and the middle class-based Conservative party. In comparison to the British Labour and Conservative parties, the two dominant American political parties are less distant ideologically and have more heterogeneous social bases.[20] Nonetheless, the Democratic party has relatively close connections to organized labor and lower income and occupational status groups, while the Republican party is generally viewed as being more responsive to the interests of capital or business and upper income and occupational status groups.[21] Other things being equal, we would therefore expect to observe a downward movement in the unemployment rate during the tenure of Democratic and Labour governments and an upward movement in the unemployment rate during periods of Republican and Conservative rule in the United States and Great Britain, respectively.

In order to evaluate this proposition rigorously, we need a model that permits estimation of the hypothesized effects of government macroeconomic policies on the unemployment rate, net of trends, cycles and stochastic fluctuation in the unemployment time-series observations. In contrast to more conventional approaches, I have used the "intervention analysis" scheme of Box, Jenkins and Tiao.[22]

[18]Robert J. Flanagan, "The U.S. Phillips Curve and International Unemployment Rate Differentials," *American Economic Review,* 63 (1973), 114–31. For additional evidence on cross-national variation in Phillips curves, see Ronald G. Bodkin et al., *Price Stability and High Employment: The Options for Canadian Economic Policy* (Ottawa: Economic Council of Canada, 1967).

[19]Of course leftist governments have not been equally effective in this regard. For example, British Labour governments have been much less imaginative in developing macroeconomic policy (and have pursued a more centrist political strategy) than Swedish Social Democratic administrations. See the perceptive comparative analysis in Andrew Martin, *The Politics of Economic Policy in the U.S.: A Tentative View from a Comparative Perspective* (Beverly Hills: Sage Professional Paper in Comparative Politics, 1973). The best treatment in English of the archetypal Swedish model is probably A. Lindbeck, *Swedish Economic Policy* (Berkeley: University of California Press, 1974).

[20]See, for example, Robert Alford, *Party and Society* (Chicago: Rand-McNally, 1963).

[21]For an argument that organized labor and the Democratic party in the United States are interpenetrated in a way that is at least partially equivalent to Socialist party-labor union alliances in much of Western Europe, see J. D. Greenstone, *Labor in American Politics* (New York: Alfred A. Knopf, 1969).

[22]See G. E. P. Box and G. M. Jenkins, *Time Series Analysis; Forecasting and Control* (San Francisco: Holden-Day, 1970), part III; and G. E. P. Box and G. C. Tiao, "Intervention Analysis with Applications to Economic and Environmental Problems," *Journal of the American Statistical Association,* 70 (March 1975), 70–79. The scheme of Box, Jenkins, and Tiao

Box-Jenkins or Box-Tiao models represent time-series observations on the endogenous variable (in this case unemployment) as the realization of a linear stochastic process of autoregressive, moving average, or mixed, auto-regressive-moving average form. The auto-regressive-moving average (ARMA) model provides ˉa stochastic benchmark against which intervention-induced changes in the slope and/or level of the endogenous time-series are assessed. Intervention occurrences (in this case partisan changes in government) are represented by binary variables (0, 1) or by related coding schemes (e.g., +1, −1), and the effects of interventions are specified by simple "transfer functions."

Regarding the problem at hand, the most plausible hypothesis is that shifts in the political orientation of governments during the post-war period in Great Britain and the United States will be associated with *gradual* changes in the net *levels* of the British and American unemployment rates. The intervention models therefore take the general form

$$U_t = \frac{\beta}{1 - \delta L} G_{t-1} + \frac{\theta_0 + \theta_q(L)}{\phi_p(L)(1-L)^d} a_t \qquad (1)$$

where: $U_t =$ the percentage of the civilian labor force unemployed (quarterly data);

$G_t =$ +1 during Labour or Democratic administrations; −1 during Conservative or Republican administrations;

$\beta,\delta =$ parameters describing the effects of shifts in G_t on U_t;

$L =$ lag operator such that $LU_t = U_{t-1}, L^i U_t = U_{t-i}$, etc;

$(1-L)^d =$ a lag difference operator such that $(1-L)U_t = U_t - U_{t-1}, (1-L)^2 = (1-2L + L^2)U_t = U_t - 2U_{t-1} + U_{t-2}$, etc.;

$\theta_q(L) = 1 - \theta_1 L - \theta_2 L^2 - \ldots - \theta_q L^q$
$\phi_p(L) = 1 - \phi_2 L - \phi_2 L^2 - \ldots - \phi_p L^p$
are moving average and auto-regressive polynomials in L of order p and q, respectively;

---

is contrasted with the conventional structural equation approach in Douglas A. Hibbs, Jr., "On Analyzing the Effects of Policy Interventions: Box-Jenkins and Box-Tiao vs. Structural Equation Models," in *Sociological Methodology 1977*, ed. D. Heise (San Francisco: Jossey Bass, 1977), pp. 137–79.

$\theta_0 =$ a constant indexing a deterministic time trend of degree d in U_t; and

$a_t =$ a sequence of independently distributed random variables with mean zero and variance σ_a^2.

Equation (1) simply expresses the proposition that–net of trends, cycles, and stochastic fluctuation in the unemployment time-series, which are captured by the autoregressive-moving average terms in the model[23]–we anticipate a gradual rise in unemployment levels under Conservative and Republican governments and, conversely, a gradual decline in unemployment levels during Labour and Democratic administrations. If a partisan change in government, occurring, for example, at time n, was sustained indefinitely (e.g., $G_t = +1$ for all $t \geqslant n$), the unemployment rate would eventually fluctuate about the steady state or equilibrium value $\beta/1-\delta$. The rate of adjustment to the new equilibrium depends on the magnitude of the dynamic parameter δ. Since we assume that the macroeconomic policies of a new government are not introduced or implemented instantaneously, the intervention term G_t is specified with a one period (quarter) delay or lag.[24]

The British Unemployment Model. The first step in the model building process is to develop a preliminary specification of the stochastic or ARMA component of equation (1) by analyzing the sample autocorrelation and partial autocorrelation functions of the endogenous variable (i.e., unemployment).[25] The sample autocorrelation function[26] r_k for seasonally unadjusted quarterly observations on the Brit-

---

[23]The cyclical or seasonal component of the model is not represented explicitly by the ARMA terms of eq. (1).

[24]The one quarter lag on G_t may be too short, especially for the United States. However, since the intervention function allows U to respond gradually to shifts in G, this is not an important problem.

[25]The ARMA model building process is systematically reviewed in Hibbs, "On Analyzing Policy Interventions," and developed in great detail by Box and Jenkins, *Time Series Analysis*.

[26]Sample autocorrelations are simply the correlations between observations separated k periods in time and are given by:

$$r_k = \frac{\Sigma(U_t - \overline{U}_t)(U_{t-k} - \overline{U}_t)}{\Sigma(U_t - \overline{U}_t)^2} \qquad r = 1, 2, \ldots$$

Thus r_1 denotes the correlation between U_t and U_{t-1}; r_2 denotes the correlation between U_t and U_{t-2}; and so on.

ish unemployment rate over the 1948(1) to 1972(4) period is graphed in Figure 4.[27] The sample autocorrelations decay steadily as the lag k increases, which indicates that a low-order autoregressive process is compatible with the British unemployment observations. Since the partial autocorrelations (which are not reported here) are insignificant for $k > 1$, we tentatively entertain a first order autoregressive specification:

$$U_t = \phi_1 U_{t-1} + e_t, \text{ or} \tag{2}$$

$$(1 - \phi_1 L) U_t = e_t.$$

Figure 5 presents the sample autocorrelations of the residuals $\hat{e}_t$, that is the autocorrelations of the transformed data $U_t - \hat{\phi}_1 U_{t-1}$. The autocorrelations exhibit distinct peaks every fourth quarter—at $k = 4, 8, 12, 16 \ldots$—which suggests a strong seasonal dependence between unemployment rates of the same quarter in different years. This depen-

[27]The British unemployment data (wholly unemployed as a percentage of the civilian labor force) were obtained from the *Ministry of Labour Gazette,* various issues. In view of the unprecedented exogenously imposed economic crisis facing advanced industrial societies since 1973, the time series analyses are intentionally not taken beyond the fourth quarter of 1972.

dence comes as no surprise, since it is well known that unemployment is influenced by seasonal factors and the British data were not available in seasonally adjusted form. The seasonal dependence identified in Figure 5 shows no tendency to die out as the lag k increases, and therefore, four-quarter, seasonal differencing is called for. Hence we propose the model:

$$(1 - L^4) e_t = \theta_0 + a_t, \text{ or} \tag{3}$$

$$e_t = \frac{\theta_0 + a_t}{(1 - L^4)}.$$

Substituting (3) into (2) yields the following expression for the stochastic component of the general intervention scheme given in (1):

$$(1 - \phi_1 L) U_t = \frac{\theta_0 + a_t}{(1 - L^4)}, \text{ or} \tag{4}$$

$$U_t = \frac{\theta_0 + a_t}{(1 - L^4)(1 - \phi_1 L)}.$$

Adjoining (4) to the intervention function proposed in (1) to represent the hypothesized net impact of partisan changes in government on the unemployment level, we arrive at the equation:

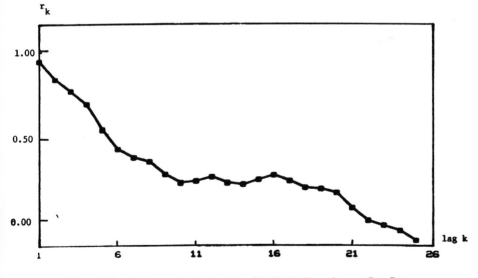

r_k

Figure 4. Sample Autocorrelation Function of the British Unemployment Rate Data, 1948(1)–1972(4)

$$U_t = \frac{\beta}{1-\delta L}\, G_{t-1} + \frac{\theta_0 + a_t}{(1-L^4)(1-\phi_1 L)} \qquad (5)$$

where: U_t = the percentage of the civilian labor force wholly unemployed in Great Britain quarterly 1948(1)–1972(4);

G_t = +1 during Labour governments; −1 during Conservative governments;

and all other terms are as previously defined.

A second intervention term should be added to the British unemployment model in order to take account of an important change in the British unemployment compensation scheme which was initiated in October 1966. Until 1966, the unemployed in Great Britain received a relatively flat-rate benefit that was not tied to previous earnings. The change in the unemployment system initiated by the Labour government in 1966 provided for an "earnings-related supplement" equal to about one-third of the unemployed person's previous average weekly earnings between £9 and £30. This represented a substantial increase in benefits for most wage earning groups.[28] As a result, unemployed workers were under less financial pressure to accept unattractive jobs and presumably spent more time in searching for new employment. It is therefore widely believed that the new compensation scheme increased the rate and duration of unemployment.[29] Thus we define a

[28]For example, it is estimated that the earnings-related benefits increased the unemployment income of a typical married male worker with two children from about 40 percent to 60 percent of average employment income. See OECD, *Manpower Policy in the United Kingdom* (Paris: OECD Publications, 1970).

[29]Unfortunately the picture is complicated by the fact that a number of other macroeconomic policy changes were implemented during the 1965–67 period. These policy changes are reviewed by Bowers et al., in "The Change in the Relationship Between Unemployment and Earnings Increases: A Review of Some Possible Explanations," *National Institute Economic Review* (November 1970), 44–63. However, the survey-based analysis of D. MacKay and G. Reid in "Redundancy, Unemployment and Manpower Policy," *Economic Journal* (December 1972), 1256–72, leaves little doubt that the new compensation law had a significant effect on the duration (and thus the rate) of unemployment. Also see the discussion by M. Feldstein, "The Economics of the New Unemployment," *Public Interest*, 33 (Fall 1973), 3–42.

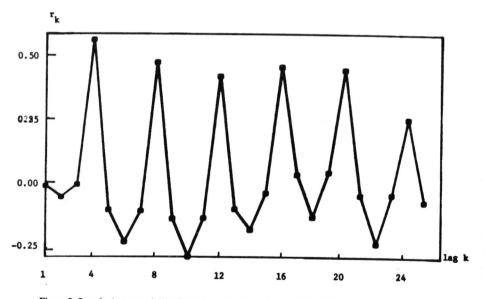

Figure 5. Sample Autocorrelation Function of the Transformed British Unemployment Rate Data
$(1-\phi_1 L)\, U_t, 1948(1)-1972(4)$

new variable C_t taking a value of 0 prior to 1966(4) and a value of +1 otherwise, and specify the revised model:

$$U_t = \frac{\beta_1}{1-\delta_1 L} G_{t-1} + \frac{\beta_2}{1-\delta_2 L} C_t$$

$$+ \frac{\theta_0 + a_t}{(1-L^4)(1-\phi_1 L)} \qquad (6)$$

The revised model in (6) allows the introduction of the new unemployment compensation system as well as unrelated interparty differences in macroeconomic policy to alter gradually the level of British unemployment.

Table 2 reports the estimation results for equation (6).[30] All coefficients (except the constant or trend term θ_0) are substantially larger than their estimated standard errors and therefore are significant by conventional statistical criteria. Before considering the implications of these estimates, let us first evaluate the adequacy of the fitted model. Figure 6 shows the actual and predicted levels of the unemployment time series.[31] The predicted unem-

ployment observations track the actual data quite well, which of course is expected in view of the highly significant parameter estimates and small residual variance reported in Table 2. Diagnostic checks applied to the residuals provide more convincing evidence of the model's adequacy. Figure 7 presents the residual autocorrelations $r_k(\hat{a}_t)$ for lags 1 through 25. The autocorrelations exhibit no systematic patterns and, except for $k = 4$, fall within the approximate ±2 standard deviation limits.[32] The mean of the residuals is $\bar{a} = .0000003$ and the estimated standard error $\sigma_{\hat{a}}^2 = .023$. The sample evidence strongly suggests therefore that the a_t are independently distributed random variates with zero means.

Returning to the parameter estimates in Table 2, interest centers on the intervention coefficients $\hat{\beta}$ and $\hat{\delta}$. The coefficients associated with the unemployment compensation dummy variable C_t ($\hat{\beta}_2$, $\hat{\delta}_2$) indicate that the additional unemployment benefits available since October 1966 produced a net increase of about 0.86 percent in the equilibrium level of unemployment, that is,

$$+ \frac{\hat{\beta}_2}{1-\hat{\delta}_2} = \frac{+.511}{1-.407} = 0.86.$$

In view of the fact that the dynamic response parameter $\hat{\delta}_2 = .407$, the steady state effect of

---

[30] The models in this section were estimated with Kent D. Wall's ERSF program, which provides Full Information Maximum Likelihood estimates of Rational Distributed Lag Structural Form equations. Details are given in Wall, "FIML Estimation of Rational Distributed Lag Structural Form Models," Working Paper No. 77 (Cambridge: National Bureau of Economic Research, Inc., March, 1975).

[31] The predicted level data are obtained by summing the predicted four-quarter difference series, i.e.,

$$\hat{U}_t = U_0 + \sum_t (1-L^4)\hat{U}_t.$$

The summation operator Σ is the inverse of the difference operator $(1-L)$ in the same way that integration is the inverse of differentiation in continuous time problems.

[32] The lag 4 autocorrelation is of course significant and therefore the model might be improved by specifying $a_t = (1-\theta_4 L^4) v_t$ where the v_t are $N(0, \sigma_v^2)$. Since the $k=4$ autocorrelation was essentially induced by the seasonal differencing (which overcompensates for the four-quarter seasonal dependency), and we are primarily interested in predicting the level unemployment series, modification of the model in this way is not advantageous.

Table 2. Estimation Results for the British Unemployment Rate Model (Eq. 6)

	Parameter Estimates	Standard Errors
G_{t-1}	$\hat{\beta}_1 = -.094$	.035
	$\hat{\delta}_1 = +.692$	.118
C_t	$\hat{\beta}_2 = +.511$	.115
	$\hat{\delta}_2 = +.407$	.228
Trend (4 quarter)	$\hat{\theta}_0 = +.002$	.023
Autoregressive	$\hat{\phi}_1 = +.773$	.071
	Residual Variance, $\hat{\sigma}_a^2 = .045$	$R^2 = .95$[a]

[a] The R^2 reported here pertains to the level data rather than to the four-quarter difference data. The four-quarter difference R^2 is .85.

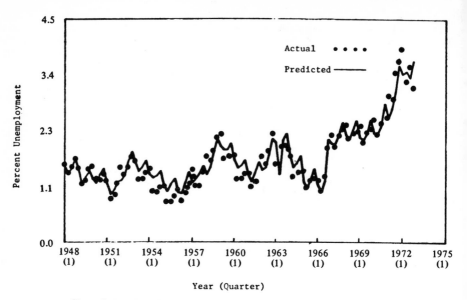

Figure 6. Actual and Predicted Values from the British Unemployment Rate Model (Eq. 6)

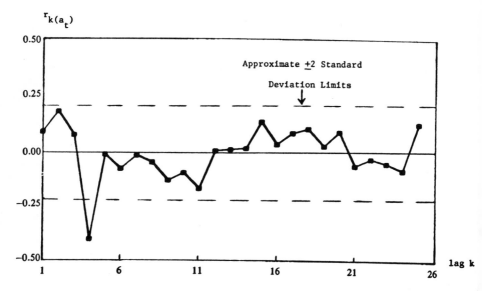

Figure 7. Residual Autocorrelations from the British Unemployment Rate Model

0.86 percent was fully realized rather quickly— after only four or five quarters. However, effects associated with the C_t term, although sizable, are only of incidental interest in this study.

More important for our purposes are the maximum likelihood estimates of β_1 and δ_1 which clearly support our initial proposition concerning the impact of partisan change on the British unemployment rate. Net of the effects attributed to the new unemployment compensation law, and independent of trends, seasonal dependencies, and stochastic fluctuation in the time series, the unemployment rate appears to be driven downward during the tenure of Labour governments and to move upward during periods of Conservative rule. The estimated steady state effects are ±0.31 percent, that is:

$$\pm \frac{\hat{\beta}_1}{1-\hat{\delta}_1} = \pm \frac{.094}{1-.692} = \pm 0.31,$$

which implies a difference of about 0.62 percent between the equilibrium unemployment levels associated with Labour and Conservative governments. Holding fixed the C_t variable and the stochastic ARMA terms in the model, we see that the expression $U_t =$

$\dfrac{\hat{\beta}_1}{1-\hat{\delta}_1 L} G_{t-1}$ implies $U_t = \hat{\delta}_1 U_{t-1} + \hat{\beta}_1 G_{t-1}$, which upon repeated substitution gives:

$$U_t = \hat{\delta}_1^t U_0 + \hat{\beta}_1 \sum_{i=0}^{t-1} \hat{\delta}_1^i \, G_{t-1-i} . \qquad (7)$$

Imposing the arbitrary initial condition $U_0 = 0$ and applying the coefficient estimates $\hat{\beta}_1 = -.094$, $\hat{\delta}_1 = .692$, we obtain the dynamic time paths of the unemployment rate that can be attributed to Labour and Conservative macroeconomic policies by simulating (7) for G_t held at +1 and −1, respectively. Figure 8 depicts the unemployment time paths for regimes of 20 quarters (5 years) duration. Notice that the steady state values of ±0.31 percent are fully realized after about 16 quarters or 4 years.

An interparty difference of just over one-half of one percent in government-induced unemployment levels may seem small by American standards, but, if evaluated against Great Britain's average postwar unemployment rate of 1.67 percent, it is by no means trivial. Applied to the British civilian labor force, which has averaged 24.1 million workers during the postwar period, the effects graphed in Figure 8 translate into about 149,000 jobs. Since British unemployment data are compiled by the regis-

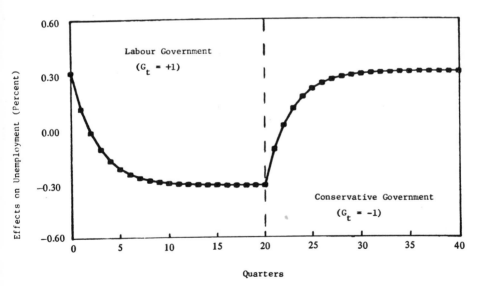

Figure 8. Simulated Net Effects of Labour and Conservative Governments on the Unemployment Rate

tration method, the measured unemployment rate tends to be biased downward relative to that of the United States, which is based on labor force survey data. Adjusting the British data to the American definition therefore permits more accurate comparisons to be made with the U.S. experience. Myers estimates the adjustment factor to be 1.51.[33] Applying this to the British data yields an interparty steady state difference of 0.94 percent, or about 226,000 jobs.

Nonetheless, the estimated effect of Labour versus Conservative macroeconomic policies on the equilibrium level of unemployment is perhaps smaller than one might have anticipated from the earlier discussion of left-to-right cleavages regarding various economic goals. Indeed the ideological distance between the Labour and the Conservative parties on the full employment issue is undoubtedly not as great as that implied by the general scheme introduced previously in Table 1. Throughout the postwar period the Conservatives have made great efforts to disassociate themselves from the mass

[33]R. J. Meyers, "The Unemployment Problem: What We Can Learn from European Experience," in *Measuring Employment and Unemployment* by the Joint Economic Committee of the U.S. Congress (Washington, D.C.: Government Printing Office, 1963).

unemployment of the 1930s by repeatedly emphasizing their commitment to the full employment goal, although in practice it was sometimes viewed as necessary to induce increases in unemployment in order to fight inflation. However, it should be recognized that, unlike the United States, Great Britain is very much an open economy and the macroeconomic policies of both Labour and Conservative governments have been severely constrained by the necessity of maintaining a satisfactory external trade balance. Political authorities of both parties had to insure that the country did not inflate at a rate exceeding that of its principal trading partners in order to maintain the competitiveness of British exports in world markets. In view of the international economic constraints facing all British governments, the estimated interparty difference of 0.62 percent (0.94 percent adjusted to U.S. concepts) does not appear quite as modest in magnitude.

The U.S. Unemployment Model. The impact of Democratic versus Republican administrations on the U.S. unemployment rate is also estimated by developing an ARMA-intervention model. The model building procedure is the same as that outlined in the course of the British analysis. Figure 9 shows the sample autocorrelation function for seasonally adjusted

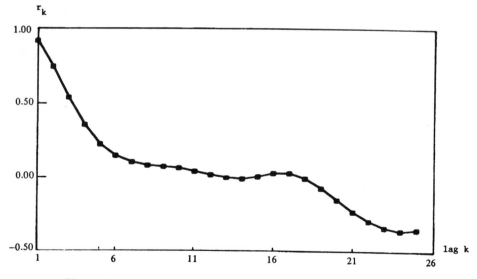

Figure 9. Sample Autocorrelation Function of the U.S. Unemployment Rate Data, 1948(1)–1972(4)

quarterly observations on the U.S. employment rate over the period 1948(1)–1972(4). The autocorrelations exhibit mild oscillations and decay as the lag k increases–properties which are characteristic of a low-order autoregressive process. Partial autocorrelations (which are not reported here) are significant for $k \leqslant 2$, and therefore we propose a second-order process for the stochastic component of the intervention model:[34]

$$U_t = \theta_0 + \phi_1 U_{t-1} + \phi_2 U_{t-2} + a_t, \text{ or} \quad (8)$$

$$U_t = \frac{\theta_0 + a_t}{1 - \phi_1 L - \phi_2 L^2}.$$

Adjoining (8) to the intervention function introduced previously in (1) yields the estimating equation:

$$U_t = \frac{\beta}{1 - \delta L} G_{t-1} + \frac{\theta_0 + a_t}{1 - \phi_1 L - \phi_2 L^2} \quad (9)$$

where: U_t = the percentage of the civilian labor force unemployed in the U.S. quarterly 1948(1)–1972(4);

G_t = +1 during Democratic administrations, −1 during Republican administrations;

and other terms are as previously defined.

In its present form, the model in equation (9) is unlikely to provide a very good estimate

[34]Equation (8) is nearly identical to the model developed by C. R. Nelson for quarterly U.S. unemployment data over the period 1948(1)–1966(4). Nelson's model, incidentally, outperformed the MIT-FRB-Penn econometric model in short-term forecasting experiments. "The Predictive Performance of the FRB-MIT-PENN Model of the U.S. Economy," *American Economic Review* (1972), 902–17.

of the net effect of Democratic versus Republican macroeconomic policies on the U.S. unemployment rate. An important omitted variable, which is not likely to be captured by the autoregressive terms in the model, is American intervention in the Korean and Vietnamese civil wars. The enormous fiscal stimulus to the domestic economy (not to mention the sizable number of young men withdrawn from the civilian labor force) generated by American participation in these conflicts shows up clearly in the steadily declining unemployment rates of the war years. (The same can of course be said about the contribution of World War II to the recovery from the Great Depression.) Indeed the United States experienced its lowest postwar unemployment rates during the peaks of these wars. Since American involvement in the Korean and Vietnamese conflicts occurred during (covaried with) Democratic administrations, it is necessary to include an additional "war" term in the model in order to disentangle the party effects of interest from the war effect. Therefore we introduce an additional variable W_t taking a value of +1 during the Korean and Vietnamese wars and a value of 0 otherwise, and specify the revised model

$$U_t = \frac{\beta_1}{1 - \delta_1 L} G_{t-1} + \frac{\beta_2}{1 - \delta_2 L} W_t$$

$$+ \frac{\theta_0 + a_t}{1 - \phi_1 L - \phi_2 L^2}. \quad (10)$$

The specification of the W_t term in (10) is identical to that of the G_t term, except that the war variable appears without a delay or lag. The revised model therefore allows the economic stimuli accompanying American intervention in Korea and Vietnam as well as non-war-related interparty differences in macroeconomic policy to alter gradually the level of unemployment.

Estimation results for the U.S. unemployment model of equation (10) are presented in

Table 3. Estimation Results for the U.S. Unemployment Rate Model (Eq. 10)

	Parameter Estimates	Standard Errors
G_{t-1}	$\beta_1 = -.071$	.020
	$\delta_1 = +.974$	.017
W_t	$\beta_2 = -.179$	.145
	$\delta_2 = +.513$	.320
Autoregressive	$\phi_1 = +1.49$	.072
	$\phi_2 = -.718$	.071
	Residual Variance, $\hat{\sigma}_a^2 = .085$	$R^2 = .94$

Table 3.[35] The coefficient estimates associated with the administration term G_{t-1} ($\hat{\beta}_1, \hat{\delta}_1$) and the estimates of the autoregressive parameters ($\hat{\phi}_1, \hat{\phi}_2$) are substantially larger than their respective standard errors and thus easily satisfy the usual criteria of statistical significance. However, the coefficients associated with the war term W_t ($\hat{\beta}_2\hat{\delta}_2$), although larger than their respective standard errors, are not significant by conventional standards, and therefore we cannot place very much confidence in these parameter estimates.[36] In view of the collinearity

[35]Since the unemployment data did not exhibit a trend over the observation period, all variables were deviated from their means and the model was estimated without a constant term. θ_0 therefore does not appear in Table 3.

[36]The t ratio of $\hat{\beta}_2$ = 1.23 and of $\hat{\delta}_2$ = 1.60; both are insignificant at the .05 level. Computation of the implied dynamic response of the unemployment rate to American involvement in the Korean and Vietnamese civil wars is therefore problematic. Robert Solow has suggested to me that since the effects of both the war term and the administration term work through the actual tax, expenditure, and monetary actions of the government, the model might be better specified by constraining $\delta_1 = \delta_2$. However, estimates obtained by imposing this constraint did not alter the results reported in Table 3 and graphed below in Figure 12 appreciably: the war coefficient remained insignificant, $\hat{\delta}_1 = \hat{\delta}_2$ = .969, and $\hat{\beta}_1$ = −.091.

between W_t and G_t noted earlier, it is not surprising that $\hat{\beta}_2$ and $\hat{\delta}_2$ exhibit relatively large variances. However, we are primarily interested in securing an unbiased estimate of the net response of the unemployment rate to interadministration differences in macroeconomic policy, and hence the war term should be retained in the model in order to insure that the administration effect is not confounded with the war effect.

The actual and predicted values of the unemployment time series are graphed in Figure 10. The fitted values track the actual data very closely and errors do not appear to exhibit any systematic pattern. The residual autocorrelations reported in Figure 11 confirm this observation. Except for $k = 8$, all of the $r_k(\hat{a}_t)$ fall within ±2 standard deviations from zero, suggesting that the a_t are independently distributed random variates.[37] Finally, the average of the residuals is $\bar{a}$ = −.034 and the estimated standard error is $\sigma\frac{2}{\bar{a}}$ = .030, which indicates that the residual mean is not significantly different from zero.

[37]The negative residual autocorrelation at $k = 8$ $(r_8(\hat{a}_t)$ = −.253) indicates that there is a modest, negative two-year (8 quarter) dependency between U.S. unemployment rates. This is compatible with the

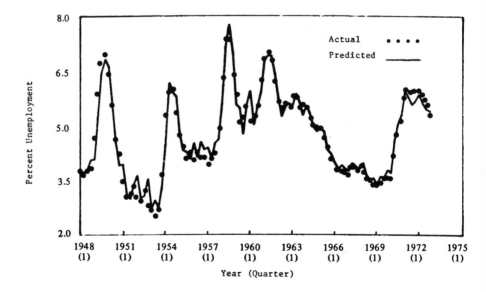

Figure 10. Actual and Predicted Values from the U.S. Unemployment Rate Model (Eq. 10)

Having established the overall adequacy of the model, we focus on the substantive implications of the administration parameters $\hat{\beta}_1$ and $\hat{\delta}_1$. The estimates reported in Table 3 give strong support to the basic hypothesis: Democratic administrations appear to engineer downward movements in the U.S. unemployment level, whereas the reverse is true of Republican administrations. The estimation results indicate that the steady state effects are on the order of ±2.73 percent, that is:

---

political-electoral business cycle argument of Nordhaus, Tufte and others, in which unemployment tends to fall before Presidential elections and to rise thereafter in response to administration efforts to engineer favorable economic conditions just prior to elections and to postpone austerity measures until after elections are safely over. [Nordhaus, "The Political Business Cycle;" and Edward Tufte, *Elections and Economics: Macroeconomics Under Conditions of Political Competition* (Princeton, N.J.: Princeton University Press, forthcoming).] If this pattern was strong and more or less uniform across four-year presidential administrations, we should observe a sizable negative autocorrelation at $k = 8$ (two-year intervals) and a positive autocorrelation at $k = 16$ (four-year intervals). Although the focus of this study is on long-run patterns in macroeconomic policies and outcomes that distinguish left- and right-wing regimes, attempts were made to build an electoral unemployment cycle of this sort into the model. However, elaborations of the model along these lines did not yield significant results.

$$\pm \frac{\hat{\beta}_1}{1 - \hat{\delta}_1} = \pm \frac{.071}{1 - .974} = \pm 2.73,$$

which implies an interadministration difference of about 5.46 percent in the long-run, equilibrium level of unemployment. In view of the fact that the (seasonally adjusted) U.S. unemployment rate has varied between 2.6 percent and 7.4 percent during the 1948 to 1972 period, an interadministration difference of this magnitude is simply not plausible. Note, however, that this is a steady state figure, that is, it gives the implied, net difference in unemployment levels if one and then the other party were to govern nationally for an indefinitely long period of time. Since the dynamic adjustment parameter $\hat{\delta}_1$ is estimated to be .974, convergence to equilibrium is very slow and would not be fully realized until a given party had held office for more than 100 quarters or 25 years.[38] However, neither political party in the

[38]This is readily confirmed by evaluating the expression $\hat{\beta}_1 \sum_{i=0}^{\infty} \hat{\delta}_1^i G_{t-1-i}$ over the index i for fixed G_t. Unlike the British results, which implied convergence to steady state after only 16 quarters, the U.S. steady state is not reached until the index i is taken to well over 100 quarters.

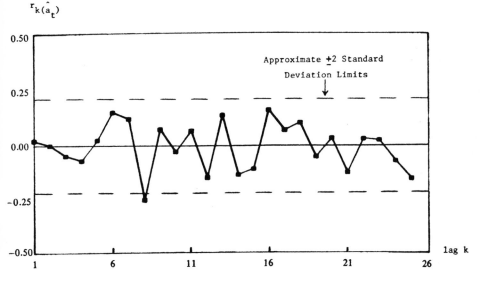

$r_k(\hat{a}_t)$

Figure 11. Residual Autocorrelations from the U.S. Unemployment Rate Model

United States has held the presidency for more than two terms in succession during the postwar period, and therefore it is sensible to restrict the interpretation of the estimation results to 32 quarters or 8 years.

Figure 12 shows the dynamic time paths of the unemployment rate implied by the G_t component of the model for Democratic and Republican administrations, respectively.[39] Notice that after 32 quarters (i.e., two presidential administrations) the estimated administration effects are on the order of ±1.18 percent and hence the interadministration difference in government induced unemployment levels is about 2.36 percent. This estimate is of course much more compatible with the postwar U.S. experience than the long-run, steady state difference

[39]The results graphed in Figure 12 were obtained in the same way as described earlier for the British case, i.e., by simulating

$$U_t = \hat{\delta}_1^t U_0 + \hat{\beta}_1 \sum_{i=0}^{t=1} \hat{\delta}_1^i G_{t-1-i}$$

for G_t held at +1 and then −1 over regimes of 32 quarters (8 years).

of 5.46 percent reported earlier. A comparison of the U.S. results in Table 3 and Figure 12 to the corresponding results for Great Britain in Table 2 and Figure 8 also indicates that the ultimate impact of an administration on the rate of unemployment accumulates much more slowly in the United States than in Great Britain. In other words, the results suggest that the effects of government macroeconomic policies on the unemployment rate are processed much more quickly through the British system than through the American system. These inferences are entirely reasonable in view of the fact that the political and economic environment facing macroeconomic policy makers in the United States is considerably more decentralized and heterogeneous than that facing macroeconomic policy makers in the parliamentary system of Great Britain.

Discussion

The estimated interparty difference of 2.36 percent in the unemployment performance of Democratic versus Republican administrations is perhaps best illustrated historically by con-

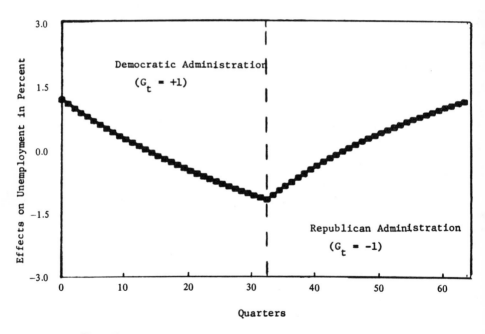

Figure 12. Simulated Net Effects of Democratic and Republican Administrations on the Unemployment Rate

trasting briefly the macroeconomic policies of the Eisenhower, Kennedy-Johnson and Nixon administrations. The principal economic goals of the Eisenhower administrations were a balanced federal budget and a reduction in the rate of inflation.[40] Despite repeated contractions in aggregate economic activity (the "Eisenhower recessions"), full employment and economic expansion never became primary goals. Indeed the emphasis on price stability and a balanced budget was so great that federal expenditures were actually decreased during the 1953–54 recession and budget outlays only barely exceeded receipts during the recession years of 1957–58 and 1960.[41]

The excessive caution exercised by the Eisenhower administrations in dealing with recession and the great weight placed upon price stability were of course roundly attacked by liberal Keynesian economists, organized labor, and others. In his memoirs of this period Eisenhower responded to such criticism by noting that "critics overlooked the inflationary psychology which prevailed during the mid-fifties and which I thought it necessary to defeat. . . . The anti-inflation battle is never-ending, though I fear that in 1959 the public was apathetic, at least uninformed, regarding this issue."[42] The consequence of this never-ending battle against inflation was an economy that was chronically in stagnation and an unemployment rate that regularly exceeded six percent.

The Kennedy-Johnson administrations' posture toward recession and unemployment stands in sharp contrast to Eisenhower's. The most significant manifestation of the greater importance attached to full employment and

economic expansion by these Democratic administrations was the 1964 tax cut. First proposed publicly by Kennedy in June 1962, introduced in Congress in January 1963, and signed into law by Johnson in February 1964, the Revenue Act of 1964 injected a ten billion dollar fiscal stimulus into a sagging economy. This represented a clear break with the budget balancing ideology of previous Republican administrations (although the rhetoric of the balanced budget lingered on) and, in view of the economic outlook at the time and the historical periodicity of U.S. recessions, undoubtedly helped prevent a serious economic contraction in 1964–65 and thereby contributed to the prolongation of the longest expansion in postwar U.S. history. Johnson defended government initiatives on the employment front by arguing that "the number 1 in priority today is more jobs. This is our dominant domestic problem and we have to face it head-on."[43]

The basic economic priorities associated with the Eisenhower era were reestablished during the Nixon and Ford administrations. Although Nixon-Ford macroeconomic policies were more interventionist than those of earlier Republican administrations, high employment once again was sacrificed for the sake of restraining inflation. It is generally agreed that the 1970–71 recession was deliberately induced by the Nixon administration to check inflation, though this policy was later jettisoned in an attempt to stimulate a pre-election boom. In most respects the short-lived Ford administration was a replay of the Eisenhower years. The macroeconomic game-plan called for running the economy at considerable "slack" to reverse "inflationary expectations," and repeated attempts by the Democratic Congress to pass measures promoting a more rapid economic expansion were vigorously opposed.

Macroeconomic outcomes, then, are not altogether endogenous to the economy, but obviously are influenced to a significant extent by long- and short-term political choices. The real winners of elections are perhaps best determined by examining the policy consequences of partisan change rather than by simply tallying the votes.

[40]See, for example, O. Eckstein, "Economic Policy in the United States," in *Economic Policy in Our Time*, Vol. II, ed. O. Eckstein et al. (Amsterdam, North Holland, 1964), pp. 1–88; and especially H. Stein, *The Fiscal Revolution in America* (Chicago: University of Chicago Press, 1969), Ch. 11–14.

[41]Many analysts argue that Eisenhower's fiscal policies not only did little to combat the economic contradictions of the period but were also important causes of the 1957–58 and 1960–61 recessions. See W. Lewis, *Federal Fiscal Policy in the Postwar Recessions* (Washington, D.C.: The Brookings Institution, 1962); and Stein, *The Fiscal Revolution in America*.

[42]D. Eisenhower, *Waging Peace, 1956–61* (Garden City, N.Y.: Doubleday, 1965), pp. 461, 462.

[43]Cited in F. R. Dulles, *Labor in America* (New York: Crowell 1966), p. 394.

12

THE FULFILLMENT OF PLATFORMS

Gerald M. Pomper with Susan S. Lederman

The proof of the pudding remains in the eating. It may be true that platforms are prepared well, consist of the right ingredients in proper proportions, and seem palatable to the voters. But, how are they digested? After the elections, do platforms prove to be attractive but insubstantial, like empty pastry shells, or is there some filling inside?

Indirect influence of voters on public policy is possible if two conditions are met. First, there must be some meaningful identification of parties with specific programs. The evidence of the last chapter indicates that this condition is generally satisfied. Second, the parties must fulfill their pledges to a reasonable extent. The platforms would be useless to voters in promoting their specialized interests unless the party documents actually presaged action. Similarly, the parties would not be truly anticipating and meeting voter needs if their pledges were unredeemed. Popular support of a party is a meaningful intervention only when this support has observable policy consequences.[1] In this chapter we will examine the parties' performance on their pledges. A high degree of fulfillment of platforms will be a further indication of the indirect effects of elections.

Platforms are usually considered unrelated to government action. As David Truman authoritatively writes: "The platform is generally regarded as a document that says little, binds no one, and is forgotten by politicians as quickly as possible after it is adopted. . . . Considered as a pledge of future action, the party platform is almost meaningless and is properly so regarded by the voters." [2] Since platforms are allegedly unimportant, much of the effort to reform our parties has been directed toward increasing their importance and the degree of fulfillment. [3]

There are many reasons to expect platforms to be disregarded. Written as electoral documents, they are obviously different from a legislative program. Often, platforms represent only the view of the victorious faction at a national convention. Opponents may be defeated at the convention, but still retain the power to block implementation of party promises. The many checks and balances of American government are a further restriction on platform fulfillment.

Given these obstacles, it is noteworthy that politicians do in fact devote some attention to their platforms. In House debate on the Medicare bill in 1965, for example, party spokesmen agreed that election commitments had decided the issue. Democrat Ray Madden concluded that "the greatest testimonial for this legislation, coupled with the educational legislation passed several weeks ago, was the returns of the recent election of November 5, 1964. By a majority of over 15 million, President Johnson and Vice-President Humphrey won an unprecedented victory and the principal plank in their platform was education and medicare."

Regretfully, Republican Thomas Curtis agreed to the potency of platform pledges: "It is obvious that this House is not in a mood to deliberate. The decision which was made outside of the well of the House, outside the deliberative process, is going to prevail. . . . Is it not obvious, Mr. Chairman, what has happened? The Congress of the United States has become a rubber-stamp." [4] A party victory in the 1964 election was interpreted as an endorsement of party program. Indirect voter influence over policy was achieved.

Platforms are also used as standards by which parties approvingly measure their own performance and condemn that of the opposition. A generation of Republican speeches has been based on a comparison of New Deal deficit spending to the Democrats' 1932 promises to reduce federal expenditures and balance the budget. More recently, Democrats have found their platform a source of inspiration rather than embarrassment. As President Carter took office, his staff compiled a list of campaign promises as a guide to legislative action. The achievement of these pledges would become the basis of his reelection effort. [5]

These partisan evaluations are obviously self-serving and cannot be accepted without more thorough analysis. Nevertheless, they do demonstrate that parties at least place some importance on claims that they have fulfilled or neglected the platform. Politicians perceive their electoral interest to lie in performing on their promises—or at least seeming to perform. Other factors may prevent fulfillment, but apparently some efforts will be made. We must now try to judge to what extent these efforts succeed.

TESTING PARTY PERFORMANCE

We begin by stating a precise hypothesis: "Platform pledges are fulfilled." [6] As a second step, we define (or "operationalize") our terms specifically, in order to eliminate ambiguity or inconstancy in our language. We must specify the meaning of "pledges" and "fulfillment." (Full details of the methods used in this chapter are provided in the appendix.)

Platform *pledges* will be defined as all statements in the third through sixth categories of future promises. As designated in the last chapter, these include pledges of continuity, expressions of goals and concern, pledges of action, and detailed promises. For all eighteen platforms, this definition provides 3,194 pledges, which is 58 percent of all commitments and 30 percent of all statements in the platforms. National policy also is affected by the general social values included in rhetorical and general statements, and by party evaluations of the past. Since it is difficult to see the detailed policy implications of these provisions, however, we will confine our analysis to specific commitments.

To explore *fulfillment,* our other term, is even more difficult. A promise and an action are inherently different. In an ideal world of platform fulfillment, each pledge could be matched to a specific action. In reality, pledges and actions are too discrete for such simple matching. Platforms, lengthy and specific though they may be, are unrelated to a large proportion of governmental actions. The parties deliberately evade pledges on some issues; others require knowledge too specialized for either politicians or voters; and others arise only after the presidential election.

Much of the output of Congress, such as providing for an increase in the District of Columbia's borrowing authority to finance capital improvements, is too limited to receive attention from a national convention. Congress severely restricted federal Medicaid funding for abortions in 1977, approved President Carter's plan for selling sophisticated jet fighters to Saudi Arabia, and abandoned agricultural parity prices for the more flexible target supports, although none of these actions was specifically supported in the party manifestos. The President and the bureaucracy are even more active than Congress, and most of their work is necessarily independent of platform provisions.

In testing fulfillment, there are questions of degree as well. Must a pledge be kept in full to be considered kept at all? The Democrats in 1976 pledged "a complete overhaul of the present tax system, which will review all special tax provisions to ensure that they are justified and distributed equitably among our citizens." [7] Was this pledge kept by the $18.7 billion tax cut bill passed in 1978, which did provide some income tax cuts for the working poor and middle-class taxpayers? Only a few "loopholes" were eliminated, and upper-class taxpayers benefited most from the reduction in capital gains taxes. Definitions of fulfillment are, then, of necessity methodological rather than legal. The "special provisions" were indeed reviewed in the process of debate on the legislation—the spirit of the pledge, however, was only partially fulfilled. Similarly, the means of fulfillment may vary. Passage of one law may make another law unnecessary, or a presidential action may substitute for legislation.

Fulfillment is here considered some substantial governmental action of the kind and in the direction promised. There must be the realization of a pledge, not only an attempt at realization, and the achieved result must be clearly akin to the promise. No judgments are made of the adequacy or desirability of the action taken.

Fulfillment can be achieved in one of four ways: (1) *Full action* is the passage of a law (or section of a law) directly related to the platform provision. A very close correspondence must exist between the promise and the statute. Compromise legislation that differs significantly from an explicit pledge, as in the case of tax reform, is not included. (2) Another means of fulfillment is presidential or other *executive actions* that directly accomplish commitments. (3) Pledges may not be fulfilled directly, but *similar actions* may be taken by either Congress or the executive branch. (4) Finally, there is a category of *negative fulfillment*. An important proportion of promises are pledges *not* to act, to maintain the status quo. Where the party has been true to its promise to leave a situation undisturbed, this is also considered adequate performance. [8]

There are two means by which a pledge may be unfulfilled. In one situation, an attempt may be made to accomplish the goal, but the attempt is *defeated*. Such results occur when a presidential measure is killed in committee, a proposal loses in a floor vote, or the President successfully vetoes a bill. Second, platform commitments may fail of accomplishment simply because there is *no action*. The pledge is ignored or, in rare instances, the opposite action is taken. This last category also includes nonpresidential bills that are buried in committee.

Judgments on fulfillment were made after comparing the pledges in both party platforms for a given election to the legislation and other actions of the following four years. (For the 1964 platform, only the events of 1965 and 1966 are included; similarly, only 1977 and 1978 events are counted for the 1976 platform.) This task involves the separate organization of platform promises and official policies and then itemized comparisons between the two categories. The procedure, along with other methods employed in this chapter, is detailed in the Appendix for this chapter.

The judgments used may become clearer through the following examples of pledges from the 1976 Democratic platform and corresponding governmental response: [9]

FULL ACTION

Platform: Strip-mining legislation designed to protect and restore the environment and encourage careful coal mining.

Action: Passage of the 1977 strip-mining-control law.

EXECUTIVE ACTION

Platform: To aggressively involve black Americans in foreign policy decisions affecting African interests.

Action: The appointment of Andrew Young as U.S. ambassador to the UN.

SIMILAR ACTION

Platform: Complete overhaul of the present tax system, with a review of all special tax provisions.

Action: 1978 tax cut eliminates some loopholes, but is not comprehensive.

NEGATIVE FULFILLMENT

Platform: No erosion of social security benefits.

Action: No action.

DEFEATED

Platform: Protect the right of construction workers to picket a job site (common situs picketing).

Action: The House rejected the bill in March 1977 by a 205–217 vote.

NO ACTION

Platform: Move the U.S. Embassy in Israel from Tel Aviv to Jerusalem.

Action: No action.

THE RECORD OF FULFILLMENT

Tables 8.1 and 8.2 present the degree of fulfillment of party pledges by election years and by topics. Separate columns are provided for promises by the Democrats and Republicans, by both parties, and by factions in and out of the White House. Separate totals are also shown for the years 1944–66 and 1968 through 1978.[10] (Fuller details may be found in appendix table 8.1.)

The most important conclusion to be derived from the mass of figures is that pledges are indeed redeemed. In the earlier two decades, over half the commitments met by direct congressional or executive action were fulfilled. When similar actions or appropriate inactions are included, nearly three-fourths of all promises were kept. During the last decade of government action, almost two-thirds of all promises were fulfilled in some fashion, with 30 percent directly enacted through congressional or executive initiations. In the 1944–66 period, only 10 percent of partisan pledges were ignored. The more recent political era shows greater disregard of partisan promises—almost one-third not acted upon. This recent decade, however, has been witness to particular political upheavals. The Republican presidents have had to contend with overwhelmingly Democratic Congresses. The 1972 Democratic platform—the largest in history—promised, in great detail, many benefits that only a minority of the Democratic party endorsed. Finally, President Carter, in his first two years in the White House, lacked experience in forging legislative majorities for his program and faced an increasingly independent and cantankerous Congress bent on flexing its legislative prerogatives. Given the political turmoil of the 1968–78 decade, it is remarkable that such attention to platform pledges was being paid.

The bipartisan aspects of American government are evident. When the parties agree in their positions, some action is almost certain. Three-fourths of the bipartisan pledges of the recent decade were fulfilled, as were 85 percent of the 1944–66 period. It is also noteworthy that the party out of power, even though without the resources of the executive branch, has been able to redeem better than half its own pledges, while sharing in performance on bipartisan planks. A party will not be completely frustrated even if it loses the Presidency. The Democrats did extremely well in the first four years of the Nixon administration—slightly outperforming the Republicans in the percentage of platform pledges fulfilled. With control of Congress and an apparent adoption of some Democratic foreign and defense policy stances by the President, two-thirds of the Democrats' promises were carried

TABLE 8.1

FULFILLMENT OF PLATFORM PLEDGES, BY ELECTION YEARS
(in percentages) [a]

Election Year	Demo-cratic	Repub-lican	Bipar-tisan	In-Party	Out-Party	Total
1944: Full Action	11	33	66	11	33	40
Executive	0	3	7	0	3	4
Similar	45	17	0	45	17	15
Negative	0	14	7	0	14	10
Total Action	*56*	*67*	*80*	*56*	*67*	*69*
Defeated	33	24	20	33	24	24
No Action	11	9	0	11	9	7
1948: Full Action	48	10	58	48	10	46
Executive	4	0	11	4	0	6
Similar	6	30	4	6	30	9
Negative	7	5	4	7	5	6
Total Action	*65*	*45*	*77*	*65*	*45*	*67*
Defeated	27	45	23	27	45	28
No Action	8	10	0	8	10	5
1952: Full Action	28	45	67	45	28	43
Executive	3	8	0	8	3	3
Similar	10	16	8	16	10	11
Negative	12	11	0	11	12	9
Total Action	*53*	*80*	*75*	*80*	*53*	*66*
Defeated	29	10	18	10	29	21
No Action	18	10	7	10	18	13
1956: Full Action	32	42	53	42	32	42
Executive	3	4	8	4	3	5
Similar	13	19	7	19	13	13
Negative	6	18	12	18	6	10
Total Action	*54*	*83*	*80*	*83*	*54*	*70*
Defeated	28	13	14	13	28	20
No Action	18	4	6	4	18	10
1960: Full Action	46	31	69	46	31	51
Executive	14	5	7	14	5	9
Similar	16	16	10	16	16	13
Negative	5	6	6	5	6	7
Total Action	*81*	*58*	*92*	*81*	*58*	*80*
Defeated	14	24	7	14	24	14
No Action	5	18	1	5	18	6
1964: Full Action	54	12	79	54	12	40
Executive	10	6	0	10	6	6
Similar	14	15	6	14	15	13
Negative	5	7	15	5	7	7
Total Action	*83*	*40*	*100*	*83*	*40*	*66*
Defeated	16	21	0	16	21	16
No Action	1	39	0	1	39	18

TABLE 8.1 (continued)

Election Year	Demo-cratic	Repub-lican	Bipar-tisan	In-Party	Out-Party	Total
1968: Full Action	30	23	54	42	61	31
Executive	8	11	8	19	17	9
Similar	26	28	18	50	54	26
Negative	2	3	3	6	3	2
Total Action	*66*	*65*	*83*	*37*	*30*	*68*
Defeated	7	7	0	13	14	6
No Action	27	28	17	50	56	26
1972: Full Action	16	26	36	26	16	21
Executive	5	11	10	11	5	7
Similar	24	29	22	29	24	25
Negative	6	9	9	9	6	7
Total Action	*51*	*74*	*77*	*74*	*51*	*60*
Defeated	5	4	2	4	5	4
No Action	44	22	21	22	44	35
1976: Full Action	20	12	13	20	12	15
Executive	11	3	7	11	3	7
Similar	23	25	39	23	25	27
Negative	7	16	12	7	16	12
Total Action	*61*	*56*	*71*	*61*	*56*	*61*
Defeated	5	5	5	5	5	5
No Action	34	39	24	34	39	34
Total: 1944–66						
Full Action	40	30	64	46	26	45
Executive	8	5	6	9	4	6
Similar	14	17	7	16	15	13
Negative	6	10	8	8	8	8
Total Action	*68*	*62*	*85*	*79*	*53*	*72*
Defeated	22	21	13	16	27	18
No Action	10	17	2	5	20	10
Total: 1968–78						
Full Action	20	19	32	22	18	22
Executive	8	8	8	11	5	8
Similar	25	27	28	26	25	26
Negative	5	10	9	6	8	9
Total Action	*58*	*64*	*76*	*66*	*56*	*63*
Defeated	5	5	3	5	5	5
No Action	37	31	21	29	39	32
Number of Pledges	(1,437)	(1,026)	(731)	(1,069)	(1,394)	(3,194)

[a] *Within years, last three figures in each column add vertically to 100%.*

TABLE 8.2

FULFILLMENT OF PLATFORM PLEDGES, BY POLICY TOPICS
(in percentages of Total Action) [a]

Policy Topic	Demo-cratic	Repub-lican	Bipar-tisan	In-Party	Out-Party	Total
Foreign						
1944–66	76	47	96	76	53	79
1968–78	51	67	67	66	51	61
Defense						
1944–66	86	62	86	91	53	74
1968–78	66	77	100	67	75	73
Economics						
1944–66	68	66	95	84	53	73
1968–78	74	67	100	75	66	73
Labor						
1944–66	39	50	64	54	26	50
1968–78	45	48	100	49	44	48
Agriculture						
1944–66	69	76	100	91	57	81
1968–78	60	74	69	62	67	66
Resources						
1944–66	84	72	96	90	62	84
1968–78	64	70	77	74	61	69
Welfare						
1944–66	66	56	97	73	54	72
1968–78	51	59	83	65	49	58
Government						
1944–66	54	60	44	74	43	55
1968–78	60	58	76	62	58	62
Civil Rights						
1944–66	50	62	63	67	50	60
1968–78	59	69	50	68	58	61
N Total, 1944–66	(517)	(418)	(464)	(432)	(503)	(1,399)
N Total, 1968–78	(920)	(608)	(267)	(637)	(891)	(1,795)

[a] *Full details can be found in Appendix Table 8.1.*

out. The lowest out-party figure is for the Republicans after 1964. This result is a reflection of the unusual character of their platform and their reduced representation in the 89th Congress.[11]

Winning the Presidency made a considerable difference in platform fulfillment in the first two and a half decades under study. In all categories, the in-party achieved about four-fifths of its program, half again as much as the losers. During the 1968–78 years, the difference in winning the White House added an average of only 10 percent to the record of program attainment.

The record of the in-party is superior after all elections but 1944 and 1968. In 1944 the winning Democrats made only nine specific pledges, too small a number for meaningful analyses. The 1968 Republicans were slightly overshadowed by the Democrats' record of fulfillment— the party controlling Congress had a total action score one percentage point higher than that of the party controlling the White House. The importance of the White House can also be seen in the topical distribution. Generally, in each policy area, the in-party achieves a greater proportion of its pledges. In the earlier time period, the differences between in-party and out-party policy achievement is greater than between Democrats and Republicans for each topic but foreign policy. Clearly, during this political era, control of the White House was crucial. Not so in the 1968–78 decade. Although generally the party that controlled the White House was more likely to succeed in translating its promises into programs, in some issue areas the out-party had a higher degree of success. In defense policy, the nonpresidential party succeeded in adopting three-quarters of its program, compared with two-thirds of the presidential party's success ratio; and in agriculture the out-party had a slightly higher record of fulfillment than the executive's party. The most dramatic impact of presidential control during the last decade was in the area of social welfare. Whereas the Republican and Democratic records of achievement are similar, the in-party was able to achieve close to two-thirds of the promises, compared with just less than half of the out-party's welfare program. Voter endorsement of one party in presidential elections does make a difference in future policies, providing the power necessary for governmental action. This impact is strengthened when the majority of Congress and the President are of the same party. This finding is consistent with the conclusion of our historical study in chapter 5.

In each of these areas, the parties tended to appeal to distinct and recognizable minorities, such as unions, governmental reformers, and blacks. When pledges are made, they are often in response to and in imitation of an interest-group appeal. To win the support of unions, the

Democrats endorsed repeal of the Taft-Hartley Act. To indicate their support for reduced spending, the Republicans proposed a constitutional amendment for an item-veto on appropriations bills. To appeal to the urban North, both parties backed a strong civil rights program.

These specific platform pledges were made to enhance the party's electoral appeal. However, the interests involved were too weak to ensure fulfillment. In some cases, opposing groups resisted the platform provision. Although these issues were contentious, the parties did not resort to platform vagueness in an effort to satisfy the contending groups. Some definite appeals were made to one interest or another. The existence of opposition did make fulfillment more difficult, however.

Conflict has tended to be particularly intense on labor and civil rights, for these issues raise both material and ideological stakes. Pledges appealing to one group are likely to arouse vehement opposition from another, so that action is prevented. The same pattern has been evident on some governmental issues, such as home rule for the District of Columbia. However, on most issues of government the problem has been quite different. Because issues such as an item-veto or electoral college reform are abstract, supporters were unlikely to be intense, and these proposals were most likely to be simply presented and then forgotten.

Accomplishment varies considerably by policy topic. In the 1944–66 period, performance was notably poor in the three designated areas: labor, government, and civil rights. In these cases, legislation directly to redeem a platform pledge had been particularly unlikely, with executive, similar, and negative actions more feasible. In all three cases as well, bipartisan pledges fared badly in comparison to the record or other topics. These similarities were due both to the nature of the issues and the distribution of political power in the United States during that political period.

In the recent political era, only one issue area stands out with an unusually low record of fulfillment: labor. One must realize that organized labor continues to be a well-organized interest group, especially important at election time in informing its members and getting out the vote. Thus the Democrats continue to pledge to repeal section 14(b) of the Taft-Hartley Act. Membership in labor unions, however, is declining as a percentage of the work force, and support for "right to work" seems to be growing. Although civil rights promises are not redeemed at a higher rate than they were during the 1944–66 period, the record of fulfillment compared to issue areas of the more recent era is similar.

Governmental promises had a higher fulfillment score in the 1970s, perhaps because the tenor of these promises changed. The bulk of government pledges dealt with intergovernmental relations and restructuring government operations—sunset laws, accountability, and the like. Whereas government pledges may have been esoteric in the early era of our study, they are now the *nouvelle mode*.

What does this degree of fulfillment indicate? Is it significant that two-thirds or three-fourths of all pledges are kept in some way? Or is it more significant that over a quarter to a third of all pledges are not redeemed? Whatever measurement is employed, it is notable that platforms are considered at all, for the party manifestos have usually been scorned, not respected. To find any fulfillment of party pledges is remarkable, in the light of the conventional wisdom.

There is no absolute standard with which to compare party performance. Even the promises of the Delphic Oracle were subject to interpretation, and human vows are necessarily less reliable. All married persons have solemnly pledged to "love, honor and cherish," but over a third of all marriages end in divorce. Should parties be more faithful?

If platform pledges were only endorsements of undisputed values, such as Motherhood and Country, fulfillment would not be significant. We have therefore restricted our attention to the more specific statements. However, parties may not be promising and accomplishing important programs. Legislating a raft of trivia does not compensate for failure to deal with the vital issues of the time. Yet, an overall reading of platforms indicates that they deal with specific important issues.

Moreover, we have found distinctly superior performance by the party in the White House. The power of the Presidency is not needed to accomplish bland programs. It becomes valuable only when a party seeks to accomplish policies in dispute. We have also found variations in fulfillment by topic, with lessened achievement in policy areas in which positions are conflicting and entrenched. Such opposition would not exist unless vital interests were at stake in attempts to redeem platform pledges.

THE CHARACTER OF THE PARTIES

In choosing a party to control the government, voters can influence official action. The character of the winning faction is crucial, for its concerns and initiatives form the basis for governmental programs. Through further analysis of platforms, we are now in a position to assess the character of American parties.

There are two different models of what the parties are or should be. According to one model, Democrats and Republicans are virtually identical, one "Tweedledee" and one "Tweedledum." They say the same things to the same people, and there is no real basis for policy choice between them. Moreover, the parties are weak, decentralized, and undisciplined. "The parties are unable to hold their lines in a controversial public issue when the pressure is on. This condition," wrote the dean of American students of politics, "constitutes the most important single fact concerning the American parties. He who knows this fact, and knows nothing else, knows more about American parties than he who knows everything except this fact." [12] Partisanship therefore will have little relation to government, and party pledges, particularly on the most contentious issues, are unlikely to be fulfilled.

Other writers wish the situation were different. The model they would prefer is one of "party government," in which there are clear programmatic differences between Democrats and Republicans. The differing policies would then provide the voter with "a choice, not an echo." [13] Strong centralized and disciplined parties would direct governmental action. The platform of the majority party would constitute the agenda of the President and Congress, and its pledges would be redeemed by a cohesive national organization.[14] Platforms provide material for judging the empirical reality of these opposing models. Let us examine the degree of similarity and conflict in platform pledges and the nature of party action in Congress.

If the parties are duplicates of one another, a large proportion of their pledges will be similar, or bipartisan promises. If they are fit for "party government," a large proportion of pledges will be in conflict. Fitting neither model would be a situation in which the promises of Democrats and Republicans were neither identical nor conflicting, but only different. To resolve the question, 3,194 relatively specific pledges were compared. The percentage distribution of pledges, by election year and policy topic, is presented in table 8.3.

There is only limited conflict in the planks; there is greater, but still only moderate, bipartisan agreement. For the most part, the parties are simply different and fit neither of the models. The parties do not duplicate one another, but appeal to distinct groups of voters. On infrequent occasions, their varying appeals bring them into direct opposition. Less than one-tenth of all pledges involve party conflict. These occasions are important, but they do not constitute the major proportion of American party activity. Only in the intense campaigns of 1952 and 1964 did the proportion of conflicting pledges approach the proportion of bipartisan commitments.

Conflict between the parties varies among the topics. In general, conflict is higher on issues in which the benefits are divisible and tangi-

TABLE 8.3

SIMILARITY AND CONFLICT IN PLATFORM PLEDGES
(in percentages of pledges and designated year or topic) [a]

Year or Topic	(N)	One-Party Pledge Only	Bipartisan Pledges	Conflicting Pledges
Election Year				
1944	(102)	70	28	2
1948	(124)	51	42	7
1952	(205)	52	29	19
1956	(302)	61	34	5
1960	(464)	51	39	10
1964	(202)	70	19	11
1968	(457)	77	16	7
1972	(698)	83	13	5
1976	(640)	76	17	7
Policy Topic				
Foreign	(509)	60	34	6
Defense	(166)	74	22	4
Economics	(397)	76	15	9
Labor	(180)	65	17	18
Agriculture	(243)	66	27	7
Resources	(338)	69	22	9
Welfare	(696)	71	19	10
Government	(441)	78	18	4
Civil rights	(225)	63	35	2
All Pledges	(3,194)	69	23	8
N Total	3,194	2,218	731	245

[a] *Rows add horizontally to 100% for the three columns.*

ble, and contending groups exist. These are material issues in the broad sense, including benefits to specific groups involved in economic policy, labor, agriculture, resources, and social welfare. Even in these categories, bipartisan pledges predominate, but there is a greater likelihood that the parties will clash directly. The parties react to the voters' stress on their particular interests. Competition in the form of conflicting pledges is greatest on those issues we have found to be most important in influencing the electorate. A similar stress in the specificity of pledges was observed in the last chapter.

Bipartisan agreement on platform pledges had been exceptionally high on issues of foreign policy and civil rights prior to the Nixon regime. Since 1968, there has been a marked decline in the bipartisan focus on these issues, which were markedly volatile in the 1960s and '70s. In most issue areas each party carries out a distinct position, one that is different from the opposition. In 1976, for example, in dealing

with the economy the Republican party focused on inflation while the
Democrats addressed the problem of unemployment. The percentage
of directly conflicting pledges has decreased, as has the percentage of
bipartisan promises. The platforms, in the last decade, have continued
to appeal to distinct interests.

Further evidence of the applicability of the two models of parties is
possible through analysis of performance on conflicting pledges. If the
parties have any meaningful identity, we would expect them to display
their character on these questions. If, to the contrary, the parties are
shapeless, they would be unable to present a united front on the most
contentious issues. Analysis of congressional roll calls was employed
to assess the degree of party solidarity. Through procedures detailed in
the Appendix, seventy roll calls of the 1944–66 period and twenty-three
roll calls of the 1968–78 period were selected as directly related to the
issues presented by platform conflicts.[15]

If platforms have any significance in Congress, we would expect the
parties to differ on these ''conflict roll calls.'' They would then constitute party-unity votes, in which a majority of Democrats take a position
in opposition to a majority of Republicans. In all postwar administrations, this expectation is largely met. Of the relevant roll calls, 89
percent of the Truman years and 87 percent in both the Eisenhower and
Kennedy-Johnson periods were of this type.

In the first Nixon administration, 75 percent of the conflict roll calls
were party-unity votes, and 78 percent of the Nixon-Ford years' conflicts fit this model. The first two years of Carter's administration produced a 67 percent party-unity vote on conflicting pledges.

By comparison, of all congressional roll calls in the early period,
only about half split the two parties. Specifically, 58 percent of the roll
calls in the Truman years, 46 percent of the Eisenhower administration,
and 49 percent in the Kennedy-Johnson sessions found a majority of
the parties in opposition to each other.[16] During the 1970s, less than
two-fifths of the recorded roll calls produced party-unity votes. In the
first Nixon administration, 35 percent of the roll calls divided the two
parties, while 41 percent in the Nixon-Ford congressional session, and
40 percent of the votes in the first two years of the Carter Presidency
produced partisan voting splits. The national parties' representatives
and senators act in accord with their national pledges, resulting in
greater than normal conflict for Congress. Election disputes are not
forgotten when Congress convenes, but carry over into legislative voting.

We can also measure the degree of unity within each party on these roll calls and the extent of similarity between Republicans and Democrats. Internal solidity is gauged by an "index of cohesion," which varies from 100, when the party is completely united, to 0, when it is completely divided. Similarities between the parties are shown by an "index of likeness," which varies from 100, when the parties duplicate one another, to 0, when they are completely opposed. For purposes of comparison, these measures are calculated both for "conflict roll cails" and for all congressional votes. The latter roll calls are also divided into party-unity votes and bipartisan votes, in which a majority of both parties takes the same position. Table 8.4 presents the average indexes of cohesion and likeness for each presidential era.

The degree of cohesion on the controversial platform pledges is similar to that which exists in Congress generally. The most relevant comparison is that between "conflict roll calls" and all party-unity votes. Both are cases of partisan conflict, and the degree of party cohesion is similar. Unity of the parties does tend to be somewhat higher on the platform votes, and this finding is significant. Given the visibility, pressures, and importance that attach to these votes, relatively high party solidarity indicates that a large portion of the party stands behind its pledges. Party unity does not melt in the heat of controversy. It is maintained, and even some increased fusion of the party can be observed. At the same time, to change the image, platforms are seen as one sector in a general field of party battle, for cohesion on these issues is similar to that on all party votes. The platform conflicts are not special cases. They are, rather, the most obvious and dramatic instances of larger differences between the parties.

The parties also vote differently from one another. The index of likeness is usually lower for platform conflicts than for all votes in Congress, indicating greater differences between the parties on these issues. The typical platform vote would find the two parties opposed, with somewhat less than one-fifth of each faction joining the opposition. In all congressional votes, however, the parties would be relatively similar to one another, and actually in agreement on half or more of the roll calls.

Roll calls on conflicting pledges are again found to be similar to all party-unity votes. Whenever the parties differ, the extent of their difference is comparable to their differences over platform issues, and there is actually somewhat greater conflict in the votes related to party promises. The platform is again seen as related to congressional behavior. It is associated with party conflict and is seen as an indication

TABLE 8.4

PARTY COHESION AND LIKENESS
(average indexes for presidential terms)

Period	House Cohesion		Senate Cohesion		Likeness	
	Demo-crats	Repub-licans	Demo-crats	Repub-licans	House	Senate
1948–50						
Conflicts	54	86	39	45	30	64
All Roll Calls	63	67	60	55	68	64
Party unity	60	64	60	54	38	43
Bipartisan	66	70	60	56	98	98
1953–59						
Conflicts	66	66	66	67	35	37
All Roll Calls	60	64	56	65	74	77
Party unity	56	60	52	62	42	43
Bipartisan	64	68	60	68	98	96
1961–66						
Conflicts	56	74	58	50	35	50
All Roll Calls	73	67	60	62	66	74
Party unity	64	64	56	58	36	43
Bipartisan	82	70	64	66	94	99
1969–72						
Conflicts	39	44	49	38	66	58
All Roll Calls	64	68	56	57	89	85
Party unity	42	46	44	44	56	56
Bipartisan	72·	76	62	64	98	99
1973–76						
Conflicts	56	54	42	62	57	54
All Roll Calls	64	61	66	57	80	77
Party unity	50	58	53	46	51	50
Bipartisan	73	69	73	63	98	95
1977–78						
Conflicts	42	56	27	22	54	76
All Roll Calls [a]	66	66	52	55	78	75
Party unity	45	54	47	41	50	56
Bipartisan [a]	80	76	60	60	98	100

[a] *Includes 1977 roll calls only.*

of the character of this conflict, rather than as an independent source of contention. "Conflict roll calls" relate to fundamental group differences.

In general, our evidence indicates that neither model fits American parties well. Pledges do not duplicate one another, nor are they commonly conflicting. Party lines hold in Congress on votes relating to platform conflicts, but many congressmen and senators cast their ballots with members of the opposition. Platform pledges, particularly those of the party in power, are redeemed, but there are many opportunities for the minority to win on some issues, or to block all action. Democrats and Republicans are not "Tweedledee" and "Tweedledum," but neither are they practitioners of "party government."

PARTIES, PLATFORMS, AND POLICIES

The evidence of this and earlier chapters suggests another model, that of parties as competing coalitions. These coalitions are not under the discipline of a centralized leadership, but neither are they meaningless entities. Parties are social formations, which are united to a noticeable extent in the quest for victory.[17] The quest for victory becomes involved with issues of public policy in two ways. Party leaders and candidates have their own programmatic objectives, and their election will mean popular endorsement of their aims. In addition, parties use programs and issues as one means of attracting the votes necessary to win office. In responding to popular demands, or anticipating them, politicians provide a means for indirect popular influence on governmental action.

The platform may be seen as a useful indicator of the nature of the party coalition. The parties do not copy each other's pledges, but make divergent appeals, thereby pointing to the differences in their basic composition. Union support for the Democrats is reflected in pledges to repeal Taft-Hartley, while business endorsement of Republicans is evidenced in GOP concern with the deregulation of business. Party voting in Congress on platform issues is another indication. The degree of internal cohesion and interparty difference on "conflict roll calls" is similar to that on other contentious issues. Attitudes on platform issues reflect the more general attitudes of the parties.

The platform is important, but not as an inspired gospel to which politicians resort for policy guidance. It is important because it summarizes, crystallizes, and presents to the voters the character of the party coalition. Platform pledges are not simply good ideas, or even original ones.[18] In their programs, Democrats and Republicans are not typically breaking new paths; they are promising to proceed along one or another path that has already become involved in political controversy. The stands taken in the platform clarify the parties' positions on these controversies and reveal the nature of their support and appeals.

Thus, the party manifesto is Janus-like, both retrospective and prospective. After issues have arisen, the platform indicates the party's future intentions. If victorious, the party coalition will pursue its programs. Endorsement of a proposal in the platform provides evidence of its suitability for governmental action and an argument in its behalf. The many obstacles of American institutions may prevent action, however. Fulfillment of platform pledges is common, but it is not required.

The pattern of Medicare is illustrative. National health insurance had been proposed during the Truman administration but was defeated in Congress. Proposals for a more restricted program of hospital insurance for the aged through social security began to be heard in the mid-1950s. It became an important issue in Congress, but the House Ways and Means Committee, which had jurisdiction over the measure, refused to approve it. Supporters then sought its endorsement in party platforms. The Democrats included Medicare in their 1960 platform, and it became a primary item on the agendas of Presidents Kennedy and Johnson. The Senate voted on the measure three times, finally approving it in 1964, but the House still refused to act. In 1964 the Democrats again endorsed Medicare and, following the Johnson victory, it became law in 1965. The platform did not force party action immediately, but it did indicate the character of the Democratic coalition.

The party coalition needs popular support in order to accomplish its aims. Our findings on the fulfillment of platforms demonstrate the superior position of the victorious party in regard to policy achievement. The in-party is better able to meet its platform commitments, particularly on those issues in dispute with its opposition. Popular intervention provides the lever of power for a group of politicians that seeks to move the government.

To win power, parties must also serve the interests of voters. Party responsiveness to or anticipation of popular desires can provide a means of indirect electoral influence over policy. Such influence requires both meaningful platform commitments and the fulfillment of these pledges. We have found that platforms are relatively specific. Moreover, and contrary to the conventional wisdom, these platform pledges are redeemed. Legislation or executive action directly fulfills close to half the planks, and some definite action is taken in two-thirds to three-fourths of the cases. Achievement is even greater for the party in the White House. The vote for party is also a vote for policy.

The influence of the electorate is most evident in regard to voters' particular material and tangible interests. The political theorists defending elections were most concerned with the protection of personal interests. The evidence in this and the last chapter consistently indicates that elections are in fact most likely to provide such protection. The platforms' most specific appeals are related to tangible and distributive rewards, and conflict between party pledges is most common on such issues. The parties are relatively coherent and distinct in fulfilling these pledges, and the effect of party victory is particularly evident in fulfilling tangible promises. In giving their support to one party, voters are bringing to power a group with a definable set of policies that are especially significant in relation to the personal interests the voter wishes to project and promote.

Popular intervention in government does not mean direct and complete control over policy. The parties are insufficiently cohesive, and American institutions insufficiently centralized, to permit even a good imitation of "party government." Elections do make a difference, however, by installing a coalition with specific commitments, relevant to voters' interests, and likely of fulfillment. Voters can make a more meaningful choice than that between "Tweedledee" and "Tweedledum," and also can serve their own interests and secure their own protection. Platforms, then, are a meaningful guide to party action, not because of their binding quality, but because they contain the commitments and appeals of the parties. Party programs thereby permit indirect voter influence.

The significance of party platforms has received increasing attention in recent years. Analyses of the platforms have been extended backward through American history, revealing distinctive patterns. The platforms change their focus drastically at important junctures in American history. Major value changes in the nation, such as the shift from a concern with morality to an emphasis on wealth and well-being, are reflected in the platforms.[19] Changes in the political agenda of the United States are also evident in the platforms, such as the replacement of the earlier attention to national integration by a focus on economic development. Significantly, these changes in the platform correspond in time with critical party realignments. A new issue brings with it a new party coalition to deal with that issue.[20] Important changes in the content of public policy then result.[21]

Platforms have been found to constitute "a form of national planning," for the party documents are "taken very seriously by federal officials who occupy positions on the White House staff, the Bureau of the Budget, and elsewhere." [22] Their growing importance is further indicated by changes made by the political parties in the past twelve years. The platform committees have been reconstituted to be more representative of voter population. These committees now convene long before the national conventions, hold public hearings around the nation, and write drafts of particular planks long before the party's presidential nomination is made. The Democratic party now holds regular midterm conferences to reconsider its programs; and the platforms themselves have become longer, more detailed, and broader in their range.

Campaign promises have been found to be significantly fulfilled in a number of forums. Promises in regard to social security have been consistently redeemed, in keeping with the nature of the parties' commitments to their basic coalitions and their propensity to emphasize material benefits.[23] Among the states, some positive action has been found in as many as half of all party pledges.[24] In another analysis, closely paralleling ours, Grogan examined the fulfillment of campaign promises by Presidents Johnson and Nixon. He found that both chief executives delivered either fully or partially on a majority of their pledges (Johnson on 64 percent, Nixon on 60 percent). Furthermore, of those presidential promises that required congressional support, Johnson was able to win nearly nine-tenths of those he endorsed, and Nixon three-fifths. As parties honor their pledges, candidates honor their contracts with the electorate.[25]

Academic research thus underlines political practice. We should take platforms seriously—because politicians seem to take them seriously. One President, responding to critics of his program, stated a common theme: "I made it abundantly clear that I ran on a platform that contained my commitments; that I expect to carry them out to the extent of my ability; that I appreciated their cooperation to the extent that they could in good conscience give it to me." [26] Surprisingly, American party leaders usually agree.

Notes

1. Performance of pledges is also necessary to achieve both party-rationality and voter-rationality, as discussed in the last chapter. See also Anthony Downs, *An Economic Theory of Democracy* (New York: Harper & Row, 1957), pp. 103–9.

2. David Truman, *The Governmental Process* (New York: Knopf, 1951), pp. 282–83.

3. See American Political Science Association, Committee on Political Parties, "Toward a More Responsible Two-Party System," *American Political Science Review* 44 (September 1950): supplement. Proposals made in this report include biennial conventions, shorter platforms, a small party council to interpret the document, and mandatory acceptance of platform pledges by party candidates.

4. *Congressional Record,* vol. 111, 89th Cong., 1st sess. (April 7, 1965), pp. 6947, 6976.

5. *The New York Times,* March 19, 1977, p. 19, summarizing a 111-page compilation.

6. In this case we are dealing only with a statement of association. If we were dealing with a causal statement (e.g., "Platforms lead to party unity"), it would be best to cast

our statement in such a way that we prefer it to be disproven. In social science we can rarely expect to prove a statement. The best we can usually do is to disprove an opposite statement. We can then console ourselves that we have increased the probability that our preferred statement is true. See Morris Cohen and Ernest Nagel, *An Introduction to Logic and Scientific Method* (New York: Harcourt Brace Jovanovich, 1943). For application to statistical tests of significance, see Linton Freeman, *Elementary Applied Statistics* (New York: Wiley, 1965), pp. 149–56. See also chap. 6, pp. 112–113 of this book.

7. 1976 Democratic Platform, *1976 Congressional Quarterly Almanac* (Congressional Quarterly), p. 857.

8. In the previous chapter, such pledges were considered in the same manner as those promising some innovative action. "Negative fulfillment" does not apply to situations in which an existing law must be extended to remain in force, and the law then is continued without change. When any activity is required, such action falls outside of this category, which is reserved for promises literally to do nothing. For those satisfied with the status quo, such promises are significant and often crucial.

9. All statements from the 1976 platforms are from 1976 Democratic Platform, "Contract with the People," *1976 Congressional Quarterly Almanac*, pp. 855–71.

10. For the definition of bipartisan pledges, see p. 204 below.

11. The low out-party proportion after the 1948 election is probably a reflection of the vague Republican platform, which contained only twenty specific pledges. Republican gains in the 1966 congressional election did not result in the later passage of the party's program, but rather in the blocking of new administration programs.

12. E. E. Schattschneider, *Party Government* (New York: Holt, Rinehart & Winston, 1942), pp. 131–32. These sentences are italicized by Schattschneider. Other writers defend this model. See Pendleton Herring, *The Politics of Democracy* (New York: Norton, 1940); and Edward C. Banfield, "In Defense of the American Party System," in *Political Parties U.S.A.*, ed. Robert A. Goldwin (Chicago: Rand McNally, 1964), pp. 21–37.

13. For an excellent analysis of candidate differences and similarities, see Benjamin Page, *Choices and Echoes in Presidential Elections* (Chicago: University of Chicago Press, 1978).

14. Schattschneider has been one of the foremost advocates of "party government." For similar views, see APSA, "Toward a More Responsible Two-Party System." For a fuller discussion of party models, see Judson L. James, *American Political Parties in Transition* (New York: Harper & Row, 1974), chap. 1.

15. There were 45 issues involved in the 136 conflictions platform pledges of the first political period, and 44 issues in the 109 conflictions pledges in the 1968–76 period. In other words, because of issue duplication, there was an average of 2.75 platform provisions to every issue.

16. The percentage of party-unity votes among all roll calls is taken from the relevant volumes of *Congressional Quarterly Almanac*. All roll calls in the congressional sessions in which platform votes occur were used for this comparison. There were no "conflict roll calls" in 1945–47, 1951–52, 1960, 1964, 1970, 1974, and 1975. Consequently, these years are not included in calculations of general congressional voting.

17. See Neil A. McDonald, *The Study of Political Parties* (Garden City, N.Y.: Doubleday, 1955), chap. 2.

18. Minor parties are often credited with originating new ideas, but the evidence is mixed. See V. O. Key, Jr., *Politics, Parties and Pressure Groups* (5th ed.; New York: Crowell, 1964), chap. 10; William Hesseltine, *Third-Party Movements in the United States* (Princeton: Van Nostrand, 1962); and Daniel Mazmanian, *Third Parties in Presidential Elections* (Washington, D.C.: Brookings Institution, 1974).

19. J. Zvi Namenwirth and Harold D. Lasswell, *The Changing Language of Ameri can Values: A Computer Study of Selected Party Platforms* (Beverly Hills: Sage Professional Papers in Comparative Politics, No. 01-DO1, 1970).

20. Benjamin Ginsberg, "Critical Elections and the Substance of Party Conflict, 1844–1968," *Midwest Journal of Political Science* 16 (November 1972: 603–25.

21. Benjamin Ginsberg, "Elections and Public Policy," *American Political Science Review* 70 (March 1976): 41–49.

22. Paul T. David, "Party Platforms as National Plans," *Public Administration Review* 31 (May/June 1971): 304.

23. John D. Bradley, "Party Platforms and Party Performance Concerning Social Security," *Polity* 1 (Spring 1969): 337–58.

24. Richard C. Elling, "State Party Platforms and State Legislative Performance," *American Journal of Political Science* 23 (May 1979): 388.

25. Fred J. Grogan, "Candidate Promises and Presidential Performance, 1964–1972" (paper prepared for the annual meeting of the Midwest Political Science Association, 1977), tables 3, 5.

26. Lyndon Johnson, replying to criticisms by Democratic governors after the party's mid-term defeats. *The New York Times,* December 22, 1966, p. 24.

ECONOMIC ISSUES

The history of economic doctrines in the past essentially took place in a context in which the search for laws and tendencies represented a kind of immutable activity; with people "actors" in scripts written by "nature" or "history." With the advent of John Maynard Keynes, economics as a function of policy became the norm. His *General Theory* provided a basis for a new way of viewing the relationship of wages to prices and profits to production; more significantly, it showed how the manipulation of economic indicators changes so-called immutable outcomes. Not only did "government" become an essential element in doing economics, but it became an essential mechanism for creating the kind of economic outcomes that produce desirable ends such as social equity, full employment, and racial, ethnic, and sexual parities. The new economics, with its emphasis on forms of planning and goal-oriented tasks, made policy-making an essential—perhaps the quintessential—ingredient in the new economics, whether of "mainstream," "monetarist," or "Marxist" varieties.

As Ward appropriately indicates, comparative analysis, especially of economic systems, is inherently policy-oriented, since the relationship between economic systems is a matter of choice and has been so conceived since the days of utopian analysis. Ward outlines the alternatives in both utopian and empirical settings, believing the appraisal of alternative systems is still a major ground for future policy. He also sees a shift in policy resulting less from socialist than from ecological models, the least developed utopia in the arsenal of comparative economic policy-making. Moving from the realm of alternative models to a welfare model sensitive to policy shifts, Van Loon sees policy-making as deeply sensitive to broader political and economic factors. Policy-making thus becomes a battleground for reform-minded welfare advocates and budget-minded political officials. The Canadian case is clearly typical of the Western style of policy-making in an economic restrictive environment. Horowitz's article is an effort to locate the limits-of-growth debate in a policy context of egalitarian demands on one side and declining resources on the other. He sees the policy shift from social stratification to economic equilibrium as potentially risky, since it invites not simply stagnation but risks of polarization. While the declining power of the American economy on a world scale is recognized, the policy mechanisms employed to deal with such decline can be reduced to a zero growth formula only if a set of corollary assumptions about stratification and polarization are also accepted. For as long as economic equality remains an essential social goal, a policy of growth rather than no-growth will probably be on the national agenda.

13

COMPARATIVE ECONOMIC SYSTEMS
Changing Times—Changing Issues

Benjamin Ward

The fundamental question asked in the field of comparative systems is: What is the opportunity cost of capitalism? That is, what is the best possible alternative structure of economic interactions for a society? Of course, the question can be answered in various ways: One can concentrate on the values and goals appropriate to an economic system; or one can concentrate on modeling, on generating the logical implications of particular patterns of interdependence; or one can concentrate on facts, restricting the scope of the question to actually existing societies and so to the description of their structure and performance. And, as one might expect, many individual practitioners may never offer a complete answer to the question, but orient their research to rather specific partial answers. Even so, the big question lurks continuously behind the little answers, providing a kind of vision that has been central to the field throughout its existence.

Author's Note: *The author would like to thank Gregory Grossman and Thomas Meyer for critical comments and the Institute for International Studies, University of California, Berkeley, for clerical assistance.*

I

A brief history of this field may well begin with the utopian novels of the later nineteenth century and the communes whose existence both influenced and was influenced by them. Generally, the experimental communities were inspired by the notion of brotherly love, or, as an economist might say, by the belief that humans naturally have strongly interdependent utility functions, in which one person's satisfaction is strongly and positively affected by the level of others' utilities. If brotherly love—solidarity—is not so apparent in the larger society, it is purportedly because of the distortion of that natural tendency by the materialism and self-seeking forced on individuals by the structure of capitalism.

The communes tended to be short-lived.[1] They also suffered from a perhaps more serious defect from the point of view of an economist: there was no way to establish a genuine commune for a large population. Perhaps the most interesting attempt to deal with this problem in the utopian literature is Edward Bellamy's *Looking Backward.*[2] Through his novel Bellamy argued that solidarity can be inculcated partly through education, but mostly through the connection between solidarity and equality. Each citizen was provided the same sum of money each year with which to order needed goods, while employment in less desirable jobs was stimulated partly through voluntary service and partly by reducing the hours of work in such jobs to the level that would balance supply and demand. Offering a number of proposed solutions to economic problems of interest from the point of view of economic analysis, Bellamy's utopia seriously addressed central issues which must be resolved before the utopia of brotherly love could be made a reality.

A second line of utopian writing is reflected in William Morris' *News From Nowhere*, which combines anarchy with a vision that the essence of the good life consists of man engaged in harmonious strife with nature.[3] Production was to be highly decentralized, with emphasis on the aesthetic quality of goods in daily use and the quality of a society in which the institutional bases of coercion had been completely dismantled. Perhaps less realistic than Bellamy, Morris' novel nevertheless seems to have caught some of the spirit that informs the ecological movement today.

A third line of utopian argument is reflected in Theodor Hertzka's novel, *Freeland*.[4] In Hertzka's world the market provides the instrument which makes basic resource allocation decisions. Capital is made freely available to groups of users, and workers may freely join any work group they wish. The proceeds of a work group are shared among the members of that group, thus with a single stroke providing full employment and an incentive both to work and to associate oneself with activities that produce goods in public demand. Political decisions were made democratically in a series of limited-interest parliaments. Hertzka's novel fired the imaginations of a large number of people in the early 1890s, and associations were formed which intended to emigrate and establish their utopia in Kenya. Though the colonies were not formed, the blueprint remains as a defense of the human potential in the market economy.

These three types of utopia—the world of competitive man, taking basic pleasure in the struggle to achieve relative to other humans; the world of ecological man, taking his deepest pleasure in interaction with nature; and solidary man, taking his deepest pleasure in relations with other humans—seem to exhaust the primary human orientations that have informed answers to comparative systems' fundamental question. They have undergone very different levels of development in economics over the past century, as we will see.

One might have expected the first great controversy in economics over socialism to have involved Marxism in a central way. However, things did not turn out that way. Marx did not have very much to say about socialism, his work being devoted essentially to the appraisal of capitalism. Economic analysis of socialism is entirely lacking in Marx—for example, it is not clear how or even whether Marx intended his theory of value to apply to a socialist economy. Marxism has had surprisingly little to say on the major economic issues associated with the nature of socialism.

The first great controversy in comparative economics probably grew out of the rather general interest in utopias of the last century, bursting out around the turn of the century and at least smoldering in the literature ever since.[5] It is often called the socialist controversy, since it involved explicitly the comparison between socialism and capitalism. However it was an economist's argument, couched in the language of the new marginalist economic theory of the time and emphasizing the role of scarcity in analyzing the economic aspects of justice. The key intellectual device in the discussion was the model of competitive capitalism. This model is structured around the concept of equilibrium, the situation in which all participants in an economy are in a state in which no one can improve his or her position legally or without coercion. For example, consider a market economy in which each participant has a stock of resources and in which voluntary exchange is the only method by which resources can be transferred among individuals. Mutually beneficial trades are made until no one can find another deal which he or she is willing to make and another participant is willing to accept. At this point the best of all possible worlds has been reached in a very specific and limited sense: no one can be made better off without making someone else worse off.

This is the heart of the competitive model. It can be generalized to include production activities as well as the exchange of already existing goods and still possess that same optimality property. Furthermore, prices serve to define an important additional property of equilibrium. Given the initial distribution of resources and the set of prices of all goods and services associated with the equilibrium, individuals, acting on competitive capitalist markets, will choose the Pareto optimal equilibrium point without any coercive interventions from outside agents such as governments. The equilibrium prices, then, measure the relative values of goods and services, including labor, in the optimal situation. In a limited sense prices become moral measures that determine the worth of a good to the economy's members: Equilibrium prices measure the amount of some goods *each* member of the economy participating in a given market is willing to give up in order to acquire a unit of the good sold in that market.

The notion of Pareto optimality was closely intertwined with the idea of capitalism. Private ownership of all resources, including means of production, was assumed, and the extended use of markets was the most obvious manifestation of the new capitalist societies that emerged during the course of the nineteeth century. Perhaps some analysts could be forgiven for arguing that this model demonstrated the superiority of capitalism over all possible competitors. However, the socialist controversy was initiated, not when critics pointed to the substantial deviations from reality which are built into the model, but when they pointed out that the model can be reinterpreted to charcterize the socialist ideal. Suppose, they argued, that one assumes that the means of production are under social control. Prices are set for these socialized goods following rules equivalent to those employed in the competitive capitalist model. Then a new equilibrium is reached which has the same property of Pareto optimality as its capitalist counterpart. However, it has one additional property: Since the profits of capital are now under social control, they can be used in part to promote equality in income distribution, altering that initial distribution of resources from which the system of voluntary, market-mediated transfers begins. Thus, they argued, socialism provides the best of two worlds, equaling the efficiency property of capitalism but providing a specific mechanism for avoiding the gross inequalities of that system.

Once engaged, this argument, as noted, has continued to the present day without any decisive resolution. The argument can continue because of the elements of idealization present in the set of underlying assumptions. How much damage does monopoly do to the efficiency argument? How do environmental issues, which are inconsistent with the assumption of mutual independence of the individual production and consumption units, affect the relative outcomes generated by the two systems? A host of issues are suggested by this controversy, and have had their impact on later developments. One might only note that implicitly two of the three basic utopian ideal types have been left by the roadside, the arguments in the context of the socialist controversy implicitly accepting the Hertzkan competitive-man utopia as the framework for the comparisons.

Apparently, it was during the 1930s that comparative systems were officially inaugurated in the sense that textbooks first began to be written for the field. The early texts tended to be as much comparisons of ideologies as of actual or theoretical economies.[6] The three principal ideologies in those days were capitalism, fascism, and socialism. Socialism tended to be represented not by the Soviet Union but by Marxian conceptions of that system; fascism by the protagonists of the corporatist state, of which the early New Deal might be considered a somewhat distant cousin;[7] and capitalism by something very like the competitive model. Though accompanied neither by careful descriptions of existing economies nor by much economic analysis of the proposed systems, this orientation did bring out a somewhat different aspect of comparative economics, namely the role of historical forces. The socialist controversy interpreted the fundamental question rather literally: Given that we are to make a rational decision between socialism and capitalism, which shall we choose? That is perhaps a naive view as to how revolutions come about. At any rate, this ideological genre emphasized the longer-run historical forces that may tend to push social structures in particular directions. Of course, a leading candidate in the thirties was stagnationism, the argument that capitalism could no longer naturally generate sufficient demand for goods to move the economy, by means of voluntary market interactions, to the vicinity of full employment. This of course created a major argument for socialism, in which managed aggregate demand might more easily be achieved, and also created the Keynesian counterattack that capitalism could be saved from stagnation by suitable application of fiscal policy.

The rise of the Cold War in the early postwar period generated a new thrust to the by now well-established field of comparative economics. Competition with the Soviet Union, combined with the Stalinist Iron Curtain rung down on the publishing of economic data, stimulated efforts at careful study of the institutions and performance of that economy. Substantial support from government and foundations was forthcoming for the study of a topic that now was of central policy relevance, and research institutes were established, especially at Harvard and Columbia, that were to train the lion's share of students of the Soviet economy, as well as to produce research that provided a firm basis for appraisal of that economy.

The first order of business was the appraisal of Soviet statistics. Stalin had once said that statistics were instruments in the class struggle, and there were plenty of suspicions as to the reliability of many Soviet claims regarding the growth of their economy during the plan era after 1928. A massive survey was made of Soviet sources in order to collect all available input and output statistics, and a variety of systems of aggregating that data were carried out in order to determine how well, relatively and absolutely, the Soviet economy had performed and just what its current capabilities were. The net result of all this effort was a clearer picture of Soviet performance, but still one fraught with mysteries and controversies. It seems that the Soviets under Stalin did little outright fabrication of data at the central level, though there was a good deal of withholding of unfavorable statistics and some very misleading interpretations of data. However, participants lower down in the system had a variety of incentives to misreport their own performance (much as the composer of a capitalist income tax return does), and the leadership may not always have assiduously rooted out such inflated claims. It turned out, of course, that the Soviets had successfully transformed their economy into the world's second largest industrial complex, at the expense of maintaining very low levels of consumption and of the extraordinary backwardness of the agricultural sector.[8]

The second main task was to develop some understanding of Soviet economic institutions and decision processes. Extraordinary secrecy surrounded the operation of the Soviet economy, and visiting and talking with economists and industrial managers and officials was impossible. However, it turned out that under careful analysis the Soviet press revealed a good deal more than one might expect about this range of issues. Furthermore, there was a considerable number of former Soviet citizens who had remained in the west after World War II and who had

had some experience with prewar economic management. Interestingly enough, two studies of industrial management—one emphasizing the former, the other the latter of these two data sources—produced very similar pictures of the operation of the system (Berlinger, 1957; Granick, 1954). Similar work produced a better understanding of trade, the budgetary system and finance, and agriculture. By 1960 Soviet economic institutions had been substantially demystified.

Some 15 or 20 scholars, most of them Americans teaching in universities, led this massive effort. Naturally, it had a considerable effect on the teaching of the subject of comparative economics. Courses in the Soviet economy proliferated, while courses in comparative systems gave increasing emphasis to that economy. Interest in the field shifted toward the description of institutions and the analysis of quantitative data on performance. New centers of Soviet research sprang up, many at universities, but also elsewhere, as at the Rand Corporation (Air Force-sponsored) in Santa Monica, California. As the Cold War pressures toward conformity and secrecy diminished in the United States, Washington became a rapidly increasing center of scholarly research; even the CIA began releasing some of its studies to scholars.[9]

However by the early 1960s new issues and problems had begun to reshape the field. The first aspect of change came from the Soviet Union itself in the form of the Thaw, which for our subject meant a substantial increase in the amount of information available about the Soviet economy, a renewal of long-missing contacts with Soviet economists and Soviet reality, and the renewal of Soviet economic science itself. The first of these did not dramatically change the already emerged picture of the Soviet economy, but of course did add new dimensions of detail. Oddly enough, it seems that Soviet economists too had been largely denied access to much general information about the workings of their own economy. Their newly acquired information, and their reading of Western studies of the workings of their economy, gave a large number of them, especially the younger ones, a strongly reformist orientation. Led by the influential academician Nemchinov, by the long silenced economist V. V. Novzhilov, and by the mathematician (and mathematical economist) L. V. Kantorovich, this group set about to reform the Soviet economy and Soviet economics. They had rather more success in the latter than in the former activity; curricula were revised, quantitative studies based on techniques substantially developed in the West began to be used in research and planning, and new journals instituted to spread the new message. This aspect of reform has now grown to exercise great influence in Soviet economics, and Western and many Soviet economists now speak essentially the same professional language.[10]

The reform of planned economies was a different story however, and one in which the Soviet Union's own economy was not at the center of interest. Actually the first major reform of a centrally planned socialist economy had occurred in the early 1950s when Yugoslavia, boycotted by the Cominform countries, abandoned central planning for a worker managed, market socialist economic system (at least in industry and large scale trade). Following Khrushchev's 1956 speech, which formally inaugurated the Thaw, a number of Eastern European economies began cooling at a rapid rate. Once the Polish and Hungarian revolts had been contained, however, and the pace of change had apparently been brought under firm political control, economic reform was allowed to continue. This made the 1960s the era of reform, whose main thrust was the need to decentralize substantially the more routine economic decisions and to design incentive systems which would generate decentralized decisions of a kind that the leadership would approve. Economists in Eastern Europe as well as the Soviet Union enthusiastically embarked on this venture. No economy in the area, except for Albania, was unaffected by this activity. In Hungary the reform finally adopted was quite substantial, turning basic responsibility for short run industrial decisions over to a set of large industrial combines (associations of factories under a single head), with the planning commission serving more as a guide than as a director of the economy—at least that was the intent. In other economies the reforms were much more modest, though all moved in the same general direction, usually accompanied by a massive reform of the structure of prices.[11]

By the late 1950s another socialist giant had emerged with a track record in need of serious study, namely China. Once again considerations of policy meant both government and foundation support were available for the effort, and the apparently successful model for the study of the Soviet Union seemed a good one to follow. Institutes for the study of modern China, with considerable emphasis on the economy, were established at a number of universities, the most important probably being those at Harvard, Michigan, and Berkeley, with economic research at Rand and in Washington again playing an important role. However China study had a much bumpier road to travel than its Soviet counterpart. The drying up of data after the failure of the Great Leap of the late fifties was followed by the Cultural Revolution in the later sixties and the splitting of the academic community induced by the Viet Nam war and the rise of radical student movements on campus. The community of China scholars was also split, no doubt partly under the influence of those disrupted times, but also because of a major controversy within the field as to the nature and level of achievement of the Chinese economy. During the 1950s the Chinese clearly had borrowed heavily from the Soviets, not only in terms of factories and technology, but also in form and operation of their economic institutions. The Chinese claimed to have made a sharp break with these experiences after the conflict with the Soviet Union surfaced in 1960, and by the later sixties to have established essentially new and more nearly socialist forms of socioeconomic relationships. Some foreign visitors lent credence to these claims in reporting on their trips. Others were not so sure, and there was no way to check so long as the Chinese press was as reticent as it had become and visitors so restricted in their observations. Since the changes were assertedly of very recent vintage, the reactions of emigrés, such as those who had left it in considerable numbers shortly after the Great Leap of the late 1950s, were not really relevant. This time around, in sharp contrast with the experience of economic research on the Soviet Union, scholarship did not produce consensus.[12]

In addition to the study of China and of economic reforms, a third major thread of research in comparative economic systems emerged in the 1960s: neoclassical theory of socialist economies. Despite the fact that the socialist controversy had been conducted almost entirely within the framework of the central core of neoclassical economics, the theory that included the analysis of competitive equilibrium discussed above, the field was a bit tardy in the postwar period in bringing economic analysis to the fore. This was probably because of the concentration of attention on issues of institutional description and of the generation and revision of time series and of index numbers. But the groundwork for a new theory of planning had already been laid by economic theorists outside the field in the 1950s. Students of competitive equilibrium theory developed mathematical theorems which gave new life to the old idea that central planning might be carried out successfully using prices to aid in testing alternative plans. For example, the solution of complex models of an economy had to be carried out in a series of iterations, each of which moved one a bit closer to the optimal economic outcome, as defined by the modeller. This approach could be considered as equivalent to the actions of a planner, armed with a mathematical description of the production possibilities for his economy, and also with a criterion for deciding which outcomes were to be preferred, groping his way on the computer to the optimal plan. American theorists, it seemed, were showing the Soviets the way to improve the working of their own economy, namely by adopting the techniques the Americans were developing.

Another thread of theory involved neoclassical theorizing about the nature of the firm under socialism and of the interactions among enterprises and other economic units. The early descriptive studies of the Soviet enterprise had suggested an approach: Assume that the production environment was very similar to that of an American business but that the criterion of performance, and the institutional constraints on that performance were different.[13] This produced some interesting theorizing about the problems of the Soviet firm; however its most successful development occurred in analyzing the situation suggested by Yugoslav laws and experience. In this case the market environment which had inspired the creators of price theory in the first place was preserved, and the major change was to assume that worker managed firms would try to maximize, not profits, but profits per worker. This produced a number of interesting deviations from the results of conventional neo-classical theory and offered many opportunities for the application of conventional theory, including to some extent even macroeconomics.[14]

II

Today the field of comparative economic systems would not be widely regarded among economists as one of the central fields of their discipline. To some extent this may reflect a certain parochial focus by the profession on the problems of the American economy. However there are more substantive reasons. In the postwar period economics has become thoroughly dominated by neoclassical economic theory, divided into its two basic departments of micro- and macroeconomics. Furthermore applied fields have tended to draw the structure of their problems from theory itself. Armed with models derived from a common store of theory and applying econometrics as the major tool for relating the theory to the real world of observations, there is a strong tendency within the profession to judge the centrality of any field by the extent to which it employs these tools and enriches them in its work. On this score comparative systems cannot receive high marks.

Nevertheless, as our historical survey has shown, the field has developed rapidly over the last three decades. The range of problems under consideration has certainly grown, as have the number of practitioners. Most every economic department teaches courses in the subject at the undergraduate level and most graduate programs now accept it as a field for the Ph.D.

But does it possess any real unity in theory or problem orientation? To what extent do practitioners interact with one another, at least reading the research reports of their colleagues? What is its relation to the wider discipline of economics itself? We turn now to these questions before discussing the prospects of the field.

At the heart of comparative systems as it has developed in the postwar period is the study of the major socialist economies. This continues to be true today. However the seventies have seen a major shift of emphasis in the location of research activity oriented toward understanding the operation of specific socialist economies. The 1970s have been an era of decline of university-based area studies centers. They have also been an era of rapid development of scholarly activity in area studies that is government financed, and which is undertaken with increasing frequency in government agencies. This trend is largely a product of declining foundation support for area studies and of increasing government support. Of course financial control by the latter tends to keep the research oriented toward current-policy-related issues. What about the effect on scholarly quality?

The first thing to note is that university based students of socialist economies have not formed a cohesive intellectual group. The students of the Soviet Union tend to be off in one corner of a campus, the students of China off in another, perhaps even using separate libraries. And the students of East European economies may be even more fragmented, there being many countries to study, each with its own language and relatively few students. Students of Yugoslavia in particular have gone their separate way. The study of economic reforms and of planning theory in the 1960s served as an integrating topic for the Slavists, but did not affect Sinologists. And the handful of students of Cuba have tended to be quite separate within the discipline's pattern of social interactions. On this dimension government sponsorship has not caused any harm and by providing a sort of central place for research and its reporting may have contributed a bit to greater unity in interaction.

Substantively it seems clear that the new level of government involvement has had some unifying effect on the field. This has come about largely through the impact of the series of Joint Economic Committee volumes which have been published on a regular schedule during the 1970s. Currently every three years this Congressional body sponsors a volume on one of the three main areas (for example, *Chinese Economy Post-Mao* in 1978, *East European Economies Post-Helsinki* in 1977, and *Soviet Economy in a New Perspective* in 1976). These are rather massive collections of papers providing broad coverage describing and analyzing developments in the area in the recent past and appraising trends. The volumes are of generally high quality, using specialists from universities and government to provide the papers. The results are widely read and are beginning to form a sort of factual basis which practitioners generally rely on in their own research and teaching. A principal role in organizing and developing these volumes has been played by John Hardt. The further opening up of the CIA has led to the publication of an increasing number of studies of scholarly relevance under the research direction of Maurice Ernst, and these too have contributed to a greater unity in the knowledge base of practitioners of comparative economic systems.

The question naturally arises as to whether this perhaps permanently increased role of government in research on socialist economies has an effect on the range of questions asked within the field. If one is simply to make the contrast between university-based and government-based research on socialist economies as it has occurred in the United States, the difference is not particularly significant for the Slavists, for the questions the two groups have tended to ask have been very similar. However the issue may be more serious for China. Though students with a relatively friendly orientation toward the PRC are not excluded from the pages of the Joint Economic Committee volumes, they are not exactly present in bulk. Also the range of questions that might be asked by someone seriously interested in a socialist form of economic organization as an alternative for his own presently nonsocialist regime, tend not to be asked. Given the current disarray in the ranks of those who have been sympathetic toward China, this does not pose any serious short run problem of distortion. Over the longer run there might be cause for more worry.

A comparison of the topics dealt with in these volumes with their counterpart research of a decade or so ago indicates a good deal more current emphasis on international trade, resource issues, especially energy, and defense economics. Much less attention is given to economic reform and domestic organizational structure. These changes in research emphasis reflect real changes in the structure of policy issues in these economies, and in our own. Issues such as participation, the structure of power and influence, and long-run dynamics are clearly given reduced weight. Here again, these changes reflect changes that are paralleled among university researchers. Probably the test of the effect of the change in research location and sponsorship will only come when we can observe the response of the research community to a change in interests away from those of current governmental policy relevance.

A second factor affecting the unity of the field has been the increased emphasis on abstract neoclassical analysis, especially by the younger generation of researchers. This of course provides a basis for communication across area specialties and might be expected to have a strongly unifying effect. In certain areas, perhaps especially the study of international trade relations, that has been true. However so far this unifying effect is not terribly pronounced. For one thing, the bureaucratic structure of centrally planned economies does not seem to lend itself well to economic analysis. Too much information remains imbedded in the bureaucracy; furthermore too many decisions tend to have an ad hoc basis, to be the product of localized influence and information structures about which we do not at present have sufficient information for analytic purposes. Basically economic theory has been developed to explain market phenomena, as noted earlier. And macroeconomics deals with variables, particularly monetary variables, that have a different and less central role in the economic control of centrally planned economies.

For reasons such as these, students of Yugoslavia have continued to go their own ways in economic analysis. And the China field has been little penetrated by these developments because of the mystery that continues to surround operation of its basic economic institutions and the continued weakness of the quantitative data base.

In sum the two major changes in orientation that have occurred in the 1970s have not yet had a major impact in altering the orientations and efforts of practitioners, though they have clearly contributed to a broadening of our understanding of these economies. Let us turn very briefly now to select reference to areas of recent development and their prospects.

III

Developments of planning theory in the 1970s have not realized the promise of the 1960s. Large scale computation has turned out to be less easy to carry out than had been hoped. The planning models that have seemed to be computable tend to be too simplistic in their assumptions with great difficulties emerging when one shifts to more complex and realistic economic models. General equilibrium remains relatively impervious to analysis under conditions of externalities, (roughly, environmental effects) while such phenomena have tended to become relatively more salient in the real world. And the addition of uncertainty to the theory, while adding realism and generating some results, makes very heavy data demands, and is still hampered by lack of understanding of the appropriate attitude toward risk to use in modelling real world situations. It seems to be an area in which research continues but where, barring a breakthrough, near term prospects are for at best modest progress.[15]

A second analytic area that underwent rapid development in the 1960s is the modeling of the cooperative or worker managed enterprise and of the economy in which all enterprises are managed by the workers with a view to serving their own material interests. Development has continued in the seventies, and as with planning theory, the theory of the cooperative has been enriched by recent attempts to deal with the role of uncertainty in affecting enterprise behavior. However there too the progress made has also been rather limited and the theorems seem to be of relatively weak compass and implication. Furthermore the assumptions of these models clearly differ substantially from Yugoslav reality, so that attempts to apply the theory to the environment have not produced any decisive results. One might also suspect that the economic theory of cooperation has become largely an exercise in the application of economic theory rather than a serious attempt to appraise an alternative form of economic system.[16]

A third area of development is in applied quantitative work. If the 1950s were the era of recomputing industrial production series and the 1960s the era of studying the productivity of the economy's major inputs, labor, capital and technical change, then the 1970s may be considered the era of applying econometric tools to the study of socialist economies. Of course the earlier work continued, with data appraisal efforts concentrated on China and productivity studies on the Slavic economies. But serious macroeconomic study of Yugoslavia is a product of our own decade, as is the development of large scale models of the Soviet economy. In a related development there has been some econometric study of inflation and of trade interactions in Soviet-type economies.[17]

The growing interaction among these economists who apply conventional economic techniques in the study of socialist economies has been accompanied by a more or less tacit assumption that there is a unique animal loose in the world of comparative systems, namely the Soviet-type economy, which has a structure and dynamic quite different from that of capitalism. The similarities and differences among these economies has yet to be appraised with a view to explicitly testing the hypothesis of systemic unity, but I suspect that will come; interest in the idea is strengthened not only by the prospect it offers for joint study of several socialist economies, but also because of some indications that China probably belongs in the same box. At any rate this is a hypothesis with the capacity to have a considerable shaping effect on the comparative systems of the eighties.

There have been two recent attempts to provide essentially a treatise of comparative economics, a volume which in some sense codifies results and procedures for the field (Montias, 1976; Wiles, 1977). They are very different in structure and thrust. Montias' work is essentially a plea to turn comparative systems into a full-fledged branch of conventional economics, applying tools of the trade to those problems that are amenable to this sort of treatment. Wiles is more oriented toward institutions and tends to emphasize the ad hoc and shifting nature of problems in the field; on the whole it is a much more eclectic approach. It is also a very personal one, reflecting a level of erudition and insight that cannot be trained into students in a routine manner. In short, comparative systems seem to resist codification at the moment and one suspects that though the 1980s will bring a continuing shift in emphasis toward neoclassical lines of work, the modest achievements of these efforts so far will still leave a number of practitioners attempting to apply other approaches.

IV

In conclusion let me return to the fundamental question of comparative systems and a personal reaction to the current state of the field. I believe the fundamental question must continue to inform the general thrust of the field if it is to serve as a genuinely distinct branch of economics. This is the only place where one seriously asks the question: What are the prospects for economic systems which are substantially different from our own in their organizational structure? Even for those who believe that capitalism, especially developed capitalism, has no worthy competitor, the question is useful. In a time of social crisis it can be of considerable help to know that the alternatives of this kind have been carefully surveyed and found wanting. And of course the question is even more important for those who believe that other alternatives *are* relatively promising—and who are also serious in the sense that they believe a careful appraisal of the prospective performance of alternative systems should precede their adoption. The question has not lost its cogency for the 1980s.

Marxists were once the great protagonists of socialism. They are noticeable by their rather sparse membership in the current community of students of comparative economics. This I think is partly a consequence of pressures within Marxism itself. There have been the usual political pressures not to discuss the alternative too precisely—as all politicians know, that is a good way to lose votes. There has been considerable disillusionment with existing socialist economies. Their performance with respect to growth, to attention to the needs of consumers, and to freedom to pursue one's own interests, including political interests, seems inadequate to compensate for their somewhat better distribution of goods and services than their capitalist counterparts.[18] But, perhaps more important, Marxist economists have not only failed to develop analytic methods for dealing with the issues associated with the functioning of the economy in a solidary society, they have increasingly come under the sway of neoclassical economics. Today most of the writings of radical American economists involve the use of techniques developed by their neoclassical confreres. This means that in fact they seem to have given up the ghost with respect to developing any serious and positive analysis associated directly with the fundamental question.

That is especially true because of the central thrust of neoclassical economics. As was noted earlier, it is essentially structured to deal with only one of the three ideal types of utopias. In the competitive utopia individual actors pursue their own interests; efficiency almost requires them to ignore direct interactions among established agents engaged in economic activity. Modeling of socialist economies uses these competitive-utopian assumptions, looking to the individual interests of the participants in the system in theorizing about behavior. Consequently the fundamental question is used within comparative economics only to appraise alternative "competitive" utopias. This may be a seriously narrowing structure for the field.

Which brings us back to the ecological utopia, the least developed utopian ideal within economics. If there is any substantial clientele within the United States today prepared to consider dramatically different forms of economic organization than the one we have, surely it comes from the large and relatively young group of participants in the various strands of the environmental movement. These groups are not well served by existing economic analysis to the extent that they are willing to contemplate seriously such dramatic, as opposed to marginal, changes in the directions they desire.

If comparative economic systems is to serve this group it must build on the very weak heritage of analysis of ecological associationism as an economic alternative to the solidary and competitive utopias.[19] Just what sort of analysis might be appropriate cannot be inferred by reference to the existing comparative systems literature, but the prospect is by no means excluded that it may serve to define a major change of course for this field in the 1980s.

NOTES

1. On the history of communes see Rexroth (1974) and Roberts (1971).

2. First published in 1887 in Boston.

3. First published in 1891 in London.

4. First published in 1891 in Vienna.

5. For surveys of the controversy see Bergson (1948) and Ward (1976).

6. The first popular textbook seems to have been Loucks (1938). For another sample of the genre see Halm (1951).

7. In the sense that in both systems big businesses were expected to collaborate with one another rather than compete, with government serving as an overall controller.

8. Much of this work was led by Bergson and carried out first at Columbia and then at the Russian Research Center at Harvard and the Rand Corporation in Santa Monica, California. For a short survey of the key results see Bergson and Kunets (1963).

9. It may be noted that the McCarthy era was not an era of repression of Soviet studies, even in Washington.

10. For a survey of the rise of neoclassical economics in the Soviet Union see Zauberman (1967); a volume of translations of the fascinating work of Soviet economists during the 1920s has been prepared by Spulber (1964), and Grossman has covered the difficult intermediate period in "Scarce Capital and Soviet Doctrine" (1953).

11. Feiwel (1968) provides a survey of research on the economic reforms. For an account of the Yugoslav experience see Horvat (1977).

12. Chen and Galenson (1967) summarize much American research to that date. Gurley (1976) provides a more positive appraisal of the Chinese experience in this series of essays.

13. Thornton (1976) provides some recent examples of this sort of modeling.

14. This line of research began with Ward (1958).

15. For a more enthusiastic appraisal see Conn (1978).

16. The key work in this area is Vanek (1970). The latest effort at introducing uncertainty to the analysis is Neary (1978).

17. For examples of this research genre see Tyson (1976), Green and Higgins (1977), and Portes (1977).

18. See Wiles (1974) for an argument that British income distribution may actually be less skewed than that in the Soviet Union.

19. For an interesting contemporary attempt to spell out aspects of this ecological utopia see Lutz and Lux (1979). Clearly, cooperation plays a central role in this orientation. However, I think the attempt to build it around the economic theory of worker management is a mistake; the latter is too firmly imbedded in the assumptions of the competitive utopia to serve as a base. For a few hints as to the ingredients that might work see parts 3 and 5 of my *What's Wrong with Economics* New York, 1972).

REFERENCES

BERGSON, A. (1948) "Socialist economics," in H. Ellis (ed.) Survey of Contemporary Economics, Vol. 1. Philadelphia.

——— and S. KUNETS (eds.) (1963) Economic Trends in the Soviet Union. Cambridge, MA: Harvard Univ. Press.

BERLINER, J. (1957) Factory and Manager in the USSR. Cambridge, MA: Harvard Univ. Press.

CHEN, N-R. and W. GALENSON (1967) The Chinese Economy Under Communism. Chicago.

CONN, D. (1978) "Economic theory and comparative economic systems: a partial literature survey," J. of Comparative Economics (December).

ELLIS, H. [ed.] (1948) Survey of Contemporary Economics. Philadelphia.

FEIWEL, G. [ed.] (1968) New Currents in Soviet-Type Economies: A Reader. Scranton.

GRANICK, D. (1954) Management of the Industrial Firm in the USSR. New York.

GREEN, D. and C. HIGGINS (1977) SOVMOD: A Macroeconomic Model of the Soviet Union. New York.

GROSSMAN, G. (1953) "Scarce capital and Soviet doctrine." Q. J. of Economics.

GURLEY, J. (1976) China's Economy and the Maoist Strategy. New York.

HALM, G. (1951) Economic Systems, A Comparative Analysis. New York.

HORVAT, B. (1977) The Yugoslav Economic System. White Plains, NY.

LOUCKS, W. (1938) Comparative Economic Systems. New York.

LUTZ, M. and K. LUX (1979) The Challenge of Humanistic Economics. Menlo Park, CA.

MONTIAS, J. M. (1976) The Structure of Economic Systems. New Haven, CT: Yale Univ. Press.

NEARY, H. (1978) "The labor-managed firm: monopolistic competition, implicit contracts and uncertainty." University of California, Berkeley. (mimeo)

PORTES, R. (1977) "The control of inflation: lessons from East European experience." Economica (March).

REXROTH, K. (1974) Communalism: From its Origins to the Twentieth Century. New York.

ROBERTS, R. (1971) The New Communes. Englewood Cliffs, NJ: Prentice-Hall.

SPULBER, N. (1964) Foundations of the Soviet Strategy for Economic Development. Bloomington, IL.

THORNTON, J. [ed.] (1976) Economic Analysis of the Soviet Type System. Cambridge, MA: Cambridge Univ. Press.

TYSON, L. (1976) "The Yugoslav economy in the seventies," in U.S. Congress, Joint Economic Committee, East European Economies Post-Helsinki. Washington, DC: U.S. Government Printing Office.

VANEK, J. (1970) The General Theory of Labor Managed Market Economies. Ithaca, NY.

WARD, B. (1976) The Socialist Economy. New York.

——— (1972) What's Wrong with Economics? New York.

——— (1958) "The firm in Illyria: market syndicalism." Amer. Econ. Rev.

WILES, P. (1977) Economic Institutions Compared. New York.

——— (1974) The Distribution of Income East and West. Amsterdam.

ZAUBERMAN, A. (1967) Aspects of Planometrics. New Haven, CT: Yale Univ. Press.

REFORMING WELFARE IN CANADA

Rick Van Loon

From 1973 to 1978 a major review of welfare policy in Canada aimed to improve social-insurance programs, inaugurate a "Community Employment Strategy," provide better funding for personal social services, expand existing demogrant programs and, most important to its planners, introduce a program of income supplementation for the working poor. The review was begun partly because of problems within the welfare system but in large measure because of broader political considerations. Its outcome too was largely determined by external considerations, most notably the fiscal restraint of the late 1970s: a modest start at income supplementation was won in late 1978—paradoxically—as part of a rapidly contrived program of expenditure reduction. Welfare reformers must apparently be constantly ready to use whatever opportunities arise to further their aims.

Introduction

In April 1973 Canada's Minister of National Health and Welfare published a series of major welfare-reform proposals. The document, entitled *A Working Paper on Social Security in Canada,* is popularly known as the "Orange Paper" and the policy review that it inaugurated as the Social Security Review. As the principal authors, the Minister of Health and Welfare Marc Lalonde and his Deputy Minister A. W. Johnson wrote in the Preface:

> We have sought, in developing our proposals, to comprehend the whole sweep of social security policy and to develop a comprehensive, logical, and hopefully imaginative approach to this field. We have sought, too, to exercise our ingenuity in

From Rick Van Loon, "Reforming Welfare in Canada," 27(4) *Public Policy* 469-504 (Fall 1979). Copyright 1979 by the President and Fellows of Harvard College. Reprinted by permission of John Wiley & Sons, Inc.

finding new, and if necessary radical, federal–provincial or constitutional arrangements, in order to achieve the kind of integrated social security system which will best serve the needs of the Canadian people.

The list of programs to be examined was extensive. Included were federal Family Allowances, the joint federal–provincial cash-assistance and personal social-service programs, the whole range of programs provided to the elderly, Unemployment Insurance, and several job-creation programs. Planning was to be completed within two years and implementation within five.

But as time went on, the reform proposals that were launched with such optimism traveled an increasingly rocky road. By April 1978, at the end of the scheduled reform period, the basic outlines of Canada's social-security system remained much as they had been in 1973. Expenditures had certainly grown and many clients, particularly among the elderly, were better off, but the cornerstone of the reform exercise, an income-supplementation program for the working poor, remained in limbo. A new personal Social Services Act had vanished from the parliamentary order paper and the last vestiges of a "Community Employment Program" had disappeared in a round of federal cost cutting. No major new program could be said to have appeared during a period intended to "achieve the kind of integrated social security system which will best serve the needs of the Canadian people." Yet paradoxically in August 1978, as a result of a series of events apparently unrelated to welfare reform, and indeed ostensibly quite inimical to it, the door was opened on what is potentially one of the most important changes in the history of the Canadian welfare system: a federally operated, refundable child tax credit.

What can we conclude from this story and from the unexpected events of 1978? Was the Review exercise a failure? Is welfare reform whimsical, exempt from the strictures of rational planning? And whatever the answers to these questions, what lessons can be gleaned concerning the potential for welfare reform?

Our conclusions can be stated fairly simply. They corroborate what many students and practitioners of social reform have long believed: social policy and particularly welfare reform are very much governed by factors external to the welfare system. Reforms that seemed easy and logical in the expansive atmosphere of the late 1960s and early 1970s became unthinkable in the worried climate of the later 1970s. Yet these factors can take strange twists and even in an atmosphere that appears inhospitable to welfare reform, significant changes can take place.

To arrive at these conclusions, we will begin by summarizing the key factors that precipitated the Social Security Review. The second section describes briefly the initial proposals while a subsequent section considers the evolution and eventual disposition of the proposals and examines the policy process itself. The conclusions are then set forth.

I. The Political and Social Policy Situation

THE OVERALL WELFARE "PROBLEM"

The relative size and growth rates of the welfare sectors in Canada and the United States are roughly comparable. In 1967 Canadian federal cash-transfer and personal social-service expenditures accounted for about 4.4 percent of GNP. By 1971 that figure had risen to 5.9 percent and by 1975, the mid-point of the Review process, to 7.5 percent.[1] In both countries aggregate state, provincial, and local expenditures accounted for another 3 to 4 percent of GNP.[2]

The income distribution in the two countries is also comparable.[3] In Canada the share of income received by the poorest one-fifth of family units has remained between 5 and 6 percent throughout the 1970s; the situation is similar in the U.S.[4] The semi-decile ratio (the ratio of family income at the 95th decile to

[1] Canadian figures are adopted from Statistics Canada, *Social Security, National Programs*, Ottawa, 1976, pp. 20, 21, 23. They exclude expenditures on public health insurance, public housing, manpower training programs, and municipal relief, which in 1975 would add about another 4 percent of GNP.

[2] United States federal figures are from Barry L. Friedman and Leonard J. Hausman, "Welfare in Retreat: A Dilemma for the Federal System," *Public Policy*, Winter 1977, pp. 27–28.

[3] Harold Wilensky, *The Welfare State and Equality*, Berkeley, University of California Press, 1975.

[4] Both Statistics Canada and the U.S. Bureau of the Census regularly report these figures. In Canada they are publicized in sources such as *The Financial Post, The Financial Times*, and *The Globe and Mail, Report on Business*.

that at the 5th decile) for Canada is 12.0, for the U.S., 13.3. By contrast it is 3.0 in Sweden, 4.5 in Czechoslovakia, 5.9 in the U.K., and 6.0 in Denmark and the USSR.[5]

When one looks more closely at the U.S. and Canadian welfare systems, however, significant differences in the nature of programs and in the causes for expenditure growth emerge. The Canadian income-maintenance system depends in large part on a series of demogrants financed from general revenues. Only the Canada Pension Plan and, in part, Unemployment Insurance, are based on social-insurance principles. These demogrant programs together accounted for 3.8 percent of GNP and about 50 percent of federal welfare expenditures in 1975 in Canada.

Moreover, the reasons for the rate of growth of welfare programs in Canada and the United States are rather different. In the U.S., growth in the most visible of welfare programs, AFDC, resulted primarily from increased numbers of recipients, and it was growth in that program that appears to have been responsible for most of the welfare backlash.[6] In Canada much of the expenditure increase can be attributed to increasing levels of benefits, particularly in the Old Age Security, Family Allowance, and Unemployment Insurance Programs; only the last of these programs, which has also shown a steep increase in the number of claimants, has produced a significant backlash.[7]

The cumulative result was an increase in total cash-transfer-program costs from 5.0 percent of GNP in 1968 to 7.3 percent in 1973, when the Review began.[8] Yet, with the exception of Unemployment Insurance, there was little perception before the Review in either Ottawa or the provincial capitals that welfare costs

[5] From Peter Wiles, *Distribution of Income; East and West,* American Elsevier, 1974, cited in Robert Haveman, "Poverty, Income Distribution and Social Policy: The Last Decade and the Next," *Public Policy,* Winter 1977, p. 14.

[6] Any number of U.S. sources document this with respect to American programs. See, for example, B.L. Friedman and L.J. Hausman, *op. cit.,* p. 28.

[7] Statistics Canada, *Social Security, National Programs,* p. 272. Figures on caseloads and numbers of recipients are notoriously unreliable. It appears that in the late 1960s and through the 1970s the number of cases increased but the number of recipients decreased or was relatively stable. Thus from 1970 to 1976 the number of cases grew by 23 percent but the number of recipients per case declined by at least 20 percent. This complex issue is examined in detail in *"Trends in General Assistance Expenditures and Caseload, 1967–1977,* Policy Research and Strategic Planning Branch, National Health and Welfare, February 1978, mimeo.

[8] *Social Security, National Programs,* p. 236.

were out of control, and no Canadian equivalent of the near panic
induced among U.S. policy makers by the burgeoning AFDC caseloads of the late 1960s.[9]

What, then, did precipitate the largest federal–provincial policy-
making exercise in Canadian history? The question is crucial, for
social policy concerns were not necessarily the primary factors in
the minds of many of the major actors at the outset of this exercise. To see why we must look to the broad political situation.

THE POLITICAL PROBLEMS

The major immediate cause for the Social Security Review was the
collapse, in the summer of 1971, of a major attempt to rewrite
and "patriate" the Canadian Constitution.[10] A series of federal-
provincial meetings over the period 1968-71 had apparently led to
basic agreement on a patriation and amending formula and a Bill
of Rights.[11] All that remained was formal legislative approval by

---

[9] Christopher Leman, *The Collapse of Recent Reforms: Political Institutions, Policies
and the Poor in Canada and the United States* (Cambridge, Mass., MIT Press, forthcoming),
suggests that the composition of caseloads in the AFDC Program and Canadian Social
Assistance has much to do with the lack of concern in Canada about rising costs. In the
AFDC, single mothers—particularly black single mothers—are isolated in a highly visible
program. In Canada, single mothers, widows, the blind, and the disabled are all handled
under a single program. The "deserving" poor (in the public view) are thus grouped in
Canada with the "undeserving" (single parents) to the benefit of the latter.

This suggestion is less appealing on closer examination. First, the simple fact of burgeoning AFDC caseloads, whatever their cause, may be all that is necessary to explain
the attention attracted by that program. Second, Canadians do not typically consider
single parents "undeserving." A survey taken in 1975 by National Health and Welfare
also indicated the Canadian public tends to lump single mothers with the handicapped
and elderly as deserving of public support, and detailed discussions of an "employment
availability test" during the Social Security Review revealed that no jurisdiction was considering any form of compulsory work requirement for single parents of primary-school-
aged children.

[10] The current formal Canadian Constitution is the British North America Act, an act
of the British Parliament and amendable only by it. Canada is thus the only nation unable to amend its own Constitution, a source of constant (if fairly minor) concern to
many Canadians, including Pierre Trudeau.

[11] For a complete description of the Constitutional Review of 1968-1971 see Donald
Smiley, *Canada in Question*, McGraw–Hill–Ryerson, Toronto, 1976, pp. 41-49. Further
evidence of the link between social policy and the Constitution can be found in the
careers of the key actors Marc Lalonde and A. W. Johnson. Lalonde was deeply involved
in the 1968-71 review as Principal Secretary to the Prime Minister. He then became
Minister of National Health and Welfare where he was formally responsible for the whole
Social Security Review. After its termination and after the election of a separatist provincial government in Quebec he became Minister of State for Federal–Provincial Relations and, subsequently, Minister of Justice, in which post he is responsible for the latest

the federal and provincial governments—usually a foregone conclusion in Canada—when the Premier of Quebec, Robert Bourassa, declared that his province would be unable to support the so-called "Victoria Charter." The charter failed to provide for a jurisdictional settlement in the field of social policy, and social policy was basic to the Quebec government's determination to foster a strong French culture in North America.[12] Hence no patriation of the Constitution would be possible until those concerns were satisfied.

The need for a review was reinforced by the state into which federal–provincial relations over social policy had fallen in 1972. In Canada provincial governments retain the bulk of the jurisdiction over the costly field of social policy while the federal government has the superior taxing authority. Cooperation is obviously essential. Yet in 1971 vast changes were made in the Unemployment Insurance program virtually without consultation with provincial governments. In 1971-72 a proposal to change Family Allowances from a demogrant to an income-tested program, again with potentially significant effects on provincial social policy, was proposed to Parliament with almost no prior federal–provincial consultation. Extensive discussions of social policy during the abortive constitutional talks of 1968-71 had revealed little agreement. A conference of Provincial Welfare Ministers in 1972 requested unanimously that the federal government convene a federal–provincial meeting to develop better mechanisms for consultation and to unsnarl the jurisdictional tangle. Federal officials and the federal Cabinet recognized that they would have been ill-advised not to comply.

Other factors related only in part to the welfare system strengthened the demand for review. In 1970 the extensive *Report of the Quebec Commission on Health and Social Welfare* (the Castonguay–Nepveu report) had proposed a major re-structuring and integration of the health and social-security systems in Quebec.[13] The

---

round of Constitution writing. His principal assistant during the Social Security Review was A. W. Johnson, the Deputy Minister of Welfare. Johnson had been the principal federal authority on social policy during the 1968–71 Constitutional Review.

[12] Communiqué, Office of the Premier of Quebec, June 23, 1971 (mimeo).

[13] Government of Quebec, *Report of the Commission on Health and Social Welfare*, Quebec, 1970.

ideas in the report were very popular in Quebec but it was by no means certain that the reforms could be financed under existing federal–provincial financial arrangements.

Quebec insisted that its proposals in what was, after all, an area of provincial jurisdiction should not be inhibited by federal laws and policies. Indeed, for the province of Quebec, the review came to be viewed as a means of winning piecemeal the concessions the province had failed to gain in the 1968–1971 Constitutional Review.

More important from the federal government's perspective, the publication of the highly innovative Castonguay–Nepveu report left social-policy initiative in Canada squarely with the Government of Quebec, a situation that was difficult to countenance for members of the federal government. The Social Security Review and particularly the Orange Paper was intended to help regain the initiative for the federal government.[14]

Finally, the minority Liberal government had agreed, at least informally, to reconsider social programs and particularly to expand demogrant programs as partial return for the support of the New Democratic Party in Parliament after the 1972 election.

Another obvious factor precipitating the review was simply the large amount of money being spent. Because of this "fiscal visibility," the extensive review of social policy is an almost continual process in both Canada and the United States. Reinforcing this concern, changes in Unemployment Insurance had led to dramatic cost increases (from $700 million in 1971 to $1.87 billion in 1973)[15] that played a large part in reducing the Liberal government to a minority position in the 1972 election.

In sum, the Social Security Review was initiated in an environment where welfare programs were in many respects a surrogate for broader political issues, a situation that left the reform process very much open to control by larger political and social forces.

[14] A similar pattern was observed in 1964 during the development of the Canada and Quebec Pension Plans with near disastrous consequences for Confederation. See R.E.B. Simeon, *Federal-Provincial Diplomacy;* Kenneth Bryden, *Old Age Pensions and Policy Making in Canada,* Queen's–McGill Press, Montreal, 1974.

In one of those minor footnotes to history, Claude Castonguay resigned as Minister of Social Affairs in Quebec in 1973 and was promptly hired as a consultant by the federal government, whose principal policy advisers had great respect for both Castonguay's ideas and his influence in Quebec.

[15] Unless otherwise indicated, all figures cited are in Canadian dollars.

Nevertheless, the Review did focus on social policy. Important and exciting innovations were proposed and were certainly relevant to the outcome of the process. Many of the political and bureaucratic actors involved in the Review were deeply committed to social reform, and they used an opportunity precipitated largely by factors external to social policy to attempt to achieve it. Moreover, as time passed the focus of attention of everyone directly involved in the Review turned more and more to the proposals themselves—until the external factors reasserted themselves with a jolt. We turn now to a consideration of those proposals and then to consideration of what happened when they met the factors outside the welfare system.

II. The Social Policy Considerations and Reforms

THE IDEAL SYSTEM

The *Working Paper on Social Security in Canada* provides the clearest guide to the social-policy objectives of the reformers:[16]

> For people who are of working age, and are able to work, there would be employment at at least a living wage. To ensure that a living wage is paid, the state would legislate a minimum wage. If the minimum wage were sufficient to support small family units only, income supplements would be available to meet the costs of child-raising in larger families whose incomes fell at or near the minimum wage.

> To meet the contingencies of life—temporary unemployment, sickness, injury, and disability—and to provide for retirement, everyone would save a portion of his or her income, and contribute these savings to an insurance plan. The basic insurance plan, and insurance above these basic levels would be provided for privately.

> To meet large and unforeseen expenditures, such as medical

---

[16] They are also rather strikingly like the ideal welfare system of most other mainstream North American welfare reformers of the 1970s. Witness, for example, Jimmy Carter's message to Congress of Aug. 6, 1977.

and hospital bills, special or universal hospital and medical insurance plans would be established by the state.

If someone somehow failed to receive an adequate "income through employment" (with supplementation of family income for low income earners), or "income from savings" (social insurance), additional income support measures would be available. These would be required when employment was not available for a person, or when he/she was not suited for the jobs which were available. Such measures would be required, too, when a person had been unable by reason of his/her income to save for retirement or for the contingencies of life. These supplementary income support measures would be associated with the social and employment services needed to assist in returning to employment those who were able to do so—services such as training, placement, rehabilitation and counselling. They would be accompanied, too, by any special or institutional services required, such as nursing homes, or child care facilities.[17]

THE PROBLEMS OF THE CURRENT SYSTEM

When the existing Canadian welfare system is compared to this ideal it is found to have a number of problems requiring more or less radical treatment.[18]

First, the system was built upon an assumption of full or nearly full employment and on the assumption that when unemployment did rise, macroeconomic policies would be for the most part sufficient to correct the situation. The authors of the Orange Paper, and by implication the Cabinet which approved it, now felt differently.

---

[17]Marc Lalonde, *Working Paper on Social Security in Canada,* pp. 6–7. The authors of the Orange Paper were ambivalent on the question of whether radical or incremental reform was needed. They spoke in the Preface of the possible need for radical action, yet they ended it by asserting "It must not be thought. . . that the launching of such a critical review is a sure sign that Canada's present social security system is fundamentally unsound and in need of total transformation, for this is simply not the case. . . ." A. W. Johnson later wrote of their "incremental" approach in "Canada's Social Security Review: The Central Issue," *Canadian Public Policy,* Autumn 1975 (1:4).

[18]In Canada, Colored Papers such as the *Working Paper on Social Security* are approved by the Cabinet before release. Hence the implication can be drawn—indeed *was* drawn by the principal actors—that the government agrees with the diagnosis and the proposed cures.

Second, income from employment was frequently inadequate, particularly in larger families. The family-allowance program provided only $72 to $120 per year and child-related tax exemptions did not begin until a couple earned over $3000. In any event those were exemptions, not tax credits. Moreover, the working member of a family might hold only part-time or intermittent employment yet not qualify for either Unemployment Insurance or social-assistance payments.

Third, there was little incentive to get off social assistance once one was on it. In 1973, average social-assistance cash payments for a couple with three children were more generous than the minimum wage in every province except Quebec, as were occupational-training program allowances and wages provided on government-sponsored job-creation projects. "Fringe benefits" were available to social-assistance recipients and if one did find part-time employment, social-assistance payments were generally reduced by a dollar for every dollar of employment income after a small "work expenses" exemption.[19]

Fourth, benefit levels varied widely in different jurisdictions and under different programs. As a result, payments often depended more on the recipient's category or on the place of residence than on financial need. In March 1973, a couple with three children received annually in social assistance, on average, $3480 in Quebec and $5064 in British Columbia.[20]

Fifth, social-insurance plans were inadequate. In particular, the rates of contributions and pay-out in the Canada and Quebec pension plans were relatively low.

Sixth, the various elements of the income-security system lacked coordination. Often it was up to the citizen to coordinate

[19] These second and third problems will be familiar to those acquainted with U.S. welfare problems. They were the primary motivation behind the Nixon Family Assistance Program (FAP) proposals of 1969–72 and Carter's 1977 proposals. The authors of the Orange Paper were well aware of U.S. work in this area and the principal draftsmen of the Working Paper had been strongly influenced by Daniel P. Moynihan's *The Politics of A Guaranteed Annual Income.*

[20] The Orange Paper recognized that to some extent this problem is indigenous to a federal system. In any event the differences were less than in the U.S., where in July 1974 the range of annual benefits for a one-parent, three-child family ran from $2210 in North Carolina to $5470 in Wisconsin (Department of Health, Education and Welfare, Social and Rehabilitation Service, Assistance Payments Administration, *Characteristics of State Plans,* cited in C. Leman, *op. cit.*).

an array of programs for which he or she might be eligible—a task governments themselves were quite unable to achieve.

Seventh and *eighth* were the stigma of social assistance and the real or perceived abuses of the system by clients. Although the Orange Paper minimized the extent of abuse of social assistance, that, to some degree, begged the issue, for when Canadians think of welfare abuse they are more often thinking of Unemployment Insurance.[21] On that score the Orange Paper was less assertive, reflecting both a lack of data and the government's concerns that the program really was subject to abuse.[22] Indeed, the August 1978 fiscal-restraint programs launched by the federal government significantly restricted the Unemployment Insurance program.

Such were the major social-policy problems that the Review was intended to rectify. To anyone familiar with the history of U.S. welfare reform, it is clear that before the Social Security Review the problems in the two countries were similar; it is a commentary of sorts that in 1979 they still are.

THE PROPOSED SOLUTIONS

The potential solutions to these problems were embodied in five "strategies" encompassing fourteen "propositions" to be considered by federal and provincial governments.

The Employment Strategy was "to provide people with jobs—with income through employment rather than income through social assistance"; its main tool was macroeconomic policy. But whatever hopes governments may entertain of dealing with cyclical unemployment through fiscal and monetary policy, those tools

---

[21] C. Leman, *op. cit,* cites evidence from public-opinion polls that suggests Canadians share Americans' feelings about welfare abusers. There have been few national polls on this subject in Canada, however, and those have not typically differentiated between social-assistance and unemployment-insurance programs. Evidence cited above (fn. 9) suggests that Canadians differentiate sharply between "deserving" and "undeserving" poor and that they tend to consider all categories covered under social assistance deserving.

[22] *Working Paper on Social Security in Canada,* p. 16. The Department of Health and Welfare was not responsible for the Unemployment Insurance Program. At the time the Orange Paper was written, that responsibility belonged to a semi-independent commission called the Unemployment Insurance Commission which reported to Parliament via the Minister of Manpower and Immigration.

are not sufficient to deal with seasonal and structural unemployment and with the employment problems of many of the disabled,
so other measures were required. The employment strategy was
summarized in three propositions:

Proposition #1: That the income security system should
remove any disincentives which may exist to discourage people
who are on social assistance from taking advantage of the
training and employment opportunities available to them, and
thus from becoming wholly self-dependent. It should also take
care to eliminate any incentive which may now exist for
people to shift from employment to social assistance, by
reason of the higher benefits which might thus be obtained.

Proposition #2: That governments should do a better job of
finding employment in the general labour market for people
who have been unemployed for an extended period of time,
and of helping them to equip themselves for such employment.

Proposition #3: That as a means of meeting social needs
that are now neglected or inadequately met, governments
should consider the establishment of a community employment programme. Its purpose would be to provide socially useful employment to people who have been unemployed for an
extended period of time, either by reason of the lack of jobs
in the areas in which they might reasonably be expected to
look for work, or by reason of the "employability" of the
people concerned.

The Social-Insurance Strategy demonstrates as much the drafters'
heavy commitment to an income supplementation program as to
social insurance principles.

Proposition #4: That government should continue to encourage people to save to meet the contingencies of life, and
to provide for retirement, through social insurance plans. The
benefits from these plans, like income from employment,
should be supplemented where required from an income
supplementation plan.

No other formal propositions concerning social insurance were offered. As the review progressed significant changes were made in the Canada and Quebec Pension Plans, but these were not the deepest concerns of the planners.[23]

The Income-Maintenance Strategy formed the core of the review.

> *Proposition #5:* That federal family allowances should be increased from their present average of $7.21 per child per month to an average of $20.00 per child, and be made taxable (included in the income of the parent claiming the child as a dependent). Further, that the level of the allowances should be reviewed from time to time in the light of changes in the consumer price index. Subject to a national minimum, and assuming the development of a consensus along the lines suggested in Propositions #12 and 13, the precise amount to be paid for individual children would be left to the provinces to determine: Whether the allowances should be varied according to the age of the child, or whether, as some have advocated, they should be varied with family size.

Provincial variations in the Family Allowance Program, a venerable cornerstone of Canada's social-security system, were novel. They were partly a concession to Quebec's desire to gain further control over social policy and partly a response to a 1972 request from all provincial welfare ministers. Only Quebec, Alberta, and Prince Edward Island, however, took advantage of this provision.[24]

The central propositions of the entire review were numbers 6 and 7.

---

[23] Changes included a commitment to increase the yearly maximum pensionable earning (YMPE), on which benefits and contributions are calculated, at a rate of 12.5 percent per year until it reached the median industrial composite wage. Since the industrial composite actually rose faster than 12.5 percent for two years, the gap did not close quickly. But, assuming a 10 percent annual increase in the composite, equivalence should be achieved in the mid-1990s. For 1977 the YMPE stands at $10,400. Other changes included an increase in earnings exemptions to 10 percent of income, full escalation of benefits in line with the consumer price index, and full vesting of benefits at age 65 without any retirement or earnings test.

[24] Changes in Family Allowances occupied much of the time and attention of policy makers in the early stages of the Review. For a full description see Simon McInnes, *Family Allowances and Federal Provincial Relations in Canada,* Ph.D. dissertation, Carleton University, 1978.

Proposition #6: That the incomes of those who are working but whose incomes are inadequate by reason of family size (even after the increase in family allowances proposed above) or by reason of the nature of their employment (low-paying self employment or intermittent or partial employment) should be supplemented under a single general income supplementation plan, with built-in work incentives.

Proposition #7: That a guaranteed income should be available to people whose incomes are insufficient because they are unable or are not expected to work, namely the retired or disabled, single parent families, and people who are not presently employable by reason of a combination of factors such as age, lack of skills, or length of time out of the labour market. The guaranteed income would be paid in the form of an additional income supplement over and above the general income supplementation available—thus taking account of the fact that these people either do not have or are relatively unable to earn their own income—with the guaranteed income being set at levels appropriate to the different groups of people involved. The additional income supplementation should provide some advantage to the single parent families and the aged and the disabled who have income from savings or who choose and are able to earn income from work, and a positive incentive to those who are not presently employable to take advantage of the training, rehabilitation, and counselling which would make them employable.

Many questions are left unanswered by these propositions, questions such as eligibility, guarantee levels (the level of benefits at zero income), reduction rates (the rate at which benefits are reduced as income rises), the definition of family unit, the payment and accounting periods (the length of time between payments and the period over which income and benefits are reconciled), and the relationship with social insurance, other income-support systems, and the taxation system. The answers to these and other seemingly technical questions would determine the whole nature of the program and its costs.

Clearly the planners were determined to avoid what they viewed as the major flaw in Nixon's then recently deceased Family Assistance Program—the excessive costs of using one benefit structure to provide adequate benefits for those with no other income and at the same time adequate work incentives for those with income insufficient to meet needs. For example, if the guaranteed income for a family of four is $5000 and additional income is taxed at 33 percent (roughly the level considered necessary to preserve work incentives), families with incomes up to $15,000 will then receive supplementation, a result that the federal planners judged unacceptable in Canada in 1973.

To avoid this problem the propositions suggested a "two-tier system," with one guarantee level and reduction rate for those receiving income supplementation and another for those "unable or unexpected" to work.[25] The figures in the backs of federal planners' minds were a guarantee level of $4800 for a family of four with a reduction rate of 75 percent after a $50 monthly exemption for those with no other income. For those with other income from employment, the guarantee level was $1800 and the reduction rate 37.5 percent, creating a break-even point (the point at which all benefits ceased) of $7200.[26]

We will return to the trials and tribulations of the income-supplementation proposal shortly. In the meantime it is useful to consider other propositions, not least because expenditure increases generated by dealing with them were ultimately important in the disposition of the supplementation proposals.

> *Proposition #8:* That the old age security programme should be continued with the universal payments under that

[25] This solution was in effect the same as that adopted in the Carter reform proposals in 1977. The term "support" was used in both proposals to describe the benefit structure available to those not expected to work. The U.S. equivalent of income supplementation was "work benefit." The maximum guarantee levels appear higher in the Canadian version but probably would not have turned out to be so in practice since the Canadian levels were the maximum amounts for which the federal government would share costs with the provinces, whereas the Carter proposals envisaged that many states would supplement what were exclusively federal payments with shared cost "top-up."

[26] Since proposals always envisaged a considerable degree of provincial flexibility (up to some maximum level of benefits), actual dollar figures were seldom mentioned in public and cost estimates were generally prepared using several sets of figures. See Federal-Provincial Working Party on Income Maintenance, *Background Paper on Income Support and Supplementation,* available from Policy Research and Strategic Planning Branch, National Health and Welfare, Ottawa.

programme being considered as a base on top of which any guaranteed income plan for the aged would be built. Further that the present guaranteed income supplement programme should also be continued, but with people who are over 65 and who have low incomes being given the option of choosing between it and any new guaranteed income plan—depending upon which is the more advantageous of the two.

Proposition #9: That, while income supplementation along the lines provided for in Propositions 6 and 7 would remove the great majority of people from social assistance as it now stands, a supplementary or "last resort" programme would be required to meet special situations as they arose (as is now provided for under the Canada assistance plan).

During the review the level of benefits under these two programs rose considerably (as much in response to automatic indexing introduced to cope with inflation as to any increase in the benefit base) until they stood at $6753 per year for a couple in the first quarter of 1979.

The Personal Social-Services Strategy encompassed two propositions.

Proposition #10: That the broad spectrum of social and employment services required to make the employment and income supplementation strategies fully effective and efficient should be extended and improved—training, counselling, placement, rehabilitation, special work situations, homemaker and child care services.

Proposition #11: That the costs of special services including nursing home and child care, which cannot be met by the individual out of his/her income, including income supplementation, should be covered through special measures under the general social security system.

Social and employment services were considered at the outset to be essentially secondary to the income-maintenance strategy, a reflection of the views of those federal planners most centrally involved in the early stages of the review process.

The Federal–Provincial Relations Strategy reflected the original impetus for the Review in the failure of the constitutional reform efforts of 1968–71. The chief architects of the Social Security Review were well aware of the difficulties imposed by the jurisdictional issue and in this case proposed to deal with the problem in part by avoiding it—at least at the outset. Hence the Orange Paper declared:

> It would be premature to seek to discuss which government should do what under such a system. For our first obligation as governments is to seek to design a system which will be best for individual Canadians. Only then should we move on to consider which government should administer which elements or parts of the system.[27]

The issue, however, could not really be avoided, and two innovative propositions were advanced under which provinces could utilize the vast funds in previously sacrosanct federal programs such as Family Allowances to shape their own social-security programs. At the same time they would be subject to a set of minimum national standards.

> *Proposition #12:* That the levels of income guarantees and supplementation should be chosen by the individual provinces, and that the provinces should further be given the power to vary the levels of universal and other allowances paid under federally administered programmes (excepting wage-related social insurance measures).
>
> Where any province were to seek a reduction in the federal allowances under one particular programme, the moneys saved by such a reduction would be transferred to increase the allowances paid under another federal or federally-financed income support programme, as requested by the province.
>
> This provincial flexibility in setting the income support

---

[27] *Working Paper on Social Security in Canada,* p. 36.

levels within each province would be subject to three conditions. First, the provinces would be bound to observe the minimum standards set by the Parliament of Canada in respect of the income support programmes administered or financed by the Government of Canada. Secondly, the provinces would not be free to use this flexibility in such a way as to increase net federal payments to any province—whether to the people or to the government of the province, and whether by increases in federal payments or reductions in federal tax revenues—beyond what would have been paid under the "programme norms" legislated by Parliament to determine total federal contributions to the programme. Thirdly, the provinces would be required to contribute to the social security system the amount they would otherwise have contributed prior to any changes in the system, and before any changes in the levels of federal allowances or income support payments under any new "flexibility formula."

Proposition #13: That in the interest of combatting poverty by way of a fair distribution of income between people across Canada, and in the interest of promoting national unity through avoiding extremes in income disparities, national minimums should be set by the Parliament of Canada in the levels of the allowances administered and financed by the Government of Canada. Further, that "norms" should also be legislated by Parliament in respect of the payments under such programmes, when such norms are required in order to determine the total contributions Parliament is prepared to make under the programmes.

This proposal was widely viewed at the time as an attempt to gain the support of Quebec by permitting that province greater control over a key element of social security, the Family Allowance program. To a degree it appears to have succeeded, for Quebec was basically cooperative throughout the Review and Claude Castonguay, the still-influential former Minister of Social Affairs in that province and the author of the Castonguay–Nepveu report, acted for a time as a consultant to the federal government. Alberta and Prince Edward Island also took advantage of the proposal.

III. The Outcomes: Social Policy and Political Reality

Just as the Orange Paper had divided the reform proposals into a set of strategies, so the reform process was pursued by three interrelated federal–provincial working parties. They consisted of a variety of officials and reported to federal and provincial welfare ministers through a frequently convened forum of federal and provincial deputy ministers. One working party dealt with the employment strategy, another with the personal social services, and the third with income maintenance and social insurance. Most of the bureaucratic "big guns" of the Review process served on the third working party, which was generally considered to be at the core of the whole Review.

In this section we will look at the work of these groups and at the impact upon their work of the larger context within which the Review process took place.

THE EMPLOYMENT STRATEGY

The employment strategy component of the Social Security Review had sunk without a trace by mid-1978. The primary responsibility for macroeconomic policy lay with the Department of Finance, while labor market intervention at the federal level was the domain of the Department of Manpower and Immigration. Political and bureaucratic reality demanded that the latter be declared the "lead department" with respect to employment strategy, even though the major actors in the Social Security Review were in the Department of National Health and Welfare. But a combination of the usual interdepartmental jealousies, a consequent lack of interest and enthusiasm for the Review process in the Department of Manpower and Immigration, and a certain amount of bureaucratic infighting within that latter department between promoters of the "Community Employment Strategy" and those responsible for the older job-creation programs all combined to ensure that the department primarily responsible for the employment strategy part of the Review was unable to further it. The jurisdictional tangles in the provinces were similar. Not surprisingly, few of the major actors at either level of government were able or eager to spend time or effort untangling such snarls when they had bigger games to play.

In any event, the primary interests of the key federal actors in the Review lay with the income-transfer aspects of the process. The employment strategy had been primarily aimed at making the major propositions more salable in the face of a real or apprehended welfare backlash.[28]

To be sure, an expenditure of $50 million over the 1974–77 period was approved for the Community Employment Strategy by the federal Cabinet. Few proposed projects ever got beyond the planning stage, however, and the funding was progressively reduced in the later 1970s and disappeared entirely in the largest round of budget cuts in August 1978.

SOCIAL SERVICES

No such simple fate awaited either the personal social-services or the income-maintenance aspects of the Review process. Both are political versions of the Perils of Pauline, with the hapless welfare heroine thrust from one misadventure to another with the shifting winds of political fortune.

The Working Party on Social Services. The social-services saga starts out rather slowly. A federal–provincial working party labored for over a year to produce its first "interim" report. The federal and provincial deputy ministers received it "with thanks," and promptly ordered the working party to remain "quiescent" until further notice; the first report was also the last.

The Shared Cost Proposal. The whole social-service issue was then put aside for nearly a year. But by early 1975, the income-maintenance strategy had lost much of its momentum and an alternate focus was required if the Review was to be kept alive. So it was that early in 1975 the federal deputy minister and his senior adviser on social-service programs sat down virtually alone and very rapidly drafted a proposed outline for a new cost-sharing arrangement. Services were divided into categories according to whether they should be universally available without cost to the user (crisis intervention and referral), free to those who needed them because of some long-standing problem (rehabilitation), or

[28] A. W. Johnson, *op. cit.*, p. 465.

income-tested (residential care, day care, and some forms of home care). The proposal was extensively discussed with provincial welfare officials and ministers, and an unusual degree of harmony was achieved. Two years and nine legislative outlines later a new Social Services Bill was before the federal Parliament and although the bill died on the federal parliamentary order paper at the end of the session in Spring 1977, it was expected to be revived and passed later the next year.[29]

The Block-Funding Proposal. The next chapter is thus at first glance very surprising. In August 1977, as virtually his last act before leaving Health and Welfare to become Minister of State for Federal–Provincial Relations, Marc Lalonde informed provincial welfare ministers that the bill would be replaced by a proposal to provide each provincial government with an essentially unconditional block grant in lieu of social-service financing—a grant not even contingent on the money being used for social services.[30]

Many provincial welfare ministers were not pleased—particularly at the fact that after the extensive consultations involved in the Social Security Review, they had not been directly consulted about this latest move.[31] But if provincial ministers were not pleased, neither were they terribly surprised. To see why we will again have to consider the impact on social policy of variables lying largely outside of the social-policy system.[32]

Canada's personal social-service and universal public medical-insurance system were largely built on the financial foundation of shared-cost programs. The federal government could thereby use its power to raise and spend money to ensure a basic standard of services in areas such as health and welfare that lie largely within provincial jurisdiction. At the same time, however, shared-cost programs are, for the federal government, an unpredictable drain on revenues, for it is liable virtually without limit for a propor-

---

[29] The legislation is described in detail in the Communiqué of the Federal and Provincial Welfare Ministers' Conference, June 1976, available from the Information Directorate, National Health and Welfare, Ottawa. The legislation was Bill C–57.

[30] The letter was made public on Sept. 15, 1977.

[31] See the Communiqué from Provincial Welfare Ministers, Sept. 22, 1977.

[32] For a more extensive treatment of this topic with respect to other social programs see R. Van Loon, "From Shared Cost to Block Funding and Beyond," and D.V. Smiley, *Canada in Question.*

tion (usually one-half) of the costs of designated programs. More-over, federal Treasury officials believe that provincial governments have little tendency to economize for under such a system provinces can buy a dollar of program for just 50 cents of their own money. That price may be worth paying in expansive times and in order to get programs started. But when the major programs are already in place, when costs begin to rise at alarming rates in some sectors, and when public opinion becomes .hostile to increased government spending, the shared-cost instrument becomes much less attractive.

This federal unease is matched at the provincial level among those in premiers' offices and treasuries who resent the way the federal 50-cent dollars skew their priorities. Departments responsible for program delivery, of course, find that those same 50-cent dollars give them a favorable lever at budget time so they are considerably more favorably disposed toward them than are their brethren in central agencies.

By mid-1976, the balance had tipped against shared-cost programs, particularly in the area of publicly financed health insurance. Many in the federal government believed that those programs were sufficiently well established that provinces would continue to operate them even if funds were provided *en bloc* or by a transfer of "tax room" rather than after an audit of expenses; that method would allegedly make federal expenditures in this area more predictable. Thus in March 1977 partial block-funding for medical insurance became a reality, with the rest of the program funds accounted for by a transfer of tax room from the federal to provincial governments.

Given the precedent of block-funding in another major area of social policy, it seemed reasonable that it should also apply in social services. Social services are an area of provincial jurisdiction, argued several of the larger and richer provinces, and hence provincial governments should decide on expenditure priorities. Federal Treasury authorities felt that more predictable expenditure estimates were desirable, and the senior federal officials in Health and Welfare were in any event increasingly dubious about the administrative complexities of the new Social Services Bill and about the ability of the federal government to shape provincial priorities in this area. The result was the withdrawal of the Social

Service legislation and its replacement by the block-funding proposal.

Until the early summer of 1978 it appeared certain that the Social Services block-funding provisions would pass the federal Parliament by mid-autumn of that year. In August of 1978, however, the political and economic context once again derailed what had appeared to be a certain measure of welfare reform.

The Demise of Block-Funding. This time the outside event was an expenditure-reduction exercise. On Aug. 1, 1978, Prime Minister Trudeau, in a nationally televised message, declared that his government would reduce projected expenditures for 1979–80 by about 5 percent, or $2.5 billion; many hitherto secure programs were suddenly at risk.

Since transfer payments to the provinces account for over 21 percent of federal expenditures, they were a logical target. Several programs were fingered for possible cuts, but most transfer payments were protected by legislative guarantees that the provinces were most reluctant to change. That fact increased the vulnerability of proposals that had not yet been enshrined in legislation. The proposed block-funding of social services was just such a proposal and since it represented an increase of $225 million in federal expenditures, it was highly vulnerable. After considerable debate in Cabinet, the federal Minister of Health and Welfare, Monique Bégin, was forced to announce to her provincial colleagues that the proposal was dead. Its death was not entirely lamented by provincial welfare ministries, many of whom preferred the old arrangements which gave them a bargaining lever with their own Treasuries. Nor is its death likely to be long lamented in Ottawa, where there is growing suspicion that block-funding is the worst of all worlds: the federal government must raise the money, reaping public discontent about taxes, then transfer the money to the provinces, which claim full credit for the successful programs while happily blaming the federal government for any problems that arise.

Social-services financing is thus left on a rather uncertain footing; few are happy with current arrangements but few care to face another round of reform proposals in view of the outcome of the last two rounds. Given the vicissitudes of reform proposals in this area, few would dare to predict what will happen next.

INCOME MAINTENANCE

The Original Proposals. As noted above, the income-maintenance propositions of the Orange Paper raised more questions than they answered. To give shape to the proposals, a 96-person policy-analysis unit, devoted mainly to various aspects of income-maintenance and social-insurance problems, was established within the federal Department of Health and Welfare. It fed much of its work into what was viewed as the senior of the federal–provincial working parties, that for income maintenance. From an academic point of view the income-maintenance discussions and related research were interesting and, given the data limitations, of high caliber; they provided much of the background that eventually went into firmer proposals. From the perspective of those directly responsible for policy—ministers and deputy ministers—the issues were often technically complex and hence difficult to comprehend.

The discussion also lacked focus; in Canada no less than in the United States, really concrete intergovernment discussion requires that there be something on the table to bargain about.[33] Hence most provincial governments engaged in the Review hung back, waiting for the federal proposal they felt certain would come.[34] At the same time the federal representatives hesitated to produce any complete package beyond what was already in the Orange Paper lest the "cooperative" nature of the Review be compromised.

Work on some other aspects of the income-maintenance strategy, particularly Family Allowance increases and changes in the Canada and Quebec Pension Plans, moved ahead much faster since concrete federal proposals had already been made in the Orange Paper and had met wide acceptance.[35] As a result, by the time the

[33] For a slightly different point of view that suggests that the process is more akin to diplomacy than bargaining, see Richard Simeon, *Federal–Provincial Diplomacy.*
[34] Significant exceptions have included the government of Quebec on virtually all aspects of social policy and the Province of Alberta with respect to natural-resource policy. The ability of larger provinces to do policy research has increased significantly since the mid-1960s.
[35] Simon McInnes, *op. cit.,* describes the earlier Family Allowance changes in detail.

large income-supplementation proposals were brought to the federal Cabinet, the Review had already led to a substantial increase in income-security expenditures, a situation that was to have a damaging impact on the later proposals.

By mid-1974 it became obvious to federal planners that the Review could move forward only if a firm federal proposal for income support and supplementation was made. Final work therefore began on the preparation of detailed proposals for consideration by the federal Cabinet and subsequent presentation to the provinces. At this point, Health and Welfare officials saw no reason to anticipate any difficulty with the income-supplementation proposal or with its $2 billion annual price tag. After all, the major changes in Family Allowances, costing over $1 billion annually, had faced no problems, nor had $1 billion in Old Age Security increases. An equally large increase in Unemployment Insurance had moved easily enough through the Cabinet machinery three years before. But therein, of course, lay the rub: the money was all gone.

By the autumn of 1974, a detailed "memorandum to Cabinet" was in preparation, outlining six basic options for the provision and administration of the income-support and supplementation plans.[36] Three options based on the number of children in the family unit were quickly dropped, on the grounds that they were relatively poorly targeted. A single-tier system with one benefit structure applicable to all and essentially similar to Nixon's FAP was discarded for cost reasons. The two favored proposals were both two-tier systems, as described earlier, with broad eligibility for the supplementation program and with an employment-availability test for the higher guarantee level "guaranteed income" program. The difference between the two proposals lay in whether the supplementation program should be delivered via refundable tax credits or via transfer payments not tied to the tax system. The former implied a federally delivered system, the latter a provincial one. It was assumed that the income-support program for those not expected to work would be provincially delivered.

---

[36] Memoranda to Cabinet are generally treated as confidential or secret documents in Canada. The *Background Paper on Income Support and Supplementation* closely parallels the original submission to Cabinet and contains virtually all of the technical information which was placed before Cabinet.

Not all provincial governments agreed with the two-tier proposal. The New Democratic Party governments in Manitoba, British Columbia, and Saskatchewan favored a single-tier system much like FAP, as did Quebec early in the Review. The federal position eventually was accepted by a Federal–Provincial Welfare Ministers' Conference, although the three NDP provinces were reluctant converts at best.

Regardless of difficulties with the provinces, federal Health and Welfare planners were strongly predisposed to favor the two-tier system with at least the supplementation segment delivered via refundable tax credits. Federal–provincial relations were a stumbling block, however. Given the commitment to provincial flexibility in the federal–provincial relations strategy, no uniform federal program could be imposed without very broad provincial agreement. While it was possible to deliver a program with provincial flexibility via the tax-credits mechanism, it would be difficult. In addition, federal Department of Finance officials were reluctant to use the tax system as an income-transfer mechanism on two grounds: (1) it would impugn the purity of what was intended as a revenue-gathering mechanism; (2) the tax system, which had recently been extensively reformed, could take no more major changes at that time. Moreover, since some provinces, particularly Quebec, wished to maintain control of as many social programs as possible, provincial program delivery seemed the only practical route. For the moment, at least, federal–provincial relations and the preservation of the tax system dominated. Although both Marc Lalonde and A. W. Johnson may have felt uncomfortable with the compromise, they recommended to the Cabinet an income-support and supplementation program could be provincially delivered on a shared-cost basis.

The costs of the program would, of course, depend on eligibility and on the benefit structure. The parameters recommended to Cabinet specified eligibility for those over 30 with minimum supplementation reduction rates of 37½ percent and support reduction rates of 75 percent. A maximum support guarantee level of $4800 for a 2-audit, 2-child family and a maximum supplementation level of $1700 were also felt to be reasonable and cost-conscious choices. The combined federal and provincial costs for such a system were expected to be about $2 billion above current costs;

the federal government would assume about two-thirds of this total.

Cabinet Consideration. Health and Welfare officials saw no reason why the Cabinet would not agree to this program. They were thus little prepared for the lightning that struck.

At that time a program proposal passed through two stages in federal Cabinet: detailed consideration by a committee of Cabinet and approval by full Cabinet. Once committee approval had been secured, full Cabinet approval was usually assured. In this case, committee approval was obtained with little more than the normal opposition of Department of Finance and some Treasury Board officials, whose job it is to worry about costs. But in the full Cabinet meeting the decision was quite different. Cabinet declared that the Government of Canada remained highly committed to the *concept* of income supplementation and approved the *concept* of delivery of supplementation via provincial transfer payments, but implementation would have to be delayed.[37] In government, delay is but one step from death. For the moment, at least, income support and supplementation seemed very near death.

In retrospect, the original income-supplementation proposal was delayed by the political necessity of extensive federal–provincial consultations and made less attractive by meager information about program impacts and costs. Losing momentum, it succumbed to the nascent politics of government restraint and the perpetual politics of redistribution. Although the complication of a federal–provincial constraint is not universal, the rest of the story is familiar to students of social reform throughout the world.

In 1973 the atmosphere in the federal government had been expansive; revenues were rising, the economy was healthy, and, perhaps because the government had nearly been defeated in the recent election, a sense of reform was afoot. By early 1975, the environment that had been supportive of social reform and of major new spending programs had turned hostile. But if the

---

[37] Bureaucrats are present and participate in Cabinet committee meetings. No bureaucrat except the Clerk of the Privy Council is present in full Cabinet meetings. Nonetheless it is frequently possible for an enterprising journalist to piece together from his favorite ministerial sources what happened in a contentious full Cabinet session. The account here is substantially as reported by John Grey in a series of articles in the *Ottawa Citizen* in late February 1975.

federal–provincial niceties made delay inevitable, and if the patient was weakened by scant data and a chill in the fiscal atmosphere, the kill was administered by the politics of redistribution. The conservative forces within the federal government are normally represented by the Minister of Finance and many of his departmental officials and by that budgetary watchdog, the Treasury Board and its Secretariat. In 1975, the Minister of Finance was John Turner, then clearly the predominant English-speaking voice in the Cabinet and a politician with a personal following rivaling that of the Prime Minister. Turner was clearly and publicly disgruntled about the rapidly rising expenditures of the federal government—and had muttered darkly about resigning over the issue. He and some of the other ministers were most unhappy with the prospect of a new $2 billion program that would also have had very significant redistributive effects. Still others, prompted by their own departments, opposed the new program because it would preclude expansion of their own programs. When Turner spoke forcefully against the program in a meeting of the full Cabinet, his arguments fell on sympathetic ears. After a long and reportedly very heated debate between Lalonde and Turner, the decision was reached to delay implementation indefinitely.

The Minister of Health and Welfare may have been unaware of the depth of opposition to his proposals; certainly his officials were. Too, they may have become mesmerized by the features of the reform proposal itself, losing track of its context and of the need to build a supporting coalition within government. The Minister may also have counted on the Prime Minister's support but this did not materialize to the required degree. On some issues, most notably language rights and national unity, the Prime Minister does take sides. But on many others he prefers to allow the debate to range widely before he sums up the consensus of the meeting. This time the consensus was not favorable to a vast new social program. The decision was lost.

The Proposals Amended. Marc Lalonde and his senior officials were thus forced, however reluctantly, to present a federal proposal for a provincially delivered income-supplementation system without saying anything about the date of implementation. The failure to offer a firm dollar commitment did not go unnoticed among the provincial welfare ministers; only by an intense personal effort were Lalonde and Johnson able to hold the Review together in the ensuing months. They did so in part by changing the focus to personal social services and in part by continuing to wrestle with the technical details of a plan that might never be implemented.

In July 1975, A. W. Johnson was succeeded by Bruce Rawson, a former provincial Deputy Minister from Alberta. Rawson and Lalonde recognized that there was no chance in the foreseeable future of Cabinet approval for a $2 billion plan. A pared-down version was prepared, with eligibility restricted to families with children and those 55 to 65; the price tag was generally assumed to be in the $240 million range.

In spite of the stated federal policy of restraining expenditure growth, Cabinet approval was won early in 1976. John Turner had by then left politics, and his replacement, Donald Macdonald, was more sympathetic to income redistribution and to this particular program. More important, it was very much smaller than the original proposal. The new President of Treasury Board, Jean Chrétien, was either unable to block the program or not interested in doing so. Again no firm implementation date was specified but apparently the tenor of the discussions was quite different: this time Lalonde was sufficiently sure of his support that 1978 became generally understood as the implementation date.

Lalonde presented this proposal to provincial welfare ministers in February 1976. Considerable support was expressed and it was therefore a surprise when, a week before the June Ministers' meeting, it became evident that welfare reform had struck still another snag: a consensus to implement the program would not be reached. The Ontario Cabinet flatly rejected the program—in part because of opposition to any new shared-cost programs, in part because of a feeling that the program should be federally delivered via the tax system, in part because of a reluctance to take on any new expenditures, and in part because of inherent conservatism. Without Ontario's support, over one-third of the Canadian population could not be reached by the program. While no other province opposed the proposal in principle, only British Columbia enthusiastically endorsed it and only three or four provinces held out any hope of implementing it in the near future. That proposal, too, appeared to be dead.

This surprising outcome is attributable to much the same factors as the failure in the federal Cabinet of the larger 1975 proposal. The same expenditure restraints that hit the federal government in 1975 were also being felt in the provinces. The debate between Turner and Lalonde was doubtless repeated in most provincial capitals 16 months later—and with the same result. In general, the endorsement of a program by ministers of line departments cannot be taken as an endorsement by a government; the central agencies may feel quite differently and their views have recently tended to prevail.

At the June 1976 federal–provincial ministers' meeting, Lalonde was confronted by a groundswell of apathy and, on the part of Ontario, with outright opposition. He suggested that the federal offer be left on the table, with provincial welfare ministers providing their "final answers" to him over the summer. He also indicated that he would think seriously about a federally operated refundable tax-credit mechanism to deliver the supplementation program. Such a suggestion would have produced screams of disapproval from many provincial governments two years earlier. It produced no overt opposition in 1976—but no ringing endorsements either.

At that point the income-supplementation proposal dropped from center stage in the Canadian social-policy scene. The only visible sign of life was a federal task force (the Tax-Transfer Integration group) which reported to Cabinet early in 1977 that a tax-system delivered supplementation system was technically feasible. But by late 1977 the forces of expenditure restraint held an even more powerful position within the federal government.[38] Marc Lalonde had ostensibly left the welfare-reform scene and turned to broader issues. As the new Minister of State for Federal–Provincial Relations, he was fully occupied by the situation in Quebec, where the Parti Québécois had recently been elected. The social-policy concerns that had seemed so vital in 1973 no longer held such imm diacy for the government. Income supplementation appeared to be dead.

[38] The report has since been published as *The Integration of Social Program Payments into the Income Tax System,* Department of Finance, November 1978.

Born Again. But the reader has been warned; just as the train was about to grind slowly over Pauline she was once again snatched from the tracks.

The federal expenditure-restraint exercise of August 1978 has already been described; one of its major casualties had been the proposed Social Services block-funding arrangement. But no government likes to cancel proposed programs while offering nothing in return—especially with an election in the offing. What better way to resolve this dilemma in a time of restraint than to replace part of a universal and poorly targeted program with a more sharply targeted income-tested program? If the times make it impossible to establish any new bureaucracy to implement the program, then why not utilize an already existing system to deliver it? And if you can experiment a bit with new forms of program delivery, in accord with the task-force report on tax and transfer program integration, then why not proceed that way?

Suddenly, in a period of expenditure restraint, the time for welfare reform was ripe! Within three weeks after it was proposed to Cabinet by a senior adviser to the Prime Minister and the Department of Health and Welfare, Cabinet approved an $800 million reduction in the Family Allowance program, elimination of some special child-related tax deductions, and the implementation of a refundable Child Tax Credit delivered via the federal income-tax system. The credit is valued at $200 per child (indexed for inflation) and is fully payable to families with incomes up to $18,000. Above that level, benefits are reduced at a 5 percent rate as income rises. A full supplementation program it is not, but it is an important beginning for it foreshadows sharper targeting of social programs and pioneers tax-credit delivery.

The legislation passed Parliament with little difficulty; scarcely a provincial voice was raised in dissent. The first benefits are payable in early 1979. Part of what planners had failed to gain through the lengthy Social Security Review they won, with apparent ease, through a conjunction of forces largely outside the welfare system after the Review was over.

Their success may, of course, be attributed in part to the fact that the Review had accustomed people to the idea of income supplementation and refundable tax credits. In Canada, as elsewhere, social-policy ideas are likely to be around a long time before they are implemented. They tend to start as small programs—perhaps first in a few provincial jurisdictions—and then grow slowly to prominence.[39] Kenneth Bryden quotes Bernard Hennessy in suggesting that policy concepts in Canada move through a series of stages in public view from "sacrilege" through "idea," "proposal," and "policy," and finally to "tradition."[40] Old Age Security has moved through all these stages, as has the Family Allowances Program and publicly financed Medical Insurance. Income-supplementation and tax-credit delivery systems appear to be launched on the same route. The Review itself may have been responsible for taking the concept from "sacrilege" to "proposal"; if the Hennessy paradigm is correct that was an essential preliminary to achieving the status of "policy."

Typically, too, in Canada, when implementation does come, it comes quickly. Most major social-policy changes in Canada have suffered through long periods of gestation before being snatched off the shelf and moved quickly through Parliament by a government suddenly faced with a social crisis or eager to display a dramatic new policy. A small start, accompanied by a good deal of ballyhoo, is then typically followed by a slow evolution into a large program. There is no reason to expect otherwise with income supplementation.

There is an obvious moral to this part of the story. Policy planners had continued work on income supplementation even when all appeared lost. A second generation of supplementation advocates had taken over at Health and Welfare. Essentially unbloodied by the 1975 defeat, they kept the idea alive and under development, and were thus able to ensure that when the climate was right for reform their ideas would be paramount.

Monique Bégin, who had replaced Marc Lalonde, continued to advocate income-supplementation programs even though the idea had apparently lost it popularity; although no longer Minister of Health and Welfare, Lalonde remained an active and persistent advocate of tax-credit supplementation. No one could predict

---

[39] Christopher Leman, "Patterns of Policy Development: Social Security in the United States and Canada" (*Public Policy*, Spring 1977), contrasts the gradualism of Canadian policy development with the "big bang" image of policy development in the United States.

[40] Kenneth Bryden, *op. cit.*

when the time for reform would come but when it did everything had been done to ensure that the proposal would not be overlooked.

IV. Conclusions

It is tempting to conclude that the Social Security Review itself was largely a failure; certainly that was the prevailing interpretation in the segment of the press that pays any attention to social policy. The income-supplementation program was not implemented during the Review, and when it did come it was child-based and much smaller than originally foreseen. Moreover, the Social Services were funded on exactly the same basis at the end of 1978 as they were in 1973. It is also tempting to draw conclusions that point the finger at major actors—Marc Lalonde, A. W. Johnson, John Turner, or Pierre Trudeau—some for not being sufficiently adroit at manipulating the policy process, others for being too conservative, and still others for cynically raising the hopes of the poor and then dashing them again. It is tempting but it is facile, and it obscures the appropriate conclusion and lessons.

From many perspectives the Review was not a failure, even if its "rational" plans were not implemented in the time allotted. The Canada and Quebec Pension Plans were significantly changed. The levels and escalation rules for Old Age Security and the Guaranteed Income Supplement were revised. The level and basic structures of the Family Allowance Programs were fundamentally changed. And it could be argued that in a period that saw increasing government expenditure restraint the best defense for social policy was a good offense.

At least equally important, it must be kept in mind that one of the most fundamental reasons for the Review was to improve federal–provincial relations in the social-policy field; in this it appears to have succeeded. Finally, although the Refundable Child Tax Credit was not formally implemented within the Review period, it seems likely that without the groundwork laid during the Review, neither would it have been implemented in 1978.

As for the policy process itself, the major actors performed in accord with the roles defined by their positions. Finance ministers and Treasurers are generally supposed to be fiscally conservative; Welfare ministers and their senior officials are expected to be advocates on behalf of their clientele and to fight for redistribution of incomes. Prime Ministers who ultimately must hold a Cabinet together are certainly well advised to stay out of highly divisive arguments and to promote reform only when a constellation of forces seems more favorable to change. It may be that the Minister of Health and Welfare failed to build the requisite coalition in February 1975 and that his provincial colleagues did the same in 1976—but it may equally be that the creation of such coalitions was not possible at that time.

More important, however, is the way in which the process and particularly the timing of change was governed in largely unpredictable ways by variables that lie outside social-policy concerns per se. Federal–provincial relations and a change in the attitude toward government expenditures were the most crucial of these. Only hindsight would allow us to claim that an expenditure-restraint exercise would lead to what is potentially a crucial change in the direction of Canadian welfare policy.

The experience of welfare reform in Canada in the 1970s may also allow us to comment on the hypothesis that advocates of income redistribution in Canada and the U.S. are in a perpetually losing position. Certainly the current distribution of incomes suggests that this is the case, and theoretical models predict continuing failure no matter how much we tinker with delivery mechanisms. If, for example, redistributive outcomes result from a process characterized by a centralized decision-making system, an aggregated demand pattern, and low information costs, then the probability of significantly redistributive policy in Canada seems extremely limited.[41] The poor in Canada are, to an even greater extent than in the United States, almost totally unorganized and collectively inarticulate.[42] Data on distribution of incomes

---

[41] Theodore Lowi, "Four Systems of Policy, Politics and Choices," *Public Administration Review*, July–August 1972, pp. 298–310; and R. Salisbury and J. Heinz, "A Theory of Policy Analysis and Some Preliminary Applications" in I. Sharkansky, *Policy Analysis in Political Science*, Chicago, Markham, 1970.

[42] There is only one national interest group consisting of poor people, The National Anti-Poverty Organization. The National Council of Welfare, an advisory committee to the federal minister, has representatives of the poor and acts as a spokesman for them.

and characteristics of poverty in Canada are scant and unreliable.[43] And to characterize Canada's tangle of federal–provincial and interdepartmental jurisdictions as a fragmented decision system is to understate the case.

This hypothesis is reinforced by the fact that the progress made in August of 1978 was effected by an *ad hoc* decision system put in place following an apparently unilateral decision about expenditure restraint by the Prime Minister and characterized by an unusual concentration of economic decision-making power in the hands of the Prime Minister and his personal staff. It is further reinforced by the fact that many of the successful federal proposals for new social programs have come from or been promoted by central agencies and, most particularly, the Prime Minister's office. Medical Care Insurance, the Canada Pension Plan, and the Canada Assistance Plan were worked out in detail by Health and Welfare officials. But the impetus for the final decision to implement came from elsewhere and all were driven into place over varying but substantial degrees of provincial opposition.

That is a fairly gloomy hypothesis if one has a commitment to social-policy development; it should be tempered by the main theme of this paper: If advocates of policy reform persist, they have a considerable chance of success even in a period of expenditure restraint. Indeed opportunities that were not available in more affluent times may well be available now. Improved program targeting such as was achieved by the Child Tax Credit is but one example. After all, both Canada and the U.S. spend enough in what are allegedly welfare programs virtually to eliminate any poverty gap, but both nations share a predilection for distributing the bulk of "welfare" funds to middle-class citizens. Under the banner of restraint the latter may be persuaded to take somewhat less themselves in transfer payments in return for reduced taxes— with a highly beneficial spill-over for the poor.

The other large national interest group is the Canadian Council on Social Development. It is primarily a middle-class organization of social workers and others interested in social policy.

[43] *The Report of the Senate Special Committee on Poverty* (Ottawa, 1971) expresses a constant concern with lack of data. Documentary material collected during the Review by the Policy Research Branch of Health and Welfare for the Working Party on Income Maintenance partially filled the gap but almost none of this was made public.

One conclusion stands out above others. Welfare reform depends—like so much else—on opportunism, on being ready and in place to take advantage of opportunities when they occur. It requires a great deal of work on policy proposals and a great deal of persistence, even when the chance of success sometimes appears remote indeed. If there is a moral to what is a very long and complex story, that surely is it.

15

ECONOMIC EQUALITY AS A SOCIAL GOAL
Policy Implications of the "Limits to Growth" Thesis

Irving Louis Horowitz

The Club of Rome's discourse on the limits to growth has been transformed into a free-for-all on the limits to equity. Simply put, analysis of technological limits to further progress has been supplanted by renewed examination of sociological limits to the egalitarian model that has governed Western society and law in this century.

Equity Demands

The limits to growth debate has led certain commentators to conclude, in no uncertain terms, that "without rather radical changes in the consumption patterns in the rich countries, any pious talk about a new world economic order is humbug" [Myrdal 1976, p. 5]. The trouble is that discussion of changes in consumption is often coupled with talk about the finite nature of physical and productive capabilities [Forrester 1973, pp. 129–32]. Onto this balance sheet must be placed increased demands for radical changes in the distribution of wealth. When all these elements are calculated, the result is a new equation: the more limited the levels of production, the less inhibited are demands for redistribution of present wealth.

The marshaling of data to support special interests is an old and vener-

The author is Hannah Arendt Distinguished Professor of Sociology and Political Science, Rutgers University, New Brunswick, New Jersey.

From Irving Louis Horowitz, "Economic Equality as a Social Goal: Policy Implications of the 'Limits to Growth' Thesis," XIV(4) *Journal of Economic Issues* 937-958 (December 1980). Copyright 1980 by Irving Louis Horowitz. Reprinted by permission.

able lobbying technique; the mobilization of such information by have-nots is less venerable, but no less compelling. Since these outsider groups have the benefit of social science forces that, if anything, are more sophisticated than older lobbies in collating data for their clientele, the impact of their demands is even greater [see Miller and Hoops 1976, pp. 582–83]. As long as the clamor for a greater share of the mythical "pie" occurs in a context of zero or limited growth, such demands on the larger society are potentially volatile. In the past, U.S. society met incremental demands by outsiders (that is, blacks, women, youth, ethnic groups, and so forth) by expanding both productivity and consumption. Now, such demands are accelerated, while productivity is curbed by class interests, and consumption is curbed by environmental interests. Some examples of this phenomenon are in order.

There is a newfound struggle between the snowbelt and the sunbelt—between those states of the Midwest and Northeast that are experiencing population decline or stagnation with no corresponding decline in demands for services. These states are beginning to organize to retrieve some of the region's federal tax money from the sunbelt states of the South and West. Citing federal tax and spending policies which are shifting an enormous flow of wealth from the North to the South, former Governor Daniel Walker of Illinois said that the time is over for federal subsidies to southern and western states. He was joined by the former governor of Wisconsin, Patrick Lucey, in his call for "a common cause with the Northeast" [Los Angeles Times 1976].

The voice of small town and rural people also is being heard, asserting a demand for more equity. These groups constitute 31 percent of the nation's population, account for 44 percent of the poor and 60 percent of substandard housing, yet receive only 27 percent of federal outlays for welfare and poverty. Critics add that rural America contains 29 percent of the national labor force but receives only 17 percent of federal outlays for employment and manpower training programs. The list of complaints and demands for redress of grievances is unending, but generally accurate [*Rural America* 1976, p. 1]

Another phenomenon has been the growth of special interest centers, such as the Center for American Women and Politics. It cites facts and figures indicating that women constitute more than 50 percent of the voting population and 40 percent of the U.S. labor force, but hold only 4 to 7 percent of all public offices. Few women serve in cabinet posts; no women have ever been appointed to the Supreme Court; and very few women have been governors or senators. These patterns of discrimination, the center claims, hold at the level of county, city, and state commissions as well [Center for the American Woman and Politics 1975, pp. 6–7]. Again, the demands and appeals for equity are perfectly justifiable on statistical grounds.

In short, there is an overriding pattern of accelerated demands for equity. Because demands for zero growth in industry and population are occurring at the same time, one must expect an intense struggle for the redistribution of the American pie. As the nation slows or stops its creation of a larger pie, concern inevitably shifts to the slices.

Limits to Growth or Limits to Equity?

Recommendations of the Club of Rome indicate how clearly the sociological message of the limits to equity underlies the technological rhetoric of the limits to growth. First, the club presents an image of a "fixed pie," which assumes nonrenewable or limited resources for further growth. As a result, there are few mechanisms available to prevent the rich from growing richer, or the poor from becoming poorer. Second, it assumes diminishing returns in the sense that new technology and additional capital investment necessary to extract marginal resources will vastly increase pollution and exhaust resources. Diminishing marginal returns require an effort toward zero growth to reestablish the "natural" balance. Third, the club assumes that the rapidity of change involves growth in the complexity of problems; hence, the resolution of conflicts is difficult, and the management of resources is impossible. The club recommends simplifying issues and centralizing decision making, even if that entails limiting democracy. Fourth, the club presents the notion of uncontrollable expansion in population, which presumably doubles every thirty years. This, too, will mean exhaustion of resources and an inability to cope with the distribution of goods and services. As in so many areas, the Club of Rome's views about population are analogous to stopping the action on a film; they do not argue for the alternative—redistribution of the gross world product. Fifth, the club strongly hints that progress may postpone the need for immediate drastic action, but the final collapse is inevitable. Furthermore, its arrival may be hastened and its effects made even more severe by our efforts to forestall it. Again, the demand is for restraint, even cutback. Sixth, income gaps are widening, rendering worldwide class war or political warfare imminent. Again, the club postulates freezing the current situation, and that means the current inequities, rather than redistributing or redividing wealth. The Club of Rome's recommendations range from maintaining the status quo, to planning controlled growth, to implementing harsh and even repressive measures to prevent worse actions in the future.

To date, the social science literature primarily concerns the debate about whether the energy crisis is a reality or a fabrication. Only recently has there been a realization that sociological issues emerge from genuine shortages, and that at stake are ideological issues beyond those concerning inequity. The environmentalists have been slow to take into account the social and economic effects of the policies they support. An important social science conference recently constructed a list of 200 areas in which the energy crisis affects society and that require research [Landberg 1974]. The conference attempted to exchange views with environmentalists who, for the most part, saw little value in the social science itinerary and were skeptical of an economic view of the energy crisis. The environmentalists believed the solution would come from hard scientific data, that is, from the biological and natural sciences.

Other parties to the dispute, namely, special interest groups demanding equity, have tended to discount the current energy crisis. Leon Keyserling [1975, p. 9] notes that oil shortages and high electricity costs have resulted from policies of economic scarcity—tight money and fantastically high and rising interest rates—which bears down especially harshly on public utilities. Other groups fail to connect the limits to growth with the limits to equity and see the problem as temporary, as the result of current governmental and industrial policy making.

From a political viewpoint, what has taken place is a fragmentation of old coalitions at the mass as well as the intellectual level. Economic clusters, from factory workers to factory owners, see the environmental coalition as a veritable conspiracy to prevent the exercise of free enterprise, free markets, and free labor. The relative reluctance of blacks and other working-class minorities to participate in the environmental alarums are indicative of how intense is the difference in feelings. A body of folklore has grown up that blames the environmentalists, the Arabs, and the oil companies for the higher costs of fuel to operate and maintain automobiles and to heat homes, costs that are more readily borne by environmental interest groups drawn from the middle class than by economically hard-pressed groups within the working class.

For the most part, environmental groups have labored long and hard to convince sectors of the population that environmentalism means new jobs, above all in poor neighborhoods, and that higher costs are relatively temporary and, even so, worthwhile. Beyond that, they argue that they are drawing attention to problems, such as oil and fuel shortages, so that solutions may be found to prevent the breakdown of the social system.

The recent discussion of the limits to growth and the limits to equity is original. Its contribution to the literature of stratification is to take far greater cognizance than in the past of the costs of equity programs, as well as the benefits of growth programs. Equity becomes a goal rather than a reality, albeit one that in absolute terms is unreachable.

The Development of Equity Concepts

However fervent the sociological debates of the 1950s about the tragedy of human inequality, in retrospect there was a virtual consensus that stratification was a permanent feature of all economies. Hence, the issue was not so much one of establishing egalitarian principles as it was of lessening the extremities of inequality [see Davis and Moore 1945, pp. 242–49; and Tumin 1953, pp. 415–27].

The 1960s witnessed an almost equally unanimous repudiation of this position, arguing that social equality is both realizable and a practical necessity. Movements pleading for equity and justice employed an array of statistics showing the income and occupational lag of racial, sexual, and religious minorities and made veiled threats that equity might entail parity of wealth, goods, and services [Gans 1968, 1973; and Miller 1968].

The 1970s witnessed neither a return to an earlier imagery of inequality nor abandonment of the goal of perfect equality. What took place was a clarification between what is and what ought to be, between the facts of inequality and the goals of equality. The appreciation intensified that equality is a costly process and, like growth itself, is subject to constant refinement. If equality can be guaranteed only by growth, and growth can be secured only by differential rewards and specialized incentives (at least within market economies), then the problems of stratification and equality are dialectically intermixed. This fact may contribute to the inability to forge new policies that anticipate new contingencies.

If there is a trend for the 1980s and beyond, it is clearly toward the universal acceptance of equality as a goal and the parallel delegitimation of inequality. Earlier principles of self-regulation and self-interest have clearly fallen on hard times. Even those who still maintain a fervent belief in individualism as a way of life admit the need for state regulation and social interests. The practical legal issues invariably concern how much regulation, how much supervision. In a most perceptive observation, Fred Hirsch [1976, p. 12] has called attention to this peculiar dialectic.

The principle of self-interest is incomplete as a social organizing device. It operates effectively only in tandem with some supporting social principle. While the need for modifications in laissez-faire in public policies has been increasingly accepted, the need for qualifications to self-interested behavior by individuals has been increasingly neglected. Yet correctives to laissez-faire increase rather than decrease reliance on some degree of social orientation and social responsibility in individual behavior. The attempt has been made to erect an increasingly explicit social organization without a supporting social morality. The result has been a structural strain on both the market mechanism and the political mechanism designed to regulate and supplement it. In this way, the foundations of the market system have been weakened, while its general behavioral norm of acting on the criterion of self-interest has won ever-widening acceptance.

Thus, we have a social system that generates strong contradictions without providing mechanisms for conflict resolution. In this context, making the stakes of success smaller, arguing that "small is beautiful," and urging limits to growth have the overriding effect of reducing tensions without necessarily altering structures. Let us see, then, how the new egalitarianism confronts the new conservatism.

Herbert Gans [1974, pp. 20–21] emphasizes that the black movement provided a model for equality demands. He presents three major causes of the new egalitarianism originating from the black movement:

1. First, many Americans are now beginning to realize that the frontier, by which I mean the opportunity to strike out on one's own and perhaps to strike it rich, is closing down. 2. Second, as people have voiced more political demands, they have also become less patient with political inequality, particularly with their increasing powerlessness as bureaucracies and corporations continue to get bigger. 3. Third, the affluence of the post-World War II era has enabled many Americans to raise their incomes to a point where they are no longer occupied solely with making ends meet. As a result, new expectations have emerged, not only for a higher standard of living but also for improvements in the quality of life and for greater power to control one's destiny.

These three points are important, but they actually are precipitating factors made possible by underlying structural changes. These precipitating factors require further elaboration, but before doing so we must examine the underlying changes that brought them about and gave them force.

The foremost structural change in twentieth-century U.S. society has been in the size, role, and legitimation of state power. The federal government has become a large, complex organization, and most of its growth has taken place in this century. Growth in size alone would not provide a structural basis for delegitimation of state power, but the changing role of the state and changing bases of legitimation have been important factors. Initially, the major responsibility of the federal government was to provide an environment for business activity. The first action taken in pursuit of this goal was the creation of a stable currency and a stable legal order to ensure the rights of exchange and contract. After establishing this basic framework, government also provided services and facilities, such as national roadways and waterways, for economic activities that individuals and firms could not provide for themselves. Government supports may include indirect subsidies, such as protective tariffs and import quotas, and direct subsidies, such as those for the railroads. This legal-rational government provides a predictable environment for the growth of business and capitalist activity. The government legitimated itself by presenting its activities as favorable to economic growth and industrial expansion. As Calvin Coolidge said, "the business of government is business." Even reform groups, such as the Progressives, sought to use the state to provide a better business atmosphere. Antitrust legislation was intended to check the evils of monopoly in relation to business activities.

During the Great Depression and the New Deal, the role of government began to change. In its new framework, it sought not only to improve business conditions, but also to better the condition of the population as a whole. Government not only created a framework for business activity through which individuals could benefit by upward mobility, but also attempted to intervene more directly into the economy to uplift entire groups. The first such actions were to recognize labor unions and pass laws favorable to their activities. Another indicator of this change was the growth of social welfare programs during and after the New Deal. By these actions, the state indicated that inequality did not result from individuals' failure to take advantage of opportunities but from social factors beyond their control. The state began to legitimate itself not only by acting as the protector of the business community, but also by assuming a responsibility for improving the status of all groups. The presentation of its goals in these terms further delegitimated existing inequalities by implying that they are not natural and hence are correctable.

Alice Rossi [1974, p. 212–27] has shown that there is a movement from the lowest or "pluralist" level to the highest or "hybrid" level as equality demands increase. Most equality movements create rising expectations. In describing these patterns, Rossi shows their effects upon not only women, but also racial and ethnic minorities.

1. *Pluralist model*: This model anticipates a society in which marked racial, religious, and ethnic differences are retained and valued for their diversity, yielding a heterogeneous society in which it is hoped cultural strength is increased by the diverse strands making up the whole society.
2. *Assimilation model*: This model anticipates a society in which the minority groups are gradually absorbed into the mainstream by losing their distinguishing characteristics and acquiring the language, occupational

skills, and life-style of the majority of the host culture. 3. *Hybrid model*: This model anticipates a society in which there is change in both the ascendant group and the minority groups—a "melting-pot" hybrid requiring changes not only in blacks and Jews and women, but white male Protestants as well.

Previously, equality movements were directed against individual firms, groups, or opposing classes in society. The best documented example is the working class union movement. Unions directed their activities against corporations or businesses by means of strikes, organizing campaigns, or product boycotts. Initially, unions feared and opposed government intervention into this conflict. Today, women, blacks, and others seeking equality attempt to achieve their aims through the state more than any other part of society. The women's movement is trying to achieve equality through legislation or judicial review, by means of lobbying or electoral politics. Action against firms is not taken directly, as unions did, but through a third party, the government, by means of the courts or human rights commissions. When steps are taken directly against a firm, this is often done to provoke the state into action. It is not the closing of opportunities that creates strains resulting in demands for equality, but the opening of the state as a new avenue for equality demands.

S. M. Miller and Pamela Roby [1970, p. 10] have stated that power is an important aspect of the drive for equality.

In the "welfare state," in particular, many important elements of the command over resources become available as public services. The distribution and quality of these public services affect the absolute and relative well-being of all individuals. Considerable inconsistency *may* exist between the incomes and basic services of persons or groups. While the two are fairly closely linked in the United States, poor basic services are *not* associated with low income in Sweden. A larger issue is also involved. As Marshall has argued, the welfare state approach breaks the link between the market and well-being.

As the state attempts to legitimate itself as a service organization, political power enters into the equation as a factor in inequality.

Associated with the rise of state power and questions of equality are the expansion of citizenship to the lower classes and the participation in the state of more groups. Initially, it was believed that this expansion of citizenship would introduce a new era of political democracy and consensus, an "end of ideology." Paradoxically, while a nonideological period may have prevailed for a limited time, these developments laid the foundation for a new ideological period [see Huntington 1975, p. 10].

The increased role of the state as mediator of class claims, rather than as the simple legal expression of the dominance of one class over others, converted the state from a superstructural reflex to an initiator. The class state yields to the service state, and the delegitimation of inequality in this way sets the stage for greater political struggle as the arena shifts from the factory or the workshop to legislatures and the community. In short, if economic exploitation remains the source of inequality, the democratic state must become the source of relief from such conditions.

Economic Dysfunctions and the
Social Cost of Inequality

It has been a central premise of sociology and economics that inequality is a functional necessity for any society. Even Marxism states that classes are necessary for capitalist development and hence are a precondition for the development of socialism. In sociology, the basis of this argument has been presented by Kingsley Davis and Wilbert Moore [1966, p. 247]: "The main functional necessity explaining the universal presence of stratification is precisely the requirement faced by any society of placing and motivating individuals in the social structure. As a functioning mechanism, a society must somehow distribute its members in social positions and induce them to perform the duties of these positions." A similar view is found in neoclassical economics. Within a market system, inequalities in rewards are necessary. Without them, people would lack motivation to incur the costs involved in leaving present positions and taking on socially important positions that are unoccupied. It is thought that unequal rewards motivate economic growth by spurring investment and entrepreneurship and hence a better society. Neoclassical economists cite the cost of equality in terms of declining efficiency. Attempts to achieve more equality, the neoclassicists believe, result in a less efficient economy due to a decline in motivation, a drop in investment funds, and the rise of costly bureaucracies to ensure equality.

Most arguments against inequality have generally relied upon assumptions about the moral or ethical value of equality or, in its Marxist form, the iron laws of history (the Marxist argument also carries with it a moral vision). Most of these arguments cite the impoverishment or deprived condition of the lower classes and speak of the right to happiness or to a better life. A quotation from Christopher Jencks [1972, p. 9] exemplifies this type of argument: "Why, after all, should we be so concerned about economic equality? We begin with the premise that every individual's happiness is of equal value. From this, it is a short step to Bentham's dictum that society should be organized so as to provide the greatest good for the greatest number."

Another argument against inequality, one which avoids the pitfalls of moral dictums or assumptions about historical laws, is to point out that while inequality *may* be functional, it is also dysfunctional. There are disadvantages not only for those who hold unequal positions, but also for society as a whole. Most arguments concerning inequality, whether pro or con, fail to cite its possible costs in the social as well as the economic realm.

Despite arguments to the contrary by Davis, Moore, and others, inequality may lead to malintegration in a society. As John Goldthorpe [1974, p. 136] points out, "the existence of inequality, of an extreme, unyielding, and largely illegitimate kind, does mitigate seriously against any stable normative regulation in the economic sphere—because it mitigates against the possibility of effective value consensus on the distribution of economic and other resources and rewards."

The malintegration that is associated with inequality is not simple Marxist class conflict; it is far more complex. There is no clearer example of this complexity than the area of crime. Although the literature does not agree about what is meant by class or status, a standard proposition in criminology is that certain types of crime, particularly violent kinds, are negatively correlated with class or status. The lower the class or status, the higher is the incidence of violent crime: "A 1960 Milwaukee study indicated that the slum or inner core area of the city, comprising 13.7 percent of the population, had 38 percent of the arrests for burglary, had 69 percent of the aggravated assaults, 47 percent of other assaults, 60 percent of the murders, 72 percent of the arrests for commercial vice, 22 percent of the drunkenness, and 67 percent of the narcotics arrests" [Chalfant 1974, p. 201]. In a similar vein, larger cities have a higher rate of violent crime than small ones. Large cities are more likely to contain concentrations of poor and minority groups. These higher crime rates are an indicator of the relationship of crime and inequality.

Differences between smaller and larger cities cannot be explained simply by greater objective inequality in larger urban areas. Goldthorpe spoke of illegitimate inequality, which raises the concept of relative deprivation. As Jackson Toby [quoted in Schur 1976, p. 266] states: "Analyzing the relationship between objective deprivation is more complicated than was at first thought. Poverty cannot cause crime but resentment of poverty is more likely to develop among the relatively deprived of a rich society than among the objectively deprived in a poor society." A sense of relative deprivation is more likely to form in large heterogeneous cities than in small homogeneous ones. In larger cities, interaction among groups is more likely to take place, allowing for the formation of reference groups and the delegitimation of one's own lower status.

From 1960 to 1973, numerous social changes and social movements were taking place in the United States. The two most important were the black movement and the War on Poverty. Both questioned the social order and gave rise to "new minorities" with rising expectations and new equity demands, who in general did not accept existing inequalities.

The easiest way to measure the cost of crime resulting from this delegitimated inequality (and not from poverty alone) is the cash value of damage done by crime and expenditures by government in combating or correcting the damage [Bureau of the Census 1975, p. 158]. These costs and their relationship to inequality become clearer when the businesses affected are controlled for location. By establishing the categories of ghetto, nonghetto (inner city), and suburbs, one can almost create a scale for levels of inequality. The lowest level is the ghetto, where the greatest economic inequality and racial discrimination exist. Next are nonghetto areas, with economic inequality but a generally white population. The last group, the suburbs, does not necessarily consist of W. Lloyd Warner's upper-upper class, but it is the most prosperous of the three [Warner 1960, 1964]. As one moves up this scale, crime decreases in most categories. This supports our proposition about the relationship between inequality and instances of crime [Bureau of the Census 1975, pp. 159–60]. As inequality becomes delegitimated, its cost increases. Other costs of crime are federal outlays for crime reduction ($2,839 million in 1975) and state and local police expenditures ($6,535 million in 1973) [Bureau of the Census 1975, pp. 160–61].

These indicators only take into account the direct monetary costs of crime. Two other costs should be considered. The first are opportunity costs incurred in the expenditure of funds as a result of crime. Government funds are limited, and monies spent on criminal justice programs and police activities cannot be used for other programs. The second cost is noneconomic, namely, the social disruption resulting from crime. Emile Durkheim may have been correct—some levels of crime are functional by virtue of their shock value and reinforcement of social norms—but present crime is far beyond this level. The existing high crime rate inflicts costs in terms of fear among noncriminal members of society. These costs are hard to quantify, but included are such manifestations as the fear of leaving home after dark, crowding in the middle cars of subway trains, and lost sleep from the strange noises outside a window at night.

Another dysfunctional effect of inequality is felt in economic production. The disadvantages of inequality in the workplace have been obvious since Marx's writings on alienation and class conflict. Although no class consciousness or large-scale class conflict as described by Marx exists in the United States, inequalities still impose costs upon the production of goods and services. Workplace inequalities are not defined only by income, but in other terms. Ely Chinoy's study of automobile workers [1955] demonstrated that workers rank their positions by income plus type of work done, physical demands, health and safety conditions, and authority relations. There are numerous sources of inequality in such multidimensional work. Since these inequalities were pointed out by the workers, their legitimacy is in question.

The consequences of workplace inequality are obvious. One easy means of measuring the cost is work hours lost due to labor disputes [Bureau of the Census 1975, p. 374]. Work stoppages for various causes, ranging from general wage dissatisfaction to plant administration, indicate the degree to which differential rewards lower economic output, quite apart from the "ethical" question of differential payment for different kinds of work.

Other costs of inequality in work are harder to measure. Examples are the inefficiency and poor quality of work resulting from discontent among producers. An indirect measure of these costs is time lost from the job due to illness. Of importance here is the difference between *disease* and *illness*. Charles Kadushin [1966, p. 407] notes that "disease is an abnormal structure or function; illness is the feeling of discomfort which arises out of disease." Kadushin shows that there is little or no association between social class and *disease*, yet there is a high correlation between social class and *illness*. What is important is the relationship between income and time loss for illness [Kadushin 1966, p. 411]. A plausible hypothesis to explain the greater absenteeism among lower as opposed to other income groups is discontent with work and its inequalities. There are other costs, such as sabotage on assembly lines, general apathy regarding the quality of products manufactured, and a breakdown of creative performance as a result of routinization.

There is little empirical work on the effect of no-growth policies upon employment or of increased employment upon the environment. Environmentalists and those supporting increased employment live in different ideological realms and have little contact with one another. Environmental groups view problems in terms of biology and physics and have little insight into the social consequences of their policies. Proponents of full employment and increased equality believe the world has infinite resources.

Many economists concerned about the environment stress the negative effect of growth upon "spaceship earth" and show little interest in the consequences of no-growth upon employment patterns and equity demands [Daly 1971]. In contrast, Bayard Rustin [1976, p. 13] thinks we are facing an historic national crisis.

> There is mass unemployment, a sizable and expanding black underclass comprising persons whose lives were scarcely touched by the civil-rights revolution, and a declining standard of living for millions of working people. Yet many of those who profess concern about unemployment and poverty also actively support the concept of limiting economic growth in order to protect the environment. That notion, if translated into conscious policy, would measureably worsen the nation's—and the world's—economic plight. And its promoters would bear the responsibility for having shattered the hopes of those who have never had a normal role in the world economy, among whom the darker-skinned people of the world rank most prominently.

Clearly, the line between problems of production and consumption is thin indeed. Perhaps it would be more fruitful to conceptualize the issue as one of redistributing present products and consumer patterns.

Environmental protection policy has a direct and an indirect effect upon employment and equality: The direct effect is felt when an operation or industrial plant is closed due to violation of pollution laws. This results in lowered employment and economic depression in the surrounding area. A major example is the Environmental Protection Agency's closing of an ore processing plant that was depositing chemical waste into Lake Superior. The cost of correcting the problem was beyond the profits of the operation, and the local economy suffered severely. Older industrial cities bear the brunt of environmental laws. They generally have the worst air and water pollution problems, and hence the laws are enforced stringently. These cities have also become centers for low income and minority populations. Industries in the area either must add expensive pollution control devices or move to communities where incremental increases in emissions have less affect upon air and water quality. The result is limited increases or actual decreases in employment in the older city. It should be noted that the jobs lost are generally unskilled or semiskilled entry level positions.

The indirect effect of environmental policy has been manifested through structural changes in the U.S. economy. The shift, as outlined by Daniel Bell [1973; 1976], has been from energy-intensive productive industries to knowledge-intensive service industries. No-growth in manufacturing, in contrast to accelerated growth in service industries, is a social fact. As Bell states, this process is already going on, and environmental laws will only hasten it. There are several implications for employment and equality. First, high level positions in service industries require considerable skill and knowledge; entry into them requires certified education and professional standing. The result will be a small professional elite and a vast class of unskilled workers with little opportunity for advancement. Second, concerning the wage structure and productivity of service industries, that sector suffers from low productivity and lacks the means for increasing it. Since wage gains will not be connected to productivity gains, they will be harder to obtain. This is particularly true when the employer is the government, and the wages are drawn from taxes. Third, there will be a relative decline of labor unions, which historically have been a force working for equality. With the decline of the industrial sector, where they are strongest, the relative power of unions will diminish.

Other Characteristics and
Consequences of Inequality

Thus far we have been discussing costs of inequality in a limited circumstance, that is, when existing inequalities are perceived as illegitimate. Both crime and work conflict are costs inflicted by actors who perceive their inequality as being unnatural or wrongly and unjustly imposed upon them. There are other costs that do not require either the delegitimation of inequality or the conscious action of those in unequal conditions. These costs center around the less than optimal distribution and use of resources for which there is an inelastic demand. They are particularly important in a world of limited resources and economic growth, and they are highest for a market economy. Mark Kelman [1973] presents this case in terms of medical services, the demand for which is virtually inelastic, yet the supply of which is limited. Consequently, physicians and hospitals are located in high income areas, and low income areas suffer from a lack of services. A direct cost to society is the general rise in the price of all medical services due to this pattern. In high income areas, large sums of money are spent upon nonessential services, such as cosmetic surgery. This drain of resources and personnel raises the cost of essential and life-sustaining services for all users.

An equitable policy for the distribution of funds for medical care would limit demand for nonessential services and increase the supply of resources and personnel for other important uses. Growth alone would not reduce medical costs, but might increase them. Given a product with inelastic demand, such as medical care, economic growth without redistribution of purchasing power would only increase the demand for medical services across all groups. There would be greater demand for nonessential services, and resources would be drained off from essential services. This may be the reason that the United States has the most used (some claim the most overused) medical system, and yet the most costly and inefficient delivery system. Kelman's model [1973] of the social costs of inequality can also be applied to other limited resources with inelastic demand. A few examples are energy, food, and certain environmental amenities. All are in limited supply, yet high income groups demand and can command a greater share of them: heated pools, higher quality protein, and quiet neighborhoods. The limited supplies mean higher costs across the board.

For the most part, questions related to equity have been considered within a domestic context. Increasingly, a group of economists and sociologists, among whom Gunnar Myrdal is typical, have argued that a more appropriate framework for the discussion of these issues is the international arena, and that problems of redistribution of wealth can only be understood within that larger scope [Myrdal 1976, p. 4].

> The blunt truth is that without rather radical changes in the consumption patterns in the rich countries, any pious talk about a new world economic order is humbug. It is legitimate for an economist to analyze the rational inferences in regard to economic policy based on what is in people's true interests and their acclaimed ideals. But if, instead, we raise the problems of what is actually going to happen, it is difficult to believe that rational policy conclusions will be followed in the practical policies of the developed countries. In the tradition of Western civilization we are quite well trained to combine base behavior with high ideals.

Leaving aside the feasibility of Myrdal's solution based on "rational national planning," which has as its end product a "curtailment of consumption," the fact that such desperate theorizing is taking place highlights the reemergence of Malthusian doctrine.

The current stratification of nations is being questioned. This means not only the creation of a Fourth World, a *lumpenproletariat* of nations, but also major shifts in relations within and between the other three worlds. Relations based upon ideology are being reevaluated, and dependency relations are being reversed. The major characteristics of this neo-Malthusian world are the growth of power based upon raw materials and the decline of power based upon technology or military position. Ideology no longer functions either as a basis of or a barrier to alliance.

The Organization of Petroleum Exporting Countries (OPEC) is a case in point. All its members have Third World social organization, yet they differ in many other respects. Although we generally consider OPEC to be an Arab cartel, it includes such non-Arab countries as Iran, Indonesia, and Venezuela. Members represent not only diverse religions and cultures, but also ideologies. Even among the Arab members are radical Algeria and conservative Saudi Arabia. Norman Girvan [1975, p. 146] has outlined the dynamics of this emerging phenomenon: "Nor is Third World economic nationalism seen as stopping at attempts to control prices for the primary products upon which the export incomes and the economic livelihood of these countries depend. Market power is seen as only one component in a general strategy for securing control over marketing and ultimately over production of the natural resources that sustain the Third World economies." This philosophy is adaptable to either a socialist or capitalist economy, or to the range of mixed market systems that falls between the two.

Accompanying these new nonideological developments in the Third World has been the breakup of ideological alignments in the First and Second World. The behavior of NATO and OECD countries in response to OPEC is an illustration. These First World countries failed to agree on common action during or after the oil embargo. Similarly, the Second World, which also exports petroleum, has acted in a nonideological manner. During the embargo, the Soviet Union voiced full support of Arab actions, yet it continued to sell oil to target countries. In 1973, the year of the embargo, Soviet exports to Japan and the Netherlands doubled, and the cash value of those exports tripled [Horowitz 1975, pp. 120–38]. This represents a pragmatic nonideological world view on the part of the Second World.

More important than the breakdown of ideology has been the shift in the basis of power, until recently based upon either technology or military strength. Within this framework, the First and Second World was in a superior position to the Third World. With unlimited raw materials, industrial nations were able to set the price for those materials and finished products. The increased awareness of limited resources has altered this relationship. Japan is an example. Prior to the 1973 oil embargo, many predicted that Japan would be the power of the next century. Although heavily industrialized and technologically advanced, Japan must import both fuel and food; it was nearly destroyed by the embargo and has yet to recover fully from its economic effects. Although oil is in short supply, manufactured goods are available to OPEC nations at competitive prices. The position of OPEC nations has improved as a result of their cartel activities, but Third World nations lacking in natural resources have declined economically. The prices they pay for imports, both raw and finished, are forced upward, but the prices they receive for their limited exports are unchanged. As these rations decline, the size of the Fourth World increases.

Nathan Keyfitz [1976, p. 34] has discussed the effect on poor countries.

Price increases such as those of the Organization of Petroleum Exporting
Countries can have little overall effect on the number of middle class people in the world (although they have some effect on whether the newly
middle class will speak Spanish or Arabic or English). Who ultimately
bears the burden of such price raises is not clear. Some of the burden is
carried by poor countries that are not endowed with materials; when the
repercussions have worked themselves out, India may find it has contributed a higher proportion of its income to Saudi Arabian opulence than
the U.S. has. Certainly some U.S. fertilizer that would have gone to India
before 1973 now goes to the Middle East; German chemical-plant investments are similarly diverted. The offsetting of oil price rises by French
arms sales to Iran has everything to do with national power and little to do
with the total distribution of poverty or even the national distribution.
The main point is that only a small fraction of the world population is in
resource-rich areas.

In those countries which do have raw materials, there is a question as
to whether the OPEC model can be followed. Superficially, it appears it
may yet be feasible.

Four poor countries—Chile, Peru, Zambia, and Zaire (Congo)—supply
most of the world's exportable surplus of copper. Three others—Malaysia,
Bolivia, and Thailand—account for 70 percent of all tin entering international trade channels. Cuba and New Caledonia have well over half of
the world's known reserves of nickel. The main known reserves of cobalt
are in Zaire, Cuba, New Caledonia, and parts of Asia. And Mexico and
Peru, along with Australia, account for 60 percent of the exportable supply of lead [Brown 1973, p. 159; a rundown of world resources is also contained in Schneider 1976].

Some of these groups, for example, coffee, copper, and bauxite exporters,
are trying to form cartels and gain more control over the marketing of
their raw materials.

It is by no means clear that the policies of OPEC can be adopted successfully by other Third World countries. Petroleum is an unusual product
in that demand is nearly inelastic and substitution is difficult. A Brookings
Institution [1974, p. 28] study sets three conditions for a successful cartel:
"(a) The group must control a sufficiently large share of world exports,
world production, and, for mineral resources, world reserves; (b) the
price elasticity of demand for the commodity in question, including the
cross-elasticity with possible substitutes, must be sufficiently low; (c) the
group itself must be sufficiently cohesive to prevent individual members
from pursuing their own advantage through unilateral action in the market." Rarely can these conditions be met. Most nonfuel resources have
very elastic demand curves; they can be easily substituted for or done with-

out. Two examples are coffee and copper. Coffee can be foregone with no major effect on the life-style of the user. In contrast, for both economic and social reasons, other energy sources cannot easily replace petroleum.

What is of interest for the First World is that advanced technology does not fit this model. The power of the First World has largely rested upon its technological ability and control. Hans Morgenthau [1975, p. 43] has stated that technology is no longer the only basis. William Schneider [1976, p. 5] has shown that technology does not fit the framework discussed above in two areas: monopoly and inelasticity of demand. "(1) The United States does not have a Monopoly on advanced industrial and scientific technology. The expertise and production capability for a wide range of advanced technology products exist in most of the West European countries and Japan. Over time, the ability of a target nation to procure advanced technology from nations other than the United States is likely to increase. (2) There are few examples of advanced technology that are both essential and unique (that is, for which no substitutes are feasible)."

Since Schneider is speaking only of the United States, a third point should be noted. The First World has not been sufficiently cohesive to prevent individual members from pursuing their own advantage. Three examples of the failure of technological power are the U.S. trade embargo of Cuba; its embargo of Iran; and the UN embargo of Rhodesia. In fact, Schneider's argument for using food as an economic weapon is symptomatic of the failure of technology and industry to form a base of power in a neo-Malthusian world.

Given this outline of the effects of a no-growth policy upon international stratification, it is possible to point out major implications for both First and Third World countries: a decreased standard of living for much of the First World, and increased standards for those fortunate Third World countries able to exploit cartels. Since the Third World differs from the Fourth because of its "concept of emergence" [Horowitz 1972, p. 18], and since the possibility of emergence is limited because all Third World countries cannot play the cartel game (given their limited resources), the size of the Fourth World will expand, augmented by former members of the Third World.

Conclusion

As I have tried to show elsewhere [Horowitz 1977, pp. 1–18], the presumed "crisis" in world capitalism is largely a fictitious extrapolation from American conditions, that is, from the past disproportionate utilization of resources and energy by the United States. As we enter the 1980s, more, not fewer, nation-states are in advanced stages of capitalist development, or at least have a mixed market-welfare system that can boast of a sizable, even expanding, private sector. Hence, the limits to economic growth model is a response to the specific American situation, and it should be so perceived before the world is reduced to the manufacture of windmills.

The subtle transformation of the model from the limits to growth to the equity type has considerable dangers, and these at least should be addressed, if not resolved. First, in shifting the emphasis to economic equilibrium and away from social stratification, certain structural deformities in U.S. society are hardened, and the attendant risk of class polarization and, ultimately, class warfare is enhanced. Second, to speak of limits to equity as an absolute physical requirement invites the state to turn a deaf ear to the needs and aims of the less economically advantaged sectors of society, which also risks polarization. Third, in order to deal with such heightened polarization, it is not improbable that ever-increasing repressive measures will be used in domestic affairs. Fourth, such repression would inevitably risk a growing isolation from the international community. Fifth, the ultimate consequence of a limits to growth policy would be an absolute decline in the United States as a world power; it would mean acceptance not only of the redivision of the world's resource and energy base, but also a redistribution of profits so that new wealthy and exploiting classes on the world scene would and could act with impunity against the United States. This would aggravate the growing internal fissure between haves and have-nots in the domestic economy.

The limits to equity model is simply a mechanistic response to structural changes in the balance of forces in the international economy and technology. To accept uncritically a model that accepts the international status quo and categorically denies the major impulses that have guided U.S. society throughout the century is to invite a solution that would only sharpen the inner tensions of that society. It would be made more vulnerable to contradiction and collapse. Those who take their theorizing as axiomatic rather than problematic would do well to ponder these risks of the limits to growth ideology before seeking to impose it on U.S. society as a general theory of the future direction of its domestic and foreign policy.

References

Bell, Daniel. 1973. *The Coming of Post-Industrial Society.* New York: Basic Books.

Bell, Daniel. 1976. *The Cultural Contradictions of Capitalism.* New York: Basic Books.

Bergsten, C. Fred. 1974. "The Response to the Third World." *Foreign Policy* 17 (Winter).

Bloom, Gordon F., and Herbert R. Northrup. 1973. *Economics of Labor Relations.* Homewood, Ill.: Richard D. Irwin.

Brookings Institution. 1974. *Trade in Primary Commodities: Conflict or Cooperation?* Washington, D.C.

Brown, Lester. 1973. "Rich Countries and Poor in a Finite, Interdependent World." *Daedalus* 102 (Fall): 153–64.

Center for the American Woman and Politics. 1975. *Report of CAWP: 1974–1975.* New Brunswick: Eagleton Institute of Politics, Rutgers University.

Chalfant, H. P. 1974. "Correlates of Poverty." In *The Sociology of American Poverty*, edited by Joan Huber and H. P. Chalfant. Cambridge, Mass.: Schenkman.

Chinoy, Ely. 1955. *Automobile Workers and the American Dream.* Boston: Beacon Press.

Daly, Herman E. 1972. *Essays toward a Steady-State Economy.* Mexico City: Cidoc Cuaderno No. 70.

Davis, Kingsley, and Wilbert E. Moore. 1945. "Some Principles of Stratification." *American Sociological Review* 10, no. 2: 242–49. In this connection, also see Kingsley Davis. 1949. *Human Society.* New York: Macmillan.

Ehrlich, Paul R., and Anne H. Ehrlich. 1974. *The End of Affluence: A Blueprint for Your Future.* New York: Ballantine Books.

Epstein, Edward Jay. 1976. "Good News from Mr. Bad News." *New York Magazine* 9 (9 August): 34–42.

Forrester, Jay W. 1973. *World Dynamics*, 2d ed. Cambridge, Mass.: Wright-Allen Press, distributed by M.I.T. Press.

Gans, Herbert J. 1968. *People and Plans: Essays on Urban Problems and Solutions.* New York: Basic Books.

Gans, Herbert J. 1973. *More Equality.* New York: Pantheon Books.

Gans, Herbert J. 1974. "The New Egalitarianism." In *Social Problems and Public Policy: Inequality and Justice*, edited by Lee Rainwater. Chicago: Aldine. Pp. 247–53.

Girvan, Norman. 1975. "Economic Nationalism." *Daedalus* 104 (Fall): 146–58.

Goldthorpe, John H. 1974. "Social Inequality and Social Integration." In *Social Problems and Public Policy: Inequality and Justice*, edited by Lee Rainwater. Chicago: Aldine.

Hirsch, Fred. 1976. *Social Limits to Growth.* A Twentieth Century Fund Study. Cambridge, Mass.: Harvard University Press.

Horowitz, Irving Louis. 1975. "Capitalism, Communism and Multinationalism." In *The New Sovereigns: Multinational Corporations as World Powers*, edited by Abdul A. Said and Luiz R. Simmons. Englewood Cliffs, N.J.: Prentice-Hall. Pp. 120–38.

Horowitz, Irving Louis. 1977. *Equity, Income and Policy: Comparative Studies in Three Worlds of Development.* New York: Praeger Publishers/Holt, Rinehart & Winston.

Huntington, Samuel P. 1975. "The Democratic Distemper." *Public Interest* 41 (Fall): 9–38.

Jencks, Christopher, et al. 1972. *Inequality: A Reassessment of the Effect of Family and Schooling in America.* New York: Harper & Row.

Kadushin, Charles. 1966. "Social Class and the Experience of Ill Health." In *Class, Status, and Power,* edited by Reinhard Bendix and Seymour Martin Lipset. New York: The Free Press.

Kahn, Herman; William Brown; and Leon Martel. 1976. *The Next Two Hundred Years.* New York: William Morrow.

Kelman, Mark. 1973. "The Social Costs of Inequality." *Dissent* 20 (Summer): 291–98.

Keyfitz, Nathan. 1976. "World Resources and the World Middle Class." *Scientific American* 235 (July): 28–35.

Keyserling, Leon H. 1975. *Full Employment with Inflation.* Washington, D.C.: Conference on Economic Progress.

Landsberg, Hans H. 1974. *Energy and the Social Sciences: An Examination of Research Needs.* Washington, D.C.: Resources for the Future.

Lenczowski, George. 1975. "The Oil Producing Countries." *Daedalus* 104 (Fall): 59–71.

Lipset, Seymour Martin. 1967. *The First New Nation.* Garden City, N.Y.: Anchor Books.

Los Angeles Times. 1976. "Snow Belt Seeks More U.S. Funds." Reported in the *Washington Post,* 24 October, p. E-7.

Lukes, Steven. 1975. "Socialism and Equality." *Dissent* 22 (Spring): 154–68.

Miller, S. M., and Frank Riessman. 1968. *Social Class and Social Policy.* New York: Basic Books.

Miller, S. M., and Pamela Roby. 1970. *The Future of Inequality.* New York: Basic Books.

Miller, S. M., and John Hoops. 1976. "Work." *New Society* 36 (10 June): 582–83.

Morgenthau, Hans J. 1975. "World Politics and the Politics of Oil." In *Energy: The Policy Issues,* edited by Gary Eppen. Chicago: University of Chicago Press.

Murphy, John J. 1972. *Energy and Public Policy.* New York: Conference Board.

Myrdal, Gunnar. 1976. "On the Equality Issue in World Development." *World Issues* 1 (October-November): 3–5.

Prodi, Romano, and Allierto Clo. 1975. "Europe." *Daedalus* 104 (Fall): 91–110.

Rossi, Alice. 1974. "Sex Equality: The Beginnings of an Ideology." In *Social Problems and Public Policy: Inequality and Justice,* edited by Lee Rainwater. Chicago: Aldine.

Rural America. 1976. "Call to Second National Conference on Rural America." *Rural America* 1 (October): 1.

Rustin, Bayard. 1976. "No Growth Has to Mean Less Is Less." *New York Times Magazine* 13 (2 May): 72–80.

Schneider, William. 1976. *Food, Foreign Policy, and Raw Materials Cartels.* New York: Crane, Russak.

Schur, Edwin M. 1974. "Poverty, Violence and Crime in America." In *The Sociology of American Poverty*, edited by Joan Huber and H. P. Chalfant. Cambridge, Mass.: Schenkman.

Tumin, Melvin. 1953. "Some Principles of Stratification: A Critical Analysis." *American Sociological Review* 18, no. 4: 415–27. In this connection, also see Melvin Tumin. 1973. *Patterns of Society: Identities, Roles and Resources*. Boston: Little, Brown.

U.S. Bureau of the Census. 1975. *Statistical Abstract of the United States: 1975*. 96th ed. Washington, D.C.

Varon, Bension, and Kenji Takevchi. 1974. "Developing Countries and Non-Fuel Minerals." *Foreign Affairs* 52 (April): 497–510.

Warner, W. Lloyd, et al. 1960. *Social Class in America: A Manual of Procedure for the Measurement of Social Status*. New York: Harper Bros.

Warner, W. Lloyd, et al. 1964. *American Life: Dream and Reality*. Rev. ed. Chicago: University of Chicago Press.

Wolozin, Harold. 1974. *Energy and the Environment*. Morristown, N.J.: General Learning Corporation.

ENVIRONMENT AND NATIONAL RESOURCES

If economics is most likely the first social science to utilize a policy framework, then environmental and resource studies are probably the most recent to enter the fray. Indeed, so intimately related is the question of environment to policy that it is scarcely possible to speak of the two terms separately. It frequently appears that environmental research is intrinsically and organically connected to definite policy outcomes, such as the maximization of the earth's resources for short- and long-range periods to serve the greater (if more distant) good for the greatest number. The issue is not so much environmental policy as the economic costs of institutionalizing reforms in the areas of air quality, industrial waste management, laws of the seas, and the like. Energy in particular is now seen as a finite resource rather than a renewable resource that can be turned on or off at will. As we move from a world of presumed abundance to a recognition of scarcities, policy shifts its emphasis from protecting environment in general to allocating resources specifically; and beyond that, to evaluating the costs of preserving an environment versus the benefit of maintaining sufficiently high levels of production and consumption.

Increasingly, environmental issues have intersected with energy policies; the latter have focused in turn partly on conservation of resources. Beck's essay establishes several significant points: market factors do indeed play a large role in conservation of scarce resources, and price mechanisms are an effective deterrent against abuse of resource bases. However, he also notes a strong class component in the conservation approach that limits a policy premised solely on letting the market work out its averages. Poor people, subject to highly inelastic demand structures and limited in their income strategies, bear a disproportionate burden of a pure marketing strategy; thus, a series of carefully calibrated policies are required to distribute evenly the penalties of energy shortfalls across class lines. The paper by Regens outlines another serious constraint to an energy policy for the entire nation—namely, the uneven distribution of resources to the state level. Hence, although nearly all states have enacted policy measures to conserve energy, such initiatives are most often connected to the existing energy supply and demand system. Policy is thus closely linked to structural elements and can scarcely proceed without placing such considerations first. Orr's paper is an interesting effort to show how these energy policies provide not simply a new problem but the basis of new solutions to matters of participatory democracy—not in an ideological, sloganeering sense, but as a massive effort to organize the political process for equity-binding goals. Orr argues that since the problem is not exclusively technological, the solution cannot be framed within narrow straits. Energy policy can become a way to mobilize society as a whole to deal with the entire range of societal inequities. In this way, policy is linked to participation and ultimately to expansion of democratic opportunity.

16

CORRELATES OF ENERGY CONSERVATION

Paul Allen Beck

*Results from a study of the factors related to family energy con-
servation are employed to evaluate some assumptions of and prospects for energy policy. The study is based on a sample survey of
779 Pittsburgh families conducted in 1978. Home ownership and a
variety of attitudes and perceptions, in particular, are found to be
related to general conservation as measured by an index constructed from seventeen different conserving activities. Home
owners, middle- and upper-income families, and people who are
cost-conscious seem to have responded to higher energy prices by
conserving, thus showing the potential of market pricing for
energy. But variations in the elasticity of demand for energy by
attribute and attitude and the special hardships imposed upon the
poor as energy prices rise place limitations on the desirability of a
pure market approach for achieving conservation. The impact of
attitudes and perceptions on conservation suggests also that campaigns to persuade people to conserve voluntarily are worthwhile.
In general, this paper demonstrates how an understanding of the
factors that shape family energy conservation can contribute to
the formulation of effective energy policy.*

It is increasingly apparent that conservation must play a central
role in solving America's energy problems. The amount of energy
produced from conventional sources—oil, natural gas, coal, and
nuclear—seems unlikely to increase sufficiently in the foreseeable
future to meet the normal expansion of demand. Domestic oil and
natural gas reserves are simply not plentiful enough, while greater
reliance on imported oil and gas exposes America even more to the
caprices of the OPEC cartel in setting prices and regulating
supplies. Other problems—economic, political, and technological—
limit increased usage of coal and nuclear energy, only recently extolled as the "fuels of the future." Nor does the development of
renewable energy sources, such as solar, provide much immediate

From Paul Allen Beck, "Correlates of Energy Conservation," 28(4) *Public Policy* 451-472 (Fall 1980).
Copyright 1980 by the President and Fellows of Harvard College. Reprinted by permission of John
Wiley & Sons, Inc.

hope. They remain prospects for the future, but that future still lies decades away. Given the difficulties in increasing supplies of energy over the next few decades, the normal expansion of demand must be constrained. In one sense it will, of course, since we can not consume more energy than we have. The more efficacious approach, however, is to induce Americans to engage in voluntary conservation.

In designing policies to promote greater conservation, both a knowledge of what Americans are doing now to conserve and an understanding of the factors that have influenced this behavior are helpful. The purpose of this study is to shed some light on these matters. How residential consumers' attitudes and attributes relate to their levels of conservation is examined in a large metropolitan area. Other studies have focussed on variations in energy consumption and responses to particular short-term energy crises.[1] This study is distinctive in that it looks instead at relative conservation in energy usage, or the extent to which people engage in common conservation practices.

The Data

Data for this analysis were collected as part of a broad-gauged study of energy conservation in Allegheny County, Pennsylvania (Pittsburgh and environs).[2] This report is based on 779 personal interviews with one adult in each of a representative sample of Allegheny County households between February and April 1978. A response rate of 63 percent was achieved in the survey. Respondents were asked to report on specific energy-related activities of

[1] The leading study of national variations in overall energy usage is Newman and Day (1975). There are a number of studies of responses to energy crises such as the Arab oil embargo of 1973–74 or the natural gas shortage of 1977. Among them are Murray, Minor, Cotteman, and Bradburn (1974); Perlman and Warren (1977); Sears, Tyler, Citren, and Kinder (1978); Bartell (1976); and Gottlieb and Matre (1976). See also Craig, Dormstadter, and Rattien (1976) for a discussion of the general factors involved in energy conservation.

[2] For a full report on the study, see Beck, Doctors, and Hammond (1980). The study was funded by the Department of Energy under contract number C-77-C-01-8702. Samuel I. Doctors, Paul Y. Hammond, and I were the principal investigators. Neither the Department nor my colleagues in the project should be held responsible for the analyses and interpretations contained herein.

themselves and other members of their family.[3] Data were gathered also on factors that seemed likely to be related to household conservation. They included attributes of the residence and the respondents, as well as attitudes and perceptions about energy and conservation.

The energy conservation measure examined in the following pages is based on the number of conservation activities performed. We began with self reports on twenty common conservation practices. The consistency across these behaviors was striking: the pairwise correlations between activities were always positive and typically substantial, indicating that those who practiced the one were likely to have practiced the other. This consistency was confirmed systematically by a principal components factor analysis, which showed that seventeen activities were sufficiently intercorrelated to have significant loadings on the first or common factor. Our measure of energy conservation was constructed by simply counting the number of activities performed of those seventeen with relatively high loadings on the first factor. These activities and their relationships to the conservation index are listed in Table 1.[4]

The conservation index employed in our analysis is designed to measure conservation within the respondent's own framework for action rather than absolute usage of energy. Families who live in large homes or own three automobiles, for instance, may be heavy users of energy in an absolute sense, but they may also use energy more or less efficiently *given* their current "needs." Our focus is

[3] Since self-reports of conservation are of questionable validity (Milstein, 1977), we attempted to confirm their accuracy whenever possible by making use of more objective measures. For thermostat settings and the use of storm windows, the interviewers were able to make direct observations of behavior. For several other activities, additional information on conserving behavior was obtained from the respondent at other points in the interview. We were able to check the validity of the self-reports in some fashion for seven of the activities in our conservation index. In general, the self-reports were found to inflate actual conservation. The inflation was correlated, though, with only a few explanatory variables. Just 7 of 161 relationships between reporting error for the 7 self-reports and the 23 explanatory variables used in analysis emerged as significant at the 0.05 level. None of them were very large. Three of the seven significant relationships involved explanatory variables later found to be related to conservation. These are the instances in which our significant findings conceivably could be attributed to response error. In each case, however, the pattern of bias was in a direction that could only *deflate* the real relationship, giving us confidence that the normal exaggeration contained in self-reports of conservation has not produced relationships that would not have appeared otherwise. A similar result is reported by Perlman and Warren (1977) in their study of conservation in the wake of the Arab embargo.

[4] The index of conservation has a mean of 9.1 (on a 0 to 17 scale), a standard deviation of 2.8, and a distribution of scores that is normal in form.

Table 1. CORRELATIONS OF ACTIVITIES WITH CONSERVATION INDEX[a]

	Product moment correlation
Winterization Activities	
Use storm windows	0.41
Weatherstrip each year	0.42
Added attic insulation	0.31
Added wall insulation	0.43
Heating Activities	
Lower thermostat at night	0.33
Set thermostat at 68° or less in day	0.38
Shut off heat in unused rooms	0.38
Cooling Activities	
Run air conditioning only on hottest days	0.30
Set air conditioning above 72° in hot weather	0.23
Use fans instead of air conditioners	0.22
Appliance Usage Activities	
Keep hot water heater below high setting	0.15
Wash/dry only with full loads	0.29
Transportation Activities	
Drive at 60 mph or less on highways	0.27
Do not drive on trips of 1/2 mile or less	0.19
Own an economy car	0.31
Carpool to work	0.25
Other Activities	
Recycle newspapers or cans	0.26

[a]Entries are the correlations between the row activity, dichotomized from the original question, and the additive conservation index.

on the variations in this efficiency. Greater promise for energy saving in the foreseeable future lies, we believe, in improved efficiency in usage given one's present situation than in the severe changes in life style that shifts in absolute usage would require.[5]

[5] This distinction between energy usage and energy conservation is made also by Perlman and Warren (1977).

The objective of our study was to identify factors that are related to conservation. Four different sets of factors were specified initially as candidates for this distinction. The first set involves attributes that locate the individual and family in the social order: age, sex, race, income, and anticipated future income position. The second set characterizes the residential situation: ownership, size, and age of residence. The third set is perceptual in nature. Included are perceptions of the personal impact of both the 1978 coal strike and the energy situation in general as well as perceptions of efforts by others (a group to which they belong or Project Pacesetter, a community campaign for conservation) to induce the respondent to conserve.

The final set of factors is attitudinal. Two attitudes involve trust in government. A second pair deals with attitudes towards conservation. A third pair reflects general value orientations: how cost conscious and how materialistic a person is. Three factors were specified that involve orientations towards the energy situation itself: concern about it, pessimism about finding easy solutions to it, and understanding of its causes. The final factor reflects an attitude toward adoption of innovations.

Each of the aforementioned factors was measured using respondent reports so that is could be introduced as an explanatory variable into the analysis. Measurement of the demographic and situational factors was straightforward and requires little elaboration here, except to say that (1) anticipated income is a perception about whether future income would or would not keep up with inflation, and (2) size of residence was indicated by the number of rooms. The perceptual factors were measured by asking whether respondents had themselves experienced problems or efforts by others to influence their energy usage. Measurement of the attitudinal factors, on the other hand, requires elaboration. In eight of ten cases, the variables are indices created by counting the number of consistent responses to two or more questions.[6] In the two remaining cases, dichotomized responses to a single question are used. Table 2 specifies how each of the attitudinal variables was created.

[6] Items were identified for inclusion in each index based on similarity in their content. In most cases, significant empirical relationships appear among the items contributing to the same index.

Table 2.   COMPONENT ITEMS OF ATTITUDINAL VARIABLES[a]

Specific Political Trust: (1) Congress can be trusted to do what is necessary to deal with any energy problems (+); (2) President Carter can be trusted to do what is necessary to deal with any energy problems (+); and (3) People should be willing to do whatever the President asks to save energy (+).

General Political Trust: (1) The federal government wastes most of the money we pay in taxes (-); (2) The federal government is run by a few big interests looking out for themselves (-); (3) Many of the people running the federal government are crooked (-); (4) We can trust federal government to do what is right most of the time (+); and (5) The federal government does not seem to care about the needs of people like me (-).

Energy Sophistication: (1) The energy situation is too complicated for me to understand (-); (2) The Arabs are the major cause of America's energy problems (-); (3) The unusually cold weather of last winter is the major cause of America's energy problems (-); (4) The coal strike is the major cause of America's energy problems (-); and (5) Attempts by oil and gas companies to increase their profits are the major cause of America's energy problems (-).

Energy Conservation: (1) Being able to save electricity or gas makes me feel really good (+); (2) Before I will make more sacrifices to conserve energy, I want to make sure others are sacrificing too (-); and (3) Having to sacrifice takes the fun out of life (-).

General Conservation: (1) Sacrifice is good for people (+); (2) Most Americans are too comfortable (+); (3) I am much less wasteful than most people (+).

Energy Pessimism: (1) Scientists will find solutions to our energy problems before any serious shortages occur (-); and (2) America will never run out of energy resources (-).

Cost Consciousness: (1) I usually go to several stores to find the lowest prices for the things I buy (+); and (2) The cost of something I am buying is more important to me than its other qualities (+).

Antimaterialism: (1) A person is a success if he is able to buy a big house, a big car, and travel when he wants to (-); and (2) Improving your mind and maintaining health are more important than having things like a fancy house and car (+).

Energy Concern: (1) The energy situation in America today worries me a great deal (+).

Innovativeness: (1) I like to try out new things before other people do (+).

---

[a]Each measure was constructed by counting the number of consistent responses to the statements that follow it. A "+" indicates that approval with the statement was counted, and a "-" indicates that disapproval with the statement was counted.

The Factors Related to Conservation

We now turn to an examination of the empirical relationships between these twenty-three "explanatory" variables and conservation among Pittsburgh residents. This examination is descriptive in that it represents an attempt to identify factors that are related to conservation. Full determination of the direction of these relationships, except in the most obvious cases, and of specific theories for explaining conservation is, however, beyond the scope of this study and must await longitudinal research designs.

Two related techniques are employed to determine the relationships between the explanatory variables and conservation. First, the simple product-moment correlation between each explanatory variable and the conservation index has been calculated.[7] The simple correlation is of limited value, however, because it summarizes each relationship in a vacuum as if no other forces were operating. Other forces were present! The independent variables used in this analysis are often interrelated, so that "true" relationships may be masked or suppressed. Consequently we employ multiple linear regression analysis in order to overcome this limitation by considering simultaneously the relationship of all explanatory variables to conservation. This technique gives us a better picture of the factors that relate to conservation because it takes into account the interrelations among all variables in the model. The correlation and regression results are presented in Table 3.[8] Almost 30 percent of the variance in the conservation index is accounted for—a high figure given the normal levels of reliability of survey data and the number of factors that remain unspecified by the model.

In terms of both the correlation and regression coefficients,

[7] These correlations capture the *linear* association between the two variables. Careful analysis of the scatterplots of these relationships uncovered no theoretically meaningful curvilinearities, giving us confidence that testing for the linear relationships is the best procedure for this study.

[8] Correlation and regression analyses depend upon the relations of variances and, as a result, require that all variables be measured on an interval scale. This requirement is satisfied by all but two of the variables, and most crucially by the dependent variable. Education and family income do not satisfy the interval level of measurement assumption. For analytical purposes, we shall assume that they are measured on an interval scale, with the confidence (based on other analysis) that this does no noticeable damage to our results.

Table 3. FACTORS RELATED TO ENERGY CONSERVATION[a]

Factors	(1) Simple correlations	(2) b	(3) Beta
Demographic			
Family income	0.21**	− 0.01 (.07)	0.00
Anticipated family income	0.01	0.23 (.20)	0.04
Respondent education	0.12**	0.02 (.09)	0.01
Respondent age	− 0.09*	− 0.02 (.01)	− .013**
Respondent race	0.25**	1.70 (.35)	0.17**
Respondent sex	− 0.02	− 0.15 (.20)	− 0.02
Situational			
Age of residence	− 0.13**	0.00 (.00)	− 0.02
Size of residence	0.06	0.00 (.01)	0.00
Ownership of residence	0.39**	2.16 (.23)	0.36**
Perceptual			
Energy situation impact	0.10**	0.10 (.19)	0.02
Coal strike impact	0.13**	0.43 (.19)	0.08*
Pacesetter recognition	0.10**	0.38 (.25)	0.05
Group encouragement	0.03	0.06 (.22)	0.01
Attitudinal			
Specific political trust	0.06	0.42 (.11)	0.14**
General political trust	0.03	− 0.16 (.07)	− 0.09*
Energy sophistication	0.19**	0.30 (.09)	0.14**
Energy pessimism	0.11**	0.24 (.13)	0.07
Energy concern	0.11**	0.44 (.21)	0.07*
Energy conservation	0.16**	0.33 (.12)	0.10**
General conservation	0.07	0.05 (.11)	0.01
Cost consciousness	0.06	0.51 (.15)	0.12**
Antimaterialism	0.10**	0.37 (.17)	0.07*
Innovativeness	− 0.01	− 0.04 (.20)	− 0.01
Constant term		3.31	
			$(R^2 = 0.29**)$

[a]Column 1 contains the simple correlations between each row variable and the conservation index; column 2 the unstandardized regression coefficients and their standard errors; and column 3 the standardized regression coefficients, or betas, Significance levels: *−.05; **−.01; N = 717 to 778 (cases with missing data were eliminated on a pairwise basis).

ownership of residence bears the strongest relationship to conservation. Home owners were much more likely to conserve than non-owners, even after other variables in the model had been taken into account. Home ownership accounts for almost thirteen percent of the variance in conservation. Some reasons for this relationship are implied by our data. Renters and owners differed most in winterization activities—installing storm windows, insulating, and using weatherstripping on a regular basis. The first two of these activities are investments in the dwelling and provide no direct returns to nonowners, thus limiting the direct payoff to renter-conservers.

Owners were more conservation-oriented than renters for non-investment activities also, but the differences were small. The greater conservation of owners even here suggests that they may be more sensitive to energy costs in general. One reason is that some renters do not pay their utility bills and lack a *direct* stake in certain forms of conservation. These renters conserve less. The effect of this on the overall relationship is small, however, since most renters in the sample paid all utility bills. Even those renters who paid directly for their utilities were less likely than owners to conserve. Something about renting per se (perhaps a shorter time perspective) apparently limits conservation.

Beyond the dramatic impact of home ownership, the most substantial relationships in the regression analysis involve attitudes and perceptions. Together they account for about ten percent of the variance in conservation. Five of them are significantly associated with conservation in simple correlation terms and remain so in the multivariate analysis. Four of these variables reflect attitudes about energy usage and the energy situation in America.

The largest simple correlation is between energy sophistication and conservation. More sophisticated respondents were substantially more likely to conserve. As one would expect, sophistication bears a strong relationship to education ($r = 0.45$). Its impact on conservation, though, is not attributable to education. When the two variables are treated simultaneously in the regression analysis, it is the impact of education, not sophistication, that is reduced to insignificance. These results suggest that understanding of the energy situation heightens a sense of individual responsibility for dealing with it, thus increasing conservation.

Also more likely to conserve were those who derived satisfaction from energy conservation per se. The relationships attain significance in both the correlation and regression analyses. This variable too is correlated with education, but again the level of education cannot account for the impact of the attitude. It may seem commonplace that people who derive satisfaction from conservation conserve more. Where the linkage of attitudes to behavior is concerned, however, any positive findings are more than commonplace. Here is one attitude that may well have important behavioral consequences, although the possibility that the attitude is derived to justify the behavior cannot be dismissed.

A third attitude related to conservation is concern about the energy situation. This implies a connection between worry and individual behavior that responds to the worry. The energy concern variable is correlated with energy pessimism ($r = 0.12$), as might be expected. This correlation may well account for the fact that only one of these variables, concern, survives in the multivariate analysis even though both enjoy significant initial correlations with conservation.

Finally, those who experienced hardship because of the coal strike were more likely to conserve. In part this relationship reflects perceptions of greater coal strike impact among people with higher levels of income and education, variables also related to conservation. A reduced but still significant relationship appears once these and other variables are controlled, though, to indicate a connection between the perception per se and conservation. At first stance, it is difficult to understand why the impact of the coal strike, but not of the general energy situation, is significant. Effects of the coal strike, after all, should have been restricted to electricity usage and reflected only marginally in the conservation index. Careful reading of the interview protocols provides clues for understanding this relationship. The coal strike impact question was the initial question in the interview. Because of its position, it captured sentiment about a variety of energy crises and their impacts upon our respondents. For example, some respondents mentioned natural gas shortages, gasoline shortages, and other problems unrelated to electricity or coal when asked to specify the impact of the coal strike.

The only other attitudinal variable to remain significant in both the correlation and regression analyses is the index of antimaterialism. This variable is not linked conceptually to conservation in the direct manner of the preceding variables. Nonetheless, values and conservation have become intertwined to a substantial degree in recent years.[9] Antimaterialism was associated with conservation in our study. It should come as no surprise either that antimaterialists were pro-energy conservation in attitude and younger, even though these factors alone cannot explain the greater conservation among antimaterialists.

Three additional attitudinal and perceptual variables emerge as significant only in the regression analysis. Their impact had been suppressed by third variables in the correlation analysis and became apparent only when these third variables could be controlled. In each case, the standardized regression coefficient (beta) is at least twice the magnitude of the simple correlation.

The greatest increases from correlation to beta coefficent were recorded by the two trust variables. Specific political trust measures confidence in the energy-policy capabilities of the president and Congress. General political trust, on the other hand, refers broadly to government and policy. Even though these two indices of trust are themselves correlated ($r = 0.29$), they exhibit contrasting relationships to conservation in the regression analysis. The stronger relationship of the two shows that the higher the level of specific political trust, the *more* conservation was recorded. By contrast, higher levels of general political trust are related to *less* conservation. That theoretically and empirically similar variables should exhibit opposite relationships to conservation is puzzling, and the data contain no clues for solving this puzzle. Given this situation, it seems best to take the relationships at face value. Where trust is specifically focussed on actors in the energy policy context, it appears to induce higher levels of compliance with government pleas to conserve. Where it is generalized, on the other hand, trust may be less important and even a bit dysfunctional for conservation.[10]

[9] Some Americans seem attracted to conservation because it involves rejection of the high living standards of modern American society. Indeed, Bupp and Derian (1978) attribute some of the most potent opposition to nuclear energy to such feelings.

[10] Previous research (Miller, 1974) shows, however, that general trust in government is affected by partisanship and ideology. For example, Democrats are more trusting of

A substantial increase from correlation to beta coefficient is found also for the attitudinal measure of cost consciousness. Cost conscious respondents were more conserving in the regression analysis, as we would expect given the emphasis on conservation as being economically rational. This relationship is suppressed in the simple correlation analysis by the tendency for the less educated and poorer to be both more cost conscious and less likely to conserve. Once income and education are controlled, though, it is obvious that cost consciousness can stand on its own as an important correlate of conservation. At all levels of education and income people more attuned to cost factors conserved more.

A number of attitudes and perceptions have been found to be related to energy conservation. This result dramatizes the utility of focussing on people's cognitive orientations in order to comprehend fully their conservation actions. Had we been able to correct our relationships for the inevitable attenuation that results from unreliable survey measures of attitudes and to gauge these orientations for the full family rather than a single member of it, the attitudes and perceptions undoubtedly would have figured even more prominently in our explanations of conserving behavior. As it is, they appear to be critical contributors to energy conservation.

The discussion of the direct relationships between the demographic variables and conservation has been left for last because these variables are the least manipulable by policy-makers. While four of six relationships are significant in the correlational analysis, only two remain significant in the regression analysis. Overall, the demographic variables accounted for a very modest five percent of the variance in conservation. Family income, so often cited as an important determinant of conservation (Perlman and Warren, 1977, Chap. 7), turns out to have a relationship with conservation in our study that is accounted for by the operation of third variables, expecially home ownership and sophistication. Income seems to have little explanatory power by itself.

The impacts of age and race, by contrast, cannot be attributed to other variables in the model. Several hypotheses come immediately to mind to account for the impact of age. Younger people

---

Democratic presidents, while Republicans are more trusting of Republican presidents. This makes our inconsistent findings with the two trust variables even more perplexing.

may be more likely to conserve because their world views and life styles have been formed in an age of rising energy costs. Alternatively, the greater conservation of the young may be a life stage phenomenon that will vanish as they age. These explanations can be tested only with longitudinal data.

The relationship of race and conservation is more difficult to explain. Given our other findings, it should not be surprising that whites were much more likely to conserve. They are more likely to possess the attributes (income, education, home ownership) found to be connected to conservation. But we had fully expected the race-conservation relationship to be spurious, produced through these other variables. Instead it has second largest beta coefficient in Table 3. Whites were more likely to conserve than blacks, even after many differences between the two groups were taken into account. Since it seems doubtful that there is anything inherent in racial characteristics that relates to conservation, the only sensible conclusion is that the appropriate "third" variables remain unspecified in our model.[11]

Before moving on to consider the implications of these findings, it is necessary to stress the limitations of our data. First, these results can be generalized safely only to adult residents of Allegheny County. Similar results might be expected, though, with comparable populations in areas with the same climate, type of housing stock, transportation system, and energy mix. Second, the relationships we have uncovered hold for the winter of 1978 and cannot be generalized with confidence to other times. Too much has changed and will continue to change in the energy situation to make time of incidental importance. A final limitation is inherent in the design of our study. The analysis has established empirical relationships among important variables in a static sense. Yet the most interesting question is a dynamic one: Do changes in atti-

---

[11] A possible explanation for the racial differences in conservation, even after controls have been imposed, is that blacks have fewer options in their energy usage than whites at the same income or education levels. Blacks fell into the lowest regions of each of the income and education categories we used, making it impossible to control fully for these variables. Their choice of housing too is much more restricted due to the continuing legacy of discrimination, limiting their ability to choose dwellings that are more amenable to conservation measures. Overall it seems likely that more blacks subsist at the bare minimum of energy usage and can reduce no further. This conclusion is drawn by Perlman and Warren (1977, pp. 134–137) and finds reinforcement in the general findings on energy usage by blacks reported by Newman and Day (1975, Chap. 7).

tudes, perceptions, and other factors lead to changes in conservation? Our results can only imply answers to this question. A dynamic research design, such as that employed in a panel study, is required before we can begin to treat adequately the questions of dynamic, even causal, connection.

In spite of these limitations, this study takes an important first step towards identifying the factors related to household energy conservation. Important energy policy decisions are too often based only upon *assumptions* about the individual and situational factors that produce conservation. The empirical foundations for these assumptions require examination through studies of conservation behavior at the individual level. Not only can this examination provide tests of the views underlying current energy policy, but it can also guide policy-makers in developing strategies to increase conservation in the future. With these goals in mind, let us now consider some implications of our findings.

Implications for Energy Policy

Public policies are the operational translations of theories concerning how desired goals can be achieved. As such, they depend on assumptions about the consequences of particular actions. Rational policy-makers should be interested in testing these assumptions continually. If found to be empirically unsupportable, however attractive they might have been on a logical or theoretical basis, policy adjustments and revisions are in order. That such adjustments are not always made attests to the vested interests that arise in any policy once it is enacted. Policy rationality, after all, does not always coincide with political rationality.

One important goal of energy policy in America is to enhance conservation by individual consumers. A variety of policy approaches have been suggested for achieving this goal. The common element in all of them is a reliance upon assumptions about what factors condition energy conservation in the household.[12]

[12] Consider some examples: A policy of oil price deregulation is based on the assumption that higher prices for oil will lead Americans to cut back on its usage. Warnings of projected fuel shortages are premised on the notion that shortages can be ameliorated if citizens are advised in advance. The dissemination of information on the energy situation

The results of our study of energy conservation among Pittsburgh families can provide empirical evidence concerning some of these assumptions by identifying the factors that are currently related to variations among households in conservation practices.

Many have contended that substantially more conservation will be achieved if prices for energy are allowed to reach their market levels. This argument presumes that higher prices will restrict demand. Few people would challenge this presumption in its general form: virtually everyone agrees that aggregate demand will decline with increases in price. What is disputed instead is the tightness of the relationship between price and demand where energy is concerned. In other words, what is the elasticity of demand for energy?

While we cannot estimate this elasticity with our data, some clues about the impact of rising prices for energy in the last few years can be derived from the results of our study. A first general observation is that most people in our sample conserved to some degree, lending credence to the notion that increased prices have affected demand. But the more interesting observation is that the elasticities of demand for energy seem to have varied substantially across different groups.

Perhaps most revealing is the relationship between income and conservation in our data. It is well known that energy usage increases with income.[13] The results of our study show that con-

---

and on ways to conserve presumes that informed citizens will conserve more. Each of these assumptions may be valid or invalid. Only empirical investigation can resolve the matter. But testing of assumptions such as these is enormously difficult. One way is to monitor the overall demand for energy under different conditions. This aggregate test is too blunt for most purposes, though, since it examines only the bottom line and ignores the series of individual decisions that produced the bottom line. When many policy approaches are operating simultaneously, aggregate figures do not permit evaluation of any single approach. An alternative is to monitor directly changes in individual behavior and in components of the individual decision field. This requires longitudinal data on individuals, which is very expensive and difficult to collect. A second alternative is to derive a series of static or cross-sectional predictions from the assumptions and test them under real-world conditions. This is the approach we shall follow here. Regardless of its limitations, it is the only approach available at present that is sensitive to individual energy conservation behavior and the factors that may influence it.

[13] Newman and Day (1975, p. 88) found in their 1972–73 study that the well-off used more than twice as much energy overall as the poor—and over five times as much gasoline. The well-off were all those with a family income over $16,000, while the poor were defined by family size and income using the U.S. government levels for poor and near poor. See Newman and Day (1975, p. 91).

servation too increases with income—a relationship that appears to be explained best by the operation of intervening variables.[14] In one sense, this relationship is puzzling, because the fact that energy-related expenditures constitute a much larger portion of disposable income for the poor should force them to be more sensitive to price. In another sense, though, it is understandable. The typical lower-income family consumes energy to provide only the necessities of modern life and has precious little margin for cutting back. Middle- and upper-income families, by comparison, can pare their usage without cutting into essentials. Furthermore, lower-income families have fewer alternatives for economizing in their energy usage. For example, investments in insulation or economy cars are likely to be prohibitively expensive for them.

Several implications may be drawn from these findings. The first is that, since the elasticity of demand for energy appears to grow with income, the market approach will have greater success in stimulating conservation among middle and upper income families. The lower responsiveness of the relatively poor to energy price increases also limits the overall elasticity of demand. If some way could be found to enable them to be more responsive, American energy demand would show even greater sensitivity to energy prices.

A second and more disturbing implication is that the market approach imposes great hardships on lower income families. Given their lower levels of energy usage and their inability to make conserving investments on their own, the poor have little choice but to absorb the higher prices. It is little wonder that rationing of energy seems preferable to deregulation of energy prices among those who pay special heed to the concerns of lower income groups. Full market pricing for necessities like energy raises issues of equity. The competition between equity and efficiency should continue to lie at the center of energy policy-making.

The overall elasticity of demand for energy is affected also by the distribution of cost conscious attitudes (i.e., individual elasticities) in the public. Those people who said they paid unusual

[14] Perlman and Warren (1977, Chap. 7) report a similar finding from their three-city study: relative reductions in energy usage in response to the Arab embargo of 1973 increased with income.

attention to costs in their consumption habits were more likely to have conserved in fact in their energy usage, once other variables were held constant. Yet many of our respondents were not particularly cost conscious, making them less sensitive to rising prices. Conservation by them is more likely to be affected by noneconomic considerations.

Another limitation on the overall elasticity of demand for energy is the relative insensitivity of renters to the need for conservation. We found that home owners were much more likely to conserve than renters. Some renters do not pay utility bills and, as a result, do not see the direct costs of their energy usage. To the extent that rents are determined by supply and demand and energy costs are not passed on to renters, they may not be able to determine even their indirect energy costs. But renters who paid their utility bills were less likely to conserve as well. Because renters move even more frequently than the average American, they may have a shorter time perspective then homeowners. And the fact that they have no equity in the property limits the payoff to renters from energy-saving investments. Where energy conservation is focussed on the home, at least, the insulation of renters (who comprise about 30 percent of all households in the sample and about 25 percent in the nation) from market forces stands as another impediment to increased conservation.

Because of both problems of equity and individual variations in responsiveness to energy prices, alternative approaches have been suggested to market pricing for achieving desired levels of conservation. One approach is to persuade people to conserve voluntarily. Persuasion may reach people who are insulated from market forces— e.g., renters. Voluntary conservation, induced by this approach, has the advantage of not harming the poor. The persuasion approach is predicated upon assumptions about the relationship of attitudes and perceptions to conservation behavior and how these attitudes and perceptions can be influenced. Our data permit examination of these assumptions.

In recent years government and private groups (such as Project Pacesetter in the Pittsburgh area) have devoted substantial resources to campaigns to promote energy conservation. One assumption justifying these efforts is the notion that greater understanding of the energy situation will lead to greater conservation.

This notion receives support from our data. Respondents with a better grasp of the energy situation, those who scored high on the index of energy sophistication, were substantially more likely to conserve.

Efforts to promote conservation have gone far beyond appeals to rationality via educational campaigns. Somewhat haphazardly and perhaps even unconsciously, but nonetheless forcefully, the irrational side of the American psyche has been touched by emphasizing the crisis nature of the energy situation. Government has not acted alone in this, as is witnessed by the doomsday preaching of some conservation groups. Nor can the message of the crisis rhetoric be easily dismissed. This rhetoric is designed to produce a response of greater conservation among the American public. Our results provide circumstantial evidence that it does. Both those concerned about the energy situation and those pessimistic about our ability to resolve it easily were more likely to conserve. There is evidence also that experience is a good teacher. People who experienced some impact from the coal strike and the energy situation in general were found to be more likely to conserve, although this relationship remained significant only for the coal strike variable in the regression analysis. In sum, it appears that both crisis rhetoric and crisis experience may promote conservation.[15]

The evidence that attitudes and perceptions are related to conservation lends support to a persuasion approach at a more general level. Many of these orientations appear to contribute to conservation and, taken together, they account for an impressive amount of variation in the conservation index. Concentration on attitudes and perceptions should be a high priority of campaigns to increase levels of conservation. One strategy would be to attempt to change the distribution of the population on a particular orientation—for example, to make people more concerned or more pessimistic about the energy situation. An alternative strategy is to attempt to

[15] There is always the danger that crisis rhetoric will be overblown—like the proverbial boy who cried wolf too often. Our respondents evinced sone tendency to test rhetoric against reality during the 1978 coal strike, and more than a few concluded that the rhetoric had been exaggerated. This left them less inclined to believe crisis warnings in the future. The lessons in this are that crisis rhetoric must be moderated to fit the situation and that any failure of the crisis to materialize as predicted must be fully accounted for in post-crisis public statements.

change the extant relationship of an attitude or perception to behavior. This is best accomplished by making both the attitude and
the behavior salient, so as to force people to recognize the inconsistency between them.[16] For example, efforts to clarify the costs
of energy usage and how those costs might be reduced could
tighten the relationship between cost consciousness and conservation. As recent experience shows, achieving voluntary conservation
through persuasion is difficult. Yet it is an approach that has considerable promise, in no small measure due to the fact that it is
wholly voluntary and attracts little opposition.

Conclusion

Although there have been several attempts to formulate a comprehensive energy policy at the national level, our government does
not now follow such a policy. Rather what we have are a congeries
of energy programs, some reinforcing and others contradictory,
with little promise of complete coherence in the near future. The
formulation of comprehensive policy in the energy area has been
stalemated by a host of political problems, evidence that neither
the public nor its leaders are in agreement about the necessity for
action or the paths such action might take. Agreement on the
necessity for action can emerge only from sustained experience
with energy problems and forceful leadership at the national level.
Determination of paths for action, on the other hand, can be informed by an understanding of why people conserve. The results
of our analysis can aid in this understanding.

Many policy implications surely could be drawn from the findings of this study. We have focussed on the most obvious ones—in

[16] Social psychologists have long recognized that when two salient cognitions are contradictory, psychological pressures to resolve the contradictions often result. Making the
inconsistency salient is the key, for people handle the numerous contradictions in their
everyday lives through compartmentalization. Of course, the risk of adopting this
approach in the conservation setting, where behavior is one of the elements, is that the
attitude will be changed to fit the behavior rather than the opposite and more desirable
result. Nevertheless, the cognitive consistency approach to promoting conservation is
worthy of consideration. Evidence from our survey shows that the social pressures in
favor of conservation are strong, enhancing the likelihood that cognitive inconsistency
will be resolved through conservation. For the seminal treatment of the most familiar
form of consistency theory, see Festinger (1957).

part to demonstrate how survey data on the correlates of conservation may be useful in the development of strategies to increase
conservation. Our results are limited undeniably by site, time, and
design. Nonetheless, they provide a context for understanding individual conservation in America today. With this understanding,
effective strategies for achieving even greater conservation can be
formulated. Such strategies are necessary if the nation is to deal
with its energy problems in the future. Without this understanding,
assumptions rather than realities will guide policy making, with
the inevitable consequence that neither conservation nor equity in
sharing the burdens of conservation will be optimized.

BIBLIOGRAPHY

Bartell, Ted (1976). "Political Orientations and Public Response
to the Energy Crisis." *Social Science Quarterly*, 57: 430–436.
Beck, Paul Allen, Samuel I. Doctors, and Paul Y. Hammond (1980).
Individual Energy Conservation Behaviors. Oelgeschlager, Gunn
& Haig, Cambridge, MA.
Bupp, Irwin C., and Jean-Claude Derian (1978). *Light Water: How
the Nuclear Dream Dissolved.* Basic Books, New York.
Craig, Paul P., Joel Darmstadter, and Stephen Rattien (1976).
"Social and Institutional Factors in Energy Conservation."
Annual Review of Energy, 1: 535–552.
Festinger, Leon (1957). *A Theory of Cognitive Dissonance.* Stan-
ford University Press, Stanford.
Gottieb, David and Marc Matre. "Conceptions of Energy Shortages
and Energy Consuming Behavior." *Social Science Quarterly*, 57:
421–429.
Miller, Arthur H. (1977). "Political Issues and Trust in Govern-
ment: 1964–1970." *The American Political Science Review*, 68:
951–972.
Milstein, Jeffery S. (1977). "How Consumers Feel About Energy:
Attitudes and Behavior During the Winter and Spring of 1976–
77." Office of Conservation, Federal Energy Administration,
Washington, D.C.
Murray, James R., Michael J. Minor, Robert F. Cotterman, and
Norman M. Bradburn (1974). "The Impact of the 1973–1974

Oil Embargo on the American Household." Unpublished manuscript, National Opinion Research Corporation, Chicago.

Newman, Dorothy K., and Dawn Day (1975). *The American Energy Consumer.* Ballinger, Cambridge, MA.

Perlman, Robert, and Roland L. Warren (1977). *Families in the Energy Crisis: Impacts and Implications for Theory and Policy.* Ballinger, Cambridge, MA.

Sears, David O., Tom R. Tyler, Jack Citrin, and Donald R. Kinder (1978). "Political System Support and Public Response to the Energy Crisis." *American Journal of Political Science,* 22: 56–82.

17

STATE POLICY RESPONSES TO THE ENERGY ISSUE
An Analysis of Innovation

James L. Regens

ALTHOUGH STATE INNOVATION ADOPTION AND ITS CORRELATES HAVE
been the subject of an increasing amount of scholarly attention
in recent years (see Walker, 1969; Gray, 1973; Savage, 1978), the
very "newness" of energy as a public policy concern makes it an ideal
issue domain for examining the dynamics of policy innovativeness among
the American states. Unlike most policy areas, the current context for energy policy making reveals an emergent, but not yet dominant leadership role on the part of the federal government. As a result, states have
the opportunity to achieve the first or at least early use of those energy
policy options that they choose to implement rather than merely adopting
"wait-and-see" attitudes to comply with federal mandates.[2] Thus, the
states would appear to have the potential to formulate and implement
innovative policy responses beyond those mandated by the federal government in the energy area. This study explores the extent to which the
states have opted to pursue such an active as opposed to passive role in
energy policymaking.

[1] An earlier version of this paper was presented at the 1979 Annual Meeting of the
Southwestern Political Science Association, Fort Worth, Texas, March 28–31,
1979. Portions of the research for this paper were supported by the Southern
States Energy Board under contract number 1.0.001-7803. Stanley W. Shelton,
John M. Beard, and R. Michael Chandler assisted in the data collection. I
wish to thank Charles S. Bullock, III, Timothy A. Hall, and several anonymous readers for comments on an earlier version of this manuscript. Editor's note: SSQ reviewers were Steven Ballard, Marlan Blissett, Robert L. Savage and Ira Sharkansky.

[2] Significant federal leadership occurs in most established policy areas, usually with
grant-in-aid mechanisms attached, with state efforts largely responses to mandates
rather than actual innovations (Rose, 1973). Thus, if a policy is *mandated* by the
federal government, unless one accepts the idea that the policy need only be new to
the organization or individual considering it, then innovation at the state level is not
in question. As a consequence, this analysis is based on the assumption that state
policy responses should be relatively new (see Mohr, 1969; Downs and Mohr, 1976)
and state-initiated (see Rose, 1973) in order to be characterized as examples of innovation instead of compliance behavior. For an analysis of state compliance with
those energy policy measures that have been mandated by the federal government,
see Regens (1979).

From James L. Regens, "State Policy Responses to the Energy Issue: An Analysis of Innovation,"
61(1) *Social Science Quarterly* 44-57 (June 1980). Copyright © 1980 by the University of Texas Press.
Reprinted by permission.

AN OVERVIEW OF NATIONAL ENERGY POLICY AND THE STATES

Historically, the organizational structure for energy policy making in the United States has been diffuse (Davis, 1974; Kash et al., 1976: 28–51; Regens, 1978: 179–80), with the states traditionally establishing policy in such areas as public utility regulation and facility siting (Hall et al., 1978: 198). The 1973 Organization of Petroleum Exporting Countries' (OPEC) oil embargo, however, revealed that the traditional settings for energy policymaking under conditions of abundant, cheap energy lacked the capabilities to address problems of supply uncertainty coupled with substantial price increases (see Mancke, 1974, 1976). Early studies such as the Energy Policy Project of the Ford Foundation (1974) asserted that because of the presumed centrality of energy resource availability for maintaining industrial societies (see Meadows et al., 1972) and the weaknesses in the existing policy mechanisms, the federal government should assume a leading role in energy policy[2] (see also Hamilton, 1978). As a consequence, despite growing demands by the states for continuing and expanded participation in decision-making (Light, 1976; White et al., 1977; Hall et al., 1978), energy has been perceived largely as a policy question for the national government's agenda.[3] This new emphasis on the federal dimension has produced uncertainty about intergovernmental as well as public-private sector roles and relationships which are still stabilizing (Regens, 1978: 186).

In theory, expansion of the federal government's role in energy policy making need not necessarily be at the expense of the states. For example, the Energy Policy and Conservation Act of 1975 (EPCA, PL94-163) and the Energy Conservation and Production Act of 1976 (ECPA, PL94-385) assign major implementation responsibilities to the states in the area of energy conservation (see also Mills and Woodson, 1976; Hackbart and Patton, 1976). However, the National Energy Plan (NEP) primarily limits the states to such mandated implementation activities while restricting them to minor roles in policy formulation (Executive Office of the President, 1977; U.S. Congress, Office of Technology Assessment, 1977). Thus, the overall effect of energy becoming a highly visible policy concern has been an apparent shift in the balance between the two levels of government. The role of the federal government appears

[2] For an alternative perspective which suggests that energy policy should be left largely to market forces, see Adelman et al. (1975); Carnesale et al. (1977).

[3] Considerable attention has focused on such aspects as evolving national energy policy (Gordon, 1974; Rose, 1974; Leonard, 1976; Ball, 1977; Goldstein, 1978), trade-offs between energy and other policy areas (Caldwell, 1973; Garvey, 1972, 1975; Regens, 1978), changing public-private sector relationships (Mead, 1977; Hamilton, 1978), implications for national security (Szyliowicz and O'Neill, 1975; Blair, 1976; Nau, 1978), and comparisons of U.S. responses with those of other countries (Lindberg, 1977; Schipper, 1978).

to have expanded, at least partially, through a reduction of state authority (Hall et al., 1978: 198–99). Assessments of intergovernmental relations since the 1950s support such a "centrally directed" model of federalism (see Sundquist, 1969; Scheffer, 1975), especially with regard to environmental policies (Jones, 1974; Lieber, 1975; Ingram, 1978).

Clearly, the federal government has provided the impetus for recent activity in a number of policy areas. Yet, states originally experimented with many of the innovative policies in areas other than energy for which the federal government received the credit (Sharkansky, 1972). Similar controversy surrounds discussions of the nature of state responses to the energy issue. For example, Light (1976) suggests that a number of states had, in fact, initiated energy programs before the 1973 OPEC oil embargo in response to fairly tangible energy-related problems that they confronted (see also Hackbart and Patton, 1976). On the other hand, Cortner (1978) argues that present state responses are grossly inadequate with the states adopting a "wait-and-see" attitude instead of pursuing innovative, nonfederally mandated measures.

In spite of the controversy over the nature of state responses, there have been few systematic examinations of the extent to which states have formulated and implemented various energy policies in the absence of federal mandates. Moreover, existing analyses are largely case studies or concerned with diffusion within limited geographic areas (Griffin and Shelton, 1978; Cortner, 1978) and usually ignore reasons for policy adoption. As a result, our understanding of the degree to which the states have engaged in innovative activity as well as the determinants of innovation adoption in the energy policy area is limited. The following analysis, therefore, provides a nation-wide examination of (1) the current level of state implementation of non-federally mandated energy policies, and (2) what factors account for variation in the degree of state innovation adoption in the energy area.

PATTERNS OF STATE ENERGY POLICY INNOVATION

The data employed in this study to measure implementation of energy policy innovations are based on a comprehensive survey of all 50 state energy agencies conducted in the late spring and summer of 1978.[4] Respondents were asked to identify whether their state had implemented each of the following non-federally mandated policy measures in order to deal with their state's energy-related problems:
  (1) State funding for R & D projects.
  (2) Comprehensive energy resource development plan.
  (3) State-sponsored demonstration projects.

[4] The data were obtained using a combination of telephone interviews with and mail questionnaires directed to state energy agency directors. Alaska is excluded in this analysis because of missing data on the energy policy innovation measures

TABLE 1

Status of State Implementation of Selected Energy
Policy Innovations°

Policy Measure	Implementation %	(n)
State Funding for R&D Projects Arizona, Arkansas, California, Colorado, Connecticut, Florida, Georgia, Hawaii, Illinois, Indiana, Iowa, Kentucky, Louisiana, Maine, Maryland, Minnesota, Montana, Nevada, New Mexico, New York, North Carolina, Ohio, Oregon, Pennsylvania, Texas	51.0	(25)
Comprehensive Energy Resource Development Plan Maine, Minnesota, New Mexico, New York, Oregon, Texas, Utah	14.3	(7)
State-Sponsored Demonstration Projects Arizona, California, Connecticut, Georgia, Hawaii, Idaho, Illinois, Kansas, Kentucky, Louisiana, Maine, Minnesota, Missouri, Nevada, New Mexico, New York, North Carolina, Ohio, Oklahoma, Oregon, Pennsylvania, Tennessee, Texas, Utah, Vermont, Virginia, Washington, Wisconsin	57.1	(28)
Tax Incentives for Industry Arizona, Georgia, Kansas, Massachusetts, New Jersey, New Mexico, North Carolina, Ohio, Oklahoma, Pennsylvania, Texas, Vermont, Virginia, West Virginia	28.6	(14)
Tax Incentives for Individuals Arizona, Arkansas, California, Colorado, Connecticut, Georgia, Hawaii, Idaho, Indiana, Kansas, Maine, Maryland, Massachusetts, Michigan, Montana, Nevada, New Jersey, New Mexico, New York, North Carolina, North Dakota, Oklahoma, Oregon, South Dakota, Vermont, Virginia, Wisconsin	55.1	(27)
Forecasting/Modeling Arizona, California, Connecticut, Indiana, Iowa, Louisiana, Maine, Maryland, Massachusetts, Michigan Minnesota, Nebraska, Nevada, New York, North Carolina, Ohio, Oregon, Pennsylvania, South Carolina, Texas, Utah, Wisconsin, Wyoming	46.9	(23)
Interstate Cooperative Energy Resources Development Agreement Arizona, Arkansas, California, Florida, Maryland, Mississippi, Missouri, New Jersey, New Mexico, New York, North Carolina, Oklahoma, Oregon, Pennsylvania, Rhode Island, South Dakota, Texas, Utah, Vermont, Washington	40.8	(20)

°Excludes Alaska

(4) Tax incentives for industry.
(5) Tax incentives for individuals.
(6) Forecasting/modeling.
(7) Interstate cooperative energy resources development agreements.

Because none of the above policy options are currently mandated by the federal government, each represents a potentially innovative, state-initiated response to energy problems.

Examination of Table 1 reveals varying levels of implementation for the selected innovation measures. The states are largely willing to adopt state-funded research and development (R&D) or state-sponsored demonstration projects as well as forecasting/modeling techniques that suggest a willingness to rely on "technical fix" solutions to their energy-related problems (see Energy Policy Project of the Ford Foundation, 1974; Kash et al., 1976). Implementation of tax incentive policies, especially for individuals, suggests a similar willingness to explore the efficacy of "social fix" approaches (Tuve, 1976: 7–8). Given the tradition of interstate compacts, particularly among the western states, a substantial percentage of the states have adopted cooperative resources development agreements. On the other hand, the states have been overwhelmingly reluctant to establish comprehensive energy resource development plans, perhaps in part reflecting the political complexities of state resource management (see Mann, 1978).

Moreover, Table 2 reveals that while each of the energy policies has been adopted by at least one state, none of the states has adopted all of the measures while three states (Alabama, Delaware and New Hampshire) failed to adopt any of them. In fact, although most states tend to implement some nonfederally mandated response, they generally restrict the number of policies which they adopt. Given the nature of communication networks in the United States (Rogers, 1962; Rogers and Shoemaker, 1971; Zaltman et al., 1973), this suggests that most states are more inclined to emulate successful programs of others rather than embark on widespread innovativeness on an individual basis.

PREDICTING STATE INNOVATION EFFORTS

Clearly, a substantial proportion of the states have implemented at least one nonfederally mandated energy policy in an attempt to respond to their existing energy-related problems. This raises the question of which independent variables shape the process of energy policy innovation at the state level. Examination of the literature suggests that energy policy is potentially influenced by levels of industrialization, affluence, energy consumption by end use sectors, population size, and relative

TABLE 2
Overall Levels of State Implementation of Selected Energy
Policy Innovations

Total Adopted	States	%	Implementation (n)
0	Alabama, Delaware, New Hampshire	6.1	(3)
1	Mississippi, Nebraska, North Dakota, Rhode Island, South Carolina, Tennessee, West Virginia	16.3	(8)
2	Colorado, Florida, Idaho, Illinois, Iowa, Kentucky, Michigan, Missouri, Montana, South Dakota, Washington	22.4	(11)
3	Arkansas, Hawaii, Indiana, Kansas, Louisiana, Massachusetts, New Jersey, Virginia, Wisconsin	18.4	(9)
4	Connecticut, Georgia, Maryland, Minnesota, Nevada, Ohio, Oklahoma, Utah, Vermont	18.4	(9)
5	California, Maine, Pennsylvania	6.1	(3)
6	Arizona, New Mexico, New York, North Carolina, Oregon, Texas	12.2	(6)
7		0.0	(0)
		100.0	(49)

energy self-sufficiency[5] (see Craig, Darmstadter and Rattien, 1976; Darmstadter, Dunkerley and Alterman, 1977). Climate is also frequently suggested as a major variable related to energy use patterns and problems[6] (Olgayay, 1963; Knowles, 1974; Socolow, 1975; Harwood, 1977: 16–22). Similarly, the importance that public opinion gives to an issue can affect policy responses[7] (see Monroe, 1979). Finally, the willingness

[5] Those independent variables were operationalized as follows: (1) industrialization levels and affluence levels were measured by factor scores for each state (see Morgan and Lyons, 1975); (2) energy consumption by end use sectors (e.g., residential, commercial, industrial and transportation) was measured in 10^{15} BTUs consumed on an individual sector basis for each state (see Kidman and Barrett, 1977); (3) population size represents the natural log transformation of total state population (see U.S. Bureau of the Census, 1975); and (4) relative energy self-sufficiency measures whether the state was a net energy exporter (see Kidman and Barrett, 1977).

[6] Each state's climate was measured in terms of normal heating degree days, a unit based upon temperature difference and time, which are derived from the values for the monthly minimum and maximum temperatures and computed from the standard base 65° F. For any one day, when the temperature is less than 65° F, there exist as many degree days as there are Fahrenheit degrees difference in the temperature between the average for the day and 65° F. As the number of degree days increases, a state's climate becomes more harsh with a corresponding increase in its normal heating load in winter (see U.S. Bureau of the Census, 1976: 201).

[7] An indirect measure of aggregate public opinion at the state level about the importance of energy as a policy issue was obtained using a two-step opinion simulation

that states exhibit to intervene in new policy areas or expand their role in existing ones may reflect their relative levels of overall innovativeness[8] (Savage, 1978). In reality the decision on the part of states to adopt energy policy innovation is based on a mix of these structural factors.

Discriminant analysis is an appropriate statistical technique for predicting state energy policy innovation based on those structural characteristics (Cooley and Lohnes, 1971; Aldrich and Cnudde, 1975). In this research, the application of discriminant analysis produces a single function[9] that represents a linear combination of the set of independent variables that distinguishes adoption from nonadoption for each of the policy measures. The standardized coefficients of the loadings for the independent (classification) variables on the function measure the predictive capability of the variables and are similar in interpretation to beta weights while the eta[2] coefficient is comparable to the R^2 value in regression analysis.

Table 3 presents the coefficient patterns for the independent variables on each of the energy policy innovation measures.[10] Energy consumption

---

process (see Weber and Shaffer, 1972). In the first step, a regression equation was generated to predict individuals' opinions from their background characteristics. In the second step, aggregated mean attitudes for each state are estimated as the weighted sum of the aggregated known population characteristics of that state, with the weights provided by the unstandardized regression coefficients of the initial equation. The measure employed in this study to assess the relationship between public perceptions of the salience of energy as an issue and policy innovativeness in each state was derived from survey data originally collected by the Opinion Research Corporation under contract to the Federal Energy Administration. The data were made available by the Inter-University Consortium for Political and Social Research supported by National Science Foundation Grant No. SOC 75-20938. Neither the original collectors of the data, the sponsoring agencies, nor the Consortium bear any responsibility for the analyses and interpretations presented here.

[8] An index that measures the adoption rate of 69 new policies across the entire array of state functions (e.g., environment, health, business regulation, social welfare, criminal justice, etc.) during the period 1930–70 was employed to assess the relative level of overall or general policy innovativeness for each state (Savage, 1978).

[9] Although regression analysis and discriminant analysis produce standardized coefficients that can be interpreted in the same fashion, the two techniques have distinct theoretical objectives (see Kort, 1973; Aldrich and Cnudde, 1975). Regression focuses on minimizing error terms to predict variance for an internal dependent variable. Discriminant maximizes category separation to establish values for the function(s) that will classify each case in the most appropriate category of a noninterval dependent variable. Mathematically, the two-group discriminant function,

$$Z_i = c_1 x_{i1} + c_2 X_{i2} + \ldots + c_j x_{ij} + \ldots + c_n x_{in}$$

where Z_i is an index that places each in an adopt/nonadopt category; c_j is the coefficient in the discriminant function; and x_{ij} is the value of the independent variable j for the ith observation expresses the analysis employed in this research. In discriminant analysis, the number of functions is equal to the number of categories in the dependent variable minus one (or the number of independent variables minus one whichever is less).

[10] The interpretation of the sign for each independent variable on the discriminant functions is keyed to the sign of the group centroids for the function. The group centroids are the mean values for each category of the scores that serve as an index to

TABLE 3

Standardized Discriminant Function Coefficients for Predictors of State
Implementation of Selected Energy Policy Innovations

State Funding for R&D Projects
Policy Innovativeness	.119
Industrialization	−.568
Affluence	.619
Salience of Energy Issue	.277
Climate	−.028
Residential Consumption (ln)	1.852
Commercial Consumption (ln)	−2.226
Industrial Consumption (ln)	.500
Transportation Consumption (ln)	1.944
Population (ln)	−1.327
Energy Exporting State	−.322

Percent Cases Correctly Predicted = 75.0%   Eta² = .440

Comprehensive Energy Resource Development Plan
Policy Innovativeness	−.659
Industrialization	.037
Affluence	.041
Salience of Energy Issue	.304
Climate	−.779
Residential Consumption (ln)	.876
Commercial Consumption (ln)	1.611
Industrial Consumption (ln)	.026
Transportation Consumption (ln)	−2.540
Population (ln)	−.630
Energy Exporting State	−.561

Percent Cases Correctly Predicted = 79.2%   Eta² = .278

State-Sponsored Demonstration Projects
Policy Innovativeness	.379
Industrialization	−.350
Affluence	.460
Salience of Energy Issue	.082
Climate	.240
Residential Consumption (ln)	2.140
Commercial Consumption (ln)	−3.490
Industrial Consumption (ln)	−.064
Transportation Consumption (ln)	2.885
Population (ln)	−.972
Energy Exporting State	.106

Percent Cases Correctly Predicted = 81.2%   Eta² = .560

Tax Incentives for Industry
Policy Innovativeness	−.346
Industrialization	.010
Affluence	.323

TABLE 3.—Continued

Salience of Energy Issue	.113
Climate	−.958
Residential Consumption (ln)	1.646
Commercial Consumption (ln)	.771
Industrial Consumption (ln)	−.809
Transportation Consumption (ln)	−1.320
Population (ln)	−.251
Energy Exporting State	.890

Percent Cases Correctly Predicted = 75.0%   Eta^2 = .371

Tax Incentives for Individuals

Policy Innovativeness	.168
Industrialization	−.238
Affluence	−.014
Salience of Energy Issue	.108
Climate	−.091
Residential Consumption (ln)	−.338
Commercial Consumption (ln)	1.546
Industrial Consumption (ln)	−1.938
Transportation Consumption (ln)	1.143
Population (ln)	−.674
Energy Exporting State	.330

Percent Cases Correctly Predicted = 68.8%   Eta^2 = .360

Forecasting/Modeling

Policy Innovativeness	−.324
Industrialization	−.277
Affluence	.821
Salience of Energy Issue	−.023
Climate	.198
Residential Consumption (ln)	2.124
Commercial Consumption (ln)	−1.081
Industrial Consumption (ln)	1.565
Transportation Consumption (ln)	.065
Population (ln)	−1.945
Energy Exporting State	−.604

Percent Cases Correctly Predicted = 72.9%   Eta^2 = .430

Interstate Cooperative Energy Resources Development Agreement

Policy Innovativeness	.557
Industrialization	−.064
Affluence	.073
Salience of Energy Issue	−.402
Climate	−.973
Residential Consumption (ln)	1.041
Commercial Consumption (ln)	−.435
Industrial Consumption (ln)	−1.289
Transportation Consumption (ln)	.770
Population (ln)	−.431
Energy Exporting State	.402

Percent Cases Correctly Predicted = 76.6%   Eta^2 = .524

levels—especially in the residential/commercial and transportation sectors—relative state energy self-sufficiency, and population size are the most discriminating predictors. Moreover, the analysis succeeds in classifying correctly state policy responses for a large percentage of the cases ($\overline{X} = 75.53\%$), with good overall predictive capability. For example, energy exporting states as well as those with high levels of commercial sector energy consumption are more likely to adopt policies that provide tax incentives for industry. Climate is also related strongly to industry tax incentives, which suggests that "sun belt" states (many of whom are also energy producing states) may have linked, at least partially, their industrial development and energy policies. Policy innovativeness and affluence are also related but to a lesser extent to formulating and implementing state-initiated energy policies. Perhaps the most revealing finding is the relatively insignificant role that state public opinion about the importance of energy as a problem plays in the state energy policy innovation adoption process. In fact, with the exception of resource development policies (largely supply enhancement/"technical fix" options), public opinion seems to be largely unrelated to the actions of state energy policymakers.

Unfortunately, the policy measures are not program specific. Thus, while we are able to establish general patterns of state responsiveness to the energy issue as well as model components of the adoption process, we are unable to determine or compare the individual characteristics of a given state's response with those of other adopters. For example, because program-level budgetary data generally is not available from the states, the analysis cannot reveal whether state research and development money is going for solar, nuclear, coal, oil and gas or what. Moreover, some states may adopt particular policy measures yet fail to achieve effective program implementation. Reliance on survey data, however, does reveal that non-federal energy alternatives are available to the states, depending on the character of their resource base, industrial structure, and energy consumption requirements. Presumably, as energy policy responsibilities evolve into a more established functional area for the states, such program and budget data will become available permitting more defined analyses of the innovativeness of state responses to the energy issue.

CONCLUSION

From a policy perspective, this analysis raises some interesting implications. Clearly, a number of energy policy measures have been im-

---

classify each case into the most appropriate category of the dependent variable (see Cooley and Lohnes, 1971). In this analysis, with the exception of comprehensive energy resource development plans, a positive sign on the centroids and, thus, for the independent variables are related to adoption of the policy measure.

plemented at the state level without the impetus of federal mandates. Almost all of the states have adopted at least one of the policy innovations examined in this research, and a number have implemented multiple state-initiated policy measures. While some could expand substantially the scope of their energy policy activities and all of them might further develop their energy policymaking capabilities, these findings suggest a much more vigorous state policy role than the bleak scenario portrayed in earlier studies (see Cortner, 1978). At the same time, the extent to which states choose to develop energy policy options appears to be primarily related to their structural composition, particularly their existing energy supply–demand system. Public perceptions of the importance of energy as a problem, or rather the general absence of such perceptions, has exerted a largely negligible impact on state energy policy efforts to date. The absence of such a linkage may help to explain why efforts at both the state and federal level to address the nation's energy problem have focused primarily on "technical fix" options.

REFERENCES

Adelman, M. A., A. A. Alchinan, J. Dehaven, G. W. Hilton, M. B. Johnson, H. Kahn, W. J. Mead, A. Moore, T. G. Moore and W. H. Riker. 1975. *No Time to Confuse* (San Francisco: Institute for Contemporary Studies).

Aldrich, J. and C. F. Cnudde. 1975. "Probing the Bounds of Conventional Wisdom: A Comparison of Regression, Probit, and Discriminant Analysis," *American Journal of Political Science*, 29 (August): 571–608.

Ball, B. C., Jr. 1977. "Energy: Policymaking in a New Reality," *Technology Review*, 80 (October/November): 48–51.

Blair, J. 1976. *The Control of Oil* (New York: Pantheon).

Caldwell, L. K. 1973. "Energy and Environment: The Bases for Public Choices," *Annals of the American Academy of Political and Social Science*, 410 (November): 127–38.

Carnesale, A., S. M. Greenfield, F. S. Hoffman, E. J. Mitchell, W. R. Moffat, R. Nehring, R. S. Pindyck, N. C. Rasmussen, D. J. Rowen, J. L. Sweeney and A. W. Wright. 1977. *Options for U.S. Energy Policy* (San Francisco: Institute for Contemporary Studies).

Cooley, W. W. and P. R. Lohnes. 1971. *Multivariate Data Analysis* (New York: Wiley).

Cortner, H. J. 1978. "Formulating and Implementing Energy Policy: The Inadequacy of the State Response," *Policy Studies Journal*, 7 (Autumn): 24–29.

Craig, P. P., J. Darmstadter and S. Rattien. 1976. "Social and Institutional Factors in Energy Conservation," in J. M. Hollander, ed., *Annual Review of Energy*, Vol. 1 (Palo Alto, CA: Annual Reviews): 535–51.

Darmstadter, J., J. Dunkerley and J. Alterman. 1977. *How Industrial Societies Use Energy: A Comparative Analysis* (Baltimore: Johns Hopkins University Press).

Davis, D. H. 1974. *Energy Politics* (New York: St. Martin's).

Downs, G. W., Jr. and L. B. Mohr. 1976. "Conceptual Issues in the Study of Innovation," *Administrative Science Quarterly*, 21 (December): 700–14.

Energy Policy Project of the Ford Foundation. 1974. *A Time to Choose* (Cambridge, MA: Ballinger).

Executive Office of the President. 1977. *The National Energy Plan* (Washington, D.C.: U.S. Government Printing Office).

Garvey, G. 1972. *Energy, Ecology, Economy* (New York: W. W. Morton).
tional Background to Environmental Administration," *Public Administration Review*, 35 (July/August): 328–33.

Garvey, G. 1972. *Energy, Ecology, Economy* (New York: W. W. Morton).

Goldstein, W. 1978. "The Politics of US Energy Policy," *Energy Policy*, 6 (September): 180–95.

Gordon, R. L. 1974. "Mythology and Reality in Energy Policy," *Energy Policy*, 2 (September): 189–203.

Gray, V. 1973. "Innovation in the States: A Diffusion Study," *American Political Science Review*, 67 (December): 1173–85.

Griffin, K. N. and R. B. Shelton. 1978. "Coal Severance Tax Policies in the Rocky Mountain States," *Policy Studies Journal*, 7 (Autumn): 29–40.

Hackbart, M. M. and J. W. Patton. 1976. "State Energy Programs: An Analysis of Innovation," *Review of Public Data Use*, 4 (November): 2–9.

Hall, T. A., I. L. White and S. C. Ballard. 1978. "Western States and National Energy Policy: The New States' Rights," *American Behavioral Scientist*, 22 (November/December): 191–212.

Hamilton, M. R. 1978. "Energy Policy and Changing Public-Private Sector Relations," *Policy Studies Journal*, 7 (Autumn): 90–96.

Harwood, C. C. 1977. *Using Land to Save Enegry* (Cambridge, Mass.: Ballinger).

Ingram, H. 1978. "Future Policy Directions: Challenges for the State," *American Behavioral Scientist*, 22 (November/December): 311–20.

Jones, C. O. 1974. "Federal-State-Local Sharing in Air Pollution Control," *Publius*, 4 (Winter): 70–73.

Kash, D. E., M. D. Devine, J. B. Freim, M. W. Gilliland, R. W. Rycroft and T. J. Wilbanks. 1976. *Our Energy Future: The Role of Research, Development, and Demonstration in Reaching a National Consensus on Energy Supply* (Norman: University of Oklahoma Press).

Kidman, R. B. and R. J. Barrett. 1977. "State Energy Flow Patterns," pp. 113–46 in R. A. Fazzolare and C. B. Smith, eds., *Energy Use Management*, Vol. 11 (New York: Pergamon).

Knowles, R. L. 1974. *Energy and Form: An Ecological Approach to Urban Growth*, (Cambridge, Mass.: MIT Press).

Kort, F. 1973. "Regression Analysis and Discriminant Analysis: An Application of R. A. Fisher's Theorem to Data in Political Science," *American Political Science Review*, 67 (June): 555–59.

Leonard, W. N. 1976. "In Search of an Energy Policy," *Challenge*, 19 (May/June): 52–56.

Lieber, H. 1975. *Federalism and Clean Waters* (Lexington, Mass.: D. C. Heath).

Light, A. R. 1976. "Federalism and the Energy Crisis: A View From the States," *Publius*, 6 (Winter): 81–96.

Lindberg, L. N. , ed., 1977. *The Energy Syndrome* (Lexington, Mass.: D. C. Heath).

Mancke, R. B. 1976. *Squeaking By: U.S. Energy Policy Since the Embargo* (New York: Columbia University Press).

Mancke, R. B. 1974. *The Failure of U.S. Energy Policy* (New York: Columbia University Press).

Mann, D. E. 1978. "Water Planning in the States of the Upper Basin of the Colorado River: Challenges and Prospects," *American Behavioral Scientist*, 22 (November/December): 237–76.

Mead, W. J. 1977. "An Economic Appraisal of President Carter's Energy Program," *Science*, 197 (July 22): 340–45.

Meadows, D. H., D. L. Meadows, J. R. Randers, and W. W. Behrens III. 1972. *The Limits to Growth* (New York: Universe).

Mills, J. and R. D. Woodson. 1976. "Energy Policy: A Test for Federalism," *Arizona Law Review*, 18: 405–51.

Mohr, L. B. 1969. "Determinants of Innovation in Organizations," *American Political Science Review*, 63 (March): 111–26.

Monroe, A. D. 1979. "Consistency Between Public Preferences and National Policy Decisions," *American Politics Quarterly*, 7 (January): 3–19.

Morgan, D. R. and W. Lyons. 1975. "Industrialization and Affluence Revisited: A Note on Socioeconomic Dimensions of the American States," *American Journal of Political Science*, 19 (May): 263–76.

Nau, H. R. 1978. "Continuity and Change in U.S. Foreign Energy Policy," *Policy Studies Journal*, 7 (Autumn): 121–31.

Olgayay, V. 1963. *Design With Climate: Bioclimatic Approach to Architectural Regionalism* (Princeton, N.J.: Princeton University Press).

Regens, J. L. 1978. "Energy Development, Environmental Protection, and Public Policy," *American Behavioral Scientist*, 22 (November/December): 175–90.

Regens, J. L. 1979. "Patterns of State Compliance with Federal Energy Conservation Guidelines," in R. A. Fazzolare and C. B. Smith, eds., *Changing Energy Use Futures* (New York: Pergamon).

Rogers, E. M. 1962. *Diffusion of Innovations* (New York: Free Press).

Rogers, E. M. and F. F. Shoemaker. 1971. *Communication of Innovations: A Cross-Cultural Approach* (New York: Free Press).

Rose, D. D. 1973. "National and Local Forces in State Politics: The Implications of Multi-Level Policy Analysis," *American Political Science Review*, 67 (December): 1162–73.

Rose, D. J. 1974. "Energy Policy in the U.S.," *Scientific American*, 230 (January): 20–29.

Savage, R. L. 1978. "Policy Innovativeness as a Trait of American States," *Journal of Politics*, 40 (February): 212–24.

Scheffer, W. F. 1975. "Intergovernmental Relations and Decentralization," pp. 3–24 in W. F. Scheffer, ed., *General Revenue Sharing and Decentralization* (Norman: University of Oklahoma Press).

Schipper, L. 1978. "The Swedish-U.S. Energy Use Comparison and Beyond: Summary," pp. 47–51 in J. Dunkerley, ed., *International Comparisons of Energy Consumption* (Washington, D.C.: Resources for the Future).

Sharkansky, I. 1972. *The Maligned States: Policy Accomplishments, Problems, and Opportunities* (New York: McGraw-Hill).

Socolow, R. H. 1975. "Energy Conservation in Housing: Concepts and Options," in R. W. Burchell and D. Listokin, eds., *Future Land Use/Energy, Environmental, and Legal Constraints* (New Brunswick, N.J.: Rutgers University Press).

Sundquist, J. 1969. *Making Federalism Work* (Washington, D.C.: Brookings Institution).

Szyliowicz, J. S. and B. E. O'Neill, eds. 1975. *The Energy Crisis and U.S. Foreign Policy* (New York: Praeger).

Tuve, G. 1976. *Energy, Environment, Population and Food: Our Four Interdependent Crises* (New York: Wiley).

U.S. Bureau of the Census. 1975. *Population Estimates and Projections*, Series P-25, No. 615 (November): (Washington, D.C.: U.S. Government Printing Office).

U.S. Bureau of the Census. 1976. *Statistical Abstract of the United States: 1976.* 97th ed. (Washington, D.C.: U.S. Government Printing Office).

U.S. Congress, Office of Technology Assessment. 1977. *Analysis of the Proposed National Energy Plan* (Washington, D.C.: U.S. Government Printing Office).

Walker, J. L. 1969. "The Diffusion of Innovations Among The American States," *American Political Science Review*, 63 (September): 880–99.

Weber, R. E. and W. R. Shaffer. 1972. "Public Opinion and American State Policy-Making," *Midwest Journal of Political Science*, 16 (November): 683–99.

White, I. L., M. A. Chartock, R. L. Leonard, S. C. Ballard, M. W. Gilliland, T. A. Hall, E. J. Malecki, E. B. Rappaport, R. K. Freed, G. D. Miller, F. S. Lagrone, C. P. Bartosh, D. B. Cabe, B. R. Eppright, D. C. Grossman, J. C. Lacy, T. D. Raye, J. D. Stuart, and M. L. Wilson. 1977. *Energy from the West: A Progress Report of a Technology Assessment of Western Energy Resources Development* (Washington, D.C.: U.S. Environmental Protection Agency).

Zaltman, G., R. Duncan and J. Holbek. 1973. *Innovations and Organizations* (New York: Wiley).

18

U.S. ENERGY POLICY AND
THE POLITICAL ECONOMY OF PARTICIPATION

David W. Orr

Energy policy is commonly regarded as a highly technical subject requiring expertise in nuclear physics and other recondite disciplines. Accordingly, discussions of energy matters are commonly restricted to the technical aspects of its conversion and use. In contrast, the thesis of this essay is that energy policy most directly involves politics and ethics. In particular, much of the debate of the past several years about a national energy policy concerns which risks we as a society accept, which we avoid, who decides, and by what process. These issues, however, are seldom addressed explicitly.

In the essay that follows I will first briefly discuss what is meant by the energy transition. Second, I will examine three broad perspectives on energy policy, comparing the goals and assumptions of each. Third, I will sketch an argument for extending participation in both policy-making and policy implementation. Undoubtedly, this is not the present state of affairs nor is it generally thought to be either feasible or desirable. Nevertheless, I will argue that greater public involvement in the energy sector would broaden the public interest, promote equity in the distribution of payoffs,

° I am indebted to John S. Nelson, Marvin S. Soroos, Edward J. Woodhouse, and Frank Munger for extensive comments on an earlier draft of this article.

increase public accountability, and improve social resilience, but at the cost of a more technologically modest future. My underlying assumption is that the transition to inexhaustible energy sources over the next 50-75 years is problematic because of the unprecedented magnitude of the change required and the risks it entails. In this respect the energy "crisis" foreshadows other issues on the horizon concerning the allocation of scarce resources, adaptation to—or the attempt to expand—environmental limits, and the management of technology. Although these issues will confront us with extraordinary challenges, our institutions, political processes, and reigning philosophies were designed to deal with simpler and less portentous problems.

While the focus of this essay is confined to the relatively narrow issue of energy policy, I fully agree with Robert Dahl's recent assertion that it is time to reappraise thoroughly our system of governance.[1] A good place to begin would be to consider the effects of technology on our theories of democracy. At present we have no theory describing the relationship between technology and the political system, nor do I offer one here. What I intend to do is to sketch an argument that the issues of energy policy and the technological choices entailed present more of a challenge to our political creativity than to our technical genius.

I

The present energy "crisis" involves the early stages of transition from a declining energy base to another, more abundant one. Previous transitions from wood to coal or from coal to oil have taken earlier and simpler societies not less than half a century.[2] The causes of the transitions include the depletion of one resource base and/or the development of the technological means to exploit another. Historical evidence indicates that the shift can involve great turmoil leading to social and political disintegration. We might reasonably assume that the greater the dependence on nonrenewable energy sources (e.g., fossil fuels) and the greater the demand for energy, the more difficult the change will be. The important variables include the amount of lead-time avaliable to create and

---

[1] Robert A. Dahl, "On Removing Certain Impediments to Democracy in The States," *Dissent* 25 (Summer 1978), 322.

[2] Earl Cook, *Man, Energy, Society* (San Francisco: W. H. Freeman and Company, 1976), 164-187; John U. Nef, "An Early Energy Crisis and Its Consequences," *Scientific American* 234 (November, 1977), 140-151.

disseminate energy conversion technologies, the degree of societal adaptability, and the quality of political leadership.

Briefly stated, the present energy crisis in the United States is attributable to the fact that the production of oil and natural gas has been declining since 1970 while consumption continues to rise. New discoveries—including North Slope Alaskan oil (amounting to less than two years of present consumption)—can delay but will not appreciably alter the trend.[3] The use of coal is problematic because of its effects on human health, ecology, climate, and the high capital costs of converting it to more acceptable forms.[4] Nuclear power—once heralded as the means to produce electricity "too cheap to meter" is faced with rising capital and operating costs, unanswered (and possibly unanswerable) questions about safety, waste storage, vulnerability to terrorism, and its effects on the proliferation of nuclear weapons.[5]

Given the limits to each of the four major existing energy sources (oil, natural gas, coal, and uranium), it is clear that the energy base of the mid twenty-first century will be radically different from that of the present. As nonrenewable sources decline they must be replaced by renewable and inexhaustible energy sources including decentralized solar energy, breeder reactors, fusion, and solar power beamed to earth from space satellites. The rate at which nonrenewable fossil fuels decline will vary, with recoverable supplies of oil declining much more rapidly than those of coal. Nevertheless the overall trend is clear, even if the timing is not. Because of the high capital costs of the renewable energy options, they are to a large extent mutually exclusive.[6]

[3] The analysis of oil and gas resources and reserves is explained in *Resources* 58 (March 1978). For varying estimates the reader may compare findings of the Workshop on Alternative Energy Strategies, *Energy: Global Prospects 1985-2000* (New York: McGraw-Hill, 1977), with that presented by David A. Stockman, "The Wrong War? The Case against a National Energy Policy," *The Public Interest* 53 (Fall, 1978), 3-44.

[4] John Harte and Alan Jassby, "Energy Technologies and Natural Environments: The Search for Compatibility," in *Annual Review of Energy*, Volume 3, ed. Jack M. Hollander (Palo Alto: Annual Review, Inc., 1978), 111-117.

[5] For contrasting views see Irvin C. Bupp and Jean-Claude Derian, *Lightwater: How the Nuclear Dream Dissolved* (New York: Basic Books, 1978); Walter C. Patterson, *Nuclear Power* (Baltimore: Penguin Books, 1976); Spurgeon M. Keeny, et. al., *Nuclear Power: Issues and Choices* (Cambridge, MA: Ballinger, 1977).

[6] See the discussion by M. H. Ross and R. H. Williams, *Energy and Economic Growth*. U. S. Congress, Joint Economic Committee. (Washington, D. C.: U. S. Government Printing Office, 1977), 52-57.

The present energy transition is qualitatively different from earlier ones in at least three ways. First, we are much more dependent on energy than were earlier societies so that the prospect of energy shortages strikes at the very foundation of technologically advanced countries. Second, energy policy is made in a context of high interdependence, in which the effects of national decisions spill across political, economic, and ecological boundaries. Third, ours will be the first attempt to manage politically the transition from one energy base to another. Prospects for success, therefore, are much more dependent upon political processes and bureaucratic structures than ever before.

II

At the risk of some distortion, we can distinguish three dominant perspectives in the current debate over U.S. energy policy.

The Supply Perspective

The first of these, the supply argument, holds that we must produce our way out of the crisis, because, "The country that runs on energy can't afford to run short." The energy crisis is defined as a problem of assuring an increasing supply of cheap energy and not one of scarcity, since, "The earth's remaining supplies of known petroleum are enormous and still growing."[7] Energy demand is further presumed to be highly inelastic and tightly linked to economic growth. The alternative to continually increasing energy supply is in Hans Bethe's words, "unemployment and recession, if not worse."[8] Conservation would not only reduce the standard of living, it would stall efforts to alleviate poverty and clean up the environment.[9] In this view government intervention on the demand side of the energy equation would abridge fundamental rights and undermine the free enterprise system.

For the advocates of the supply position, the principle actors in

[7] Richard B. Mancke, *The Failure of U. S. Energy Policy* (New York: Columbia University Press, 1974), 11; Stockman, "Wrong War," 10-19.

[8] Hans Bethe, "The necessity of Fission Power," *Scientific American* 234 (January, 1976), 31.

[9] Chase Manhattan Bank, *Energy Outlook in the United States to 1985* (New York, 1972). M. A. Wright (Chairman and Chief Executive, Exxon), "The Energy Future," Address at the University of Nebraska at Omaha (May 16, 1975).

energy policy are, in order of importance, corporations, government officials, and university experts. This group corresponds to
the elite that has controlled energy policy in the recent past and
which has been described by one analyst as a "small, stable, and
closed circle of . . . petroleum, or coal, or oil, or nuclear men . . .
having a strong supply orientation, a common faith in technology,
and an 'engineering mentality.' "[10] The exclusion of the public from
policy making is an extension of the belief that citizens cannot understand complex issues. When the public does get involved, it will
". . . usually result in a misallocation of resources" because the
public ". . . simply does not have the information to relate perception to reality."[11]

The goal for the advocates of this perspective is to achieve an
inexhaustible supply of cheap energy based initially on increasing
current production of fossil fuels and eventually on the breeder
reactor and nuclear fusion. If successful, we could ". . . make a
direct attack on entropy . . . or even reach for the alchemist's dream
of elemental transmutation."[12] If we fail, the future they depict
differs in no appreciable way from that commonly attributed to
"neo-malthusians." The goal, therefore, is so vital that it requires
us to court risks of technological catastrophes, the effects of which
would be comparable to what Bethe describes as "minor wars."[13]
This result presents us with a paradox. On the one hand, technologically advanced societies are portrayed as so inflexible that
any levelling or reduction in energy consumption would cause
disaster. On the other hand, these same societies are portrayed as
flexible enough to withstand the acknowledged certainty of periodic
catastrophes, including large oil spills, nuclear melt-downs, liquid
natural gas explosions and global climate change.[14]

The Conservation Perspective

A second view of the energy crisis has been described in the

[10] Leon Lindberg, "Comparing Energy Policies," in Leon Lindberg, ed.,
The Energy Syndrome (Lexington, Mass.: D. C. Heath, 1977) 334.

[11] Chauncey Starr, Richard Rudman, Chris Whipple, "Philosophical Basis for
Risk Analysis," in *Annual Review of Energy*, Volume 1, ed. Jack M. Hollander,
(Palo Alto, Calif.: Annual Reviews, Inc., 1976), 635.

[12] Sterling Brubaker, *In Command of Tomorrow* (Baltimore: Johns Hopkins
University Press, 1975), 5.

[13] Bethe, "Necessity," 31.

[14] Herman Kahn, William Brown, Leon Martel, *The Next 200 Years* (New
York: William Morrow Co., 1976), 163-180.

"technical fix" scenario of the Ford Foundation's Energy Policy Project and later in the Carter Administration's National Energy Plan (NEP).[15] The key proposition is that the United States wastes from 30-50 percent of its total energy budget.[16] Sweden, by contrast, uses half as much energy per capita as the United States, and Switzerland only a third as much.[17] Conservation, in the words of the NEP, is "the cleanest and cheapest source of new energy" and is essential if we are to avoid the hazards of dependence on foreign sources of energy and the possibility of energy wars.

The principal assumption of those emphasizing conservation is that the historic tie between energy consumption and economic growth can be de-coupled, which need not exact a penalty in reduced economic growth.[18] Marc Ross and Robert Williams, for instance, argue that we can reach zero energy growth by 1985 while maintaining comfortable rates of economic growth thereafter.[19] Another recent study concluded, "It will be technically feasible in 2010 to use roughly a total amount of energy as low as that used today and still provide a higher level of amenities, even with a total population increasing 35%."[20] The NEP was not as optimistic, but nevertheless aimed to maintain high rates of economic growth while reducing the annual increase in energy demand to less than two percent. Despite varying estimates about the price elasticity of energy demand, each of these studies assumes that an increase in the price of energy combined with the removal of institutional

[15] Ford Foundation Energy Policy Project, *A Time to Choose* (Cambridge, Mass.: Ballinger, 1974); Executive Office of the President, *The National Energy Plan* (Washington, D. C.: 1977).

[16] Robert Socolow, "The Coming Age of Conservation," in *Annual Review of Energy*, Volume 2, ed. Jack M. Hollander (Palo Alto, Calif.: Annual Reviews, Inc., 1977), 239-289; also Denis Hayes, *Rays of Hope* (New York: W. W. Norton Co., 1977), 77-88.

[17] Lee Schipper and Allan J. Lichtenberg, "Efficient Energy Use and Well-Being: The Swedish Example," *Science* 194 (3 December, 1976), 1001-1013.

[18] See for example, "Energy Trends of Interest," *Institute for Energy Analysis News*, Oak Ridge Institute for Energy Analysis (June, 1978); Also Lee Schipper, "Raising the Productivity of Energy Utilization," in *Annual Review of Energy*, 1976, 455-517.

[19] M. H. Ross and R. H. Williams, *Energy and Economic Growth*, 2.

[20] Demand and Conservation Panel for the Committee on Nuclear and Alternative Energy Systems, "U. S. Energy Demand: Some Low Energy Futures," *Science* 200 (14 April, 1978), 151; see also John S. Steinhart, *A Low Energy Scenario For the United States: 1975-2050*, Report 83, (Madison, WI: Institute for Environmental Studies, 1977).

barriers will reduce energy demand and lead to the emergence of an energy efficient and more labor intensive economy.

In contrast to the emphasis on corporate initiatives in the first approach, the catalyst for energy efficiency is the federal government. In the words of the NEP, "The energy problem can be effectively addressed only by a government that accepts responsibility for dealing with it comprehensively."[21] Government intervention is necessary to ensure that energy is priced at its replacement level; to provide consumer incentives for conservation (e.g., tax credits, extension programs, low interest loans); and to conduct research on energy technologies not otherwise developed in the private sector. The conservation approach is epitomized by the creation of a ten billion dollar Department of Energy and a growing body of federal energy efficiency standards in transportation, residential, and industrial sectors.[22]

The goal of conservation is that of an energy-efficient society in the near term, to allow time to build a more secure energy base for the long term.[23] To this end, it is essential to eliminate obvious

[21] *The National Energy Plan,* 26.

[22] Particularly in the Energy Policy and Conservation Act (1975) and the Energy Conservation and Production Act (1976).

[23] Lee Schipper, in "Raising the Productivity of Energy," 457, for example, defines conservation as a strategy of adjusting and optimizing energy to reduce energy output (or well-being) while holding constant or reducing total costs of providing the output from these systems. Estimates of efficiency, however, vary according to the standard used to measure it. Previous standards of energy efficiency were based on the first law of thermodynamics which gives a ratio of the total energy input or work or heat output. Since energy can neither be created nor destroyed this law requires that we account for the total energy that is converted into work or heat and that which is dissipated as waste. Hence,

$$\frac{\text{energy converted to usable form}}{\text{total energy input.}}$$

The American Physical Society in 1975 recommended that efficiency standards ought, however, to be based on the Second law of thermodynamics which holds that energy, while not destroyed, flows in only one direction and cannot be recycled without incurring a higher energy cost than that in the energy recovered. Second law efficiency standards would encourage the user to match energy in quantity and quality with the quantity and quality needed to perform a certain task. Hence,

$$\frac{\text{minimum energy required by 2nd law}}{\text{energy actually consumed.}}$$

sources of waste and to utilize technical innovations and price incentives to maximize the productivity of energy. Adoption of the conservation ethic, however, entails no sweeping change either in lifestyles beyond those commonly described as "cosmetic;"[24] or in the goal of economic growth.[25] The technological goals of the conservation approach evidenced by the Department of Energy's research and development expenditures do not differ much from those of the first perspective. Between 1978 and 2000 they propose a combination of conservation and greater reliance on nuclear power and coal. Beyond 2000, they propose to phase in more exotic technologies, including coal gasification, the breeder reactor, and nuclear fusion.

In addition to the risks of economic dislocation caused by interruption of energy supplies, proponents of conservation warn of the impending exhaustion of oil reserves, mounting balance-of-payments problems, and the possibility of energy wars. President Carter has also warned that failure to conserve will lead to ". . . an economic, social, and political crisis that will threaten our free institutions."[26]

It is difficult to argue against the need for conservation and increased efficiency, but it is entirely possible that conservation may be too little, too late. Given the historic relationship between energy use and GNP, we must admit the possibility that the prospect of zero energy growth could lead to severe economic hardships.[27] Even if one assumes that supplies will be sufficient to meet demand for the next two decades, rising prices could still cause massive hardships. In short, the transition to a more energy efficient society could be far more traumatic and uncertain than President Carter and conservation enthusiasts suggest.

The Energetics Perspective

Drawing from a diverse array of thinkers, we can outline a third perspective which asserts a causal relationship between the energy basis of a society and its social, political, and economic structures. The energy crisis, in this view, is more than a problem of inadequate supply or inefficiency, it is a fundamental social and cultural crisis.

[24] See Socolow, "The Coming Age," 256-272.
[25] National Energy Plan, ix.
[26] New York Times, (November 11, 1977).
[27] Earl T. Hayes reaches this dismal conclusion in "Energy Resources Available to the United States, 1885-2000," Science 203 (19 January, 1979), 233-239.

The "problem" of energy is one of creating an energy supply system consistent with democratic values and with the physical laws governing energy.

The basic premise of the third perspective—that society is subject to the laws of thermodynamics—dates at least to the work of the British chemist turned economist, Frederick Soddy. Writing in 1922, Soddy argued that energy flows were causally linked to social and economic development.[28] Fred Cottrell expanded this theme in his *Energy and Society,* arguing, "The energy available to man limits what he *can* do and influences what he *will* do."[29] He developed the idea that the control of surplus or net energy is the key to understanding social stratification and cultural evolution. Increased energy use also creates costs including the concentration of political power, the consequent decline of democracy, and a greater possibility of international conflict.[30] Similar themes appear in the work of anthropologist Leslie White, who argued in an essay in 1949 that cultural evolution depends upon energy use per capita and the efficiency with which a society harnesses it. Although expanding energy use motivates cultural development, according to White, it again leads to the concentration of political power and international conflict.[31]

Energy determinism is even more pronounced in the work of Howard Odum, who maintains that the source of energy and its rate of flow determine societal values and the superstructure of economic and political institutions.[32] Societies—like natural systems —can be mapped as energy flows and ought to be similarly patterned to stress decentralization, diversity, and redundancy. Both natural and social systems develop until their "maintenance and

---

[28] Frederick Soddy, *Cartesian Economics* (London: Hendersons, 1922); for a brief review of Soddy and other "global" theorists, see Laura Nader and Stephen Beckerman, "Energy as it relates to the Quality and Style of Life" in *Annual Review of Energy,* 1978, 3-10.

[29] Fred Cottrell, *Energy and Society* (New York: McGraw-Hill, 1955), 2.

[30] *Ibid.,* 227-240; 267.

[31] Leslie A. White, "Energy and the Evolution of Culture," in *The Science of Culture,* ed. Leslie White, (New York: Grove Press, 1949), 388.

[32] Howard T. Odum, *Environment, Power, and Society* (New York: Wiley-Interscience, 1971), 34. See also Charles J. Ryan, "The Choices in the Next Energy and Social Revolution," paper presented to the 1977 Conference on Growth Policy, The Woodlands, Texas, October 1977); and Richard Newbold Adams, *Energy and Structure* (Austin: University of Texas Press, 1975), 279-315.

organizational costs equal their energy budgets."[33] Beyond this point, all systems decline. Thus in nature and in human affairs, energy efficiency is related to stability and survival. A second and related assumption is that energy conversion is limited by the second law of thermodynamics. To speed the pace of economic development is to hasten the creation of entropy or social disorder. In this view, the appropriate question is not whether to strive for a steady state, but how best to prolong a declining one.[34]

Amory Lovins' *Soft Energy Paths* also reflects the energetics approach, while deemphasizing its assumption of determinism. Along with the first two perspectives Lovins states that government must initiate an appropriate energy policy, but then argues somewhat ambiguously, for widespread public involvement in policy making. Thus: "Some action by central and local government is necessary to get the ball rolling, but then its mostly downhill." Elsewhere he states, "Ordinary people are qualified and responsible to make these energy policy choices . . . through the democratic political process."[35]

The goal for Lovins and others is the creation of a solar-based, decentralized, egalitarian, and participatory society along lines proposed by Jefferson, Kropotkin, and E. F. Schumacher. Energy policy is regarded as a lever to move society toward a more sustainable, if less extravagant, basis while enhancing equity and participation.

Despite the obvious appeal of the soft path, Lovins is not describing a political process, but an economic one triggered by decisions of the central government, which is not policy making as normally defined, but rather economic behavior and technological diffusion with political implications. He has to some degree depoliticized energy policy by consigning it to the realm of consumer choice. Whether this process will catalyze substantial democratization beyond the energy sector as claimed depends on who produces, distributes, and owns soft technologies, and on the degree to which energy flows are causally linked to political structures and behavior. Lovins may be entirely correct in concluding that the hard path will lead to economic, ecological, and social disaster, but

[33] Adams, *Energy and Structure,* 231.

[34] See, for example, Nicholas Georgescu-Roegen, *The Entropy Law and the Economic Process* (Cambridge, Mass.: Harvard University Press, 1974), 292-315.

[35] Amory B. Lovins, *Soft Energy Paths* (Cambridge, Mass.: Ballinger, 1977), 152; also Lovins, "Cost-Risk-Benefits Assessments in Energy Policy," *George Washington Law Review* 45 (August 1977), 941-943.

it does not automatically follow that the soft path will be a Jeffersonian utopia except by comparison.

In any event we are left to wonder how the choice of the soft path might be made. Will the elite that dominates energy policy accept a course of action that would jeopardize its position? Alternatively, would the public, given a choice between hard and soft paths, choose the latter? The advertised virtues of the soft path, including self-reliance, voluntary simplicity, ecological modesty, and neighborliness have not been tested in either the political arena or in the marketplace, Jerry Brown and E. F. Schumacher notwithstanding.

III

Each of the three positions offers different diagnoses of the crisis and different prescriptions for its resolution, as suggested in figure one. But advocates of each view agree that the situation is unprecedented for at least five reasons: (1) the great dependence of the United States on the uninterrupted flow of cheap energy; (2) the foreseeable exhaustion of easily exploitable supplies of oil and natural gas; (3) the long lead-time necessary to create a new energy base; (4) the likely irreversibility of the choices; and (5) the large-scale risks entailed in the decision.

There are, however, two areas of substantial disagreement. The first concerns the type and extent of risk involved in energy policy. The proponents of the supply perspective are peroccupied with economic risks caused by an interruption in energy supply. Advocates of the second approach have a longer list which includes, in addition to economic disruption, the problems of weapons proliferation and excessive dependence on foreign oil suppliers. From the energetics perspective, the dominant risks are those of resource exhaustion, ecological damage, climate change, and technological accidents such as oil spills, nuclear melt-downs, and liquid natural gas explosions. It would be presumptuous and beyond the scope of this paper to say how these risks ought to be weighed, but clearly we do not have the option of a risk free energy policy.

This is not to say, however, that all possible risks ought to be regarded as equally plausible. A wise choice in these circumstances will require both an open, unbiased decision process and a calculus that enables us to distinguish risks to survival from those to particular interests or to various social patterns. We must also

FIGURE 1

	1 Supply	II Conservation	III Energetics
Definition of problem	inadequate supply	energy waste	energy as cultural-social problem
Assumptions	energy growth continued (energy-economic growth linked)	energy growth slowed (energy-economic growth can be decoupled)	energy determinism entropic limits to energy conservation end of cheap energy
Primary Actors	energy corporations (Laissez Faire)	government (Leviathan)	public (Jeffersonian)
Goal/values	inexhaustible cheap energy no value change	near term: efficiency long term: inexhaustible supply small value change	decentralized solar based society radical value change
Risks to be avoided	economic disruption	balance of payments, dependence, energy wars	technological accidents resource exhaustion climate change
Ultimate Energy Source:	breeder/fusion	conservation technology-breeder/fusion	decentralized-solar, wind biomass

learn to weigh risks with allowance for the unknown, in both particular and aggregate dimensions. We currently concentrate on the risk potential from individual energy facilities, while ignoring the accumulation of risk from all sources. Presumably we might prefer to disperse some risks geographically or temporally in order to diffuse the total risk burden.[36]

Finally, we need a systematic way to identify, assess, and implement alternatives to risk-prone technologies before foreclosing op-

[36] David W. Orr, "Catastrophe and Social Order," *Human Ecology* 7 (March, 1979), 41-52; See also William W. Lowrance, *Of Acceptable Risk: Science and the Determination of Safety* (Los Altos, CA: William Kaufmann, Inc., 1976).

tions that hindsight may show were superior. For example, recent
studies demonstrating the feasibility and desirability of solar power
—including those by the Office of Technology Assessment, the
state of California, and the Department of Energy—come only after
the United States has sunk over 100 billion dollars into the nuclear
option, including some 17 to 24 billion dollars in federal research
funds and subsidies.[37]   In contrast, solar power has lagged partly
because it has had to compete with fuels priced below their replacement costs and because it has lacked an organized, highly-funded
interest group pushing its adoption despite the conclusion of the
Paley Commission in 1952 that solar power represented a viable,
large-scale source of energy that could meet as much as 25 percent
of U.S. energy demand by 1977.[38]   Typically, the identification of
policy alternatives is dominated by well-intrenched interests with
financial or professional stakes in the outcome so that debate is restricted to what is narrowly practical.

A second—and for our purposes more important—point of disagreement among the three perspectives concerns differences over
what can be broadly described as the decision-making process.   Advocates of the first perspective favor a corporate dominated approach to energy policy.   Freed from excessive government restraints
the energy market will tend toward an optimal balance between
supply and demand.   The conservation approach, in contrast, calls
for a larger government role in the energy sector in order to control
prices, manage research, limit demand, and protect long term societal
interests.   Greater government control is regarded as essential to
remedy deficiencies of imperfect markets and extend control into
areas where markets are inoperative or inappropriate.   Advocates
of the third perspective propose changes that would alter the policy
process in order to enhance public involvement.   From their perspective, utilization of diffuse solar energy promotes democracy
because it is not easily monopolized.   In this view Democracy is incompatible with certain energy technologies that are large-scale,

---

[37] Office of Technology Assessment, *Application of Solar Technology to
Today's Energy Needs* (Washington, D. C., 1978); The SolarCal Staff,
"Towards a Solar California" (1978), mimeo; U. S. Department of Energy,
Distributed Energy Systems in California's Future (Washington, D. C., 1978);
Council on Environmental Quality, *The Good News about Energy* (Washing-
ton: U. S. Government Printing Office, 1979).

[38] William Paley, Resources for Freedom: *Foundation for Growth and
Security* (Washington, D. C.: U. S. Government Printing Office, 1952).

complex, capital-intensive, risk-prone, environmentally destructive, and subject to sabotage and terrorism.[39]

The idea that technology has anything to do with democracy is itself an interesting, if not altogether novel hypothesis. But the argument also suggests that democratic participation is necessary to preserve a margin of error between expanding technological capabilities and environmental carrying capacity. This view stands in marked contrast to previous theories of democracy which were based on the belief that participation was good for the citizen or vaguely related to the health of the polity, but not important in any more functional way.

To be taken seriously, this argument must show that participation either raises the quality of public decisions or minimizes the possibility of very bad ones, or both. Although advocates of energetics perspective make no explicit case to this effect, I will argue that both are supportable if not definitive conclusions. First, however, we will consider three arguments customarily made against participatory democracy.

The Case against Participation

The first of these arguments—based largely on studies of voting behavior—shows that a high percentage of the public typically does not and presumably will not participate in electoral politics. The turnout for presidential elections seldom exceeds 60 percent, and the percentage drops sharply for state and local elections. But evidence drawn from voting studies is inconclusive. In contrast to the interpretation that the public is indifferent to politics, one might plausibly explain low turnout and non-participation as a function of (1) the lack of opportunity for meaningful involvement; (2) the lack of genuine choice; (3) the understandable belief that the political system cannot solve problems anyway; (4) the unequal distribution of wealth and consequent feelings of "low efficacy"; or (5) some combination of the four.

Moreover, studies of participation understate the extent and intensity of political involvement by generally excluding acts such as

[39] These points are made forcefully by Lovins, *Soft Energy Paths*, 147-159. The civil implications of nuclear power are described by Russel W. Ayres, "Policing Plutonium: The Civil Liberties Fallout," *Harvard Civil Rights— Civil Liberties Law Review* 10(1975), 369-443.

protest and demonstration which are not as easy to observe and measure as acts of voting.[40] The public-interest movement manifested in activism on civil rights, peace, consumerism, environmental quality, women's liberation and nuclear safety resulted from large numbers of people acting outside the normal political channels but with large effect on voting patterns and government policy. In each case, awareness of important and otherwise neglected problems was heightened, and public policy was often markedly improved in ways that are not apparent if we concentrate on voting behavior alone.

A second argument against participation is that greater participation would lead to inefficiency and chaos. According to some pluralists, not only does a sizeable majority of the public abstain from political activity but this condition is itself a necessary requisite of democratic stability. Mass involvement would signal not only the breakdown of consensus, but would also overburden the machinery of government with excessive demands. Further, it would lower the equality of public decisions because the masses lack the knowledge essential for informed opinions on most issues. Public participation therefore, is mediated through organized interest groups pursuing their own self-interest.

Samuel Huntington has taken the proposition further to argue that democracy is inherently unstable and leads to the "breakdown of traditional means of social control, a delegitimation of political and other forms of authority, and an overload of demands on government, exceeding its capacity to respond."[41] The solution Huntington proposes involves the expansion of central authority and the consequent reduction of citizen participation. For very different reasons, Robert Heilbroner and William Ophuls reach more drastic conclusions which call for the creation of authoritarian governments to resolve the coming crisis of scarcity.[42] Likewise, others, including Physicist Alvin Weinberg, propose "Faustian bargains"

[40] See the discussion by William R. Schonfield, "The Meaning of Democratic Participation," *World Politics* 28 (October, 1975), 143.

[41] Michel J. Crozier, Samuel P. Huntington, Joji Watanuki, *The Crisis of Democracy* (New York: New York University Press, 1975), 8; see also Samuel P. Huntington, "Postindustrial Politics: How Benign Will It Be?" *Comparative Politics* 6 (January, 1974), 163-192.

[42] For discussion of this view see David W. Orr and Stuart Hill, "Leviathan, the Open Society, and the Crisis of Ecology," *The Western Political Quarterly* 31 (December, 1978), 457-469.

between society and scientists to resolve energy and resource problems.[43]

The pluralist assumption that democracy can work only as long as a large majority of citizens remains apathetic and dependent upon elites is ironic to say the least. More important, elitist theories of democracy rest on a model of "rational" behavior which not only suffers from normative anemia, but may be useful as a description only under particular conditions which are seldom specified.[44] From such assumptions it is a small step for political scientists to become apologists for the status quo and for a system that, in one critic's words, entails "elite domination of the major issues salient to elites, severe limitations on protest group activity, and manipulation of the terms on which issues arise and are processed."[45] Among the casualties of the pluralist theory are the concept of the politically active citizen and the notion of a transcendent public interest as something other than a haphazard outcome of collective greed.

Finally, the belief that the survival of democratic government requires greater reliance on elites strikes a curious note in the wake of recent exhibits of their ineptitude or worse in the Vietnam War, Watergate, a medly of corporate scandals, Koreagate, the ongoing debacle of uncontrolled inflation, Three Mile Island, and the energy crisis itself. It is hard to disagree with Walter Dean Burnham's assertion that the present distrust of elites—the "democratic distemper" that Huntington and others so detest—is in very large part ". . . the natural outgrowth of decisions made by activist elites in domestic and international arenas and not by predatory publics."[46]

A third and related argument against extending participation is that many policy issues—especially those concerning technology—are too complex for the public. Issues involving highly technical tradeoffs require the specialized knowledge of policy analysts, scientists, and technologists so that democracy and expertise work at

[43] Alvin M. Weinberg, "Social Institutions and Nuclear Energy," *Science* 177 (7 July, 1972), 27-34.

[44] For critiques see, for example, Jack L. Walker, "A Critique of the Elitist Theory of Democracy," *American Political Science Review* 60 (June, 1966), 285-295; also C. B. Macpherson, *The Life and Times of Liberal Democracy* (New York: Oxford University Press, 1977), 77-92.

[45] Michael Lipsky, "Introduction," in Murray Edelman, *Political Language* (New York: Academic Press, 1977), xviii.

[46] Walter Dean Burnham, "Reflections on the Crisis of Democracy in the United States," *Trialogue* (Fall, 1976), 8.

cross purposes. There can be no question about the need for greater expertise in the policy-making process. The problem is how to strike and maintain a balance between public control and the need for specialized knowledge. The danger of overemphasizing the latter is that expertise leads to the eventual expulsion of the nonexpert citizen from the policy arena, since, in Robert Dahl's words, "Decisions as to means can also determine ends. Democracy only for general ends and meritocracy for means will soon become meritocracy for both means and ends."[47] Computer expert Joseph Weizenbaum is even more blunt in arguing that computerized expertise leads to ". . . authoritarianism based on expertise . . . pressed into the service of rationalizing, supporting, and sustaining the most conservative, indeed reactionary, ideological components of the current zeitgeist."[48]

Moreover, in many cases the nature of the issue is unclear so that it is debatable which experts are relevant. For example, nuclear power is generally regarded as the proper domain of the physicist. If, however, the fundamental issues in this instance are those of ethics, persons so trained ought to be given priority in the policy debate. In either case, once having assigned a problem by default or otherwise to a set of experts the discussion thereafter is strongly influenced by their particular disciplinary and methodological biases. Economists' use of cost-benefit analysis, for example, may cause distortions because of its inability to deal with incommensurable values, soft variables, holistic-ecological issues, questions of justice, and the interests of future generations.[49] In such cases the

---

[47] Dahl, "On Removing Certain Impediments," 323.

[48] Joseph Weizenbaum, *Computer Power and Human Reason* (San Francisco: W. H. Freeman Co., 1976), 250.

[49] Laurence Tribe, for example, has argued that cost-benefit analysis cannot deal with ". . . three categories of values and interests . . . those too widely diffused over space (or too incrementally affected over time) to be strongly championed by any single client of a policy analysis; those associated only with persons not yet existing (future generations); and those not associated with persons at all (for example, the rights of wild animals)." Laurence H. Tribe, "Policy Science: Analysis or Ideology?" *Philosophy and Public Affairs* 2 (Fall, 1972), 102; Peter Junger's critique of cost-benefit analysis applied to issues of water pollution is even more comprehensive and damning. Peter D. Junger, "A Recipe for Bad Water: Welfare Economics and Nuisance Law Mixed Well," *Case Western Reserve Law Review* 27 (Fall, 1976), 3-163; see also Eric Ashby, *Reconciling Man with the Environment* (Stanford: Stanford University Press, 1978), 29-57; Ida Hoos, *Systems Analysis in Public Policy* (Berkeley: University of California Press, 1974); Amory B. Lovins, "Cost-Risk-Benefit Assessments."

demand for rigor can lead to rigor mortis, and the avoidance of hard choices and human dilemmas in the vain hope that technique can absolve us from the responsibility of decision. Taken to its extreme, the dominance of expertise represents the triumph of method over politics and a means of avoiding public debate by disguising critical decisions beneath the rhetoric of necessity and economic efficiency.

Finally, even the claim to expertise in social policy is contestable.[50] Experts can improve the quality of public choices by gathering information, identifying conceptual problems, and by describing the probable consequences of particular policies. But many issues concern value choices for which there are no experts. In these circumstances the attempt of the "value neutral" policy analyst to imitate the physical sciences by compulsive quantification and the use of complex models represents, in Almond and Genco's words, a "historical deviation, a flirtation with mistaken metaphors" that assumes a Newtonian clockwork social universe.[51]

The pluralist critique of participation shares with policy analysis and the supply perspective a limited and distorted view of human behavior. Both the model of economic man and its derivative— the rational voter—reduce the citizen to an apathetic, self-indulgent, dull-witted, incompetent. Not only does this assumption tend to promote the very behavior that it purports only to describe, but in so doing serves as a further justification for even more elite control. Elites—whether energy company executives, technical experts, pluralist leaders, or policy analysts—thus have a vested interest of sorts in mass dependence and incompetence. The supply perspective, pluralism, and policy analysis also share the assumption that political questions can be transmuted into rational decisions analogous to market choices. But the public cannot register a preference for options not offered in the market, nor can there be a purely rational basis for value choices.[52]

---

[50] Alasdair MacIntyre, "Ideology, Social Science, and Revolution," *Comparative Politics* 5 (April 1973), 334-335; see also the provocative discussion by Paul Feyerabend, *Science in a Free Society* (London: NLB Publishers, 1978), 96-107.

[51] Gabriel A. Almond and Stephen J. Genco, "Clouds, Clocks, and the Study of Politics," *World Politics* 29 (July, 1977), 522.

[52] See the discussion of values in Richard J. Bernstein, *The Restructuring of Social and Political Theory* (Philadelphia: University of Pennsylvania Press, 1976), 45-54.

FIGURE 2

PARTICIPATION

		High	Low
Energy Systems:	Soft	Lovins' Model	elite imposed solar society; traditional societies
	Hard	Public rejects soft path Faustian Bargains	Present U. S., Supply Perspective

The Case for Participation

Classical theorists of democracy generally argued that participation contributed to the moral development and independence of the citizen as well as to the integration of the political community, but not necessarily to the enhancement of public policy. In this section we will consider four arguments supporting greater public involvement as a means to improve the quality of energy policy. In the first three arguments participation implies involvement in policymaking in ways ranging from merely improving public access to information, to means that channel information about public attitudes to appropriate authorities, to a genuine sharing of power. As Burnham describes, participation in this sense implies

. . . the emergence of mass demands on policy elites . . . with the end in view of relegitimating the political system by giving people an authentic share in shaping their own lives and destinies. [It also implies the] recasting of the political structure itself, the curbing of the power of 'technetronic' elites both official and private to overwhelm the lives of non-elites and at some point coming to terms with the need to remold the political economy along more genuinely participatory lines.[53]

The fourth argument derived from the energetics perspective holds that participation should also mean widespread public involvement in policy implementation through the decentralization of the energy production system. Although the arguments overlap, it is important to note, as suggested in Figure 2, that participation in the former sense does not automatically lead to the acceptance of

[53] Walter Dean Burnham, "Reflections," 8.

soft, participatory technologies since one can imagine an authoritarian or elite-imposed solar society. The point is that greater participation in either sense need not presume the other.

The case for increasing participation in both ways can be stated as four overlapping and partially asymmetrical propositions. The first with antecedents in the work of John Stuart Mill, maintains that participation alters the outlook and behavior of the participant and encourages awareness of the wider public interest. Participation then presumably increases the sense of political "efficacy," raises the level of knowledge about public affairs, expands the sense of community, and helps the individual relate private to public needs.[54]

Empirical evidence about the effects of greater public involvement in energy policy, however, is at best only suggestive. Aside from anti-nuclear or pro-solar demonstrations, there is only a handful of cases—mostly European—in which the public has been drawn into the policy process in any form. In most of these cases, participation broadened the concerns normally associated with energy policy and was often expressed as opposition to nuclear energy. Regardless of the pros and cons of the nuclear debate, public-interest groups consistently dissented from the view that the issue of energy supply ought to override other elements of the public interest. Whether these concerns are "rational" or whether they accurately reflect the public interest need not trouble us. The point is simply that participation has tended to widen the concept of public interest in the energy sector.

The best known example is the case of Sweden where in January, 1974, the government initiated a campaign of study groups organized by political parties, labor unions, and religious groups to debate issues relating to nuclear power.[55] The use of such groups in Sweden had roots extending back into the nineteenth century and had been originally devised as a method to encourage democratic participation. In the debate over nuclear power, the focus of the

[54] Carole Pateman, *Participation and Democratic Theory* (New York: Cambridge University Press, 1970), 110.

[55] Dorothy Nelkin and Michael Pollak, "The Politics of Participation and the Nuclear Debate in Sweden, The Netherlands, and Austria," *Public Policy* 25 (Summer 1977), 333-357; see also the discussion of participation in nuclear politics in the U. S. by Nelkin and Susan Fallows, "The Evolution of the Nuclear Debate" in *Annual Review of Energy*, 1978, 275-312; Mans Lonroth, "Swedish Energy Policy: Technology in the Political Process" in *The Energy Syndrome*, 255-284.

study groups quickly expanded to include issues such as the optimum level of energy demand, a comparison of different energy sources, and questions of safety. Although the government had initiated the study groups as a means to manipulate public opinion in order to develop support for its nuclear program, these groups tended to express strong reservations about nuclear energy. Influenced by this reaction, the government in March of 1975 presented an energy policy to the parliament that reduced the nuclear component, and proposed a decrease in the energy growth rate to two percent between 1975 and 1985, and a zero growth rate after 1990. In order to achieve these goals the government proposed higher taxes on energy, grants for retrofitting, and a large research and development program in alternative sources. Subsequently, energy issues—particularly nuclear power—played some (if undetermined) role in the defeat of the Palme government.

Conclusions from the Swedish case are limited by the fact that the process lasted for only one year and included only an estimated 80,000 (or about one percent) of the population. Moreover, the study group technique was conducted in a relatively small, homogeneous society with no major cleavages and depended upon government initiation and response since the groups themselves had no inherent power. Still, participation affected public attitudes enough to dislodge government policy from its predominately high-technology, supply orientation. In Lindberg's words: "Alternative policy criteria penetrated policy debate at the highest levels; the mass public has been mobilized and made more aware of the larger stakes of energy policy; and decisionmaking at the bureaucratic-technocratic levels has been made permeable to new actors and new perception of the problem."[56]

In other European cases, including the citizens' initiative movement in Germany and the November, 1978, Austrian referendum on nuclear energy, public involvement led to somewhat similar results —though by different processes. The rapid growth of anti-nuclear attitudes through locally organized citizens' initiatives in West Germany is particularly striking.[57] Despite having different goals, most German groups have tended to express highly informed and

[56] Leon Lindberg, "Comparing Energy Policies: Policy Implications," in *The Energy Syndrome*, 255-284.

[57] Volkmer Lauber, "A Role for Citizens in Environmental Policy: The United States, France, and Germany," (paper presented at the Third Capon Springs Conference, Arlington, VA., September 13-15, 1978), 11-14.

militant opposition to nuclear power. Although the membership of these groups exceeds that of all German political parties combined, they have not been given formal standing by the government so that is it unclear what impact they will have on West German energy policy. Similarly in the Austrian referendum of November, 1978, slightly more than half (50.5 percent) voted against nuclear power.[58] As with referenda on nuclear power in the United States in 1976 and 1978, however, the outcome was the result of the interplay of nuclear opposition, economic issues, and politics.

On the basis of the limited evidence available, one can draw only suggestive conclusions about the effects of participation. In the Swedish case, the public was involved in a relatively coherent examination of the issues of energy policy within the context of small discussion groups. In the Austrian case and in state referenda in the United States, the public was given no opportunity to debate the wider context of energy policy and could only vote on narrow issues relating to nuclear power. Judgments about public attitudes expressed in the nine state referenda on nuclear energy in the U.S. are difficult to make because of the different ways the issue appeared on the ballot and because of the distorting effects of the large amounts of money spent by the pro-nuclear side.[59] Nevertheless, despite differences in the nature and extent of public involvement, participation has led to a discernible broadening of the concept of public interest applied to the energy sector.

Even if one concedes that greater participation alters perceptions of the public interest, it does not necessarily follow that the quality of energy policy (however defined) is thereby improved. Indeed some have argued that the "emotional" anti-nuclear views characteristic of participatory movements have lowered it considerably. The second proposition partially counters this criticism by holding that participation would promote greater equity in the distribution of costs and benefits of energy policy and thereby enhance social stability. Under ideal circumstances those receiving the benefits of a policy should pay its full costs or render mutually agreed compensation to those who do, which is not the case at present in the

[58] Walter Patterson, "Austria's Nuclear Referendum," *Bulletin of Atomic Scientists* 35 (January, 1979), 6-7.

[59] For a review of U. S. referenda see Lettie McSpadden Wenner and Manfred W. Wenner, "Nuclear Policy and Public Participation," *American Behavioral Scientist* 22 (October-December, 1978), 282-308.

energy sector where the lack of participation has contributed to a marked divergence of costs and benefits. This is apparent in the use of fossil fuels in which uncompensated environmental, health, and social costs of extraction, combustion, and transmission are allocated to predominantly rural areas while the benefits in the form of profits and high quality fuels or electricity go to urban areas. Similarly those living near uranium mines, nuclear plants, reprocessing facilities, or waste disposal sites are involuntarily exposed to higher risks of accident and the chronic effects of low level radiation. The lack of participation conceals a system of winners and losers. The winners are cooled, coiffured, and entertained electrically, while the losers are stripmined, irradiated, and polluted. The argument also applies to the divergence of costs and benefits between generations. The benefits of present nuclear reactors, for example, will be confined to the next 30-40 years, but the costs and risks of dismantling reactors and storing nuclear wastes will be borne by future generations who cannot participate in the decisions and who will receive no obvious compensation.

The costs and risks of energy policy thus are not random, but fall most heavily on those least able to participate in the decision-making process—including future generations, which leads to a major quandry. The losers are a poor, disorganized minority, and in the case of posterity, politically irrelevant. (To paraphrase Stalin, "How many divisions does posterity have?") In contrast, the winners are numerous, rich, and politically powerful. Any contest between the two—democratic or not—would be one-sided at best and would probably lead to even greater inequity.

Other inequities, however, affect the whole society. Political and economic benefits are also concentrated while the costs and risks of high technology energy systems are diffused. As a result, the high technology portion of the energy sector has received large subsidies for research and development, depletion allowances, tax advantages, and accelerated depreciation, that were unavailable either in kind or magnitude to low technology energy systems, and to other parts of the economy. According to one study, federal subsidies for fossil fuels and nuclear energy total an estimated 123-133 billion dollars.[60]

[60] Battelle Laboratories, *An Analysis of Federal Incentives Used to Stimulate Energy Production* (Richland Washington, 1978), 262. The Battelle esttimate of nuclear subsidies is $17 billion. Hughes Spectrolab estimated R & D and other subsidies at $24.4 billion. For a detailed analysis of nuclear economics see U. S. Congress, House Subcommittee of the Committee on Government Operations, *Nuclear Power Costs* 2 volumes. 95th Congress, 1st session, 1977.

The federal government, in effect, pays about 20 percent of the cost of each new power plant.   Nuclear power in particular has benefited from construction work in progress allowances, "phantom" taxes which are collected from consumers but never paid to the government, subsidized fuel enrichment, and federal responsibility for waste storage.   Furthermore, utility and energy companies are buffered from the effects of accidents including nuclear meltdowns and large oil spills by de facto or de jure liability limits such as that in the Price-Anderson Act.   Full responsibility is seldom assigned for acts which individually or cumulatively lead to long term environmental damage, or climate change.   Similarly, the hazards of oil and natural gas depletion are quietly deferred to the future. Moreover, despite the growing knowledge of the adverse health effects of energy production and conversion these costs are widely distributed without much, if any, compensation.   In short, the price that the public nominally pays for "cheap" energy has not included federal subsidies, tax advantages to energy companies, environmental costs, health costs, its replacement costs, or insurance against disaster.

It is not very convincing to argue that these external costs are only a slight technical problem to be remedied by "internalization." As the scale of energy technologies has risen so have the number of unknowns; thus the full costs of a technology are seldom evident until long afterward.   But even in cases in which the costs and risks are known, well intrenched interests have opposed any reassignment of responsibility to their disadvantage.[61]

Given the fact that the present costs of high technology energy systems are diffused and must be paid collectively (but the benefits are concentrated and accrue to only a few), one can argue that the public acting in its self interest would insist upon greater equity. Said differently, a minimally rational public acting on reliable information would be less willing to subsidize the exorbitant costs of high technology in the energy sector, including those of accidents, than elites (Engler's "private government of energy") who benefit in terms of power, profit, and peer acclaim.   Only in instances of utter irrationality or where costs and risks can be deferred to succeeding generations does this principle not hold.

Critics from the supply perspective have responded that any change toward soft technologies would lead to even greater in-

[61] See Charles E. Lindblom, *Politics and Markets* (New York: Basic Books, 1977), 344-356.

equities because the growth in energy consumption is tied to economic growth, jobs, and social stability. An increasing supply of energy is necessary, they say, to improve the growing volume of energy necessary to support continued economic growth and would lead to social and economic ruin. The burdens, according to critics, would fall hardest and most inequitably on the poor, the elderly, and minorities displaced by economic decline, and unable to afford the high cost of on-site technologies.

There is, however, a large and growing body of evidence showing that on-site, renewable energy systems could meet a majority of U.S. energy needs within 50 years, and that energy use and economic growth can be de-coupled.[62] As suggested in the conservation approach, this option would require a strong effort to remove the 30-50 percent of present U.S. energy use that is wasted, as well as a transition toward a more labor intensive economy. These studies show that on-site energy technologies would create far more jobs per dollar invested than do high-technology systems.[63] But the price of this approach may include less personal mobility, less consumption, and a sizeable restructuring of the society. Knowing the fine print, would the public choose the on-site solar alternative, even if it distributed costs and benefits more equitably?

This is a difficult question to which one can only make a tentative answer, but there is some evidence that the values of community, self-reliance, and simplicity implicit in small scale energy systems are becoming more attractive to a growing number of people. This change in values is reflected in data from Harris, Gallup, and Opinion Research Corporation surveys from the early 1970s to the present. A 1978 poll on environmental attitudes conducted by Resources for the Future, for example, concluded that environmental protection has joined such issues as education and health as en-

[62] For example, Office of Technology Assessment, *Application of Solar Technology to Today's Energy Needs* (Washington, D. C., 1978); *U. S. Department of Energy, Distributed Energy Systems in California's Future* (Washington, D. C. 1978); *Domestic Policy Review of Solar Energy* (Washington, D. C., 1978).

[63] See Bruce Hannon, "Economic Growth, Energy Use, and Altruism" in Dennis L. Meadows, ed., *Alternatives to Growth/I* (Cambridge, MA.: Ballinger, 1977), 79-100; also Fred Branfman, *Jobs From the Sun* (California Public Policy Center, February, 1978); also the review by Richard Grossman and Gail Daneker, *Jobs and Energy* (Washington, D. C.: Environmentalists for Full Employment, 1977).

during and even generally non-controversial public concerns.[64]
Public attitudes toward energy technologies are less clear, although
the RFF poll showed that by 47 to 31 percent the public favored
environmental protection over increased energy production.   A
Harris survey in 1977 indicated that public support for nuclear
energy had declined by 19 percent within the previous twelve
months.   An NBC poll in the summer of 1978 showed a majority of
52 percent opposed to further expansion of nuclear energy, but the
results of the RFF poll showed that 65 percent were either "fairly"
or "very" favorable to nuclear energy.[65]   It is not clear what effect
the accident at Three Mile Island will have on public attitudes, or
how much opposition to nuclear energy spills over to other high
technology energy systems such as strip-mining, coal gasification,
oil refineries, offshore oil drilling, and nuclear fusion.   Regardless,
poll data does indicate that public attitudes toward the environment, mass consumption, and technology are changing because of
greater concern for the quality of life.

A third and related argument is that participation is essential as
a countervailing influence to offset elite biases, ensure accountability, and to prevent domination of energy policy by special interests.   The dominance of technical experts has risen with increases
in the scale, sophistication, complexity, and capital requirements of
energy technologies.   The consequences for democratic societies are
troubling.   The typical response from advocates of either the supply
or conservation perspectives is that technological developments
represent either necessity or progress.

This attitude is rooted in the belief that the development of
technology is subject to a Darwinian process of natural selection.
Technologies that survive are assumed to be more "fit" than those
that do not.   In this view the process of technological development
is as neutral as that of biological evolution.   An alternative and
more accurate approach would place technological change in its
social and political context and explain the development and adoption of a technology as the result of social values, a specific set of
economic and political payoffs, and its technical feasibility.   In this
view technological choices are profoundly political, affecting the

[64] *Resources,* 60 (September-November, 1978); see also *Resources,* 57
(January-March, 1978).
[65] As reported in *Resources,* 60; NBC Poll in *The New York Times,* November 22, 1978.

"authoritative allocation of values" or "who gets what, when, and how?"

The present emphasis on high technology in U.S. energy policy is a product of a cultural orientation characterized by anthropocentrism, and an uncritical faith in progress, technical efficiency, and economic growth. In Leon Lindberg's words, its proponents have a ". . . trained incapacity to think in terms of labor intensive technology or resource limits; methodological commitments that disaggregate and subdivide problems; and a trained incapacity to see that energy, ecology and economics form a single unified system." More important, present policy ". . . conforms closely to the long-term interest perceptions and survival imperatives of some of the most decisive social groupings in advanced industrial societies."[66] Energy policy thus represents a crystallization of the interests of the dominant class.

One need not phrase the argument in class terms, however, to see that high technologies will give rise to increasingly rigid political structures and large bureaucratic organizations presided over by a new class of technocrats and policy analysts deciding who shall bear what costs and what level of risk is acceptable for whom. It is not far fetched to imagine that democratic processes will be further sacrificed in the name of necessity, efficiency, and technique and that traditional civil liberties will be subordinated to the imperative of securing risky, vulnerable technologies.[67] As the dependence on large-scale technology grows, so does the tolerance for risks that we would otherwise avoid, and with it the power of the managers and vendors of technology.

The thesis that technology has political implications is not new. C. S. Lewis argued in an essay in 1947 that the urge to dominate nature in fact meant that some men dominated nature in order to control other men.[68] Nature in Lewis' view was simply the medium from which some men extracted economic or political leverage necessary for controlling others. Members of the Frankfurt School, including Herbert Marcuse, Jurgen Habermas, and Max Horkheimer, similarly have regarded science and technology as the expression of dominant interests. Marcuse, for example, argues, "Science by virtue of its own method and concepts, has projected and pro-

---

[66] Lindberg, "Comparing Energy Policies," 344. See also Robert Engler, *The Brotherhood of Oil* (Chicago: University of Chicago Press, 1977), 245-246.

[67] Ayres, "Policing Plutonium."

[68] C. S. Lewis, *The Abolition of Man* (New York: MacMillan 1965), 67-91.

moted a universe in which the domination of nature has remained linked to the domination of man."[69] For Habermas, likewise, the rationality of science is the "rationality of domination" which leads inevitably to the coalescence of power in a technical-administrative elite and to a pervasive technocratic ideology disguising practical problems.[70] In this perspective the technological choices involved in energy policy are political; and public oversight is necessary to broaden the range of interests brought to bear on decisions before large capital investments and irreversible choices are made.

Critics will respond that participation has its own dangers including the possibility that energy policy will be fragmented, and subject to prolonged stalemate. But it may be that in an era when vast technological gambles are made on the basis of scientific knowledge that is prone to rapid obsolescence, delay and fragmentation may have some survival value.

More seriously, if public oversight is to be meaningful, it will be necessary to consider limiting energy technologies to those which can be controlled democratically.[71] This consideration might lead to limits on technologies that are resistant to public oversight, either because they are too complex to be comprehensible or because their social and ecological effects are unpredictable. It might also be necessary to limit technologies that require longer time commitments than a democratic society with shifting public attitudes could make, applying to all choices that were irreversible over, say, 50 years. The catch, of course, is that participation implies that the public has the right to sign away its own control and to make Faustian bargains with whomever, or whatever, it pleases. Whether plausible or not, others will argue the opposite: that the public would jealously guard its oversight function and would thereby inhibit technological "progress" or stop it altogether. The belief that given the opportunity the public would reject some energy technologies, however, may be a tacit admission that we might be better off without them.

In any event, public oversight is obviously a two-edged sword. Which way it cuts depends a great deal on factors that I have not touched on, particularly those of public education. Some argue that

[69] Herbert Marcuse, *One Dimensional Man* (Boston: Beacon Press, 1964), 166.

[70] Jurgen Habermas, *Toward a Rational Society* (Boston: Beacon Press, 1970), 111.

[71] Engler, *Brotherhood*, 209-250; Feyerabend, *Science,* 96-98.

this necessarily implies limits on distorted information (e.g., advertising) broadcast over public airways. Regardless, it is unarguable that the quality of public knowledge would have to be raised substantially above its present levels.

A fourth argument, made most emphatically by Amory Lovins, holds that participation leads to greater societal resilience defined as the capacity to withstand disturbances. The three previous arguments applied directly to public involvement in policy making while the fourth applies to policy implementation. Resilience involves the decentralization of much of the energy production system to the household, neighborhood, and community levels, thereby allowing the public direct participation in the choice of operation of a variety of on-site solar, wind, biomass, and photovoltaic technologies.[72] The result would be the replacement of a relatively small number of governmental decisions about energy policy by millions of "pluralistic consumer choices."

Since solar energy is diffuse—in effect already distributed—the allocative role of government in the energy sector would necessarily diminish. The fact that solar energy can be captured and used on site without extensive processing, refining and transmission implies less federal regulation and management. The major role for government lies in managing the transition through the promotion of replacement cost pricing, life-cycle-cost accounting, the elimination of institutional barriers, and in offering assistance to consumers, manufacturers, and distributors of on-site energy systems in the form of low-interest loans, tax credits and research funding.[73]

Distributed energy systems, in contrast to highly centralized facilities with extensive transportation and transmission grids, are less vulnerable to disruption from accidents, acts of God, sabotage, terrorism, embargoes, and changing societal preferences. The reasons for this lie in the fact that a large number of small producers can absorb disturbances with less chance of collapse than a system

[72] Lovins, *Soft Energy Paths*, 52; on resilience see C. S. Holling, "The Curious Behavior of Complex Systems; Lessons from Ecology," in Harold A. Linstone and W. H. Clive Simmonds, eds., *Futures Research* (Reading, Mass.: Addison Wesley, 1977), 114-129; C. S. Holling, "Myths of Ecology and Energy" in Metzger, ed., *Future Strategies for Energy Development* (Oak Ridge RN: ORAU, 1978), 36-49; also William C. Clark, "Managing the Unknown," in Robert W. Kates, ed., *Managing Technological Hazard: Research Needs and Opportunities* (Boulder: Institute of Behavioral Science, 1977), 126-142.

[73] Barry Commoner, *The Politics of Energy* (New York: Knopf, 1979) 49-65; OTA, *Application of Solar Technology*, 59-111.

with a small number of large producers.[74] Thus on-site systems have a greater margin for error and a higher degree of flexibility and reversibility than do large-scale alternatives. They also pose less chance of massive environmental disruption and hence have less need for increased government authority to remedy mistakes.

Participation leading to resilience is thus more an engineering or design principle connoting flexibility and adaptability than it is an ethical imperative. It indicates prudence and caution rather than moral right. As with equity, it is not either/or but more-or less, suggesting the need for flexibility and the preservation of options in order to avoid excessive vulnerability to the unknown in the form of changing societal objectives, changing economic forces, or the emergence of new functional relations, including scarcity. Concern for resilience directs attention to the need to cope with uncertainty by designing a margin of error into technological systems to absorb the unexpected. In studies of ecological systems, resilience is partly a function of the degree of species diversity, which acts as a buffer against perturbations. In technological systems, diversity, redundancy, and small scale may serve a comparable function.

Conclusion

Present differences over energy policy are as much about politics as they are about technology. Attempts to confine the energy debate to the latter are inherently incomplete, misleading, and dangerous. The supply, conservation, and energetics perspectives entail different views of policy making, but only the third has attempted explicitly to relate democratic processes to the substance of energy policy. In doing so, its proponents have implicitly sketched the basis for a revision of democratic theory in a high technology society. Whether the theory can be extended beyond the energy sector is at least debatable. The possibility that widespread public involvement in energy policy is related to controlling risk, to insuring the equitable distribution of costs and benefits, and to promoting societal resilience poses an overdue challenge to elitist versions of democratic theory and to visions of a benign, but autonomous technocracy.

[74] Department of Energy, *Distributed Energy Systems,* Chapter 1.

POPULATION POLICY

Demography is a field which not long ago thought of itself as an essentially quantitative science; almost a branch of applied mathematics or social physics. But as a series of major decisions concerning allocation of scarce resources increasingly involved determinations as to the actual population in a country, city, region, or even township, demography became to that extent an essential touchstone for distribution of goods and services. From an allocational perspective, since every person does indeed count as one, as the Constitution mandates, the absence of an accurate census count, for whatever reasons, weighs heavily on the course of policy. Who gets what and why is linked to who lives where and why. Thus, although the science of demography has become more exacting than at any time in the past, instead of being removed from an atmosphere of contentiousness, its austere quantitative properties have only increased pressures for more precise methods of research and more compassionate views of the social meaning of head and body counts.

Population counts, the oldest basis for making policy, have inevitably generated more than their share of controversy. Keyfitz demonstrates that current methods of establishing the census are more exact and sophisticated than ever. Hence, efforts to manipulate results or massage the data for certain interest group ends are less workable than ever. Keyfitz's essay can be read as a statement on the limits of policy. In fact, his effort is more nearly cautionary, emphasizing the need for careful maintenance of checks and balances between administratively mandated research efforts and court-induced adjustments. If the Keyfitz paper is focused on the policy implications of artifically tampering with hard data, the paper by Adamczuk and Zagórski indicates that a careful study of microeconomic time budget data reveals a radical disproportion of people using leisure time and special non-work-related activities. Indirectly, the paper shows that systematic factors such as socialism or capitalism may be less important than occupational factors such as white-collar work versus farming in determining the utilization of cultural resources. The paper by Martin and Sehgal focuses less on whole populations than on partial populations—in their case, the problem of illegal aliens in the United States. They indicate three available options: maintain the status quo, provide amnesty for present aliens and severely restrict future migration, or convert illegal aliens into guestworkers—along the lines of foreign workers in West Germany. The authors argue against the guestworker option, although the series of dangerous consequences they anticipate can indeed be planned for. They argue that increasing the quota of legal immigration would be far superior to the present malaise, one that would taper off as a corresponding policy of aiding Mexico in its own development took root. Here is an example of researchers opting for modest and restrictive policy initiatives rather than the more grandiose approaches characteristic of an earlier generation of policy experts. Such examples are becoming more frequent.

19

STATISTICS, LAW, AND CENSUS REPORTING

Nathan Keyfitz

The first count of the 1980 Census is now nearing completion, and it makes obsolete nearly everything that has been said about the undercount and possibilities of adjusting. Expectations of incompleteness based on earlier experiences have to be drastically revised, and so do hopes of easily making corrections.

The censuses of 1950, 1960, and 1970 each turned up with 5 million fewer people than calculation showed were present. In respect of April 1, 1970, for example, the preceding births less deaths, Medicare figures, and other evidence indicated that the resident population of the United States was 208.5 million; the census counted only 203.2 million. With all that hangs on the census, the case for adjustment seemed strong. No official adjustment was made to the 1970 Census; the Bureau of the Census put out several bulletins showing the undercount, worked out from the true population as of April 1, 1970, as far as it could be estimated, but the tens of thousands of pages of published detail, as well as the machine-readable detail offered to the public and equivalent to further hundreds of thousands of pages, showed the actual counts.

The purpose of the census is not to establish the total population of the United States—that can be equally well obtained from births, immigration, and other sources—but to find the populations and characteristics of some 39,000 states, cities, and smaller jurisdictions, an even larger number of census tracts, and other geographical detail. Of course one could raise up these local units in proportion to the undercount for the country as a whole, and that would improve some counts, while others would be less accurate than the unadjusted count. Still, on the basis of the 1970 results the public demand for adjustment was strong and had some support from the courts. Supposing that the 1980 figures would be 5 million or more short, and that this undercount would contain a disproportionate number of members of minority groups, the sentiment for adjustment that persisted has seemed justified. Preliminary counts drastically undercut this argument, and the whole matter needs fresh thought.

The financial stake in the 1980 Census results is at least $50 billion per year, and in response to public concern an unprecedented effort was made in 1980 to get an accurate count. After allowing for inflation, the amount spent on field work was more than double that spent in 1970. Follow-up enumerators were paid at more generous hourly rates to track down nonrespondents; local offices were kept open months longer than in past censuses. In addition to this paid effort, a great deal of publicity was provided free to the census by public-spirited corporations and media. The equivalent of $50 million in publicity succeeded in catching the attention of varied elements of the population who in the past had not been aware of the census.

The first sign that things were going well was the larger than expected numbers who simply filled in and returned the mail questionnaire. The spontaneous return of 80 percent by mail would have been good; in fact, fully 86 percent of the population was covered by the mail-in-mail-out phase. This freed resources for the more intense follow-up of the 14 percent who did not respond.

More important is the total number of persons enumerated. On information available prior to the census—births less deaths, etc.—it appeared that the number of residents of the United States on April 1, 1980, was some 227 million. This total, calculated entirely from extra-census sources, is about as solid a figure as can be obtained, and it is all that we have for checking the completeness of the census. If the calculated omission of each of the previous three censuses, about 5 million, is subtracted from 227 million, that brings the number down to 222 million, and this is what the 1980 Census was expected to count. If one looks in the 1979 edition of the *Statistical Abstract of the United States*, the figure given for July 1, 1978, which is the latest, shows 218.5 million. This was 21 months before the census, and the current increase being about 1.8 million per year, or 3.2 million per 21 months, that brings us to 221.7 million, as a continuation of the completeness level of the 1970 Census.

As this is being written, the census count has come well above 225 million, and it could easily exceed 226 million before the work is through. In comparison with the 227 million known from extra-census sources to have been resident in the country, that means that the undercount has been driven down to less than one half of one percent.

It will be some time before the analysis of this material is complete, so that we can know just how the drastic change from past censuses has come about. Some features other than sheer efficiency of enumeration are present. The extensive publicity, together with the knowledge that one's town and state benefit financially through each person's being enumerated, engaged civic loyalty in

---

> As the courts cannot command that a perpetual motion machine be produced, so they cannot order a statistical impossibility.

---

a way that increased the response. But civic loyalty may have been excessive; the awareness by enumerator and enumerated that large payments hang on the result could make for overenumeration. The Census Bureau has checks that limit the sheer addition of imaginary people, what is called "curbstoning"; there is a strict quality control of the individual enumerator's work. But there are doubtful cases—Jones, who lives in Montana, is found on April 1 in Texas; and what about Cousin Heidi from Dusseldorf, who is staying with relatives in New York for a few weeks? Neither belongs in the census where found, yet a zealous enumerator might include them. The person who died just before the census date, or one who was born just after, if the respondent was not sure of the time, might be included. In the United States there are about 40,000 deaths a week, and about 75,000 births, so any imprecision on the date makes an appreciable fuzziness in the count. It is impossible to push hard for completeness without bringing in at least some people who ought not to be counted. The Bureau of the Census is undertaking matching studies to estimate the number of duplications and persons who for whatever reason should not have been enumerated, but it will be months before results are obtained in this tedious work.

A second group of difficulties concerns the illegal or undocumented immigrants. No one knows how many of these there are at any one time; estimates have run as high as 12 million, though more believable figures make them closer to 4 million. The extra-census calculation of 227 million presumably does not include these people. If a person is not in the birth, immigration, or Medicare records, then there is no way of including him in the calculation. The census defined undocumented immigrants as in the population and made special efforts in the minority areas where they were likely to be found. Its attempts to enumerate them undoubtedly succeeded in a

fraction of cases; certainly not all were included and not all were missed. The undercount is thus improperly reduced by whatever number of illegals were caught in the census. No one knows much about this, and no one will ever know, since the census can hardly ask people whether they are in the country legally.

Differential Completeness

In a sense all these questions are subsidiary to the main question: how does completeness compare for whites and blacks? for English-speakers and Spanish-speakers? Whether for apportionment in the House of Representatives or for allocation of revenue-sharing funds, it is the *relative* completeness that counts. If it were not for differentials no one would care much about the undercount. It could be 2 percent (or 10 percent, for that matter), and as long as it was uniformly distributed through the country it would make no difference for these or for most other purposes.

The main reason we would like a complete count is the thought that this would make differentials smaller, at least in absolute numbers. Suppose the studies for 1980 show a million people missed, of which 600,000 are white and 400,000 are black. As a percent of the population the undercount for blacks would be 2 percent, of whites 0.3 percent, so the ratio for blacks would be six times that of whites. That sounds worse than 1970, until we reflect that the loss to any community depends on the absolute number of people missed, not on the percentage. As the census pushes towards completeness it is likely that the undercount *ratios* will become larger at the same time as the *absolute amounts* of differential become smaller, and this is a gain for equity.

We will not have any idea of the number missed by race until February 1981, when the tapes have been completed and run at least once through the census computers. The count so made can be compared with the extra-census calculation for blacks. The extra-census calculation cannot be made in the same way for Hispanics, since language is not recorded on the birth certificate. The number of Hispanics missed can only be known by matching name by name from the Current Population Survey. That work is now under way and its outcome is expected by the summer of 1981.

In January 1981 one can do nothing more than speculate on how the differential will stand in the framework of a negligible undercount overall. It could be that the additional effort towards enumeration made in minority areas will have the effect of eliminating the differential altogether. Or it could be that the effort was not successful, and the whole of the undercount is among blacks, while there is an overcount of whites. Further speculation at this point is not useful; we will just have to wait and see. Differentials could also be important between cities and upstate areas. It might be that blacks in Detroit are missed, while those in rural Michigan are completely counted. No one yet knows, and the Bureau of the Census hopes to find out, but only for groups for which the undercount proves large in comparison with the fuzziness at the margin of all such calculations.

The whole issue is confounded with real population changes. The major cities of the country have lost population in the seventies as in earlier decades, at least in the East and Midwest. People have been leaving the central cities for half a century or more, and now they are apparently leaving many of the suburbs as well, headed for the open country. Some are going just beyond the boundaries of their metropolitan areas and continuing to commute; others are going much farther. Some are fleeing taxes, others seek a rural style of life. Some, like pensioners, whose numbers have increased, have incomes that do not depend on place, while others are following a footloose industry in which they work. Whatever the reasons, we are in the midst of a major redistribution of population, and one purpose of taking censuses is to show such redistributions. Those who do not like the trend are tempted to say that the census is wrong. A mayor can appeal to his constituents by asserting this and claiming that his city is not really losing population; the strength of the appeal is not much affected by what the facts are. Yet we should not take a census at all if we reject any results from it that do not accord with preconceptions.

Enter the Law

In our litigious society it is natural that many think they can benefit by bringing their case before the courts. Detroit, New York, and other cities have sued or are suing the Bureau of the Census, demanding that it adjust its figures by the best method it can devise. The Detroit court has ruled in favor of the plaintiffs and requires the census to improve the figures by adjustment. This might have made sense with a five million undercount, but now the prospect is for an undercount so small as to be within the margin of error of any possible correction. At some point a line has to be drawn between the power of the courts and the limitations of the natural world. Just as the

---

At some point a line has to be drawn between the power of the courts and the limitations of the natural world.

---

courts cannot command that a perpetual motion machine be produced, so they cannot order a statistical impossibility. The population count cannot be adjusted to make it correct; it cannot be adjusted for Detroit and New York by any method that will not make some other places worse.

If statistics teaches anything it is the universality of error. Statisticians are not primarily people concerned

with numbers; they have that in common with most other sciences. Statisticians have been getting to know more and more about error during the course of the twentieth century. The natural laws by which errors cumulate, whether in agricultural experiments, industrial production, or census taking are the pivot of their discipline. To face the fact of error is not easy—it has taken the genius of Ronald Fisher, Jerzy Neyman, and others to bring the discipline to its present position. Its results have influenced pure and applied science and engineering from agronomy through pharmacy to industrial production. The law has given much less attention to error, to the criminals who got away, to the accused who were wrongly sentenced, or to quality control of judicial activities. This may be for good reason, but it helps to explain the present impasse between a statistical agency and the courts.

Inevitable Error

The most easily written part of articles on census completeness is an exhortation to the Bureau of the Census to do better, to take the 1980 Census exactly, with no errors. Writers of such articles seem unaware that over the last forty years the Bureau of the Census has pioneered in the reduction of census error. The errors that remain are not due to negligence or ignorance on the part of Bureau personnel, who know more about errors of counting than any other group in the world. The difficulties will not be removed by change of management or adoption of any obvious new methods. It will take a very clever journalist to see more deeply into the problem of completeness than have the series of brilliant census leaders of the past forty years. Moreover, it is the Census Bureau that has told us most of what we know about the incompleteness of its counts. It has pioneered not only in the reduction of error, but in the measurement of what error it does make. Courts and municipal leaders charge the census with incompleteness, ungenerously omitting to say that the charges are based on the estimates of undercount provided by the Bureau itself.

The nagging thought persists that the census really ought not to be appreciably incomplete. If 200 passengers in an airplane can be counted exactly, with zero error, why not 200 million? The census is taken by dividing the country into small areas containing an average of 1000 persons and assigning the responsibility for each area to one enumerator. Zero error in each of 220,000 areas would mean zero error for the country as a whole. There are a number of things wrong with this commonsense view. Error is an integral part of counting a real population engaged in the varied activities of living; the difference between a precise survey and a poor one is in the amount of error, not in that one contains errors and the other does not. There is a penumbra of irremovable arbitrariness around any permissible way of taking the census.

Anyone can think of ways of taking a more nearly complete census if some of the constraints can be relaxed. If people could be required to stay home for one day, or until the enumerator calls; if people could be given a button indicating that they had been enumerated, and required to wear it; if this or some other means of showing that they had been enumerated, perhaps a card, were required for transacting such business as cashing a paycheck, drawing social security, or being attended by a doctor, everyone would have an immediate interest in being included in the census. Such devices have not been found acceptable in the United States. They might be applied in totalitarian societies, though there it turns out that other inefficiencies intervene; censuses taken in the USSR have been bad, and one even had to be abandoned before publication.

One source of definitional uncertainty is whether "population" includes illegal aliens. The issue was bitterly debated, to the point of putting the census itself in jeopardy. The Constitution as modified by the 14th Amendment orders the counting of "the whole number of persons in each State, excluding Indians not taxed." This would seem plainly to include illegal aliens, but nonetheless the census had to fight off a lawsuit demanding their omission. It was in the end sensibly decided that the question whether people *should be* here ought to be addressed to the Immigration and Naturalization Service; the census is only concerned with whether they *are* here. Of course in practice the illegals would be subject to gross omission no matter how the census set the definition.

It is hard to imagine the question of illegal aliens arising when the Constitution was framed or amended. Only

Error is an integral part of counting a real population engaged in the varied activities of living.

now, when redistributive legislation has made them important, is the matter viewed with deadly seriousness. One example—others will arise later—of what may be called the hardening of expectations concerns school lunches. When Congress first offered to pay for them, say at so much per year per child in school, no one was likely to ask whether children here illegally would partake. But once the program has been going for some time and is thoroughly incorporated in the community's receipts and expenditures, attention comes to be focused very intensively on such marginal questions.

Though undocumented aliens are the largest, and legally the most interesting, of the groups that give rise to dispute on the part of those who will benefit from a particular definition of population, there are a host of other points on which census practice could be challenged once the door is opened. A college student is to be counted where he lives while attending college, not at his parents' home, even though he may be with his parents when the enumerator calls. On the other hand, a child who is in a residential secondary school is counted in the household of his parents, irrespective of where he happens to be at the time of the census. Could a town like Exeter, New Hampshire, with a large secondary boarding school sue to have the students considered as residents?

Since there is no general definition of resident, the census has to decide where to draw its many boundary lines. The lines should be sharp and objective on the one hand, and suited to the concept of usual residence on the other. These two considerations may conflict. In many instances the sharp definition is not appropriate to the use of the results. A person who has more than one home, and divides his time between them, is to be listed where he spends the largest part of the calendar year, according to the census instructions. It would be sharper to put him where he is actually found at the time of enumeration, but this would be less in accord with the objective of finding the usual population. To the arbitrariness incorporated in the census definitions must be added the errors in implementation by the enumerator. A census is an intricate affair, hedged about by arbitrary definitions, enumerated by people who through human fallibility add their own errors to those provided them by the respondents.

Beyond all questions of definition is the matter of those who should have been included in the census and who were just not caught. About half of those omitted in 1970 were in households that were not reported on any list and not known to the post office. The other half were members of a known household but were somehow omitted from its census questionnaire. Either there was no evidence of their existence such as would put the enumerator on their trail, or there was evidence but the enumerator was delinquent. An enumerator will make one, two, three callbacks for a person not at home on the first call, but a time comes when the most devoted enumerator gives up.

Aside from all this, some social changes adverse to the census have occurred in recent decades. Housewives were the backbone of the enumerator force in earlier times, and other housewives usually answered the door bells they rang. Now the majority of housewives have regular jobs; an excellent source of census labor has dried up, so that less suitable people had to be hired, and much of the job had to be done in the evening. Where once a college-educated housewife who had taken a job as enumerator went the rounds during the daytime addressing the census questions to other housewives, now the enumerator (perhaps an unemployed auto mechanic) more often found no one at home and had to call back, which was less convenient both for him and for the respondents, as well as being more expensive.

In addition to there being more one-person households that have always been harder to find and enumerate than families, people are more mobile, more suspicious of government, more concerned about their privacy. There are more laws, and hence more people have something to conceal—all the way from lodgers in a zone where they are prohibited to workers enjoying unreported incomes. Surveys are no longer a novelty, and people are more

---

The 1980 Census is apparently the most complete ever taken.

---

impatient with questions, commercial as well as governmental. Registration of youth for the armed forces, ordered by President Carter two months before the census date, may have caused some reticence.

Against all these handicaps, the Census Bureau applied new techniques, spent more money, and improved its organization. The newly added procedures have more than offset the greater difficulties, and the 1980 Census is apparently the most complete ever taken.

The unavoidable arbitrariness of the census does not end with the definitions as specified in the instructions, nor with the (one suspects highly variable) interpretations of these by respondents and enumerators. It continues through the processing of the census schedules. In 1970 some 4.5 million individuals for whose existence there was more or less evidence, but for whom no information on characteristics was reported, had to be incorporated in the tabulations by some kind of calculation. The convenient way of doing this that has been used since 1960 is to duplicate the record for the next person enumerated whose characteristics were reported. Thus the Bureau of the Census takes advantage of any homogeneity of local areas in respect to income and other features, since residential segregation of many kinds is still a fact. When data are missing for a number of consecutive individuals, the computer searches beyond the nearest person completely enumerated; the U.S. Bureau of the Census (USBC) rules do not permit duplication of one individual more than three times.

Such duplication of characteristics is preferable to retaining "not stated" entries through the tabulation to the published volumes. As was pointed out as early as the 1940s by Deming, Hansen, and others, "not stated" entries are both costly to the printing and provide very little information. The user is saved trouble, the printing bill is reduced, and accuracy is served if the nearest known case is duplicated. Aside from the 4.5 million, all of whose characteristics were obtained in this way, many

others lacked information in one or a few questions. Income was often omitted, and it is important in many allocation formulas; it was duplicated for some fifteen percent of cases.

Yet few users of the census need to refer to these fine points, which affect the margins of the count, not its core. Think of the typical questions asked of the census: Are people marrying younger than they did? Do the rich have fewer children than the poor? Which service occupations are declining, which increasing, as we move into the postindustrial society? Enumeration error, or the arbitrariness of the definitions, matter hardly at all for these. Error is tolerable, and it would be wasteful to enumerate everyone; the error of a five percent sample is perfectly acceptable.

None of this latitude is so readily accepted when the census is used for allocation of billions of dollars. Each person missed can cause a municipality to lose $1000 over the course of the ensuing decade. Hence the undercount and its incidence by areas become of crucial importance. Yet from another point of view the emphasis on exact figures, concern about a small fraction omitted, is misplaced. That fact emerges clearly as soon as we drop the accounting viewpoint, and ask the *purpose* of the legislation that distributes federal funds.

Equity and Expectations

For each item of allocative legislation one can offer a clear (if somewhat abstract) criterion for how the census ought to be carried out. Insofar as people constitute costs for a jurisdiction, that is where they should be counted. When Congress allocates funds for a school breakfast program, its intention is best served if the funds are given to jurisdictions according to the number of their school children poor enough to need the breakfast. Funds for supplementary benefits to the unemployed ought to be distributed in proportion to the number of longterm unemployed, etc. One need only say this to realize what a crude instrument the usual allocation formula is. When Congress allocates funds according to population and a few other measurable variables, deviations from its target of hundreds of percent are easily possible. Based on the formula a city may get an allowance for something it does not need at all. This does not mean that the hundred or so federal laws covering support for education, health, transportation, housing, manpower, and other programs are misconceived; they are necessarily targeted by some determinate simple formula that is only more or less related to need.

An undercount in which individuals are omitted at random would do little harm, and would inspire little pressure to adjust the census. The concentration of omissions in certain regions and racial groups is more difficult, for it produces a distribution of federal funds different from what Congress intended. Often it is the very groups

Congress aimed most clearly at helping that are under-stated. The problem is to rectify the distribution but not to overturn the census in so doing.

Unanticipated random error has to be accepted. If to the true apportionment there were added a random component of expected value zero, this would be no worse for states than the sort of random variation that any jurisdiction is subject to from many causes. It would be comparable with bad growing weather in Kansas or a tourist boom for Plains, Georgia, produced by one of its son's becoming president. The common run of random events that reduce income or force expenditure are not in general thought to require federal compensation.

It is non-random variation, that is known in advance, which arouses just resentment. It seems only fair that the census results should be adjusted for that, in the simplest possible way that will achieve the intentions of Congress. One such way is to increase not the census figure but the payment, in accord with the relative understatement. If the net undercount is estimated at 1.9 percent of the number enumerated for whites and 7.7 percent for blacks, the payment for blacks would be raised by $7.7 - 1.9 = 5.8$ percent, which might be rounded to 6 percent. In such a census as that of 1970 a municipality would be given a bonus of 6 percent for its blacks to offset relative census

---

A statistically acceptable adjustment must take account of whatever evidence is at hand and not go beyond that evidence.

---

incompleteness. We know less about the understatement of the Spanish-speaking population, and the same bonus could be given to it.

Such an adjustment has the advantage of unpreten-tiousness—no one would make the mistake of thinking it produced correct figures in each locality. The net adjust-ment for about 45 of the states would have been less than 1 percent. It would not reduce the incentive to complete enumeration in any one jurisdiction. One hopes it would be temporary, and the USBC would in due course attain sensibly equal completeness for the several social groups.

Once the essential matter is settled—that payments will be made in proportion to population—then negotia-tion shifts to marginal variations in the definition and count of populations. An incentive is offered to seek out any part of the census procedure that could be made to seem wrong, an incentive amounting to millions of dol-lars in the case of a medium-sized city, to hundreds of millions in the case of New York. The dynamics here could destroy the best census in the world. All possible census procedures contain arbitrary elements, and it is in the nature of census-taking that no census can stand up to such partisan examination.

Every piece of the legislation we are concerned with has a target, and it needs a convention that will provide a reasonable approximation to the target. That a conven-tion can be accepted that everyone knows is only a rough approximation to the target is shown by the 200-year history of apportionment in the House of Representa-tives. Alabama was actually given 7 representatives on the basis of the 1970 census, but USBC figures, cor-rected by methods beyond challenge, using the previous census and other data, would entitle it to 8; and Califor-nia would give up 1 of its 43. After most censuses at least one state turns out to be so deprived because the conven-tion (in this case the census count as published by the USBC) is not quite on target. Yet no one says that American democracy is frustrated by California having one seat too many and Alabama one too few.

Determinacy versus Precision

On apportionment of funds the problem is to choose among conventions. The choice involves a conflict be-tween determinacy and precision that may be illustrated by post-censal adjustments. One convention is to take the published count at the last preceding census and stay with it for 10 years. The advantage of this convention is that each jurisdiction would know near the start of the decade what it was to get, and could make plans for disbursement. But some jurisdictions could protest that they had been growing and were likely to grow in the future, so the "last census" formula would give them less than Congress intended them to have. The point might be met by saying that every jurisdiction would get the straight-line projection of its population from the last two censuses. This would have the same advantage of being immediately-known and calculable, and would not discriminate against the growing parts of the country. The future is sufficiently unknown that this does not discriminate against anyone in any obvious way statable in advance.

Intercensal estimates are not the present subject and I cite them only to bring out some of the issues, in par-ticular to illustrate the choice to be made between accord with the objective of the legislation and accuracy. For clearly anyone can do better than the straight-line projec-tions by taking account of such supplementary material as building permits, city directories, or local counts made after the last census. But these would depend on how the person making them chose among various items of ancillary data. Is a straight-line extrapolation, that gives exactly the same number irrespective of who makes it, preferable to a professional estimate that de-pends on someone's decision to trust building permits rather than a city directory? The user who wants deter-minacy, simplicity, and objectivity above all will take the first; the one who wants precision and fidelity to the object of the legislation will take the second.

To adjust the census or not to adjust it is far from a symmetrical choice. The unadjusted result that comes

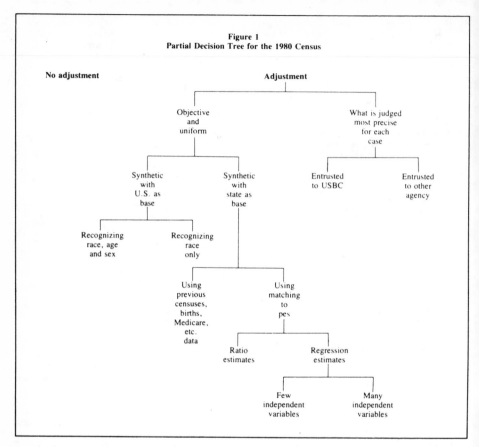

Figure 1
Partial Decision Tree for the 1980 Census

out of the standard and traditional procedures of the USBC is a single possibility; adjustment is many possibilities. Once adjustment is decided on it would have to be decided further whether (1) to use an objective and uniform, though admittedly inaccurate, method, or (2) a subjective method that would give greater precision. Figure 1 shows part of the decision tree that would be required if there is to be adjustment.

It might be decided to match with the post-enumeration survey (pes), find the people included in the pes that were missed in the census, identify their characteristics, and correct the count for each jurisdiction by regression. But the size of the pes sample would not suffice to provide data for individual jurisdictions. Hence the ratios or regressions would have to be obtained for some larger area, perhaps states or regions, and applied to all individual jurisdictions within the larger area—the procedure has come to be called synthetic. To decide

how large the area from which the coefficients would be obtained should be necessitates a tradeoff between sampling error—which grows greater as one attempts to derive coefficients from smaller areas—and appropriateness of the coefficients—which grows greater as the area from which they are derived becomes smaller. Beyond this is the question of what characteristics shall be recognized in the regressions: would one go beyond race to age and sex, and beyond that to income, size of dwelling, etc? The decision diagram shown as Figure 1 contains only a small part of the choices that would have to be made once we start down the road of adjustment.

Beyond the decisions indicated in the tree are other choices. Would the census be adjusted for all purposes, down to the finest tabulations? This could be done consistently very easily by computer. For example, if it were decided that each black enumerated was to count for 1.06, then that could be incorporated individual by individual in programming the tabulations, which would then come out consistent with one another. (The alternative of multiplying up the finished tables to adjust to the new total has the disadvantage that different cross-tabulations would not be consistent with one another.)

Such a diagram as suitably expanded would provide a framework within which each person could find his or her preference; that is both the good and the bad of it. In

> Given the superior quality of this census, it is ironic that 1980 was the first year in which the courts insisted on adjustment.

a sense it is guilty of complicating the task, suggesting different numbers for different users. Some will want a straightforward method that anyone can verify from published census figures on his own scratch pad; others will seek every last gain in accuracy, even at the cost of great complexity.

What is the role of knowledge in all this? A demographer can use outside information to ascertain that the census is short and could be brought closer to the truth by some kind of correction. It is little more trouble to do this separately for whites and nonwhites. Such calculations, using births, social security, Medicare, and other noncensus data according to the judgment of the particular demographer and with the degree of incompleteness of 1970, can produce results better than the census. The cost of this would be a few thousands of dollars worth of a demographer's time.

But what about the Spanish-speakers? Unlike the white-nonwhite division, the Spanish-speakers cannot be identified in consistent fashion on past birth and death certificates, and this makes the extra-census calculation much more elusive than that for whites and nonwhites. the USBC has tried to see what it could make of aggregate statistics; its resulting Bulletin does not lay claim to any dazzling result. Since the matter is important enough, resort will be had to a sample in the field, already taken for purposes of measuring unemployment and known as the Current Population Survey (CPS). When this was done with the population as a whole for 1970, it came up with a fraction missed less than the demographic calculation using outside sources, but this time a more substantial effort is being made. For the Spanish-speakers there would be greater difficulties than for native whites, so we should hold modest hopes of estimating the undercount by matching to an independent survey.

All this is at the national level. For individual jurisdictions some kind of synthetic method is inevitable—using either the undercount ratio for the United States as a whole or that for a region or state. Some experimenting has been done on the error of a synthetic estimate, and more would be useful. But work on this would share a feature common to all research—no one can be sure in advance that it will succeed in producing usable results.

A statistically acceptable adjustment must take account of whatever evidence is at hand and not go beyond that evidence. Numbers only become evidence when they are unlikely to have arisen by chance out of sampling and other features of the method of measurement. The usual statement is significance at the 5 percent level—we would say that the country or state is undercounted if there is less than 1 chance in 20 of the revealed shortfall having arisen through random causes associated with the way the data were selected. Two states are significantly different if they show measured shortfalls whose difference could have arisen by chance with a probability of no more than 1 in 20. It will be a number of months before the evidence on such points is available, and no one can now say how sharp it will be.

The calculation by which we have known the undercount in the past is not capable of measuring as small a quantity as the undercount of 1980 now promises to be. The largest uncertainty in the calculation is in migration; we know nothing of the illegal part of immigration and not much about emigration. Travellers from the United States do not have to pass any official who counts those among them who are residents leaving to take up residence in other countries.

If the undercount is large, the error with which migration and other components can be estimated does not prevent its calculation. To oversimplify somewhat, in 1970 the emigration estimated by immigration records of other countries and similar sources could be used to estimate what the census population should have been. In 1980 census completeness may have risen to the point where the census count could give an indication of the amount of emigration from the country.

Given the superior quality of this census, in which the undercount is barely large enough to be estimated with any degree of confidence, it is ironic that 1980 is the first year in which the courts insist on adjustment. They are apparently making their decision on the basis of the large sums of money legislated during the 1970s and riding on the 1980 Census, combined with the (supposedly) known undercount of 1970. This strange combination of elements out of the past presents the Bureau with some of the most puzzling dilemmas that statisticians have had to face. □

Nathan Keyfitz is Andelot Professor of Sociology and Demography at Harvard University. His numerous writings on the mathematics of population include Applied Mathematical Demography.

20

THE TIME BUDGET
IN SOCIO-DEMOGRAPHIC STATISTICS

Lucjan Adamczuk and Krzysztof Zagórski

ABSTRACT. The paper describes a Polish time budget survey conducted in 1976 on a rotation sample of the whole (non-agricultural and agricultural) adult population. Different time budget indicators are presented and their linkages with other statistical data and usefulness for social policy formulation and evaluation are discussed. Some new time indicators, not used in previous surveys, are recommended. Usefulness of time budged surveys for assessing an account of labor force and investigating of the social distribution of labor time as well as leisure time is underlined. The possibility of using time budget data for analyses of the social distribution of some welfare outlays in the field of cultural participation and consumption is also indicated. The paper is concerned with some methodological problems and the applicability of time budget research, rather than a comprehensive presentation of survey results.

1. AIMS AND SCOPE OF THE PAPER

The aim of this paper is to discuss possible ways of utilizing time budget survey results treated as an element of socio-demographic statistics. Different types of time budget indicators may be arranged in different types of accounts, to serve the particular needs of social policy makers and evaluators. Full utilization of time budget data requires some linkages with other social statistics. Such linkages will be discussed below. An attempt to integrate time budget data with official statistical data concerning different social and demographic issues may be treated as a part of international efforts to integrate and systematize socio-demographic statistics (U.N., 1976).

2. METHODOLOGY AND ORGANIZATION OF POLISH TIME BUDGET SURVEYS

Experience gained so far in Poland and other countries in the field of time budget surveys of large populations proved to be most satisfactory when applying the rotation sampling method with the full 24-hour rotation. This method was applied in the 1969 and the 1976 surveys conducted in Poland by the Central Statistical Office (Wnuk-Lipinski, 1971; Adamczuk, 1978).

From Lucjan Adamczuk and Krzysztof Zagórski, "The Time Budget in Socio-Demographic Statistics," 8 *Social Indicators Research* 423-439 (1980). Copyright 1980 by D. Reidel Publishing Co., Dordrecht, Holland, and Boston, U.S.A. Reprinted by permission.

Both surveys were based on the representative sample of households for the family budget (income and expenditures) survey.

The survey carried out in 1976 examined 9966 households where individual time budgets were registered for 21 819 persons ages 18 and over. The sample consisted of;

- employee housholds   5438; 11 660 persons surveyed
- pensioner households   1445; 2090 persons
- farmer households   1622; 3893 persons
- employee-farmer households   1461; 4176 persons

The rotation survey method requires establishing a time limit for the survey, i.e. the number of days surveyd. A one-year period (365 days) would be the most advantageous from the point of view of the subject-matter and statistical purposes. Organisational and financial limitations prohibited such solution. In connection with this, a yearly survey was realized on the basis of four seasons' 'representation'. Each season of the year was represented by four contiguous weeks, i.e., 28 days. Thus, a one year period was represented by 112 days (4 ×28 = 112). The following months: April, September, November and February — represented the four seasons, respectively. The household sample was randonly distributed in time, to assure an equal number of households surveyed each day. Due to this there were 112 daily (24-hours) sub-samples which underwent rotation for the duration of the survey. A daily sub-sample had 89 households (195 persons on an average).

One of the basic conditions for obtaining error-free results in rotation survey is minimization of the number of units deleted from the investigation. This requires an efficient organization of the survey and highly skilled inter-viewers. The Central Statistical Office has a permanent survey network which conducts the systematic surveys of household budgets. There are several hundred interviewers and inspectors located in all regional administrative units (i.e. voivodships) through the country. These interviewers were trained in advance in the different methods of statistical and sociological surveys and were also specifically trained to conduct the time budget survey.

Prior to each of the four survey periods the C.S.O. sent them computer prepared lists of the households to be surveyed during particular days. An interviewer was scheduled to arrive in each household one day prior to the day of completion of the questionnaires, in order to instruct people how things were to be registered, to fix the date of the time budget self-registering by all adult household members, and finally, to collect additional information on each adult, on the household and the place of residence. Each household received a special booklet with instructions on how to fill out questionnaires. The day after the questionnaire was due to be filled out the inquirers visited the household again, checked the questionnaires, made corrections where necessary, and sent them on to the control centers, where all of the questionnaires were collected. The control centers checked them again (in the logical and formal sense), and then sent the questionnaires to the C.S.O. computing center for computation.

The survey was carried out with competence since out of the 9984 households included in the sample, 9966 (99.8%) households compiled the time budget. The 112 sub-samples were maintained, as expected, by nearly 89 households daily, which means that the results may carry only minimum sampling errors. It should be stressed, however, that the sampling error might arise earlier, during the sampling of households for the household budget survey, since some of them refused to be included in the sample. Moreover some households dropped out from the household survey before the time budget was completed.

The fundamental technique used in the survey was autochronography (self-registration) with the use of special survey tools like chronocards, which enabled each person to mark the duration of the 47 typical activities performed during 24-hours, exact to 15 minutes. A chronocard allowed for easy control of registering the duration of time spent on activities by summing them up and checking whether the total time was equal to 24 hours. It also made possible the registration of the duration of 'accompanying' activities, that is activities which were performed in conjunction with the main activities. The division into main and accompanying activities was done by respondents.

The problem of accompanying activities will not be discussed in this paper, so all empirical material must be treated as simplified to some extent. This burden is not a significant one, however, if such basic activities as work, physiological needs satisfaction, reading, theatre and movie attendance etc., are under consideration.

3. BASIC TIME BUDGET INDICATORS

The easiest way to include time budget surveys into the broader frame work of socio-demographic statistics serving social politicians and planners is to take into account the indicators characterizing time consumed by the population for work, cultural activities, other forms of recreation, etc. These indicators belong to the group of social indicators concerning individual spheres of social policy.

Three basic types of indicators concerning the time budget are used by most researchers from different countries (see Szalai, 1972):

(a) The average daily duration of particular activities $(\bar{\bar{y}})$, calculated for the whole surveyed population or whole subgroups of this population defined by the researcher, (e.g. age groups, sex groups, educational or socio-occupational groups etc);

(b) a number of persons performing a particular daily activity (n') expressed as a percentage of the total number of persons investigated or of the number of persons belonging to particular subgroups distinguished by the researcher;

(c) The average daily duration of a particular activity performed by persons indicated by the parameter n', (i.e., only persons performing this activity) $(\bar{y})$.

Table I presents all three kinds of indicators calculated separately for the population living in urban and rural areas. Due to lack of space 47 detailed categories of activities which were distinguished in the original survey are aggregated in this table into main groups, with only work and leisure time remaining disaggregated.

Only the joint examination of all three indicators allows one to reach the conclusion that the average duration of work is longer among rural than among urban adult populations only because of the greater ratio of employment (economic activity) of the former, since working persons in towns spend more time at work. The greater length of daily leisure time for the urban population is caused, on the contrary, both by the greater percentage of people having free time during one average day and by the longer duration of leisure of people who enjoy it.

Such statements may have important implications for some social policy issues like economic activization, organization of work or providing leisure facilities.

The treatment of time budget survey results, discussed above, leads to the inclusion of time indicators into a broader set of social indicators (or socio-demographic statistics) but not to the integration of time budget with other statistical data. Some possibilities of such integration will be presented below.

TABLE I

Twenty-four-hours time budget of the adult inhabitants of urban and rural areas in Poland in 1976

Activities	Urban areas			Rural areas		
	Average duration of activities/all persons $\bar{\bar{Y}}$	Average duration of activity performed $\bar{Y}$	Daily Participation of persons in performing activity N'	Average duration of activities/all persons $\bar{\bar{Y}}$	Average duration of activity performed $\bar{Y}$	Daily Participation of persons in performing activity N'
ACTIVITIES DURING 24-HOURS – TOTAL	24.00	x	x	24.00	x	x
TIME FOR PHYSIOLOGICAL NEEDS[a]	10.02	10.02	100.0	10.05	10.05	100.0
DURATION OF WORK	4.06	7.36	54.0	5.26	6.49	79.9
Work for compensation – main, not connected with an agricultural holding	3.45	7.39	49.9	2.07	7.45	27.3
Secondary additional work for compensation	0.06	3.35	2.8	0.10	4.59	3.5
Agricultural field works/or in the garden/	0.06	3.18	2.8	1.15	4.47	26.2
Looking after livestock and poultry	0.03	1.37	2.9	1.10	2.09	94.0
Farm maintenance, repairs, etc.	0.01	2.27	0.7	0.16	2.38	10.3
Other activities connected with work	0.02	1.27	1.9	0.28	1.39	18.5
COMMUTING	0.53	1.11	75.0	0.49	1.19	61.8
HOUSEHOLD ACTIVITIES OUTSIDE HOME[b]	0.43	1.27	49.5	0.32	1.36	33.1
HOUSEHOLD ACTIVITIES (IN HOME)[c]	3.08	3.46	83.4	3.18	4.31	73.1
LEARNING	0.32	5.47	9.1	0.17	6.12	4.5
LEISURE TIME	4.36	4.50	95.2	3.33	3.55	90.7
Social work and activities	0.04	2.03	3.1	0.03	2.04	2.0
Reading newspaper and magazines	0.18	0.46	38.8	0.11	0.48	22.5
Book reading	0.14	1.18	17.6	0.06	1.20	7.1
Watching TV	1.40	2.17	72.9	1.16	2.07	60.8
Listening to the radio	0.05	1.05	7.5	0.06	1.07	8.4
Listening to the music on records or tapes	0.01	1.00	2.2	0.01	1.08	1.0
Active participation in cultural activities	–	1.27	0.3	–	2.10	0.1
Theatre performances	0.01	2.26	0.8	0.01	3.10	0.2
Cinema projections	0.04	2.04	3.0	0.01	2.07	0.8
Meetings, visits, plays and social games	0.43	2.37	27.8	0.35	2.45	21.1
Walks, watching sports events	0.19	1.39	19.4	0.04	1.32	4.3
Active practicing sports	0.03	2.57	1.6	–	1.37	0.5
Hobbies	0.05	1.42	4.8	0.02	1.30	2.5
Religious activities	0.08	0.59	13.6	0.11	0.54	19.6
Talks with family members	0.10	0.49	20.1	0.11	0.54	20.4
Talks with other persons	0.05	0.52	10.2	0.08	0.57	14.1
Other leisure time activities	0.08	1.24	10.0	0.07	1.24	8.1
Passive resting	0.28	1.23	33.5	0.31	1.32	33.8

[a] Sleep, personal hygiene and meals.

[b] Shopping, use of services, dealing with offices and other institutions.

[c] Cooking, washing, sewing, cleaning, household appliances repair, child or elderly people care, etc.

4. TIME BUDGET AND MANPOWER ACCOUNTS

Manpower accounts are drawn up so that one part characterizes manpower potential, while the other characterizes its use. In both, an individual is an accounting unit. This approach is useful for examining the socio-demographic structure of the population. On the basis of this type of analysis we get information on the number of people (by sex and age) employed in different divisions of the national economy, at schools and higher education establishments, or outside employment and education.

This type of information does not say much about real involvement in work processes, particularly when referring to employment in agriculture. In many economic papers it is stressed that, contrary to some non-agricultural branches of the national economy where duration of women's work is more or less equal to that of men's, the involvement of women in work in private agricultural holdings is much smaller than that of men. In many countries extensive employment in agriculture surpasses actual needs and is possible only on the condition that the duration of women's or older persons' work becomes shorter. S. Kuznets (1971) assumes that women employed in agriculture spend effectively at work on a farm only one fifth of the time devoted to work by men. Such an assumption can be verified in particular countries and in particular socio-economic systems only by careful examination of time budget data. In order to make a proper evaluation of the economy, for comparison purposes and for the evaluation of real amounts of work done by specific population groups, it is necessary to examine average daily duration of working time, by sex and age groups, and socio-economic categories. In addition to that, it is important in Poland to find out the degree of commitment in work outside agriculture and in agriculture by members of farm families who, working outside agriculture, help to run an agricultural holding. The Polish social structure includes a great number of such persons.

The data obtained from the last survey in Poland shows that a man economically active outside agriculture spends approximately 6 hours and 39 minutes daily for work for compensation while women spend 5 hours and 45 minutes, that is 86% of the time devoted to work by men. The data concern both principal and overtime jobs, as well as other additional work, excluding work in an agricultural holding owned by a family. The number is an average yearly value including Sundays and holidays, but excluding days on sick-leave and vacation. The values quoted differ but slightly according to age. The length of time devoted to work outside agriculture is not much influenced by additional activities in an agricultural holding.

Working time in a private agricultural holding is much more differentiated, as shown in Table II.

According to microcensus data (after corrections have been made according to the estimated error) in Poland in 1974 there were 5 million 375 thousand individual farmers [owners and helpers] and 2 million 434 thousand persons whose main work was done outside an agricultural holding, but who belonged to households using an individual agricultural holding. On the basis of indicators in Table II we can convert these data into numbers showing employment in individual agriculture in an accouting unit which is equal to the effective employment of man-farmer up to 64 years of age (i.e. *'full-time employment unit'*). In this way we obtain 4 million 753 thousand full-time employed individual farmers.

This example shows how the data on the number of economically active men and women can be transferred into data on 'full-time employees', when integrated with time budget data.

TABLE II

Worktime in a private agricultural holding by various categories of the economically active population (daily averages)

Categories of persons according to type of main job	Hours and minutes	Ratio (a person working full-time = 1)
Private farmers/owners and family members who help:		
Men up to 64 years of age	7.07	1.00
Men aged 65 and over	6.26	0.90
Women up to 64 years of age	4.28	0.63
Women aged 65 and over	3.24	0.48
Members of agricultural families whose main job is outside the private farm:		
Employed mainly in other jobs in agriculture:		
Men	2.26	0.34
Women	0.36	0.08
Employed mainly outside agriculture:		
Men	2.14	0.31
Women	0.52	0.12

Having at our disposal fully representative data on time budgets we can, apart from converting the number of employees into 'full-time employees', make a nation-wide *account of work* with the estimation of *gross work* in the society. An attempt can be made to relate the time of real work to the national income (on a nation-wide scale) or to production in particular branches of the national economy. This would be a new approach to the problem of productivity.

A socio-occupational distribution of the working population is not the same as the distribution of the total time of work since the length of work varies from one group to another. So the question may arise, how much do particular socio-occupational groups contribute to the national economy, not in terms of number of employed persons, but in terms of the amount of work they do?

An index reflecting the relationship of participation level of a given group in the work time of the whole society to the participation of the same group's members in the labor force reflects the relative involvement of this group in economic activity.

This index may be calculated in two ways. One may calculate it by dividing the percentage of total work time of the entire society which is contributed by a particular socio-occupational group by a percentage expressing the number of members of this group in the whole labor force. This index may contain a substantive rounding error, if rounded percentage values are used for computation. Sometimes more exact results may be obtained by dividing an average daily work time of the group under investigation by an average daily working time of the whole economically active population. Arithmetically the results should be the same, if calculated with enough accuracy. Such an index may be called the relative duration of work.

The representativeness of time budget samples and especially the reflection of the socio-occupational structure of the total population is very essential for this kind of analysis. Since unfortunately neither the representativeness of the 1976 household budget survey (used to investigate time budgets, also) nor the socio-occupational structure of the 1976 working population were known, all time budget data were weighed to make the structure of the sample identical to the socio-occupational structure of the population investigated in Poland by microcensus in 1974. The assumption was made that the use of time did not change during the two year period from 1974 to

1976. Estimates of work time, social distribution, and the distribution of time devoted to other activities in 1974 resulted from this procedure.

Estimates presented in Table III indicate among other things that individual farmers who constitute 30.4 percent of the labor force utilize only 26.6 percent of the time spent at work by the whole working population. This difference results first of all from a great number of women who spend much less time working on their farm than their husbands and who divide their working time between the farm and the household (see Table II also).

On the other hand, agricultural workers and specialists, as well as transport, communication and non-industrial service workers contribute to the total work time of the economically active population about 1.2 times more than

TABLE III

Elements of worktime balance of economically active Polish population (Estimates for 1974)

Socio-occupational groups [a]	Structure of labor force (%)	Average duration of daily worktime [b] $(\bar{\bar{y}})$	Social distribution of total worktime (%)	Relative worktime duration
Total	100.0	6.19	100.0	x
Administrative and office workers	9.5	5.58	8.8	0.95
Specialists in technical occupations	4.8	6.26	4.8	1.00
Specialists in non-technical occupations	5.8	5.58	5.4	0.90
Transport, communication, trade and personal [c] service workers	11.3	7.16	12.7	1.16
Industrial and construction workers	27.3	6.57	29.3	1.10
Specialists in agricultural occupations	0.5	7.34	0.6	1.19
Agricultural workers	2.4	7.43	2.8	1.20
Individual farmers	30.4	5.36	26.6	0.87
Other and unknown	8.0	6.53	9.0	1.09

[a] Socio-occupational groups are defined by the character of job, not by the branch of national economy.
[b] Average daily duration of all days, including weekends and holidays. (All Sundays but only one Saturday each month are free in Poland.)
[c] Housemaids etc. excluded.

would be expected by group size. The contribution of industrial and construction workers to the total work time is also greater than their share in the total labor force but the difference is not very great in this case.

5. TIME BUDGET, THE GROSS NATIONAL PRODUCT AND PRODUCTIVITY INDICES

We have no data available now on the part of national income produced by particular socio-occupational groups and we have no data on the time budget of workers of particular branches of the economy. The efficiency of one hour of work done by a member of a socio-occupational group or a worker in an economic branch (i.e. productivity index) could be calculated if the data mentioned above were available. Availability of additional data on wages and salaries of particular groups may allow us to calculate financial rewards received by members of different groups for one hour of their work and to calculate a ratio of one hour salary to one hour of product. Such data are indispensable for an analysis of the interrelations between social distribution of work and income. Very little has been done till now by sociologists or other scientists interested in social indicators in this respect, in spite of the importance of such analyses for social and economic policy.

The concept of national product used most often in Poland as well as in other socialist countries is not suitable for calculating the work efficiency of the whole working population, since, according to the assumptions of the so called 'Material Product System' (M.P.S.), it comprises only the value of material production, services excluded. Most Western estimates of gross domestic product in East European countries, (taking into account both material production and services), are very crude because of a lack of appropriate, detailed basic statistical data which are necessary for such estimations. Fortunately the value of gross national product including services (S.N.A. i.e. the 'System of National Account' concept) was carefully calculated in Poland by the Central Statistical Office for 1974 (GUS, 1976). This value is expressed both in Polish zlotys and U.S. dollars. The dollar-zloty ratio was estimated according to the real purchasing power of both con-sumption and investment goods and was based on several previous international comparisons (INSEE-GUS, 1975; ICP, 1975).

According to the analyses mentioned above, the Polish gross domestic product amounted in 1974 to 1503 billion zlotys or 73 billion dollars. The

Polish economy employed at the same time 17.7 million persons. (The last figure may differ from some official publications, because it concerns both full and part-time employees and is corrected according to the estimation of microcensus error.) The comparison of both figures indicates that each economically active person produced on a average in 1974 in Poland material goods and services of a value of 84 900 zlotys or $4100. It must be underlined that if the dollar-zloty ratio seems to be not very realistic to those who know conditions in both countries from their personal experience as tourists, it is so because the costs of many social services (health and education included) are much lower in Poland than in U.S.A. Low costs of these services causes also a relative lowering of the aggregated value of the gross national product.

The time budget survey indicates that each economically active person spends daily 6 hours and 19 minutes at work. This is an average of working days and weekends in all four months under investigation, but does not take into account those persons who left their families at the time of the survey for a yearly holiday leave, and the sick. It must be stressed moreover, that state and religious holidays took place mostly in the periods not covered by the survey. So to estimate the number of work hours in the whole year, an average daily work time should be multiplied by less than 365 days. We have no good statistical data indicating a proper number of days, so we may only make an arbitrary assumption. If we take only 330 days, which seems to be below a reasonable minimum, the value of the gross national product produced during an average work hour would be 40.6 zl. If we take 355 days, which – on the contrary – seems to be above a reasonable maximum, the value would be 37.8 zl. The difference is not very great so we may conclude that one average work hour of a Polish economically active person produces about 40 zl. ($2) of the gross national product.

6. TIME BUDGET AND THE ACCOUNT OF INCOME AND EXPENDITURE OF THE POPULATION

The data on the income of the population come from the two statistical sources: family budget surveys (micro data) and the data from the economic statistics on the distribution of national income (macro data). The macro data can hardly be disaggregated in such a way as to show the incomes of small population groups as suggested in the previous section. It is possible, however, to define the value of income from different sources, in specific socio-economic categories of households due to family budget surveys (micro data). When possessing such data we can compare the expenditure of labor by households to the income from work. In this way we can evaluate the 'remunerativeness' of work in worker-, peasant- and intellectual-families, in urban and rural areas, etc.

TABLE IV

Average duration of leisure time activities on Sundays and working days, by yearly expenditure on cultural services, education and recreation per head in a household

Activity	Total	Up to 200 zl	201 – 400	401 – 800	801 – 1600	1601 – 3200	3201 – 5000	5000 and over
Sunday (hours and minutes)								
Total	7.57	7.10	7.36	7.56	8.08	8.07	8.30	8.29
of which:								
Social work and activity	0.06	0.02	0.03	0.05	0.08	0.05	0.10	0.18
Reading newspapers and magazines	0.20	0.16	0.17	0.18	0.22	0.23	0.23	0.24
Reading books	0.15	0.08	0.07	0.14	0.15	0.21	0.23	0.23
Watching TV	2.32	1.21	2.20	2.43	2.50	2.39	2.35	2.41
Listening to the radio	0.09	0.17	0.12	0.06	0.06	0.08	0.07	0.09
Theatre, concerts, operas	0.02	0.05	0.02	0.04	0.01	0.01	0.01	0.02
Cinema	0.04	0.01	0.03	0.04	0.04	0.07	0.09	0.06
Social events, visits, plays	1.44	1.41	1.49	1.46	1.38	1.48	1.39	1.53
Walks, sports events	0.36	0.11	0.20	0.32	0.42	0.46	1.04	0.45
Sports and tourism	0.05	0.01	0.01	0.03	0.05	0.05	0.17	0.18
Religious practices	0.40	0.58	0.49	0.41	0.37	0.28	0.34	0.26
Working days (hours and minutes)								
Total	3.19	2.59	3.14	3.22	3.22	3.21	3.22	3.41
of which:								
Social work and activity	0.03	0.01	0.02	0.03	0.04	0.04	0.04	0.06
Reading newspapers, magazines	0.13	0.10	0.11	0.13	0.15	0.16	0.15	0.15
Reading books	0.09	0.05	0.08	0.08	0.10	0.11	0.11	0.17
Watching TV	1.15	0.43	1.11	1.18	1.12	1.23	1.17	1.21
Listening to the radio	0.05	0.07	0.06	0.05	0.04	0.03	0.03	0.03
Theatre, concerts, operas	–	–	–	–	0.01	–	0.01	–
Cinema	–	–	–	–	0.02	0.03	0.03	0.04
Social events, visits, plays	0.25	0.26	0.23	0.24	0.22	0.26	0.28	0.36
Walks, sports events	0.07	0.07	0.05	0.08	0.08	0.08	0.08	0.11
Sports and tourism	0.01	–	–	0.01	0.01	0.01	0.02	0.04
Religious practices	0.04	0.08	0.05	0.05	0.03	0.02	0.02	0.02

On the other hand, we can also examine the relationship between the expenditure for various activities and the time used for these purposes.

Surveys on the interdependencies between the total time budget (the model of time consumption) or its elements and the general income level, affluence or expenditures, can be very interesting, as well as important for the needs of social policy.

Significance is attached to surveying the relationships between the amount of expenditure on specific purposes like cultural consumption, entertainment and recreation, and the duration of time spent on them. When examining the relations between both, the real working time and the income from work, and the expenditure on specific purposes at leisure time and the actual use of leisure time, two types of analyses can be applied:

– on the aggregated level: comparing income or expenditure of large population groups on one hand and, specific elements of the time budget of these groups, on the other. Money budget (income and expenditure) and time bugdet surveys can be realized on different samples on the condition that the samples are representative for the same general population and that the same classifications of households are applied.

– on the individual level it is possible to apply an exact matching of data from money budgets and the time budget if the survey includes the same physical units. It would permit the construction of complex tables (cross-tabulation) and the application of more refined statistical analysis of the interdependencies between income and expenditure and time economy, for example the regression and correlation analysis used in Poland.

Table IV is an example of the cross-tabulation of directly matched data from the Polish surveys on family budgets and the time budgets.

7. TIME BUDGET AND SOCIAL CONSUMPTION FUND

Most of the cultural institutions, as well as others connected with various forms of recreation in Poland, are financed from social sources, within the social consumption fund. General outlays on cultural services and recreation are considerably higher than the financing from social consumption fund since some of them are in addition paid individually by the population in the form of buying services. Some of these services are fully financed and some only partly subsidized from the social consumption fund.

Knowing the total value of the outlay or only the outlays from the social consumption fund we are now interested in the outcome. One of the ways to define effects is by an analysis of general time resources devoted by the population to specific types of activities, the financing of which is described through economic statistics. Unfortunately, this particular method creates some problems, since the activity in many fields, closely related to cultural services and recreation, is not determined by the existing possibilities only. To a great extent it depends on personal motivation. Nevertheless, this type of approach would be tantamount to an attempt to define the degree (time duration) to which the population uses the existing possibilities created by available means.

Knowing this, apart from the social consumption fund, meant for financing some of the forms of cultural activities and recreation, we would possess a 'social time fund', that is the time resources spent by the society for this kind of activity.

The next step would be to examine to what extent the total amount of time for specific types of activities is used by various population groups in the society. Thus, we could call it a survey of time distribution between various groups of the population. The assumption can be made that the distribution of time devoted to a particular activity is parallel to the distribution of financial outlays for this activity from the social consumption fund. This is a simplifying assumption, but the simplification is not great enough to make the analysis unjustified. If, for example, we make an assumption that a social-occupational group 'x', representing ten percent of the total population, consumes 20% of the total time resources in the whole population to cinema, concerts, theatre performances, etc., it would enable us to state that this group uses the resources of social consumption fund meant for these sorts of cultural activities to a greater extent than the number of persons in the group would indicate. At the same time we can, more or less, state that this group consumes 20% of financial outlays on maintaining cinemas, theatres, philharmonic halls, etc. The matter is simplified of course, but it should be stressed that, up until now, we have not succeeded in finding fully reliable data on the use of various services by the population.

Table V contains some data on the distribution of different leisure activities among the Polish adult population. Let us underline only some of the most interesting findings in this respect.

It may be seen for example, that one fourth of the reading of books, newspapers and magazines (school books excluded) done by an adult

TABLE V

Social distribution of leisure time of Polish adult population (18 years old and more) (estimates for 1974)

Socio-occupational groups[a]	Social structure of population	Social distribution of leisure time					
		Total leisure time of population	Selected leisure activities[b]				
			tv watching	Concert or stage performance[c]	Movie	Reading	
						Books	Newspapers and magazines
Total population	100.0	100.0	100.0	100.0	100.0	100.0	100.0
Economically active	73.6	63.0	71.5	62.0	65.8	48.3	65.2
administrative and office workers	7.0	6.4	7.3	9.5	12.2	9.3	7.4
specialists in technical occupations	3.5	3.8	4.3	8.2	5.9	4.6	5.2
specialists in non-technical occupations	4.2	3.7	4.1	9.5	4.8	7.3	4.8
transport, communication, trade and personal[e] service workers	8.2	7.2	8.9	7.5	11.0	5.0	7.9
industrial and construction workers	20.1	18.9	21.7	17.0	22.8	11.8	20.6
specialists in agricultural occupations	0.4	0.3	0.5	0.0[d]	0.4	0.4	0.5
agricultural workers	1.7	1.7	2.5	0.0[d]	0.9	0.6	1.6
individual farmers	22.4	17.2	16.5	6.9	3.9	6.5	13.0
other and unknown	6.1	4.6	5.7	3.4	3.9	2.8	4.2
Economically inactive	26.4	36.2	28.5	38.0	34.2	51.7	34.8
students (middle and high school or university level)	4.5	4.8	3.9	11.7	18.2	12.8	3.6
pensioners	11.8	19.2	13.9	11.5	6.7	27.8	22.8
other (housewifes included)	10.1	12.2	10.7	8.8	9.3	11.1	8.4

[a] Socio-occupational groups defined by the character of job, not by the branch of national economy.
[b] Not all activities included in the total leisure time are enumerated in the table.
[c] All kind of life music and life performance (drama and light entertainment) included.
[d] Less than 0.05.
[e] Housemaids etc. excluded.

population is in fact done by the pensioners who constitute only 11.8 percent of the population. Students who constitute less than five percent of an adult population use nearly twenty percent of the time spent by this population on movie watching and more than ten percent of the time spent on attending concerts or stage theatre performances.

The social distribution of the time spent for T.V. watching is very similar to the social structure of the total population (with the exception of farmers), but, other 'cultural consumption' time categories are distributed less evenly and professional groups (educated specialists) show a tendency for greater participation in cultural activities. It must be stressed however, that workers in industrial and construction occupations (unskilled laborers for different simple work were not included in this group) participate in most leisure activities proportionately to their number in the total adult population. Only book reading seems to be under-represented in this group.

Individual farmers constitute a group which participates in the whole leisure time of the society and in particular leisure activities much less than would be expected by its size in the total population. They also participate less than expected in the total work time. This is so because they devote much more time than other groups to different household duties, included neither in work nor in leisure time in this analysis.

We did not present and discuss here the data on average duration of particular leisure or cultural activities performed by different socio-occupational groups. Such data are more often discussed by most time budget researchers and they can be found in other publications. Our aim is to point to some new possibilities for time budget analyses which may be of use for social planners, social politicians and people interested in the evaluation of these activities.

Most of the possibilities of time budget analyses in relation to other types of social statistics (discussed above) are only survey proposals. Presently only a few elements of these proposals have been executed in time budget surveys. The Polish survey was not planned with the intention of conducting such analyses, but some of the recommendations can be realized in the course of elaboration of its outcome as they are presented on this page. It concerns the working time balance in terms of full-time employees, problems of interdependencies between expenditures on specific forms of activity and the time devoted to them, as well as the social distribution of general work and leisure time resources.

Central Statistical Office, Warsaw

Polish Academy of Sciences, Warsaw

NOTE

* This is a largely extended and modified version of a paper presented by the Central Statistical Office of Poland during the meeting of the Working Group on Social and Demographic Statistics organized by the Conference of European Statisticians, Economic Commission for Europe, United Nations, Geneva 1978. The final version was completed by K. Zagórski during his visiting professorship at the Department of Sociology, Virginia Polytechnic Institute and State University, Blacksburg, Virgina in the U.S.A. The content of this version may not in all respects reflect an official view-point of the Central Statistical Office. The authors express their gratitude to Erin Gotard who devoted a lot of her time to editing the English manuscript.

BIBLIOGRAPHY

Adamczuk, L.: 1978, Budzet czasu mieszkancow Polski (Glowny Urzad Statystyczny, Warsaw).
GUS: 1976, Studium porownawcze dochodu narodowego Polski w dolarach U.S.A. za lata 1974 i 1975, ZBSE GUS (Instytut Planowania, Warsaw).
ICP: 1975, United Nations International Comparison Project: Phase One, A System of International Comparisons of Gross Product and Purchasing Power (Baltimore).
INSEE-GUS: 1975, Porownanie cen i poziomu spozycia Polska-Francja Institut National de la Statistique et des Etudes Economiques – Glowny Urzad Statystyczny (Paris-Warsaw).
Kuznets, S.: 1971, Economic Growth of Nations (The Belknap Press).
Szlai, A. (ed.): 1972, The Use of Time (Mouton, The Hague-Paris).
UN: 1976, Toward the System of Social and Demographic Statistics (United Nations, New York).
Wnuk-Lipinski, E.: Gospodarowanie czasem wolnym i zajetym, Glowny Urzad Statystyczny (Warsaw).

21

ILLEGAL IMMIGRATION
The Guestworker Option

Philip L. Martin and Ellen B. Sehgal

The United States annually apprehends almost one million Mexicans who are illegally in the United States. Three strategies have been proposed to deal with this illegal immigration: (1) do nothing (maintain the status quo); (2) provide amnesty for aliens present and attempt to discourage future entrants; and (3) convert illegal aliens into legal "guestworkers" by issuing limited-duration work permits to Mexican nationals.

A United States guestworker program is discouraged on both conceptual and empirical grounds. Guestworkers are aliens with restricted rights and would be "second-class citizens" in the United States. The availability of foreign workers does not solve "labor shortage" problems; further, it only postpones debate and decision on the kinds of jobs and job structure the United States should have. European experience has shown that temporary guestworkers are likely to become permanent residents and that exporting labor can distort economic development processes in sending nations.

In 1978 the Immigration and Naturalization Service (INS) apprehended almost one million Mexicans attempting illegal entry into the United States and returned them to Mexico. This aggregate number conceals the fact that some individuals are caught several times in one year, but the upward spiral in gross apprehensions (from 152,000 in 1968) confirms the suspicion that Mexican nationals are illegally entering the United States at an increasing

We are indebted to Howard Rosen, Marion Houstoun, Michael Piore and Vernon Briggs for helpful comments on an earlier draft. This article does not necessarily represent the official opinion of the Department of Labor. Giannini Foundation Paper 561.

pace (Fig. 1.) Moreover, most persons attempting illegal entry are not caught. To be sure, not all of these "undocumented workers" are Mexican.[1] Estimates vary widely, but most observers agree that about three-fifths of the estimated three to six million persons currently living in the United States without visas or work permits are Mexicans.

Mexicans figure prominently in the current debate on immigration policy because the United States shares a largely open 2,000-mile border with labor-surplus Mexico. On the Mexican side live 67 million people, 31 million of them under age 15. The population is growing at a 3.4 percent annual rate, against a rate of 0.6 percent for the United States. One-third to one-half of all Mexican workers are unemployed or underemployed, driving down wages to levels that make a *day's* work in Mexico as remunerative as an *hour's* work in the United States. United States employers' willingness to hire "undocumented workers" (foreign nationals without work visas) helps encourage the northward trek, which has swelled the 1970s wave of illegal immigration into the United States.

Although information is scanty, enough is known about illegal immigration to stem the tide at least partially. But both domestic and foreign policy concerns restrict the policy options that are available. About one-half of all the Mexicans apprehended by the INS are caught around the cities of El Paso, Texas and San Ysidro, California. An October 1978 proposal to improve border fences (primarily for crime control) in these areas brought such protests in both the United States and Mexico against the erection of a "tortilla curtain" that even improvements on the existing 27-mile fence were postponed.[2] Many employers want continued access to alien labor, and some groups believe that Mexicans should be permitted to cross the "artificial" border freely, while negotia-

---

[1] Illegal aliens, undocumented workers, and deportable aliens are the terms used most frequently to describe persons who entered the United States without inspection, entered the United States with fraudulent documents, or entered the United States legally but later violated the terms of their entry permit, e.g., tourists who overstay their visas or accept employment.

[2] The Mexican press, which kept the fence improvement a "headline story" until it was abandoned, accused the United States of being inhumane because the planned repairs had a "razor-sharp" grating. The ensuing press commentary largely overlooked one fence objective: controlling the youth gangs crossing the border for petty theft. See the *Houston Chronicle,* October 28, 1978, p. 1.

Figure 1. ILLEGAL ALIENS APPREHENDED IN THE UNITED STATES, 1970–1978

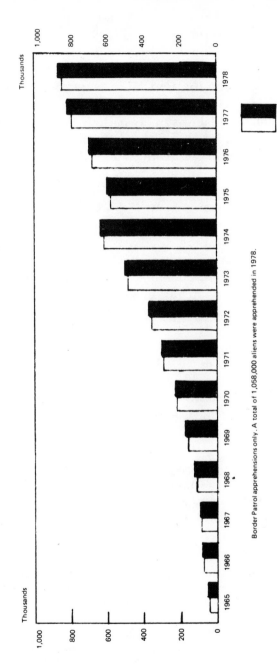

Border Patrol apprehensions only. A total of 1,058,000 aliens were apprehended in 1978.

Source: U.S. Immigration and Naturalization Service.

tions to gain United States access to Mexican energy supplies discourage the adoption of effective exclusionary policies that would alienate the Mexican government.

The increase in illegal immigration and the dim prospects for an internal solution to Mexican employment problems have prompted calls for action by the United States. Several proposals have been advanced, most of which include increasing the amount of foreign assistance to labor-surplus nations (Mexico), encouraging the development of labor-intensive industries abroad, and more vigorous enforcement of protective labor laws. The proposals differ in their treatment of illegal aliens already in the United States and in measures to prevent future entry. The simplest "option" is simply to maintain the status quo. A second would fine employers who knowingly hire aliens while offering amnesty to some aliens already in the United States. A third would convert illegals into legals by issuing temporary work permits for "guestworkers." Each option (or combination of options) has different implications for both immigration policy and the structure of American society.

Maintaining the Status Quo

The simplest policy for dealing with illegal immigration is to maintain the status quo, which permits the legal entry of about 400,000 immigrants annually. Present immigration laws encourage family reunification (three-fourths of all permanent immigrants), favor those with scarce jobs skills, and admit refugees. The family preference favors countries that have sent large numbers of immigrants to the United States, while the labor market criteria permit a professional/skilled worker bias among permanent resident aliens. The United States admitted 73,864 legal Mexican immigrants in FY 1976,[3] making Mexico the largest single source of the 400,000 legal immigrants admitted that year.

In addition to permanent immigrants, the United States annually admits about 30,000 persons for temporary employment.

---

[3] In 1977, Mexico and other Western Hemisphere nations became subject to the 20,000 immigrants per country limitation. Note that immediate relatives of adult U.S. citizens are admitted outside this 20,000 immigrants per country quota.

Under the H-2 system, similar to the now-defunct bracero program, the Attorney General usually permits foreign nationals to enter the United States after the Department of Labor certifies employer requests for foreign workers. This certification procedure is aimed at ensuring that domestic labor is unavailable and that the foreign workers will not adversely affect wages and working conditions. Many foreign nationals admitted for temporary United States employment are professionals—athletes, entertainers, scientific personnel, etc.—but about 10,000 are agricultural workers imported to pick apples and cut sugar cane. Mexico supplies virtually none of these temporary workers, in sharp contrast to its supply role under the bracero program (1942-1964), when five million Mexicans worked in Southwestern agriculture.

Ideally, many status quo advocates would prefer fewer immigration restrictions. Employers who can use alien labor get a docile work force while saving both wages and the cost of mechanizing or of restructuring jobs to attract domestic workers. Many non-employer groups also favor continued (illegal) immigration from Mexico. Some groups argue that the free movement of people is more important than national identification with either Mexico or the United States, while others limit their advocacy to assisting Hispanics already in the United States who want to regularize their status. Status quo advocates agree with proponents of other immigration options that existing wage and working condition legislation must be strictly enforced to prevent the exploitation of both natives and aliens.

Status quo advocates have effectively dominated policy making to date, thwarting efforts to tighten the border and blocking both employer sanctions and a worker identification system. Their effectiveness lies in the ambiguity inherent in any debate on illegal activities: no incontrovertible evidence exists as to their extent and impact. Status quo advocates argue that illegal immigrant estimates are exaggerated, that few aliens take jobs that would have been filled by natives, that most aliens pay taxes rather than obtain social welfare benfits,[4] and that, in any case, Mexicans have

[4] On these points, see Wayne Cornelius, "Mexican Migration to the United States: Causes, Consequences, and United States Responses," unpublished working paper, MIT, July 1978. Cornelius also argues that "it is clear that the majority of Mexicans who migrate to the United States do not want to stay here permanently" (p. 27).

as much right to enter the United States in the 1970s as Europeans did a century earlier. By preventing change, status quo advocates effectively perpetuate an immigration system that may admit as many as two illegal aliens for each legal entry.

Employer Sanctions and Amnesty

Despite our immigrant heritage, a majority of Americans apparently oppose the renewal of large-scale, nineteenth century-style immigration.[5] Regarding illegal immigration, the Gallup organization reported that 52 percent of the American population opposed the Carter administration's proposed amnesty for persons living in the United States illegally since 1970.[6] Since most illegal aliens enter the United States to work, any measure that made it more difficult for aliens to find work would presumably discourage illegal entry. Depending on the question asked, some 60 to 80 percent of all Americans favor legislation that penalizes employers who "knowingly" hire illegal aliens.[7] Twelve states already have such legislation.

In light of public opinion, the Carter immigration proposals announced on August 4, 1977 seem generous. Distaste for round-ups and deportations (as well as possible foreign relations repercussions) prompted a proposal for a two-tiered amnesty program. Individuals who could prove entry prior to 1970 (with payroll stubs, rent receipts, etc.) would become immediately eligible for permanent residence status and citizenship after five years. Those who entered between 1970 and 1977 (and stayed) would become eligible for a new status, temporary resident alien. As a temporary resident alien, an individual could continue living and working in

---

[5] Indeed, restrictionist attitudes characterize postwar American opinion. In the early 1960s, one writer noted that restrictionist views "are strongly held by so wide a segment of the American public that an argument for free immigration of the pre-1920 variety would not receive a serious hearing." Melvin Reder, "The Economic Consequences of Increased Immigration," *The Review of Economics and Statistics,* p. 222, August 1963.

[6] Reported in the *New York Times,* October 30, 1977, p. 13.

[7] Gallop Poll release, April 24, 1977 (Princeton, N.J.). Among other responses in a face-to-face survey of 1,509 persons, 45 percent of the respondents favored legislation requiring an identification card that includes a picture and fingerprints. Only seven percent of those polled favored increasing the number of legal immigrants.

the United States for five years but could not participate in federally supported welfare programs, could not bring his family to the United States, and could not become eligible for citizenship through participation in the amnesty program. During the five year period, temporary resident aliens would be free to leave and reenter the United States. Aliens entering illegally after January 1, 1977, would be subject to immediate expulsion.

Amnesty is an administrative device designed to induce aliens currently in the United States to identify themselves, thus permitting more control over a now unmanaged population. Stepped-up border patrols are intended to keep potential aliens at home. But as long as employers need workers to fill menial jobs, individuals will have an incentive to enter the United States illegally. To discourage entry and force employers to favor natives and legal aliens, the Carter proposals include provisions for employer sanctions and civil penalties of up to $1,000 for each illegal alien employed. Under the employer sanction proposal, only employers who were accused of engaging in a "pattern or practice" of hiring illegal entrants would be prosecuted. An employer who can prove that some form of identification establishing legal status (e.g., a Social Security card) was presented cannot be prosecuted. The employer need only have seen the identification; he or she is *not* obliged to determine its authenticity.

To make the employer sanction proposal effective, some observers believe that a form of identification that is widely held and not readily counterfeited should be available. A leading candidate is a counterfeit-proof Social Security card. It is a logical choice because the Social Security number is already required by most employers, it can be assigned at birth (or legal entry) and cancelled upon death (or exit), and duplicates can be quickly detected with computer checks. If used for this purpose, the Social Security card would become, in effect, a domestic "work permit."

The idea of a *mandatory* worker identification, however, is repugnant to many Americans. Civil libertarians wonder if including an individual's number in a national computer system will permit police to trace people for reasons unrelated to employment. Many observers are troubled by the "big brother" potentials of the system, arguing that illegal aliens must pose truly disruptive socioeconomic costs before such an identification system would become acceptable.

Guestworker Programs

If employer sanctions and limited amnesty present insuperable problems and if the illegal alien "problem" requires action, some observers argue that illegals could be converted into legals simply by issuing temporary work visas. Most individuals enter the United States illegally in order to work, so the issuance of one- or two-year work permits would not alter the present character of illegal immigration (i.e., it would not immediately lead to family immigration), but would permit the United States to "manage" the (illegal) alien work force better. Guestworker advocates believe that most aliens want only short-duration employment in the United States, allowing the management made possible with work permits to minimize seasonal labor market disruptions. This option—granting work permits to potential illegal aliens—has an intuitively appealing logic and a ready model, the European *Gastarbeiter* programs.[8]

A guestworker program is usually the result of a bilateral agreement that details recruitment methods, responsibilities for travel and housing, and the obligations of host governments to protect migrant workers. One program advanced would permit Mexicans to apply in Mexico for year-long, renewable United States work permits. To avoid the abuses of the bracero program, the guestworker would be free to change employers but could, under some proposals, be confined to a single geographic area or occupation [e.g., unskilled labor in one Standard Metropolitan Statistical Area (SMSA).]

Some of the other American guestworker proposals call for an adaptation and expansion of the current temporary work (H-2) system.[9] Work permits could be issued in the labor-surplus coun-

---

[8] For an elaboration on the arguments in this section, see Philip Martin, *Guestworker Programs: Lessons from Europe,* prepared for the Joint Economic Committee, June 1979.

[9] The H-2 program is designed to provide flexibility to permit the entry of nonimmigrant labor under exceptional circumstances for limited periods of employment. Workers admitted under the H-2 program may (but rarely do) bring nonworking spouses and children (H-4's) and are entitled only to wages; they do not participate in Social Security or unemployment insurance programs, for example. Given its original intent and current

try on either a first-come, first-served basis or under a priority-preference arrangement.[10] Since it is assumed that illegal entrants would rather enter the United States legally, the number of work permits could be less than current illegal entry levels (perhaps 300,000 to 500,000 permits per year) if individuals knew that a short wait for "their turn" would assure legal entry and job protections.

Under most European guestworker programs, employers must search for natives before offering jobs to workers from outside the European Economic Community (EEC). Although guestworker rights vary by country and type of labor agreement (e.g., citizens of former colonies—Algerians in France[11] and Commonwealth citizens in Britain—enjoy special rights), most host countries guarantee guestworkers rights to organize into unions, the right to vote and participate in extra-union works councils at individual enterprises, and family-unification rights after one year's employment. In Europe, guestworkers pay income taxes and participate in normally extensive social welfare programs, including social security, children's allowances, and unemployment insurance. The details vary, but the general thrust is clear—guestworkers are aliens to be integrated into the work force but *not* into an immigrant stream eventually leading to citizenship.

---

purposes, the H-2 program would have to be substantially modified to change from a process for admitting 30,000 individuals, some for no more than a month or two, to an entry device for 500,000 year-long workers. At a minimum, individual employer certification procedures would have to be altered drastically unless several thousand administrators were assigned to the task.

[10] It is almost impossible to distribute work permits honestly in sending societies where "fees" (bribes) are commonplace. Any system that rationed the number of permits would likely be accompanied by informal fees to assure an individual's place on the waiting list. Turkey tried to convert this practice into a development instrument by giving priority to emigrating workers willing to invest in newly established Village Development Cooperatives before leaving. Cooperatives were quickly formed to jump members ahead in the emigration queue, but few actually began operations and still fewer survive today.

[11] Unlike other non-EEC aliens, Algerians entering France were eligible for 10-year residence permits, did not need a job offer or work permit to enter France, and could search for work in any occupation or industry. In May 1979, the French Assembly passed a law that, *inter alia*, prevented the renewal of the Algerians' 10-year residence permits. The French action is indicative of a European-wide trend to shed foreign workers. See "French Act to Curb Flow of Immigrants," *New York Times,* May 31, 1979, and "L'Assemblee limite les internements aux seuls cas de refoulement aux frontiers," *Le Monde,* May 31, 1979.

A guestworker program, the argument runs, has multiple benefits. Mexico (and other labor-surplus nations) are allowed a labor-export safety valve until their own development efforts make emigration unnecessary. United States employers get enough labor to avoid costly job restructuring, holding down product prices and inflationary wage pressures. Individuals from developing nations can earn money to finance a socioeconomic advance at home, while their remittances and industrial training accelerate the overall pace of economic development. Since guestworkers are presumed to be a flexible work force, they can be directed to areas and industries in need of labor, minimizing the relocations required of the native population. Even if some of these benefits do not materialize, a guestworker program would only recognize the fact that aliens already work in the United States and give policy makers one instrument to "manage" better a currently "unmanageable" population.

Guestworker advocates argue that a system of temporary work permits is feasible by pointing to the postwar Western European experience with migrant workers. Between 1960 and 1975, some 30 million alien workers shuttled between homes in Southern Europe, Northern Africa, and Iberia and jobs in Northern Europe. After Italian labor reserves were exhausted (the one million Italian guestworkers are guaranteed entry into other EEC countries because Italy is an EEC member nation), the labor-importing nations began to recruit in Turkey, Portugal, Spain, and Yugoslavia (Table 1). The migrant impact was and is substantial. Migrants typically constituted six to ten percent of host-nation labor forces (30 percent in Switzerland), draining five to 15 percent of sending-country work forces. As the number of migrants rose (nearly eight million were employed in 1973), it was predicted that 15 million migrants would eventually be included in the host nations' (Europe excluding Italy) total labor forces of 100 million.

The optimistic predictions of migrant labor's future proved wrong for reasons that should be sobering to domestic guestworker advocates. Rather than continue expanding their migrant workforces, labor-importing nations abruptly halted all labor recruitment in 1973-1974. Some companies (Volkswagen) and countries (France) went further, offering "golden handshakes" of

Table 1. ESTIMATED NUMBERS OF FOREIGN WORKERS, 1977

	Austria	Belgium	France	Germany	Luxemburg	Netherlands	Sweden	Switzerland
Algeria	–	3,600	331,100	–	–	–	200	–
Austria	–	–	–	75,000	–	–	2,400	24,100
Finland	–	–	–	2,900	–	–	103,000	–
Greece	–	8,900	–	162,500	–	1,900	9,200	4,800
Italy	2,100	119,000	199,200	281,200	10,800	10,000	2,800	253,100
Morocco	–	36,000	152,300	15,200	–	29,200	600	–
Portugal	–	5,800	360,700	60,200	12,900	5,200	1,000	4,800
Spain	–	27,600	204,000	100,300	2,200	17,500	1,900	62,700
Tunisia	–	2,000	73,000	–	–	1,100	400	–
Turkey	27,000	23,000	31,200	517,500	–	42,400	4,200	14,900
Yugoslavia	131,000	–	42,400	377,200	600	8,000	25,800	25,400
Others	28,800	143,900	190,600	296,600	22,600	21,000	73,800	103,000
Total	188,900	369,800	1,584,300	1,888,600	49,100	115,300	225,300	492,800

Source:

Belgium: The SOPEMI correspondent's estimate of the active population. Frontier workers not included.

France: Based on 1975 20 percent census. May well represent an underestimation.

Germany: Defined as "working in Germany," i.e., includes frontier workers.

Luxemburg: From official sources.

Netherlands: Holders of work permits (except for the 'Italians, who are estimated separately); thus estimate nominally includes frontier workers, but in practice these are likely to be excluded as Common Market citizens. Does not include Surinamese, etc.

Sweden: Includes only those resident, or intending to reside, for six months or more.

Switzerland: Comprises the "established" and those on annual permits; thus it does not include frontier or seasonal workers.

$2,000 to 4,000 to any migrant[12] who surrendered a work permit and left the country. What had gone wrong? If guestworker programs provide mutual benefits, how were labor-recruitment nations so quickly transformed into labor-autarky fortresses? If Europe's guestworkers programs ended with such abruptness under an aura of failure, should the United States initiate its own guestworker program?

PERMANENCE AND DEPENDENCY

The most important lesson of the European guestworker experience was the explosion of the "temporary" myth: temporary became permanent for up to half the migrant work force. Many of the reasons for permanence were predictable. Some individuals quickly adapted to the work and wages in host nations and were reluctant to return to lower living standards at home. Many migrants wanted to return but were rebuffed by the same unemployment and underemployment that drove them abroad in the first place. A number of migrants tried to lead "split" lives, purchasing urban land for a house at home but working abroad every other year. Whenever political or economic pressures abroad threatened migrants' chances for reentry into the host nation, most elected to stay abroad rather than risk later exclusion. As permanence became more pronounced as migrant concentrations in industrial centers became evident and as migrants began to form families, creating new demands for goods and services and decreasing the likelihood of returning home, pressure to "do something" mounted.

With permanence came new economic, social, and political problems. Permanent guestworkers become immigrants requiring the same housing and social services as those available to natives. As migrants left their barracks (which were often on employer property) for low-cost "regular" housing, competition and tensions followed. Migrant children born abroad were citizens of their parents' country, not of the host nation as in the United States.

---

[12] At Volkswagen, *all* workers were entitled to "golden handshakes" of up to one year's unemployment compensation. Given the public role in Volkswagen management, it is clear that the plan was largely aimed at encouraging migrants to depart "voluntarily".

Migrant children had to be educated, and the dilemma of whether to teach in the native language, the host-country's language, or both resulted in millions of children left between cultures and languages.[13] Some of the children adopted the attitudes of the host country, responding to civil rights activism and shunning the menial jobs gladly accepted by their parents. Migrant children who had only visited their "home" country identified success more closely with the host nation than with their parents' homeland.

Migrant children created economic as well as social and political dilemmas. Guestworkers were originally imported to fill labor market gaps, to take assembly line and service jobs rejected by natives. They permitted continued economic expansion, thereby opening new jobs opportunities for native workers. As natives were promoted, vacating lower level jobs, more and more jobs became "guestworker" jobs that natives were reluctant to take. As long as host nations continued to import labor, these jobs were filled, and the process received little attention. When the labor recruitment ban took effect, it was widely assumed that the children of migrants could and would enter the labor market for the menial jobs. But the "second-generation" effect had put labor-importing nations on a dependency treadmill. Because migrant workers were available to fill them, "bad" jobs were not eliminated; but the children of migrants refused to follow in their parents' footsteps, requiring yet another round of labor importation. Each further round of importation produced new permanent immigrants, while perpetuating the secondary jobs that the migrants were originally imported to fill.

European guestworker programs became, in effect, de facto immigration programs whose size, characteristics, and distribution were dictated by short-term employer needs, not by any long-term population planning. This transition from temporary worker to permanent resident occurred whether the host country was tough (Germany) or lenient (France) in accommodating guestworkers.

The permanence of European migrants and the treadmill of dependency that resulted are especially important for the United

[13] See Ray Rist, *Guestworkers in Germany*, Praeger, New York, 1978. Germany elected to integrate guestworker children in German schools, even though some sending-society governments "were strongly in favor of the proposal" to establish independent schools for guestworker children (p. 191).

States debate because the permanence developed despite more or less explicit policies to avoid permanent immigration. Except for France, most countries were explicit in declaring that "we are not a country of immigration."[14] Instead, host nations intended to adopt the *Rotationprinzip*. When an individual's year-long work permit expired, he or she would be sent home and replaced by a fellow countryman. But the abstract policy of limited duration work permits fell victim to employer requests for extensions (to avoid recruitment and training costs), migrant desires to stay, and the simple humanitarian gesture of not uprooting migrants in order to import replacements simply because their work permits expired. The fact that most immigrants continued to claim that they *wanted* to return home because they missed familiar friends, language, and amenities lulled host and sending governments into complacency, even as the average duration of stay climbed to over five years.[15]

Host nations have unwittingly gained permanent immigrants who have become a subclass demanding native rights[16] and have not eliminated the labor market conditions that encouraged labor importation in the first place. Migrants remain abroad because their own countries have not developed fast enough to provide them jobs; indeed, in many instances, returning migrants would find fewer employment opportunities than when they left. Once in residence, the receiving country became responsible for the migrant's fate, losing the freedom-of action that accompanies the notion that guestworkers can be imported and exported according to domestic economic conditions.

[14] Sweden is an exception, treating guestworkers as immigrants and going to great lengths, including 240 hours of employer-paid language training, to offer foreign workers a true "choice" between remaining or returning. See Jonas Widgren, "Sweden," in *International Labor Migration in Europe*, R. Krane, Ed., Praeger, New York, 1979.

[15] Relatively few migrant workers *intend* to stay abroad. Instead, they continue to believe they will return as soon as a savings target is reached and/or job prospects appear at home. One observer notes that "almost no European migrant initially thinks of a long stay abroad, although about 50 percent stay for more than 5 years." Salustiano del Campo, "Spain," p. 158, in R. Krane, *op. cit.*

[16] Some argue that "permanent migrants" deserve preferential treatment because they entered their new homelands with restricted rights. For example, a French report argues: "One cannot repeat too often that the foreign population needs an infrastructure in the realm of schooling, health, administration and housing that is *better* than that of the French population." G. Mauco, "Les Traveilleurs Etrangers," *Le Monde*, March 25–26, 1973 (emphasis added). Similarly, a German study concluded that the "rise to equality can only be achieved by putting imigrants in a privileged position for a limited time," *Denkschrift zur Reform der Aüslanderpolitik*" (Arbeitswohlfahrt Bundesverband, Bonn, March 30, 1973).

EFFECTS ON SENDING COUNTRIES

European complacency in the face of ever-lengthening durations of stay resulted from the mistaken notion that the need for foreign labor was temporary *and* that the accelerated economic development made possible because of worker remittances and foreign training would provide an economic magnet encouraging returns. Most migrants initially went abroad with a target savings goal. But this savings goal usually reflected a desire to purchase land or consumer durables, *not* investment shares in local industries. As a result, worker remittances often led to land price inflation, especially on the urban fringe, and introduced a new dependency on foreign-made consumer durables—cars and goods purchased abroad and brought back on vacation visits or permanent returns. Despite bilateral efforts to channel worker remittances into productive investment, the "typical" returned migrant is far more likely to build a home and become a taxi driver than to enter local industry. As a result, *individual* purchasing and employment decision on return do little for a labor-sending country's long-term industrial development.

The most careful study of the impact of labor's export on a developing country is Suzanne Paine's analysis of the Turkish economy between 1965 and 1974.[17] In general, she found that the actual effects of emigration tended to be negative rather than positive. Examples abound. The exodus of guestworkers results in age polarization, especially in rural villages. As the 20- to 50-year-old rural males emigrate, land consolidation would be a logical agricultural reform. Remaining dependents often rely on remittances to purchase daily necessities, but few rural families are willing to sell or even lease their land, given the uncertainty of the breadwinner's tenure abroad. Instead of consolidation and rationalization, some of the land is left idle, forcing increased food imports because rural workers emigrated. The very uncertainty of the migrant's stay abroad makes individuals hesitant to sell or even give long-term leases on their land at home, preventing the local assemblage of acreage which could justify major agricultural investments.

[17] Suzanne Paine, *Exporting Workers: The Turkish Experience,* Cambridge University Press, Cambridge, 1974.

Just as agriculture is not often transformed by the emigration of labor, so industry can be helped or hobbled by emigration. In theory, the return of migrants accustomed to industrial life should facilitate industrial production, since domestic training costs are reduced. In practice, skill differentials widen as the more skilled work force emigrates, encouraging developing country industries to take a turn toward capital intensity because of employer uncertainty over work forces loyalty given foreign opportunities. In 1973, for example, 136,000 Turks left for foreign jobs, but an additional 1.5 million were registered to emigrate at the first opportunity. A bias toward more capital intensity may not increase domestic unemployment so long as migrants continue to go abroad, but a foreign recession can send migrants home to find their old jobs replaced by machinery. Once again, theoretical benefits can quickly turn into practical problems.

Even if industrial jobs are available to returning migrants, the "training" received in industrial countries is often irrelevant at local factories. Local producers are more likely to use "older" capital equipment, so that returned migrants must often be "retrained" to be absorbed in developing countries' industries. Belated recognition of this block to return has spurred the creation of "vocational training" programs in labor-sending nations financed by host countries seeking to rid themselves of migrants, a policy that has earned a chiding from the Council of Europe.[18]

To sum up, temporary worker programs may aid individuals, but they rarely accelerate economic growth in sending societies. As a result of sending workers abroad, many of the labor-sending nations quickly passed from agricultural to service economies, rarely stopping to build an industrial base. Instead of going into industrial investments, worker remittances went into "unproductive" land purchases and imported consumer durables, distorting rather than balancing the development process. Returned migrants preferred self-employment to industrial work, using investment remittances to purchase taxis or transport vehicles. The remitances themselves proved an uncertain source of foreign exchange, decreasing after the 1973-74 recession when they were most

[18] See the Report of an Ad Hoc Meeting of Senior Officials, *New Developments in Intra-European Migration Since 1974*, Council of Europe, Stockholm, 1978.

needed. No labor-sending country can rely on worker remittances to be a *stable* source of foreign exchange when making development plans; indeed, Turkey's current $2.9 billion foreign debt was incurred in part because of an overly ambitious development plan which placed too much reliance on worker remittances, remittances which dropped sharply when the number of Turks emigrating fell from 136,000 in 1973 to 4,000 in 1975.

Sending temporary workers abroad has not promoted job-creating development at home. Some observers go much further, arguing that international labor migration is a plot by the industrialized nations to keep the sending nations poor, to keep a reserve labor supply on tap. Describing the effects of labor exports on Yugoslavia, *New Yorker* writer Jane Kramer notes:

> . . . twenty-five years of emigration have done a lot to keep the countries of the south [i.e., of Southern Europe] underdeveloped. The emigration had a placebo effect on fundamental social and economic problems, offering temporary solutions to unemployment and encouraging illusions to domestic wealth invested unproductively.[19]

If the migrant workers' productive contributions primarily redound to the benefit of the host nation, should labor-receiving nations continue to claim the right to open and close their borders at will? "The growing realization that international migration is an inequitable and unrequited resource transfer has led to calls by poor countries for compensation."[20] The most concrete of these was a 1977 demand for the establishment of an "International Labor Compensation Facility" through which host countries would compensate sending countries.

SUMMING UP THE EUROPEAN GUESTWORKER EXPERIENCE

European guestworker programs halted under a pessimistic cloud. The slow spread of rights to migrants—most countries permit

---

[19] Jane Kramer, "Profiles: Yugoslav Workers in Sweden," *The New Yorker,* March 22, 1976. The same point is made more strongly by Mario Nikolinakos, *Polititische Ökonomie der Gastarbeiter Frage,* Rowohlt, Hamburg, 1973.

[20] W. R. Böhning, "International Migration in Western Europe: Reflections on the Past Five Years," *International Labour Review,* 118: 410, July-August 1979. The compensation facility was proposed by Crown Prince Talal of Jordan.

migrants to hold trade union offices, and Sweden permits some migrants to vote in municipal elections[21] —promises eventually to make polyglot Europe even more diverse, but the lag in extending rights threatens civil rights pressures and social tensions during the integration process. Immigration continues but now consists of dependents rather than workers. In France, for example, family members accounted for three-fourths of all non-EEC immigration in 1975, up from 30 percent in 1970. In short, European host nations inherited a permanent population and a looming civil rights problem without filling the labor market gaps that encouraged migration in the first place.

Lessons for the United States

Unless carefully planned, an American guestworker program could result in many of the same European problems and some new ones as well. A United States guestworker program would serve one of three purposes: (1) it could rectify general labor shortages; (2) it could supply alien workers to fill particular labor supply gaps ("the jobs Americans won't take"); and (3) it could be initiated to relieve unemployment pressures abroad. No one suggests that the United States currently faces a *general* labor shortage. The fate of jobs now held by illegal immigrants is the subject of vigorous debate; no one knows if employers could and would upgrade jobs now held by aliens. Indeed, if the United States government develops a guestworker program to supply workers for "jobs Americans won't take," in effect it is intervening to preserve the existing job structure; employers have few incentives to upgrade wages and working conditions if alien labor is available, widening the gap between "good" and "bad" American jobs.[22] The most frequently

[21] See Tomas Hammer, "The First Immigrant Election," *International Migration*, 4(2/3):153–155, 1977. The law permitting immigrants to vote in municipal elections was passed in December 1975, more to establish "fairness" than in response to migrant demands. In the first election (September 19, 1976), 59 percent of all "immigrants" voted, compared to the 92 percent turnout among native Swedes.

[22] Good and bad jobs vary widely in the industrialized countries. Among the major auto producers, only the United States and Japan still rely on natives for assembly line work. Mining and construction use largely native labor in the United States but rely heavily on alien labor in Europe. Hotels and restaurants tend to rely on alien workers in many industrialized nations.

voiced argument is that aliens will enter the United States in any case, and that some regulation of this inevitable alien labor flow is better than none.

European countries imported workers when their unemployment rates were near zero, to meet general *demand* pressures, not to "manage" illegal immigration resulting from (Mexico) supply pressures and some specific historical demand pressures, e.g., for braceros.[23] The causation is fundamentally different. Unemployment among the Americans most likely to compete with Mexican entrants (youth, women, and minorities) is already high; importing Mexicans can only aggravate unemployment pressures *without* changing the jobs that may be partially responsible for current unemployment levels.[24] A demographic "bust" in the mid-1980s may change this unemployment picture, but a guestworker program today can only aggravate it without, once again, eliminating current reasons for native unemployment.

Any supply-oriented guestworker program will be difficult to administer. A program that overly restricts the number of work permits available would simply perpetuate current illegal immigration, reducing the "management" rationale for beginning the program in the first place. A supply-oriented program is not sensitive to the United States business cycle: whether unemployment is high or low, guestworkers are admitted. Indeed, an effective United States guestworker program would directly link entrant levels to *foreign* rather than domestic economic conditions.

Administering a "fair" guestworker program may, paradoxically, increase both legal *and* illegal immigration. Each legal guestworker flow is accompanied by an illegal flow that varies by country of origin (supply pressures) and ease of entry. In Europe, these illegal flows are estimated at 10 to 20 percent of the legal flow. If the United States initiated a guestworkers program, demands for "fairness" may require the inclusion of Mexico and other Caribbean,

[23] Some observers argue that employers "actively recruit" immigrant workers by informing their current employees of new job openings, establishing a system of "informal recruitment." See Michael Piore, *Birds of Passage: Long-Distance Migrants and Industrial Societies,* Cambridge University Press, New York, 1979.

[24] Agriculture is one industry where, it is argued, "labor shortages" exist. But these "shortages" may be a mirage—explainable more by current wages and working conditions than some inherent distaste for farm work. It should be noted that Europe imported virtually no *Gastarbeiter* for agricultural work. In the United States, most hired farmworkers (three-fourths) are local residents, not migratory workers.

Central, and South American nations. With several countries sharing a restricted number of work permits, new countries may become sources of illegal aliens, as fellow (legal) countrymen advise those desiring entry and provide shelter to illegal entrants. Without increased border enforcement and employer sanctions, any "fair" guestworker program may increase the number of countries sending illegal aliens to the United States.

Instead of improving United States–Mexican relations in order to assure access to Mexican oil and gas, a guestworker program may aggravate bilateral tensions. The Federal government would assume the duty of enforcing wage and work condition standards for temporary workers and might also be obliged to create local guestworker assistance centers to provide language training, to handle migrant complaints, and to provide other services. American guestworkers, unlike their European counterparts, will not usually find a trade union or workers' council to handle their work place concerns.

Some guestworker advocates argue that the pending exploitation of Mexican natural resources will gradually eliminate the supply pressures that now encourage emigration. But natural resource production is inherently capital intensive, with the result that revenues generated from the sale of oil and gas must be expended on (other) job-creating projects to have any major employment impact. The history of agrarian reform and economic development in Mexico cannot make one sanguine about the potential for converting new foreign earnings into massive job-creating instruments that quickly lead to full employment.

Concern for human rights has diffused the idea that emigration is an individual right. No nation exporting labor to Europe (except Algeria in 1973) has explicitly attempted to curb the outflow of unskilled workers sought by foreign employers. Yet while emigration is becoming a human right in much of the world, immigration remains a privilege extended by the destination country. Guestworker programs, regardless of their other objectives, become an immigration avenue that eventually imposes costs on both sending and receiving societies. Rather than deferring costly adjustments at home or painful development processes abroad, labor-sending and-receiving societies might better face up to the difficulties each faces rather than postponing structural changes by transferring workers.

The Pandora's Box

America's illegal immigration is largely a supply-induced phenomenon whose magnitude and impact became apparent only in the 1970s. Little concern was expressed initially, largely because rural Texas and California have long provided at least temporary work to a variety of Mexican citizens as braceros, green carders, or undocumented (illegal) workers. As the illegal component grew and as Mexican nationals entered industrial and service jobs in urban areas, concern mounted, although the concern often came from persons not directly affected by the immigration, e.g., from population-control and environmental organizations. The unions representing workers in two directly affected sectors—agriculture and textiles—moved from anti-illegal to more ambivalent stances after they began organizing and representing undocumented aliens.

The result of these shifting positions is a policy stasis that perpetuates the status quo. Employers and Hispanic groups cannot make entry easier, but they can block attempts to change existing immigration practices. The "action" debate falls, by default, to those favoring employer sanctions to deter entry, on the one hand, and advocates of a temporary foreign worker program, on the other.

The debate on sanctions and guestworkers has just begun. The idea of sanctions immediately encounters strong opposition—from employers who do not want to assume a new duty, from civil libertarians who fear the consequences of an incipient worker identification system, and from Hispanics who fear yet another source of discrimination. Each fear is real. To compound these fears, any employer sanction system based on a counterfeit-proof identification system would affect *all* persons seeking work, not just aliens.

The combined weight of these objections has stymied Administration attempts to introduce a sanctions–identification system.[25]

---

[25] It should be noted that the administration proposals did not include a worker-identification system.

A guestworker alternative appears attractive—employers get their workers without liability for illegal hires; work permits (and their policing) are theoretically confined to noncitizens; and industries that rely on alien labor are not disrupted. But the guestworker alternative turns out to be no long-run alternative at all. Instead, it merely postpones the decisions causing controversy today without affecting the factors encouraging illegal immigration.

Given the ease of illegal entry, any United States guestworker program must issue almost as many work permits as there are potential illegal aliens; a few may wait their turn for legal entry. Once the program is accepted in principle, it must be decided whether the work permit is good in any region and occupation or just in particular areas and jobs. If the employer sanction is effective, employers must presumably police all applicants by requesting their work permits or papers providing citizenship. But even these administration problems pale alongside the longer-term issues. What if the "guests" want to remain? Do we force a "rotation" or extend permits? What about family dependents? Will they be permitted to enter at the outset, after one year, or never? If guestworkers pay income and payroll taxes, will they be entitled to benefits upon their return home? Will program regulations be the subject of ongoing negotiations (a likely prospect given oil leverage) or will they be fixed at the outset? Finally, how will the presence of guestworkers provide incentives to restructure or eliminate the menial jobs they are imported to fill?

Illegal immigration is an economic problem without a ready economic solution. Every change in current policy and practice will cause disruptions, disruptions whose net benefits are difficult to gauge. The two policy options that would change current practices—sanctions and guestworkers—have different short- and long-term consequences. Employers' sanctions may have drawbacks, but the European guestworker experience should also prompt caution about a massive temporary-worker program in the United States. A nation still struggling to provide equal opportunity for previously excluded groups would be ill-advised to choose deliberately to admit large numbers of foreign nationals as second-class citizens.

The real long-run solution for illegal immigration lies in efforts by the sending countries to promote economic development and limit population growth. If the United States wants to absorb directly some of the foreign unemployed, it could increase the number of permanent immigrants admitted, persons who are free to emigrate later. The United States has a long and enviable record of admitting and absorbing permanent immigrants. Rather than importing large numbers of foreigners for planned short-duration stays, it may be better to increase the permanent immigrant quotas of neighboring Mexico. More permanent immigration at the outset—where the United States is an unrivaled leader—may be preferable to massive ad hoc solutions to our current illegal immigration dilemma.

DEFENSE AND MILITARY POLICY

In a sense, defense and military policy is impervious to change. Actual budgetary shifts are slight over time, amounting to between two and five percent per annum; whatever administration is in power, it would seem that this area is a veritable sacred cow. But defense and military spending illustrates the very reverse. Even the most minor changes can have a cataclysmic impact. Every decision to build a new type of missile craft, or every round of arms control negotiations, has maximum impact within a global framework. What makes policy decisions in this area so momentous is the impact of mistakes or miscalculations on the symbolic conduct of international affairs. In other areas where policy recommendations are implemented, national areas in the main, even high-risk decisions do not affect the very life and death of the earth itself. But in the area of defense and military expenditures, such allocations affect issues of human survival and the terms of global survival. As a result, incremental changes in defense and military policy can have catastrophic consequences in world affairs.

Foreign policy can be viewed either as a necessity for choice, as Henry Kissinger has suggested, or as a choice among necessities. The latter is probably a more accurate expression of the domain of policy built into requirements of any nation living in the world of competing nations. In the case of the United States, a sovereign power of global influence, every bilateral, regional, or multilateral arrangement can be considered a separate policy sphere. For that reason, the analysis of U.S. foreign policy is as elusive as it is necessary.

Foreign policy may well be the most talked about and least implemented aspect of the policy process itself. Tucker's essay helps to explain why. The nation is in the throes of far-reaching policy shifts whose consequences are hard to foresee. Tucker argues that to avoid the excesses of concern and withdrawal characteristic of post-World War II foreign policy, it is necessary to carefully delineate the core and peripheral concerns of America's vital interests. For example, Middle East resources are vital to our survival; Central America's claims are rooted in geography and history. Tucker concludes by noting that American policy may or may not be accepted by allies but that disparities in power command action and yet limit the support of others. The piece by Chan can be read as a curious underwriting of Tucker's position. He argues that in the absence of multilateral policies, bilateral policies arise, with linkages between arms and oil in which major fuel consumers sell more weapons and major fuel producers buy more weapons. It is clear that industrialized nations employ arms sales for recycling petrodollars. Chan also indicates that those nations dependent on foreign energy are not discouraged in their demands for weapons. Hence, if the demand for weapons increases as a policy is pursued that is almost indifferent to the supply of energy, one can only conclude that the volatility of the international environment is increased in the absence of overall policy guidelines of the major powers. Huntington, starting from premises similar to those of Tucker, nonetheless draws very different conclusions. He admits that during the coming period American foreign policy will have to respond to diminished military capability with respect to the Soviet Union and increased dependence on external energy supplies. Yet he argues that an increased emphasis on NATO and on European defense should be the cornerstone of policy. It is Huntington's view that NATO is uniquely equipped to address a wide array of policy issues, from arms control agreements in gray areas to the means of dealing with serious threats to global areas outside NATO. Huntington concludes with the view that a greater unilateral emphasis in U.S. foreign policy would not so much set new priorities as upset old alliances.

22

THE PURPOSES OF AMERICAN POWER

Robert W. Tucker

Once again we have reached a major turning point in American foreign policy. On this, at least, there is widespread agreement. The conviction that the nation has come to a critical juncture in its foreign relations is broadly shared by those who may disagree on virtually everything else. Everywhere the signs point to the conclusion that for the third time in the post-World War II period we are in the throes of far-reaching change in the nation's foreign policy. What these signs do not divulge are the eventual scope and magnitude of the change.

Yet the same was true of the two earlier occasions in which American foreign policy underwent significant transformation. The observer in 1947 could not know from the events of that year the form that the emerging policy of containment would ultimately take. In its inception containment had no determinate outcome. Neither the external circumstances in which containment arose and which conditioned the immediate development of that policy nor the domestic reaction to these circumstances dictated the form that containment would ultimately take. It is true that in the sweeping language of the Truman Doctrine—"We must assist free peoples to work out their destinies in their own way"—as well as in its sense of universal crisis—"At the present moment in world history every nation must choose between alternative ways of life"—we can see the subsequent course of a policy that led to the equation of American security with world order, world order with the containment of communism, and the containment of communism with the conflict—Vietnam—that brought an end to the policy of global containment.

Robert W. Tucker is Professor of Political Science at The Johns Hopkins University, co-director of studies at The Lehrman Institute, and the author of *The Inequality of Nations* and other works. The author wishes to express his gratitude to David Hendrickson for his invaluable assistance in preparing this essay.

Reprinted by permission from *Foreign Affairs,* Winter 1980/81. Copyright 1980 by Council on Foreign Relations, Inc.

But the Truman Doctrine did not foreordain Vietnam, whatever the intent of its authors. Instead, it was the Korean War, and the sudden extension of containment to Asia that the war precipitated, which led to Vietnam. It was the American intervention in Korea—prompted far more by conventional balance-of-power calculations than by the universal pretensions of the Truman Doctrine—that led to the extension of containment in Asia, which was divisive from the start and never supported by more than a negative consensus.

What may be said of the policy of global containment may also be said of the policy that succeeded it in the late 1960s and early 1970s. The Nixon policy reformulation held out the promise of a foreign policy that, while preserving America's essential role and interests in the world, would be far less burdensome than the policy it presumably displaced. That promise could not be fulfilled. The logic of the Nixon reformulation, with its centerpiece of détente, was the logic of retrenchment. But this is not to say that the "new structure of peace" had from its inception an outcome that had to lead to the general decline experienced by America in the 1970s any more than the policy of containment initiated by the Truman Administration had to lead to Vietnam.

The domestic circumstances that attended the coming to power of the Carter Administration did not dictate the foreign policy that it followed during its first three years in office. In contributing to the further decline in the American global position it acted as much from internal conviction—not domestic political necessity—as the Johnson Administration did in its pursuit of the war in Vietnam.

It is worth recalling these earlier occasions today, if only to question the view that the course of American foreign policy in the 1980s is already largely dictated by the present situation. This view is shared by otherwise very divergent groups in the foreign policy spectrum. Those who believe that we must adjust our interests and behavior to the more modest position we now occupy in the world emphasize such a view as much as those who believe that we can and must recapture the position and leadership we once enjoyed. To the former, adjustment to our diminished status is a necessity we can attempt to escape only at our peril. To the latter, the reassertion of something akin to the former policy of global containment is the only safe course we can take. Otherwise we shall suffer ever more severe threats to our security, whether in our competition with the Soviet Union or, more generally, in our attempt to preserve the essential elements of a moderate international system.

If these positions are oversimplified here, the emphasis common to both is clear enough. In a darkening international landscape, the view that we must return to our pre-Vietnam role has recently gained an unexpected strength. Even so, its emphasis on the virtual absence of any other choice lacks persuasiveness. The degree of freedom in foreign policy we continue to enjoy today, once immediate security threats are addressed, may not be as broad as it once was but it is still considerable. How this freedom will be employed remains an open question.

II

How are we to account for the rising debate today over American foreign policy? To some, the debate has been largely precipitated by domestic critics who have succeeded in creating the requisite atmosphere for disaffection and debate over the nation's foreign policy. This is the view expressed most notably perhaps by former Secretary of State Cyrus Vance. To him, "much of the current dissatisfaction with the world and our role in it rests on certain fallacies." It is those who have purveyed these fallacies or myths—above all, "the pervasive fallacy that America could have the power to order the world just the way we want it to be"—who have led the way not only to much of the current dissension over foreign policy but to the "disturbing fear in the land that we are no longer capable of shaping our future."[1]

The difficulty with this view is its inversion of cause and effect. If there is marked dissatisfaction over American foreign policy today, it is not mainly the handiwork of critics but the result of events. It has been the visible decline of American power and position that has led today to a greater dissatisfaction over foreign policy than we have experienced for a decade.

If there can be little question over what has precipitated renewed debate, there can also be little question that it is a debate over American security: once again, we are "reconsidering" our security. We are doing so, moreover, against the background of an experience that led to the discrediting of the security rationale on which postwar American foreign policy had come to rest. The debate provoked by Vietnam was, like the debates of the 1930s and 1940s, over security. At issue was a broad disagreement over both the conditions, and even the very meaning, of American security interests whose vindication would justify, if necessary, the use of American military power.

But the outcome of the debate was unlike the outcome of earlier ones. Whereas the earlier ones had resulted in the triumph of the

---

[1] Speech delivered by Cyrus Vance at Harvard University, June 5, 1980, *The New York Times*, June 6, 1980, p. A12.

view held by the administration of the day, Vietnam led to the defeat of the view urged by the Johnson Administration. The succeeding Nixon Administration was careful to avoid the appearance of attempting to restore this view. Indeed, though it continued the war, it did so ostensibly on other grounds and, at the same time, seemed to accept the principal critique brought against the war by liberal and moderate opponents.

This critique denied that there were any meaningful security interests at stake in Vietnam. Clearly, it was argued, this was true of the interests for which the war was allegedly undertaken. Yet it was also held to be no less true of the interests for which the war was continued after victory had been all but openly abandoned. Vietnam had neither intrinsic nor symbolic importance for American security. Even when judged from the perspective of the containment of China, the outcome of the war was deemed largely irrelevant to the nation's legitimate security concerns. Instead, what Vietnam showed in the view of most critics were the absurd lengths to which a security rationale might be employed in circumstances that bore little relationship to those in which this rationale had once been meaningful and persuasive. In this liberal and moderate critique, then, Vietnam was above all the product of intellectual error. It resulted from a failure to understand the changes that had occurred over a generation and more, which had irrevocably altered while radically improving the American security position.

The prolonged debate that attended the war led to the belief that the world which had emerged by the middle to late 1960s, though far more complicated than the world of a generation earlier, was a much safer one—presumably, on the whole, because it had become a far more pluralistic one. Interpreted, in essence, as the triumph of nationalism, pluralism was thought to mean that communist expansion no longer carried the threat to America it had once carried. Pluralism meant, as well, that the prospect of Soviet expansion had dramatically declined. A pluralistic world might, it was conceded, be more disorderly. But in the circumstances of the late 1960s and early 1970s this seemed a reasonable price to pay if such a world also pointed to a marked decline in the need for military intervention as a means for preserving vital American interests.

Yet it was not so much the optimistic expectations generally entertained of an increasingly pluralistic world that appear so striking in retrospect, as it was the change that many, this writer included, found to have already occurred in the structure of

American security.[2] Taken alone, the appeal to pluralism as a refutation of the security rationale that led to Vietnam seemed, at best, inconclusive. But the argument that concentrated on the change in the structure of American security which had presumably occurred between the late 1940s and a generation later was another matter. It rested on the tried and true calculations that have always conditioned a nation's security—or so it seemed. On these calculations it no longer appeared plausible, let alone persuasive, to imagine an imbalance of power resulting in a serious threat to American security—that is, to our physical security, our economic well-being, or the integrity of our democratic institutions.

A wiser counsel would have cautioned—as a few did—that the persistence of a favorable power balance cannot be taken for granted, and that this particular constellation of power, like so many in the past, might also prove to be fragile and mutable. Indeed, we can now see that the foundations on which this constellation rested were beginning to erode even at the time their solidarity was being so confidently proclaimed. For the security it appeared to afford depended primarily on a favorable balance of military power that could be maintained, if at all, only by measures that were not taken.

Instead, the policy adopted by the Johnson Administration, and subsequently given formal expression by the Nixon Administration, accepted the Soviet Union as the equal—or soon to be equal—of this country in strategic military power. How this policy might be safely reconciled with the continued integrity of American vital interests and commitments in Europe, the Middle East and Asia, particularly if the United States together with its allies did not enjoy parity in conventional military power with the Soviet Union, was never satisfactorily explained. Those who made policy never persuasively addressed the central issue of what would effectively restrain the Soviet Union from taking such advantage as it safely could of an ever-improving military position.

---

[2] Robert W. Tucker, *Nation or Empire? The Debate Over American Foreign Policy*, Baltimore: The Johns Hopkins University Press, 1968, p. 32. Surveying the changes that had occurred over a generation in the structure of American security, I concluded that: "There is, in fact, no meaningful comparison to be drawn between the security position of this nation in the late nineteen-forties and its security position today. Whereas in the nineteen-forties it was still entirely possible, if not entirely plausible, to imagine an imbalance of military power that would threaten the physical security of America, today this contingency is no longer a meaningful possibility. Whereas in the nineteen-forties it was still entirely possible, and altogether plausible, to imagine an imbalance of power resulting in a security problem the solution of which would severely strain the nation's resources and jeopardize its democratic institutions, today this contingency is, at best, very remote."

Instead, they largely proceeded from the undemonstrated assumption that the Soviet Union had become—or was in the process of becoming—a status quo power, and that it could now be expected to act with growing restraint. When, in the face of contrary evidence, this assumption began to wear thin, many fell back on the argument that even if the Soviet Union was intent upon expanding its influence, and would employ its growing military power to this end, the forces of resistance thrown up by a determinedly pluralistic world would ultimately frustrate its efforts.

Applied to areas of secondary interest, which also happen to be areas that are not contiguous to the Soviet Union, the merit of this argument may not prove to be of crucial concern. When applied to areas of primary interest that are also adjacent to the Soviet Union, or very nearly so, it is. With respect to these areas, among which the Persian Gulf is the prime case, the reliance on pluralism was and is little more than an expression of hope.

The degree of security that only yesterday was commonly taken for granted also rested on the assumption that continued Western access to the raw materials—above all, energy resources—of the developing world could be assured, and on terms compatible with substantial economic growth of the industrial democracies. Ironically, Vietnam and the debate the war precipitated appeared to many to confirm this assumption. America had entered the war, it was held, largely out of an excessive preoccupation in the 1960s with the Third World. An eminent commentator articulated the new understanding in noting that by any power calculus the states of the Third World "have no vital relation to the economic or strategic position of the developed countries. They do supply raw materials. But even here the typical observation concerns not their power as sources of such supply, but rather their weakness as competitive hewers of wood in the markets of the industrially advanced countries."[3]

These words were written when the storm was already gathering. In respect to the one transcendently important raw material, oil, demand was already pressing hard on supply. Rather than choosing to increase supply, and to remain competitive "hewers of wood," the producers chose to combine and to impose a fourfold increase in the price of their oil. At the time of the increase, some producers also initiated a limited embargo against states whose policies in the 1973 Arab-Israeli war were considered objectionable. Neither of these measures provoked significant Western re-

[3] John Kenneth Galbraith, "Plain Lessons of a Bad Decade," *Foreign Policy*, Winter 1970–71, p. 37.

action. Both challenged the foundations of the postwar order as no other event had since the 1940s.

Quite apart from the constraints on economic growth that OPEC price rises placed on the industrial democracies, the failure in 1973–74 to respond to the Arab oil embargo raised from the outset the issue of right of access to the oil supplies of the Persian Gulf. Obscured for a time by the preoccupation with the economic side of the crisis, the issue of access became apparent with the Iranian revolution, which shut off most of the production of a major producer. In swift succession, the Soviet invasion of Afghanistan revealed the potential external threat to Western access, while the outbreak of war between Iraq and Iran illuminated yet another aspect of the indigenous threat to what remains of the Western position.

It is in the coalescence of these two momentous developments— a military balance increasingly favorable to the Soviet Union and the steady erosion of Western power and position in the Persian Gulf—that the essential dimensions of the American security problem are to be seen today. The point has often been made that in its origins and subsequent course the energy crisis had very little to do with the Soviet Union and that, indeed, the Soviets have been—at least, until recently—quite cautious and tentative in taking such advantage as they might have from the decline of the Western position in the Gulf. Though on balance this point is well taken, at present it is not possible to separate the issue of Western access to the Gulf from the military power the Soviet Union is able to bring to bear in order to inhibit and, it may be, to openly challenge the attempted reassertion of Western power in this vital region.

III

In light of these considerations, if we are to judge the significance of the present debate over foreign policy by way of comparison with the past, it is to the late 1940s that we must look and not the late 1960s. The prospect that was virtually dismissed by most observers only a short time ago has nevertheless materialized again. The fear that was entertained at the outset of the cold war—that the Soviet Union might succeed in extending its sway over Western Europe—is once again entertained.

Nor is this fear any less plausible today than it was in an earlier period, and this despite the great changes that have since tran- spired. The military balance was no more favorable to the Soviet Union in the late 1940s than it is today. If anything, it was less favorable then, the still prostrate condition of Western Europe notwithstanding. For if the American strategic capability then was miniscule as compared with what it is today, it was still considerable, while the Soviet capability of striking directly at the United States was nonexistent. Were the worst to have come, Western Europe would have been the helpless prey to Soviet conventional forces. At the same time, Soviet industrial and population centers would have been the helpless prey to the strategic power of a still physically invulnerable America.

True, in the late 1940s, Western Europe was not only still economically prostrate but politically and psychologically vulnerable. It was this vulnerability that some saw at the time and continue to see in retrospect as the real threat held out to Western Europe, and not the threat of Soviet arms. Undoubtedly, the ravages of a brutal war, the shock of defeat, and the pervasive conviction that Europe was historically spent, led to a profound crisis of self-confidence that found expression in an acute sense of vulnerability. Even so, an important part of Europe's sense of vulnerability could not be distinguished from the threat of Soviet arms. Nor, in fact, did most Western Europeans make the distinction.

In circumstances that in many respects are so radically changed, this sense of vulnerability has revived today. The oil crisis has accentuated it as perhaps no other factor, including the relentless buildup of Soviet arms. Were Western Europe to be denied the oil of the Persian Gulf, its economic life would come to a sudden halt. The intense awareness of this accounts for the willingness of Western European states increasingly to accept almost any economic or political terms producing countries may impose on them rather than to run the risk of being cut off from their oil supplies. There is no apparent reason to believe that this subservience would not be shown in far greater degree toward a state that controlled the oil of the Persian Gulf while, at the same time, holding a military position in Europe superior to that of the Western alliance. In the 1940s, the Soviet Union could threaten Western Europe's physical security, but only if prepared to endure American reprisals to which it could not directly respond. Today, the Soviet Union, if once in control of the Persian Gulf, could dispose of Western Europe's economic life. A militarily superior position in Europe would simply reinforce a control that the United States would be powerless to contest.

What is significant, then, about the present debate over American foreign policy is its unexpected familiarity. At issue are essentially the same security interests that were at issue in the years immediately following World War II. If the locus of the now most likely threat to those interests has shifted from Europe to the Persian Gulf, the vital interests at stake in the Gulf remain unchanged from the vital interests that were earlier at stake in Europe. None of the participants in the present debate seriously questions this, for no one seriously argues that the loss of Western access to the Gulf could eventuate in anything short of a mortal blow to the post-World War II structure of America's global interests. What is disputed is the Soviet intention to challenge Western access. But this dispute is not unlike the dispute that arose in the 1940s over Moscow's intentions toward Europe. Short of intention materializing through action, the present controversy is likely to prove as inconclusive as its predecessor.

The parallel thus apparent between the immediate postwar years and today is striking. Like any parallel, it can be pushed too far. The differences in the circumstances attending Western Europe in the late 1940s and the Persian Gulf today are also striking. Whereas Western Europe was relatively stable, despite appearances to the contrary, the Persian Gulf is a nightmare of present and potential instability. And whereas Western Europe on balance welcomed the American "intervention," the states of the Persian Gulf are still very far from doing so. It is, above all, the latter difference that has received considerable emphasis and that vitiates, in the judgment of many observers, if not the parallel drawn here then at least the prospect that a comparable response to that made in an earlier period is possible today. In this view, the states of the region hold it within their power to deny Western access and to defeat any attempt to force them to grant access to their oil supplies.

But this judgment is almost certainly misplaced. The Gulf today constitutes a power vacuum that will eventually be filled, whether by the one or the other superpower or by both. If, contrary to all reasonable expectation, this vacuum does persist, its very persistence would indeed herald a transformation of revolutionary proportions in the international system. The outcome would confirm what has now been contended for more than a decade— that certain traditional forms of power, above all, military power, have been substantially deprived of their former utility.

Were this contention to be borne out by events, the Western predicament in the Persian Gulf would very likely issue in the altogether grim prospects that have been recently outlined in these pages by Walter Levy.[4] Rather than from the Soviet Union, the great threat to the stability and security of the West would come from the very vacuum that the West must continue to rely upon but which it cannot effectively fill. In these circumstances, the military power of the Soviet Union would presumably prove as impotent as that of the West. But in these circumstances as well, the military power of the Soviet Union could in general be safely neglected. For what this power could not do in the Persian Gulf, it could also not be expected to do in Western Europe.

IV

If we instead assume the persistence of a more traditional world, we have little alternative but to respond to a conventional security threat in the way that states have regularly responded to such threats. An imbalance of military power, present or prospective, must be met by countervailing military power. We have no choice when faced by threats that, if permitted to go unmet, could result in sacrificing interests on which the nation's economic well-being and the integrity of its basic institutions depend. The purist may cavil even at this restricted meaning given to necessity in foreign policy, but short of circumstances in which an insoluble conflict between physical security and the other attributes commonly identified with security is demonstrably apparent, it will suffice.

The case for considering our immediate options *today* as very narrow is difficult to contest. Admittedly, it is still contested, as the continuing debate over America's proper policy in the Persian Gulf testifies. Even so, the shifting nature of that debate also demonstrates the compelling force of vital interest once a threat to it becomes inescapably clear. At each successive stage in the unfolding of the threat to Western access to the oil supplies of the Gulf, resistance to measures once dismissed as either unnecessary or impossible has steadily weakened. Confronted with the stark alternatives of risking loss of access, or of deploying military power to prevent such a loss, the Carter Administration had no choice in the end but to respond to a vital interest.

---

[4] Cf. Walter J. Levy, "Oil and the Decline of the West," *Foreign Affairs*, Summer 1980, pp. 999–1015, for the prospects that Levy believes await the West if there is not a very substantial change in the world's dependence on Middle East oil. Yet such change is, for all practical purposes, ruled out in the foreseeable future. In its absence, Levy concludes, "the world, as we know it now, will probably not be able to maintain its cohesion, nor be able to provide for the continued economic progress of its people against the onslaught of future oil shocks—with all that this might imply for the political stability of the West, its free institutions, and its internal and external stability." One must search diligently to find an equally bleak and forbidding assessment of the future in the almost 60 years of publication history of *Foreign Affairs*.

Its response was marked by ambiguity. In implementation, it was faltering and tortuous. But whatever criticism one may make of it, there has been a response. Moreover, under the impact of events that have left little room for doubt over the straitened position of the West in the Persian Gulf, this response gathered momentum. A comparison of the American position in the region in the fall of 1979 with the nation's position in the late fall of 1980 reveals the extent of the change that has taken place, a change that was clearly uncongenial to President Carter and that he resisted until events left him no meaningful choice.

More generally, the compelling force of vital interest has left us no meaningful choice in deciding whether or not we will respond to the continuing arms buildup of the Soviet Union with an improved military position of our own. The manner and emphasis, the pace and magnitude, of the response continue to elicit controversy. The diplomatic consequences that some fear rearmament to hold out provoke even greater controversy. These and still other considerations notwithstanding, a majority among elites and public alike now accepts the imminent prospect—if not the present reality—of an overall arms balance that favors the Soviet Union. The need to redress this actual or prospective imbalance is also broadly accepted.

The wellspring of this consensus must be traced to the growing conviction that the United States has steadily moved throughout the past decade toward an insolvent foreign policy, whether in the Persian Gulf—where commitment was not in accord with interest and where the means to sustain interest or commitment were almost totally lacking—or in Western Europe—where credibility of commitment was increasingly called into question by the growing inadequacy of the necessary means. The remedy for a foreign policy that has come close to insolvency—because the means to secure vital interests are inadequate—is plainly to restore the necessary means. In the two most critical areas of concern to the United States, the necessary means—not the only means but the necessary means—are military. This point deserves particular emphasis with respect to the Persian Gulf. Though it is here that the need is greatest, it is also here that the temptation persists to find a substitute for this need.

The experience of a decade, however, has amply demonstrated the truth that should have been apparent from the outset: there is no reliable substitute for Western power in the Gulf. The continued search for such a substitute—whether in the form of another American surrogate, of alignment with the West by means of a regional arrangement, or of collective nonalignment—is entirely vain. The conditions of domestic instability and of intraregional rivalries that characterize the Gulf render any and all of these schemes either impossible to achieve or without real value even if apparently achieved.

Nor is there any plausible reason for believing that these schemes would prove feasible and effective if a satisfactory settlement of the Palestinian issue were achieved. A settlement of the Palestinian issue would not materially lessen the need for Western power in the Gulf. It would not do so because it would not remove the many sources of conflict and instability in the region. Of the major events that have shaken the Gulf in the past two years and that have threatened Western access—notably the fall of the Shah and the Iraqi-Iranian war—none have had more than a peripheral relationship to the Palestinian issue. The continued insistence upon seeing in a comprehensive settlement of the Arab-Israeli conflict a critical part of the solution to Western vulnerability in the Gulf has become the refuge of those who do not believe there can be an effective reassertion of Western power and that, this being so, we must clutch at such straws as best we can.

A recent variation on this view holds that Arab states of the Gulf—particularly Saudi Arabia—would be more receptive to an American military presence if the Palestinian issue were to be satisfactorily resolved.[5] Those urging this view seem oblivious to the notorious fact that there is no consensus among Arab states on what a "satisfactory" solution would consist of and that such a consensus is not likely to emerge. The argument that the receptivity of the Gulf states to an American presence depends on the politics of the area is surely right. But it does not follow that the Palestinian issue is the key to a favorable attitude of the Gulf states toward a Western military presence on their territory. Instead, the key is a restoration of American credibility, a restoration that will not be furthered by an America that is seen to be pressuring Israel on the Palestinian issue *in order to* improve its standing in the Arab world. If anything, such pressure is likely to have the opposite effect from what its advocates claim it would have. The Saudis will see it not as an indication of American credibility but as further evidence of the weakness of our position.

Although the conditions of solvency have been increasingly placed in question even in Western Europe, in the Persian Gulf

---

[5] See David Watt, "The Atlantic Alliance Needs Leaders Who Face the Facts," *The Economist*, October 11, 1980, p. 26.

their fulfillment has until very recently never been seriously attempted. Now the task can no longer be avoided. Yet it is bound to prove far more exacting than the effort required for Western Europe. This is so not only because the current military advantage of the Russians in the Gulf region is considerably greater than it is in Europe, but also because the purposes for which American power might have to be employed today in the Gulf are more complex and ambiguous, and the conditions of employment more difficult, than in Europe. Whereas in Europe the purpose of American power is either to deter or to defend against Soviet armed aggression, in the Persian Gulf the purpose is to ensure access to the region's oil supplies.

This being so, we can have no single standing and identifiable adversary in the Gulf; the threat to access may arise from any number of possible sources, of which a direct Soviet armed intervention, though the most serious, is only one. More likely, a threat to access will arise primarily from developments indigenous to the Gulf, though the Soviet Union may play a peripheral role even here. The diversity and ambiguity of the circumstances in which force may have to be threatened or employed imposes both political and strategic dilemmas—political dilemmas in that the use of American power may have to be undertaken in response to internal politics of a Gulf state, and strategic dilemmas in that American forces may be required to act in circumstances impossible to foresee.

What is still more sobering is that the Western position of conventional inferiority with respect to the Soviet Union raises the issue of nuclear deterrence as it has not been raised for many years. In the limiting situation—a determined Russian assault in the Gulf—we must either rely on the threat of responding with nuclear weapons or concede that as matters now stand there is no effective response we can make. To acknowledge this unpalatable truth is not to cast doubt on the need for making a serious effort to strengthen conventional forces in the region. Without such an effort, a strategy of nuclear deterrence in the Gulf would not only encounter the now familiar problems of credibility arising from our European experience, it would meet the additional difficulty resulting from a variety of circumstances which are absent in Europe but which largely define the condition of the Gulf. In these circumstances, a nuclear tripwire would either lack credibility or simply prove irrelevant.

These considerations do not mean that there is no proper role in a Gulf strategy for the threat of nuclear escalation. Instead, they point to the conclusion that this threat must be reserved for the limiting situation. If it is argued that even here the threat will fail to carry the persuasiveness that it has carried in Europe, the reason must be either that we do not have the same interest in the Gulf that we have in Europe or that, though having a comparable interest, we do not have the conventional forces needed to give the requisite credibility to nuclear deterrence. And since the former reason cannot be sustained, given Western Europe's critical dependence on the Gulf, it is the latter that is evidently intended. But the dependence of a credible nuclear threat on a substantial conventional force structure is not questioned here. Clearly, the experience we have to date supports the need for a substantial ground presence if a nuclear threat is to be credible. What is questioned is the view that the Gulf can be successfully defended against a major Soviet assault by conventional forces. It cannot be done at present. Nor is there much likelihood it might be done in the immediate future.

A viable strategy in the Persian Gulf, then, must have as its goal the creation of a conventional force structure that can effectively deal with the contingencies that may arise short of a determined Russian assault. If such a force were established, it would still not remove the possibility of the limiting situation arising, but it would severely reduce this prospect. It would represent a very great improvement over our present position. As matters now stand, however, establishing it will prove quite difficult, largely because of the persisting obstacles to deploying conventional military power, other than naval forces, in the region.

These obstacles to the permanent stationing of ground forces and land-based aircraft, if not in, then immediately proximate to, the Gulf, are not insurmountable. They are not dictated by the unchanging "realities" of the region. Instead, they are the result of a decline in power and position that has made the kind of relationship needed to entertain such forces a liability for most governments in the area. They reflect the low estate to which American power has sunk in a decade, while making extraordinarily difficult any attempts at the effective restoration of this power within a reasonable period of time.

Whether the constraints on the deployment of American power can be overcome in the near future must remain an open question. What does seem reasonably clear is that there is no apparent way by which we can conform to these constraints and still respond adequately to the deepening crisis in the Gulf. A permanent and much larger naval combat presence in the Arabian Sea could effectively meet some of the disabilities thereby imposed, though by no means all. Even then, the creation of such a presence will itself require considerable time. This being so, we must choose either to resign ourselves to a future over which we can have but limited control, or attempt to break out of constraints that hamper a more effective response than is now possible.

V

If this is the realm of necessity for American foreign policy today, what are the implications of responding to necessity? First and foremost, what kind of relationship can we reasonably expect to have with the Soviet Union? A candid answer is that the measures required to redress the arms balance and to improve the Western position in the Persian Gulf will strain our relationship with the Soviet Union in the immediate future. Still other issues may also intervene to compound the difficulties and dangers that are now all too likely to mark the relationship. In any case, the outlook is bleak.

The principal reasons for this are clear enough. Moscow is quite likely to view a significant effort at rearmament as an attempt not merely to redress an arms balance but to reestablish an overall position of superiority. Moreover, whatever the Soviet leaders may say about their determination to match any American effort, they are bound to entertain serious doubts over their ability to do so in the longer run. They may well be skeptical over the willingness of this nation to accept for long the sacrifices substantial rearmament would entail—certainly their skepticism finds ample support in the doubts entertained by many American observers—but they must harbor no little apprehension over the results of our rearmament if given sustained public support. Even if the Soviet government were nevertheless willing and able to match the American effort, the result would severely strain the Russian economy and, in the bargain, might even produce serious domestic unrest. Yet if Moscow should fail to respond to the American effort, the result, again in Russian eyes, might well be seen as the beginning of the end to pretensions of global power status.

These considerations alone provide ample grounds for pessimism. To them, however, must be added the structural causes for conflict that are provided by the Persian Gulf. The observation has been regularly made that the instability characteristic of much of the Third World provides the single most significant, and seemingly intractable, source of conflict between the United States and the Soviet Union. But it is not the points of contention and conflict *generally* in the Third World that have brought the superpowers into potentially dangerous confrontation today; it is the growing competition in the region of the Persian Gulf that has done so. It is the Gulf that forms the indispensable key to the defense of the American global position, just as it forms the indispensable key without which the Soviet Union cannot seriously aspire to global predominance. Alongside the stakes accruing from control of the Gulf, the contest in other regions of the Third World can have but peripheral significance.

The intrinsic importance of the Gulf thus acts as a magnet that, for different reasons, neither superpower can resist. The competition for control of the area is about as certain as anything can be in politics. So long as it persists—and it probably will for some years to come—it will hold out the constant prospect for dangerous confrontations between the United States and the Soviet Union.

With the advantage of hindsight, a number of observers now find that this prospect might have been largely avoided had American policy accepted the Soviet Union as a partner in the Middle East peace process. Instead, by seeking to exclude Moscow from a Middle East settlement, we succeeded only in provoking renewed Soviet determination to improve its position in the areas around the Persian Gulf.

This argument, however, indicates an unwillingness to acknowledge that the Gulf cannot be bought by a policy conceding the form in the hope of retaining the substance. Quite apart from the notorious difficulties raised by including the Russians in the peace process, how would this inclusion have diminished their aspirations in the Gulf? Presumably including them would have been an acknowledgement of the equality upon which they are so insistent. But unless this acknowledgment could also be expected to yield tangible consequences in the Persian Gulf, it would represent in the end little more than an empty gesture. Is there any plausible reason for believing that the Soviets would have been satisfied by such a gesture, or that they might be so satisfied today?

It is, of course, the prospect of a very difficult and dangerous relationship with the Soviet Union that is the principal objection to a policy whose first priority is the restoration of American power generally and, above all, in the Persian Gulf. Yet unless one argues that such restoration is simply unnecessary there is no viable alternative to it. The risks it gives rise to can only be

weighed against those that must be run through failing to respond
to a still growing Soviet strategic and conventional arms momentum.

VI

If the risks inherent in the Soviet-American relationship today
cannot be exorcised by the simple refusal to acknowledge their
existence, is there nevertheless substantial reason to believe they
can be kept to a moderate threshold? While pursuing a restoration
of American power and position, and while once again drawing
lines which the Russians are expected not to violate, can we still
keep the relationship short of one that is under constant strain? Is
it plausible to expect a U.S. policy that will involve, in the phrase
of Robert Legvold, "containment without confrontation"?[6]

Clearly, this would be a far more attractive prospect than the
one indicated in these pages. What would a U.S. policy toward
the Soviet Union look like that might be expected to lead to this
happier relationship? Mr. Legvold argues that it must consist of
two principal elements or, in his words, "must proceed on two
tracks: one of firmness, military strength (but not by seeking
military superiority), and a will to act (requiring a public readier
for the possibility); the other of cooperation, the extended hand,
and a renewed interest in dealing with problems jointly rather
than in turning problems against each other."[7] The first track
would provide the means of a refurbished policy of containment
and draw the lines of such policy. The second track would provide
the incentive for the Soviet Union to accept, though perhaps not
without occasional lapses, the first. It would include "an economic
policy founded on cooperation," "arms control efforts as a significant and carefully coordinated element in a national security
policy that does not rely only on arming," and "a serious attempt
to open the one area of détente that never got started, namely,
crisis management."[8]

This is clearly a prescription for a return to the policy of the
early 1970s, though a return without the illusions of these earlier
years. Legvold's "sound, resurrected détente" is a détente that is
based on power and a willingness to use that power. It does not
assume that Moscow will refrain from seeking "marginal advantages" in the Third World, but rather accepts that Moscow will

---

[6] Robert Legvold, "Containment Without Confrontation," *Foreign Policy*, Fall 1980, pp. 74–
98.

[7] *Ibid.*, p. 93.

[8] *Ibid.*, p. 95.

be so tempted and that the temptation must be countered by a combination of threats, rewards and a growing recognition—encouraged by institutionalized procedures—of mutuality of interest in managing the inevitable competition. The earlier détente presumably failed because it was too soft where it should have been harder and too hard where it should have been softer. A resurrected détente can proceed on the basis of this experience and can do so without having to contend with the domestic constraints of the early to middle 1970s.

Is it reasonable to believe that Legvold's détente would enjoy a better fate than its predecessor? One must doubt that it would. This is so even if we freely grant the assumption that this détente would not suffer from the domestic constraints attending the implementation of the earlier détente. For the principal question the Nixon-Kissinger policy raised—what would induce the Soviet Union to become more moderate, one that no longer sought to exploit opportunities and take advantage of instabilities?—must also be raised by current proposals for a resurrected détente. Moreover, this question must be raised in circumstances much less auspicious than those of an earlier period.

Whereas the détente of 1972 was undertaken at a time when this country was still considered to enjoy a position of net superiority in the arms balance with the Soviet Union, today this no longer holds. And whereas the détente of 1972 was undertaken at a time when the temptations held out by the 'Third World appeared to have receded, today they have sharply risen—above all, in the one most critical area of the Third World. Finally, Soviet insistence upon being treated as an equal of America, with all that this implies in the various areas of competition, has markedly increased. The time when Moscow could be appeased or fobbed off with the symbols of equality has passed.

Against these considerations, what are the incentives that might induce Moscow to accept an American-inspired definition of moderate behavior? The belief that a more cooperative economic policy might do so is surely a slender reed to rely on. Those who continue to do so have yet to demonstrate how such a policy, once free of the Jackson-Vanik Amendment and other impediments, could promote more than a modest relationship without creating more *economic risks* than benefits for the United States. They would also have to indicate the benefits—whether in trade, providing credit facilities, or technology transfers—that the Russians do not already enjoy in increasing measure by virtue of their economic relationships with West European countries. And even if these propositions could be persuasively demonstrated, they would still have to indicate why the Soviet Union might be expected to do what it has never before done: to subordinate high policy to such benefits as an improved economic relationship might bring. In this regard, it may be recalled that the first serious test, and failure, of the promise of détente, the 1973 Arab-Israeli war, preceded the Jackson-Vanik Amendment.

The emphasis placed by advocates of a new détente on a continuing and even greater effort toward arms control is easy to understand though difficult to credit. It is easy to understand since the SALT process has come to be seen as the principal achievement of the old détente. In the course of the 1970s, this process has even been increasingly viewed as constituting the principal ongoing method of political communication with the Soviet Union, the jeopardizing of which would measurably enhance the prospects of nuclear war. Not surprisingly, this view has become the more insistent as the normal forms of communication have atrophied in the wake of Afghanistan.

Yet the emphasis placed on the SALT process remains difficult to credit. In the last eight years this process has not hindered the Soviets from pursuing substantially the same arms buildup we have every reason to believe they would have pursued in its absence. Nor did Moscow's stake in SALT prevent it from exploiting those situations in the Third World that opportunity presented. We have, of course, no way of knowing what the Soviet Union might have done in the Third World without SALT. But it is special pleading to point to Afghanistan as an example of what might have occurred earlier had it not been for Soviet interest in arms control. There are many reasons that account for Afghanistan. The Soviet calculation in late 1979 that the cause of SALT II had been lost—at least for the time being—could only have been one such reason and likely a subordinate one.

If we put aside economic policy and arms control, there remains the area of "crisis management," of dealing jointly with problems arising from superpower competition in the Third World. Without question, this has been, as Legvold and others remind us, the area in which the old détente never got started. It is also the area that more than any other proved fatal to the old détente. The reasons it did so, however, must surely tell us something about the prospects held out by a new détente, for these reasons are clearly no less relevant today than they were in the early to middle 1970s.

If the Soviet leadership was unwilling then to acquiesce in a definition of equality that, in its eyes, denied Moscow the substance of equality, it is all the more unwilling to do so today. An improved military position has given added weight to Soviet insistence upon equal rights in the Third World, while the rising opportunities for exploiting instabilities have made the claim almost compelling in its attraction.

On the American side, though the arms balance has steadily moved in an adverse direction, there is an increasing disposition to resist Moscow's claim to equal rights not only because of a general change in the climate of opinion—a change resulting in part from the experience with the old détente—but also, and more important, because of the rising fear that the claim, once acknowledged in principle, would soon be applied to regions of critical interest to this country.

In these circumstances, the prospects for crisis management must be rated as very low. Nor is it apparent why in these circumstances crisis management is intrinsically desirable, even if presently unobtainable. Clearly, it is desirable if such management may operate within a framework of state relations to which the parties can meaningfully subscribe. Within this framework, the competition of the great powers for position and advantage has been difficult enough to manage. Without it, the search for crisis management—in effect, for mutually agreed "rules of the game"—must either prove barren or lead to quite undesirable results. For the search itself necessarily presumes the basis for the desired goal, else the effort to fashion reliable patterns of mutual restraint must prove feckless. Unfortunately, the evidence that this basis exists is no more convincing today than it was in the period of the cold war. It is only the belief that it exists which has increased.[9]

VII

The renewed search for détente with the Soviet Union, this time a détente without the illusions and excessive expectations attending the old détente, reflects the fear that in its absence we will be tempted to return to something akin to the policy of containment that prevailed from the early 1950s to the mid-1960s. In turn, that fear finds a two fold expression. In one, it is that if we attempt to

---

[9] A telling sign of this belief in the past year has been the fashionable analogy drawn between 1914 and 1980, with its evident implication that the Soviet Union is today's Wilhelmenian Germany, a revisionist power, to be sure, but one whose revisionism is nevertheless limited by adherence to the same framework of state relations as its competitors. The progression of thought from the early 1970s, then, is this: whereas in these earlier years the Soviet Union was seen by many as an increasingly status quo power in the literal sense, now it is seen as revisionist, though revisionist in the conventional meaning of the term.

resurrect the containment of yesterday in the conditions of today, we may well tempt the Soviets to exploit their present position of strength in a manner that will lead to an ultimate confrontation. In the other, it is that if we attempt and even partially succeed in resurrecting the containment of yesterday, we will tempt ourselves to repeat the excesses of yesterday. Thus, whether we fail or succeed, the alternatives to a new détente are seen as forbidding.

There is no need, however, to accept these as the only alternatives to a new détente. The Soviet-American relationship may take yet other expressions and hold out less forbidding consequences, even in the short term. What American policy cannot avoid, save at the risk of sacrificing its global position and gravely jeopardizing its security, are the measures outlined earlier in this essay. But these measures form no more than a limited policy of containment. They respond essentially to the same security interests that an earlier policy of containment responded to in the years immediately following World War II. Even so, a policy of moderate containment today would necessarily differ from the moderate containment of the late 1940s because we cannot regain the relative power advantage we once enjoyed. Certainly there is no way by which we can recapture the immunity from direct attack we once enjoyed. Nor can we determine the behavior of our principal allies in the manner we once could.

These changes, not to speak of the changes that have occurred in the once-passive Third World, require us to recognize that today we could only pursue the methods and even the aspirations which characterized an earlier period of containment at very great cost and effort, and even then with no more than a modest prospect of success. If this is so, the containment of today and tomorrow, unlike yesterday's containment, will have to deal with the Soviet Union in a manner that those who presided over containment in the past were often reluctant to accept. The containment of today and tomorrow will have to make concessions and compromises in areas of contention where concession and compromise were once spurned. And if it is at all prudent, a refurbished containment will, wherever possible, avoid measures which at once sharply exacerbate the relationship with the Soviet Union and make the prospect of its future amelioration virtually impossible.

Nothing would be more likely to have these effects than a military alliance, even if only de facto, with China. Yet this is the direction in which American policy has been inexorably moving in the past year or so. If it is carried forward much more, it will soon seal the Soviet-American relationship in a fixed and truly dangerous mold by making it hostage to our relations with China. Nor will it matter that this is done from a position of growing strength rather than, as in the recent past, from a position of relative weakness.

The promise of a policy of limited containment envisaged here is not the promise of détente—even of a "sound, resurrected détente." It suggests far more competition than cooperation. It finds the sources of this competition primarily in the structural causes of conflict between the superpowers rather than in the still profoundly different visions of the world and of the state system that the two respectively entertain.

Even so, the great ideological divide that continues to separate the Soviet Union and the United States remains an important source of conflict. When combined with the structural causes, the result gives the Soviet-American relationship greater continuity with the past than is commonly acknowledged. It is, indeed, this continuity in change that prompts some to insist that a policy of moderate containment will not work and that the logic of our position requires a resurgent America in pursuit of goals reminiscent of the later period of containment.

VIII

The case for recognizing the central importance of the ideological stakes of the conflict has been most forcefully and acutely made by Norman Podhoretz.[10] It is not sufficient, he has argued, to treat the Soviet-American rivalry in the manner of conventional great power contests. The "new nationalism" that has arisen in reaction to the visible decline of American power (though needed and healthy) has a tendency to do just that. Podhoretz finds in this reaction little awareness of the deeper meaning of the conflict. Yet unless a deeper meaning is given to Soviet-American rivalry—now more serious in its implications than perhaps it has ever been—he fears that the requisite base for carrying us into and sustaining a new period of global containment will prove lacking. The threat that ought to rouse us but that is still missing from a long overdue reaction to a policy of strategic retreat is communism. Without an awareness of the all-embracing threat that the

[10] Norman Podhoretz, *The Present Danger*, New York: Simon and Schuster, 1980.

advance of communism implies, the change we are witnessing today will lack direction and purpose. He writes:

In resisting the advance of Soviet Power . . . . we *are* fighting for freedom and against Communism, for democracy and against totalitarianism. Yet it is precisely this sense of things that the new nationalism thus far lacks . . . . Without such clarity, the new nationalism is unlikely to do more than lead to sporadic outbursts of indignant energy.[11]

It is in Podhoretz's outlook that we may find perhaps the clearest advocacy of a resurgent America committed again to the goals of a policy of global containment. Directed not only against Soviet expansion, but against the coming to power of communist governments generally, this policy would be restrained only by considerations of prudence. But if the constraints of prudence are to be taken with greater seriousness than in an earlier period, they are not to be used as an excuse for a policy indistinguishable from moderate containment.

If we contrast the alternative that Podhoretz presents with the requirements of a policy of limited containment, it is apparent that in choosing between them we are destined to retrace an old argument. For they are strikingly similar to the alternatives held out in the years that followed World War II. The two principal versions of containment that vied with one another then promise to become once again the major source of contention today.

Though the earlier debate ultimately turned on two different views of the requirements of American security, it is important not to exaggerate the differences between them. The circumstances of the late 1940s made the application of containment roughly identical with a balance-of-power policy. Yet even then, containment in Europe was from the outset undertaken for reasons that went beyond security, narrowly construed. Here, as well as in the case of Japan, the intent was not only to prevent these centers of industrial power from falling under Russian control, but to ensure that they would remain—or become—democratic societies. From the outset, then, the policy of moderate containment expressed a security interest that went beyond a conventional security interest in balance-of-power terms to identify security with the internal order maintained by states. Though modest, it still implied a scheme of things that went beyond the order implicit in a balance of power. This scheme cannot be equated with the universalist

---

[11] *Ibid.*, pp. 100–01.

pretensions of the Truman Doctrine; but it also cannot be equated with a narrow and traditional conception of security.

In a word, the differences between the two initial views of containment were relative, not absolute. Had this not been the case, it would have been much more difficult than it was to move from the narrower and more conventional view of security characteristic of the early years of containment to the broader view that came to prevail in the period following Korea. Still, these relative differences were important. They carried distinctive implications not only about the kind of world we needed for our security but also about the kind of world we wanted. Indeed, in both views, it was virtually impossible to distinguish need from want.

This inability to separate need from want in the evolution of containment is scarcely unusual. It is a common characteristic of all great nations. For the latter, the ultimate expression of security can rarely be found in its physical or economic dimensions, but must instead be found in the moral-psychological—or, if one prefers, the spiritual—dimension. What else can explain the insistence that security cannot be limited to "mere" physical security? And what else can explain the insistence that although the nation's physical being may remain inviolate and its economic base secured, the nation "itself" may not survive? In failing to take these questions seriously, we misunderstand the meaning not only of great power behavior, but of our own as well.

In abandoning isolationism in the 1930s, we responded not only to a perceived threat to our physical and economic security. We also recoiled from the prospect of a world in which America's political and economic frontiers would become coterminous with her territorial frontiers, a world in which societies that shared our institutions and values might very possibly disappear—in sum, a world in which the American example and American influence would become irrelevant. In such a world, it was argued, America could no longer realize her promise, since a hostile world from which America was shut out would inevitably affect the integrity of the nation's institutions and the quality of its domestic life. The issues of physical security and economic well-being apart, it was to prevent this prospect from materializing that the nation abandoned its interwar isolationism, intervened in World War II, and, in the years following the war, adopted a policy of containment. And it has been to prevent this same prospect from materializing that we have been willing to incur the risk of physical destruction through nuclear war, rather than to abandon interests which would not jeopardize our physical existence if once lost.

This experience does indeed indicate that the initial and indispensable stimulus prompting the exercise of American power has been a perceived threat to the nation's physical security or material well-being. But it also points to the inadequacy of conventional security calculations in sustaining the exercise of American power. Once the initial threat has brought forth a response, America has needed a broader rationale for the effort and sacrifice required to sustain the exercise of power. When it has not been forthcoming or when it has been discredited, the result has been drift and uncertainty. So it was that in the early stages of containment the response that was initially evoked, largely as a result of conventional security considerations, was sustained and even expanded by what came to be a still broader motive for policy. When that broader motive was discredited, as it was by Vietnam, even the narrower and conventional security policy became difficult to sustain.

IX

The American experience would thus appear to support the view that our alternatives today are either a policy of a resurgent America intent once again on containing wherever possible the expansion of Soviet influence—as well as the expansion of communism generally—or a policy of moderate containment that may prove inadequate to sustain the power and discipline even to protect interests on which our essential security depends. For if the latter is less demanding, it is also considerably less appealing in the promise it holds out: not of a world moving progressively under American leadership toward the eventual triumph of liberal-capitalist values, but of a world in which America would have to abandon expectations that only yesterday she confidently held. We would have to reconcile ourselves to the prospect of a world of which a large, and perhaps increasing, part outside the industrial democracies would resist American influence.

If that prospect is viewed with alarm, it is not only so viewed by the proponents of a resurgent America. Even those who decry the call for a resurgent America and insistently remind us that we no longer have the power to shape the world according to our desires appear uneasy over accepting the prospect of a world in which American influence would decline. This, at least, is what they have repeatedly declared. The officials of the Carter Administration, including the President, were no doubt quite sincere in expressing the desire to see the developing world move in a manner that would ultimately prove congenial to us. To be sure, they advocated the need for America "to get on the side of change." But they did so presumably in order to guide and to manage the great changes they found sweeping the world. Through different and more congenial methods than those that were often employed in the past, they nonetheless aspired to achieve the goals of the past.

This strategy inevitably failed. The goals of the past could not be achieved while foreswearing the methods that once attended those goals. Even a policy of moderate containment cannot escape incurring the risk of intervention. Clearly, it cannot do so in the Persian Gulf; and circumstances there may prove even more ambiguous than those attending past interventions. It will not do, then, to charge that a resurgent America will be an interventionist America. Any policy of containment must accept the risk of intervention, and in circumstances that we may find in many ways undesirable.

Still, there are risks and risks, and it would be disingenuous to deny that the risks, and costs, likely to attend a return to something resembling the former policy of global containment would be anything less than considerable. The circumstances in which such a policy would have to be undertaken today are much less auspicious than they were a decade and a half ago. Nor is it reasonable to expect a substantial change for the better until the military measures discussed earlier have been successfully undertaken. This will require several years, though, and even then the outcome will not necessarily yield advantages in the overall military balance that a policy of a resurgent America would require. For that policy presupposes a position of clear military superiority; it cannot be prudently undertaken from a position of parity or even from a position of slight advantage.

What might the Soviet Union be expected to do in the face of a policy that wherever possible intends to resist its every move, and that undertakes to develop the necessary means to do so? I am not speaking here of a policy intent on preserving interests outside this hemisphere, which for the United States are indispensable to its entire position in the world, such as the Persian Gulf. For the Soviet Union these interests are indispensable as the key to global predominance. The measures required to implement such a policy are not without risks. Confronted even with these measures, the Soviet leaders must anticipate the time when they will no longer enjoy their present military position. Moreover, they can have no assurance that, having once taken these measures, we will forego the temptation to achieve a position of military superiority. But if the risks inherent in the attempt to redress the present military balance are substantial, how much greater would they be if accompanied by a commitment to a policy of global containment?

In the present circumstances, then, a return to the expansive version of containment, if seriously intended, is likely to place us on the most dangerous of courses with the Soviet Union. For that policy must in effect convey the message to Moscow that the clock is to be set back at least 15 years, that the status of equality accorded the U.S.S.R. by the late 1960s is henceforth to have a largely honorific significance, and that the United States no longer intends to accept the Soviet Union as a global power. Quite apart from the reaction of Soviet leaders to what they would see as a renewed determination to treat them as a regional power, what effect would this have on our principal allies?

If the experience of the past year is any indication, the answer is reasonably clear. At best, it would further exacerbate the existing crisis in the Western alliance. At worst, it might lead to an open rupture and to the greatest diplomatic defeat for this country in the postwar period. Disagreement within the Atlantic Alliance has almost always been greatest over issues that have not been specifically European. In truth, the alliance has seldom effectively functioned as an alliance with respect to these issues, even when the issue in question has vitally affected alliance interests. Of these, the energy crisis and ensuing differences over the proper Western policy to be pursued in the Middle East afford the most dramatic and important examples.

Of course, one may argue that these differences are largely the result of a markedly declining confidence of Western Europe in American leadership, discipline and will, and that a resurgent America dedicated again to global containment would, in demonstrating these qualities, restore this badly impaired confidence. Without question, a more consistent and resolute American leadership would restore a measure of European confidence and elicit a greater degree of cooperation. It is, after all, scarcely surprising that given the character of American policy in recent years, Western Europe did not greet the hardened position toward the U.S.S.R. in 1980 with enthusiasm. If this shift were to prove' abortive, or if it were not to be followed up, America would risk losing a great deal. But Western Europe would risk losing everything.

In these circumstances, and with a vivid memory of the American record since the mid-1970s, what is perhaps surprising is that West European resistance to shifts in American policy this past year was not more pronounced. At the same time, the effective reassertion of American power and leadership may yet prompt a quite different reaction—and sooner than is commonly expected. It will do so, however, only if the Europeans are persuaded that the United States is pursuing a policy that does not risk confrontation with the Soviet Union over interests deemed extraneous to the Western alliance. This task of persuasion has been difficult enough in the Middle East, where Western Europe's interests are manifest but where American policy has been seen to jeopardize those interests because of Washington's position on the Arab-Israeli conflict and—to a lesser degree—even on the Soviet invasion of Afghanistan. Yet how much greater would European opposition be to a policy that, in seeking to deny the extension of Soviet power and influence in areas of no intrinsic concern to Western Europe, threatened to take Europe back to the conditions of the 1950s?

To the risks that a policy of a resurgent America would likely incur must be added the costs. How great those costs would be, when added to those of a more modest policy, is difficult to assess. Certainly they would be substantially greater, if only because a policy of global containment implies military superiority over the Soviet Union. They would also be substantially greater because this more ambitious policy holds out a greater promise of intervention. It would be reckless to assume that interventions in the future will prove less costly than those in the past. The Third World has not become more passive since the 1960s. Instead, it has become almost everywhere more resistant to great-power attempts to exercise the control or even the influence that was once part of the order of things.

This being so, the risks of intervention, when measured in terms of domestic support, have not diminished but, if anything, increased. They have increased not because of the many, though dubious, "lessons" that have been drawn from our experience in Vietnam but because of one indisputable lesson. It is that success is the great solvent of serious public disaffection over foreign policy, and particularly over military intervention. Had the intervention in Vietnam succeeded within a relatively brief period, it is reasonable to assume that significant opposition to the war would not have arisen. Unless future interventions can find a justification in security interests that the public finds compelling, they will have to enjoy relatively quick and cheap success. Yet the prospects for satisfying these requirements are today less favorable than ever.

Given these considerations, could a policy reminiscent of the later period of containment be expected to command the necessary support at home? Could it elicit the broad domestic consensus required to sustain it over the long term? There are no easy answers to these questions. It is reasonably clear, however, that the domestic support required for a return to the policy of a generation ago does not yet exist. Instead, in the emergence of a "new nationalism" we find a public that at once rejects the guilt and withdrawal of the post-Vietnam period while reluctant to embrace again the enthusiasms of the pre-Vietnam period. Though it has become increasingly supportive of greater defense efforts, it has also remained cautious of the purposes for which American arms might be employed. Accordingly, though it is supportive of existing commitments, it has also remained cautious over endorsing new commitments—witness the less than overwhelming public response evoked by the Carter Doctrine.

To date, then, the new nationalism appears thoroughly self-interested. It is precisely this trait that leads observers like Norman Podhoretz to conclude that the new nationalism lacks "a sense of things." Yet what it lacks is not an anti-communist disposition as such, but the anti-communist disposition of yesterday and, of course, the willingness of yesterday to act on the basis of that disposition.

Whether the prevailing public mood of today can be sustained remains to be seen. It may be that it cannot. Expressing as it does an outlook supportive of a modest policy and based on calculations of self-interest, it is, as already noted, different from our experience since World War II. To this experience, moreover, must be added the attractions of investing great significance in conflicts that bear only marginally on our core interests. If, however, the new nationalism could be sustained, if it could avoid the disenchantment and withdrawal that followed Vietnam as well as the enthusiasm and involvement that preceded Vietnam, it would not need the intellectual guidance that many believe it must have. Indeed, the foreign policy elites might well benefit by taking their cue from the new nationalism rather than by endeavoring to instruct it. The essential elements of a viable consensus on foreign policy need not be further sought after. For the moment, at any rate, they are apparent in the prevailing public mood.

X

If a domestic consensus can be sustained in support of a policy of moderate containment, as outlined earlier in these pages, what is the great objection to its acceptance? Though described as moderate, it is not, after all, an inconsiderable enterprise. To redress the overall arms balance, to ensure Western access to the oil supplies of the Persian Gulf, and generally to restore confidence abroad that America has the understanding and the discipline to maintain a solvent foreign policy, seems a substantial enough undertaking. Why, then, should we consider taking on more unless it can be shown that the more is essential to our security?

These questions bring us back to the difficult, perhaps even insoluble, distinction between need and want. It is clear what we generally want to happen in the Third World (and it is the Third World that we are talking about). Yet it is also in much of the Third World that our distinction between need and want has often been the most tenuous, just as it is here that containment in the past has enjoyed the least success. The issue a refurbished policy of global containment must raise is not whether it should be applied to those areas where need is or should be apparent to all, as in the region of the Persian Gulf, but where it is plausible, at best, only if unverifiable assumption is piled upon unverifiable assumption.

The argument may be illustrated by reference to an area, Central America, that seems almost certain to provoke rising concern and controversy in the coming period.[12] In Central America there are no vital raw materials or minerals whose loss might provide the basis for legitimate security concerns. Yet Central America bears geographical proximity to the United States, and historically it has long been regarded as falling within our sphere of influence. As such, we have long exercised the role great powers have traditionally exercised over small states which fall within their respective spheres of influence. We have regularly played a determining role in making and in unmaking governments, and we have defined what we have considered to be the acceptable behavior of governments. In Central America our pride is engaged as it cannot possibly be engaged in Africa or in Southeast Asia. If we do not apply a policy of a resurgent America to prevent the

[12] In considering the Central American example, I have benefited much from conversations with my colleague, Professor Piero Gleijeses. These conversations were all the more instructive in that Professor Gleijeses reflects the perspective of the Left, while I of the Right.

coming to power of radical regimes in Central America, we have even less reason to do so in other areas where conventional security interests are not apparent. Reasons of pride and historic tradition apart, it is here, if anywhere, that we enjoy clear military superiority and may expect to retain such superiority in the future. In Central America, then, one risk of an ambitious containment policy would be absent.

Would a return to a policy of the past work in Central America? Providing that we exercise some care in defining what we mean by "work," there is no persuasive reason for believing that it would not. The measures required to ensure success may prove unwelcome and embarrassing today since we can have no assurance that indirect methods of intervention will prove sufficient. We have now passed the period of overthrowing an Arbenz in Guatemala, when disposing of governments to which we took offense was a quite easy undertaking. Today we must expect to deal with a far more determined and effective opposition. The price promises to be markedly greater, and it will have to be paid not only in the actions we take but in the reaction of others— particularly, though not only, in Latin America—to our actions.

Moreover, this price cannot be trimmed by halfway measures, that is, by an opposition to radical movements that still fails to prevent their taking power, or, more important, that fails to remove them should they achieve power. The expected result of such halfway measures will only be to create the conditions for another Cuba. Radical movements or radical regimes must be defeated. Yet even if we pay the necessary price for defeating them, we cannot be sure how long our success will endure. Success is likely to prove precarious not only because the defeated may well continue to enjoy broad support, but because the victors will have to do what has to date been impossible for them to do— enlist the support of centrist elements. Unfortunately, these elements no longer exist in Central American states. Right-wing governments will have to be given steady outside support, even, if necessary, by sending in American forces.

It can be done. But why should we do it? If one replies that our security requires doing it, we still have to determine the nature of the security interests at stake. One presumably relates to Mexico. Is it reasonable to assume, however, that the course of Central America will seriously influence the course of Mexico? Most outside observers think not, believing instead that Mexico's future will be determined by that nation's internal policies. Certainly the

Mexicans do not think so, else it would be difficult to explain their current policy toward Central America. It does not seem unreasonable in this instance to accept the Mexicans' assessment of their interests.

There remains, it is true, the broader relationship-of-interests argument. If, it runs here, the Soviet Union observes our passivity to events in our own backyard that signal the loss of American control, what conclusions might it draw about our probable passivity in other, far more difficult, areas? The argument cannot simply be dismissed. Yet its persuasiveness depends, in the final reckoning, on what we do or fail to do in areas where vital interests clearly are at stake. If we remain passive in these areas, what we do in Central America will have only marginal significance. The eagle that kills the deer in Central America will not frighten the bear in the Middle East.

It is not need that would prompt this course but want—a want, moreover, which the Soviet Union would not only accept but probably endorse, since it would be seen to help legitimize much of its own behavior. The only other coherent policy is to observe a hands-off position toward the events now occurring in Central America, a position that implies stopping military aid to El Salvador. Should further radical regimes come to power, we would accept the outcome. More, we would give them reason to maintain a normal relationship with the Soviet Union, rather than to follow in the footsteps of Cuba. Such inducement, of which the present economic aid to Nicaragua forms an example, may be seen as a mere euphemism for blackmail. I have no objection to the term. But then blackmail is a commonplace in the relations of states. Having put up with the spectacular instances of it that we have seen in the past decade, to balk here would truly be a case of straining at the gnat while swallowing the camel.

If we were instead to swallow the gnat, and perhaps a few others as well in the years to come, it would not signify that we liked this diet. It would only mean that we recognized at last that we are in a position where we can afford to view changes we do not welcome with the equanimity they deserve.

What we cannot view with equanimity is that the states of Central America enter into a relationship with the Soviet Union that resembles the relationship with Cuba. Geographical proximity has not lost its significance. At issue, then, is not whether Central America continues to form a part of this nation's sphere of influence. Instead, it is the nature of the influence we should seek to exercise within our sphere and how best such influence may be preserved. It is between those who define our sphere of influence to include the internal order of states, and those who do not, that there is a clear difference in principle. That difference ought not to be confused with the preeminently practical judgment on the policy best suited to prevent the kind of intrusion by an outside power we should clearly aim to prevent.

In the Central American case, our claims are rooted in geography and history. If these claims ought not to extend to the internal order of states here, there is still less reason for extending them elsewhere in the Third World. The strictures earlier made with respect to the Persian Gulf do not contradict this conclusion. In the Gulf, we are necessarily concerned with internal order because this issue cannot be separated from a vital interest in access to oil supplies. The same vital interest bids us oppose the extension of Soviet influence in that region. Were it not for this interest we could view changes in the internal order and, for that matter, the extension of Soviet influence, with relative detachment. Not with utter indifference, but with the relative detachment that holds out the best promise of avoiding the excesses which have characterized American foreign policy in the past.

XI

There is no fate that decrees we must repeat these excesses of concern and withdrawal. Having experienced the consequences of both in the past two decades, we ought to have learned that the result of both is to lead to the insolvency of policy. A period of withdrawal and of passivity has come to an end. If it is to be succeeded by a period of an America everywhere resurgent and activist, we will only risk jeopardizing interests that are critical to the nation's security and well-being.

The restoration of those interests will prove no small task. Once done, the great object of American foreign policy ought to be the restoration of a more normal political world, a world in which those states possessing the elements of great power once again play the role their power entitles them to play. In the case of our principal allies, this disparity between latent and actual power has, if anything, grown rather than diminished. If not substantially reduced, the disparity is almost certain to lead to still greater difficulty in alliance relationships, and this quite apart from the manner in which America conducts her foreign policy.

For the principal difficulty that characterizes alliance relationships today goes much deeper than issues of style or even of substance. It reflects instead the frustration, and resentment, of those who are now able to assume responsibility for their security but have yet to do so. If they were at long last to do so, the political world as we know it today would be transformed. A third of a century after World War II, that transformation is surely long overdue.

23

THE CONSEQUENCES OF EXPENSIVE OIL
ON ARMS TRANSFERS

Steve Chan

This article examines the short-term effects of expensive oil on the supply and demand patterns for conventional weapons. It pools the cross-section and time-series data on petroleum and arms trade, and uses a crossed-error regression model to estimate these effects for three groups of countries. The results offer some tentative support for several widely shared impressions. They indicate a linkage between oil and arms trade, thus providing the necessary although not sufficient condition for proving that weapons have been used by the Western industrialized nations to recycle petrodollars from the OPEC countries. They also show that dependency on foreign fuel, increasing trade deficits, and low per capita GNP do not restrain the demand for weapons by those countries that are both oil and arms net importers. Most of these countries are developing nations, and their demand seems to be relatively inelastic in the short term.

The consequences of expensive oil on arms transfers

The sharp increases in oil price during the 1973-74 period presented very difficult balance of payment problems for many nations, including some oil exporting countries that were suddenly faced with major investment decisions for their unexpectedly large surpluses (Willrich 1975: 136). This article examines one aspect of efforts to cope with these problems by the petroleum importers as well as exporters, namely, the short-term effects of oil price hikes on the supply and demand patterns for conventional arms.

We begin with a presentation of views on the dynamics of arms transfers which we

* I would like to thank Robert Bernstein, Davis Bobrow, Charles Doran, James Dyer, John Kringen, and several anonymous reviewers for their helpful comments. An earlier version of this research was supported in part by the Defense Advanced Research Projects Agency of the U.S. Department of Defense and was monitored by the Office of Naval Research under contract no. N00014-75-C-0846. The views and conclusions contained in this document are those of the author and should not be interpreted as necessarily representing the official policies, expressed or implied, of the Defense Advanced Research Projects Agency or the U.S. government. The computer time for this analysis was provided by a grant from the Texas A&M University.

wish to check, at least in part, in the subsequent empirical analysis. In this presentation, we shall attend to factors that appear to be pertinent to countries occupying different positions in the international oil trade relationship. The sample and data used to verify these expectations are then described and explained in the next section. Finally, the test results and the regression procedures that generated these results are discussed.

Rationales for arms transfers

The supply of conventional weapons by the industrialized nations has received much attention in popular as well as scholarly discussions on recycling petrodollars (e. g., Bobrow 1977; Ray 1976; Willrich 1975). Many of these discussions imply that arms sales offer an attractive solution to these nations' trade deficits caused by the sharp increases in oil price.[1] This trade imbalance is difficult to alter in the short term by such measures as adjusting domestic oil supply and demand, or developing alternative sources of energy.[2] Moreover, efforts to curb the adverse effects of expensive imported fuel through such policies as restricting foreign imports in general, devaluing currency to facilitate exports, increasing deficit spending, or inviting foreign investment in the domestic economy of the affected countries entail some rather unpleasant consequences. They include foreign retaliation against import restrictions or agitation against export dumping, consumer revolt against inflation, and public outcry against foreign takeover of domestic business. Arms sales, on the other hand, tend to be a relatively unobtrusive issue for most voters.[3] And, while it is a competitive business, the number of suppliers is relatively small and there is no shortage of demand for weapons.[4] Thus, it seems to provide a relatively expedient and politically safe way to redress current or anticipated trade imbalance.

It has also often been suggested that important market mechanisms are working to perpetuate vigorous and expanding arms trade (e. g., Gelb 1976-77). The competitiveness among suppliers reduces inhibitions against selling; self-restraint becomes less compelling given the reasoning that 'if we don't sell, others certainly will.' Additionally, local rivalry among arms recipients tends to cause an escalation of demand over time, thus sometimes resulting in regional arms races such as in the Middle East and South Asia. The ever expanding global demand for imported weapons promises increasing business for all the major suppliers, since the technological base necessary for modern arms manufacturing limits their number.[5] They can also more confidently expect to capture a stable share of this growing market to the extent that the buyers are interested in diversifying the sources of their arms imports, given the uncertainties about potential supply interruptions.

Even without the oil crisis, strong economic and political incentives exist to export weapons. The economic reasons include the high overhead costs for the research and development of new weapons systems, and the diminishing marginal costs for additional units of production. Thus, except for the superpowers, modern arms industries cannot depend on internal demand alone if they are to operate economically. For the major suppliers such as the United States, overseas sales have traditionally served the function of relieving obsolescent stocks and over-

coming slacks during times of peace.[6] More recently, the value of these sales has increased tremendously, since they now often involve very sophisticated weapons systems.[7] Even if payment is spread out over several years, these sales offer substantial income. They also usually create opportunities for selling other kinds of goods and services to develop the recipients' 'support infrastructure' for the imported weapons.

As for political reasons, concern about maintaining friendly client states and East-West competition has always operated to encourage arms transfers, whether they are in the form of grants, loans, or sales. In the post-Vietnam era, local recipients of U.S. arms have been even more prominently cast in the role of proxies to check Soviet influence (e. g., Egypt, Saudi Arabia and, until recently, Iran). Furthermore, arms exports may have been motivated by the desire to placate foreign allies and domestic critics who are alarmed by the diminishing U.S. military presence abroad and an apparent resurgence of Soviet influence in the Third World.[8] The domestic climate that discourages direct U.S. foreign intervention could have an opposite effect on the Soviet Union and its allies; they have mounted more vigorous programs of weapons exports in support of their local clients (e. g., Afghanistan, Angola, Ethiopia, Vietnam).

The oil crisis was not responsible for these forces promoting arms sales, but rather compounded them. Heavy dependence on foreign fuel has led many West European countries to sell weapons to the Arab oil producers as a way of improving the security, if not the pricing, of their energy supply. Given their voracious appetite for Western technologies and mounting bills for imported petroleum,[9] the East European countries need to earn extra revenues by pushing one of their few viable exports: arms.[10] As for the United States, weapons sales to both the Arabs and Israelis have ostensibly been used as a leverage for mediating the Middle East conflict.[11] Finally, the oil crisis has accentuated concern about nuclear proliferation. According to one rationale for exporting U.S. weapons (Gelb 1976-77), it is better to sell conventional weapons to others than to have them purchase or develop a nuclear capability. Incidentally, those countries that have major security incentives for developing this capability also appear to have much to gain from a more independent source of energy in nuclear power, since their fuel supply is quite vulnerable to political or economic coercion in the form of embargoes or price hikes (e. g., Israel, South Africa, and, to a lesser extent, Taiwan and South Korea).

The arms importers constitute a rather heterogeneous group. While the majority of these countries are members of the Third and Fourth World, some net importers of weapons are industrialized nations (e. g., Japan, Australia, Denmark). Consequently, the dramatic rise in oil price had somewhat different short-term effects on their economic performance. In the period immediately after the energy crisis (1974-75), the economic growth rate slowed down more for the industrialized nations than for the less developed nations (Bobrow et al. 1977). The developing countries were less hurt by this adverse development in part because their economies were more insulated from the world economy and it took some time for the ripple effects of an economic slowdown in the developed countries to reach them.

It is not clear how the oil crisis and its economic consequences would affect the demand for weapons by the oil importers. The developed countries in this group are more dependent on foreign fuel, and are thus more vulnerable to its shortage and expensiveness. On the other hand, they are also less sensitive to these adversities in the sense that they are in a stronger position to cope with economic shocks. In addition to their relative wealth, the industrialized nations would presumably possess greater managerial skills in government and the private sector to adjust to the new economic situation (Bobrow et al. 1977). Thus, the data on oil dependency and its economic consequences may not bear any simple and direct relationship to the decisions to import weapons by these countries.

It is also possible that expensive petroleum had only a marginal effect on the demand for imported weapons by the poorer countries. A number of these countries have received OPEC loans or grants to ease the effects of oil price hikes. Additionally, perceived foreign threats and domestic interest alignments in some countries may perpetuate and perhaps even increase military spending. Therefore, in the short term there may be some income inelasticity in their demand for arms, regardless of the deteriorating trade positions of these developing countries in Africa, Asia, and Latin America.[12]

The oil exporting nations represent another subset of the arms importers. While as a group their increased oil revenues have obviously enhanced their ability to purchase weapons, three factors appear to be germane to their individual decisions to actually import arms. The oil crisis has increased the strategic, economic and symbolic importance of these countries, both in their own eyes and in those of others. Military modernization may be pursued by some of these countries as an effort to narrow the gap between their real strength and their new self-image as emerging powers. It may also result from a recognition of the changed perceptions of others, which can in turn create a sense of vulnerability, and thus induce them to engage in policies designed to improve their self-defense capabilities. Of course, their aspirations for grandeur and perception of foreign threat may or may not correspond to reality. But they are nevertheless important for understanding their decisions on defense spending.

Second, oil revenues have spurred rapid socioeconomic change in these countries, at a rate much faster than for others at a comparable stage of development. This situation is likely to induce an enhanced elite concern with the possibility of internal instability. Although the modern weapons purchased may not in themselves be useful for dealing with civil unrest, they are important for assuring the loyalty and support of the military establishment, without which it would be difficult for the ruling elites to maintain their dominance. This concern would seem to apply with greater force to traditional regimes such as those of Saudi Arabia, Kuwait, and Iran under the Shah.

Third, the availability of ready cash is likely to affect decisions to invest heavily on weapons. This condition is tied to the capital absorption capacity of the individual oil producing countries (Abolfathi et al. 1977). And, as regards their sensitivity to perceived external and internal threats, this factor is more relevant for the large producers with huge oil revenues but a small population.[13] Thus, we would again expect to find differences in the behavior of the members of the petroleum exporting community in acquiring weapons.

Sample and data

In order to test some of the above views, we use a sample of 56 countries with annual observations for the 1971-76 period (that is, for three years before the oil crisis and three years after it). Since we shall be using pooled cross-section time-series analysis, there are 336 cases representing country-years. The sampled countries belong to three categories: (1) the industrialized nations that are arms exporters and oil importers $(N = 9)$; (2) the oil exporting nations that are also arms importers $(N = 10)$; and (3) those countries that are both oil and arms net importers $(N = 37)$.[15] Appendix A identifies the countries in each group.

Several factors have influenced the selection of countries for this analysis. First, the problem of missing data has resulted in the exclusion of a number of less developed countries. Second, centrally-planned economies have been excluded, because they were only marginally involved in the international petroleum market.[16] Moreover, the conversion of their economic data into dollar equivalents involves difficult estimation problems. Third, countries with less than $200 million gross national product or one million population have not been included in the sample, since we are interested in the

behavior of the larger states. Finally, Canada, Mexico, Colombia, Norway, and Egypt have been excluded. Canada was in a relatively unique position of being both an oil and arms exporter, while the Egyptian oil fields in the Sinai were under Israeli control during the period under investigation. The other three countries have changed their status as a net oil importer or exporter during the same period.

As they were initially developed with somewhat different intentions, the arms transfer data used in this analysis have some important limitations.[17] They are estimates made by the U.S. Arms Control and Disarmament Agency (ACDA 1978). An arms transfer is defined as an 'international transfer under grant, credit, or cash sales terms of military equipment usually referred to as "conventional," including weapons of war, parts thereof, ammunition, support equipment, and other commodities considered primarily military in nature' (ACDA 1978: 23). It excludes the value of such activities as training, servicing, and construction. Moreover, the data are 'estimates of the value of goods actually delivered during the reference year, in contrast to the value of programs, agreements, contracts, or orders which may result in a future transfer of goods, or to the actual payment made for such deliveries' (ACDA 1978: 23).

These data characteristics raise several troublesome validity questions for the analysis. First, the exclusion of service, training, and construction costs depresses the amount of arms-related sales. If they were included, the figures would be much higher. The value of U.S. exports would be increased by as much as 30 % to 50 % (Cahn 1978). An underestimation of French arms transfers by the ACDA data has also recently been reported by Kolodziej (1979). However, we do not know whether this bias affects the figures for all countries to the same relative extent, and an investigation to clarify this question is beyond the scope of this study.

Second, the arms transfer data include

grants and loans. We cannot control for this factor, since a breakdown of the data according to grants, credits, and cash sales is not available for *all* the countries in the sample. But as already mentioned, grants have declined to a rather small share of total arms transfers in recent years. Thus, we underestimate the concomitant relative rise in sales by using these total figures for drawing overtime comparisons, and our assessment of the effects of the oil crisis on these sales tends to err on the side of being too conservative.

Third, the time lapse between the contracting for and delivery of weapons and between their delivery and payment means that these actions do not necessarily occur in the same year. Thus, for example, the post oil crisis figures may include some orders placed before or during 1973. Again, we lack the necessary data to control for this complication. But since the buyers usually have the option of cancelling their orders,[18] acceptance of the delivery of a previous year's order may be interpreted as equivalent to a decision to purchase these weapons in the year of delivery.

Finally, with respect to the timing and method of payment for arms — which can be financed through a variety of means such as barter arrangements, third-party loans, and partial debt forgiveness, we have to assume that the acceptance of arms delivery indicates an elite's expectation of its country's ability to pay for it (whether immediately or at some future date), and that this expectation bears some objective correspondence to the country's current financial capabilities and obligations. While this is obviously not a completely satisfactory solution to the problem, we shall simply have to accept the data imperfections if we are not to be totally immobilized by them. Knowledge about their existence, however, should alert us to the limitations of this analysis.

Method and analysis
The small number of cases in two of our categories — the arms exporting-oil import-

ing nations and the arms importing-oil exporting nations — poses another methodological problem. To ameliorate this problem, we combine the cross-section (56 countries) and time-series (6 years) data in our analysis, which gives us a total of 336 country-year cases. This decision in turn means that our dependent variable is the level of a country's participation in the weapons trade. In other words, it is the absolute dollar amount of the weapons sold by an exporter or bought by an importer.[19] This decision to capture the behavior of countries with considerable diversity in their background in a single analysis assumes that their weapons decisions are subject to similar economic and political influences. In effect, the regression equation we present later is an attempt to explain the arms transactions among the noncommunist countries, as they are influenced by forces on both the supply and demand sides.

As we have mentioned earlier, a variety of influences are at work in determining the volume of arms transfers. In our attempt to assess the relative importance of these different influences, we include eight independent variables in the regression equation. Four of these are dummy variables, and the rest are (1) the amount of oil trade,[20] (2) GNP per capita, (3) overall trade balance, and (4) military personnel per capita. To control for inflation, all dollar measures are in 1975 constant U.S. dollars.

The oil trade variable is intended to tap the relative dependency on foreign fuel for the importers, and the relative dominance of the petroleum market for the exporters. The per capita GNP variable is used as an approximate measure of the ability to absorb the economic shock induced by fuel inflation for the importers, and the inability to absorb surplus capital for domestic investment for the exporters. Albeit an imperfect measure, this variable is also indicative of two factors relevant to the arms exporters: the industrial base required for the manufacture of sophisticated weapons systems, and the existence of a global dealer network in the form of multinational corporations for promoting and servicing foreign sales. The trade balance variable does not distinguish between individual pairs of trading partners, but rather sums up the figures for each country with respect to all its trading partners. It does discount the value of arms transfers; that is, it indicates the size of a nation's surplus or deficit if it had not been involved in arms sales or purchases. For the oil exporters, a large surplus could again be indicative of possible limits to a country's capital absorption capacity. Finally, we employ military manpower proportionate to population as a surrogate measure of national perceptions of security threats. This variable has the advantage of reflecting not only an elite's recent conflict experience, but also its anticipation of possible future crises. This security concern applies to both the arms importers and exporters. It would presumably encourage the latter countries to arm their allies in order to deter possible aggression by their common adversaries.

We do not expect the independent variables specified above to behave in a straightforward manner with respect to the dependent variable. As in any empirical analysis, the same independent variable can reflect different aspects of reality. For instance, in the case of the arms exporters per capita GNP can indicate a country's relative ability to withstand the energy shock and, at the same time, its ability to manufacture and sell advanced weaponry. Thus, countries with high scores on this variable may have less need but more ability to export arms. Conversely, for the non-OPEC countries with high per capita GNP, there may be greater ability but less incentive to buy arms. Their need to import weapons may be diminished by a more secure domestic or international environment and a greater indigenous capability to produce weapons. And, for the OPEC countries, a high per capita GNP figure can indicate both a capability and willingness to purchase weapons, to the extent that this variable measures their relative wealth and inability to absorb

additional capital in their domestic economies.[21] We hope to disentangle somewhat these various plausible expectations in the subsequent discussion, especially for countries that import both arms and oil. We are not sure about how their relative dependency on foreign fuel and the resulting trade deficits for most of them would affect their decisions to buy weapons. As already mentioned, the energy crisis might have diminished the ability of these countries to purchase weapons, but not necessarily their incentives.

In addition to the variables already mentioned, we use two dummy variables to label country types, with the arms exporting-oil importing nations and the arms importing-oil exporting nations being coded 1 for these respective variables. Countries that are both arms and oil importers are coded 0 for both of these variables, and serve as a 'control' group for drawing comparisons with the other two groups. The other two dummy variables are time (with 1 for after and 0 for before the 1973 oil crisis), and war (with 1 for participation and 0 for nonparticipation in an armed conflict).[22] We use the former variable to determine possible differences in the demand and supply patterns for weapons before and after the energy crisis, and we use the latter variable to control for the influence of wars on arms demand. These variables help us to separate the effects of the oil crisis from those related to the replacement or stockpiling of military equipment as a result of or in anticipation of armed combat.[23]

The nature of our research design suggests that the ordinary least-squares approach to analyzing the data will be inappropriate. Our data violate the nonautoregression condition, which assumes that disturbances at one point in time are uncorrelated with any other disturbances. Furthermore, the use of a single error term as provided by the OLS approach will in our case produce estimates that are biased, inconsistent, and inefficient, because the relationship between errors of a single country at two points in time would be different from the relationship between errors of two countries at the same point in time. Accordingly, we shall rely instead on the generalized least-squares estimation procedures to determine the regression parameters for arms transfers. Additionally, since our analysis combines cross-section and time-series data, it is necessary to distinguish between these two sources of error in the regression estimation. We shall adopt a crossed-error model to decompose the regression residual into parts that are due to cross-section, time-series, and error variances (Drummond & Gallant 1977a, 1977b). The variance components are determined by the 'fitting-of-constants' method (Searle 1971), and are used to transform the data so that the results of our regression estimation will be unbiased and efficient (Fuller and Battese 1974).

The regression results produced by this method are reported in Table I. The top section of this table presents the regression parameters and the statistics for testing their significance. The bottom section provides the estimates for the variance components. These estimates show a much smaller time-series component than cross-section component, suggesting that the model has been able to capture most of the overtime changes in a country's arms imports or exports. On the other hand, it performs less well in ex-

plaining the differences in the import or export levels of various countries at the same point in time.

In assessing the parameter estimates, we rely on the values provided by the second and third columns in the top section of Table I. 'T for H: $B = 0$' gives the t statistic for testing the null hypothesis that the parameter is equal to zero. With 327 degrees of freedom, we need a t value of 1.96 or larger to reject the null hypothesis at the .05 level of confidence. The other column, 'Prob>|T|', assesses the chances of obtaining a larger value of t if the parameter is really equal to zero. A very small value for this probability implies that the independent variable makes a significant contribution to the model.

Using these criteria, we find that some of the views expressed earlier are not strongly supported. Specifically, military personnel per capita — used here as a surrogate for an elite's concern with domestic or foreign threat — is not significant in determining decisions to import or export weapons. After controlling for the effects of oil trade, trade balance, and GNP per capita, the b coefficient for this variable is in fact slightly negative, thus implying that there is perhaps a tradeoff in an elite's relative emphasis on manpower as opposed to imported weapons in its defense calculations.

Additionally, the t tests for the dummy

Table I. Regression results.

Source	B Value	T for H: B=0	Prob>|T|	Std Err B
Intercept	—146.01	—1.47	0.14	99.02
Oil trade	1.55	2.83	0.00	0.55
Trade balance	0.00	0.44	0.66	0.00
GNP per capita	0.04	2.07	0.04	0.02
Military manpower per capita	—0.96	—0.22	0.83	4.33
Time	11.99	0.38	0.70	31.45
War	1023.60	4.42	0.00	231.79
Arms exporter - oil importer	422.03	1.96	0.05	215.42
Arms importer - oil exporter	57.80	0.30	0.77	194.43

Degrees of freedom for T statistic = 327.

Variance Component for Cross Section	251498.49
Variance Component for Time Series	1043.59
Variance Component for Error	20591.20
Transformed Regression Mean Square Error	21320.18

variable of time are not encouraging, although its b value does indicate more weapons transfers in the post-1973 period than in the pre-1973 period with an average increase of 12 million dollars. Thus, while we do find a positive shift in the supply and demand patterns for weapons in the period subsequent to the oil crisis, this shift is not statistically significant at the .05 level. The same conclusion applies to the dummy variable indicating a country's status as an arms importer and oil exporter. While its b value is again in the expected direction — it indicates that the petroleum producing nations imported an average of 57.8 million dollars of weapons more than the petroleum consuming nations, the t tests caution against its acceptance.

Table I also shows that a country's balance of trade does not influence its decision to import or export weapons. The b coefficient for this variable is close to zero, and the t tests for it also do not inspire confidence. However, this contradiction of our previous discussion is more apparent than real. The absence of a significant relationship in this case is due to the different effects of trade balance on the weapons decisions of the oil importing and exporting nations. When we disaggregate the data according to country types, there is a negative association between these two variables for the arms exporters-oil importers ($r = -.46$) and the arms importers-oil importers ($r = -.39$). Thus, a trade deficit tends to encourage the export of weapons by the Western industrialized nations, and it does *not* impede the import of weapons by countries that are both oil and arms net consumers. Most of the latter countries are developing nations, and the result suggests that a deterioration in their trade position does not in itself curb their appetite for foreign arms. In fact, countries with larger deficits tend to purchase more weapons.[24] The relationship between trade balance and arms imports is positive for the OPEC countries ($r = .36$). This finding is, of course, congruent with the suggestion that a trade

surplus tends to spur weapons purchases by these oil exporters. However, the positive correlation for this group of countries is cancelled by the negative correlations for the other two groups of petroleum importing nations, thus resulting in a b coefficient for the balance of trade that approaches zero.[25]

The above interpretation receives indirect support from the finding that the volume of a country's oil trade has an important influence on its decision to import or export weapons.[26] The b value for the former variable is 1.55 and is significant at the .05 level of confidence. This indicates that as a country increases its oil imports, it is likely to increase its weapons exports — a finding that is understandable in view of the fact that the large oil consuming nations are also the big industrialized nations, which in turn have traditionally been the major sources of arms supplies.

Conversely, the more a country exports petroleum, the more it imports weapons. Again, this finding confirms the impression that the leading OPEC producers are the largest arms purchasers. What is not intuitively obvious is that our result also implies that dependency on foreign fuel does not dampen the demand for weapons by the third and numerically largest group in our sample, most of which are developing countries.

The t tests are significant at the .05 level for GNP per capita, although its b coefficient is quite small. This result may again be due to the differences in the relationship between national wealth and arms transfers that characterize our three groups of countries. The simple correlation coefficients between these two variables are .13, —.09, and .10 for the three groups. Thus, these correlations are all quite low. Nevertheless, they indicate that the wealthier industrialized nations tend to export more weapons, whereas the wealthier oil consumers tend to import more weapons. The negative correlation for the OPEC countries indicates that the wealthier oil producers tend to import less weapons in absolute terms. This finding becomes more understandable when we realize that small countries such as Kuwait tend to rank high on the GNP per capita measure, and that these countries tend to rank low in their defense need to import weapons and in their ability to make use of the imported weapons.

The dummy variables of war and status as arms exporters-oil importers show huge b values. They indicate that those countries that have participated in a foreign war imported or exported an average of 1023.6 million dollars more weapons than those that have not engaged in a conflict, and that the value of weapons supplied by the exporters exceeded by an average of 422 million dollars the value received by the importers in our sample.[27] We note that both of these findings are influenced by the United States as an outlier in the data distribution; it is by far the largest arms supplier in this study.

Conclusions

This analysis has focused on a brief time period, and has not dealt with other sorts of foreign sales (e. g., wheat, minerals, consumer goods) that may be equally important in affecting a country's balance of payments. Moreover, the various data limitations cau-

tion against any definitive conclusion. Our results do, however, provide some empirical support for several widely accepted qualitative assessments of the impact of expensive fuel on weapons transfers.

We have found some evidence indicating a linkage between arms and oil trade, with the major fuel consumers selling more weapons and the major fuel producers buying more weapons. Moreover, the volume of weapons trade has increased since 1973, and the oil exporting countries have spent more on foreign arms than the oil importing countries. These findings provide the necessary although not sufficient condition for confirming the view that the Western industrialized nations have used arms sales as a means for recycling petrodollars.[28]

Our analysis also indicates that dependency on foreign energy and relative national poverty do not seem to discourage the demand for weapons by countries that are both oil and arms net consumers, most of which are developing countries. Also, this demand is insensitive to the deteriorating trade positions of these countries. Consequently, it does not easily adjust in the short term to the changed economic situation facing them.

APPENDIX A

Country cases

Arms Exporter - Oil Importer	Arms Importer - Oil Exporter	Arms Importer - Oil Importer	
Belgium	Ecuador	Argentina	Korea, South
France	Indonesia	Australia	Malaysia
Germany, West	Iran	Austria	Morocco
Italy	Iraq	Brazil	New Zealand
Netherlands	Kuwait	Chile	Nicaragua
Sweden	Libya	Costa Rica	Pakistan
Switzerland	Nigeria	Denmark	Panama
United Kingdom	Saudi Arabia	El Salvador	Philippines
United States	Tunisia	Finland	Portugal
	Venezuela	Ghana	Singapore
		Greece	Spain
(N = 9)	(N = 10)	Guatemala	Sri Lanka
		India	Sudan
		Ireland	Tanzania
		Israel	Thailand
		Ivory Coast	Trinidad and Tobago
		Jamaica	Turkey
		Japan	Zaire
		Kenya	
		(N = 37)	

NOTES

1. There are also some who would posit a reversed causal relationship between increases in oil price and arms transfers. For example, interviews with former senior officials of the U.S. government in a recent *Sixty Minutes* program of the CBS television network (May 3, 1980) have produced allegations that the Nixon - Kissinger administration tacitly approved, or at least did not actively oppose, the Shah's decision to raise oil price. According to these allegations, the United States was interested in increasing the military capability of Iran under the Shah. The intention was to make that country a bastion against possible Soviet aggression, in view of the impediments to direct U.S. military involvement abroad in the aftermath of Vietnam. But since the U.S. Congress was unlikely to approve massive military aid to Iran, a price hike in oil appeared as an expedient way to enable the Shah to finance his weapons purchases. Kissinger declined to appear in this television program to rebut his critics.

2. The United States has a special position in this respect. Compared to many other countries, it is less dependent on foreign fuel and has more abundant coal reserves. Also, since a very large portion of its energy demand is for private consumption as automobile fuel, there is greater flexibility in curtailing demand without hurting economic performance.

3. That is, most voters are unconcerned about the moral issues connected with the charge of 'merchants of death'. If anything, for communities with a heavy concentration of arms-related industries (e. g., Los Angeles, Seattle), voters and elected officials are more likely to be concerned about the adverse implications for employment if weapons exports are curtailed. For a general discussion of these topics, see Sampson (1977).

4. The volume of arms trade has increased 60 % between 1967 and 1976, after controlling for inflation. It was about 13 billion dollars in 1976, the last year for which figures were available at the time of this research.

5. However, recently a number of less industrialized nations (e. g., Israel, Greece, Spain, Yugoslavia) have joined the arms trade race as suppliers. They have been able to capture a small but growing share of the market. Thus, while 95.5 % of the world's arms supply came from the ten leading exporters in 1967, their share had fallen to 90.1 % in 1976.

6. Therefore, arms exports serve a very important purpose of keeping the production lines open and active, which would make the task of gearing up for wartime production easier.

7. This demand for sophisticated weapons systems has created some opposition to arms sales within the supplier countries in that it impinges on their ability to satisfy the needs of their own defense establishments. For example, it has been pointed out that foreign sales have compelled U.S. armed forces to share current production lines, thus possibly contributing to a loss in their combat effectiveness (Gelb 1976-77: 8).

8. Of course, these motivations for supplying arms may not have the desired effects. Empirical research suggests that arms exports by the United States have not been totally successful in gaining influence abroad (Sylvan 1978), and that sharp increases in arms imports may in themselves induce a more antagonistic foreign policy posture on the part of the recipients (Sylvan 1976).

9. The Soviet Union, the major supplier of petroleum for East Europe, has adjusted its oil price to reflect the increasing cost of OPEC fuel.

10. As the Soviet ability to export energy diminishes (CIA 1977), it is also likely to place more emphasis on arms sales for earning additional foreign revenues.

11. For a discussion that challenges the view that arms sales can be used effectively to influence Israeli behavior, see Wheelock (1978).

12. One development, however, tends to curtail the amount of weapons transfers to these countries. In view of their own trade deficits, the arms suppliers are likely to be more reluctant to offer weapons on a grant or credit basis. The share of military assistance in total arms transfers has declined steadily and sharply in recent years, thus making it more difficult for the poorer countries to acquire foreign weapons. In the case of the United States, military aid to other countries fell from a high of 5.7 billion dollars in 1952 to under 600 million dollars in recent years (Gelb 1976-77: 7). Proportionately, grants constituted about 2 % of U.S. arms transfers during the mid 1970's, compared to about 75 % during the period between 1950 and 1967 (CDI 1978: 3). Moreover, the U.S. Congress has mandated the termination of the entire military assistance program.

13. Iran under the Shah was a prominent exception to this generalization.

14. Arms exporters are defined as those countries that have exported more than 250 million 1975 constant U.S.dollars during 1967-76.

15. As mentioned earlier, some of the countries in this category are industrialized nations. Also, given our focus on the status of a country as a net importer or exporter of weapons, some of these countries (e. g., Israel, Brazil) do supply arms to foreign clients. However, the amount of their imports always exceeds the amount of their exports. Finally, we focus on the aggregate amount of a country's weapons imports or exports without attempting to examine the volume of this trade between individual pairs of nations, since preferences for particular buyers or sellers are not relevant to the concerns of this analysis.

16. The barter arrangements for trade between these countries also complicate our analysis, if they are to be included. Because of these arrangements, it is more difficult to estimate the value of their trade. We should also point out that recipients of arms from these countries are not necessarily excluded from this analysis.

17. For a comparison of the merits of the different existing data sets on arms transfers, see Laurance and Sherwin (1978).

18. Of course, this option would usually invoke some financial penalty. Cancellation may also reduce the value of those parts of a weapons system that have already been imported. Thus, in these cases the marginal costs for purchasing additional parts tend to diminish while their marginal benefits tend to rise.

19. Ordinarily, we would prefer to separate imports from exports. However, due to the small number of cases for two of our groups of countries, a consideration already mentioned, we do not differentiate the signs of the figures for arms transfers. If we were to conduct separate analyses for each group, the low degrees of freedom would render their results suspect. Moreover, an attempt at group-specific analysis would limit the range of variation for some of the variables (e. g., GNP per capita, oil import levels), which could cause an understatement of the relationships between these variables. We should also explain the decision to use levels of arms transfers as the measure for our dependent variable. This means that we are not controlling for base figures, and thus the results are likely to be influenced by outliers such as the United States and Iran. We have chosen to use this measure in part because of its sensitivity. It is, for example, difficult for a measure such as percentage change to vary very dramatically after a certain point. That is, it is unrealistic to expect a country to continue to increase the proportion of its previous weapons imports, defense spending, total trade, or GNP for arms purchases beyond a certain threshold. More importantly, we settle for the level rather than the rate of change in arms transfers, because the expectations derived from our previous discussion relate to the former and not latter measure.

20. This variable, measured in millions of metric tons, is based on the United Nations (1978, 1977).

21. The same complexity holds for some of the other independent variables. For example, it is possible that a high ratio of military personnel to the civilian population indicates a defense strategy stressing manpower rather than modern weapons, thus implying less reliance on arms imports for the countries concerned.

22. The belligerent states are the United States, India, Israel, Pakistan, Portugal, and Turkey.

23. Participation in wars may either increase

(e. g., U.S. arms supply to Israel after the Yom Kippur war) or decrease (e. g., U.S. arms embargo against Turkey in the aftermath of its invasion of Cyprus) the import of weapons.

24. The reverse interpretation — that trade deficits are caused by arms purchases — is ruled out, because the figures for military transfers have been excluded in the calculation of trade balance.

25. For an explanation of our decision to eschew separate analysis for each group of countries, see note 19.

26. The product-moment correlation coefficients between a country's trade balance and its participation in oil trade are —.30 for the arms exporters-oil importers, .78 for the arms importers-oil exporters, and —.05 for the arms importers-oil importers. These results conform to our general expectations. A careful reader may ask whether the b coefficient we obtained for oil trade is possibly distorted due to its different effects on our three groups of countries, as in the case of trade balance just discussed. Specifically, it may be argued that a greater involvement in the oil trade will spur arms transfers for the arms exporters and oil exporters, but will dampen the demand for weapons on the part of countries that import both arms and oil (since money spent on oil cannot be used to finance weapons). Our results do not support the latter contention; the correlation coefficients for oil and arms transfers are .62, .49, and .05 for the three groups respectively. Thus, dependence on foreign sources of energy has a slightly positive impact on weapons purchases for the third group, comprised of countries that are both arms and oil importers. In other words, it does not discourage their appetite for imported weapons.

27. This result is understandable since many clients of the arms suppliers in our sample have not been included in this study. By the same token, the import figures for the recipients can include weapons supplied by countries not included in the sample (e. g., the Communist states).

28. Incidentally, the results reported here are also unable to discriminate between the rival hypotheses concerning the direction of causal relationship between increases in oil prices and weapons sales, as discussed in note 1.

REFERENCES

Abolfathi, A., G. Keynon, M. D. Hayes, L. A. Hazlewood, and R. Crain, 1977. *The OPEC Market to 1985.* Lexington, Mass.: Lexington Books.

Arms Control and Disarmament Agency. 1978. *World Military Expenditures and Arms Trans-*

fers: 1967-76. Washington, D. C.: Government Printing Office.

Blair, J. M. 1976. *The Control of Oil.* New York: Pantheon.

Bobrow, D. B. 1977. 'Realities in North-South Relations.' Presented at the conference on 'Power and Responsibility of the Developed Countries,' Tokyo, October 13-18.

Bobrow, D. B., R. Kudrle, and D. Pirages. 1977. 'Contrived Scarcity: The Short-Term Consequences of Expensive Oil.' *International Studies Quarterly 21* (December), 619-45.

Cahn, A. H. 1978. 'ACDA's Comment.' *Armed Forces Journal* (November), *37.*

Center for Defense Information. 1978. 'U.S. Weapons Exports: Can We Cut the Arms Connection?' Washington, D. C.: Center for Defense Information.

Central Intelligence Agency. 1977. 'The International Energy Situation: Outlook to 1985.' Washington, D. C.: Central Intelligence Agency.

Choucri, N. 1976. *International Politics of Energy Interdependence.* Lexington, Mass.: Lexington Books.

Doran, C. F. 1977. *Myth, Oil and Politics.* New York: Free Press.

Drummond, D. J. and A. R. Gallant. 1977a. 'TSCSREG: A SAS Procedure for the Analysis of Time Series Cross Section Data.' Raleigh, N. C.: Institute of Statistics, North Carolina State University (mimeo. series no. 1107).

Drummond, D. J. and A. R. Gallant. 1977b. 'The TSCSREG Procedure,' pp. 155-167 in J. T.Helwig (ed.), *SAS: Supplemental Library.* Raleigh, N. C.: SAS Institute.

Fuller, W. A. and G. E. Battese. 1974. 'Estimation of Linear Models with Crossed-Error Structure.'

Journal of Econometrics 2 (May), 67-78.

Gail, B. 1978. 'The Fine Old Game of Killing.' *Armed Forces Journal* (November), 37-39.

Kolodziej, E. A. 1979. 'Measuring French Arms Transfers.' *Journal of Conflict Resolution 23* (June), 195-227.

Laurance, E. J. and R. G. Sherwin. 1978. 'Understanding Arms Transfers through Data Analysis,' pp. 87-106 in U. Ra'anan, R. Pfaltzgraff, Jr., and G. Kemp (eds.), *Arms Transfers to the Third World.* Boulder, Colo: Westview Press.

Ray, G. F. 1976. 'Impact of the Oil Crisis on the Energy Situation in Western Europe,' pp. 94-130 in T. M. Rybczynski (ed.), *The Economics of the Oil Crisis.* New York: Holmes and Meier.

Sampson, A. 1977. *The Arms Bazaar.* New York: Viking Press.

Searle, S. R. 1971. 'Topics in Variance Component Estimation.' *Biometrics 27,* 1-76.

Sylvan, D. J. 1978. 'Arms Transfers and the Logic of Political Efficacy.' Carlisle Barracks, Penn.: Strategic Studies Institute, US Army War College.

Sylvan, D. A. 1976. 'Consequences of Sharp Military Assistance Increases for International Conflict and Cooperation.' *Journal of Conflict Resolution 22* (December), 609-36.

United Nations. 1978. *World Energy Supplies: 1972-1976.* New York: United Nations.

United Nations 1977. *World Energy Supplies: 1971-1975.* New York: United Nations.

Wheelock, T. R. 1978. 'Arms for Israel: The Limit of Leverage.' *International Security 3* (Fall), 123-38.

Willrich, M. 1975. *Energy and World Politics.* New York: Free Press.

24

AMERICAN FOREIGN POLICY
The Changing Political Universe

Samuel P. Huntington

During the coming decade, American foreign policy will have to respond to significant changes in the U.S. position in the world. These include, among others, diminished military capability relative to that of the Soviet Union, increased dependence on foreign sources of energy, and the heightened sensitivity of the American economy to external influences. During the same decade, American foreign policy will also inevitably reflect the changes in the American political system that have occurred in recent years. These changes are in part a product of the upheavals associated with Vietnam and Watergate, in part a reaction against what those upheavals produced, and in part the consequence of longer-term social and demographic trends in American society. These changes have been of sufficient magnitude to lead at least some perceptive observers to speak of "the new American political system" that emerged in the 1970s.[1] The central issue, of course, concerns the congruence between the changes in the domestic politics of the United States and the changes in the international position of the United States. Will the former facilitate or even permit a foreign policy capable of dealing with the latter? The purpose of this paper is to identify some of the key developments on the U.S. political scene that seem most relevant to foreign policy and to suggest what some of the implications of these changes may be for U.S. foreign policy, with particular reference to the needs of NATO in the 1980s.

Any description of current political trends should also, however, be accompanied by a caveat as to the extreme volatility of contemporary American politics. Five years ago it would have taken an extraordinarily prescient observer to have identified the trends dominant today, and what seems important today may well be drastically changed by tomorrow.

THE CONSERVATIVE ASCENDANCE[2]

Few things are more striking in American politics during the past five years than the shift to the Right. This has manifested itself in public opinion polls, in election results, in the issues that top the political agenda, and in the appeals and actions of political

Samuel P. Huntington is the director of the Center of International Affairs, Harvard University.

Published by permission of Transaction, Inc. from THE WASHINGTON QUARTERLY, Vol. 2, No. 4. Copyright © 1979 by The Center for Strategic and International Studies, Georgetown University.

leaders. This trend is most notable with respect to public attitudes towards governmental spending, but it is also apparent with respect to social issues. It is manifest within both political parties. As Arthur Schlesinger, Jr. likes to complain, Jimmy Carter is the most conservative Democratic president since Grover Cleveland. He became president, however, precisely because his anti-Washington, anti-big-government appeal distinguished him from his more liberal competitors in the 1976 Democratic primaries. In the Republican party, President Ford only *narrowly achieved* renomination over Reagan and did that, in part, by shifting to the Right. The 1978 primaries and elections—ranging from the victory of Proposition 13 in California to the defeat of Don Fraser in Minnesota and the election of Ed King in Massachusetts—seemed to indicate that the conservative tide was still in full flood. With the obvious and important exception of Ted Kennedy, all the leading American political leaders today are in the conservative half of the political spectrum, judged by the standards of the past 20 years. The popularity of Kennedy, however, is more probably a sign of the public's yearning for leadership than of its liking for liberalism, and in 19/9 Kennedy himself began to emphasize his identification with conservative issues (e.g., deregulation of airlines and trucking).

That opposition to government is the hallmark of American opinion today has been documented again and again in public opinion polls. In 1959, for instance, 14% of the public identified "big government" rather than "big business" (41%) or "big labor" (15%) as "the biggest threat to the country in the future"; in 1978, 47% of the public gave big government this honor, compared to 19% each for big business and big labor.[3] As Samuel Beer has demonstrated, the "public philosophy" of the New Deal, which dominated American politics for so long, has passed into history.[4] A conservative public philosophy may now be taking its place. Ideas and issues which were once thought "far out" on the Right are increasingly coming to be viewed as main stream. Most significantly, there has been a conservative intellectual renaissance, with conservative think tanks, conservative journals, conservative social critics and commentators now dominating public debate as their liberal counterparts did only a few years ago. During the 1950s, for instance, American intellectual life was enlivened by a "New Conservative" movement, just as it is by a "neoconservative" movement today. There are, however, major differences between the two. The earlier movement was essentially an effort to import into the United States an almost totally alien Burkeian type of conservatism linked to tradition, hierarchy, and social order. It remained the fad of a handful of intellectuals. Today's neoconservatives, on the other hand, are foursquare in the American tradition of individualism, free enterprise, and limited government. Conservatism is now not only intellectually respectable, it is also interesting and relevant. And that is a revolutionary development in post-1933 American politics.

The conservative trend in the United States would appear to be congruent with current trends in public and intellectual opinion in other Western societies, particularly Canada, Britain, and France. In the American context, the pertinent question is whether this trend represents merely a temporary shift away from the liberalism that has dominated American politics since the New Deal, or whether it represents the permanent displacement of the New Deal philosophy by a new approach to public affairs. Arthur Schlesinger, Sr. interpreted American politics in terms of a cyclical alternation of liberal and conservative phases. Applying his theory to the current scene would suggest that the current conservative swing—dating from 1969—may be nearing its end and that it should be superceded by a new liberal surge in the 1980s. The causes of the current conservative mood, however, suggest that such a swing is by no means inevitable. The present conservatism is, in part, a reaction to the tremendous expansion of domestic-spending programs in the 1960s and to pervasive inflation, produced by that expansion, and rising energy costs in the 1970s. In the minds of the public, inflation is the single continuing most important issue confronting the country, and, so long as that is the case, the instincts of the country are likely to be conservative. The roots of conservatism are also found, however, in longer-term social and demo-graphic trends. The bastions of liberalism have been the Northeast, the central cities, the labor movement, youth, and racial minorities. The Northeast is declining relative to the South and the West. The central cities are declining relative to the suburbs. Organized labor is a declining proportion of the American working force. As the "pig in the python" that swelled the ranks of protest in the 1960s approaches middle age, those between 18 and 30 will become a declining sector of the population. Among the traditional sources of liberalism, only the racial minorities will continue to grow in relative numbers and political importance. Unless traditional liberalism can find new constituencies, it is difficult to identify the bases for its political renaissance.

HARDENING ATTITUDES ON FOREIGN POLICY

The 1960s witnessed, of course, the breakup of the foreign policy consensus that had crystallized after World War II. During the Vietnam decade, 1965-75, the prevailing attitudes of both elites and the general public on foreign policy took a very different tack from those that existed earlier. Since 1975, however, the attitudes of the general public on foreign policy, particularly East-West issues, have changed again and significantly hardened towards the Soviet Union. This does not mean a total return to Cold War attitudes—detente and a SALT (Strategic Arms Limitation Talks) treaty still receive overwhelming approval—but it does mean a significant modification in those attitudes which prevailed during the Vietnam War. This shift manifests itself in several ways.

First, and probably prerequisite to the other changes in mass opinion, is the public's perception of the decline of U.S. influence and power in the world, particularly in comparison with the Soviet Union. In 1978-79, 56% of the American people thought that the United States was less powerful as a world leader than it was 10 years earlier, and 66% thought the United States had been falling behind the Soviet Union in power and influence.[5] Similarly, between December 1976 and November 1978, the propor-tion of Americans believing that the United States was militarily stronger than the Soviet Union declined from 23% to 15%, while those thinking that the United States was militarily weaker rose from 30% to 43%.

Second, the general public is clearly unhappy with this decline and wishes the United States to reassert itself in world affairs. In 1974, for instance, 33% of the public wanted the United States to play a more important role in the world; by 1978, this proportion had increased to 55%. In similar fashion, the willingness of the public to support the use of U.S. troops to defend its principal allies against Soviet attack has also significantly increased. "There is," as the Chicago Council on Foreign Relations summarized it, "a continuing reluctance to make commitments *everywhere*, but at the same time a greater willingness to honor selective commitments *somewhere*."[6] This strengthening of commitment on the part of both U.S. elite and public opinion is most notable with respect to the North Atlantic Treaty Organization (NATO). In 1974, for example, 39% of the public supported the use of U.S. troops in the event of a Soviet attack on Western Europe; in 1978, 54% of the public did so. This trend among the American public would seem to parallel the increased popularity of NATO among European publics.

Third, there is renewed support for the military forces and related instruments necessary to support a firmer stand against the Soviets. Public opinion during the 1950s and very early 1960s generally favored more, rather than less, defense spending. This situation reversed itself drastically in the late 1960s and early 1970s. In the past five years, however, the balance has again changed. In 1974, for instance, 32% of the public thought that the United States was spending too much on defense and 13% thought that it was spending too little, with 47% thinking the current level was about right. In 1978, 15% thought defense spending was too high, 32% thought it was too low, and 45% thought it was about right. Defense was the only one of seven major government-spending programs with respect to which public opinion shifted from a net negative stance in 1974 to a net positive stance in 1978. Somewhat similarly, support for conscription has also increased, with 43% of the public supporting the draft in 1979 as compared to 24% in 1974.

While mass opinion shifted in the direction of a firmer anti-Soviet line and stronger defense, elite opinion remains more ambivalent. Leaders in the formulation of foreign policy are less likely than the general public to believe that the United States is falling behind the Soviet Union in power and influence (39% vs. 56%). The more educated people are, the less likely they are to think that communism is the worst form of government, and the less likely they are to see communist governments in Japan, Western Europe, Africa, or Latin America as threats to the United States. In line with this belief, the more educated are less likely than the less educated to believe that the United States should be stronger than the Soviets: in a 1979 poll, for example, 35% of those with college educations thought that it was necessary for the United States to be stronger than the Soviet Union, as compared with 47% and 59% of those with high-school and eighth-grade educations. Consequently, those with more education are much more favorably disposed to cutting the defense budget than are those with less education: in 1974, for instance, 60% of those with postgraduate educations and 28% of high-school graduates supported a defense-spending cut. Foreign policy leaders are also more in favor of cutting the defense budget than the general public is (28% vs. 16%).

These and other data reveal significant differences between the outlooks of elites and the masses with the former being less hostile to communism, less likely to see the Soviet Union as a threat, less likely to believe the United States is weaker than the Soviet Union, less likely to believe that the U.S. should be stronger than the Soviet Union, and more likely to favor cuts in defense spending. As a result of these differences, the general trends in public opinion toward a harder foreign policy line are not likely to be quickly or automatically translated into such a policy. An inverse relationship exists between influence on foreign policy decisions and hardness of foreign policy attitudes. The trends are, however, unmistakable and they undoubtedly account in part for the toughening of the attitudes of the Carter administration with respect to East-West relations as well as the virtual unanimity of Republican party leaders on these issues.

COMPETITIVE BALANCE BETWEEN PRESIDENT AND CONGRESS

For 20 years after World War II, Congress generally supported presidential initiatives on foreign policy. For a decade from the mid-1960s to the mid-1970s, Congress reasserted its own independence and power in foreign policy, and at times seemed almost automatically to oppose the president. During the last few years, however, a new pattern of executive-legislative relations has emerged. The president can now count on neither automatic support nor automatic opposition from Congress. The initiative in foreign policy rests generally with him. Where congressional approval is required, however, he has to work for it. During 1978-79 the administration had five major battles over its initiatives in foreign policy: the Panama Canal treaty; the Middle East arms sale; military assistance to Turkey; the defense bill veto; and normalization of relations with the People's Republic of China (P.R.C.). In each case, the administration confronted supposedly powerful interest groups: right-wing nationalists; the Israeli lobby; the Greek lobby; the military-industrial complex; the China lobby. In each case, powerful congressmen opposed the administration's policy. In each case the administration had to expend tremendous amounts of time and energy—including those of the president—to win support in Congress. But, in each case, the administration did win out in the end, although often by fairly narrow margins and in some cases by compromising and by making concessions in other areas. Senate consideration of the SALT treaty has followed a similar course.

This combination of presidential initiative with congressional participation and approval thus seems to be the dominant pattern of legislative-executive relations at the present time. When compared to automatic support or automatic opposition, there is much to be said for this system, and it probably approximates about as closely as is possible in the modern world the sort of relation between president and Congress that the framers of the Constitution thought should exist. It also does not differ a great deal from the relation which existed for much of pre-World War II American history. There is, however, now one important distinction. In the nineteenth and early twentieth centuries, major U.S. initiatives in foreign policy were relatively rare. A president might go to Congress to secure its approval of such an initiative—acquisition of new territory, declaration of war, major tariff legislation, major new treaty, change in military or naval force postures—perhaps once or twice in a four-year presidential term. He thus could afford to devote the time, energy, and political capital necessary to secure its approval (although even then, of course, he did not always succeed—witness Grant's effort to annex the Dominican Republic and Wilson's disaster with the Versailles treaty). Now, however, the president is continuously going to Congress to secure its approval for his foreign policy actions. No longer, as during the 1950s, can the president simply ask three or four major leaders in the House and Senate to marshal an existing majority to support his policy. Instead, a new and different majority has to be put together on each issue. The drain on presidential and staff influence, time, and resources is enormous. It also means less presidential attention to domestic issues and, quite possibly, sacrificing presidential positions on some of those issues in order to win support on the foreign policy issues.

The restrictions that Congress imposed on executive action during the Vietnam decade still remain, but the political impetus to enforce them vigorously seems to have weakened. Nor does it now appear that Congress will go out of its way to block presidential actions in foreign policy which clearly fall within his legal authority. Indicative of this change was Congress's reluctance to challenge—or even to criticize significantly—President Carter's decision in March 1979 to sell $390 million worth of weapons to Yemen. The Arms Export Control Act requires the president to place sales of more than $7 million before Congress for 30 days, during which period Congress can veto the sale if it so desires. In this case, however, the president invoked a waiver provision in the act that enables him to bypass Congress if "an emergency exists which requires such sale in the national security interests of the United States." This was the first time this Waiver provision had been invoked, and it is quite inconceivable that, a few years earlier, any president could have thought he could get away with handling such a major innovation in arms sales and U.S. commitments by this means. Yet, while a few senators and representatives did criticize the president's handling of the sale, no major effort was launched in Congress either to challenge it or to reverse it. Just as the presidential dispatch of 500,000 men to Vietnam represented the extreme of a policy shift in one direction, so also the congressional veto of U.S. involvement in Angola represented the extreme of the shift in the other direction. Neither is likely to be repeated in the immediate future.

A YEARNING FOR LEADERSHIP

In the late 1960s, public opinion mobilized for an assault on the "Imperial Presidency" and other manifestations of excessive power. The dominant trends of the 1960s were towards, simultaneously, the expansion of governmental activity and the weakening of governmental authority.[8] At the end of the 1970s, the dominant trends are almost in the opposite direction. The movement to cut back governmental activity has been paralleled by the development of a yearning for more powerful and authoritative leadership. Five years after the resignation of President Nixon, the more frequent criticism of President Carter was not that he acted in arbitrary fashion but that he fails to act in decisive fashion. The columnists who denounced Nixon as a "strong bad" president came to express almost equal unhappiness over Carter as a "weak good" president. As we have suggested, the yearning for leadership accounts for the otherwise hard-to-explain popularity of Kennedy, and it also explains why, despite two strikes against him, John B. Connally was to make such progress as a candidate for the Republican nomination. Both Kennedy and Connally convey what Carter does not: an image of vigorous, muscular leadership, and that is what the country seems to crave at the moment.

This change in public attitudes is clear. Equally clear, however, is the fact that the social changes, attacks on authority, and political upheavals of the 1960s have left an objective situation in which the exercise of leadership by anyone is extraordinarily difficult. Anthony King has perceptively described the prevalence of "atomized politics" in the United States and contrasted it with the emergence of corporatist politics in Britain.[9] The 1960s saw the dismemberment of leadership structures in the United States. Political parties disintegrated as meaningful organizations. Power became diffused within Congress. Hierarchical control in the executive branch evaporated. These developments were, in part, the result of the political spirit of the times, the overwhelming opposition to the exertion of authority in any form, but they were also, in part, the result of changes in social structure and education. Groups which had previously been outside the political system now became vigorously participant. The revolution of rising expectations was, in Daniel Bell's phrase, converted into the revolution of rising entitlements.[10] In Congress, the diffusion of power was in large part simply the result of the diffusion of expertise: congressmen were better educated and, under the ministrations of their growing staffs, better informed on the issues. A president can exercise leadership at the national level only if there are institutional, bureaucratic, local leaders with whom he can deal at the subnational level. It is through such a system rather than through broad appeals to public opinion that presidents have achieved the policy results they desire. Vigorous and responsible national leadership requires a network of petty tyrants. The dissolution of the network deprives the incumbent president of a major resource and significantly weakens him in comparison with his opposition. In its absence, even the most dramatic appeals to public opinion by the most charismatic of presidents will yield little in the way of action.

A situation thus exists where there is a subjective craving for leadership, but the absence of the objective conditions which make such leadership possible. A new president could relatively easily set forth an inspiring vision, but he could not so easily reconstitute a network of institutional relationships and reciprocal obligations. Over time, it is possible that the objective conditions for leadership can be restored and that a new system of authoritative subnational leaders can come into existence. In the meantime, however, the gap between the leadership that people desire and the leadership that the system permits further discredits those in leadership positions and, thus, in vicious circle fashion, makes it still more difficult for them to act. In this situation also, it is more difficult for an incumbent to appear to have the desirable qualities of leadership than it is for someone out of office to appear to have them. It is also more difficult for someone in the middle of the political spectrum to appear as a muscular leader than for someone closer to an extreme. And it is more difficult to exercise leadership in domestic policy than it is to exercise it in foreign policy.

A middle-of-the-road incumbent president thus faces major difficulties. Given the evisceration of the leadership networks, he will have much more difficulty exercising effective leadership in domestic policy than in foreign policy. The record rather conclusively demonstrates, for instance, that it is easier for the president of the United States to get the agreement of the president of Egypt and the prime minister of Israel to a peace treaty than it is for him to get the agreement of the House and the Senate to meaningful energy legislation. To exercise leadership, in other words, a president is almost driven to look abroad. What is significant here is the nature of President

Carter's foreign policy successes. His triumphs—Panama Canal, Middle East, SALT II, P.R.C. normalization, the Tokyo round—have been almost entirely triumphs of negotiation, compromise, mediation, and accommodation. Foreign policy triumphs in the sense of victories in confrontations with other states are notably absent. The administration has, indeed, rather carefully avoided opportunities for confrontations with both the Soviet Union and the Organization of Petroleum Exporting Countries (OPEC). It cannot be assumed that this pattern will necessarily continue in the future. Given a popular yearning for muscular leadership, and given the difficulties of providing such leadership in domestic policy, a future president might well see it to his and to the national advantage to pursue a more vigorous and assertive foreign policy, taking greater risks of confrontations with other states.

THE END OF THE ESTABLISHMENT?

In 1973, President Nixon, commenting on his Watergate problems, expressed the view that "The Establishment is dying . . .". Two years later, Henry Kissinger argued that the people who had helped John Kennedy shape and implement U.S. foreign policy had had "no adequate replacements" and that "The Establishment that carried our foreign policy has been both disintegrated and demoralized." In the summer of 1976, Hamilton Jordan predicted that neither Cyrus Vance nor Zbigniew Brzezinski would occupy top foreign policy positions in a Carter administration: "That's not going to happen. You're going to see new faces, new ideas. The Government is going to be run by people you have never heard of."[11]

These reports of the death of the Establishment would appear to be exaggerated. Yet the decline of the foreign policy Establishment is also clearly a fact. Its founding fathers of the years immediately after World War II are either dead or retired. The consensus and the confidence that once characterized it disappeared in the Vietnam decade. In their place are uncertainty and division. The principal initial foreign policy officials in the Carter administration are Establishment progeny. Yet they are also divided into three generations with significantly different outlooks produced by Vietnam. The first generation, represented most notably by Vance and Warnke, were in their 40s and held responsible positions in the Johnson administration during the Vietnam War. In the Carter administration they have espoused a softer, more conciliatory position with respect to the Soviet Union. The second generation, represented by Brzezinski and Schlesinger, were in their late 30s and held, if any, less important positions in the Johnson administration. In the Carter administration they took a much tougher line with the Soviets. The third generation, represented by almost any assistant secretary of state, were foreign service officers in their late 20s in the Johnson administration and, more often than not, resigned their positions in the Nixon-Kissinger years. The Vietnam War was the traumatic event of their early professional life and they also tended to take a softer position towards the Soviets. The foreign policy of the Carter administration, at least on East-West issues, can in large part be understood as the struggle of generation two against a coalition of generations one and three.[12] The Vietnam War thus left a legacy of significant differences, at least within the Democratic sector of the foreign policy Establishment. To complicate the situation further, there are now signs of a fourth generation beginning to appear, to whom Vietnam is history and the Soviet threat reality, and who consequently share much of the perspective of generation two. Nonetheless, despite its divisions, the eastern foreign policy Establishment retained its grip on the foreign-policy-making processes during the Nixon, Ford, and Carter administrations.

This situation poses two questions. First, how long can it endure? The locus of economic, demographic, and political power in the country is shifting from the Northeast to the South and West. (Of the seven leading figures in the 1980 presidential race, six come from the South and West: two southerners, two Texans, two Californians.) The Nixon White House was dominated by southern Californians, the Carter White House by Georgians. Yet the National Security Council (NSC) and the State Department remained curiously insulated from these currents, recognized, albeit grudgingly, as the special preserve of Wall Street lawyers and Ivy League professors. Nine of the 11 individuals who have held the positions of secretary of state since 1949 and national security advisor since 1961 have come from New York and Massachusetts (the other two were Dean Acheson and Brent Scowcroft). Yet, in the coming decade, is not American foreign policy—like American politics generally—more likely to bear the imprint of Texas and California than of New York and Massachusetts?

Second, if the eastern Establishment does wither away, what difference will it make for foreign policy? One crucial function which such an Establishment performs is the education of its members in the received wisdom of what are perceived to be the realities of the outside world, and the effective ways of dealing with the outside world. That received wisdom is the product of the collective accumulation and exchange of experience and understanding among its members over a sustained period of time. If the products of the Establishment have anything distinctive, it is presumably this awareness of what motivates other people and nations, how the international game is played, what the costs, risks, and benefits of alternative strategies and approaches may be. The weakening of the Establishment was, in some measure, signaled by the extent to which some of the early foreign policy initiatives of the Carter administration, such as those on arms transfers, negotiations with the Soviets, troop withdrawal from Korea, had a certain "naivete" about them and seemed to deviate substantially from Establishment conventional wisdom. A new administration, particularly a more conservative Republican one, might well demonstrate a more nationalistic, more assertive, more unilateralist naivete of its own in its initial foreign policy thrust. Without an Establishment or with a much weakened one, the constraints on foreign-policy decision makers will be less than they have been in the past, opening the way for dramatic initiatives, dramatic achievements, and dramatic disasters.

IMPLICATIONS FOR U.S. FOREIGN POLICY

Various changes and potential changes in U.S. domestic politics do not in themselves presage major shifts in U.S. foreign policy. They will also not necessarily prevent such shifts if these seem demanded by other extraneous forces. They are, however, compatible with what could be the emergence of a loose, general consensus on U.S. foreign policy for the coming years. Obviously, any such consensus could only be couched in generalities, but generalities can also be realities both in terms of what they prescribe and what they omit. The following might be included as elements in this emerging consensus:

1. Inflation and energy should be the principal concerns of policy. Foreign policy concerns are second to these and possibly other domestic issues. To combat inflation, the most urgent need is to reduce governmental spending. A rough order of priorities among the principal elements of "the great equation" would be: (1) a balanced budget, (2) tax reduction, (3) defense programs, (4) domestic programs. This order of priorities, it might be noted, is precisely the reverse of that historically espoused by the Democratic party in the 1950s and 1960s, and is roughly identical to that then pursued by the Republican party.[13]

2. Within the foreign policy area, no single goal, such as the containment of communism, deserves overriding priority. Foreign policy is a complex matter involving the pursuit of a variety of goals in a variety of arenas (or chessboards). Conflicts among these goals should be resolved in an ad hoc manner in individual cases.

3. Consonant with the above, U.S. foreign policy should not be "Russia obsessed." On the one hand, the claims of competition with the Soviet Union should not necessarily override all other goals in other areas (e.g., southern Africa); on the other hand, it should not be assumed that Soviet cooperation is a prerequisite to dealing effectively with major issues (e.g., the Middle East).

4. U.S. foreign policy has to reflect the realities of global politics and the needs of national security, but it also has to be rooted in basic U.S. liberal and democratic values.

5. The United States should attempt to cooperate with the Soviet Union with respect to arms control, economic relations, and other matters. At the same time, the United States must accept the facts of competition with the Soviet Union and the need to maintain at least overall equivalence in military capabilities with the Soviet Union. The latter goal requires real increases in military spending of three to five percent over the next several years.

FIGURE 1

Two Dimensions of U.S. Foreign Policy

Relations with the Soviet Union	Relations with allies and others	
	Unilateral	*Multilateral*
Cooperative	D	B
Competitive	C	A

6. Not all instabilities or aggression in the world challenge U.S. vital interests; where U.S. vital interests would be affected, however, the United States must make clear its determination to defend its interests and maintain, in cooperation with its allies, the military capabilities to do so. In addition to the Western Hemisphere, Western Europe, Japan, and Korea, the United States now also has vital interests in the security and stability of the Middle East-Persian Gulf area.

Within this broad range of consensus, obviously there can be shifts of emphasis in one direction or another. Two key dimensions of U.S. foreign policy, for instance, involve the relative emphasis on cooperation vs. competition in U.S. relations with the Soviet Union and the relative emphasis on a unilateral vs. a multilateral approach in U.S. relations with its allies and other countries. Historically, the Cold War consensus put the emphasis on competition and multilateralism (Figure 1, quadrant A). During the years of detente, the multilateral stress was more or less maintained, but the balance in connection with the Soviet Union shifted in the cooperative direction (quadrant B). In 1972, George McGovern appeared to want to lead U.S. policy into a mix of unilateralism and cooperation (quadrant D). In fact, as we have emphasized, the actual shift has been back towards more emphasis on competition with the Soviets. It would, however, be quite compatible with the trends we have discussed in American politics for policy now not only to become more competitive but also to become more unilateral (i.e., shift towards quadrant C). A conservative, assertive nationalism certainly cannot be ruled out, although again there are clear institutional and political constraints on how far such a foreign policy shift might go.

The overall U.S. commitment to the security of Western Europe and to the existing levels of U.S. forces devoted to that purpose are buttressed by the prevailing perceptions of the Soviet threat. This widespread support for NATO is not likely to be weakened except in two circumstances.

First, if it is widely perceived that the European members of NATO are not doing their share of providing for the common defense, then the desire to cut government spending could lead to a recrudescence of Mansfieldism. At present, for instance, it would appear that the GNP of the non-U.S. NATO nations is slightly more than that of the United States, but their defense spending is only about 70% of that of the United States. Any increase in this sort of disparity could generate political pressures to reconsider the large allocations of U.S. defense dollars to NATO purposes. More seriously, perhaps, the argument can be made—and is being made by some people—that the alliance has been very slow in adopting to the changing power relationships among its members. It is still shaped in the mold that was fixed when the United States was overwhelmingly powerful and European countries economically devastated. The change in the European-U.S. balance dictates a change also in their contributions to NATO.

A second way in which NATO could come to the fore in U.S. domestic politics in the coming years is in connection with the vigorous debate which will undoubtedly take place in the early 1980s over the reinstitution of the draft. Those who oppose the draft will almost inevitably have to argue in favor of smaller U.S. military forces, and, given the heavy commitment of U.S. ground forces to NATO purposes, this almost inevitably will require them to challenge the desirability and need of such a commitment.

In the coming years, NATO will also face the need to develop common approaches to many issues which are either new or which it has in the past generally tended to ignore. These include: (1) negotiating arms control agreements for gray-area weapons systems; (2) finding substitutes (theatre nuclear modernization, conventional force build-up, offensive conventional strategy) for the decreasing credibility of the U.S. strategic deterrent; (3) developing the means to deal with serious threats to NATO security outside the North Atlantic area; and (4) creating more effective mechanisms by which the NATO nations can capitalize on their economic and technological advantages in their dealings with the Soviets. To be dealt with successfully, all of these issues will require extensive intra-alliance consultation, negotiation, and accommodation. Any domestic political currents that gave a greater unilateral emphasis to. U.S. foreign policy would obviously greatly complicate the resolution of these issues. It is in that way that the exigencies of U.S. politics are most likely to conflict with the needs of NATO in the coming years.

NOTES

1. See Anthony King, ed., *The New American Political System* (Washington: American Enterprise Institute, 1978).

2. Except as otherwise noted, the terms "conservatism" and "liberalism" are used here in their American, not their European, meanings.

3. *Public Opinion* 1 (Nov.-Dec. 1978), p. 29.

4. Samuel H. Beer, "In Search of a New Public Philosophy," in King, *The New American Political System*, pp. 5-44.

5. This and other public opinion data in this section come from polls reported in *Public Opinion*, March-April 1978 to June-July 1979, and from the Chicago Council on Foreign Relations study, *American Public Opinion and U.S. Foreign Policy 1979*, edited by John E. Rielly.

6. Rielly, op. cit., p. 27.

7. This section is drawn from my paper, "The U.S. Government and International Relations, Or Why the U.S. Is at Times an Unpredictable Opponent and an Infuriating Ally," prepared for the first Argentine-American Forum, sponsored by the Gerogetown School of Foreign Service and the Pinero Pacheco Foundation, St. Michael's, Maryland, May 1979.

8. See Samuel P. Huntington, "The United States," in Michel Crozier, Samuel Huntington, and Joji Watanuki, *The Crisis of Democracy*, New York: New York University Press, 1975, pp. 59-118.

9. King, op. cit., pp. 388-95.

10. Daniel Bell, *The Cultural Contradictions of Capitalism*, New York: Basic Books, 1976, pp. 232-236.

11. Kirkpatrick Sales, *Power Shift: The Rise of the Southern Rim and Its Challenge to the Eastern Establishment*, New York: Random House, 1975, p. 4; U.S. Department of State *Bulletin*, May 12, 1975, p. 607; Robert Scheer, "Jimmy, We Hardly Know Y'All," *Playboy Magazine*, Vol. 23, November 1976, p. 192.

12. This struggle was often described in the press as a struggle between the State Department and the National Security Council. But that was inaccurate because there were many generation three people in the NSC staff; what made it seem like an interdepartmental rather than intergenerational rivalry was the total absence of any generation two people in the State Department-ACDA complex.

13. See Samuel P. Huntington, *The Common Defense* (New York: Columbia University Press, 1961), pp. 264-67.

URBAN AFFAIRS

The field of urban affairs has reached a policy-making zenith because of the high concentration of people in heavily populated regions who are short on work, have limited savings, and share a list of authentic needs ranging from education to health. Policy is intended to bring urban regions up to par with suburban or even rural areas. There was a time, before World War II, when rural areas were deemed underprivileged and most in need of federal, state, and local support. But this perception has changed dramatically with the decline in agrarian regions vis-à-vis industrial regions. As urban regions have grown old and overpopulated, services that were deemed adequate have become in desperately short supply; such vital services as transportation from home to job have deteriorated as the costs of replacement services and supplies have increased; problems of new housing in the poor and marginal sectors in the inner city have grown sharper as the middle classes have become suburbanized. Now that urban regions have to contend with new immigrants, new language groups, and new levels of retired individuals, older problems have been compounded. Who will pay for innovations in old cities, from housing to transportation, becomes a national issue, one hardly helped by the exodus of the wealthy and their replacement by marginal economic actors.

The Vaughan, Pascal, and Vaiana study shows how federal urban policies often work at cross purposes and sometimes generate quite different outcomes than those intended. The authors call this the "harmful helping hand." The economically disadvantaged were encouraged to become and remain big-city dwellers; other policies such as capital investment, procurement, tax structures, and regulations encouraged many others to leave the city. While the influence of federal policies in the urban sector is pervasive, its outcomes are not necessarily uniform or desired. Since many programs harmful to cities are irreversible, it might be best to reconsider the area of urban policy-making as supplemental to ongoing trends rather than to initiate new trends or reverse those unpalatable to any given special interest group. As Wolman and Reigeluth note, the energy crisis has highlighted new trends in urban affairs, specifically the need for a public transportation alternative to private vehicular traffic. The resistance of individuals to public transportation options is only slowly evaporating. Here we have an excellent illustration of the "harmful helping hand" principle, with only marginal results from vast public transportation policies. Still, as the crisis in energy matures, the efforts in this area are likely to increase. In this connection, the Frieden essay is of exceptional importance. For too long urban policies have been made for urban dwellers rather than by them. Who should decide, who should make policy, and how much or what kind of housing is satisfactory become central issues. And with large numbers of people content with housing, cash payments rather than indirect housing allowances may be a more equitable way of securing the urban poor in large projects, whether in housing or transportation. The priorities of the poor rather than the policies of administrators ought to be viewed as the ultimate arbiter in Frieden's view, which brings forth a serious set of questions about who should make policy and who should implement it.

25

FEDERAL URBAN POLICIES
The Harmful Helping Hand

Roger J. Vaughan, Anthony H. Pascal, and Mary E. Vaiana

The period since World War II has seen a disheartening decline in the fortunes of many of our nation's cities. Shrinking population, job losses, and fiscal weakness are interwoven features of the cities' plight. Firms have abandoned central city factories to build near suburban freeways. In 1948 suburbs had a third of metropolitan employment; they now contain more than half. Moreover, a major demographic shift is in progress. New businesses are choosing to locate in the Sunbelt rather than in traditional areas of economic concentration. The most distressed cities as measured by employment and per-capita income trends are heavily concentrated in the old manufacturing belt—New England, the mid-Atlantic states, the East North Central states. Affluent families have moved into sprawling suburban developments, leaving the central cities to a growing concentration of the poor. Forty-four of the largest American cities lost at least 10 percent of their population between 1950 and 1975; in the same period, central cities lost 3.4 million white inhabitants and gained 1.2 million nonwhites so that the latter now constitute 25 percent of all city residents. Local taxes have spiralled. In 1953 in the average state, non-federal taxes absorbed about 8 percent of personal income; by 1975, the bite was about 13 percent.

Those living in declining cities have no doubt about the existence and seriousness of the urban problem. Families face rising crime rates and pay rising property taxes; their children attend deteriorating schools. Firms operate in old buildings, have increasing difficulties locating skilled labor, and suffer from inadequate transportation services. Public officials are caught between

From Roger J. Vaughan, Anthony H. Pascal, and Mary E. Vaiana, "Federal Urban Policies: The Harmful Helping Hand," III(4) *Taxing & Spending* 27-39 (Fall 1980). Copyright 1980 by Institute for Contemporary Studies. Reprinted by permission.

declining tax bases and growing demands for public services. They have little patience with those who ask whether the urban problem

Federal policies, designed to achieve other objectives, are accelerating the decline of the central city.

is a federal issue. Enough places and people are affected to make the problem national in scope. Moreover, leaving the problem untended makes us all worse off because inattention often impels cities into a self-sustaining spiral of decline.

Much of the decline in central cities is due to changes in consumer preferences and production technologies, and is therefore, in some sense, "natural." What is neither natural nor well known is the extent to which federal policies, designed to achieve other objectives, are accelerating the decline of the central city. That this should be a largely untold story is all the more troubling in light of continued, increasing demands for new federal action. If the problem of the central cities is not primarily the result of federal policies, at least the public should be aware of the extent to which those policies and programs are accentuating current difficulties.

Urban troubles do not necessarily mean that there should be a federal policy to "save" cities; for one thing, help for distressed cities might impose costs on other locations. When a middle-income family, for example, leaves a central city for a suburb, the move may represent a loss to those remaining behind. But to the suburb the move brings improvements in markets, labor pool, and tax base. The very fact of the move suggests that the family itself has gained (or at least expected it would).

Thus, to the extent that urban decline reflects household preferences for surburban living and for commercial exploitation of the technological advantages of dispersed locations, the case for a major federal effort to save cities—as opposed to helping people who happen to live in cities—must depend on an explicit judgment that the values of urban life justify the costs of the effort. However, if, as argued here, urban decline is not simply a "natural" phenomenon, but has been partly stimulated by the largely inadvertent anti-urban bias of federal policies, then a case exists for federal urban assistance to redress the bias.

The federal role in urban affairs for the past two decades has changed along with definitions of the urban problem. Many federal programs aimed at big-city problems had insignificant effects. Other programs stimulated growth but over time injured the big cities or the Northeast or both. Still others had no particular urban objectives but worked to the disadvantage of America's central cities. The following abbreviated history highlights the essential problems.

How the federal government has treated cities

In the 1950s, urban problems were commonly defined as crowding in the central cities contrasted with inadequate infrastructure in the suburbs to accommodate their rapid growth. The interstate highway program was an important response to that definition of the problem as it could be used to disperse population for civil defense, among other purposes. Urban renewal was also designed to improve the physical conditions of cities and to increase the supply of housing for low-income residents. But it displaced many residents from their original housing and moved them to marginal areas (often bordering the original slum), where the cycle of low rents and disinvestment often led to a new round of deterioration and eventual abandonment.

During that period, however, principal attention was directed to alleviating poverty and stimulating growth in rural areas and the South rather than to aiding cities, except insofar as those programs obviated the need to migrate. Huge water projects were undertaken to open landlocked southern cities to supplies of raw materials and to the benefits of international trade. The Appalachian Regional Commission, established at the end of this period of rural focus, built highways and industrial parks in small towns and funded training programs to help local industry and to staunch the flow of rural migrants northward. Such problems as cities did experience were regarded as transitory. Rapid national growth would erase urban poverty and unemployment.

To some extent, these beliefs were justified. Northern cities generated jobs for the majority of their immigrants, and rapid suburbanization eased problems of overcrowding. However, by the mid-1960s, it became apparent that national economic growth would not eradicate the swelling pockets of urban poverty and decay. Many large metropolitan areas had stopped growing. The disparity between affluent, white suburbs and poor, black central cities became a major political concern. One policy response was the "War on Poverty" fought on several fronts: improved social services, education and training programs, anti-discrimination efforts, and, later, increased transfer payments. The policies were "urban" primarily because so many economically disadvantaged people lived in cities. On the other hand, the problems of declining urban *economies*—their needs for capital, infrastructure, market access—received little attention. In fact, most of these programs helped the poor where they lived: public housing was built in central cities; urban areas offered more training programs, social services, and public transportation subsidies; city governments actively pursued minority hiring. As a result, the economically disadvantaged, who once might have located elsewhere, were encouraged to become, and remain, big-city dwellers.

The economically disadvantaged were encouraged to become, and remain, big-city dwellers.

By the end of the 1960s, programs to upgrade the tangible capital stock of cities had regained prominence. Model Cities funds began to be used to clear areas of dilapidated housing adjacent to central business districts, and to build commercial structures and, often, middle-income housing. The Urban Mass Transit Administration provided grants for new rail systems. The Economic Development Administration funded inner-city industrial parks. But these programs were much too small in relation to the magnitude of the economic problems which needed solving.

In the early 1970s, the Nixon Administration's "New Federalism" shifted responsibility for problem solving back to local governments. Encouraged to assume more program control, local decisionmakers used the resources primarily to relieve burdens on their own taxpayers. Through programs such as the Comprehensive Employment and Training Act (CETA), Community Development Block Grants, and General Revenue Sharing, federal funds were channeled through local rather than state governments.

However, even while the more physically oriented urban programs were being dismantled, and federal funds were flowing to local officials through formula grants, federal influence in other areas was being dramatically strengthened. Environmental regulations, supervision of occupational safety and health, affirmative action programs, and Justice Department school segregation initiatives began to shape urban development—but in a far less conscious manner than had, for example, the Model Cities program.

The disappointing results from the parade of conscious federal attempts to aid cities, and the revelation of the vulnerability of central cities during the mid-1970s recession, spurred reconsideration of how the federal government influences urban conditions. Spokesmen for the cities' interests pointed to an "implicit" or "hidden" urban policy, which, through a broad spectrum of federal activities designed with other, often worthy ends in mind, were having deleterious and unanticipated side effects on cities. The message was clear: an anti-urban bias was increasingly recognized in federal programs affecting cities.

This conclusion was confirmed in our recent Rand study: federal policies have definitely, in specific ways that we traced, contributed to urban problems.

The Rand study

To analyze the effects of federal policies on cities, the Rand researchers first divided the nebulous concept of "the city" into its active components—local public, business, and household sectors. Each is run by a different decision-making unit—local government, the firm, and the household. And each sector is influenced directly by a distinct subset of federal policies.

In addition to these direct influences, a given sector also responds indirectly to many other forces, including, importantly, the behavior of the other two. For example, when local businesses receive a new federal procurement order, they will fill job openings. Rising local wages may increase labor-force participation and attract workers from more depressed areas. The increase in workers expands the local tax base and raises demand for schooling and new housing. And the increased demand for goods and services stimulated by the swelling population may lead to further labor-market expansion.

The effects of federal policies on each sector were determined through a common-sensical approach, in four parts.

First, we distinguished the major outcomes in each sector. Since these outcomes reflect a given sector's behavior, taking them into account is of crucial importance to federal and local officials, not to speak of concerned citizens. For example, when we examine the effects of federal policies on the business sector, the outcomes of primary interest are employment, wages, output, and investment. These outcomes reflect the level and growth rate of economic activity. In the residential sector, principal outcome variables are population, size, composition, and spatial distribution, and the quality of available housing. In the local public sector, the main outcomes are the level and mix of public services and the magnitude and composition of the tax burden.

These outcome measures can be used to show how development has differed among groups of cities. For instance, how has employment growth differed among Snowbelt and Sunbelt cities? How do central city and suburban households differ in ethnic and demographic characteristics? How does the tax burden differ between large and small cities?

Second, we identified the channels through which various policies affect the outcomes for each sector. Most federal policies influence incentives, and thus outcomes, indirectly.

Third, we explored interconnections among the sectors, which are often very complex. For example, local business depends on the local household sector because households affect demand for goods and services and also because they provide the labor force. Local governments influence firms through taxation and through the quality of public services such as training programs, loan programs, and sewer, water, and transportation services. But the influences flow both ways. Households respond to the local business sector by migrating toward good jobs and high wages. The local public sector relies on businesses to foot some of the tax bill.

Finally, we examined each determinant to find out what policies would be most influential. For instance, the price and availability of labor are influenced by federal transfer payments such as welfare and unemployment compensation, by training programs, and by direct federal hiring. Both personal and business tax structures also influence the labor-market operation. Personal income taxes affect labor costs relative to capital—which affects hiring. Regulations such as the minimum wage law, safety and health requirements, and affirmative action measures also influence hiring.

We undertook this analytic process for each of the outcomes in each sector. However, our ability to identify the outcome determinants differed significantly among the sectors. Determinants of employment growth and industrial location, for example, are relatively well known, but less is understood about what influences where people choose to live. And very little is understood about the factors that affect local government decisionmaking. Because of such unavoidable limitations, each of the three sectors had to be studied differently, and in the most difficult cases we were able to identify the direction but not the magnitude of effects.

This analytical framework made it possible for us to synthesize the findings of many studies that analyzed small pieces of the overall network, even though few of those studies dealt directly with the impacts of federal policies. For example, to connect federal transportation policies with regional shifts in employment, we integrated two bodies of research: analyses that linked transportation policy to changes in transportation costs, and analyses that related transportation costs to the distribution of economic activity.

Market forces and federal policies hand in hand

The studies which this report summarizes confirm the hypothesis that federal programs have stimulated employment and population growth in the Sunbelt and West at the expense of the Northeast, and in suburbs and smaller urban areas at the expense of large central cities. Federal policy has also contributed to a growing concentration of the poor in central cities. In addition, federal policy, overall, has contributed to local fiscal problems.

Market forces originated the trends that these federal effects have exacerbated. The major market forces have been technological change, rising incomes, and changing world trade patterns.

The most important technological changes are the decline in transportation costs, linked to increased use of truck and automobile transportation; modern production techniques, which utilize single-story factories that call for cheap suburban land; more complex products that use component parts rather than raw materials, thus allowing firms to move away from raw-material sources in the Northeast toward markets in the South and West; the now ubiquitous use of air conditioning, with its corresponding freedom of climate choice; and, finally but most consequentially, the communications revolution. Computer technology has reduced the cost of transmitting, storing, and processing information to a fraction of its former level. These innovations have reduced the need for face-to-face contact and for proximity among firms, service suppliers, and customers. They have also reduced the need for clerical workers, freeing firms from the necessity of locating in high-density population centers.

Rising incomes, and concomitantly rising levels of education, create changing demands. Many people move to the suburbs, seeking clean air, fewer people, more safety, and better recreation. Many also choose the more attractive Sunbelt climate. On the other hand, high-income households may choose to shun suburbia and seek city living, where special amenities can be combined with huge savings in commuting time. The proliferation of "non-normal" households—multiple jobholders, no children—has in some areas spurred a return to central-city residence; rising suburban land prices will eventually stimulate such behavior in other places.

Changing world trade patterns have particularly hurt Northeast and North Central urban areas producing goods that compete with imports—the comparative advantage for many products, especially in the auto and steel industries, has shifted abroad. In contrast, areas producing export goods, such as computers and advanced electronics, have grown rapidly. A disproportionate number of these high-technology firms are located in the South and West.

The intruding leviathan

Federal policies may not be as "primal" as market forces, but the Rand study found their role to be significant. For purposes of analysis, we considered the federal role according to our three-sector grouping. For the economic sector, we traced the deconcentration of jobs. For the residential sector, we focused on the selective deconcentration of households. And for the local public sector, we studied the fiscal problems that result from federal intervention.

Federal policies—capital investments, procurement, the tax structure, and even regulation—have encouraged the movement of jobs from the Northeast toward the South and West, and from central cities to suburbs and even nonmetropolitan areas. This consistent pattern of influence has resulted, in large part, from implicitly or explicitly favoring growth and new development over rehabilitation and repair. As a result, businesses in growing areas have been stimulated to grow more rapidly, and firms have been encouraged to move away from older central cities into these more favored areas—although it is largely a myth that the Northeast has been badly hurt by the migration of firms. Less than one job loss in 50 in the Northeast is attributable to migration; most have disappeared through the contraction or disappearance of local companies.

The most obvious channel of federal assistance is capital investment, particularly the interstate highway systems, which involved substantial interregional subsidies. Without this system, many areas in the South and West would remain inaccessible. Massive Corps of Engineers waterway projects have opened up many southern cities to the benefits of international trade. Government spending makes a big difference too. The rapid growth of defense payrolls has contributed significantly to economic development in areas remote from the old manufacturing belt.

Tax and regulations have greatly influenced regional economic development— usually inadvertently.

However, there are other nationally applied policies, including the tax structure and certain regulatory activities, that have had a distinct regional impact on economic development even though economic development has not been their primary goal. The tax structure, for example, favors growth in three ways. First, investment in new construction has traditionally been accorded more generous tax treatment than comparable investment in rehabilitation (this differential was substantially reduced in the Tax Reform Act of 1976). Second, tax-free industrial development bonds reduce the cost of constructing the infrastructure necessary for new expansion. Finally, investment tax credits subsidize expansion in the already growing areas where most investment is undertaken.

There is evidence that certain forms of regulation, however unwittingly, also affect the geographic distribution of employment. For instance, holding natural gas to a price below the market rate has led to curtailed supplies in the Northeast. This has encouraged firms that are heavy users to relocate in gas-producing states in the South and Southwest where supplies are more certain.

Regulation of transportation rates and routes has also led to deconcentration by artificially raising the cost of long-haul relative to short-haul transport, and by subsidizing shipping on less-used routes at the expense of those more intensively used. As a result, manufacturing plants have tended to move closer to their markets, redistributing themselves regionally in the process.

The policies that worked to move employment out of certain regions also encouraged the rapid growth of employment in suburban or even non-metropolitan areas at the expense of central cities. Again the chief mechanism has been implicit and explicit subsidies to new investment. Federal subsidies help support the construction of roads, industrial parks, sewers, and the electrification of rural areas.

However, the most important influences have been inadvertent. For example, in computing business-tax liabilities, land cannot be treated as a

---

Helping out, federal style

In 1974, Congress established the Community Development Block Grant program to provide housing rehabilitation, road paving, garbage pickup, health care, and other services to more than 650 cities and counties across the country. Cities had almost total control over how the money was spent. But the Department of Housing and Urban Development decided that cities were spreading their funds too thin. Last year, HUD restricted the grant money to the poorest neighborhoods in an area, and required a "substantial impact" within a "reasonable period." To comply, cities were forced to cut the number and size of neighborhoods in which they could use the funds, and as a result large residential areas in borderline neighborhoods, which had succeeded in stabilizing decline, now show signs of worsening decay. The arbitrary division of neighborhoods without regard to natural boundaries left some streets lined with new curbing and gutters on one side, and broken-down tenements on the other. Residents of Hunting Park, Philadelphia—where such a scenario occurred—had hoped that the HUD grant money would help reduce the "white flight" from their area. Instead, under the new restrictions, it has only sped up the process.

—LP

only for very low-cost housing, typically unavailable in the suburbs. At the same time, local building codes prevent the construction of cheap new suburban housing that might have provided, at comparable cost, alternatives to older units in the city.

The absence of uniformity in welfare payment levels and eligibility criteria has led to the concentration of the poor in cities offering high benefit levels. There is no evidence that high benefit levels have encouraged poor households to move to a city—jobs have usually been the goal—but nontransferability and high benefit levels do appear to deter those who have been unable to secure employment from moving to more promising labor markets.

Federal programs and policies have considerable influence on local fiscal balance—tax base, tax effort, and service demands. Policies that directly affect revenues include federal grant programs and federal tax expenditures. Local expenditures are affected by imposed definitions of local responsibilities and by the cost-sharing features of grant programs.

Local revenues are influenced by federal actions in various ways. For instance, the federal government may subsidize ongoing local programs (as in the case in general revenue sharing), or it may assume full program cost (as it did for the Supplemental Security Insurance program), or it may offer cities inducements to assume new local responsibilities. The larger cities in particular depend heavily on federal aid. The fiscal situation is also affected by the form of aid (block or categorical, lump-sum or matching); by the formula for distribution; and by accompanying state actions (control of "pass-through" funds, assumption of local programs, withdrawal from local programs funded directly by the federal government).

Federal income-tax policy provides important, if implicit, subsidies to local and state government. More than $18 billion per year, or 26 percent of the volume of overt grants to state and local governments, arise from the deductibility of state and local taxes from federally taxable income and from the tax exemption of municipal bond interest. Localities are able to collect more revenues because they need not impose the full cost of collection on their residents—that is, there will be less resistance to a rise in property tax to the extent that payments are deductible. However, only a fraction of the federal tax expenditure translates into additional state or local revenue. The remainder provides benefits to individual taxpayers, particularly the high-income households to whom any given deduction is worth more.

Finally, there are several areas in which federal regulatory programs have imposed spending obligations on local governments or raised the cost of local public services. Notable examples in the first category are environmental protection, where federal aid for construction of water-pollution-control facilities pays only part of the cost of meeting water-quality standards, and treatment of the handicapped, where Congress and the courts have established rights to service without providing enough aid to defray increased costs. In the second category, federal actions that have direct effects on local-service costs include depreciable asset. Therefore firms seek sites in areas where land prices are low—a move that has typically meant a suburban or nonmetropolitan location. This incentive is reinforced through the favorable treatment of capital gains relative to ordinary corporate income, which has led firms to purchase large lots in areas where land prices are rising.

Federal policies have spurred the deconcentration of the urban population as well as the deconcentration of jobs. But the incentives engendered have not operated on all groups equally. The result: a growing share of the population of older cities is poor, unemployed, and nonwhite. It is instructive to note how this sad result was achieved.

First, on the question of deconcentration we found that federal income-transfer payments have facilitated residential movement from region to region. Through Social Security, the elderly have become less dependent on their families and have moved from the Snowbelt to more temperate areas. Interstate highways and flood-control projects have opened previously inaccessible areas to residential settlement. Federal support for recreational facilities has been concentrated in the South and West. Placing disproportionate numbers of military bases in the South has also led to household relocation.

Selective suburbanization has been federally stimulated by encouraging the migration of more affluent households and discouraging the migration of the poor.

The departure of the affluent has been furthered in a number of ways. While auto ownership has been growing, federally funded highways have expanded the commuting range. Water and sewer grants have reduced the cost of developing newly accessible land. The tax system subsidizes homeownership by allowing the deduction of mortgage interest and local property taxes from income-tax obligations and by excluding the imputed value of owner-occupied housing from taxable income. This subsidization has reduced the cost of homeownership for middle- and upper-income households, i.e., those who itemize deductions. New homeowners have shown a marked preference for a spacious residential environment and have moved away from densely populated central cities. Supplementing these pro-homeowner policies are Federal Housing Administration and Veterans' Administration mortgage guarantees, under which nearly one in four of all new homes have been purchased. The subsidies arising out of guarantees have been limited to new housing, which has meant, in effect, suburban housing.

Finally, there is mounting evidence in many big cities that enforced school desegregation through busing has speeded up the suburbanization of white households. "White flight" results in blacker central cities.

Meanwhile, federal policies have inadvertently worked to keep the poor in place. Since most public housing has been built in central cities, poor households have been discouraged from moving to the suburbs. Subsidies to low-income groups to promote homeownership have generally been available regulation of energy prices and the requirement, under the Davis-Bacon Act, that "prevailing wages" be paid on federally aided construction projects.

What this means for federal policies

The evidence pieced together in this study suggests that a federal urban strategy must recognize three paramount facts:

1. The influence of federal policies over urban development is pervasive, and extends to almost all departments, agencies, and programs.

2. In formulating policy there is a tendency to neglect the fallout from "non-urban" policy and to concentrate on consequences of consciously "urban" policy. Among the most influential determinants in "non-urban" policy are many "non-budget" programs, such as tax expenditures and regulations, which are not typically thought of as development policies and which are seldom subject to regular Congressional scrutiny.

3. There is still a great deal we do not know about the urban impacts of federal policies. We have uncovered no secret store of potentially pro-urban programs. It has become clear that if federal policymakers anticipate how policies will shape development in the future, we must undertake further research on the geographic effects of federal actions.

On August 16, 1978, President Carter took a small but significant step toward improving the federal government's ability to understand the urban impacts of proposed new initiatives. Executive Order H-116 requires that:

Urban and community impact analyses are to be prepared on proposed major policy and program initiatives identified by each agency. All types of initiative should be considered candidates for this type of analysis, including new programs, expansions in budget outlays, program changes leading to shifts of resources among recipients, program changes affecting state and local governments, changes in tax provisions, new regulations, new regulatory authorities, and other changes in policy or program direction.

Two basic questions about Urban Impact Analyses (UIAs) spring to mind: First, is the Executive Order the right way to raise federal urban consciousness? And second, how should UIAs affect policy decisions?

UIAs have been criticized on two main grounds: they are prepared by the agency advocating the new initiative and might therefore be self-serving, and they are not public documents and may disappear during the budgetary negotiation process.

There are certainly grounds for fears that the analyses may be self-serving. Impact analyses performed by the Corps of Engineers for its major projects have notoriously underestimated costs and overstated benefits. The staff at the Office of Management and the Budget charged with the responsibility for reading and evaluating UIAs may not be sufficient for the task. As an alternative, it has been suggested that a separate executive office, similar in structure to the Council of Economic Advisors, be established to analyze urban effects.

The fear that UIAs will not enter the policymaking process should prove less serious. Generally, UIAs promise a more informed debate, and may well lead to the discovery of important but inadvertent consequences before they occur. However, we should recognize that the cost of more light may be more heat. Additional information can sharpen the debate between intended beneficiaries of the "non-urban" programs and representatives of the cities threatened by adverse impacts; the result may be deadlock. Congressmen, for example, will be interested in how new policies influence location decisions of households and firms and will call upon Urban Impact Analyses during committee hearings on new initiatives. Unfortunately, many of the more important policies are not subject to regular Congressional oversight, such as IRS procedures, enforcement strategies for environmental regulations, and court decisions on school busing.

Given that our analysis of the harmful effects of federal urban policies is correct, the question is: What should be done? Obviously, we cannot hope to create "spatially neutral" policies. Not only is this impossible, but we believe it is also undesirable. Social policies have many goals other than ill-defined "balanced growth." Many of the federal programs were expressly designed to accommodate revealed preferences of large segments of the citizenry by fostering suburbanization, homeownership, and new construction. For example, even if we had understood in advance the full ramifications of decentralizing population and jobs by way of the highway program, we would probably have done little to reshape it. Cold War fears, and concern about overcrowded urban housing in the 1950s, dictated a more dispersed population and a transportation network alternative to the railroad. And it may well be the case that the harmful effects of air pollution fully justify the deconcentration of polluting activities.

Many programs harmful to cities are irreversible.

Many of the programs that we have identified as harmful to central cities are not reversible. We can neither close down highways nor demolish suburban housing developments financed through federally guaranteed mortgages, tax-free development bonds, and income tax provisions. We must hope that, in the future, awareness of the geographic effects of policies may help us alter them sufficiently to reduce their undesirable and often unnecessary effects on business- and household-location decisions. For example, now that nuclear families make up a smaller fraction of households, it may be politically possible to extend to renters the favorable tax treatment traditionally provided to homeowners. Regulation of freight rates could be modified to reduce antirail bias. Tax incentives encouraging urban sprawl could be reduced to accord with emerging desires for environmental protection. Grants that fund only new public facilities could be extended to subsidize the rehabilitation of existing facilities.

These changes will be neither rapid nor extensive enough to provide a panacea for troubled cities. However, they may slowly reduce the critical problems faced by many policymakers, and provide them with more time to adapt to structural changes caused by inevitable processes of development and decay.

What can be done locally

Movements of jobs and people are closely interrelated. Household migration decisions are often based upon a desire to improve employment and income prospects; at the same time, firms seek to locate where demand is growing and labor available. Within this interactive system, household migration is also influenced by non-economic considerations—climate, clean air, and recreational facilities. Thus, although Detroit gained population because of the location of the auto industry, Miami grew first in population and only subsequently in economic activity to service its new retired residents, who were more concerned with local amenities than with the types of jobs available. More and more, we found, these non-economic considerations outweigh economic ones. Jobs tend to follow people rather than the reverse. The implication is that local economic-development efforts may not be successful if they focus entirely on trying to attract or retain businesses. They must be coordinated with efforts to attract or retain households who can stimulate local demand and provide skilled labor: a city park may be as powerful a development magnet as an industrial park.

Surprisingly, there is little evidence that local taxes play a critical role in determining industrial location or economic growth. However, there is some evidence that less quantifiable aspects of the local public sector, such as the diligence with which regulations are enforced and the attitude of local officials, may matter more. While this finding may be of some comfort to administrators in high-tax locales, it also implies that the rather expensive tax holidays that some areas have offered to footloose businesses may be wasteful.

One should think of federal policies not as originating forces but as important supplements— for good or ill.

Household behavior responds to local government actions. Cities offering generous services and welfare payment levels have, as we have seen, experienced a growing concentration of the poor. Suburbs have proliferated to accommodate homogenous groups of households who seek, among other advantages, to avoid redistributive local tax payments. The implication: if social segregation along jurisdictional lines is to be avoided, redistribution of income and social services for the poor must be funded at a level above that of the local government.

New policy cannot and ought not try to reverse all the ramifications of trends in tastes and technology. However, careful problem diagnosis and attention to locational incentives can prove beneficial. It is helpful to think of governmental policies not as originating forces, but as important supplements—for good or ill. Learning how federal policies have been affecting our urban problems, which this study went far toward accomplishing, is a crucial prerequisite for reforming the helping hand that presently does harm.

&

26

FINANCING URBAN PUBLIC TRANSPORTATION
Policy Implications for the U.S.

Harold Wolman and George Reigeluth

There is a tendency to view the financial problems of urban public transportation as unique to the United States. Surely, it is commonly assumed, the public transportation systems of the western European countries do not suffer from the same kinds of problems.

Our study, however, suggests that they do. The transit financing problems of the European cities appear to be quite similar to those of U.S. cities although the problems in U.S. cities have existed for a longer period of time and tend to be more extreme than in the European cities.[1]

The dynamics affecting transit financing in nearly all of the cities we examined appear to be much the same. Increasing automobile ownership and usage, combined with suburbanization, have resulted in decreased transit ridership. Transit operating costs—labor costs in particular—are rising rapidly. There is public opposition to fare increases which, except in rare cases, are lagging far behind operating costs. Transit operating deficits are large and, in most cases, increasing.

Fare Increases
It might be assumed that given U.S. economic and social philosophy, its cities and their transit systems would rely primarily on the first solution— rising fares. We would expect transit fares in the U.S. to cover a greater portion of operating costs and to have increased more rapidly than has occurred in western Europe. Such an assumption would be inaccurate. Fares in the U.S. covered only 50 percent of operating costs in 1978 (45 percent in the 26 largest metropolitan areas in 1976)[2] compared to 76 percent in London, 61 percent in Munich and 58 percent in Hamburg. Fares covered 46 percent of operating costs in Paris, but only 35 percent in Vienna and 31 percent in Stockholm. It must be that fares cover such a relatively low percentage of costs in the U.S. because ridership so low. If this is the case, part of the response to the transit financing dilemma in U.S. cities should be to actively encourage increased ridership, a strategy which was not entirely successful until the energy crisis intervened. Relating cost coverage to ridership levels and capacity utilization seems a promising subject for future research.

U.S. transit systems have been slow to increase fares as a means of covering increasing deficits. During the five year period from 1974-78, average fares per passenger trip decreased in real terms by 10 percent in the U.S. In London average real fares per passenger trip increased by 29 percent for bus and 41 percent for underground. In Paris the increase was one percent, in Stockholm there was a real decrease of four percent, in Munich of six percent. Only in Vienna, where real fares increased by 17 percent, did fare increases lag behind those in the U.S.

The reluctance of transit agencies in the United States to increase fares undoubtedly reflects public opposition to such action. Studies of price elasticity of demand for transit in various U.S. communities yield results clustering in the -.3 to -.5 range.[3] These are generally similar to elasticities found in transit demand studies of European systems[4] and suggest that fare increases, at least to the extent undertaken by the cities we visited, could have been justified by economic criteria. However, transit systems in the U.S. are primarily publicly owned and fare increases require the approval of public bodies responsible to the electorate. Since this is also the case with cities we visited, we can assume that public opposition to fare increases was stronger—or was perceived to be stronger—in U.S. cities than in European ones, a conclusion which we would not have predicted.

Rationalization

One of the most frequent responses we found in western European cities to the financing dilemma was an effort to reduce costs through rationalization—that is, an effort to provide the same level and quality of service at reduced cost. London Transport, for example, converted a portion of its bus fleet from two-man to one-man operations. In Vienna and Munich fare collectors were removed from the second and third cars of the trams and an "honor system" instituted. In Munich, many tram lines have either been eliminated, as the subway system has been phased in, or improved so that they operate on their own rights of way. In many of these cities, poorly utilized and uneconomical services have been eliminated or reduced.

It is, of course, difficult to determine the degree to which these actions result in greater efficiency and the degree to which they result in lower service quality. Obviously the reduction or elimination of poorly utilized, uneconomic routes results in a reduction of service for those passengers who did utilize them, even though it may reflect greater efficiency for the system as a whole.

Nonetheless, the net result of these rationalization efforts has been a reduction in personnel and an improvement in the ratio of operating capacity, as measured by vehicle kilometers or seat kilometers, to personnel, one possible measure of efficiency. Thus, in London, personnel operating buses decreased by 23 percent (from 28,355 to 21,922) between 1968-1978, while bus miles operated decreased by 16 percent.[5] In Munich, transit system personnel decreased by 36 percent between 1973-1977, while vehicle kilometers decreased by 9.3 percent. In Hamburg, transit personnel fell by 13 percent between 1965-1978, while vehicle kilometers increased by eight percent. And in Vienna, the number of personnel per seat kilometer dropped by 19 percent between 1965-1975. In the U.S., however, transit employees have increased by eight percent between 1974-1978 (from 153,000 to 162,510) while total vehicle miles increased by less than three percent. Stockholm was the only city we visited which also experienced personnel increases: 45 percent between 1971-1978, while vehicle kilometers increased by 29 percent.

The above discussion suggests that U.S. transit systems either do not have the same scope for personnel reduction and efficiency improvements or have, for whatever reasons, not undertaken them. Assuming that some scope for productivity improvement through rationalization does exist, one possible explanation for the failure of this to take place in U.S. systems may be the existence of Section 13(c) of the Urban Mass Transportation Act of 1964 which, in effect, mandates that employment for existing transit personnel cannot be affected adversely by the receipt of federal assistance. Some further examination of management practices and labor-management relations in an international context seems called for.

Reduction of Service

The easiest response, politically, to the financing dilemma is the reduction of service levels and quality to defer maintenance. It is largely an invisible response and one which, within limits, can be undertaken unilaterally.

It is difficult to assess the degree to which cities, whether in Europe or the U.S., have responded to their financial problems by cutting service. As we have noted, the number of vehicle miles operated has been reduced in several cities which indicates a decline in service level. The interviews we conducted in the cities we visited also yielded comments about declines in service quality and frequency.

Cuts in the levels of service and quality have undoubtedly been most pronounced in the United States where the financing problems have been evident for a prolonged period, where public support for transit is low, and where public transportation quality has thus far not been an important public issue.

Subsidies

Subsidies are the remaining response and the one to which the U.S. systems have predominantly resorted. Between 1970-1978, federal, state and local government subsidies to cover transit deficits increased from $200 million to nearly $2.3 billion. Nearly all of these subsidies have been provided to the largest transit systems. (In 1976, eight large systems—New York, Boston, Chicago, Philadelphia, Cleveland, San Francisco-Oakland, Detroit and Washington, D.C.—accounted for approximately 70 percent of all subsidy payments.)[6]

While in absolute amounts subsidies have increased for all transit systems we examined, the percentage of operating costs covered by subsidies has actually decreased in London and Munich and has remained relatively constant in Hamburg. However, this percentage increased by nearly 25 percent for the U.S. systems between 1973-1977, approximately the same amount by which it increased in Stockholm (26 percent) and Vienna (27 percent). Results from our survey indicate an increase in the portion of operating costs covered through subsidies occurred in most of our responding cities (17 out of 23). The increase for U.S. cities was exceeded by that of only seven others.

Somewhat surprisingly, the increase in subsidization of operating costs for the U.S. has occurred primarily from federal rather than state and local government funds. In cities in most other countries, however, local (usually) and state (in some cases) governments are the primary, if not the sole, source of operating subsidy. (The U.K. and The Netherlands are conspicuous exceptions.) Local and regional sources in the U.S. have traditionally been the primary subsidy source. However, while they continue to provide the greatest share of operating subsidies (44 percent in 1978), the federal share has been increasing rapidly (21 percent in 1975, 31 percent in 1978). Federal grants for operating subsidies increased by $388 million (from $301.8 million to $680.9 million) between 1975-1978 compared to $278 million from local sources and $158 million from state sources.[7] Commitments for Section 5 grant funds, nearly all of which are used by local governments for operating costs, amounted to in excess of $1 billion for 1979, nearly double the 1977 level.

Examining the 26 largest metropolitan areas we find a particularly dramatic increase in federal subsidies between 1973-1978 ($567 million compared to $508 million from regional sources). Indeed, Pucher remarks: *In general, the responsibility for financing transit has been shifted to higher and higher level government—from the city to the region or state, and from the region or state to the federal government.*[8]

Our discussion indicates that the U.S. has relied particularly heavily on service reduction and federal subsidies in response to its operating deficit problems. This differs from the responses on many of the foreign systems we studied.

We believe the primary factor accounting for the differences in the responses to the transit financing dilemma is the low degree of local citizen (and thus politician) support and sympathy for public transportation in the U.S. compared to cities in other countries. A high degree of local citizen support for a quality public transport system, such as exists in most other countries, will permit (although not necessarily without difficulty or opposition) reasonable fare increases and/or a high level of local subsidization. Without public sympathy or, at least acquiescence, both of these responses become politically unfeasible. As a consequence, U.S. systems have had to resort more than foreign systems to cuts in service quality and deferred maintenance and to an increased amount of subsidy from the federal as opposed to local level.

The relative lack of citizen support for public transportation in the U.S. compared to cities in other countries undoubtedly reflects both the greater extent of automobile ownership and usage in the U.S. and the composition of transit patrons. Only three percent of all urban trips in the U.S. are made by transit but, if New York City, where public transportation accounts for 56 percent of journey to work trips, is excluded, no American city exceeds 40 percent and most larger ones are less than 25 percent.[9] This compares to an average of approximately 70 percent of journey to work trips made by public transportation in the European cities we visited. In short, the quality of public transportation is not a major concern for most people in the United States simply because they do not use it. Not using it, they also resent paying through their local taxes for the small number who do. Particularly in larger cities, the small number who use the system tend to have disproportionately low and moderate incomes. They are least able to absorb fare increases and are thus resistant to them.

It is, of course, possible that public support will increase. The energy crisis has induced both increased ridership and a feeling among the broader public still not riding transit that public transportation is an important component of an urban transportation system.

Once public sympathy and support exists, moderate fare increases and substantial local subsidies become possible. The question of how to finance local subsidies becomes less a political question and more a technical one. In the absence of such support, technical questions become subordinate to political ones. Thus local subsidies become more politically feasible to the extent their source of financing is hidden or relatively invisible to the public, to the extent collection and payment are relatively simple, and to the extent that the level and source of subsidy can be isolated from year to year vagaries of politics and the budgetary process.

It is in light of these criteria that we turn to the question of political transferability of the innovative mechanisms we have examined.

Regional Mechanisms

Regional transportation agencies are not uncommon in U.S. metropolitan areas (e.g. Chicago, Cleveland, St. Louis, Los Angeles, Atlanta, Denver, San Diego, Boston, Philadelphia, Minneapolis, Buffalo, Milwaukee, Miami, etc.), but it appears that regionalism per se does not necessarily solve financing problems. If the region does not have a tax or other revenue source whose receipts are earmarked for public transportation *and* are sufficient to meet its needs, then the regional agency must still depend upon contributions from the various local governments or subsidies from higher levels.

Although it is relatively easy to justify them economically, particularly if there is a high suburban transit usage, regional taxes are highly controversial politically, as the Chicago RTA situation demonstrates, and are quite difficult to institute. Nonetheless, region-wide sales taxes, at least a portion of which are dedicated for transit, do exist in Chicago, Cleveland, St. Louis, Los Angeles, Atlanta, Denver and San Diego.[10] In addition, the absence of a regional tax does not necessarily invalidate the rationale for regional financing. Both Hamburg and Munich, for example, have regional financing systems without regional taxes; the local authorities involved each contribute a portion of the system's operating deficit, based on a formula negotiated and agreed upon every several years. This is not dissimilar to Washington D.C. where the share of the operating deficit to be contributed by the various local jurisdictions is set by a negotiated formula. However, the formula is renegotiated annually, thus creating a great deal of uncertainty. In addition, since the local taxes are not dedicated to transit the yearly local contribution must come from the general revenues of the local jurisdictions. As a result, the payment of local contributions is frequently caught in budget fights and political changes which create, for at least some of the jurisdictions, doubt concerning the extent to which they will be able to meet their required contribution. Again, this is a question of public support.

A Dedicated Tax

Paris and Vienna both have revenue sources earmarked solely for transit, while a substantial portion of the Stockholm regional tax is, for all practical purposes, also dedicated to public transportation. Locally earmarked transit taxes are relatively common in the U.S., particularly for larger cities. An Institute for Public Administration study found that 18 of the 25 largest urban areas in the U.S. had some local tax wholly or partially dedicated to the transit system's operating deficit. The local sales tax (10 cities) was the most prominently used earmarked tax, followed by the property tax (5 cities).[11]

Does the employer payroll tax, on the Paris model, hold promise for American cities? The economic rationale for the payroll tax is obvious: employers benefit since public transportation provides them access to a geographically broader labor market.

However, the political difficulties for the widespread adoption of an employer payroll tax dedicated to transit seem quite substantial. The payroll tax is a quite visible one to employers (although less visible to employees on whom the final burden is likely to rest). Second, payroll taxes in the U.S. are already quite high; the federal Social Security and Medicare tax on employers is currently 6.3 percent on each employee's earnings up to a maximum of $22,900 (and an equal tax is paid by the employee). Other payroll taxes which vary from state to state—unemployment insurance, workman's compensation—increase this rate. The social security payroll tax itself is coming under increasing opposition due to the burden it imposes and legislation to reduce it is under consideration. Imposition of an additional payroll tax at the local level would meet heavy opposition from employers for fear of placing their community at a competitive disadvantage relative to communities which did not impose such a tax.

Other earmarked taxes—whether on a regional or local level—may be more feasible particularly if they are relatively invisible. The existing use of the local sales tax in this regard suggests the possibility for extending this device to other cities. However, many states—24 as of 1978—do not permit their localities to levy a general sales tax. In addition, there is little economic rationale for applying the receipts of a general sales tax to transit operations. Motor vehicle fuel and exise taxes are perhaps more logical candidates for earmarking, since they pass the test of relative invisibility and perhaps can better be justified on economic criteria. (Automobile drivers receive benefits in terms of reduced congestion from transit systems and the full cost of operating an automobile is not reflected in the operating costs paid by the driver. A subsidy from the automobile to transit would help correct this underpricing.)

A Utility Cross-Subsidy

Vienna and Munich both provide very substantial cross-subsidies from their municipal utility (gas and electricity) companies to their transit companies. Springfield, Missouri is the only city in the U.S. of which we are aware where such a cross-subsidy exists at the municipal level. However, in New Orleans and perhaps in a few other localities where private utility companies operate the transit system as well as other utilities, a similar cross-subsidy does occur,

The utility cross-subsidy certainly passes the tests or relative invisibility and ease of collection, although as we have noted in chapters 4 and 5 it has little conceivable economic justification. However, there are relatively few cities in the U.S. with municipally owned utility companies and even fewer which have municipally owned transit systems *and* municipally owned utility companies (Pensacola, Florida; Alexandria, Lafayette and Monroe, Louisiana; Duluth, Minnesota; Columbia and Springfield, Missouri; Lincoln, Nebraska; Jamestown, New York; Cleveland, Ohio; Memphis,

Tennessee; San Antonio, Texas; and Seattle and Tacoma, Washington). However, in these and other cities with municipally owned utilities there are exceedingly strong political pressures to keep utility rates low, if not to subsidize them as some cities have done. Raising gas and electricity rates to help pay for public transportation would not be highly popular or politically advantageous.

As far as privately owned utility companies are concerned, the Public Utilities Holding Act of 1935 required utility companies to divest themselves of their transit holdings except under special circumstances. New Orleans is one of these special circumstances, but one which, without change in federal legislation, cannot legally be replicated in other cities.

CONCLUSION

On the basis of visits to six European cities and responses to our survey from 23 cities, it is clear that further work has the potential of generating important policy lessons on several topics of concern to the financing of urban mass transit systems. First, many of the cities visited have been able to reduce the rate of increase of operating deficits through successful efforts to increase productivity and to rationalize service delivery. Second, further study of the institutional organizations and political systems used by European countries and cities to deliver urban transit service might also provide useful policy lessons for U.S. cities. Finally, additional study of the effects of the specific innovative financing mechanisms described in this paper would indicate the costs and benefits of transferring such mechanisms to a U.S. setting and what some of the obstacles to successful transfer would be.

However, we would caution that the transit financing problem in the United States results in part from the low value the public places on the role and importance of public transportation. It is, therefore, a political problem as well as a technical one. As a consequence, it becomes more easily solved as the public recognizes the importance of an effective, high quality public transportation system. It is here that U.S. cities have, in the past, differed most significantly from European ones. The response to the energy crisis suggests that the level of public support for transit is on the rise in the U.S. and that the political environment may now be more propitious for adopting innovative urban public transportation financing mechanisms.

1, 6, 8, 10.   John Pucher, "Losses in the American Transit Industry," Technical Report No. 2, MIT Center for Transportation Studies, January 1978.

2, 3, 9, 11.   Institute of Public Administration, *Financing Transit: Alternatives for Local Government* (Washington, D.C., 1979).

4   In a study of transit systems in European countries, Webster and Bly report that "the statistical analysis indicated that a 10 percent increase in real fare levels was related to a 3 percent reduction in patronage." See D.V. Webster and P.H. Bly, *Op. Cit.*, p. 172.

27

HOUSING ALLOWANCES
An Experiment That Worked

Bernard J. Frieden

ONE of the biggest social experiments ever undertaken, the Department of Housing and Urban Development's experimental housing allowance program began with great fanfare in 1973 and is ending quietly in 1979-1980. It has involved more than 25,000 families in 12 metropolitan areas, at a cost that is expected to add up to $160 million. As is true of most ambitious programs, it owes its origin to the convergence of several different lines of thought on how government should cope with a problem. The problem in this case was how to improve housing conditions for low-income people. Two key ideas prompted the experiment. One was that the best way to help families who needed better housing was to give them money that they could use on their own, instead of building subsidized housing for them. The other was that the best way to learn how a new approach would work in practice was to conduct a large-scale social experiment, following a systematic design and using control groups to check the validity of the results.

Six years later, the data coming off the computers do not provide clear-cut answers to all the questions that were investigated, since the realities of human behavior turned out to be more complicated than the designers of the experiment had assumed. But the experi-

Reprinted with permission of the author from: THE PUBLIC INTEREST, No. 59 (Spring 1980), pp. 15-35. © 1980 by National Affairs, Inc.

ment produced unexpected results that challenge the traditional conception of low-income housing problems and reveal a sharp conflict between the priorities of federal officials and those of poor families.

Troubled subsidy programs

The underlying cause of the housing allowance experiment was widespread disillusionment with the conventional approach to subsidizing housing for the poor.° Ever since the mid-1930's, housing reformers and their political allies had favored a construction strategy. This meant using federal subsidies to build new housing which was then made available to poor people at below-market rents. A series of housing acts from 1937 through the mid-1960's had established first low-rent public housing and then several variations of it, all following essentially the same approach. Yet the flooding tide of housing legislation produced only a trickle of housing. The main problem with this strategy (as has also been said of Christianity) was not that it had been tried and found wanting, but that it had never been tried—at least not on a scale large enough to put it to a real test. Then, in the special political climate of the late 1960's Congress enacted the landmark Housing Act of 1968, interpreted by many as a memorial to Martin Luther King. This' act set up two important construction programs backed by the usual federal subsidies. One (known as Section 236) offered rental housing, and the other (Section 235) offered home-ownership opportunities for low- and moderate-income families. Both were designed to attract developers and investors in the hope that private sector involvement would generate a high volume of construction commensurate with the country's needs. The 1968 act, in fact, set a target of 2.6 million subsidized housing units to be built within 10 years.

Beginning in 1969, HUD Secretary George Romney gave top priority to putting the new programs into operation and meeting the

° Many individuals associated with the organizations responsible for the housing allowance experiment generously gave of their time and made available reports and other information. I would like to thank especially Jerry J. Fitts and Howard Hammerman of the Department of Housing and Urban Development, Ira S. Lowry of the Rand Corporation, and Clark Abt and Helen Bakeman of Abt Associates.

Full documentation, including citations and tables, of the findings discussed in this article are presented in my Joint Center Working Paper No. 62, "What Have We Learned from the Housing Allowance Experiment?" (M.I.T.–Harvard Joint Center for Urban Studies, Cambridge, Massachusetts, 1980). That version will be published also in *Habitat International*, Volume 5, No. 1-2 (1980).

ambitious targets of the 1968 act. Between 1969 and 1972, the federal government sponsored more subsidized construction than in
the preceding 35 years combined. Yet as the HUD programs, together with their rural counterparts in the Farmers Home Administration, grew to a volume of 400,000 starts per year, both their
financial and political costs became troublesome. The new housing
required annual federal contributions to help the residents pay the
rent or the cost of home ownership. By the early 1970's, yearly outlays began to approach 2 billion dollars. Although this figure was
no more than one-fifth of the total cost of federal tax benefits given
to middle-income homeowners, it was a natural target for a conservative administration looking for places to cut the federal budget. In addition, poor administration of these programs led to widespread corruption within the Federal Housing Administration that
escaped full notoriety only because Watergate created a bigger
scandal. President Nixon's annual report on national housing goals
for 1972 complained about the rapid growth of future housing subsidy commitments, then estimated at some $12 billion merely
to cover housing already approved. These programs were expensive, and getting more so. Worse still, the President's report also
noted that the programs were failing to reach the lowest-income
families.

Housing experts sponsored by the House of Representatives Subcommittee on Housing were also finding serious faults with these
large-scale programs. A group of researchers at M.I.T. estimated
that from one-fifth to one-half the total federal subsidy was not
reaching the residents of the new housing, but went for federal
and local administrative expenses and for tax benefits to investors. The same study found that subsidy arrangements were regressive, with greater assistance going to families at the upper
end of the eligibility range than to low-income families at the bottom. The programs were serving mainly families above the poverty
level in lower-middle-income brackets. Further, the families themselves had little freedom of choice in deciding where to live. To
get federal housing assistance, they had to move to a designated
development whose sponsor had been selected by the local FHA
field office. As a result, the allocation of subsidized housing to communities across the country did not correspond as much to the
needs of low-income residents as it did to the energy, activity, and
political muscle of local sponsors.

An underlying reason for these problems was that the programs
were designed to achieve two different purposes that were par-

tially in conflict with each other. One purpose was to encourage new construction; the second to give financial help to families who could not afford good housing on their own. The construction objective overrode the housing assistance purpose at many critical points. The high cost and the generous payments to middlemen were part of the construction strategy. So, too, was the reliance on local sponsors to make key decisions about where to locate projects and whom to admit. Ceilings on the subsidy per family made it hard to bring the cost down low enough for the very poor, and therefore tipped the balance of effort toward families who were better off.

The logic of this critique of production subsidies led toward the conclusion that direct cash payments to low-income families might well be a more effective form of housing assistance. Direct payments to the poor would bypass the project sponsors and other middlemen who were draining off so large a share of the federal housing dollar. Families with cash in hand would be able to make their own decisions about where to live, instead of being limited to designated projects or locations. Rather than having to use their money for costly new housing, they could shop around to find less expensive existing homes. Eligible families would not have to be excluded because they happened to live in communities where developers were not making use of federal housing programs. In addition, direct cash payments could be scaled according to a family's income, rather than following the complicated and regressive formulas that resulted from an attempt to stimulate new construction.

Other analyses presented to the House Subcommittee on Housing pointed in the same general direction. The New York City Rand Institute had made some startling discoveries in its detailed analyses of the New York City housing market during the 1960's. From year to year, a large volume of sound housing was deteriorating in quality and more than 30,000 units per year were being taken off the market through demolition, conversion to non-residential use, or outright abandonment. Between 1965 and 1968, housing losses were greater than new construction by a substantial margin. The main reason for this rising volume of deterioration and abandonment was that a large number of the city's low-income families were unable to pay enough rent to cover the rising costs of operating and maintaining rental property. Landlords who were unable to earn a competitive return were cutting back on maintenance, and, in time, walking away from their buildings.

Ira S. Lowry of the Rand Institute staff concluded from the Rand studies that the most effective way to meet the housing needs of low-income families in New York City was to raise the level of maintenance in existing buildings while they were still in good condition. He estimated that a rent increase of from $400 to $700 per year was needed to support moderate renovation and good maintenance in typical older apartments. Even these small increases, however, were beyond the means of low-income families. Lowry accordingly proposed a housing allowance plan that would make available rent certificates at an average cost of little more than $600 per family.

Proposals for a housing allowance program were timely not only because of disappointments with the prevailing approach to low-income housing, but also because the housing allowance idea had already caught the attention of top policy makers. President Johnson's Committee on Urban Housing (the Kaiser Committee) in its 1968 report had argued the case for housing allowances. The Committee was concerned, however, that a massive housing allowance system could lead to inflation in the general cost of housing and also doubted whether housing allowances would work effectively without parallel measures to counter racial discrimination and provide effective consumer education. It proposed an experimental program to find out. One reason for caution was that the public welfare program, which provided families with cash income intended to cover housing costs as well as other expenses, had many of the characteristics of a housing allowance program. Yet a national survey showed that welfare families had severely inadequate housing, a majority of them living in either substandard or overcrowded conditions. The low level of welfare support did not fully explain this situation. Other families in the same income brackets lived in better housing than those on welfare. It was possible, therefore, that money given to poor families through transfer payments might not open up the same access to housing markets that most people already enjoyed.

Limited trials of the housing allowance idea began in 1970 under the auspices of federally funded Model Cities programs in Kansas City, Missouri and Wilmington, Delaware. The Department of Housing and Urban Development began preliminary studies and designs for a systematic national experiment in 1970 and 1971, and then organized its Experimental Housing Allowance Program.

In January 1973, the Nixon Administration suspended almost all existing federal housing subsidies for the poor and announced its intention to search for more effective programs. The housing allowance experiment, then getting under way in 12 selected cities, took on special importance as part of that search. Meanwhile, Congress enacted a new subsidy program, known as Section 8, to replace those that had been suspended. The new program was a hybrid, based on a flexible financing arrangement that could be used either to promote new construction or, in the manner of a housing allowance, to help people pay for existing houses that met program standards.

Debating housing strategies

While the housing allowance experiments were enrolling families and collecting data, but long before any results were available, policy analysts were carrying on a lively debate over the merits of housing allowances. One school of thought held that housing markets were so restricted and defective that making more money available would still not enable poor people to find decent housing. Others believed that housing markets would respond to a moderate boost in rent levels by increasing the supply of decent, well-maintained housing.

Among the skeptics was Chester Hartman, a long-time critic of federal housing programs, who contended in an article with Dennis Keating that "the shortcomings of the past programs inhere in the nature of the housing market itself." The key assumptions were that little housing is available for the poor, markets are non-competitive, and landlords are dominant. In Hartman's view, the housing allowance approach "pays insufficient attention to the vast shortage of decent, moderate-rent housing in most urban and suburban areas, particularly for groups the market now serves poorly, such as large families." Because of this shortage, he contended, "few doubt that the introduction of housing allowances into a static supply of housing will lead to rent inflation (on a short-term basis at least), not only for recipients, but also for other low- and moderate-income households competing for the same units."

In contrast to this view of a captive market, a series of empirical studies in the 1960's found that landlords were in a precarious position themselves, caught between increasing operating costs and limited rental income. George Sternlieb's study of Newark (*The Tenement Landlord*) and Michael Stegman's study of Baltimore (*Housing Investment in the Inner City*) went a long way toward revising the stereotyped image of the powerful slum landlord who reaped great profits by milking his properties and plundering his tenants. As Stegman described the situation, "Many inner-city landlords are today as victimized as are those to whom they provide inadequate shelter."

Although a casual look at inner-city rent levels might indeed suggest that landlords were succeeding in charging exorbitant and discriminatory rents while giving little service, Stegman found the reality to be different. Inner-city landlords were incurring high operating costs as a result of such factors as non-payment of rent, high vacancy rates, and vandalism to their property. These costs were much higher than in middle-income areas and helped to explain why prevailing rent levels were neither profitable to most landlords nor adequate to provide good maintenance:

> Over 10 percent of cash inflow—an amount equal to about 80 percent of net income—is dissipated on expenditures that do not contribute directly to maintaining or improving resultant flows of housing services. This is why apparently high rents with respect to housing quality can result in little or no profit to the investor. In part, this also explains why housing quality in the inner-city is inferior to that obtainable elsewhere in the city at comparable or only slightly higher rents.

The shortfall between rent collections and maintenance demands suggested that lack of rent money was one of the most important reasons why inner-city housing markets were failing to meet the needs of the poor. Stegman's careful analysis of Baltimore led to conclusions remarkably similar to those of the New York City Rand Institute. Although Stegman himself did not endorse a housing allowance strategy, his findings gave strong support to the view that inner-city housing markets were not locked under the control of powerful slumlords and that public-policy initiatives could indeed create more effective incentives for responsible property management.

In designing the rent allowance experiment, the Department of Housing and Urban Development was concerned with specific questions about how poor families would make use of their housing allowances, how local housing markets would respond to the increased demand generated by direct cash payments, and how different administrative arrangements would influence the results. Accordingly, the program was divided into three parts—a demand experiment, a supply experiment, and an administrative-agency experiment.

In the demand experiment (conducted in Pittsburgh and Phoenix), the research focused on the extent to which eligible families took part in the experiment, changes in housing expenditures for participating families, the choices people made with respect to the quality and location of their housing, and their satisfaction with these choices.

The supply experiment (in Green Bay, Wisconsin and South Bend, Indiana) was designed to test how a large-scale infusion of housing allowance dollars in a single housing market would affect the cost and quality of housing, the behavior of landlords and realtors, and patterns of residential mobility. The supply experiment offered open enrollment to homeowners as well as renters whose incomes were within the established ceilings, and set no limit on the number of families that would be permitted to enroll. (Other parts of the experiment were open to renters only, and the number of participants was limited in advance.)

The administrative-agency experiment selected eight different agencies to carry out housing allowance programs—local housing authorities in Salem, Oregon and Tulsa, Oklahoma; metropolitan government agencies in Jacksonville, Florida and San Bernardino County, California; state community-development agencies in Peoria, Illinois and Springfield, Massachusetts; and the state welfare departments in Durham, North Carolina and Bismarck, North Dakota. In these communities, research focused on the administrative performance of such functions as screening and enrolling applicants, certifying eligibility, providing counseling, and making household inspections.

In all areas, however, the basic requirements were the same. The program was open to families of two or more people and to single individuals who were elderly or handicapped. To receive a housing allowance, a family had to have an income below a ceiling that took into account the local cost of adequate housing and the size of the household. For a family of four, the upper income limit was generally below $7,000. Allowance payments in most cases were set to equal the difference between the estimated cost of adequate housing and one-fourth of the family's income; payments averaged $75 per month. Families in the program were free to spend more or less than the estimated amount for rent, but they had to live in or move to housing that met minimum quality standards set for each part of the experiment. The last requirement was relaxed only for two experimental groups in Pittsburgh and Phoenix that could receive the allowance without meeting any standards of housing quality. Despite the different purposes of the three parts of the experiment, it is possible to consider the twelve demonstration areas as a source of general information on policy issues that cut across the individual experiments.

Did housing allowances reach those with greatest needs?

The housing allowance experiment, like other federal housing programs, established income ceilings and payment formulas intended to cover only people who could not afford the cost of decent housing on their own. In other programs, however, project sponsors and local administrators have often screened out those families likely to be most troublesome or most costly to house and have favored people from the high end of the eligible range. As a result, a chronic complaint has been that few of the benefits reached people who were most seriously disadvantaged: the very poor, racial minorities, female-headed households, welfare recipients, large families, and the elderly.

The housing allowance program has had great success in reaching these groups, particularly in comparison with earlier federal housing programs. The average income of families that received housing allowances was about $4,000 (1976 dollars). In contrast, the big subsidy programs of the early 1970's helped mostly lower-middle-income families rather than the poor. The current Section 8 existing-housing program, which has many of the features of a housing allowance, also reaches the poor: In 1977, median income for families in this program was $3,500.

Opponents of housing allowances argued that many families were "hard to house" because of discriminatory practices, and that they would be unable to use housing allowances effectively for this reason. Yet the housing allowance experiment was conspicuously successful in including minority groups, female-headed families, and people on welfare, which meant that a large number of "hard-to-house" people were able to find places of acceptable quality as required by the program.

Minority families—defined here as black or Hispanic—took part in the program fully in proportion to their eligibility. Female-headed families and those getting welfare assistance were the main participants in the housing allowance program. Households headed by women were about half the eligible families, but were half to three-quarters of those receiving payments in the various cities. Welfare families in the experimental cities ranged from 13 to 31 percent of the eligible families, but accounted for one-fifth to one-half of all those who received housing allowances. Large families with limited incomes are also hard to house, but they took part in the housing allowance program in proportion to their eligibility. Only the aged participated in lesser proportion than were eligible, possibly because they are less likely to move than other groups.

Housing allowances not only reached the groups with greatest needs, but they also provided more generous subsidies to those families with the least resources of their own. The big federal housing programs of the early 1970's were criticized for using regressive subsidy structures, with greater benefits for better-off families than for those in the lowest income brackets. Housing allowance payments, in contrast, took into account both income and family size, with larger payments going to lower-income and bigger families. In the eight cities of the administrative experiment, the average monthly payment to families with incomes under $1,000 was $114, while the average payment to families with incomes of $5,000 or more was $53.

Did housing allowances reduce excessive rent burdens?

Housing deprivation can take several different forms, and to reach a fair judgment of the effectiveness of a housing program it is important to look at its impact on each type of deprivation. Governmental concern for the housing of the poor was originally directed at the unhealthy and demoralizing living conditions in the crowded slums of American cities early in the twentieth century. The traditional focus of low-income housing policy since then has been on the substandard physical conditions of slum housing—such as poor ventilation and inadequate plumbing—and on the crowding of families into cramped quarters. More recently, housing conditions have improved for most families, and the supply of low-cost, low-quality apartments has been shrinking steadily. As a result, many people live in housing that meets reasonable physical standards but they spend a third or more of their income for rent—either because low-cost slums are no longer available as an option for the poor or because they have chosen to make financial sacrifices in order to live in better houses.

Low-income families who took part in the housing allowance experiment were originally spending an exorbitant part of their income for housing. Among the 12 cities in the entire program, the median share of total income committed to rental payments varied from 34 percent to 53 percent.

Housing allowance payments did succeed in reducing the share of family income going for rent. In almost all cities, the median rent burden for families who received housing allowances was below 25 percent, with the median in individual cities ranging from 17 to 30 percent. But even with the allowance payments, about half the participating families still spent more than the generally accepted norm of 25 percent of gross income for rent.

The rent burden came down because most families who received housing allowances chose to stay where they were already living and decided not to spend much of the allowance money for improved housing. In order to qualify for housing allowance payments, families had to find housing that conformed to the minimum quality standards established for each part of the experiment. A substantial majority of the families who met these requirements did so without moving from the places where they were living before they enrolled. Of these families that were able to join the program without having to move, most were living in apartments that met the quality standards as soon as they were inspected, but a minority had to make repairs (or get the landlord to make repairs) in order to pass the inspection. The proportion of housing allowance recipients who stayed put, with or without repairs, ranged from 55 percent in the eight cities of the administrative experiment, to 83 percent in the two cities of the supply experiment. Families who stayed where they were paid only minor rent increases.

This pattern of decisions meant that people in the program were using housing allowances mainly to substitute for money of their own that they formerly spent for rent, rather than using it to make a substantial boost in their housing outlays. In Pittsburgh, families in the program used only 9 percent of their payments for rent increases above the normal increase paid by a control group; and in Phoenix, 27 percent of the housing allowance dollars went for housing expenditures above normal increases. The great bulk of the payments went to free family income for other expenses.

Did the program improve housing quality?

A central purpose of the experiment was to find out whether housing allowances would bring about improvement in the quality of the housing supply. Although a high proportion of participating families lived in housing that met the program's quality standards from the beginning, a majority did not and either had to make repairs or had to move in order to qualify. In the eight cities of the administrative experiment, an average of 57 percent of recipients either moved or upgraded their prior housing; in Pittsburgh and Phoenix, 61 percent either moved or upgraded, and in Green Bay and South Bend, 48 percent either moved or upgraded.

The housing standards that families had to meet varied somewhat in different parts of the experiment, but they were generally in line with local housing codes, model codes recommended by building code administrators, and standards developed by public health organizations.

In order to meet these standards, most families in the program did improve the quality of their housing, either by moving or by repairing their current residences. The substantial minority who upgraded without moving did so mainly by making minor repairs at low costs. Typical repairs involved fixing windows or installing handrails on stairs; some work was also done on structural components, plumbing, and heating systems. In Green Bay and South Bend, landlords and tenants split the work about evenly, using professional contractors for only about 10 percent of repairs. Three out of four below-standard dwellings that were brought up to an acceptable level involved cash costs of less than $25 in Green Bay and less than $30 in South Bend.

In Pittsburgh and Phoenix, tenants and landlords also divided the work of bringing failed units up to standard. Residents typically painted and papered the inside, while landlords did the bulk of the work on plumbing and heating equipment and general repairs. The mean cash cost of the improvement was $92. A control group of families in these cities who did not get housing allowances reported almost the same outlays for repairs, however, and about four-fifths of those in both the experimental and control groups reported that their landlords also made improvements. The main difference was in the kinds of repairs. Families getting housing allowances were more likely to have their houses brought up to "standard" condition as required by the program.

Very few families managed to use their housing allowance payments to switch from rental housing to home ownership. In Green Bay and South Bend, about 300 families who enrolled as renters bought homes while they were in the program; these were less than 3 percent of the renters enrolled. Yet in these cities almost half of the participants in the experiment were already homeowners. Many of these had undoubtedly bought their homes at times in the past when their incomes were higher. But however feasible ownership may be for low-income families, it is clear that housing allowance payments did not raise incomes or assets enough to enable families to improve their housing by becoming homeowners.

A survey of how participating families in Pittsburgh and Phoenix felt about their housing shows that they valued the quality improvements resulting from the program, but it also reveals a deep-seated reluctance to move in order to get quality improvements. Of the families who failed to meet housing standards at the beginning, the most satisfied of all were those who later met them by improving the places where they already lived: 70 percent of these families were "very satisfied" with their housing. But the second most satisfied group were the families who stayed where they were and failed to meet the standards for receiving housing allowances: 45 percent of these were "very satisfied," compared to 30 percent of those who moved and passed and 19 percent of those who moved and failed. The families in the program were strongly attached to their homes. They were pleased if they could make them better at small cost, but giving them up for higher physical standards somewhere else yielded little satisfaction.

For those who could not easily meet the standards where they were, the program required a move that was often unwelcome and unsatisfying. The program's objective of bringing everyone into housing of standard quality was out of touch with the preferences and priorities of many of the families who took part.

Neighborhoods, housing costs, and program expense

Earlier housing programs usually offered a very restricted choice of neighborhood location, since people who wanted to use the program had to move to designated projects, and as a result of local political pressures the projects were usually concentrated in the worst neighborhoods of the city. The housing allowance strategy, in contrast, promised to open much wider options for neighborhood choice. People in the program could search out moderate-cost housing wherever it was located, and families moving one-by-one were unlikely to arouse the political protests that kept subsidized projects out of many desirable neighborhoods. A general reluctance to move undercut chances for widespread neighborhood mobility, but a sizable minority of families did move: 45 percent in the administrative experiment cities, 39 percent in Pittsburgh and Phoenix, and 16 percent in Green Bay and South Bend.

The housing allowance experiment produced only scattered information on neighborhood conditions, but what there is shows that people who moved tended to go into better neighborhoods than the ones they left. As the Rand Corporation's report summarizes the experience in Green Bay and South Bend, "the worst neighborhoods in each site lost program participants who moved, on balance, to better neighborhoods."

Similarly, in the administrative experiment cities, most people who moved went into census tracts with a higher socioeconomic-index rating (based on resident income, education, and employment) than the places they left. And 39 percent of black households who moved, moved to areas with lower minority concentrations than their original neighborhoods. Black families in the program lived in areas that had an average of 56 percent minority population at enrollment, and moved to areas with an average of 40 percent minority population at the time they got their first payment. In Phoenix and Pittsburgh, black movers also went into neighborhoods with lower black concentrations. The mean reduction was 4 percent in Pittsburgh and 3 percent in Phoenix.

The housing allowance program did not add significantly to opportunities for poor families to live in suburbia. In Pittsburgh, 18 percent of the families originally in the central city moved to the suburbs, and 12 percent of those originally in the suburbs moved to the city. In Phoenix, 33 percent moved from the city to the suburbs, while 6 percent went from the suburbs to the city. In both areas, however, control households with similar incomes who had no housing allowances showed almost exactly the same pattern of movement.

Housing allowances, then, may have widened the locational options open to poor people, but very few took the opportunity to move to different neighborhoods and most families in the program chose not to move at all. For those who did move, the program did not improve access to the suburbs, but it did help them move to better and less segregated neighborhoods in the cities.

The most troublesome fear raised by the idea of a housing allowance program was that pumping new money into malfunctioning central-city housing markets would drive up housing costs both for people in the program and for low-income renters in general. The supply experiment in Green Bay and South Bend was organized above all to investigate the possible inflationary effects of a housing allowance. All those who were eligible in terms of income were invited to apply, the availability of housing assistance was well publicized, and payments were assured for a full ten years. The intent was to saturate both housing markets with housing allowances and then to analyze changes in rent levels.

The results were clear and unequivocal: there was virtually no effect on housing costs. Rents in Green Bay and South Bend increased less rapidly than either regional or national rent averages. Gross rents in Green Bay increased by an average of 7 percent a year from 1974 through 1977, and in South Bend by 5 percent. Higher fuel and utility costs accounted for most of the change in both places.

With hindsight, it is easy to see why housing allowances had no inflationary impact. The tendency of families to stay in their previous homes, plus their reluctance to spend more for rent, meant that allowance payments injected few new dollars into local housing markets. In addition, even with open enrollment in Green Bay and South Bend, relatively few families took part in the program. About 20 percent of the households in the two areas were eligible in terms of income, but only about half the eligible families were enrolled at any given time, and about 80 percent of those enrolled actually met the requirements to receive payments. As a result, even in the supply experiment, housing allowances went to only 8 percent of the households in the area.

In the ten cities for which information is available, allowance payments per family averaged from $888 to $1,632 per year. Administrative costs averaged from $152 to $429 in addition, excluding the cost of research and analytical work commissioned for the experiment. The average cost per household was about $1,150 in 1976 dollars—$900 in cash payments and $250 for administration.

The average cost of $1,150 compares very favorably with the cost of the two earlier programs for comparable income groups, in which public housing cost an average of $1,650 per family, and rent supplements $1,310, both in 1972 dollars. HUD's current Section 8 program is also more expensive than housing allowances. By 1976 estimates, the Section 8 existing-units program—which is most comparable to housing allowances—cost $1,500 per family, and Section 8 new-or-rehabilitated-units cost more than $4,000. HUD budget projections for 1980 placed the cost of Section 8 existing-units at $2,700 per family and new-or-rehabilitated-units at more than $4,500 per family.

Where did housing allowances fall short of expectations?

To the surprise of many housing experts, less than half the families eligible for housing allowances actually participated in the program.

There are many plausible reasons why poor families who were eligible for housing aid failed to enroll for it, or once enrolled failed to qualify for payments. Case studies indicate that some people who were attached to their homes doubted whether they could

pass inspection or whether the landlord would agree to rent to
people in the program. Others avoided the program out of pride:
They viewed housing allowances as something like welfare, or they
feared the agency staff would treat them in demeaning ways.
Searching for a new place to live was almost always troublesome;
it usually meant having to arrange for baby sitters, getting listings,
finding transportation, and dealing with landlords. Often the search
had to be completed quickly while places were still available in
the local program, and many people had little free time. Even
people in the selected groups that were not required to meet any
housing standards still had to agree to be interviewed from time
to time and to file reports on their finances and their housing. Some
people were unwilling to go through the administrative procedures
and some were overwhelmed with other problems. One woman who
applied but never completed her enrollment told an interviewer
later: "I was working hard, I was pregnant and having a nervous
breakdown. My two kids had decided to live with their father. I
just couldn't get involved in anything else."

Families who were able to meet the housing standards where
they were already living had the best prospects for getting payments once they enrolled. In a few cities, many families never did
succeed in meeting the housing standards, perhaps confirming the
view of critics who had argued in advance that supply shortages
would prevent housing allowances from working satisfactorily. In
Pittsburgh, 78 percent of the families failed to meet housing standards when they first enrolled, and of these 73 percent still failed
to meet them two years later. In Phoenix, 80 percent failed to meet
the housing standards at enrollment, and 54 percent of these still
did not meet them two years later. The pattern in these cities was
not typical, however, and may reflect special enrollment procedures
in which people entered the program by invitation instead of on
their own initiative. Also in Pittsburgh and Phoenix, moving to another house did not necessarily help people meet the standards.
In Pittsburgh, of those not meeting standards at enrollment, 15
percent moved and passed but another 28 percent moved and
failed again. In Phoenix, 32 percent moved and passed, and 25 percent moved and failed. Again, however, the experience in these
cities was not typical of the entire program.

An important factor influencing participation in the housing allowance program was the severity of the housing standards families had to meet: the tougher the standards, the fewer families
took part. In Pittsburgh and Phoenix, one group of participants was

not required to meet any housing standards at all: Once enrolled on the basis of income eligibility, they automatically received payments. With no standards, 78 percent of the eligible families in Pittsburgh and 90 percent in Phoenix got the payments. In Green Bay and South Bend, where housing standards were moderately demanding, about 40 percent of the eligible renters received payments. In Pittsburgh and Phoenix, in the group forced to meet the most stringent housing standards, only 30 percent and 45 percent of those offered enrollment actually received payments. The most likely explanation for this trade-off between standards and participation is that most low-income families are reluctant either to pay higher rent or to move in order to upgrade their housing conditions.

One group—minority families—had an especially hard time qualifying for payments. In the administrative experiment, minority families were less likely than other enrollees to meet the standards for payment. On the average, only 53 percent of the black households enrolled (but 79 percent of Hispanic households) eventually got housing allowances, compared to 77 percent of non-minority families. In the severely segregated city of Jacksonville, Florida, only 21 percent of black enrollees got allowances during the first enrollment period, compared to 54 percent of others.

This minority experience partly confirms the views of skeptics who argued that shortages of standard housing and discrimination would offset the value of cash payments to the hard-to-house. But there was also minority experience to the contrary. In Pittsburgh, eligible blacks enrolled to a greater extent than other eligible families, and once enrolled did as well as others in meeting program standards. In Phoenix, minority families (mostly Hispanic) enrolled in proportion to their eligibility, and once enrolled did better than others in qualifying for payments. Since the minority pattern was mixed, it is possible to conclude either that the glass was half empty or that it was half full.

It is also true that almost all social programs for the poor operate far below their authorized levels, because many people who are legally eligible for benefits do not apply. Further, most new programs have increasing enrollment in the first few years before they reach a steady rate of participation. In Green Bay and South Bend, 26 percent of all eligible households took part in the first year, 37 percent in the second year, and 40 percent in the third year. These figures are not out of line with participation rates in other programs for the poor. In New York City, for example, only 52 percent of families eligible for all categories of welfare actually took part in welfare programs in the early 1970's. And participation in the national food stamp program ranges from 12 percent in North Dakota to 58 percent in California, with a national average of 38 percent. Once again, it is an open question whether the glass is half empty or half full.

Before the housing allowance experiment, conventional wisdom held that increases in the income of poor families would lead to nearly proportional increases in their housing expenditures—that a 10 percent increase in income would generate a 10 percent increase in rent payments. A recent Rand Corporation study, based on surveys of a sample of all households in Green Bay and South Bend, estimates the income elasticity of housing demand at only .19 for renters and .45 for homeowners. In these communities, a 10 percent increase in income for renters would lead to only a 1.9 percent increase in rent payments. Elasticities estimated for other cities in the housing allowance program were also low.

An implication is that if families who receive housing allowances are free to decide how much of their payment to spend for housing, they will not increase their rent outlays very much above the prior level. But if rent payments do not increase, giving cash to the poor is not likely to prompt landlords to spend much money for property improvements or better maintenance, as Lowry had anticipated when he proposed housing allowances as a solution to New York City's problems of deterioration and abandonment. Letting consumers make their own decisions regarding how much to spend for rent works against the goal of improving the quality of housing.

The housing allowance program was truly exceptional in allowing families to set their own priorities between spending on housing or spending on other items. Most housing programs sponsor construction to a predetermined standard and require the families involved to use most of their subsidy to pay for a level of housing quality chosen by an administrator. In the case of housing allowances, federal officials expected the typical family to move to better accommodations and to spend most of its subsidy for higher rent. The reality was that most families stayed put, made minor repairs if they were required to meet program standards, got marginally adequate housing if they did not have it to begin with, and used most of the payment to free their own funds for non-housing expenses. As a result, the program had only limited impact on the quality of the housing supply and on mobility; but these were unavoidable consequences of respecting the wishes of families in the program.

Learning from a social experiment

The housing allowance experiment did not fully resolve the debates about the nature of inner-city housing markets. The results certainly did not bear out the skeptics' fears of widespread inflation and unavailability of housing. Contrary to their predictions, the hard-to-house were able to find adequate housing through the allowance program or had already found reasonable places earlier. Female-headed and welfare families especially were able to make good use of housing allowances. But there were also results to confirm the skeptics' doubts. In some cities enrolled families had severe problems finding adequate housing, depending to a great extent on the standards they had to meet. And minority groups in many cities did not fare as well as others, bearing out the argument that discrimination would blunt some of the desired effects of cash payments for housing.

Housing allowance proponents can take satisfaction in the program's ability to reach and help families with serious housing problems. Yet this success in reaching families with marginal incomes and heavy financial burdens also insured that participating families would be reluctant to increase their rent outlays. Hard-pressed to come up with rent money to begin with, and living in the inflationary economy of the mid-1970's, they used their payments in ways that did not live up to the advocates' hopes of stimulating reinvestment in older housing.

It turned out that letting the poor make their own decisions led to results that ran counter to the goals of federal housing administrators. The Department of Housing and Urban Development has traditionally given top priority to improving the quality of housing, both for the country at large and for the people who take part in its programs. Marc Bendick, Jr., and James P. Zais of the Urban Institute began their own assessment of the housing allowance experiment by noting the goals former Secretary Patricia Harris set for HUD in a recent budget submission: the revitalization of urban areas, the maintenance and expansion of the supply of housing, and the provision of freedom of opportunity in housing. (Freedom of opportunity might conceivably include the freedom to live in housing of marginal quality in order to save on rent, but for HUD they note that this goal implies facilitating the "movement of low-income families outside areas of lower-income, minority concentration.") They argue persuasively that housing allowances do not serve the stated goals of HUD policy: "[T]hey have failed to generate substantial expansion of the housing stock, dramatic revitalization of cities, or major increases in freedom of choice in housing."

Similar results of another housing program are putting HUD's traditional commitments to the test. The Section 8 existing-housing program has many of the characteristics of a housing allowance, and also allows families to use federal subsidies in existing apartments that meet prescribed standards. About half the participants in Section 8 existing-housing do not move from where they lived before, and they use their financial assistance mainly to reduce their rent burden. This program has had great success in reaching the poor, female-headed families, minorities, and the elderly; but it has done little to improve the quality of the housing supply. Not surprisingly, HUD has begun to slow down the existing housing program and to shift most of its housing assistance activity to a different Section 8 program for new construction or substantial rehabilitation.

The housing allowance experience reinforces other analyses that have shown high cost replacing slum conditions as the major housing problem facing the urban poor. If the problem has changed, the search for solutions should not be held captive to HUD's traditional organizational mission. HUD should have a mission that encompasses the range of housing problems, and a capacity to use the right tool for each purpose. There is still need for construction programs, since they are likely to be more effective than housing allowances for such purposes as helping minority families in tight housing markets or opening up the suburbs to the poor. But housing allowances are the right tool for many problems, such as the emerging concern for the victims of "gentrification." The widely heralded rediscovery of city neighborhoods, which is prompting affluent families to refurbish charming brownstones and town houses, is also pushing many poor renters out of their homes. Housing allowances would probably be highly effective in helping these families find other places to live nearby while coping with rising rents.

The most valuable contribution of social experiments may be that they raise new and troublesome questions about the purposes of public policy. A series of education experiments, for example, tried to find ways of helping disadvantaged youngsters learn more in school. Instead of revealing the most promising teaching techniques, these experiments led analysts to question more carefully how to measure learning and how to define what kind of learning we want to achieve. Similarly, the housing allowance experiment began by trying to find answers to questions about the design of a national program of cash assistance for housing. But its operation brought to the surface a serious conflict between the priorities of the poor and those of housing-program administrators.

The poor do not give housing *quality* the high priority that program administrators do. In the long history of housing reform in the United States, this is the first time the beneficiaries of a program have been able to make their views known on how the money should be spent. The views of the reformers have always dominated; in fact, we know almost nothing about whether earlier generations of slum-dwellers would rather have had the cash than either model tenements or public housing projects. But the poor of this generation, at least, have spoken clearly through the housing allowance experiment. Their main problem, as they see it, is cost, not quality. Interestingly, a household survey commissioned by HUD just before the housing allowance experiment began also suggested that housing quality was not a serious problem for the urban poor. In three cities surveyed in 1972, fully 84 percent of the households with incomes below $5,000 rated their housing units as "excellent" or "satisfactory." The housing allowance experience confirms and amplifies this finding. The poor still have serious housing problems, but they are not the ones most public programs address.

The real test of whether the housing allowance experiment was a success will be whether policy makers re-examine the purposes of government action in the light of its unexpected results. An important question for the next wave of housing programs is: Who should decide how much housing a family ought to consume and where it ought to live, the family or an administrator who sets the standards? (And the higher the standards are set, the fewer people will take part.) There may conceivably be public benefits involved that would justify overriding the preferences of the poor themselves and requiring them to pay for better housing than they would otherwise choose to do. If that is so, federal officials have a responsibility to present the case for setting aside the wishes of the poor.

At a minimum, the housing allowance experiment calls into question those housing goals that are based mainly on the weight of tradition or on the organizational mission of an established federal agency. It offers instead a rare opportunity to recognize the changing needs of the clients.

CRIME AND CRIMINAL JUSTICE

A policy area that cannot be bounded by geographic region is the treatment and definition of crime. Increasingly, problems of robbery, assault with intent to commit bodily harm, and homicides have spread throughout the nation's more affluent regions. Aided and abetted by a rise in drug use among youth, alcoholism among women, and gambling among the elderly—problems which in the past were confined to urban regions—the issue of crime has taken on an alarming new dimension. At the same time, the question of the criminal justice system has taken on unique dimensions as well. Agreement about what constitutes a crime—or at least a punishable offense—has changed drastically in recent years. Which communities will absorb new houses of detention, what decisions are to be made about "victimless" crimes, whether mere possession of illicit drugs or only their sale constitutes a punishable offense—all of these issues have thrown into sharp relief patterns of criminality that service a large and supposedly noncriminal population, as compared to those aspects of crime, such as homicide, which are more uniformly condemned. Policy in this area becomes interlaced with definition. In turn, definition has become linked with ideology, or definitions of whose ox is being gored. Which policies are to be recommended for what individuals is a problem that has made the criminal justice system increasingly empirical and less confined than in the past to matters of deductive routine and precedence.

Questions of crime and criminal justice are increasingly being viewed against a backdrop of reform rather than punishment. For Toby, the problem of school violence is a central concern motivating the growth of busing and the expansion of private schools. Hence, the solution recommended involves isolating those school districts of highest crime, those ages contributing the greatest threat to student safety. Control mechanisms are seen not in terms of punitive policies but in terms of expulsion policies. Schools must be seen as places of learning, not as repositories of random individual youths. Toby also argues the need for an overall national strategy which does not now exist and for a higher level of parental involvement, although it is not clear that schools with such involvement fare uniformly better. Smaller numbers of students per class might help, but then costs become a factor. Toby sees a correlation of high violence with weak control. Woodson sees this approach as part of the "punishment lobby," arguing instead for a policy that emphasizes neither altering the behavior of the child nor social conditions generally: a policy which calls for increasing the stake young people have in themselves and in this society's institutions. The Yondorf essay, relying on the West German experience, argues that a policy of legalization and credentialization of prostitution has the effect of controlling prostitution, preventing such abuses as child prostitution or street solicitation. The policy is to convert prostitution from a criminal to a civil sanction and to establish officially sanctioned zones in which prostitution can be conducted without punishment or penalty. Quite apart from the intrinsic interest of the German approach is the vast shift underway in industrialized nations from a theory of criminality to one of deviance, to a midpoint of crimes without victims as nonpunishable, to an advanced stage of sanctioning behavior under strict controls formerly identified as illegal or illicit. In this way policy can inform the substance of crime, not merely serve as handmaiden to punitive techniques.

28

CRIME IN AMERICAN PUBLIC SCHOOLS

Jackson Toby

I
N the early 1970's Senator Birch Bayh's Subcommittee to Investigate Juvenile Delinquency heard alarming reports of violence and vandalism in American public schools—not just occasionally or in the central cities but chronically and all over the United States. Partly in response to these hearings, partly because of increasing preoccupation with school crime by newspapers, magazines, and television, the 93rd Congress passed an amendment to an education bill in 1974 requiring the Secretary of the Department of Health, Education, and Welfare to conduct a survey to determine the extent and seriousness of school crime.

The study was an elaborate one. Principals in 4,014 schools in large cities, smaller cities, suburban areas, and rural areas filled out questionnaires and returned them to Washington. Then 31,373 students and 23,895 teachers in 642 junior and senior high schools throughout the country were questioned about their experiences with school crime—in particular whether they themselves were victimized and, if so, how. From among the 31,373 students who filled out anonymous questionnaires, 6,283 were selected randomly for individual interviews on the same subject. Discrepancies between questionnaire reports of victimization and interview reports of victimization were probed to find out exactly what respondents meant

Reprinted with permission of the author from: THE PUBLIC INTEREST, No. 58 (Winter 1980), pp. 18-42. © 1980 by National Affairs, Inc.

when they answered that they had been attacked, robbed, or had property stolen from their desks or lockers. Finally, intensive field studies were conducted in 10 schools, schools that had had especially serious crime problems in the past and had made some progress in overcoming them.

In January 1978, the 350-page report to Congress, *Violent Schools —Safe Schools,* was published by the National Institute of Education. Though a scientific report, inevitably it had political overtones. Public schools with reputations for crime and violence tended to be located in the inner cities and to enroll high proportions of minority students from low-income families; average reading and mathematical levels were usually one or more grades behind national norms. Was there a causal relationship among high crime rates, low academic achievement, and a high proportion of minority students? Were parents with middle-class values enrolling their children in private or parochial schools out of fear of crime as well as out of desire for better academic instruction for their children? And, if so, did the problem of school crime explain an appreciable amount of middle-class flight from inner-city schools?

Perhaps because of the sensitivity of these issues, the report handled the data cautiously, drawing attention to some differences in the incidence of school crime and skipping lightly over others. The report showed that the crime problem was worse in junior high schools than in senior high schools, but it required careful examination of a table in an appendix to find statistics demonstrating that students in urban schools were robbed and assaulted more frequently than students in suburban or rural schools. (These statistics are reproduced in Tables I and II, below and on the next page, respectively.) But the differences are not as great as some of us might have expected. Statistics on the victimization of teachers, presented in Table III on page 22, were reported in an early chapter and showed unequivocally that urban teachers were more likely to be victimized than suburban or rural teachers—especially teachers in

TABLE I. *Percent of Students Who Reported Being Robbed within the Past Month**

	URBAN SCHOOLS	SUBURBAN SCHOOLS	RURAL SCHOOLS
Junior High Schools	9.5%	7.5%	7.1%
Senior High Schools	3.9	2.4	3.5

* SOURCE: *Violent Schools — Safe Schools,* Appendix A, pp. A6–A7.

Table II. *Percent of Students Who Reported Being Assaulted within the Past Month°*

	Urban Schools	Suburban Schools	Rural Schools
Junior High Schools	8.2%	7.2%	6.2%
Senior High Schools	4.0	3.0	3.4

° Source: *Violent Schools – Safe Schools*, Appendix A, pp. A6–A7.

the largest cities. But the report tells us more than that, and we will present its findings in the form of answers to key questions on school crime.

Answered and unanswered questions

1. *How much real crime is there in the schools? Does it consist mostly of juvenile mischief given the alarming labels, "crime" and "violence," by exaggerated newspaper accounts, or is school crime mostly acts that adult perpetrators would be arrested and prosecuted for?*

Schools are plagued with real crime, according to the study. *Violent Schools—Safe Schools* was not mainly concerned with mischief or with foul language—although it mentioned in passing that a majority of American junior-high-school teachers were sworn at by their students or were the target of obscene gestures within the month preceding the survey. The report was concerned mainly with illegal *acts* and with the fear those acts aroused, not with language or gestures. Both on the questionnaires and in personal interviews, students were asked questions designed to provide an estimate of the amount of theft and violence in public secondary schools:

> In [the previous month] did anyone steal things of yours from your desk, locker, or other place at school?
> Did anyone take money or things directly from you by force, weapons, or threats at school in [the previous month]?
> At school in [the previous month] did anyone physically attack and hurt you?

Eleven percent of secondary-school students reported in personal interviews having something worth more than a dollar stolen from them in the past month. A fifth of these thefts involved property worth $10 or more. One-half of one percent of secondary-school students reported being *robbed* in a month's time—that is, having property taken from them by force, weapons, or threats. One out of nine of these robberies resulted in physical injuries to the victims.

Students also told of being assaulted. One-and-a-third percent of secondary-school students reported being attacked over the course of a month, and two-fifths of these were physically injured. (However, only 14 percent of the assaults resulted in injuries serious enough to require medical attention.)

These percentages probably underestimated the true volume of student victimization. They were based on face-to-face *interviews* with students. The same questions asked of samples of students by means of anonymous *questionnaires* produced estimates of victimization about twice as high overall, and in the case of robbery four times as high. (Tables I and II are based on student questionnaires rather than on interviews.) Methodological studies conducted by the school-crime researchers convinced them that the interview results were more valid than the questionnaire results for estimating the extent of victimization; some students might have had difficulty reading and understanding the questionnaire. On the other hand, fear of crime kept some students from attending school. In reply to the question, "Did you stay at home any time in [the previous month] because someone might hurt you or bother you at school?" 8 percent of the students in big-city junior high schools said "yes," as compared with 4 percent in rural junior high schools and 5 percent in suburban and smaller-city junior high schools. Since the students who had an opportunity to reply to this question were those attending school on the day the questionnaire was administered (or on a subsequent make-up session), students in the sample who failed to fill out their questionnaires may have contained a higher proportion of victims of school crime and a higher percentage of those frightened into truancy.

The report also contained data on the victimization of teachers, data derived from questionnaires similar to those filled out by students. (There were no teacher interviews, perhaps because teachers were presumed more capable of understanding the questions and replying appropriately.) Table III on page 22 shows that an appreciable proportion of teachers reported property stolen, but that only a small proportion of teachers reported robberies and assaults. However, robberies were three times as common in inner-city schools as in rural schools, and assaults were nine times as common. Even in big-city secondary schools, less than 2 percent of the teachers surveyed cited assaults by students within the past month, but threats were more frequent. Thirty-six percent of inner-city junior-high-school teachers reported that students threatened to hurt them, as did 24 percent of inner-city high school teachers. Understandably,

Table III. *Percent of Teachers Who Reported Being Victimized within the Past Month: Thefts, Robberies, Assaults**

Community Size	Kind of Victimization		
	Thefts	Robberies	Physical Attacks
Cities of 500,000 population or more	16.7%	1.3%	1.8%
Smaller Cities	15.8	0.6	0.7
Suburban Areas	12.0	0.5	0.4
Rural Areas	9.5	0.4	0.2

* Source: *Violent Schools — Safe Schools*, p. 68.

many teachers said they were afraid of their students. Twenty-eight percent of big-city teachers reported hesitating to confront misbehaving students for fear of their own safety, as did 18 percent of smaller-city teachers, 11 percent of suburban teachers, and 7 percent of rural teachers.

Principals were questioned about a variety of crimes against the school as a community: trespassing, breaking and entering, theft of school property, vandalism, and the like. Based on these reports as well as on data collected by the National Center for Educational Statistics in a companion study, *Violent Schools—Safe Schools* estimated the monetary cost alone of replacing damaged or stolen property as $200 million per year.

2. *Are intruders from the outside community responsible for a major portion of school crime, or are the students themselves the main perpetrators of thefts, assaults, robberies, and vandalism? And, if the perpetrators are students, which students?*

According to the report, the notion that intruders are responsible for a great deal of school crime is a myth:

> Preventive strategies designed to keep "intruders" from entering the school assume that offenses in the school are usually committed by outsiders; relative safety is believed to require keeping students inside the school and others who do not belong there outside.
>
> Our data, however, suggest that rather than locking most offenders out, these strategies seem to lock the offenders in with their potential victims. Except for trespassing and break-ins, the great majority . . . of all reported offenses for which information about offenders is available were committed by current students at the school in question. . . . Even in the case of breaking and entering, slightly more than half (56 percent) of these offenses were committed by current students.

Another belief about perpetrators that the report called into question was that older students preyed on younger students. Although

younger students were disproportionately victimized, three-quarters
of those who attacked or robbed them were roughly the same age,
according to estimates of the victims themselves.

Schools in which a majority of students were from minority backgrounds had rates of assault and robbery against both students and
teachers twice as high as schools where white students predomi-
nated. But the data did not explain this finding. The issue is *what*
characteristics of minorities make them more likely to engage in
school crime. Here the report offered tantalizing hints that educational failure was causally implicated in school crime, but nothing
conclusive. Teachers who said that they taught a majority of low-
ability students were five times as likely to report being attacked
and twice as likely to report being robbed as teachers who said that
less than a third of their students were of low ability. Teachers who
said that a majority of their students were "underachievers" were
three times as likely to report being attacked and about 50 percent
more likely to report being robbed than teachers who said that less
than a third of their students were underachievers.

Staff members of the National Institute of Education had anticipated that students would prove to be the main perpetrators of
school crime and had planned to include on the student questionnaire questions about crimes the students themselves had committed.
This would have provided valuable information about the characteristics of student perpetrators and, inferentially, about perpetrators
generally. But boards of education resisted; questioning students
about their own crimes, even anonymously, was likely to arouse objections from parents, students, and perhaps from community groups.
The plan was dropped.

The report did offer impressions about perpetrators based on its
field studies in 10 schools—that is, on extensive observation over a
period of at least two weeks in each school, and on intensive interviews with school counselors, school aides, security personnel, parents, and representatives of community organizations. Professor A. J.
Ianni of Teachers College, Columbia University, the director of the
field studies, had this impression of school-crime perpetrators:

> There was general agreement among respondents in many of the
> schools that a small percentage of students—the figure 10 percent was
> frequently cited—form a hard core of disruptive students who are re-
> sponsible for most of the vandalism and violence in schools. While this
> troublesome group did not seem to be identifiable in terms of any spe-
> cific racial, ethnic, or socioeconomic status background, school staff
> commonly described them as students who were also having difficulty

academically, were frequently in trouble in the community, and tended to come from troubled homes. These students were easily identifiable and generally seemed to be known both to staff and other students because of the frequency with which they were in trouble. These same respondents indicated that in their experience this group of troublesome students could find allies among the other students when specific issues, situations, or problems arose. Violence and disruptive behavior is thus described as interactive with a small group of students frequently causing problems and at times setting off a chain reaction among other student groups.

3. Do attacks on and robberies of students occur mainly during classes or mainly before, after, and between classes?

Not surprisingly, violence directed at other students was less likely to occur during classes than at other times. Thus, the presence of teachers seemed to protect students against violence. Apparently, hallways and stairs (where teacher supervision was weak) were the sites for about a third of the violent acts, and other poorly supervised places—toilets, cafeterias, and locker rooms—the sites for another third.

The report did not ask whether violence on the way to and from the school building was a special problem. If the trip to and from school were dangerous for students in the inner cities, such schools would continue to be perceived as dangerous even though violence might be adequately controlled inside the school building itself.

4. Who are the main victims of school crime?

Younger students and the youngest, least-experienced teachers were most likely to be attacked or robbed. However, *male* students were more than twice as likely to be victims of both forms of violence than *female* students. And male teachers were somewhat more likely to be attacked than female teachers, although less likely to be robbed. The most likely explanation for the fact that schools are more dangerous for males than for females is that since males are the main authors of violent crimes, their victims tend to be the other males with whom they associate. Propinquity, both physical and psychological, increases the likelihood of victimization.

Propinquity between perpetrators and victims also explains the higher rate of victimization of students and teachers from minority backgrounds than of white students and teachers. Minority students and teachers were more likely to be attacked and robbed because their schools tended to be urban schools with high crime rates.

5. What are the causes of school crime?

The word "cause" does not appear in the index of the report. This was not an oversight. The safe-schools study was designed to

describe the crime problem in American public schools during a
short period of time (1976 to 1977), not to probe causes. However,
Congress expected that the study would show how school crime
could be prevented. And this objective implied some knowledge of
causes. The report waffled. It spoke of "potential contributions" to
school crime and of "several factors that appear likely to have general explanatory value with respect to school crimes."

But more explicit concern with the causes of school crime would
have made possible greater realism about what could be explained
and what could be done. For example, even though the report suggested on the basis of other studies that levels of school crime had
increased from the 1960's to the 1970's, the safe-schools study itself
collected no data on trends in school crime; hence, it could not
throw light on causes of the *increase* in school crime. Furthermore,
it could not explain why some youngsters committed crimes and
others in the same schools did not; it had not collected data from
offenders, only from victims. All the study could do was to contrast
the crime rates in some of the 642 schools of the sample with those
of others and to attempt to identify characteristics of high-crime and
low-crime schools. The report did this. Thus, high levels of violent
crime occurred in schools with above-average proportions of children from families of low socioeconomic status and in schools located in high-crime neighborhoods. But its authors were extremely
cautious in interpreting the associations in causal terms.

There are hints one can trace out. Among all the schools in the
survey—urban, suburban, and rural—a strong relationship existed
between laxness in enforcing school rules, as judged by teachers and
students in the school, and rate of violent crime. But surrounding
neighborhoods of low socioeconomic status and high crime resulted
in lax rule enforcement only in urban schools, not in suburban or
rural schools. Perhaps in high-crime communities of low socioeconomic status the enforcement of school rules was difficult for
teachers and principals but not, as the rural and suburban data
showed, impossible. Perhaps an urban school with sufficiently creative leadership could also enforce rules despite its adverse socioeconomic environment.

6. *Did the report suggest anything that the federal government
can do to reduce crime in the schools?*

There *were* recommendations in the concluding chapter of the
report, lots of them—but they were not recommendations for Congressional action nor indeed were they National Institute of Education recommendations. They were suggestions from school princi-

pals, teachers, and students, for controlling school crime. Principals and teachers were asked to write in their own words replies to the following question: "What measures would you recommend to schools having problems with vandalism, personal attacks, and theft?" Students were asked to make recommendations by means of a similar question: "If a school had a problem with personal attacks, theft, and property destruction, what could be done to make it safer?" The answers by principals, teachers, and students were grouped in the same eight categories: 1) security devices, 2) security personnel, 3) discipline and supervision, 4) curriculum and counseling, 5) training and organizational change, 6) physical-plant improvement, 7) parental involvement and community relations, and 8) improvement of school climate. Within each category, responses were carefully coded into subcategories to facilitate statistical tabulation. Although the victims and potential victims of school crime are not necessarily qualified to devise effective solutions, it may be worth noting that "discipline and supervision"[1] was the most popular recommendation of students and teachers as well as of principals.

The report also described—based on questionnaire responses from principals—efforts made by schools to cope with crime, and discussed the modest success (in the opinion of principals) of these different efforts to reduce "vandalism, personal attacks, and thefts." Big-city principals reported the highest proportion of successful practices, mostly in the areas of "security devices" and "discipline and supervision"; Table IV shows that, except for paddling—a measure more popular in rural and suburban schools and in smaller cities—schools in the big cities made the most serious disciplinary and control efforts. Aside from the impressionistic judgments of the principals, the report did not attempt to evaluate the effectiveness of these disciplinary efforts.

Social changes and school crime

The report described the current situation rather than attempting to explain how a less orderly school environment developed. The report did not consider social trends in American society that made it more difficult for public schools to control predatory, violent, or malicious student behavior.

---

[1] The responses classified under this heading included "enforcement of rules, suspensions, etc.," "restitution, payment," "special classes, expulsion," "monitoring, watching," "controlling student movement, I.D.," and others.

TABLE IV. *Percent of Schools Using Various Discipline and Control Procedures, by Location**

TYPE OF PROCEDURE	LARGE CITIES	SMALL CITIES	SUBURBAN AREAS	RURAL AREAS
Students must show I.D. card to authorized personnel when requested	6%	3%	3%	2%
Students must carry hall passes if out of class	41	23	20	18
Visitors must check in at the office	67	56	49	39
Suspension	47	36	33	27
Expulsion	6	3	4	4
Paddling	17	34	33	42
Assignment to special day-long class for disruptive students	10	7	7	5
Transfer to another regular school (social transfer)	35	19	7	3
Transfer to special school for disruptive students	10	7	4	2
Referral to community mental-health agency as disruptive student	40	29	20	17

* SOURCE: *Violent Schools — Safe Schools,* p. 147.

Historically, the development of American public education increasingly separated the school from the students' families and neighborhoods. Even the one-room schoolhouse of rural America represented separation of the educational process from the family. But the consolidated school districts in nonmetropolitan areas and the jumbo schools of the inner city carried separation much further. There were good reasons why large schools developed. The bigger the school, the lower the per-capita cost of education tended to be. The bigger the school, the more feasible it was to hire teachers with academic specialties like art, music, drama, and advanced mathematics. The bigger the school, the more likely that teachers and administrators could operate according to professional standards instead of in response to local sensitivities—for example, in teaching biological evolution or in designing a sex-education curriculum. But the unintended consequence of large schools that operated efficiently by bureaucratic and professional standards was to make them relatively independent of the local community. The advantages of autonomy were obvious. The disadvantages took longer to reveal themselves.

The main disadvantage was that students developed distinctive subcultures only tangentially related to education. Thus, in the 1950's Professor James S. Coleman showed in his book, *The Adolescent Society*, that American high school students seemed more preoccupied with athletics and personal popularity than with intellectual achievement. Students were "doing their own thing," and their thing was not what teachers and principals were mainly concerned about. Presumably, if parents had been more closely involved in the educational process, they would have strengthened the academic impact of teachers. Even in the 1950's, student subcultures at school facilitated misbehavior; in New York and other large cities, fights between members of street gangs from different neighborhoods sometimes broke out in secondary schools. However, Soviet achievements in space during the 1950's drew more attention to academic performance than to school crime and misbehavior. Insofar as community adults were brought into schools as teacher aides, they were introduced not to facilitate control over student misbehavior but to improve academic performance.

Until the 1960's and 1970's school administrators did not realize that order is chronically problematical when many hundreds of young people come together for congregate education. Principals did not like to call the police, preferring to organize their own disciplinary procedures. They did not believe in security guards, preferring to use teachers to monitor behavior in the halls and lunchrooms. They did not tell school architects about the need for what has come to be called "defensible space," and as a result schools were built with too many ways to gain entrance from the outside and too many rooms and corridors where surveillance was difficult. Above all, they did not consider that they had lost control over potential student misbehavior when parents were kept far away, where they could not see or know how their children were behaving. The focus of PTA's was the curriculum, and it was the better-educated, middle-class parents who tended to join them. In short, isolation of the school from the local community always means that if a large enough proportion of students misbehave, teachers and principals cannot maintain order. It was not until the 1960's and 1970's, however, that this potentiality became a reality in many American schools, especially inner-city schools. The following paragraphs come from a case study of a particularly disorderly New York high school reported in *Violent Schools—Safe Schools*:

When the student turmoil in the late 1960's led to frequent fires started by students' dropping matches into other students' lockers, all the lockers, with the exception of those in the gyms, were closed and remain so. As a result, students must carry lunches and other belongings, and these are sometimes stolen when they are left out. Vandalism, while not nearly as dramatic or widespread as it was during the time of the disruptions, still presents problems. The cost to the school in 1976 for repainting or cleaning off graffiti was approximately $5,000. The principal explains that graffiti and the breaking of windows are a constant problem both because of the size of the school and the reduction in the custodial staff.

Another trend helping to explain how a less orderly school environment developed was the continuing pressure to keep children in school longer—on the assumption that children needed all the education they could get to cope with a complicated urban industrial society. The positive side of this development was rising educational levels. Greater proportions of the age cohort graduated from high school and went on to post-secondary education than ever before. The negative aspect of compulsory-school-attendance laws and of informal pressure to stay in school longer was that youngsters who didn't wish further education were compelled to remain in school. They were, in a sense, prisoners; understandably, some of them became troublemakers. When they became insolent, violent, or criminal, there was little the public schools could do about them. (The private schools simply expelled them—that is, sent them to public schools.) Since society now believes that public schools are ultimately responsible for primary and secondary education for all children—those with special physical, emotional, or behavior problems are diverted to special schools only as a last resort—public schools are less able to control their students than they used to be.

Discovering children's rights

A third trend indirectly affecting the school-crime problem was the increasing sensitivity of public schools to the rights of children. A generation ago, it was possible for principals to rule schools autocratically, to suspend or expel students without much regard for procedural niceties. Injustices occurred; children were "pushed out" of schools because they were disliked by school officials. But this arbitrariness enabled school administrators to control the situation when real misbehavior occurred. Assaults on teachers were punished so swiftly that they were almost unthinkable. Even disrespectful language was unusual. Today school officials are required to observe due process in handling student discipline. Hearings are necessary. Witnesses must confirm suspicions. Appeals are provided for. Greater democratization of schools means that unruly students get better protection against school officials, and most students get less protection from their classmates.

Related to this third trend is a fourth: the decreased ability of schools to get help with discipline problems from the juvenile courts. Like the schools themselves, the juvenile courts have become more attentive to children's rights and less willing to exile children to a correctional Siberia. More than a decade ago the Supreme Court ruled in the *Gault* case that children could not be sent to juvenile prisons for "rehabilitation" unless proof existed that they had committed some crime for which imprisonment was appropriate.

The *Gault* decision set off a revolution in juvenile-court procedures and fostered a growing reluctance on the part of juvenile-court judges to send youngsters "away." Furthermore, a number of state legislatures restricted the discretion of juvenile-court judges. In New York and New Jersey, for example, juvenile-court judges may not commit a youngster to correctional institutions for "status offenses"—that is, for behavior that would not be a crime if done by adults. Thus truancy or ungovernable behavior in school or at home are not grounds for incarceration in New York and New Jersey. Many experts believe that the differentiation of juvenile delinquents from "Persons in Need of Supervision" is a progressive reform. But one consequence of this reform is that the public schools cannot easily persuade juvenile courts to act in school-problem cases. Student abuse of teachers, for example, is more difficult to cope with.

These social changes provide background for understanding the most important change of all: the erosion of the authority of the classroom teacher. If run-of-the-mill teachers could control effectively the behavior of students in their classes, in hallways, and in lunchrooms, there would be considerably less school violence— though theft and vandalism still might be problems. Nowadays some individual teachers can control their classes through personal charisma. But what has changed is that the *role* of teacher no longer has the prestige it once did for students and their parents, and so less forceful, less experienced, or less effective teachers cannot rely on the prestige of the role to maintain control. They are on their own in a sense that the previous generation of teachers was not. The most visible symptom of loss of automatic respect is assaults on teachers, mainly from students—but occasionally from parents themselves!

According to the report, somewhat more than 1 percent of American seventh-, eighth-, and ninth-grade teachers were assaulted by their students *every month*. Male teachers reported being attacked more frequently than female teachers, younger teachers more often than older teachers, inexperienced teachers more than experienced teachers, minority teachers more than white teachers.

What happened to erode the almost sacred status of teachers? This question was not dealt with in the report. Doubtless, lessened respect for teachers is related to fundamental cultural changes by which many authority figures—parents, police, government officials, military leaders, employers—have been removed from psychological pedestals. In the case of teachers, however, the general demythologizing process was amplified by special criticism. Best-selling books of the 1960's like John Holt's *Why Children Fail*, James Herndon's *The Way It Spozed to Be*, Jonathan Kozol's *Death at an Early Age: The Destruction of the Minds and Hearts of Negro Children in the Boston Public Schools*, and Herbert Kohl's *36 Children*, portrayed teachers, especially white middle-class teachers, as the villains of education—insensitive, authoritarian, and even racist. The failure of large numbers of children in inner-city schools to learn as much as they ought to have learned by national standards was interpreted as a responsibility of the schools and of the teachers. These books did not pretend to be quantitative surveys. They made no estimates of the percentages of American teachers who resembled the anecdotal examples the authors provided. But the consistency of the illustrations created an image of American teachers as, at best, inept and unfeeling.

The authors probably intended to exonerate youngsters for lack of academic success by portraying them as victims of failings in the educational system. *The effect on readers was to blame teachers for the poor results.* To be sure, few inner-city residents read these books. Yet the anti-establishment ideas that they contained percolated through American society as the clichés of television interviews and college education courses. Because the 1960's witnessed an enormous growth of enrollments in higher education, especially of minority community-college students, the notion that teachers could not be trusted spread from these books to college classrooms to American families, including minority families. Striking a teacher might almost appear to be a deserved punishment. Of course, only a tiny percentage of students and their parents subscribed to this ideologically extreme position. Even among parents and students who assaulted teachers, momentary anger rather than ideological conviction was probably the predominant motivation. Nevertheless, ideologically motivated attacks had symbolic impact. They suggested to children who witnessed them or heard about them that distrust of teachers must have *some* basis. Why else were people so angry? Thus ideological extremism fed on itself, increasing the mutual suspicions of students and teachers in inner-city schools and motivating some teachers to retire early and others to leave the teaching profession for other occupations.

Another indication of the erosion of teacher authority has been the decline of homework in secondary schools. When teachers could depend on all but a handful of students to turn in required written homework, they could assign homework and mean it. The slackers could be disciplined. But when teachers can no longer count on a majority of students doing their homework, the assignment of homework becomes a meaningless ritual, and many teachers give up. Of course, when homework is negligible, classroom instruction is less effective. The decline of homework also suggests that teachers lack authority to induce students to do *anything* they don't want to do: to attend school regularly, to keep quiet so an orderly recitation can proceed, to refrain from annoying a disliked classmate. Indeed, there are American public schools where one-third of the enrolled students are absent on an average school day. In the classrooms of such schools, teachers cannot build on information communicated and presumably learned during the previous lesson, because so many members of the class missed it.

To sum up: I believe school crime can best be understood in the context of social changes that separated secondary schools from effective family and neighborhood influences, that have kept older adolescents enrolled in school whether they craved education or not, that made it extremely difficult for schools to expel students guilty of intractable and even violent behavior, and that reduced the authority of classroom teachers.

Why care about school crime?

School crime receives attention mainly because individual teachers and students are assaulted and their property stolen or because the school's property is stolen or damaged. A more pernicious aspect of school crime, however, is that it reduces the effectiveness of public education, particularly in large cities.

Crime and the anticipation of crime in the past decade reduced teacher and student commitment to the educational process. Teachers in high-crime schools became less ready to demand from students in-class and out-of-class effort: Learning is work, and many teachers grew afraid to insist on what students regarded as unpleasant. They also became afraid to intervene when students fought or attacked another teacher. Some teachers found their role so different from what they had expected that they abandoned the teaching profession entirely or transferred to safer ("better") schools. Some older teachers chose to retire early. Most teachers—having invested too much in a professional career to quit—continued to serve, but with low morale. Students began to reject the educational process. They cut classes more than previous generations of students, and they took unauthorized absences of days and sometimes weeks. They complained that they weren't learning much in school—and they were right.

Those parents aware of the inadequate progress of their children in reading and arithmetic sometimes tried to correct the situation. For families with the economic resources to do so, the easiest way was to transfer their children to private or parochial schools or to move to suburban communities with reputations for good schools. Parents without the means to transfer their children could only attempt to make the local schools better, possibly by joining the PTA. But, in truth, parents could not have much impact, given the organizational and geographic isolation of the school from the local community.

The effect of this process of deterioration was to alter the role of the public school in underprivileged neighborhoods of big cities. American public schools have traditionally taught basic skills that all persons need to know in order to participate effectively in a complex industrial society. But they also served to select for post-secondary education youngsters whose native abilities and personal motivation prepared them for responsible and prestigious occupations. "Opportunity" was an incentive legitimizing the school in the eyes of the parents as well as students, and thereby justifying teacher authority. However, as crime grew more serious in big-city schools, they became less and less functional as a channel of social ascent for able students from disadvantaged backgrounds; they became traps instead of springboards. (The relentless support of the NAACP for busing to promote racial integration in public education should be understood against a background of disorder in big-city secondary schools that increasingly serve a minority clientele. Whatever else busing accomplishes, it promises to enroll minority students in safer and educationally more effective schools than they would otherwise attend and thus to return public education to its mobility-promoting function.)

Controlling violence in urban schools is thus not only desirable for its own sake, but also for the possibility of ameliorating two of the intractable problems of American education: 1) the draining away of better students and the consequent increase of racial segregation in the public schools of the largest central cities, and 2) educational ineffectiveness in those schools so serious as to prevent even intellectually able students from learning enough. To put the matter more dramatically, failure to control the violence problem in big-city schools means that urban public schools cannot propel youngsters from disadvantaged families toward successful occupational careers.

One way to avoid this conclusion is to assert that the causal order is not from violence to educational ineffectiveness to the flight from high-crime schools by better students, but rather that schools that arouse frustration and resentment in their students erupt in school crime. This is essentially the thesis of the Children's Defense Fund. According to the Fund, American schools are excessively arbitrary, especially with minority students, and suspend and expel students from school for trivial reasons unrelated to the educational process. The Children's Defense Fund refers to the "pushout problem" and argues that the disproportionate representation of black youngsters among those suspended or expelled is evidence at least of arbitrary standards and probably of racism on the part of school officials. The Fund's position is that schoolchildren need advocates to protect their legitimate interests against the oppressive authority of teachers and principals, and that more "due process" rather than less will reduce student frustration and therefore violence. Partisans of the youth-advocacy approach to crime reduction in the schools convinced the Senate Subcommittee to Investigate Juvenile Delinquency of the correctness of this approach. The Subcommittee's 1975 report, *Our Nation's Schools—A Report Card: "A" in School Violence and Vandalism,* put it this way:

> One common thread of particular interest to the Subcommittee running through many of the underlying causes of school violence and vandalism is what may be called the crisis of due process. Quite naturally schools, like other institutions, are compelled to issue rules and regulations concerning the conduct of persons within their jurisdiction. It is clear that without fair and meaningful control and discipline the schools would quickly lose their ability to educate students. Increasingly, though, educators and administrators are finding that the extent of stu-

dent conduct which is sought to be regulated, as well as the methods of regulation, are causing more problems than they are controlling. A 1975 NEA study interviewed a large number of students from different schools and found that "many students spoke of the need for consistent, fair discipline."

For example, the Subcommittee found that in numerous institutions across the country, students, administrators and teachers are embroiled in constant ongoing disputes over restrictions on hair style, smoking, hall passes, student newspapers and a myriad of other aspects of school life.

According to the Senate Subcommittee, the schools' failings in the area of due process incite students to violence, as do arbitrary expulsions and suspensions. The Subcommittee Report made the connections as follows:

> At first glance it might appear that the expulsion, suspension, pushout, force out and truancy phenomenon [sic], although certainly tragic for those involved, might at least create a somewhat more orderly atmosphere for those remaining in school as a result of the absence of youngsters evidently experiencing problems adjusting to the school environment. The opposite, however, appears to be the case. The Syracuse study, for instance, found that in schools where the average daily attendance was lower, the disruptions, violence and vandalism rates were higher. This may be explained by the fact that the vast majority of students who are voluntarily or compulsively [sic] excluded from schools do, in time, return to those schools. In many instances their frustrations and inadequacies which caused their absence in the first place have only been heightened by their exclusion and the school community will likely find itself a convenient and meaningful object of revenge.

It is not possible to dismiss the arguments of the Children's Defense Fund, the Subcommittee on Juvenile Delinquency, and the various proponents of youth advocacy out of hand. Nonetheless, it seems more plausible that school violence lowers the effectiveness of the educational process through the fears that it arouses than that arbitrary school rules so enrage students that they rob and steal from each other and teachers, and perpetrate assaults and vandalism. Conceivably though, some students seek revenge on teachers, on the school building, and on their fellow students for perceived unjust treatment.

Violent-Schools—Safe-Schools asked students and teachers questions about their perception of the fairness of school rules; a scale of perceived school fairness was constructed. Did schools where students and teachers felt the rules were unfair have higher levels of violence than schools in which students and teachers thought the rules were fairer? Apparently not in the urban junior and senior high schools where the violence problem is most acute. The tendency for "less fair" schools to have higher violence rates virtually disappeared when other co-varying causal factors were statistically removed. Thus, in addition to being implausible, the hypothesis that student resentment of unfair rules contributes substantially to school violence did not stand up under empirical test.

How to reduce school crime

Reducing school crime requires a long-run strategy rather than a search for panaceas. Informal influences, such as greater parental involvement, might prove useful in controlling school crime. Informal social controls are a factor in human behavior generally—and certainly in adolescent behavior in schools. To fail to utilize informal controls is to throw the entire burden of preventing school crime on *formal* agencies of control: security guards, teachers, principals. But channeling informal influences is more complicated than hiring security guards or buying stronger locks. Time and effort must be devoted to developing practical programs.

Parents and other neighborhood adults are already employed in urban *elementary* schools as teacher aides; they are supposed to increase the effectiveness of classroom teachers. They may also contribute to a more orderly classroom atmosphere. But in *secondary* schools teacher aides are rare. (Paraprofessionals seem less useful for helping the teacher of specialized subjects.) If it could be arranged, the routine presence of parents in junior and senior high schools might have appreciable effects on crime rates and on the fear of crime, whether or not parents make a direct contribution to academic achievement.

But how can the presence of neighborhood adults in school buildings be justified? One possibility is to hire them to perform useful services that justify their being in lunchrooms, halls, stairways, offices, and even classrooms. Hiring parents for their indirect impact on school crime is expensive. And, indeed, the informal control resulting from a parental presence in secondary schools might be achieved more cheaply. Schools are already used for adult-education courses in evening hours. Such courses could be scheduled for the school day. If crime reduction were attained at the price of increased congestion and of reduced autonomy for teachers and principals, most people would consider the tradeoff worth it.

Greater efforts could be made to involve another informal influence, the peer group, in the control of school crime. This has already been done, reportedly with success, in vandalism control. The cost of vandalism for a previous year is calculated, and the student body collectively is given the monetary equivalent of the reduction in property damage for the current year. There have also been efforts to heighten the consciousness of students about school crime through public discussions. Although these steps are in the right direction, they do not seem to mobilize strong peer sanctions against more serious crime. What is needed is sustained thought and experimentation to discover the most effective way to motivate students to disapprove of predatory behavior. Again, a long view is required.

But along with a long-term perspective for school-crime reduction there must be a set of priorities. For not even the federal government can deal with *all* school crime in *all* of the urban, suburban, and rural areas of 50 states and the District of Columbia. Some types of school crime, while undesirable, are not major threats to public education. Marijuana and alcohol use on school premises probably belong in this category; perhaps vandalism and after-hours burglaries are also bearable costs in an affluent society. On the other hand, violent crimes at school are serious threats to the viability of public education. Controlling them should be the first priority of a safe-schools strategy.

School violence is most serious in big-city junior high schools, where assaults and robberies are more than twice as frequent as in senior high schools. Furthermore, a major factor in junior-high-school crime is that junior highs are pressed to keep troublesome students because of compulsory-school-attendance laws. Expulsion is theoretically possible, but difficult in practice. A junior-high-school student who attacks a teacher may be given a five-day suspension, whereas a high school student committing the same offense would be expelled. High schools have greater proportions of voluntary students. True, some high school students are trapped by the school-attendance laws in the ninth or tenth grades, but they are outnumbered by students legally free to drop out—and therefore possible candidates for expulsion for misbehavior. These considerations explain why the problem of coping with school violence is more difficult in junior high schools than in other public secondary schools.

Can violence be controlled in big-city junior high schools? "Youth advocates" believe that designing more intriguing curricula and selecting more stimulating teachers will reduce violence. Yet no curriculum is universally intriguing, and no teacher can be stimulating all the time. Public schools may not be responsive enough to their clienteles, as proponents of youth advocacy allege, but responsiveness or lack of it is only marginally relevant to the problem of violence. Rural schools are the least responsive and the safest; some of them paddle students and conduct strip-searches for drugs. *What makes violence likely is weak control.* Big-city junior high schools have high rates of assault and robbery because they contain a handful of violent students whom they cannot control and cannot extrude, and because they have not devised credible rewards and punishments for the larger group of potentially violent youngsters who are susceptible to deterrence. Addressing these two weaknesses of control will enable big-city junior high schools to reduce violence. But coping with these weaknesses involves painful measures, not the cost-free "solutions" suggested by youth advocates.

First, to rid the junior high schools of the small percentage of violent students who have proved that they cannot be controlled by anyone, the public schools should be allowed to use expulsion more freely. This means recognizing that the limits to the right of students to remain in school for educational purposes are reached when their presence jeopardizes the education of classmates. Expulsion is a drastic remedy. Though home instruction and alternative schools will be available for expelled students, the likelihood is that expelled students will not make much further academic progress. That is sad. Nevertheless, society must be permitted to give up on students who are threatening the educational opportunities of their classmates.

Milder sanctions

The second remedy is linked to the first. It may be possible to devise innovative lesser punishments for misbehavior provided that more drastic punishments (such as expulsion) are available should the lesser sanctions fail. Suppose, for example, that a student subject to expulsion for slapping a teacher is offered the option of working 14 hours every weekend at the school—painting, scrubbing, polishing—for three months. Supervision is given by paid college students from the local community working alongside the offender. The offender receives no pay; he is being punished, not rewarded by participation in an employment program. Perhaps the assaultive student prefers expulsion to hard work on his "free" weekends. (Experience with coerced community service in New Zealand—called "periodic detention"—demonstrated that some offenders preferred jailing for a period of time to labor-punishment on the installment plan.) On the other hand, his parents may prefer that he remain in school; they press him to accept the weekend penalty and, reluctantly, he agrees. But what happens if he does not show up for his weekend drudgery? In New Zealand the failure to report for weekend work without a medical excuse results in a bench warrant being issued, and the youngster goes to jail. Were magistrates unwilling to issue bench warrants, periodic detention could not succeed; periodic detention is not a Quaker work project. In order for coerced community service to be effective as a sanction for controlling school crime, boards of education would have to expel youngsters who dropped out of the program.

The parallel is not exact. Expulsion from school may be perceived by offenders as not wholly undesirable. The New Zealand experience is with jail, not with expulsion from school. Only experimentation can show whether expulsion is a sufficient threat to motivate the majority of offenders to abide by a lesser penalty. If not, the cooperation of juvenile courts would be necessary. Since school violence is delinquency, and legally subject to the juvenile or criminal courts, judges can stand behind school-imposed disciplinary measures with the more drastic threat of incarceration. To be sure, mention of expulsion or incarceration in relation to school crime horrifies "youth advocates," and the hope, of course, would be that these fairly severe sanctions need rarely be used. Experimentation is necessary to find out whether the threat of such sanctions is sufficient to ensure compliance.

Experimentation is also necessary with more palatable forms of influencing student behavior: rewards for good behavior rather than punishment for bad. Psychologists say that "positive reinforcement" is more effective than punishment, and positive reinforcement does not involve denying some students educational opportunities in order to preserve educational opportunities for others. Unfortunately, it is difficult to hook all students on the rewards offered by principals, teachers, and conforming students. According to sociologists, the basic social reward is approval, but teachers cannot easily bestow approval upon students who are uninterested in the curriculum and flout the behavioral rules of the classroom. Furthermore, such students are likely to receive approval for their disruptive behavior from close friends and to weigh this approval against the disapproval of teachers, principals, and the majority of the student body. Consequently, as desirable as it is to search experimentally for rewards that will help control violent crime in big-city junior high schools, the likelihood is that punishments will also be necessary, and that to protect the educational process the penalties of expulsion and referral to the juvenile-justice system will have to be used for the foreseeable future.

Americans are not patient or fatalistic. Given a national problem as unpleasant as school violence, our tendency is to attempt to do something about it—fast. Unfortunately, a crash program may not ameliorate the situation; it may even make the problem worse. School violence has not triggered our usual activist response. There have been stories in the mass media, hearings in the Congress, studies by the Department of Health, Education, and Welfare, but surprisingly little in the way of systematic national effort to reduce school crime. Part of the reason that school violence has been handled gingerly is the American tradition of local control over education. The main role for the federal government has been to supply funds for school programs that the Congress and the President deem worthy. Another reason is the concentration of the problem in big cities—where it is entangled with other difficult problems. So far about all that has happened is that urban school districts have improved control over entry to and exit from school buildings and have stationed security guards in the schools. *Violent Schools—Safe Schools* summarized the situation:

> More than one-third of all big-city schools employ trained security personnel; more than half of the big-city junior high schools have them, as do two-thirds of all big-city senior high schools. In suburban areas the proportion is much lower (7 percent), and in rural schools their use is negligible (1 percent).

Meanwhile, other efforts at control illuminate ironic twists of "children's rights" in practice, as when big-city school systems attempt to move violent students from one school to another. The rationale for such transfers is that youngsters may start fresh in a new school where they do not have a bad reputation. But the case study of one inner-city junior high school, called "Rogers" in the report, shows how this system of musical chairs works in practice:

> Since it is not legally possible to expel students considered disruptive, it is customary at Rogers as in other schools, to transfer students to other schools. By board regulation, the school is not permitted to inform the receiving school of the reason for the transfer or to provide any disciplinary records. "This can present some real problems," the dean says of the confidentiality requirement: "We had a kid last year who slashed another kid's throat with a razor blade and we finally had to transfer him to one of the intermediate schools, but we couldn't tell them officially what he had done or even that they should keep an eye on him because he was potentially violent."

No one knows whether transferring violent students from school
to school reduces the total amount of violence in big-city school systems. Yet in any case humane considerations suggest that after a
student has committed violent acts against students or teachers in a
school, they ought not to have to encounter him in the corridors day
after day. (In point of fact, it is at least as common for victims—both
teachers and students—to transfer out voluntarily as it is for perpetrators to be compelled to transfer.)

What is being done?

On August 30, 1978, the Office of Juvenile Justice and Delinquency Prevention of the Law Enforcement Assistance Administration announced in the *Federal Register* a national initiative to combat school crime. Proposals were invited for a National School Resource Network; one grant of as much as $2,500,000 would be made
for an initial 15-month period to finance the successful proposal.
The presumption was that further grants would be made to maintain the School Resource Network if it seemed promising. Here is
how the solicitation justified the new initiative:

> At the present time, there is no overall or resource strategy to assist
> schools in meeting the challenge of serious school crime. Resources are
> minimal and fragmented with little capacity to develop new resources
> to meet this challenge. The development of a nationwide school re-
> source network dedicated to systematic advocacy, reform, and a safer
> environment on behalf of students and teachers is needed to provide
> overall direction and coordination of existing and new school resources.
> The promotion of due process, fairness and consistency in school secu-
> rity, and disciplinary policies and practices is important in assisting
> schools to develop and operate crime prevention and control programs.

The words have a pleasant sound, but it was not obvious what the
School Resource Network was supposed to do. Later in the solicitation, the strategy of John M. Rector, then Administrator of the
Office of Juvenile Justice and Delinquency Prevention, became
clearer. Rector's approach was to move information from schools
that had learned to cope with crime to schools that had not. Rector
explained in a paragraph included under the heading, "technical
assistance":

> The grantee shall produce technical assistance packages containing a
> variety of information materials on serious school violence and vandal-
> ism prevention. Sufficient copies of each package shall be produced to
> allow dissemination to appropriate technical assistance specialists in
> the national school resource network system. The information materials

to be included in each package shall include, but not be limited to, the Office of Juvenile Justice and Delinquency Prevention publications and materials such as the national evaluation reports, model school crime prevention programs and research reports, abstracts, bibliographies, grant project summaries, brochures, directories, and pamphlets. Materials developed and compiled should take into account regional, local and ethnic minority differences.

The dissemination of information about school violence will be helpful. But in order for improved communication to serve as the cornerstone of a national strategy for the control of school violence, some schools must be markedly more successful at coping with school violence than others. All that would then be necessary is to package the secret and send it around the country. But if, as is true especially in the inner cities, all schools are groping more or less ineffectively, a national strategy for coping with school crime should stress the systematic search for new approaches.[2]

The National School Resource Network is currently the main effort of the federal government, and local school systems are planning no new initiatives of their own. Nevertheless, school violence may diminish somewhat. The decline of births that began in the 1960's is likely to help. Junior-high-school enrollments have begun to fall. With smaller numbers of students, teachers and security guards are better able to defuse potentially explosive situations. Furthermore, teachers and principals have learned from their difficult experiences of the past decade; they know what to expect. They are less likely to become demoralized than the missionary-teachers who streamed into big-city schools in the 1960's—and streamed out again when they discovered that the role required less a guru than a policeman. Waiting passively for school violence to go away means relying on the happenstance of demography and other natural forces to cope with the problem. There is another possibility: that parents will become indignant enough about violent schools to make safer schools a political issue. Let's hope so.

---

[2] The failure of Mr. Rector's solicitation to include a research-and-development component was partly personal idiosyncracy. A lawyer by training, Rector was doubtful that social-science research could demonstrate the usefulness of an approach that practitioners were not already using—*somewhere*. This prejudice forced the School Resource Network to rely on what little was known about the control of school violence; Rector's strategy was to get the pamphlets in the mail. Rector was dismissed as Administrator in June 1979. Whether his successor will try to extricate the National School Resource Network from its presently-designed role is not yet known.

29

PREDATORY CRIME AND BLACK YOUTH

Robert L. Woodson

There is an increasing national display of concern by journalists, social workers, and criminologists over what they view as a growing phenomenon on the American scene—the hardbitten, alienated youth criminal who preys without mercy on the poor and the wealthy alike, the sick, the aged, the healthy, family or strangers, as often for kicks as for profit.

For the most part, the writers rely on newspaper headlines and information taken from researchers who purportedly possess authoritative knowledge of youth behavior. The common, recurrent theme in these writings is that a harder line must be taken; respect for punishment must be restored; a tougher policy toward violent youth will deter crime. In tandem with this is the call for the lowering of the jurisdictional age limit, thus bringing youth accused of committing more serious offenses into the adult system, where if convicted he or she would be given more severe sentence in an adult institution.[1] These proposals appear to be raised with little thought given to the policy implications of moving in such a direction. The most frightening prospect is a return to the practices and policies of precolonial America when children could be incarcerated for disrespect to their parents, and even sentenced to death.

Others believe that violent youth and other acts of criminality can only be prevented and controlled by addressing the so-called root causes of crime, and that improving social and economic conditions within the environment in which the youth live will reduce delinquency.

The theory behind this approach maintains that delinquency can be controlled and prevented by: (1) altering the behavior of the child through various techniques of mental health intervention such as psychotherapy or counseling, or (2) by altering the social conditions within the environment that influence the youth's behavior.

Neither behavior modification strategies nor systems change strategies have proven effective in reducing and preventing youth crime among the waves of violent youth which have inhabited the cities over the past several decades.

It is this author's contention that one possible solution lies in efforts to increase the stake young people have in themselves and in this society's institutions. The failure to do so portends some very grievous consequences, as pointed out by Berger and Neuhaus: "When the political order becomes detached from the values and realities of

FIGURE 1
Causes of Death: Black Males in Philadelphia, Ages 15 to 19 Years

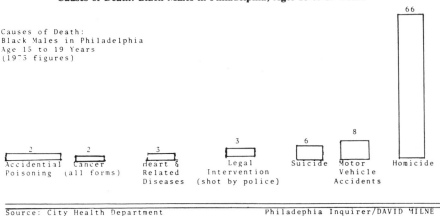

Source: City Health Department   Philadephia Inquirer/DAVID MILNE

individual life, deprived of its moral foundation, the political order is delegitimated. When that happens, the political order must be secured by coercion rather than by consent. And when that happens, democracy disappears."[2] The need to find the means to reach youngsters charged with predatory crimes is most important given the current direction of federal policy, as expressed in programs currently being funded by the Office of Juvenile Justice and Delinquency Prevention (OJJDP), under the Department of Justice. While the office was established to find solutions to youth crime, emphasis is being given to nonchronic offenders and those charged with less serious infractions of the law.[3] Little or no attention is given to the source of concern of the American public.

If this trend is allowed to continue and go unchallenged, blacks and other minority people will be passive participants in the declaration of war against our young people, as the following profile of the youth population will reveal.

PROFILE OF THE YOUTH POPULATION UNDER STUDY

Researcher Frank Zimmering, in a recent report for the Twentieth Century Funds, makes the following observations:

> Males between the ages of 13 and 20 comprise 9 percent of the population but account for more than half of all property crime arrests and more than a third of all offenses involving violence.

Violent crime by the young has increased.

Most violent crime by the young is committed against young victims; about 10 percent of all robbery of young offenders involves elderly victims.

Most young offenders who commit acts of extreme violence and pursue criminal careers come from minority ghetto and poverty backgrounds; so do their victims. [4]

(See Figure 1.)

In an earlier study commissioned by OJJDP, Zimmering predicted that youth crime rates will slowly abate over the next decade because of the decline in birthrates in the general population. However, he found that birthrates for minorities will decrease substantially. In fact, the number of young urban black males between the ages of 18 and 20 will increase by eight percent over the next 15 to 20 years. [5]

Blacks in America are the victims of urban deterioration and the social-psychological forces leading to legal deviance. And, for this reason, concern with crime in the city is often a concern with black crime. Relative deprivation and social disqualification are thus dramatically chained to despair and delinquency. [6]

Dr. Wolfgang, in his landmarked study of violent crime and the birth cohort, [7] found that of the total birth cohort of 9,946 boys studied in the city of Philadelphia, over half of the black youngsters born in the same year were delinquent, as compared with 28.64 percent of white youngsters. Only 6.4 percent of the entire cohort accounted for over half of all the delinquencies.

Dr. Wolfgang states:

> Under the generally accepted assumption that these index offenses (author's note: violent offenses and serious property crimes) are the most serious and the ones to reduce in any deterrence of prevention program, and that most of the other forms of delinquency are relatively trivial, the pivotal point of social cost reduction appears to be when juveniles have committed their first offense. To produce delinquency desisting at this stage in the biography of the child might thus be considered the most efficient procedure. More non whites go on after the first offense, and perhaps the major concern should be with this racial group.

Reasons and Kaplan gave a graphic profile when they wrote the following:

> In 1960, one out of every twenty-six black men twenty-five years old was in jail or prison, compared to one of one-hundred-sixty-three whites. On any day in California in 1970, one out of eight black men between twenty and twenty-four years of age was in prison, in jail, or on probation, compared to one of thirty whites. Extrapolation suggest that, during a one-year period, one of four black men in his early twenties, spends some time in prison or jail or on probational parole, compared with one of fifteen whites. [8]

A report of the Philadelphia Department of Health indicated that the leading cause of death in that city for black males between the ages of 15 and 19 was homicide.[9] (See attached Figure 1.)

In a recent testimony, Peter Edelman, director, New York State Division for Youth, commenting on the preventive services for delinquent youth, stated the issue clearly:

> I believe we should take a hard look at what our dollars are buying, to ensure that they are serving children who are most in need, and especially children who are most at risk of getting into trouble with the law.[10]

In a recent report that summarized the findings of seven research studies on serious juvenile offenders, it was concluded that the one consistent feature of serious offender population was the composition predominately of males at the upper limits of juvenile court jurisdiction, from inner city areas, and disproportionately of minority-group youths.[11]

While it is generally recognized that blacks and other minorities are overrepresented as both crime victims as well as those arrested for the commission of predatory crimes, blacks are underrepresented in framing the issues that address solution. Millions of dollars have been spent on research by the Office of Juvenile Justice Delinquency Prevention, of the United States Department of Justice, yet not one black private or public organization has been utilized in conducting research since the inception of the office in 1974. One result of the lack of minority input is that programmatic emphasis has been given to addressing the needs of nonminority and nonserious offender populations, as emphasis is given to the deinstitutionalization of status offenders.

Black institutions and black scholars must devote more time and attention to participating in the framing of the issues in the area of juvenile delinquency prevention and insist upon obtaining the resources to conduct research into the service of policy development.

Blacks must also desist from merely limiting their participation in rhetoric about *addressing the presumed root causes of crime*. This represents a form of escapism, for no responsibility can be conferred from such an approach, since the presumed causes of racism, poor education, inadequate housing, etc., are beyond the control of any one individual or organization. While we are pursuing solutions, we must engage in activities that are geared at symptom relief; geared to the elderly person who is mugged in a ghetto housing project. The input of minority researchers and policymakers becomes unique and valuable if it reflects perspectives and needs of those who more directly experience the problem.

We must challenge the notion that communities populated by poor and minority people are merely cesspools of pathology with little or no redeeming qualities. This perspective on individual pathology is reinforced by sociologists such as Daniel Moynihan and Edward Banfield, who provide "data" in support of the negative social impact of family decline. James Q. Wilson refers to Moynihan's works, in part, to explain the disproportionately high crime rate among poor and minority people. These writings are required reading in police training academies throughout the country.

There is a need to move away from these pathology/deviance principles that frame much of the research in juvenile delinquency and refocus our inquiries on strengths that exist within minority communities. Examples abound that demonstrate the willingness and the capacity of inner-city neighborhoods to become restored through the utilization of their own "antibodies." Most of these activities are ignored by nonminority researchers, and, therefore, seldom do these neighborhood activities find expression in an idiom that permits understanding by the larger spheres of social life.

Minorities conducting such research must study the problem from within, in an attempt to understand the dynamics of the problem by penetrating the motives, self-interpretations, and values of the individuals in the communities under study.[12]

Over the past decade, and currently at the American Enterprise Institute's Mediating Structure Project, this author has monitored the activities in several cities throughout the country, where community members themselves have used their own resources to deal with the problems of youth violence and have successfully prevented delinquent behavior. In many of these cities, adults are working closely and successfully with young people, to the point where youth who were once an anathema to community stability are protecting their neighborhood and communities. The basic ingredients to the successful approaches in these communities appear to be principles of youth development, fostered by establishment of a strong sense of "family."

The underlying ideology of these programs is the belief that the neighborhoods and communities in which young people grow up have many natural human resources, which, if properly tapped, can be effective in addressing the community's most complex problems. These development theories emphasize community resourcefulness and human strengths as the primary resources for the resolution of human problems. The community is viewed as a viable organism. When it suffers acute breakdown, it is basically able to fight off threats to its existence. This logic is analogous to the resource which exists within the human body and provides resistance to disease and the maintenance of health. Once the body experiences some injury or disease, antibodies are immediately drawn to the point of injury, and the healing process begins. Dr. Frederick Green, of Children's Hospital in Washington, D.C., draws this analogy between the natural resources of the community and the flow of blood within the body. Once a blood vessel is blocked, the body automatically establishes a corollary path around the point of blockage, enabling the blood to flow, and the natural healing process begins. Neighborhoods and communities also contain similar self-healing agents—antibodies that serve to heal deficiencies and injuries to the neighborhood. For example, during the riots of the mid-1960s in Baltimore, Maryland and Memphis, Tennessee, for three or four days the police and the community escalated the violence on both sides. However, peace and calm were restored within three hours once some community leaders surfaced and asked the police and the national guard to withdraw to enable them to counsel their peers against the implications of continued violence. Calm was restored and order prevailed.

The ''punishment lobby'' must not be allowed to prevail, since black children are its prime targets. Our lives and those of our children are at stake. The American public needs effective solutions to the question of how best to make our streets safe again. None of us can afford to allow our personal security to become the object of an ideological or rhetorical debate of the liberal vs. conservative approach, nor can we place our faith solely in the assumed competence of academia.

We cannot look to any large institution, in or out of government, to design for us a formula for survival. Such institutional resources, where they exist, must be brought down to join hands with people in the neighborhoods in an atmosphere of parity. There is much that can be learned from those who are directly experiencing the crime problem. Just as the body marshals its antibodies to confront its own disease, the neighborhoods possess their own resources for life.

NOTES

1. The legislative bodies in the states of New York and Illinois recently lowered the jurisdictional age limits to age 14.

2. Berger, Peter L. and Neuhaus, Richard John, *To Empower People*, American Enterprise Institute for Public Policy Research, 1977, p. 3.

3. Woodson, Robert L., ''A Report on the Office of Juvenile Justice Delinquency Prevention,'' prepared for the Subcommittee on Crime, United States House of Representatives, November 1978.

4. Zimmering, Franklin E., *Confronting Youth Crime*, Twentieth Century Fund, task force report on Sentencing Policy Toward Young Offenders, Holms and Meer, 1978, p. 4.

5. Zimmering, Franklin E., ''Dealing with Youth Crime, National Needs and Priorities,'' Office of Juvenile Justice (LEAA), 1975, p. 21.

6. Wolfgang, Dr. Marvin E., University of Pennsylvania, ''Youth and Violence,'' HEW, 1970, p. 42.

7. Ibid.

8. Reasons, C.E. and Kaplan, R.L., *Some Functions of Prisons, Crime and Delinquency*, October 1975, p. 370.

9. Milne, David, *Philadelphia Inquirer*, July 5, 1973.

10. Testimony before the New York state assembly's Committee on Child Care, January 16, 1978.

11. Office of Juvenile Justice and Delinquency Prevention, Law Enforcement Assistance Administration, proceedings at a national symposium, September 19 and 20, 1977, Minnesota.

12. Sudakass, Niora, ''An Exposition on the Value Premises Underlying Black Family Studies,'' *Journal of the National Medical Association*, May 1975, pp. 235-239.

30

PROSTITUTION AS A LEGAL ACTIVITY
The West German Experience

Barbara Yondorf

This paper examines the West German experience with legal prostitution, exploring in detail three questions of particular interest to American policy analysts and public decision makers: (1) How does legal prostitution affect associated social concerns? (2) What are the advantages and drawbacks of alternative ways of zoning prostitution? (3) Are civil sanctions as effective as criminal ones in the regulation of legal prostitution? The author concludes that, if the West German experience can be taken as a guide, the United States should seriously consider legalizing prostitution.

Legalized prostitution is becoming an increasingly serious possibility in the United States. Currently, prostitution is a criminal misdemeanor in every state except Nevada, where it is restricted to legal houses of prostitution in nonurban areas.[1] The rationale for and desirability of laws against prostitution have been brought into question as a consequence of both legal developments and social trends. Laws regulating sexual behavior have been relaxed, including some on fornication, homosexuality, and topless dancing. Many states have decriminalized such so-called victimless crimes as public drunkenness, gambling, vagrancy, and loitering. Throughout the

This paper is based on research carried out while I was a guest of state of the government of West Germany. I would like to extend special thanks to my translators and to Wilma Bradley of the West German consulate in Seattle for their assistance in my research.

1. For an excellent examination of the legal regulation of prostitution in Nevada see Richard E. Symanski, "Prostitution in Nevada," *Annals of the Association of American Geographers* 64 (September 1974): 357–77.

country, the incidence of legal challenges to prostitution laws has increased significantly.[2] At the same time, premarital sex has become increasingly acceptable and the feminist movement has spawned concern over a woman's right to control her own body. Finally, in the face of the rising incidence of violent crimes, the most efficient allocation of scarce police resources has become a central public policy issue.

While these developments suggest that laws banning prostitution may be outdated, moves to decriminalize prostitution in the United States have been stymied over the problem of identifying a satisfactory policy alternative. The public is unclear, and policy analysts disagree, about the expected outcomes and desirability of different legal prostitution policies. Should prostitution be zoned, taxed, or licensed? Should streetwalking be allowed? If prostitution is legalized, will there be an increase in crimes associated with prostitution (such as robbery, drug abuse, or assault)? Will the venereal disease rate increase? If houses of prostitution are allowed, will organized crime move in? Should pimping be allowed?

For the most part, discussions about whether and how to legalize prostitution in the United States have not taken account of the experiences of other countries. Since the American policy of prohibiting prostitution is the exception rather than the rule worldwide, to ignore the foreign experience seems a significant oversight. Some Western, industrialized nations where prostitution is legal are Australia, Denmark, England, Holland, Italy, Mexico, Norway, Sweden, and West Germany.

Policy analysts tend to be understandably wary of using foreign experiences as the basis for the formulation of domestic policies. With respect to prostitution, however, such an approach seems not only valid but indeed essential. On the issue of validity, there is little question that important lessons can be drawn, for instance, from attempts in other countries to zone, license, tax, certify, or allow only certain kinds of prostitution. On the question of essentialness, lack of experience with legal prostitution in contemporary, urban America has forced policy analysts to place heavy reliance on economic,

2. See Daniel E. Wade, "Prostitution and the Law: Emerging Attacks on a 'Women's Crime,'" *UMKC Law Review* 43, no. 3 (1975): 413–28. See also Marilyn G. Haft, "Hustling for Rights," *The Civil Liberties Review* 1 (Winter/Spring 1974): 3–26.

sociological, or psychological theory for predictions about the consequences of legalizing prostitution in the United States.[3] Needless
to say, both the theories and the predictions have been hotly debated. Analysts need to look at the foreign experience for additional
information.

This paper examines the West German experience with legal
prostitution.[4] I have chosen West Germany for in-depth examination for two reasons. The first is that, as a result of certain distinctive characteristics of West German policy toward prostitution,
several questions of particular interest to American policy analysts
may be explored.

- How does the legalization of prostitution affect associated social concerns (such as the public nuisance aspect of prostitution, the size of the prostitute population, or the prevalence of
  the pimp)?
- What are the advantages and drawbacks of alternative ways of
  zoning prostitution?
- Are civil sanctions as effective as criminal ones in the regulation
  of legal prostitution?

The second reason is that, like the United States, West Germany is
a modern, Western, industrialized nation with a federal system of
government. This reinforces the relevance of the West German experience to the United States.

Material for this paper comes primarily from personal observations and interviews in the Federal Republic of Germany, undertaken in the course of research for my dissertation analyzing Amer-

3. See Edward M. Davis, "Victimless Crimes—The Case For Continued
Enforcement," *Journal of Political Science and Administration* 1 (March
1973): 11–20. See also G. Thomas Gitchoff et al., "Victimless Crimes: The
Case Against Continued Enforcement," *Journal of Political Science and
Administration* 1 (1973): 401–08.

4. For a review of legal prostitution in other countries see Jacqueline
Boles and Charlotte Tatro, "Legal and Extra-Legal Methods of Controlling
Female Prostitution: A Cross Cultural Comparison," *International Journal
of Comparative and Applied Criminal Justice* 2 (Spring 1978): 71–85. See
also Gilbert Geiss, *Not the Law's Business?* Crime and Delinquency Issues
Monograph Series (Rockville, Md.: U.S. Department of Health, Education,
and Welfare, National Institutes of Health, 1972), pp. 173–221; and Elizabeth and James Vorenburg, "The Biggest Pimp of All," *Atlantic Monthly*,
January 1977, pp. 27–38.

ican policy toward prostitution. During December 1976, I conducted in-depth interviews about West German prostitution in Munich, Bonn, West Berlin, and Hamburg with police chiefs and officers, health authorities, representatives of the Federal Ministry of Justice, criminologists, social workers, prostitutes, tax authorities, women's prison personnel, and several members of the West German parliament.

HISTORY AND THE LAW

Prostitution has always been legal in West Germany.[5] Until 1974 those who broke the laws regulating legal prostitution were subject to criminal sanctions. In 1974 many of the legal codes of West Germany were revised and updated, including several laws on prostitution. As a result, minor infractions of laws and regulations on prostitution are now treated as civil or administrative offenses rather than as criminal ones. (I examine the effectiveness of this new policy later.)

Current West German federal law says the following about prostitution and related activities:

- Prostitution may *not* be banned in towns of over 20,000 inhabitants. Each city may, however, regulate the practice of prostitution by local ordinance.
- Pimping and procuring are illegal.
- Prostitution is not allowed in schools, churches, cemeteries, or houses where people are under eighteen years of age.
- Prostitutes must be eighteen years of age or older and must be citizens of West Germany.
- Boys between the ages of fourteen and eighteen may purchase the services of a prostitute only with parental permission.
- Each of the eleven *lande,* or states, that comprise the Federal Republic of West Germany is responsible for public health control, including venereal disease (VD) control. The West German health department interpreted this to mean that the states are responsible for doing regular VD checks on prostitutes.
- Income from prostitution is subject to taxation. Unlike other

5. For an early history of prostitution in Germany see Richard J. Evans, "Prostitution, State and Society in Imperial Germany," *Past and Present* 70 (February 1976): 106–29.

employed, tax-paying West German citizens, however, prostitutes are not eligible either for unemployment compensation or for social security benefits, nor are they covered by the country's national health insurance program.

Neither prostitutes nor prostitution establishments are specially licensed, registered, or certified as such in West Germany. The only monitoring of prostitution that does occur is that done by local health authorities. Prostitutes are required to register with the local health department and must be checked for VD at regular intervals, as prescribed by local law. In some cities prostitutes are required to get a VD check twice a week, in others once a week, or every two weeks. All prostitutes must carry special health cards that indicate their last visit to a doctor. Police, social workers, and health officers may, at any time, ask to see a prostitute's health card. The cost of diagnosing prostitutes for VD is covered by the government.

As noted earlier, federal law in West Germany allows each city to regulate the practice of prostitution by local ordinance. Some cities have a multiple-zone prostitution policy. In Munich, for instance, streetwalking is restricted to nine designated areas of the city. In two of these areas, streetwalkers may ply their trade at any time of the day. In the other seven, prostitutes are allowed on the streets only between 8 P.M. and 6 A.M. Prostitutes who solicit and negotiate off the street may practice at any time of day in any part of Munich, except in the city center (a two-square-block area) and the cemetery, where all types of prostitution are forbidden.

Other cities have adopted a no-zone prostitution policy. In West Berlin, for example, prostitutes may practice their trade in any part of the city. Still other cities follow a single-zone policy of strictly limiting all types of prostitution to one area. In Hamburg this is the famous St. Pauli district, an adult entertainment zone that measures about half a square kilometer. Among other entertainments, it has sex shows, bars, striptease joints, bordellos, and houses of prostitution.

PROSTITUTION IN GERMANY TODAY

Prostitutes in West Germany range in age from fourteen to sixty, though the average prostitute is about twenty-four. Prostitutes come from all social classes; some are married. While there is little male prostitution in West Germany, any and all forms of female prostitution may be found. There is also some transvestite prostitution. Most women have pimps.

The majority of houses of prostitution are small houses of seven to twenty women. Prostitutes usually rent rooms in these houses for between $28 and $40 a day. This arrangement is advantageous to both the owner and the prostitute. The owner avoids all the paperwork associated with having "employees" and makes money on rent and selling drinks. The prostitute can negotiate separate fees with each of her customers and need not worry about being thrown out of a house, as long as she pays her rent. Many West German prostitutes work eight-hour days. When business is slow, a prostitute may accept as little as $12 for straight sex; $24, however, seems to be the typical base price (or was as of December 1976).

In every West German city some prostitutes are properly registered with the local health authorities and some are not. Table 1

TABLE 1. SIZE OF REGISTERED PROSTITUTE POPULATION IN SELECTED WEST GERMAN CITIES

City	Population (in millions)	Number Registered Prostitutes
West Berlin[a]	2.0	3000
Hamburg[a]	1.8	2400
Munich[a]	1.3	800
Cologne[b]	0.866	1150
Dusseldorf[b]	0.680	300
Frankfurt[b]	0.660	1250

[a] Estimates by local police authorities interviewed between 6 and 17 December 1976.

[b] Josef Scharbert, "Kommunale dirnenwohnheime—lösung des dirnenproblems?" [Local residential homes for prostitutes—answer to prostitute problems?] *Kriminalistik* 28, no. 8 (1974): 338.

shows, for West Germany's largest cities, the numbers of registered prostitutes. No one is sure just how many unregistered prostitutes there are. The Hamburg police estimate about 2500 unregistered prostitutes in Hamburg. In Munich the police put the number at about 300. Unregistered prostitutes are believed to include primarily runaways, those wanted by the police, and those who don't want to be known as prostitutes.

From the American perspective, several issues related to legalized prostitution are of particular concern. These include the effect of legalized prostitution on—

- the incidence of associated crime;
- public expenditures and revenues associated with prostitution;
- the size of the prostitute population;
- the incidence of venereal disease;
- the prevalence of the pimp;
- the public nuisance aspect of prostitution;
- the prevalence of juvenile prostitution.

I examine each of these briefly below. I do not examine the relationship between legalized prostitution and drugs and between legalized prostitution and organized crime—two major areas of concern in the United States—as neither drug use nor organized crime is a significant problem in West Germany.[6]

Associated Crime

Much concern has been expressed in this country about crime associated with prostitution. According to West German police, legal prostitution is not a significant source of police problems.

To the extent that prostitutes are involved in criminal activities, the crimes are minor ones. In Hamburg the crime most commonly committed by prostitutes is cheating a customer; second-most common are stealing and robbery (stealing with threat of violence). In Munich, the police estimate that of the crimes associated with prostitution and committed either by the prostitute or the pimp, 90 percent are committed by pimps and 10 percent are committed by prostitutes. The West Berlin police report that only a "minor number" of prostitutes are involved in crime and note that in their experience prostitutes do not want to become involved in crime, as it would hurt their business.

This observation contrasts sharply with the American prostitu-

6. Frankfurt apparently does have a problem with drug use and prostitution. I did not have an opportunity to investigate prostitution in Frankfurt, however.

tion scene. In the United States, especially among streetwalkers and bar girls, petty larceny is a significant source of income for many prostitutes. This is not surprising, since in the illegal American market there is a strong disincentive for the client to report the theft and almost an incentive for the prostitute to steal, as the sentence for petty larceny is often lighter than the sentence for prostitution.

It is not clear to what extent the presence of prostitution creates a climate conducive to crime by those not involved in the business —drug dealers, robbers, or muggers. While the West German police do not believe this to be a major problem, no studies compare the incidence of crime in prostitute and nonprostitute areas of a West German city. The consensus, however, seems to be that because prostitutes and their customers often carry large sums of cash, they tend to attract those interested in selling illegal goods, stealing, or robbing. As in the United States, streetwalkers and their customers are most likely to be victims of crimes; call girls and their customers, the least likely.

Recognizing this problem, the West Germans have taken several steps to combat it. The Munich police have recently decentralized prostitution into a number of smaller zones, away from gambling establishments. They believe that by not allowing a concentration of prostitution traffic in any single area they have reduced the incidence of crimes associated with prostitution. In Hamburg, a force of 120 police officers patrols the adult entertainment zone where prostitution is allowed. The area is well-lit, and women working in the houses appear to have a good relation with the police, often volunteering information about crimes by others. In almost all the houses in West Germany, there are silent alarms in each room, which the prostitute may activate if she is assaulted or threatened.

Few cities in West Germany keep statistics on crimes associated with prostitution. There is, however, the following data from West Berlin for the eight-month period between 1 October 1974 and 15 July 1975:

Procurement of minors	9
Procurement of prostitutes generally	127
White slave trade	8
Pimping	85

Perjury by a prostitute regarding
her complaints against a pimp or
another   5

The West Berlin police do not have data on robberies by or of prostitutes. Statistics on crime by occupation are not collected by the government.

Josef Scharbert, in an article on prostitution in Munich, reports that, between 1962 and 1972, 20 prostitutes were victims of violent deaths; and between January and December 1973, 30 Munich prostitutes were victims of armed robbery and 801 were victims of theft.[7]

In summary, prostitution-related crime does not seem to be a serious problem in West Germany. The crimes associated with prostitution are largely minor ones, perpetrated primarily against the client and the prostitute by pimps. Unlike the United States, West German police are as concerned with the protection of the prostitute as they are with her clients and the public generally.

Public Expenditures and Revenues

Clearly, compared with the United States, West Germany realizes great savings from not arresting, prosecuting, trying, or incarcerating prostitutes. The public coffers are also somewhat swelled by the taxes collected from the bars, houses, and other establishments that have income from prostitution. One Munich house of about 100 women pays approximately $400,000 per year in taxes.

The increased revenues from treating prostitution as a legal, taxable source of income include almost no revenues from individual income taxes on the earnings of prostitutes; although prostitutes are supposed to pay taxes, almost none do. West German tax authorities note several difficulties in collecting taxes from prostitutes: no one knows for sure how much money any given prostitute actually makes; prostitutes move around a great deal, so that it is difficult for local tax authorities to keep track of them; legitimate business deductions for prostitutes are hard to define; tax authorities are not sure whether they should be taxing the prostitute or the pimp. There

7. Josef Scharbert, "Kommunale dirnenwohnheime—lösung des dirnenproblems?" [Local residential homes for prostitutes—answer to prostitute problems?] *Kriminalistik* 28, no. 8 (1974): 339.

is also the problem that, while they are supposed to pay income tax, prostitutes are not eligible for some of the major benefits of being taxpaying West German citizens. They do not receive social security benefits or unemployment compensation, nor are they covered by national health insurance.

While legalization of prostitution would mean some major expenditure savings and some increased tax revenues, it would also entail some new costs. In West Germany the government covers the costs of diagnosing VD among prostitutes and making sure that prostitutes get their regular VD checks. The health clinic in Hamburg responsible for monitoring prostitution is staffed by two doctors, four nurses, four administrators, two social workers, and one lab technician. Police resources are also needed to protect, monitor, and control the prostitution business. In Hamburg's St. Pauli district, 120 people staff the local police station.

Prostitute Population

Since we do not know the current number of prostitutes in the United States, it is impossible to predict what kind of percentage increase or decrease in prostitution might occur if it were legalized. The German experience, however, suggests a possible *upper* bound on the amount of prostitution to be expected if prostitution is legalized. Hamburg is the best indicator of this upper bound.

Hamburg is a port city of 1.8 million through which hundreds of thousands of foreign sailors pass each year. It is world famous for its St. Pauli adult entertainment district, which, in its busiest season, has more than 40,000 visitors each night. In this city where one would expect the greatest demand for prostitutes in West Germany, police and health authorities estimate that there are between 5,000 and 7,000 prostitutes. While we do not know how many prostitutes there are in any American city today, we do know that in 1975 Chicago made 6,923 arrests for female prostitution; New York City, 2,339; and Los Angeles, 2,335.[8]

Incidence of Venereal Disease

There has been a continuing debate in the United States as to the expected effect on the VD rate of legalizing prostitution. Some ar-

8. These statistics were made available by Paul A. Zolbe, Chief Uniform Crime Reports, FBI, Department of Justice, November 1976.

gue that if prostitution is legalized, prostitution-related VD will be reduced; others argue exactly the opposite. The West German health authorities I interviewed were in unanimous agreement that the only way to handle the VD problem is to legalize prostitution, require prostitutes to get regular health checks, and have the government pay for those checks.

Statistics on venereal disease in Hamburg indicate that, among the 2,300 prostitutes the Hamburg health clinic saw monthly in 1976, thirty to forty cases of gonorrhea and from one to five cases of syphilis were diagnosed each month. Whenever a prostitute tests positive for VD in Germany, she is referred to a private doctor for treatment and her health card is confiscated by the health authorities until she is treated.

German health authorities place great stress on the need for VD control among prostitutes, especially since VD is asymptomatic in so many women. The head of the Munich clinic recommended that the state pay for the treatment of VD among prostitutes. A Hamburg public health physician seconded this, saying that when health care for prostitutes is not covered by the state, the women are much less likely to get treatment, especially if their pimps are unwilling to give them the money required to get care.

Prevalence of the Pimp

All the available evidence suggests that pimps are as prevalent under West Germany's system of legal prostitution as they are in the illegal American prostitution market. In my interviews, West German estimates of the number of prostitutes having pimps ranged from 80 to 95 percent. In a small but rather significant number of cases, these so-called pimps are lovers, friends, or even husbands who "manage the affairs" of their girlfriends or wives. Usually pimp and prostitute are from the same social class. Pimps in West Germany, unlike those in the United States, rarely have "stables" of women working for them. While pimping is a felony under German law, as it is in the United States, convicting a pimp is difficult unless a prostitute is willing to register a strong complaint against him.

Why most prostitutes have pimps even though prostitution is legal, and what exactly the pimp's role is in West Germany, is not clear. West German officials familiar with prostitution offered various explanations. A University of Cologne criminologist argued that it is primarily lower-class prostitutes who have pimps, as a result of their "personality structure" and need for security. The head of the Munich police felt that prostitutes have pimps largely of their own accord, rather than as a result of external pressures; while a West Berlin social worker maintained that prostitutes need pimps for protection. In Hamburg, the physician-director of a VD clinic for prostitutes saw four reasons why most prostitutes have pimps: for protection; because the pimps threaten them; to represent their interests in quarrels with other prostitutes and in disputes with business establishments; or because they love as well as hate them. And a Hamburg police official offered this opinion: If you want to get rid of the pimp, you must change the nature of prostitutes; the prostitute is both exploited by the pimp and depends on him for support.

The West German experience, then, does not resolve the issue of whether the primary function of the pimp is as a protector and business manager to "be available when "things happen,' " as Winnick and Kinsie suggest; is a "psychosexual" role as "lover and recipient of the prostitute's money," as Benjamin and Masters suggest; or is an exploitative-oppressive role.[9] It may be that if prostitutes were to receive greater police and social insurance protection from the state, fewer of them would have pimps. All we know for certain is that, although prostitution is legal in West Germany, prostitutes there continue to have pimps.

Public Nuisance

People in the United States frequently express concern about prostitution as a public nuisance: prostitutes do unwanted soliciting, are noisy, litter, or interfere with other businesses. This is not a significant problem in West Germany—in part because prostitutes' times and places of business are usually regulated; in part because, *whether zoned or unzoned,* street prostitution tends to be limited to adult entertainment areas. Prostitutes look for customers where many are likely to be found—namely, around bars, sex shows, and adult bookstores. Furthermore, to control possible public nuisance aspects of prostitution, the West Germans use such mechanisms as regulations on advertising, laws against disturbing the peace, and

9. Charles Winnick and Paul Kinsie, *The Lively Commerce* (Chicago: Quadrangle Books, 1971), p. 109; Harry Benjamin and R.E.L. Masters, *Prostitution and Morality* (New York: Julian Press, 1964), p. 215.

the restriction of street prostitution to after shop hours, instead of making prostitution altogether illegal.

I should note that prostitution in the larger West German cities appears just about the way it does today in most major American cities, with the exception of New York. That is, prostitution in West Germany is less obtrusive, less offensive than it is in New York City. This is largely because most soliciting and prostitution in West Germany takes place off the streets rather than on them; prostitutes need not parade themselves in order to advertise their services.

Juvenile Prostitution

West Germany appears to have the same problems with juvenile prostitution as does the United States. How prevalent juvenile prostitution is in West Germany is unknown. Health clinic social workers report that many juvenile prostitutes are runaways. Most young prostitutes either work the streets or have pimps who seek out customers for them. To avoid trouble with police and health authorities, prostitution establishments try to avoid hiring under-age girls.

Social workers and health clinic staffs interviewed in the course of this study noted the difficult position they are in when dealing with juvenile prostitutes. On the one hand, they feel obligated to report juvenile prostitutes to the proper authorities (in some cities this is the police, in others it is another social agency). On the other hand, they are concerned that juvenile prostitutes not avoid the counseling and health care that the social workers and clinic staffs can provide them, out of fear of being reported to the authorities and sent back home. Clinic staffs in Munich and West Berlin reported that they try to give juvenile prostitutes health and birth control counseling and often work with these girls to find them other types of employment.

ZONING PROSTITUTION

Local regulation of pornography in the United States has, in recent years, highlighted the problem of whether and how to zone adult entertainments. The possibility of legalizing prostitution raises this same issue. The West Germans have tried three different approaches to prostitution zoning: multiple zones, no zoning, and a single zone.

Multiple Zones

Munich offers a good example of a city with a multiple-zone policy. There prostitution is allowed in nine different areas of the city, not including the city center. Most of the zones are one- or two-block stretches. In the majority of them, street prostitution is only allowed in the evening when most other businesses in the zone are closed.

The advantage of the multiple-zone approach, as emphasized by the chief of the morals division of the Munich police, is that prostitution cannot concentrate in any one area of the city. When, in earlier years, prostitution was concentrated in a few areas nearer the center of the city, there were more problems of associated crime, more complaints about noise, and a greater tendency for gambling to be linked with prostitution. Health authorities prefer zoning such as that in Munich to the lack of prostitution zoning that characterizes West Berlin. Where prostitution is zoned, health authorities can more easily find, check, and register prostitutes than where prostitutes may be found in any part of the city.

A drawback of the multiple-zone plan one sees in Munich, and indeed the single-zone plan one sees in Hamburg, is that police time must be spent making sure that prostitutes do in fact practice in the legal zones. This is not to say prostitution outside the prescribed zones is a significant police problem. In fact, it is not. The creation of zones tends to become self-reinforcing, since customers naturally gravitate toward the areas where prostitution is publicly known to be available and legal. Nonetheless, several police officers in the cities of Hamburg and Munich spend a significant amount of their time patrolling nonprostitute areas to make sure that prostitution does not go on there.

No Zoning

West Berlin has no zoning for prostitution. Interestingly enough, this has created few problems in terms of prostitution in residential neighborhoods or of the city becoming known as a "sin center." What one finds in West Berlin is that prostitution tends to locate where there is other adult entertainment, especially along the famous *Kurfurstendam,* one of the city's major avenues. Some prostitution does exist in residential neighborhoods, though this seems to be limited to house prostitution. One very well-to-do West Berlin neighborhood has in its midst a fine old residence that is now a "house." Only a handful of women work in this house; it is extremely exclusive and has had no complaints from its neighbors.

A significant advantage of Berlin's no-zone policy is that police time is not spent making sure prostitutes are in the zone. Lack of zones also means that prostitution does not concentrate in any single area. The drawback to the Berlin arrangement is the difficulty authorities have in finding and registering prostitutes.

A Single Zone

Hamburg offers one of the most famous examples of the single-zone approach to prostitution regulation. There, as noted earlier, all adult entertainment is restricted to the St. Pauli district.

The single-zone approach has the advantage that police and health authorities know exactly where the prostitutes are; they are in the St. Pauli area. It also has the advantage of limiting what many believe to be an undesirable activity to one area of the city. In Hamburg's case this is an area clearly apart from the city's business, residential, and legitimate entertainment districts.

The single-zone approach also has some significant drawbacks. The drawbacks are similar to those seen in Boston's experience with its adult entertainment "combat zone."[10] Most notably, the creation of a single zone for adult entertainment tends to link prostitution to a number of other vice activities. (Out of concern for exactly this sort of problem, Munich created nine separate prostitution zones where gambling is not allowed.) Another disadvantage of the single zone is the increased power it gives the pimp. Because women who work as prostitutes must be in the zone, it is clear when a new prostitute comes into the area. Consequently, a pimp can rather easily identify a new prostitute.

Zoning and Organized Crime

The foregoing discussion suggests that, if the West German experience can be taken as a guide, zoning offers a viable alternative for prostitution control; what sort of zoning is "best" depends on local circumstances. Having said this, I should note that the applicability of the West German experience with prostitution zoning to

10. See "Boston Combat Zone Ops Rap Police For Breakdown in Law," *Variety Newspaper,* 8 December 1976, p. 71.

the American situation is limited in one important regard. Unlike the United States, West Germany has no serious problem with organized crime. To the extent that there is organized crime, it is involved almost exclusively in international crimes, such as drug smuggling and stolen cars. Certainly a primary concern in legalizing and zoning prostitution in the United States is that organized crime will move in and take over the business.

Although organized crime has not presented a serious threat to the regulation of prostitution in West Germany, the West Germans have taken several measures to reduce the possibility of a linkage between prostitution and organized crime. Most important, brothels are forbidden. No individual or establishment may legally collect all or any fraction of a prostitute's fees or earnings. The establishments in which prostitutes conduct their business may only charge rental fees for the use of the facility.

CRIMINAL VERSUS CIVIL SANCTIONS

The West German police and community in general feel that civil sanctions are as effective as criminal sanctions in controlling legalized prostitution and certainly cost less to use. Police report that, since the prostitution statutes were moved from the criminal to the administrative code in 1974, they have not had any more trouble controlling prostitution than they did prior to 1974. A member of the Bavarian criminal police division in Munich noted when interviewed that, now, under civil sanctions, by the time the state fines a prostitute as much as $320 for her third or fourth violation, it is no longer worth her while to violate the law.

According to several West German authorities, most prostitutes now view themselves as being engaged in a legitimate business transaction and have a vested interest in not developing criminal records. Social workers I interviewed noted the importance of the use of civil rather than criminal sanctions in their efforts to encourage prostitutes to leave the profession. The social worker's job is made easier to the extent that the women with whom they work do not have criminal records.

CONCLUSION

As I noted at the outset of this paper, the policy analyst must always be skeptical of foreign experiences. In this case, no discussion will certify that West Germany is enough like the United States for us to follow its example or, more important, since prostitution is a local problem, that Hamburg and Munich are enough like Seattle or Boston to warrant using what happened in those West German cities as a guide to policy here. At the same time, West Germany does offer a wealth of good information about a variety of approaches to handling legal prostitution. Indeed, this paper might be viewed as the front end of an issue paper by a local policy analyst who would fill in the local experience.

An analysis of the drawbacks and advantages of the alternative zoning methods used in West Germany indicates that no one zoning approach is better than the others. Munich is happy with its multiple zones, West Berliners have few complaints about their no-zone policy, and Hamburg is proud of its famous St. Pauli district. This suggests that the United States might do well to follow West Germany's example of leaving prostitution zoning to local discretion.

The West German experience also suggests that if prostitution in the United States is legalized, laws regulating its practice should be part of a civil rather than a criminal code. The former is as effective as the latter and requires fewer public resources.

Legal prostitution is an accepted policy in West Germany. It is not seen as a significant criminal, health, or social problem. West Germans are convinced that the only sensible way of handling prostitution is to legalize and regulate it. What the West German experience suggests is that legal prostitution can be no more, and might indeed be less, a problem than illegal prostitution now is in the United States.

CIVIL LIBERTIES AND EQUAL RIGHTS

The areas of civil liberties and equal rights are so organically linked with issues of urban blight, flight, and criminal sanctions that to distinguish this as a separate framework for policy is itself a statement that all is not right in the world. As egalitarian and libertarian goals have become universalized, the policy goals have become all-embracing. Policy in this area has a more clear-cut mandate than in other areas, because equity and liberty have become so forcefully defined as achievable goals. Increasingly, policy has moved on a variety of fronts: from the broader spheres of overcoming inequities in wages, housing, and education for minorities; to overcoming inequities in salary differentials between men and women, young and old; to even more refined areas of the population, such as policies for the physically disabled and decisions that life chances of rural and urban populations should be equalized. As policy moves toward maximizing egalitarian aims, new issues emerge concerning the role of social differentiation in maintaining and increasing productivity and morale. Hence, hidden in policy approaches to civil liberties and equal rights is the status of social stratification, achieved characteristics of occupation and status, and ascribed factors of race and sex. The limits of policy are confronted boldly in this area by those arguing for the limits of intervention in the natural affairs of people. In the meantime, new policies invite new interest groups, which articulate yet higher levels of sophisticated demands. Rights and liberties remain in uneasy alliance mediated by a policy apparatus seeking to be responsive to social groups while avoiding intrusion upon private liberties.

Despite the policy agencies' concerted efforts to eliminate systematic discrimination between races and sexes, differences remain. Some groups are more widely hired, promoted, and retained than others. The Hoffman-Reed article is an effort to examine how one corporation engaged systematic researchers to discover why differences persist. It would appear that high job motivation correlates with marriage in men, while a similar life decision decreases motivation for corporate achievement in women. The "XYZ" corporation showed a higher rate of voluntary self-demotion in women, who chose family demands over new locales in much high proportion to men. The Hoffman-Reed paper would indicate that policies aimed at abolishing sex discrimination must take into consideration a wide array of variables related to lifestyles and non-career choices if such policies are to prove effective. The Lawrence-Howard piece also lends credence to the dangers involved in mechanical application of policies to areas. In arguing the case for greater distribution of funding in the health area, these authors discuss the tendency of research on blacks to focus on pathology, to assume a uniform black experience, to manufacture black-white comparisons without justification, and to set agendas in an abstract way without regard to equal rights in specialized areas. In this section I have chosen to deal with specific segments rather than general themes. The case of rehabilitating the severely disabled is a good example of how equal treatment can be denied through the erosion of an economy and unequal intergovernmental cost sharing. The essay by Noble seeks to show how the European experience in treating the disabled is hampered by a generally low rate of economic growth and high unemployment. As pressures for existing positions increase, the situation of the elderly will become more difficult, and conventional instruments of public policy such as antidiscrimination legislation will prove inadequate. Efforts at a policy of sheltered work or make-work may prove too costly, and jobs programs for which there is a real market demand and which are targeted to the needs of various social segments are more complete than general policy guidelines.

31

SEX DISCRIMINATION?—THE XYZ AFFAIR

Carl Hoffmann and John Shelton Reed

GROUP differences in occupational success are a stubborn fact of American life. The legislative attack on discrimination which culminated in the federal civil rights legislation of the 1960's was intended to remove that component of these differences brought about by systematic discrimination against individuals on the grounds of race, sex, religion, and other group memberships. But it remains the case that, in many situations, members of some groups are still more often hired, retained, and promoted than others. The resulting shift of emphasis from equality of opportunity to equality of result, adumbrated in Lyndon Johnson's Howard University speech of 1965, has led to the emergence of two distinct schools of thought regarding the remaining differences between what have come to be called "protected groups" and everyone else. Nowhere has the contrast between these two views been sharper, or the debate more heated, than with regard to the occupational status of women.

On the one hand, some argue that the persisting imbalances result from continuing bias and discrimination on the part of employers, more subtle than the simple refusal to reward qualified women, to be sure; it may even be unintended. Such less-than-rational ways of doing business as seniority systems, or fixed lines of progression with no opportunity for transfer between lines, or irrelevant re-

Reprinted with permission of the authors from: THE PUBLIC INTEREST, No. 62 (Winter 1981), pp. 21-39. © 1981 by National Affairs, Inc.

quirements of education or prior experience may well put unjustifi-
able barriers to advancement in the way of groups of employees or
would-be employees, groups which may be disproportionately female. Proponents of this view argue that we cannot know to what
extent parity would result from market processes until, in fact,
parity is established. Differences in the attitudes and behaviors of
men and women are seen as reflecting women's perceptions that
the opportunity structure is closed to them. Affirmative action,
"goals," and quotas are necessary to undo the "effects of past discrimination" and start things over on an equal footing. The implicit
assumption is that, thereafter, equality of result should follow.

Another view, however, has it that even after all discrimination,
blatant and subtle, is eliminated, "imbalances" will persist as a result of the tendency of men and women to make different choices—
even when given the same range of alternatives to choose from.
Women, in other words, are likely to seek out and to remain voluntarily in different sorts of jobs than men. Those who argue this
position point to one or more of three factors (though seldom to all
three) to support their conclusion.

In the first place, although it has become impolite to say so,
there are at least some biological differences between men and
women. Such differences explain why no women play for the
Pittsburgh Steelers and none ever will (except perhaps as a place-
kicker) unless the Steelers are subjected to involuntary "guidelines."
It is at least possible that other occupations are wholly or partially
closed to women for similar reasons, although the burden of proof
should no doubt rest with someone who wants to assert that there
is a performance-related, innate difference between men and
women.[1]

A second factor sometimes adduced is that the early socialization
of men and women tends to prepare them for different sorts of occupations. This fact may be deplored, but few would deny that it
is at present and has always been a fact. For the time being, at least,
sex-role socialization includes a strong occupational component. Men
and women consequently enter the labor market with different
abilities and aspirations (although this may be changing).

Finally, some point to the effects of traditional family roles on
the job-related attitudes and behavior of husbands and wives (or
those who expect to become husbands and wives). The traditional

---

[1] It is considerably easier to demonstrate—or to assume without challenge—that
the social fact of gender is job-related than to demonstrate that the biological
fact of sex is. One thinks, for example, of washroom attendants.

division of labor in the home will handicap even highly motivated and well-trained women, while it gives their husbands the freedom—indeed, the obligation—to seek occupational success. Particularly in a home where the husband is the only breadwinner, he is expected *to win bread.* And his wife is expected to support his efforts to acquire training and advancement.

These differences are especially acute when children are present. Rearing children is a compelling social function for women, one which competes with the demands of a job. Although this role is available to men, they are less likely (whether for biological or social reasons) to accept primary resposibility for it, and are more likely to be regarded as deviant if they do. *Their* responsibility to their children is likely to be seen and felt as one of providing material well-being, a responsibility quite consistent with striving for occupational success.

Whatever the basis for this view—whether it emphasizes biology, socialization, or current family roles—its implications are quite different from those of the view that sees most imbalance as resulting from discrimination of some sort. It implies that it is unreasonable to expect occupational parity between men and women soon, if ever, and that we should strive for equal treatment of individuals rather than equal results for men and for women. In particular, goals and timetables and all the rest will be and remain unwise and, in fact, illiberal. They will not have the desired effects, even in the very long run; they will undermine the economic organization of enterprise, by rewarding ascription rather than achievement; they will force employers to disregard not only their own interests but the desires of individual employees—desires the employer did nothing to produce.

Unlike the view of quotas as requiring, at most, a temporary sacrifice of economic rationality and fairness to individuals, this view has it that the sacrifice is permanent, for all practical purposes. The law should open opportunities and expand the range of choices for individuals—not interfere with rational business practice, individual decisions, or the fundamental institutions of society.

The policy debate

Clearly, in one view, employers are responsible for existing imbalances, ought to do something about them, and *can* do something without more than temporary and limited ill effects. In the other view, the situation results from factors outside employers' control, and (remediation aside) there is little employers can do that does not involve considerable and lasting cost to them, and injustice both to them and to individual employees. Obviously, it is important to know which view is more nearly, and more often, correct.

The Equal Employment Opportunity Commission and the Office of Federal Contract Compliance Programs, the two federal agencies principally responsible for enforcing the law, have in effect assumed an answer. Their original and continuing interpretation of the law has been to require parity of results in hiring, promotion, pay, and so forth—even when no wrongful action has been demonstrated. If, for instance, the proportion of women among a company's supervisors is significanctly lower than the proportion among those from whom they are drawing, a *prima facie* case for discrimination exists, and the employer can be obliged to demonstrate either that the statistics are inaccurate or that the imbalance results from differences in other factors, such as education or prior experience. This last demonstration has sometimes been challenged successfully on the grounds that these "other factors" are not actually related to job performance.

In general, the courts have upheld the legality of this procedure and, both through approving the application of affirmative action procedures and through giving massive injunctive relief to aggrieved employees—requiring organizational and procedural changes on the part of employers—have appeared to agree with the view that parity is the "normal" outcome of a fair process. (On the other hand, the courts have recently upheld in some cases segmented labor forces, seniority systems, and the loose and amorphous standard of "business necessity"—decisions rightly seen as setbacks in the struggle for parity, if not for justice.)

Whatever the position of the federal agencies and the courts, however, it is not at all clear what measure of imbalance can reasonably be expected once all vestiges of illegal discrimination are removed. Will it be negligible, as their implementation of the law implies? Or will it be substantial, as several other lines of thought suggest?

It is difficult to answer the question empirically in even a single case, since the advocates of affirmative action are quite correct in their assertion that most companies have organizational features and practices that allow at least the *possibility* of discrimination against women. Few companies have internal labor markets with complete freedom of lateral movement: Most put employees into operative, clerical, professional, or management tracks and expect them to stay there; others have union agreements to the same effect. Even fewer companies feel obliged to inform all employees of all openings within the company. Fewer still hire on the grounds of basic skills and potential ability, without regard to formal education or previous experience. And very, very few hire only at the bottom and fill all management positions from below with people who began in clerical or operative positions.

If such a company could be found, then the contentions of the two schools could be put to the test. If men and women advance in the company at different rates, if they are found in different proportions at different levels, then it must be the case that this results from differences they bring to their employment, not from discrimination. As it happens, we have just such a company, and have conducted just such a test.

In August 1978, the XYZ Corporation,[2] a Fortune 500 company, approached Hoffmann Research Associates,[3] a North Carolina consulting firm, to conduct a study of its personnel practices. The company's motive was not altruistic: A sex discrimination suit had been filed in one of its divisions, and it stood to lose a lot of money. The division of XYZ in question was one with considerable sales and clerical responsibility. It employed roughly 6,000 persons, of whom 5,500 were in entry-level clerical positions, and 500 in supervisory and management positions, ranging from assistant supervisor to senior vice-president.

The charges of discrimination had been filed by several female clerks who pointed to the fact that, while 82 percent of the entry-level jobs were filled by women between 1971 and 1978, female clerks were only 74 percent of those promoted in 1978 and only 61 percent of those promoted in earlier years. Promotion at XYZ was always from one level to the next. Men were obviously much more likely than women to be promoted at this first level (although at higher levels in the company there was no difference in the promotion rates of men and women).

XYZ made no attempt to dispute these figures, but its management could not explain them. Discrimination was forbidden; an entire district supervisory staff had once been dismissed for such practices; XYZ's management was sure employees were treated

---

[2] The company has asked that it not be identified. Otherwise, no restrictions have been placed on our analysis or our reporting on it.

[3] Carl Hoffmann is the president of Hoffmann Research Associates. John Shelton Reed served as a consultant to HRA during the later stages of data analysis and in the writing of the report. They gratefully acknowledge the various contributions of Rachael Tayar, Hunter Hughes, and Herbert Hyman.

fairly. There were no differences in education, training, or experience that could explain the differences, and seniority was not a factor. Management insisted that only knowledge of the job, performance, and leadership played a part in promotion, but never asserted that there were differences between men and women in these respects. The president of the company had started in an entry-level job in this particular division. The management of XYZ was genuinely puzzled.

Their choice of Hoffmann Research Associates (HRA) to conduct the study may speak to their belief in their own innocence. The research firm came to the attention of XYZ because of its work for plaintiffs—in support of cases very much like the one against XYZ. The research task was to determine the reasons for the lower rate of promotion for female than for male clerks, and to study another pattern that management had noticed, that of women being less likely than men to apply for lateral transfer within the company.

Trained interviewers conducted private, personal interviews, on company time, with independent samples of 363 female clerks, 283 male clerks, and 204 supervisors (102 male and 102 female). The samples were drawn randomly and proportionately from some 20 offices in all parts of the continental United States.[4] The questions of particular interest to HRA were embedded in a lengthy "job satisfaction" questionnaire.

Promotion-seeking behavior

Somewhat to the researchers' surprise, data analysis quickly made it clear that male and female clerks at XYZ were promoted in almost exactly the same proportions as they expressed interest in promotion. On the face of it, the difference in promotion rates for men and for women did not result from practices and policies that discriminated against women, but from a pattern of behaviors and attitudes that led male clerks more often than female clerks to seek and to accept promotion.

In the year prior to the survey, twice as many men as women (28 percent compared to 14 percent) had asked to be promoted, and the company's response was, if anything, more positive toward the women who asked than toward the men (See Table I on page 27; the difference is not statistically significant). Similarly, equal pro-

---

[4] Possible sampling error of plus or minus 5 percent should be allowed for the samples of clerks, and somewhat more for the samples of supervisors. Added methodological information is available on request from author Hoffmann.

portions of men and women had been asked if they were interested in promotion, but among those asked, men were nearly twice as likely as women to have indicated that they were interested. Altogether, 39 percent of the male clerks had indicated, in one way or another, that they would like to be promoted; only 21 percent of the female clerks had done so. (In earlier years, the difference had been even greater: Among those who had been with XYZ in 1977 and before, 46 percent of the men and 19 percent of the women said they had indicated their interest between 1971 and 1977.)

These ratios predict almost perfectly the relative rates of promotion for men and for women. Thirty-five percent of the clerks who expressed interest in promotion before 1978 were male, compared to 39 percent of those who were promoted; in 1978, 29 percent of those who expressed interest in promotion, and 26 percent of those who were promoted, were men. For both periods, the differences are small, and well within expected sampling error.

It seems reasonable to suppose that promotions will be offered more often to those who have indicated their availability, or at least not indicated that they are not interested. In fact, those who reported that they had sought promotion were twice as likely as the others to report that they had actually been offered promotion at some point.

We have one other indication of the behavior patterns that led to the observed differences in promotion. Ambitious clerks might stay well-informed about opportunities for lateral transfers, some of

TABLE I. *Self-Reported Promotion-Seeking Behavior, 1978 and Before.*[1]

| | 1978 | | 1977 OR BEFORE [2] | |
	MEN	WOMEN	MEN	WOMEN
Percent who requested promotion	28%	14%	30%	11%
Of those, percent reporting positive response	55	70	51	55
Percent asked whether interested in promotion	36	34	41	33
Of those, percent who expressed interest	74	43	69	35
Percent who indicated interest either way	39	21	46	19
(N)	(283)	(363)	(218)	(226)

[1] Source: Hoffmann Research Associates survey of XYZ employees.
[2] Asked only of respondents employed before 1978.

which offer more pay, responsibility, or opportunity. At XYZ, notices of openings are posted, and employees encouraged to "bid" on those that interested them. Twenty-five percent of the male clerks, compared to 10 percent of the female clerks, indicated that they followed the posted openings closely. If actual bidding practices reflected this ratio of interest, we would expect roughly 35 percent of all bids to have been from males. In fact, between 1973 and 1978, according to company records, 36 percent of the 5,708 bids by clerks were from men.

It appears, then, that male clerks at XYZ were promoted more often than female clerks to the same extent that they more often exhibited interest in promotion and engaged in promotion-seeking behavior.

Perceptions of discrimination can, of course, vary independently of actual practices. It would not be unprecedented to find a situation where some category of workers was subjected to systematic discrimination without being aware of it. Nor, in the present case, would it be surprising to find a widespread belief that female clerks were being discriminated against, particularly given the undeniable and striking differences in promotion rates and the present litigious climate.

But, as Table II on page 29 shows, although a good many respondents of both sexes were dissatisfied with various aspects of their jobs, only a negligible proportion complained about discrimination of any sort—sex, race, religious, or age—and males were more likely than females to complain. Female clerks were less likely than males to indicate that their own individual chances for promotion were "excellent" or "good," but when asked why they had not in fact been offered promotion, they were much more likely than males to indicate that they were known to be uninterested or that they were not qualified.

These data do not in themselves establish the absence of discrimination—any more than would widespread perceptions of discrimination establish its existence. But they do reinforce the evidence in the earlier analysis of even-handed treatment.

Aspirations and motivation

If, as we believe we have demonstrated, the difference in promotion rates between male and female clerks was not due to company policy or practice, the differences in behavior which did produce it remain to be explained. The explanation appears to lie in the fact that female clerks were likely to have lower aspirations than male clerks, less likely to have had the time or to have felt they had the ability for higher-level positions, more likely to have seen their employment as a "job" rather than as a stage in a career, and more likely to have sought better working conditions rather than advancement.

TABLE II. *Ratings of XYZ Promotion Policies and Perceived Reasons For Not Being Offered Promotion, By Sex.*[1]

	MEN	WOMEN
Percent saying "good" or "excellent"—		
Transfer policy	72%	80%
Policy of promoting from within	68	70
"An individual's" promotion chances	43	42
Own promotion chances	34	29
(N)	(281)	(360)
Reasons for not being offered promotion—		
Discrimination	3%	1%
Known not to be interested	27	41
Personality, personal history	19	10
Not qualified	14	25
(N)[2]	(230)	(300)

[1] Source: Hoffmann Research Associates survey of XYZ employees.
[2] Asked only of those not offered promotion in 1978.

Table III on page 30 presents some of the evidence on aspirations. Female clerks, it appears, were more likely than male clerks to have sought a clerical job specifically. Men were more likely to report that they were ready to accept any position that was open, evidently viewing their first position as simply an entree to the company. Men were also more likely to indicate an initial interest in a marketing job, while those women who did not seek to be clerks were more often looking for positions as secretaries or service workers. Men were somewhat more likely to desire to move from their present positions, and they thought of such moves in terms of promotion, while more than half of those women who wanted a change preferred to move laterally, to a position as a clerk of some other sort.

When we asked what these clerks' ultimate ambitions were, we found that women were twice as likely as men to be content with their present positions, and those who did aspire to higher positions set their sights lower than men: Only 14 percent sought positions above the level of supervisor, compared to nearly half the men.

In short, the women's ambitions, both for immediate advancement and long-term success, were more limited than the men's. This difference was present when they were hired; it was not something the company created.

TABLE III. *Past and Present Aspirations of Male and Female Clerks.*[1]

	MEN	WOMEN
Originally sought present position	45%	66%
Would like different position	67	57
Other clerical position	10	24
Supervisor, assistant supervisor, market representative	42	22
Ultimate aspirations Present position	21	39
Supervisor, assistant supervisor	12	27
Chief supervisor, manager	25	9
Executive	21	5
Other, don't know	20	20

[1] Source: Hoffmann Research Associates survey of XYZ employees.

TABLE IV. *What Promotion to Supervisor Would Mean, Responses by Sex.*[1]

	MEN	WOMEN
Would have' to work more hours	63%	62%
Flexibility of hours would decrease	53	54
Harder to find someone to cover hours	73	70
Less access to desired shifts	47	44

[1] Source: Hoffmann Research Associates survey of XYZ employees.

Resource commitment and career

For most clerks, the first step up is promotion to assistant supervisor, a position which carries a modest increase in salary ($65.00 a month at the time of the survey), longer hours, rotating shifts, and a considerable increase in responsibility. Male and female clerks agreed (see Table IV, on this page) such a promotion would impose a number of burdens that they did not have to carry in their present positions. Unless one sees it as a step toward higher, and substantially more rewarding, positions—or unless one has few other commitments—there would seem to be little incentive to accept such a promotion if it were offered. We have seen already that men are more likely to see promotion in this light; it appears also they are likely to view other commitments as less inhibiting.

Table V on page 32 shows a number of attitudes and behaviors which bear on this question. Male clerks were willing or able to give up more, in general, to obtain promotion. They would have been more likely to accept a transfer, more likely to give up an optimal shift assignment. They were more likely to indicate that they had the time to devote to the job. While nearly half of the women said they would prefer to work only part-time, if that were possible, only 18 percent of the men shared that view; male agents were more likely to have worked substantial amounts of overtime.

For many more female than male clerks, the question of promotion was of little importance, because they did not intend to remain employed. Although the great majority of both male and female clerks planned to remain in the labor force, and had been in it without interruption, female clerks were significantly more likely than male clerks to plan to drop out, at least for a while, and more likely actually to have done so in the past. The most frequent reason given by men who had dropped out or planned to do so was to obtain additional education or training; a majority of the women indicated that their past or anticipated withdrawal from the labor force was for "family reasons."

Women, more than men, were unwilling or unable to make a number of sacrifices which, they recognized, career advancement requires. Moreover, a pattern of discontinuous employment, reflecting commitments other than to one's career, was more common among women than among men. Finally, women were substantially more likely than men to believe they lacked the ability to fill higher-level positions (see Table V). While the perceptions of female clerks—or, for that matter, those of male clerks—may be inaccurate, they can have the same effects as a real difference in abilities.

Table V also shows a composite index of motivation: Those who reported that they aspire to higher-level management, that they would give up a preferred shift schedule for promotion, and that they have the time and ability to be a chief supervisor are labelled "highly motivated." Men fell in this category twice as often as

TABLE V. *Trade-Offs Against Promotion, For Male and Female Clerks.*[1]

	MEN	WOMEN
Would prefer optimal shift assignment to promotion	33%	45%
Would not accept transfer to obtain promotion	12	28
Would prefer to have part-time job, if possible	18	44
Do not have time needed for chief supervisor's position	12	30
Expect to leave labor force for significant time before retirement	4	10
Worked less than 10 hours overtime per month last year	71	83
Voluntarily out of labor market for significant time in past	5	13
Do not have ability for chief supervisor's position	8	26
Composite index of motivation (see text)—"highly motivated"	61	31
(N, range)	(279-283)	(354-363)

[1] Source: Hoffmann Research Associates survey of XYZ employees.

women; 61 percent compared to 31 percent. This difference in motivation goes a long way toward explaining the observed difference in promotion-seeking behavior. As Table VI on page 33 shows, there was no difference between men and women with low motivation: Neither group was likely to have sought promotion. Those with high motivation were much likely to have done so—twice as likely if they were women, three times as likely if they were men.

Effects of marriage and parenthood

But why were women who were apparently motivated to seek promotion less likely than men actually to have done so?

The breakdowns by marital status which appear in Table VI suggest an answer. The differences between unmotivated men and women were relatively small, as were those between highly-motivated, *unmarried* men and women. *The largest difference between men and women in the table is that between highly-motivated married men and highly-motivated married women. Marriage appears to increase promotion-seeking among highly-motivated men and to decrease it among highly-motivated women.*

The male and female respondents were about equally likely to be married: 47 percent and 48 percent respectively. But while 21 percent of the males were married men with dependent children, only 10 percent of the women were married, with children at home.

TABLE VI. *Promotion-Seeking Behavior By Motivation, For Male and Female Clerks, Married and Unmarried.*

| | PERCENT SEEKING PROMOTION (N) | |
	MEN	WOMEN
Low motivation	16%	16%
	(114)	(249)
Unmarried	14%	20%
	(65)	(127)
Married	20%	12%
	(46)	(122)
High motivation	53%	33%
	(172)	(111)
Unmarried	47%	36%
	(88)	(61)
Married	60%	30%
	(84)	(63)

[1] Source: Hoffmann Research Associates survey of XYZ employees.

Evidently, female clerks were more likely either to have deferred child-bearing or to have dropped out of the labor force while they had dependent children. It may well be that the effects of marriage and parenthood on women would be even more pronounced than they appear to be if the sample of mothers were not self-selected to comprise those most committed to their jobs or most able to cope with conflicting demands of job and family.

For nearly all of our measures of motivation, commitment, promotion-seeking, and perceived ability to meet the demands of a new position, the effect of marriage—marriage *per se,* without the added complications of child-rearing—was to reduce the likelihood of promotion for women, on the average, and to increase that for men. Nevertheless, the company appears to have inquired about interest in promotion with an even hand: Among the unmarried, 32 percent of both male and female clerks reported that they were asked whether they were interested; among the married, who tended to be older and more experienced, 40 percent of the men and 36 percent of the women reported inquiries.

One implication of this analysis is that married male clerks were more likely than married female clerks to come from households where their job was seen as the principal career within the family. Table VII (page 34) confirms this. The demands of male clerks' jobs were usually seen as determining; female clerks had more often to compromise between the demands of their jobs, on the one hand, and those of their husbands' jobs and their own household responsibilities, on the other. These women were most often economic equals with their husbands, while their male colleagues usually had *the* economically important jobs in their families.

Thus, though practically none of the male clerks would have given up his job with XYZ if his spouse's career required a move, roughly half of the female clerks would have done so (but not all, by any means). Similarly, nearly all of the male clerks would expect their wives to follow them, if their XYZ jobs required a move; about half of the female clerks would expect their husbands to move with them. While nine out of ten male clerks said that their job was the most important in the family, female clerks were more evenly divided, and frequently volunteered that their jobs and their husband's jobs were equally important.

TABLE VII. *Indicators of Occupational Primacy Within Family, By Sex (Married Respondents Only).*[1]

	MEN	WOMEN
Would give up XYZ job if spouse's job required a move	4%	53%
Spouse would give up job if respondent's job required a move	92	55
Respondent's job more important to family than spouse's	90	34
Spouse's job more important	4	50

[1] Source: Hoffmann Research Associates survey of XYZ employees.

These impressionistic data are confirmed by a look at income figures. Female clerks, on the average, earned only slightly less than their husbands (about $400 a year) and 45 percent earned more. But 92 percent of the male clerks earned more than their wives, and the average income difference was substantial—especially, of course, for the 34 percent whose wives were not in the paid labor force at all. (Less than 1 percent of the married female clerks had husbands who were not in the paid labor force.)

Marriage means different things for male and female clerks. Most often, a married male clerk finds himself with a household primarily or even completely dependent on his present and future earnings. He usually expects that his family will adjust to the demands of his career. Those demands are in a strong position in the competition for his time and attention, and he faces no choice between his family role and his job: To a large extent, his family role *is* his job. But female clerks showed no consistent pattern of either primacy or subordination in the economic lives of their families. Their career decisions often required compromises, which need not go against their career interests, but would not necessarily favor them either.

The effects of parenthood were like those of marriage, only more so. It increased men's desire for promotion and their efforts to achieve it, and decreased both among women. The male and female clerks in our sample did not differ in their desire for additional children: 43 percent of the women and 42 percent of the men intended to have them. But the effects would be quite different: 17 percent of the women who planned to have children did not intend to remain in the labor force until retirement; only 4 percent of the men who planned to have children expressed an intention to leave, a figure virtually identical to those for male and female clerks who did not plan to have more children. Similarly, 28 percent of the female clerks who had children had been out of the labor force in the past, compared to 3 percent of the fathers in our sample. Childless female clerks, and male clerks with and without children were likely to have worked overtime and reported that they were available for any shift assignment; but mothers of children under 18 years, not surprisingly, reported less flexibility.

While parenthood, like marriage, means added responsibilities for both men and women, the responsibilities of wives and mothers conflict with their on-the-job behavior in ways that those of husbands and fathers do not. In this case, it limited women's ability to devote extra time, perhaps at unusual hours, to their jobs—an ability which these clerks recognized is required of supervisors.

Female supervisors

Many female clerks resolve the conflict between their household responsibilities and their husbands' careers, on the one hand, and their own careers, on the other, by lowering their levels of aspiration and by avoiding the added responsibilities that would accompany promotion. Another possibility, of course, would be to remain single, or childless, as had many female supervisors who sought, were offered, and accepted promotion. Although they were roughly the same age as male supervisors, only 46 percent were married, compared to 81 percent of the men, and only 9 percent had children under five years old, compared to 34 percent of the men.

Married female supervisors were much more likely than married female clerks to report that their job was the more important one in their household. Although only 22 percent of the female clerks consistently reported that their jobs were more important than their spouses', 42 percent of the female supervisors did so (compared to 78 percent and 77 percent of male clerks and supervisors, respectively). Sixty percent of the female supervisors earned more than their spouses, compared to 45 percent of the female clerks (and 92 percent and 94 percent of male clerks and supervisors, respectively). Six percent reported that their husbands are full-time homemakers, a response given by only one of 175 married female clerks.

In these respects, male clerks, in general, already "looked like" male supervisors: Nearly all of both groups came from households where their economic responsibility was, both psychologically and in fact, the principal one. Female clerks, as we have seen, were much less likely to be in that situation. Female supervisors, though, fell somewhere in between.

The pattern is repeated when we look at Table VIII on page 38. In nearly every respect, supervisors differed from clerks of the same sex in those characteristics that we have identified as important for promotion—characteristics that male clerks were more likely than female clerks to display. But notice two things about the table: In the first place, male clerks by and large thought and behaved more like supervisors than did female clerks (an implication of our earlier analysis). In the second place, and importantly, female supervisors differed relatively little from male supervisors. They displayed comparable levels of motivation, similar attitudes, and similar behaviors—and they had been rewarded for that with promotion.

Some, as we have noted, did this by avoiding marriage and parenthood, others by entering into marriages where the principal economic responsibility was theirs. In general, our data showed that the effects of marriage on the attitudes and behaviors of female supervisors were usually negligible, and as often in the direction of increasing motivation and promotion-seeking behavior as of decreasing it—a striking contrast to the situation for female clerks.

In short, those women who sought and accepted promotion at XYZ were disproportionately women who, whether willingly or through force of circumstances, had avoided the pattern of aspirations, values, and behavior which led many of their female co-workers to choose not to compete for promotion. They displayed characteristics which resembled those of male clerks and supervisors, and which set them off from many female clerks. In part, this is because many had remained unmarried, and few of the married women had small children. But even those who had married showed high levels of the promotion-related characteristics we have been examining: Marriage simply appears to have had less of an inhibiting effect on their aspirations and behaviors than on those of female clerks generally. The reason seems to be that they were more likely to have a household division of labor like that of their male co-workers, in which their occupational success played an important, even a primary, part.

Discrimination?

Did the relatively low proportion of women among those promoted reflect discrimination? Clearly the answer is no. It reflected differences in the behaviors and attitudes of male and female clerks —differences the company and its policies had no part in producing. These differences decrease as one moves up the organizational ladder, reflecting self-selection at each step: Those women who are prepared to seek and to accept responsibility are as likely to be promoted as men who do so.

Even at the supervisory level, though, some of the differences persisted, as we have seen. It should come as no surprise to learn, then, that XYZ's records show a much higher rate of voluntary self-demotion among female supervisors than among their male colleagues, and that the reasons given by women usually involve family demands or moves to a new locale required by their husbands' jobs.

If this survey had not been conducted, XYZ would almost certainly have lost the lawsuit, paid million-dollar damages, and been subjected to injunctive procedures setting up goals and timetables for the elimination of discrimination. If that had happened, it would have had unfortunate consequences for nearly everyone concerned.

In the first place, and obviously, male clerks who otherwise would have been promoted would have been passed over. Perhaps less obviously, female clerks who neither sought nor desired promotion might have faced pressure to accept it, resulting either in inadequate performance in higher-level positions or in stresses and forced changes in their family lives.

From the company's point of view, perhaps the worst feature of such an outcome would be the resulting deformation of its present structure of opportunity and rewards. XYZ Corporation has been the most successful company in its industry for years despite—or because of—the fact that it does not have a "management track." The excellence of its management depends on a screening process

TABLE VIII. *Promotion-Related Characteristics, By Sex, Among Agents and Supervisors.*[1]

| | AGENTS | | SUPERVISORS | |
	MEN	WOMEN	MEN	WOMEN
Prefer promotion to desired shift	67%	54%	88%	86%
Aspire to higher management	79	60	88	82
Summary index of motivation "high"	61	31.	75	75
Would not prefer part-time job	82	56	75	78
Household responsibilities do not restrict hours available	96	92	95	98
Worked overtime in past year	91	86	91	93
Have expressed interest in promotion	39	21	63	61
Follow postings of transfers	25	10	21	6
Would accept promotion to assistant supervisor	66	52	•	•

[1] Source: Hoffmann Research Associates survey of XYZ employees.
• Not applicable, since supervisors have already accepted a promotion.

at all levels of the organization that identifies talented people, committed to the company, and rewards them for initiative, leadership, knowledge of the job, and competitive spirit. Promoting people on the basis of group membership would be as alien to the company's way (and, management believes, as damaging to morale) as promotion on the basis of seniority or some other arbitrary standard.

If, as a result of the suit, XYZ were obliged to promote women less qualified or less committed than those employees who are now promoted, it might be necessary either to lower performance standards for all supervisors or for female supervisors separately—inviting either an overall deterioration of performances or difficulties when promoting out of the ranks of supervisors. If it maintained its present standards for supervisors, it would find either much higher rates of voluntary demotion among women (aggravating a pattern that already exists) or it would be necessary to invite another lawsuit by demoting more women involuntarily. A sorry mess all around.

Whatever happened, the consumers of XYZ's services would face higher prices to pay for the settlement, and would pay for the injunctive relief through the deterioration of service, if not through higher prices.

In short, equality of opportunity and equality of result appear to be antithetical at the XYZ Corporation. Those who argue for the latter rather than the former are eager to tamper with a complex, competitive system, and their search for simple solutions to complex problems may upset the engine of our prosperity—which relies on individual initiative and competition for rewards. In the long run, family structure, sex-role socialization, and child-rearing practices may change to accommodate women's participation as equals in the paid labor force. If so, they may attain equality of position, power, and reward in the economy. But while the family, socialization, and child-rearing may change, scarcity and competition and the need for economic growth and increased productivity will not.

We are not arguing against the application of the Civil Rights Act where discrimination truly exists. We argue here against the criteria for discrimination applied by the Equal Employment Opportunity Commission and the Office of Federal Contract Compliance Programs, the agencies charged with enforcing the act. A criterion of parity, the insistence that a category of individuals is entitled to rewards proportionate to its numbers and not to its members' performances, does not serve the common good. It is, in fact, antithetical to the social contract, implicit in the American tradition: An individual is entitled to the fruits of his labor, and group membership—whether in a hereditary nobility or a "protected group"—does not entitle him to benefits. This argument against the ideology of quotas is not new; it has been put better by others before, but it does not seem to be prevailing. It should.

What is a company's obligation to its female employees? It is obliged to offer them the same opportunities as men, and to reward them in proportion to their productivity. No more. It cannot, indeed *should* not, compensate women—or anyone else—for effort expended in the service of other commitments. The inequities (if such they are) of early socialization or of the division of labor in the American household are not the responsibility nor the business, in any sense of that word, of an employer.

If a company is so moved, however, it might reasonably seek to rationalize both its internal labor market and its relations to the external market—examining its seniority systems, lines of progression, training programs, and so forth. In these areas, employers may find that they can serve the interests of their employees from "protected groups" while serving their own as well, by expanding the range of opportunities for *individuals,* and rewarding those who seize them.

32

POLICY IMPLICATIONS OF MENTAL HEALTH RESEARCH FOR BLACK AMERICANS

Lawrence E. Gary and Cleopatra Howard

In general, research can be viewed as systematic activities directed toward solving a particular problem. However, all problems cannot be solved by means of a research approach for problem resolutions are fundamentally related to policy decisions.

Within this content, politics has a tremendous impact on the research industry, as well as selected aspects of the research process. As the political climate shifts, one can see changes in research priorities and treatment modalities.[1] Since monies are necessary to support research, including mental health research, one can imagine how competition, conflict, and power interact with each other within the framework of public policy and the research funding process.

In this paper, we plan to document the relative significance of the mental health research industry, and to examine the extent to which black scholars are involved in this important industry. In elaborating on these objectives, major consideration will be given to policy implication for assessing the impact of this industry on black communities.

FUNDING FOR MENTAL HEALTH RESEARCH

In the past seven years, there have been several comprehensive studies of the research enterprise of which mental health is a major component: the 1976 report of the President's Biomedical Research Panel; 1974 Institute of Mental Health Research Task Force Report; the 1977 National Academy of Sciences—National Research Council Report on Personnel Needs and Training for Biomedical and Behavioral Research; and the 1978 President's Commission on Mental Health which had a subpanel on mental health research.[2] In addition, there have been other reports, documents, and congressional testimonies on the nature and consequences of the research industry in American society.

Such interest in research supports the notion that science is an important value in this society. Moreover, the relatively high status of science is reflected in the amount of funds allocated for research. For example, in 1977 it was estimated that $40.8 billion was spent for research and development (R&D).[3] The federal government has played a significant role in providing financial support for R&D efforts. For fiscal year 1977, it was estimated that the federal government spent $23.5 billion for the research function. Industrial firms

---

are the recipient of 52% of the federal expenditures for R&D; universities and colleges received 11% of the funds; 11% went to other organizations; and the remaining funds of $6.1 billion or 26% were used by the federal government through its intramural research program.[4]

Although there is not a consensus of what constitutes mental health, it is estimated that between 10 to 15% of the American population needs some form of mental health services and over $17 billion is expended per year for the direct cost of providing such services.[5] Looking specifically at mental health research, one will also find a serious problem with respect to the definition of mental health research. Nonetheless, according to the best estimates, in fiscal year 1976, $317 million was allocated for mental health research funding.[6] It is interesting to note that in 1976, private foundations spent approximately $11.3 million on mental health research or 3.6% of the total funding for this effort. Moreover, the federal government was the source of funding for about 88% of mental health and behavioral science research.[7] The six leading federal agencies in support of mental health research expenditures were: (1) National Institute of Mental Health ($102 million in fiscal year 1977); (2) National Institutes of Health ($54 million in fiscal year 1976); (3) National Institute of Drug Abuses ($35 million in fiscal year 1977); (4) National Science Foundation ($18 million in fiscal year 1976); (5) Department of Defense ($14 million in fiscal year 1976); and (6) National Institute on Alcohol Abuse and Alcoholism ($11 million in fiscal year 1977)[8] (See Table 1.)

A range of other federal agencies such as Office of Human Development, Veterans Administration, Departments of Justice, Health Resources Administration, and so forth has supported mental health research. It has been difficult to develop a national mental health research policy due in part to the diversity of agencies that support research in this area. Without such a policy one can speculate that there must be massive overlaps or duplication of efforts, lack of coordination, unnecessary competition, and perhaps resistance to change on the part of the federal government. Another consequence of not having such a policy is that our research capacity on behalf of the mentally ill and disabled has been impaired. While federal support for mental health research has increased, it is rising at a slower rate than in previous years. When controlling for inflation, it is estimated that almost half of the nation's mental health research capacity has been erased by inflation in the last decade.[9] This has not been the case for other health research areas located in the National Cancer Institute and National Heart, Lung and Blood Institute.

Although mental health research receives substantial financial support from the federal government, there is a need to develop appropriate policy alternatives directed at reversing the impact of inflation on this support. Since mental health research activities are scattered throughout the federal government, there is also a need to develop a standardized format for the collection of expenditure data so that a more realistic assessment can be made as to the extent and nature of federal assistance to this important area. Both of these efforts will provide the general public including the black community with the necessary information for monitoring the ongoing research activities and for expanding the opportunities for getting financial support for relevant research projects.

TABLE 1
Global "Anatomy" of Mental Health Research Funding,
FY 1976

	AMOUNT ($ millions)		PERCENT
Health, Education, and Welfare (HEW)	$220.0		69.2%
Alcohol, Drug Abuse, and Mental Health Administration (ADAMHA)[1]	(148.2		46.6)
NIAAA	10.8	3.4	
NIDA	35.3	11.1	
NIMH	102.1	32.1	
National Institutes of Health (NIH)	(53.8		16.9)
Other HEW (Office of Human Development, Health Resources Administration, etc.)	(18.2		5.7)
National Science Foundation	18.4		5.8
Veterans Administration (VA)	9.1		2.9
Department of Defense (DOD)	13.9		4.4
Other federal departments and agencies (Agriculture, Justice, EPA, etc.)	20.0		6.3
State Governments	25.0		7.9
Private Foundations	11.3		3.6
TOTAL	$317.7		100%

1. ADAMHA figures are FY 1977.

Source: The President's Commission on Mental Health,
    Task Panel Report, vol. 4, Washington, D.C.:
    U.S. Government Printing Office, 1972, p. 1615.

NIMH RESEARCH ADMINISTRATORS

As stated earlier, the federal government has invested rather heavily in mental health research. An important question is who gets these funds? To answer this question, we will focus our analysis primarily on the National Institute of Mental Health (NIMH) since it has the largest budget supporting mental health research. In general, the major elements in the research funding process for NIMH include (1) the administrators, (2) the review committee, and (3) the principal investigators. Each of these elements will be discussed for each makes important decisions which are very much related to the politics of public policy and programming for mental health research.

Although many NIMH administrators will say that they have little influence over policy, the direction of their programs, or who gets grants, this is not the case. The administrators develop program statements, prepare forward plans, solicit proposals, provide technical assistance, recommend people for the review committees, and have personal and professional relationships with committee members, and so forth. Therefore, these administrators play a significant role in the research funding process. Who are these administrators? They represent a range of academic disciplines and specialized skills. By reviewing program procedures, it was possible to identify the top 24 NIMH administrators who had significant influence over the funding of research projects in 1976.[10] Of this number, five or 20.8 percent were females; 19 or 79.2 percent were males. We were able to identify only two minorities or 1% of the total research administrators at NIMH. Unfortunately, we were not able to get additional information, such as professional specialties, education, age, career patterns, and so forth about these administrators. However, our preliminary observations suggest that the administrative set up at NIMH is essentially a white, male-dominated club. Since 1976, there probably have been some changes; however, it is assumed that the basic assertion still holds.

REVIEW COMMITTEES

After a proposal has been submitted and assigned to a program unit, the administrator will send the proposal to members of the Initial Review Committee. According to a NIMH publication:

> Initial Review Groups are panels of the best qualified, primarily non-government consultants chosen for their expertise in a given field . . . Initial Review Groups review, evaluate, and rate research grant applications. Each committee has between 10 and 15 members.[11]

In an essay on research grants, Greenberg reached a different assessment of the peer review process. He states:

> Peer review, a process virtually unknown outside the scientific community, is the sacrosanct ritual of the grant business, involving as it does, panels of specialists, mainly from universities, to grade the applicants and their proposed research projects. Sensible on the face of it, and routinely touted as instilling a competitive spirit into research, the system, however, is frequently assailed as an invitation to backscratching and a boon to scientific conversation. Critics contend, for example, that reviewers with their own scientific regulations to protect are not likely to be sympathetic to mavericks proposing research that does not harmonize with their own scientific perceptions; peer review is to inbred . . .[12]

This is an interesting commentary on the federal research funding system. However, several recent reports on the peer-review systems at the National Institutes of Health have challenged the assumption of the "old boy" network in regards to who gets governmental grants.[13] These research reports concluded that (1) the peer-review system is relatively free of cronyism, (2) scientists generally believe the system is equitable, (3) there is no evidence of bias in favor of established investigators, and (4) there is little bias against the young scientists. As one could expect, women and minority groups scientists have questioned these conclusions primarily because these studies did not deal in any meaningful way with sexual and racial biases in the peer-review system.[14]

There is no question that the initial review committee is the key element in the funding process. Given this assertion, it is important to know the profile of persons on these committees. Gary analyzed the composition of all NIMH review committees, except the National Advisory Mental Health Council, as of July 1977.[15] According to this study, there were 310 persons on the NIMH review committees, although the number authorized was 363. With respect to disciplines, 35% were psychologists, 26% were psychiatrists, 12% were sociologists, and 27% represented other disciplines. Further analysis of these committees revealed these committees were dominated by males; that is, 71% or 220 were men and 90 or 29% were women. It is estimated that there were 32 blacks on these committees, representing 10.3% of the total. Of the blacks on the committees, 40.6% were women and 59.4% were men. With respect to disciplines, 56.3% of the blacks were either psychologists or psychiatrists. These data suggest that the NIMH review committees are dominated by white male psychologists and psychiatrists.

The regional representation on these committees was not even; for example, the East Coast and West Coast (mainly California) were overrepresented. Furthermore, members on these committees are affiliated with a range of colleges and universities. The majority of these institutions were the large state-supported universities such as Te as, Michigan, Minnesota, UCLA, and elite private institutions such as Columbia, H rvard, Duke, Yale, and Chicago. Except for Howard University, very few representatives were associated with black colleges and universities.

THE PRINCIPAL INVESTIGATOR

When looking specifically at who gets the funds, one begins to see the relationship between the composition of the review committee and who is funded. For example, in 1976 the breakdown of the disciplines of principal investigators supported by NIMH research grants shows the following: 40% were psychologists, 23% psychiatrists, 12.9% social scientists, 11% biologists, and 14% other scientists.[16] In other words, 63% of NIMH supported researchers were psychologists or psychiatrists. As one may recall, 60% of the members of the NIMH review committees in July 1977 were either psychologists or psychiatrists.

Although it is difficult to get relevant information on principal investigators such as sex, race, age, publication record, and so forth, recently NIMH was able to identify known minority principal investigators who had active research projects as of July 1977.[17] Out of a total of 1,148 active research grants, there were only 83 known minority principal investigators. Of these 83 persons, 36 received their grants or funding from the

Center for Minority Group Mental Health Programs. In other words, excluding the Minority Center, only 4% of the principal investigators who received financial support for research from NIMH were minorities. Two agencies, the Center for Studies of Crime and Delinquency and the National Center for the Prevention and Control of Rape, did not have any known minority principal investigators. These data would suggest that minority scholars do not have meaningful access to federal research funds.

Black scholars interested in research at black colleges and universities are particularly disadvantaged. Robinson analyzed 522 minority research projects funded by the federal government.[18] He found that 48% of these projects used black subjects. Out of 552 projects, 388 (70.3%) were carried out at colleges and universities, but only 18 projects (3%) involved traditionally black colleges and universities. Moreover, in fiscal year 1974, some data showed that the federal government only spent $21.328 million on R&D efforts at these schools although federal obligations to non-black institutions were $2.085 billion for the same period.[19] To relate more specially to mental health, for fiscal year 1974, the Alcohol, Drug Abuse, and Mental Health Administration, which includes NIMH, spent $80.591 million for research and development at colleges and universities, but only $719,000 went to black colleges and universities.[20] In an article, "The Significance of Research for the Survival of Black Colleges," Gary concluded that the federal government, including NIMH, has not supported research at black colleges and universities even though many of these institutions have the capabilities for developing quality research programs.[21]

MANPOWER AND TRAINING

We have clearly documented that mental health research is a major business industry with a significant financial investment on the part of the federal government and that the major disciplines of principal investigators receiving funds are psychology and psychiatry. A relevent question is how many blacks are there with terminal or professional degrees in these fields? Although it is somewhat difficult to assess black manpower in the disciplines closely associated with mental health, data are being developed which will shed some light on relevant manpower and training issues, especially at the National Institute of Mental Health.

According to a 1977 National Science Foundation report, less than 2% of all doctoral psychologists and social scientists are black.[22] Based on the 1977 American Psychological Association survey, there were 287 blacks (190 males and 97 females) with doctorates in psychology representing 1.4% of respondents, 20,443.[23] The Black Psychiatrists of America conducted a survey of black psychiatrists in the United States. It is estimated that out of about 17,000 psychiatrists in this country, 500 are black (400 males, 100 females).[24] Data on nursing and sociology are very limited. Finman et al. reported that 47 black nurses had doctorates.[25] It is estimated that there are 275 blacks with a Ph.D. in sociology. Finally, of the 95,103 social workers in 1974, it was estimated that 10,372 were black. A membership survey conducted by the National Association of Social

Workers in 1975 reported that 7.6% of the 35,630 respondents were black.[26] Apparently, black social workers have a larger proportional representation than any other black social and behavioral science group in this country.

In 1977 a comprehensive study was conducted on minorities and women who received doctorates between 1973 and 1976.[27] This study should provide additional insight into the potentials of black scholars involved in family research. The data show that during this period out of 132,673 Ph.D.s awarded, blacks received 4,245. Since the National Science Foundation's report in 1973, there has been an important increase in the number of black doctoral psychologists and social scientists, although the percentage of these degrees being awarded to blacks was less than 4% of the total. Only in the fields of social work and home economic education did blacks receive over 10% of the doctoral degrees awarded during this period, and this fact holds true when we look specifically at degrees awarded to women.

NIMH provides traineeships for doctoral students with an interest in research. Unfortunately, it is very difficult to obtain data on the number of blacks who have received such assistance. However, for a special minority research workshop, NIMH was able to gather some preliminary data on this problem for 1972-1974.[28] Of the 2,056 research traineeships in 1974, only 221 or 10.8% were given to blacks. What is worth noting is that the percentage of research traineeships going to blacks has decreased from 12.5% in 1972 to 10.9% in 1974. Data were not available for 1975-1977. Even though there is a serious shortage of black doctoral scientists, NIMH's commitment to solving this problem has not been consistent and this neglect has had negative consequences for the involvement of black scholars and students in the research industry in this country.

These data clearly suggest that blacks are underrepresented in the disciplines which receive large-scale funding for mental health research. In addition, even within these disciplines, many blacks do not follow research careers. Therefore, these data support the notion that a major policy problem facing the black community is how to get more black students interested in research careers in the major social and behavioral science disciplines. Gary has discussed this problem and suggested that more emphasis be placed on analytical courses in undergraduate programs, especially at black colleges and universities, and the establishment of research centers at some of these colleges which have graduate levels of instruction in the social and behavioral sciences.[29]

CONCLUSION

In this article, consideration was given to examining the mental health research industry, the structure of the funding process at NIMH, and the involvement of black scholars in the research funding process. Through secondary sources, we have shown that there are substantial funding resources for supporting mental health research. Unfortunately, black scholars have not received their fair share of the funds in this important area. There is a need to develop policy alternatives which would make the pathway to funding more accessible to black scholars. It will be necessary to foster policies which would change or significantly modify the structure of the research funding process. More specifically, we need an affirmative action plan at NIMH for increasing the number of top black research administrators and of black scholars on review committees. Some progress is being made in these areas, but more pressure is needed from community groups as well as scholars to assist NIMH in developing a more rational mental health policy plan.

In conclusion, we are very much aware of other significant policy issues in the mental health research area. Some of the issues are (1) the tendency of research on blacks to focus on pathology or weaknesses (victim-centered perspective) rather than on strengths; (2) the tendency of many researchers to assume a uniform black experience (not recognizing the diversity within black communities); (3) too much emphasis on comparative research paradigms where blacks are always compared to whites without a theoretical justification for such a practice; (4) the relative balance between biomedical research and social problem–oriented studies; that is, priority setting; (5) institutional racism, as projected through the generation of conflict among minority groups for limited research resources and opportunities; (6) the need for a more effective information system; (7) differential impact on changing federal policy with respect to training support on the black community; that is, the shift from pre-doctoral to post-doctoral financial support; and (8) confidentiality, privacy, and human experimentation. However, it was not possible for us to cover all the issues. In the future, black researchers must become more assertive in helping to shape policy decisions in these and other areas which have a tremendous impact on the quality of mental health care for the black community.

NOTES

1. Fieve, Ronald R., *Moodswing: The Third Revolution in Psychiatry*, New York: William Morrow & Co., 1975; Gary, Lawrence E. (ed.)., *Mental Health: A Challenge to the Black Community*, Philadelphia: Dorrance & Co., 1978; Soloman, Barbara B., *Black Empowerment: Social Work in Oppressed Countries*, New York: Columbia University Press, 1976; Yette, Samuel F., *The Choice: The Issue of Black Survival in America*, New York: Putnam, 1971.

2. National Institute of Mental Health, *Research on the Service of Mental Health: Report of the Research Task Force of the National Institute of Mental Health* (DHEW Publication No. (ADM) 75-236, Rockville, Maryland: National Institute of Mental Health, 1975; The President's Commission on Mental Health, *Report to the President, Vol. 1*, Washington, D.C.: U.S. Government Printing Office, 1978; The President's Commission on Mental Health, *Task Panel Report, Vol. 4*, Washington, D.C.: U.S. Government Printing Office, 1978.

3. National Science Foundation. *National Patterns of R&D Resources; Funds and Manpower in the U.S., 1953-1977*. Washington, D.C.: U.S. Government Printing Office, 1977.

4. National Science Foundation. *Federal Funds for Research Development and Other Scientific Activities*. Washington, D.C.: U.S. Government Printing Office, 1976, p. 7.

5. The President's Commission on Mental Health. *Task Panel Report* (Vol. I), op. cit., pp. 4, 8.

6. The President's Commission on Mental Health. *Task Panel Report* (Vol. IV), op. cit., p. 1615.

7. Ibid.

8. Ibid.

9. Ibid., p. 1594.

10. U.S. Department of Health, Education and Welfare. *National Institute of Mental Health Research Support Program and Activities* (DHEW Publication No. (ADM) 76-322. Washington, D.C.: U.S. Government Printing Office, 1976.

11. Ibid., p. 9.

12. Greenberg, Daniel S. "The Edgy, Competitive World of Research Grants" *Washington Post*, October 18, 1977, p. A18.

13. Roark, Anne C. "How Much Cronyism in Federal Peer Review?" *The Chronicle of Higher Education* Vol. XVI (February 27, 1978), p. 5.

14. Ibid., p. 5.

15. Gary, Lawrence E. "The Politics of Funding Research on Black Families: Generating New Funding and Illuminating New Concepts." A Paper presented at a Conference on Black Families sponsored by the National Urban League, Chicago, Illinois, November 2-4, 1977.

16. The President's Commission on Mental Health. *Task Panel Report*, Vol. IV, op. cit., 1635.

17. Ibid., p. 1647.

18. Robinson, T.N. "Minority Research Studies," unpublished paper, 1971.

19. Federal Interagency Committee on Education. "Federal Agencies and Black Colleges" FY 1974, *FICE Report*, Vol. 3, No. 2, July 1976, p. 8.

20. Ibid., pp. 8, 9.

21. Gary, Lawrence E. "The Significance of Research for the Survival of Black Colleges." *Journal of Black Studies*, Vol. 6 (September 1975), pp. 35-53.

22. National Science Foundation. *Women and Minorities in Science and Engineering* (NSF-77-304), Washington, D.C.: Government Printing Office, 1977.

23. William Willie S.; Ralph, James R.; and Denham, William. "Black Mental Health Work Force," in Lawrence E. Gary (ed.), *Mental Health: A Challenge to the Black Community*. Philadelphia: Dorrance & Co., 1978, pp. 294-313.

24. Ibid.

25. Finman, Byron G., Peter G.; Willen, D.L.; and Sinnett, J.D. *Development of Quantitative Indices of Institutional Change with Regard to Racial Minorities and Women in NIMH External Programs*. A report prepared for the Center for Minority Group Mental Health Programs, NIMH, Rockville, Md., 1977.

26. Williams, et al., pp. 294-313.

27. Gilford, Dorothy, and Snyder, Joan. *Women and Minority Ph.D.'s in the 1970's: A Data Book*. Washington, DC.: National Academy of Sciences, 1977.

28. Office of the Director, National Institute of Mental Health. Data taken from computer files. Information developed for a special minority research workshop, December 12, 1977.

29. Gary, "The Significance of Research for the Survival of Black Colleges," pp. 35-53.

30. Gary, Lawrence E. "A Mental Health Research Agenda for the Black Community." *The Journal of Afro-American Issues*, Vol. IV (Winter, 1976), pp. 50-60.

33

REHABILITATING THE SEVERELY DISABLED
The Foreign Experience

John H. Noble, Jr.

Abstract. This paper sets forth a model for examining the relationships between fourteen policy and politicoeconomic variables, and the social benefits and costs of rehabilitation. Based on discussions in early 1977 with scholars, ministry officials, trade unionists, and politicians in several northwestern European countries, as well as on documentation relating to the rapid growth of disability expenditures and the factors thought to influence it, some "lessons" are presented for policymakers in the United States and other countries. In general, current trends are seen as depressing the post-service earnings of individual rehabilitants, limiting the stabilizing effects of rehabilitation on labor market turnover, and increasing available time for unpaid work in the home and elsewhere. Unequal intergovernmental cost sharing in the provision of benefits and services, it is argued, seems likely to promote inefficient allocation of scarce rehabilitation resources with negative consequences for goal attainment. The high rates of inflation which prevail in the United States and in many northwestern European countries are causing the immediate costs of providing rehabilitation services to rise and simultaneously increasing the opportunity costs of spending for rehabilitation. The net effect of these cost increases is a reduction in the overall benefit/cost ratio that results from investments in rehabilitation. A number of predictions are made about how the United States will shape its disability and rehabilitation policies in the course of the next twenty years.

A West German correspondent of mine recently wrote:

Our Social Security System is in deep trouble right now. It was based on a high rate of economic growth, low unemployment, and rather strong wage increases, none of which is true for some time. Instead of the basic reforms, patch-work is being done in order to meet short-run problems arising from low revenues. Likely as not, this will be a matter of considerable political controversy before too long. The high degree of independence of the different subsystems makes it impossible to set any overall priorities, and reform consists of filling

The views expressed in this paper are solely those of the author. The paper is a revision of one presented at a seminar on current disability policy issues, sponsored by the Disability and Health Economics Research Section of Rutgers University, February 28, 1978.

the holes in one subsystem by creating new holes in another one. Political infighting enters into it, i.e., the shifting of responsibilities between the Federal Government and the State Governments. Rehabilitation activities are, alas, affected by it since responsibility for large parts of it are shifted from Old Age Insurance (which is centralized) to Health Insurance (which is decentralized) and to Unemployment Insurance (which is strongly centralized). Rehabilitation centers and spas find themselves in deep trouble. It's quite a mess and ways to solve it do not seem in sight. [1]

Except for the institutional details about where responsibility lies for administering unemployment insurance, the West German social security system scenario painfully reminds us of our own. Just recently, the U.S. Congress applied some bandaids to the ailing American social security system in order to forestall imminent bankruptcy. The pundits predict that bandaids will not do the job of a tourniquet; Congress will have to undertake major revisions by 1985 if disaster is to be averted. Even Congressman Al Ullman (D-Ore.), Chairman of the House Ways and Means Committee and chief architect of the compromise social security legislation that was passed, admits to the need for further revisions.

Discussions in early 1977 with scholars, ministry officials, trade unionists, and politicians in the Netherlands, West Germany, Sweden, Norway, Denmark, the United Kingdom, and with officials of the Commission of the European Communities, as well as documentation relating to the rapid growth of disability expenditures and the factors thought to influence it, all point to lessons which policymakers in the United States and other countries should heed. There is truth in the oft quoted advice that we must learn from each other's experience—if only to avoid the same mistakes.

Overview of conditions and policies

In early 1977, the countries of northwestern Europe were all experiencing recent rapid growth both in the number of persons receiving transfer payments because of disability and in the amount of expenditures. There was universal concern about the economic consequences of these trends. Compared to the United States, these countries place considerably more emphasis on "collective security" and permit much less of the burden of ill health, accidents, unemployment, or low income to fall on the individual citizen. As Table 1 shows, social insurance coverage against the major threats to economic security is more nearly complete than in the United States.

Automatic indexing of benefits has been adopted by these countries far in advance of the United States, thus protecting recipients of fixed

Table 1. Social Security Systems Compared, 1975

Country	Old Age, Invalidity and Death	Sickness and Maternity	Work Injury	Unemployment	Family Allowances
Denmark	Multiple universal pension, assistance, and social assistance systems	Dual universal (medical benefits) and direct provision (cash benefits) systems; maternity covered	Dual universal (medical benefits) and direct provision (cash benefits) systems; compulsory insurance with private carrier (disability pension)	Subsidized voluntary insurance system	Universal system
Federal Republic of Germany	Social insurance system; special systems for self-employed persons (compulsory or voluntary), miners, public employees, and farmers; separate systems for wage earners and salaried employees with equal benefits	Social insurance system; maternity covered	Compulsory insurance with semiprivate carrier	Compulsory insurance system	Universal system

Table 1 *(Continued)*

Country	Old Age, Invalidity and Death	Sickness and Maternity	Work Injury	Unemployment	Family Allowances
Netherlands	Social insurance system; special system for public employees	Social insurance system (separate but interlocking program of cash and medical benefits); maternity covered	Social insurance system	Dual industry and general compulsory insurance systems	Dual universal and employment related systems
Norway	Dual universal pension and social insurance systems; special systems for seamen, fishermen, foresters, railroad workers, and public employees	Social insurance system (cash and medical benefits); maternity covered	Social insurance system	Social insurance system	Universal system
United Kingdom	Dual social insurance and social assistance systems; optional coverage for self-employed and non-employed with annual income less than £ 675	Dual social insurance (cash benefits) and National Health Service system; maternity covered	Social insurance system	Compulsory insurance system	Universal system

Sweden	Dual universal pension and social insurance systems	Social insurance systems (cash and medical benefits); maternity covered	Compulsory insurance with public carrier	Dual subsidized voluntary insurance system and unemployment assistance	Universal system
United States	Social insurance, except for casual agricultural and domestic workers and for limited self-employment (<$400 annual net income); voluntary coverage for non-profit organizations, state and local governments, and some clergy Special systems for railroad workers, federal employees, and many employees of state and local governments	Social insurance systems; medical benefits for disabled and persons over 65 Cash benefits in 5 states (R.I., Calif., N.J., N.Y., and Hawaii) and in Puerto Rico; maternity covered only in N.J. and $250 lump-sum in R.I.	Compulsory or elective insurance with public or private carrier	Compulsory insurance system	Means-tested federal-state benefits program for indigent families with dependent children (AFDC)

Source: Social Security Administration, *Social Security Programs Throughout the World* (Washington, D.C.: U.S. Department of Health, Education, and Welfare, 1975).

incomes against the ravages of inflation. By the same token, indexing may contribute to the rate of inflation—although not to the extent that sudden increases in the costs of such primary resources as oil and steel do. Attempts to do away with indexing seem doomed to failure. In February, 1977, the Dutch trade unions successfully struck in protest against the refusal by employers to continue indexing wages (with which social security benefits are linked) to the cost of living. Even in West Germany where the hyperinflation of the Weimar Republic is part of national consciousness, the correspondent previously quoted wrote of the little chance that the government's proposal to abolish the gross wage escalator for pensions had of passing.[2]

The causes of rapid growth in the disability rolls are thought to lie both in the medical advances which prolong life and in the general economic conditions of advanced industrial society which, through increased automation and rationalization of the processes of production, render obsolete low skilled and physically or mentally impaired workers. Representatives of GAK, the administrative organization which processes claims for the short term sickness, long term invalidity and unemployment benefits schemes for roughly 70 percent of the Dutch labor force, cited mental illness as a major problem in all of the cash benefits schemes. The stress of competition to earn and have money, as well as the threat of job loss due to lower individual productivity or bankruptcy of the whole firm, were considered destructive of mental health. Escape into invalidity provided one solution for workers threatened with the loss of work.

One study by the Norwegian scholars, J. E. Kolberg and A. Viken,[3] and several informants concluded that regional poverty and high structural unemployment due to changing labor markets, shifting enterprises, the pressure of imports, and the immediate world economic recession were causing widespread ejection from the labor force of the less able and adaptable workers. Disability transfer payment programs were thought to provide oftentimes more secure and socially acceptable, i.e., less stigmatizing, sources of income than unemployment benefits or means-tested social assistance. Officials in Denmark, for example, recognized the disability pension as more humane than continuing unemployment benefits because it enabled pensioners to escape the onus of Employment Office "control checks," which they would have had to endure as unemployment beneficiaries, and permitted them to retire and live wherever they pleased. These officials were of the opinion that such persons under the prevailing economic conditions of Denmark had little or no chance of reemployment.

In some countries, belief in the efficacy of vocational rehabilitation and retraining measures as the means of curing the disability problem had been shaken. In fact, some informants entertained the notion that spending as much as was being spent on rehabilitation was a waste, since the economy was not able to produce jobs to match the raised expectations of clients, not to mention yielding a return on the investment. But, as emphasized by one West German contact, social conscience drives the continuing investment, and memories of how the Nazis treated the infirm and handicapped makes retrenchment unthinkable. Another West German contact recently wrote, however, that the unthinkable has become thinkable: there has been a reduction in the amount of money paid to persons undergoing rehabilitation, and rehabilitation measures cannot be applied more frequently than every two years except under very special conditions.[4]

The American economist, Robert R. Haveman,[5] documented the net social costs of providing sheltered work to an increasing segment of the working age population in the Netherlands and drew sharp reactions there. Haveman estimated that the costs of producing the unmeasured economic benefits of sheltered employment were in the order of 7,500 to 10,000 Dutch guilders (U.S. $3,000–4,000) per year, and questioned whether these costs were reasonable. One Dutch economist was so frank as to deny the validity of sheltered work as a vehicle for rehabilitation into competitive employment. This view is consistent with Beatrice Reubens' observation during a period of European full employment that "the vast majority on created jobs for the severely handicapped do not succeed in obtaining regular jobs,"[6] in spite of the assumption that competitive employment will result for many. But the Dutch continue to defend sheltered work both as a substitute for institutional care of the mentally disabled and as a superior method to the dole for assuring to everybody a minimum standard of living. This is because the Dutch consider work valuable in itself and, as such, a matter of entitlement.

The political problems of alleviating the pressures that are building on disability and related programs in the northwestern European countries are accentuated by public awareness of many inequities within the existing social security schemes. Women are seeking more equal protection. Alcoholics, drug abusers, and persons perceived as "socially maladapted" want access to benefits. What is more, they are having their way. Changes in existing policies are occurring at rapid pace. In Oslo, Norwegian officials and the media were not altogether happy with the decision handed down in early 1977 by the Social Security High Court of Appeals, which held that disability benefits must be paid to alcoholics.

The remarks of Kolberg and Viken, given in the context of strikingly different disability rates which they observed among the counties of Norway, are particularly relevant: "Centralizing tendencies in Norwegian society create problems both in the periphery and in the most intensely expanding areas. There are grounds for believing that 'the second set of diners are serving themselves' from the insurance system."[7] In the context of the holding of the Norwegian Social Security High Court of Appeals, the "second set of diners" are alcoholics. But in other instances or countries, they may be drug abusers, the socially maladapted, or women.

Among the northwestern European countries, West Germany and Denmark have selected what appear to be the most direct and perhaps robust policies for managing the short and long term problems of diminished employment opportunities for the less able. In West Germany, the quota system and fines for noncompliance serve to finance an impressive array of rehabilitation and retraining centers. General provisions for apprenticeship and retraining upgrade the "human capital" of unemployed workers while marking time until the West German economy improves. To the extent that employers receive subsidies to retain and provide training for otherwise unemployable workers, the politically sensitive rate of unemployment is held down. The Danes, in contrast, recognize the near term futility of trying to move people into nonexistent jobs in an economy experiencing very high unemployment, and so have passed legislation which lowers retirement to age fifty-five for persons less able to adapt to changing labor markets.

There are, of course, great costs and certain risks attached to such policies. Some of the jobs for which people are being trained in West Germany may be redundant when the world economy improves. Some of the people in Denmark shunted to early retirement, on the other hand, may be needed later, or may fail to adapt to their new workless existence and so increase their use of health care and social services to overcome problems unrelated to income security. While making these policy choices, the officials and politicians of West Germany and Denmark recognize the absolute necessity of economic recovery to sustain the cost burden on society of an increasingly large proportion of dependent persons in the general population.

Almost all of the northwestern European countries are having difficulty implementing financial divisions of responsibility between levels of government. The tendency for one level of government to try to palm off the problem or the cost burden onto the next appears almost universal. Diagnostic labels and eligibility criteria tend to be stretched in the direction of accessible resources.

The concept of "disability" easily lends itself to such elastic use because it refers to nothing *sui generis*. Instead, "disability" refers to the disruptive effects of pathology, impairment and functional limitations—singly or interactively—on the performance of the social roles and tasks expected of "normal" members of society. The areas of life activities usually taken into account are: self care, education, family relations, work and employment, and civic and recreational functioning. Age, sex, educational status, income, and other indicators of social status do condition, either explicitly or implicitly, judgments concerning disability. The relativity of the disability concept thus makes it exceedingly difficult for one level of government to monitor the behavior of the next. The hazard, of course, is that as government and organizations pursue cost avoidance strategies, individuals will get squeezed into "solutions" that do not fit their needs.

Intergovernmental financing arrangements can encourage disability behavior. During economic recession, one level of government may label unemployed persons "disabled" both to avoid politically embarrassing high unemployment statistics and to shift the burden of unemployment compensation or public assistance onto another level of government. This happens particularly whenever responsibility for these programs is divided or the cost sharing formula offers great enough advantage. The Haveman study[8] of the Dutch system of sheltered employment, for example, shows a striking increase in the number of program participants whose disabilities are labeled as "not elsewhere classified." The program was originally designed to serve the handicapped, but generous central government subsidy of sheltered employment may have induced municipalities to enroll unemployed persons who are not disabled in the sense of suffering significant loss of physical or mental function.

This practice of distorting the concept of disability to provide income through sheltered work to the able bodied unemployed and, simultaneously, fiscal relief to the municipalities is an example of the classic problem of "displacement" that occurs in public employment programs.[9] But, in the case of sheltered work, the effects may be even more damaging: diverting scarce rehabilitation resources and opportunities from their proper use may increase the stock of needlessly dependent persons in society. In view of these intergovernmental behaviors, it is ironic how much attention is devoted in the United States to cost containment by means of such individual utilization control measures as deductibles and coinsurance and how little thought goes into discovery of more effective means of enforcing intergovernmental contracts!

Lessons to be learned

Rehabilitation takes place within a matrix of disability policies and is, in fact, one subset of the whole. Thus, variations in the structure of the set of disability policies can influence the outcomes of rehabilitation service technologies. Some combinations of policies and politico-economic conditions may be mutually reinforcing and prove productive; other combinations may simply cancel each other out; still others may be positively harmful to individuals and society.

Policy variables as they may affect rehabilitation outcomes can be crudely classified with respect to their potential for (a) immediately affecting individual decisions to behave in certain ways and (b) exerting less direct and more subtle influences. High disability pensions relative to possible wages, for example, may be a disincentive to paid work, an incentive to increased unpaid work or homemaker services, and perhaps be neutral with respect to "activities of daily living" functioning. Until more is known about the effects of policy variable structures, statements about their proximate causality and degree of influence are necessarily speculative. Theory and fragmentary evidence, nevertheless, compel explicit consideration of how these variables may influence rehabilitation outcomes. Table 2 lists fourteen variables, to which I refer in spelling out what may be learned from the northwestern European experience. These "lessons" may be regarded as testable hypotheses derived from a variety of expert opinion, statistics, and the analyses of European scholars.

The Swiss actuary, Simon Courant,[10] has documented the relationship between benefit levels and disability claims: the higher the ratio of gross insurance benefits available from long term disability insurance to previous wages, the greater the incidence of claims. As indicated by Table 3, the ratio of actual to expected claims exceeds 100 percent when the ratio of gross insurance benefits to salary reaches 60 to 70 percent, and jumps to 137 percent when the wage replacement ratio rises above 70 percent.[11] Accordingly, restoration to paid work as the result of rehabilitation services is less likely to occur as disability pension benefits exceed 60

Table 2. Variables Influencing the Outcomes of Rehabilitation

1. Wage replacement ratio of benefits
2. Criteria for judging disability
3. Community attitudes toward work
4. Timing and sequencing of rehabilitation services
5. Extent of labor market discrimination against the disabled
6. Force of antidiscrimination policies
7. Extent of demand for labor in the economy
8. Organizational pattern for distributing benefits
9. Method or principle by which disability benefits are disbursed: social insurance versus social assistance
10. Income redistribution ideologies and policies of the society
11. Intergovernmental financing arrangements
12. Amount of labor force ejection in the economy
13. Age composition of the work force and of the general population
14. Displacement effects resulting from employment of the disabled

Table 3. Ratio of Actual to Expected Claims by the Ratio of Gross Benefits to Salary: Group Long Term Disability Insurance with Six Month Deferment Period, North America, 1966–1972 (in percent)

Ratio of Gross Benefits to Salary	Ratio of Actual to Expected Claims
Less than 50	56
50	71
50 to 60	88
60 to 70	108
More than 70	137
All	83

Source: S. Courant, "The Influence of Sex and Government on Disability Experience," Paper delivered at Meeting of the Norwegian Society of Actuaries, Oslo, 10 March 1977.

percent of wages. Indeed, the size of the pension may even enter into the definition of severe "vocational" disability for purposes of judging "rehabilitative" feasibility.

The *definition of disability* as "total work incapacity" is more stringent than one which tests incapacity only with respect to usual occupation. Countries employing an occupational definition of disability are likely to experience less success in restoring people to work than those which apply a more stringent test of work incapacity as the condition for paying benefits. The size of the wage replacement ratio, however, probably makes some difference. The definition of disability establishes the threshold for eligibility, while the wage replacement ratio creates a work incentive or disincentive. Other possible influences here are community attitudes toward work and toward income redistribution. A strong work ethic, coupled with stigmatizing or punitive practices in the administration of income transfer programs, may offset to some extent both a lower disability threshold created by the chosen definition and the attraction of high benefits relative to wages.

The *timing and sequencing* of rehabilitation services can influence outcomes. If, as in the United States under social security, rehabilitation services are paid for only after eligibility for disability benefits has been established at the end of a five month waiting period from onset of illness or impairment, the success of efforts so long delayed is endangered. Similarly, to the extent that the amount of benefit is dependent on the degree of disability and is subject to contest, as is the case in workers' compensation programs or in lawsuits for negligent harm, claimants may resist or delay rehabilitation until after settlement and thereby diminish prospects for full restoration. In contrast, the Norwegian policy requiring acceptance of rehabilitation services before award of long term disability benefits appears likely to minimize work disability, provided suitable jobs for rehabilitants exist in the economy. In point of fact, the Norwegian policy which provides more generous benefits to persons undergoing rehabilitation has not worked. Because of poor economic conditions, some Norwegians claim, the majority of those undergoing rehabilitation end up on the long term disability rolls anyway.

Labor market discrimination against the disabled exists in every country that places a premium on maximizing productivity. By definition, work disability involves decrements in the capacity to function in an existing job. In many instances, residual incapacities of various kinds continue to exist after rehabilitation. Employers who hire the handicapped often incur additional production costs to make workplace modifications to accommodate certain types of disabled persons, higher absenteeism due to sickness, and the like. The developed countries have tried a variety of approaches to overcome labor market discrimination. The efficacy and force of such antidiscrimination measures can be expected to influence the outcome of rehabilitation efforts directed to restored labor force participation. Quotas, job reservation systems, educational campaigns and special projects with industry to convince employers of the benefits to be derived from hiring the handicapped, and special legislation prohibiting discrimination have all been tried.

The United States has only recently passed legislation which makes it easier for disabled persons whose rights to job opportunities and services have been infringed to seek remedy outside of the courts. Before this, the only recourse was to bring suit—a difficult, time consuming, and expensive process. Now, under the Vocational Rehabilitation Act of 1973 the federal government is required to use the economic clout of its contract and grant authorities against employers and service agencies that discriminate against the handicapped. Accomplishing the goals of the new legislation will require vigorous implementation by the federal agencies responsible for enforcement. Only time will tell whether this approach is any more effective than the quota systems of the United Kingdom, the Netherlands and the Federal Republic of Germany or the Swedish law requiring employers to petition the responsible government agency for permission to fire a disabled person.

Of the countries with quota systems, only the Federal Republic of Germany levies a stiff fine for noncompliance. The predictable result of any quota or affirmative action system is to induce employers and current employees to conspire to apply the "disability" label to as many of the workforce as possible in the effort to preserve the *status quo*. In the

United Kingdom, it is widely held that the quota system has had no greater force than "moral suasion." There is rumor of an investigation to learn why the quota system does not work better.

Little need be said about the obvious relationship between the *demand for labor* and job opportunities for the disabled. When economies are expanding and labor markets are tight, the disabled are more employable. The vocational outcomes of rehabilitation services come more easily. But during economic recession, jobs for the handicapped become more difficult to find. Even in the Federal Republic of Germany, where the quota system is enforced by fines for noncompliance, in early 1977 there were approximately 40,000 unemployed disabled persons, 75 percent of whom had been able previously to hold a job.[12] The city-state of Hamburg met only 3.8 percent of the required 6 percent hiring quota and paid a total of DM 18 million in fines. In excess of DM 400 million had been collected for the Federal Republic of Germany as a whole.

Organizational patterns may influence the outcomes of rehabilitation services, but their effects on service delivery and ultimately, on client outcomes, are extremely difficult to document. Nevertheless, manipulation of these variables holds great fascination for policymakers and administrators. The Danes, for example, are simultaneously decentralizing and integrating the delivery of social services, vocational rehabilitation, and means-tested public assistance. Many specialized rehabilitation centers are being closed in favor of integrated service delivery to generic caseloads of clients by teams of caseworkers and consultant specialists. This radical shift in organization is rationalized, partly, by the desire to make the municipality the locus of integrated service delivery and, partly, by the belief that the family (rather than individual family members) is the proper object and unit of treatment. There is also the strong possibility that cost containment is a motive. Some believe that, to the extent that municipalities must levy taxes to pay for cash benefits and services, they will exercise greater restraint than if their role is more or less simply to make referrals and fuss over the quantity and quality of the services provided by county or central governments.

Cash and other benefits may be disbursed either according to the principle of *social insurance* (i.e., coverage of certain risks as a matter of legal entitlement on the presumption of need) or according to the principle of *social assistance* (i.e., payment only on determination of actual need by means of a test of income and/or assets). Countries vary in their policy preferences for disbursing benefits according to one or the other principle. Social assistance, in imposing a test of income and/or assets to determine eligibility, has both the virtue of assigning public expenditures efficiently to the most needy and the vice of branding recipients in the minds of many taxpayers as "free loaders at the public trough." The stigma attached to social assistance causes some persons with legitimate needs to shun it and do without, thereby contributing to its reputation as "target efficient."

Rehabilitation services that do not carry the stigma of social assistance can be expected to receive higher value in countries which tend to impose a means-test before granting cash benefits than in those which adhere to the principle of social insurance. This hypothesis, of course, must be evaluated by reference to *income redistribution ideologies and policies.* Countries which view income redistribution as a positive goal may not regard means-tested social assistance as stigmatizing, whereas countries with negative views may look askance at social assistance recipients and create pressure for them to seek escape through rehabilitation.

The availability of health care and short and long term disability transfer payments as an entitlement not subject to a means-test may catch many potentially disabling conditions early and limit their effects, while protecting against severe financial losses associated with long spells of illness or impairment. In the United States, employment linked health insurance makes the person who becomes unemployed or unable to work because of prolonged illness liable to catastrophic medical bills before means-tested relief is offered. Added financial strain may aggravate and prolong illness and even impede recovery to full productive capacity. Integration of medical rehabilitation with general health care and with short and long term disability benefit schemes, in theory, could favorably influence the outcomes of rehabilitation—especially if linked to retraining and job placement services. Again, proper timing and sequencing of rehabilitation services according to an individualized case plan would be expected to promote earlier recovery and return to work.

While all these good things may happen, unless there is strict monitoring and control of the price, quantity, and quality of health services and careful case management of rehabilitation services in conjunction with disability claims processing, escalating costs will likely result. The evidence from the Federal Republic of Germany is not encouraging. Pflanz and Geissler argue convincingly that, despite generous cash benefits and health services provisions, the West German health care system is in trouble: "A combination of market factors and social policy has contributed to an enormous increase in health costs which, to the public, does not seem to have been matched by a commensurate gain in the quality of health care."[13]

Intergovernmental financing arrangements between municipalities, counties, and the central government can provide either incentives or disincentives to rehabilitation efforts. If, for example, central government matching or cost sharing formulas for rehabilitation services are less favorable than those for income transfer programs, local or county governments may find it easier to rationalize referral of more severely disabled persons to the more permanent sources of cash benefits than to spend for rehabilitation. Again, labor market demand and income redistribution ideologies probably amplify or dampen the effects of these incentives or disincentives.

The degree of industrialization and dependence of the economy on higher technology, stability of labor force participation, and the age composition of the workforce and of the general population probably interact to influence the process of *labor force ejection* and, ultimately, the success or failure of rehabilitation efforts. Highly industrialized economies, dependent on machines and sophisticated technology, have less need for unskilled labor. Increased wages due to the improved productivity of skilled labor tend to bid up the wages of everybody. Employers, in turn, seek relief from higher labor costs by further mechanizing and/or automating the production process. This results in the loss of jobs that are suitable for the less educated and even for the skilled worker who becomes disabled. Also, as women in the industrialized countries give up the traditional homemaker role to take jobs in the paid workforce, competition for the supply of existing jobs is increased, unless the economies expand fast enough to accommodate all the newcomers. Less able workers—men and women—are ejected from the workforce in favor of younger and more recently trained and mobile workers.

The Danish economist, B. R. Anderson, explains the phenomenon of labor force ejection as follows:

> The speed of the technical development and of economic growth is now so high that the mobility of the labour force cannot bring about the changes (needed to respond to shifting labor demand) . . . . Disequilibrium is the normal state of the labour market. . . . Part of the labour force is "pushed" out of their jobs. This can be done through dismissals or through changes in working procedures which cause the "weak" persons to increase their sickness absence, or otherwise. . . . This means that a rise in the number of "pushed out" persons does not necessarily indicate a growing "weakness" (e.g., physical, mental, educational "disability") in the population. It may equally well be an indicator of a growing rate of technical or economic change in the demand-structure of the labour market.[14]

Persons ejected from the labor market in this way are increasingly labeled "disabled" with often exaggerated emphasis on the medical factors that use of the term implies. The function of this usage is really to justify payment of cash benefits for short and long term disability, or to qualify people for vocational rehabilitation and job retraining programs.

The *age composition* of the workforce and of the general population may interact to ease or aggravate the process of labor force ejection and the associated burden of transfer payments for disability. Withdrawal from the labor force is expected when retirement age is reached, but generally not before except for those who attain substantial means or suffer the misfortune of serious illness or impairment. The incidence of disability increases sharply with age. The history of the social security disability insurance program in the United States since its inception indicates that the number of awards per 1,000 insured persons climbs with advancing age and leaps when . eople reach the 45–54 age group.

Except in the Netherlands, large scale withdrawal from the labor force of men in the 50–64 age group is the rule not only in northwestern Europe but in the United States, as Table 4 makes clear. But increased labor force participation by women in the same age group, as indicated by Table 5, has more than offset the loss of male workers in every country except Norway and the Federal Republic of Germany. This is not to imply that all labor force withdrawal is the result of illness or disability or even unemployment. Other population dynamics also have played a role in reducing labor force participation among the high risk age groups. A substantial drop in the total population in the 50–64 age group occurred in the Federal Republic of Germany as the result, undoubtedly, of high military and civilian casualties during World War II. The availability of income transfer payments must in itself be a contributing factor.

The need to provide transfer payments to those who give up work and to pay for retraining of those whose attachment to the labor force is weak, coupled with reduced male labor force participation, may create a greater cost burden for the economically active portion of the population in some countries more than in others. Unless the high risk age group shrinks, as in the Federal Republic of Germany, countries that replace men with women on a one-for-one or even a two-for-one basis seem likely to run into trouble. The problem arises because the social security systems of the seven countries under discussion use the payroll tax to maintain "pay-as-you-go" benefit programs for retired and disabled workers, with the exception of Denmark which pays out of general revenues.

Men qualifying for benefits generally have longer tenure in the workforce and higher wages than women and, hence, entitlement to higher levels of benefits. It will, therefore, take the taxes on the lower wages of more women, on average, to pay for the generally higher benefits of each man who retires or leaves the workforce prematurely because of ill health or disability. No relief can be expected from the taxes of younger workers unless their number is growing due to rising birthrates and/or high enough labor force participation to offset the reduced participation of older workers. This, unfortunately, is not happening. In the countries under discussion, birthrates have been on the decline for some time; and labor

Table 4. Changes in Male Population, Ages 50–64, Their Labor Force Participation (LFP), and Resulting Increase or Decline as Ratio of Expected Value of Male Population at End of Time Period, Selected Countries and Years

Countries and Years	Total Pop. Increase/Decline A	% LFP Earlier Year B	No. Expected Workers (A × B) C	% LFP Later Year D	No. Actual Workers Later Year (A × D) E	Net Increase/ Decline (E − C)[2] F	Ratio of Net Increase/Decline to Expected Value (F/C × 100) G
Denmark (1960–1970)	37,221	93.6	34,839	86.2	32,085	(2,754)	(7.90)
Federal Republic of Germany (1961–1975)	(832,839)	86.0	(716,242)	78.5	(653,779)	62,463	(8.72)
Netherlands (1960–1971)	1,445	80.9	1,169	85.1	1,230	61	5.22
Norway (1960–1970)	39,824	93.7	37,315	86.7	34,527	(2,788)	(7.47)
United Kingdom[1] (1961–1971)	403,086	98.2	395,830	95.3	384,141	(11,689)	(2.95)
Sweden (1960–1970)	70,845	90.6	64,186	85.7	60,714	(3,472)	(5.41)
United States (1960–1970)	1,891,426	87.1	1,647,432	84.6	1,600,146	(47,286)	(2.87)

Source: International Labor Organization, Yearbook of Labor Statistics (Geneva: ILO, 1966, 1971, 1973, 1976).

Notes: 1. For the U.K., 20–64 years because of reporting shifts in the age classes of the series; because the series for the U.K. does not permit isolation of the 50–64 age group, comparisons with the other countries are not possible.

2. The net increase/decline represents the difference at the end of the time period of the observed number of workers and the number that was expected on the basis of the earlier labor force participation rate applied to the later population base.

Table 5. Changes in Female Population, Ages 50–64, Their Labor Force Participation (LFP), and Resulting Increase or Decline as Ratio of Expected Value of Female Population at End of Time Period, Selected Countries and Years

Countries and Years	Total Pop. Increase/Decline A	% LFP Earlier Year B	No. Expected Workers (A × B) C	% LFP Later Year D	No. Actual Workers Later Year (A × D) E	Net Increase/ Decline (E − C)[2] F	Ratio of Net Increase/Decline to Expected Value (F/C × 100) G
Denmark (1960–1970)	34.299	32.0	10.976	47.9	16.429	5.453	49.68
Federal Republic of Germany (1961–1975)	(350.957)	31.2	(109.499)	33.7	(118.273)	(8.774)	8.01
Netherlands (1960–1971)	114.422	13.5	15.447	17.0	19.452	4.005	25.93
Norway (1960–1970)	35.427	25.0	8.857	30.8	10.912	2.055	23.20
United Kingdom[1] (1961–1971)	96.622	41.5	40.098	51.4	49.664	9.566	23.86
Sweden (1960–1970)	60.095	30.3	18.209	39.3	23.617	5.408	29.70
United States (1960–1970)	2.665.787	39.6	1.055.652	45.7	1.218.265	162.613	15.4

Source: International Labor Organization, *Yearbook of Labor Statistics* (Geneva: ILO, 1966, 1971, 1973, 1976).

Notes: 1. For the U.K., 20–64 years because of reporting shift in the age classes of the series; because the series for the U.K. does not permit isolation of the 50–64 age group, comparisons with the other countries are not possible.

2. The net increase/decline represents the difference at the end of the time period of the observed number of workers and the number that was expected on the basis of the earlier labor force participation rate applied to the later population base.

force participation among younger men has either remained constant or decreased slightly over the periods of comparison while increasing sharply among younger women. Only if these younger women remain in the workforce and obtain wages comparable to men, can some measure of relief be expected.

Last in the list of policy variables and politico-economic conditions which may influence the outcomes of rehabilitation is the tradeoff struck between labor force ejection of the disabled and the possible *displacement* effects of their employment. In an employment market where available jobs are fewer than the number of unemployed, simply providing preferential access to jobs for some may result in their gain to the detriment of others with equal or higher skills. To the extent that the less able obtain jobs through preferential access and turn out less work than those whom they have displaced, the economy will suffer a net loss of productivity. This loss must be counted as part of the social cost of employing the disabled and be evaluated against the entire array of possible benefits to be derived from their employment, including their increased satisfaction with life and possibly greater social acceptance by others in the community.

For some disabled persons, it is possible that advantage lies in employing in their stead more able workers from whose greater productivity sufficient taxes can be extracted to pay more generous income transfers to the disabled. Again, income redistribution ideology and policies will play an important role in determining what tradeoff is politically feasible. The issue deserves very careful consideration because it means denying scarce vocational rehabilitation services to some kinds of disabled persons. Such a policy should not be adopted in haste. The conditions under which displacement effects occur are hardly understood and may be quite limited.

Implications for cost/benefit analysis

How are the fourteen policy and politico-economic variables which exert influence on the outcomes of rehabilitation (Table 2) likely to affect cost/benefit modeling of public investments? Technically speaking, what are the expected signs of the regression coefficients expressing the linear relationships between these fourteen independent variables and the several dependent variables which encompass the benefits and costs of rehabilitation?

The perspective of society will be taken in analyzing benefits and costs on the grounds that public policy decisions in theory attempt to optimize net *social* benefits. The benefits and costs of rehabilitation (Table 6), while shared by individuals and families, employers, and government,

Table 6. Benefits and Costs of Rehabilitation by Analytic Perspective

	Analytic Perspective			
Benefits and Costs	Individuals and Families	Employers/ Private Sector	Government	Society
A. Benefits Increases				
1. Earnings				X
a. Net of taxes	X			
b. Taxes			X	
2. Homemaker services	X			X
3. Unpaid work	X			X
4. Satisfaction with life	X			X
5. Earnings of family members				X
a. Net of taxes	X			
b. Taxes			X	
6. Decreased medical, nursing and custodial costs $(a + b + c = 1)$	aX	bX	cX	X
7. Lower turnover in labor markets		X		X
B. Costs				
1. Case service expenditures $(a + b + c = 1)$	aX	bX	cX	X
2. Administrative and overhead expenses $(a + b = 1)$		aX	bX	X
3. Income loss/foregone earnings during program				X
a. Net of taxes	X			
b. Taxes			X	
4. Research, training and facility costs $(a + b = 1)$		aX	bX	X

Source: J. H. Noble, Jr., "The Limits of Cost-Benefit Analysis as a Guide to Priority-Setting in Rehabilitation," *Evaluation Quarterly* 1 (August 1977): 352-353.

accrue in different proportions among them. The net social benefit, on the other hand, is the surplus of benefits over costs, taking into account the monetary values attached to the benefits and losses sustained by each person affected by the investment.[15] Economists have largely adopted the societal perspective, but have been unable to document all the possible social benefits and costs of rehabilitation due to measurement problems and data insufficiencies. Although aware of their possible existence, economists avoid evaluation of such possible direct benefits to the disabled as improved capacity for self care, increased mobility, reduced pain and suffering, and increased satisfaction with life. Also not considered are the possible beneficial effects of rehabilitation on the labor force participation of other family members and on general family functioning.

As a consequence of these measurement problems, emphasis is placed on evaluating the impact of rehabilitation investments on the gross national product, with benefits defined as the lifetime earnings that would have been lost had not rehabilitation been provided to persons who are considered "disabled." As such, rehabilitation benefits represent the expected increase over some lesser amount of pay that might otherwise have been earned. To estimate the lifetime increase in earnings attributable to rehabilitation, most cost/benefit analyses have had to rely on before and after estimates of earnings without benefit of a control group against which to compare what would have actually happened if services had been withheld or if a different set of services had been administered. The present value of aggregate benefits is derived by discounting by some rate of interest expected earnings occurring over time as a probability function of survival, employment, age, sex, race, education, type of impairment, recurring disability, and average growth in the economy due to increased productivity.[16]

Earnings before and after rehabilitation are typically combined with data and/or assumptions about the annual earnings increase due to rising productivity of the workforce, unemployment and/or recurring disability, age related mortality, and the age of retirement. All of these factors except the productivity increase of wages depress forecasts of the future earnings of rehabilitants. The assumptions affecting the magnitude of future earnings vary considerably from study to study.[17]

The discount rate chosen to reduce the expected stream of future benefits resulting from rehabilitation for comparison with the costs incurred in their production is extremely important. The discount rate represents the "opportunity costs" of investing in rehabilitation rather than in some other enterprise. The appropriate decision is to invest in a rehabilitation project if its internal rate of return is greater than the expected opportunity cost rate—the latter being equal to the economy's real rate of growth if markets are perfect and equilibrium exists.[18] In theory, different discount rates should be used to reflect the different risks of different types of investments in different kinds of people. But unfortunately, as pointed out by R. W. Conley, "there is no existing or foreseeable data source that could be used to justify differential discounting of the future benefits of investing in people on this basis."[19] The proper choice of the social discount rate is important, nonetheless, because it is believed to influence the balance of investment between the public and private sectors with attendant effects on immediate and future consumption.[20]

Cost/benefit analysis does not consider payments in the form of means-tested public assistance or entitlement based disability pensions as a "cost" in the sense of using real resources which could have been invested in some alternative type of productive enterprise. Such payments instead represent the transfer of income for consumption from one segment of society to another. Also for this reason, their reduction as the result of rehabilitation is not considered a "benefit." Nevertheless, income transfer payments as a function of the wage replacement ratio can influence the likelihood that disabled persons will return to gainful employment after receiving rehabilitation services. Accordingly, they can simultaneously reduce rehabilitation benefits and increase the costs if overly generous or, alternatively, increase benefits and lessen costs if provided in proper measure.

With all this said in introduction, once more what are the expected relationships between the fourteen independent policy and politico-economic variables postulated as having an influence on the outcomes of rehabilitation and the several measures of benefits and costs? At any aggregate level of expenditure for rehabilitation, Table 7 sets forth the direction (positive or negative) of the relationships that would be expected as the result of regressing the fourteen variables on seven measures or, strictly speaking, sources of social benefits.[21]

In most instances, there is an expected tradeoff between increased individual earnings after rehabilitation and increased homemaker services and unpaid work. Time spent in gainful employment reduces availability for unpaid work in the home and elsewhere. Thus, any variable directly increasing gainful employment of the handicapped is expected simultaneously to reduce the quantity of homemaker services and unpaid work. Decreased medical, nursing and custodial costs, on the other hand, are the expected dividend of improved capacities for self-care and other non-vocational daily living activities, all of which flow from rehabilitation services independently of job opportunities and motivation to pursue gainful employment. In contrast, the increased earnings of other family members are likely to depend not only on their job opportunities and

Table 7. Expected Relationships (Positive or Negative) Between Fourteen Postulated Policy and Politico-Economic Variables and the Social Benefits of Rehabilitation

Value of Variable	Increased Individual Earnings	Increased Homemaker Services	Increased Unpaid Work	Increased Satisfaction with Life	Increased Family Member Earnings	Decreased Medical, Nursing, and Custodial Costs	Lower Labor Market Turnover
1. High wage replacement	−	+	+		−		−
2. Lenient disability criteria	−	+	+		±		−
3. Strong work ethic	+	+	+		+		+
4. Timely services	+	+	+	+	+	+	+
5. High discrimination against disabled	−	+	+	−			−
6. Weak anti-discrimination policies	−	+	+	−			
7. Weak labor demand	−	+	+	−	−	−	−
8. Centralized disbursement of benefits	−	+	+			−	−
9. Presumptive entitlement	−	+	+				−
10. Strong income redistribution ideology	−	+	+				−
11. Unequal intergovernmental cost-sharing	−	+	+				
12. High labor force ejection	−	+	+		−	−	−
13. Aging work force	−	+	+			−	−
14. High displacement effects	−	+	+			−	−

Note: ± indicates the conditional nature of the relationship: lenient criteria and low wage replacement appear likely to increase (+) family member earnings, while lenient criteria and high wage replacement would likely reduce incentive (−) for gainful employment by both the handicapped and other family members.

motivation but also on the capacities of the disabled member for self-care
and household management. Last, it is important to note that rehabilitation services often help stabilize workers in their jobs after the onset of
disabling conditions. Accordingly, the same policies and politico-
economic conditions which positively or negatively affect individual
earnings are expected to have a similar influence on that portion of labor
market turnover susceptible to the stabilizing effects of rehabilitation.

Ten of the fourteen policy and politico-economic variables (Tables 2 and
7: 1,2,5-12) directly depress post-service earnings of individual rehabilitants, limiting the stabilizing effects of rehabilitation on labor market
turnover, and increasing available time for unpaid work in the home and
elsewhere. Of the ten variables, the wage replacement ratio, stringency of
disability criteria, level of labor demand, and the rate of labor force
ejection are thought to depress the earnings of other family members.
However, the relationship between the stringency of disability criteria
and family member earnings is conditioned by the wage replacement
ratio: lenient criteria and high wage replacement seem likely to reduce
incentive for gainful employment by other family members, while lenient
criteria and low wage replacement would likely increase the incentive.

Four of the ten—labor demand, the organizational pattern for disbursing benefits, intergovernmental cost sharing arrangements, and the rate of
labor force ejection—directly affect medical, nursing, and custodial costs.
Weak demand for labor, centralized disbursement of benefits, unequal
intergovernmental cost sharing, and high labor force ejection are thought
to depress the cost limiting effects of rehabilitation. Many argue for
decentralized disbursement of benefits and services because of the greater
knowledge and sensitivity about individual needs that are supposed to
reside at the local level of government. But at the same time, unequal
intergovernmental cost sharing in the provision of benefits and
services—especially if combined with administration by the lesser paying
partner—seems likely to promote inefficient allocation of scarce rehabilitation resources with negative consequences for goal attainment. Weak
labor demand and high rates of labor force ejection by increasing
psychological distress and psychiatric impairment among persons undergoing rehabilitation can detract from the rehabilitant's perception of the
efficacy of services and lead to increased costs by virtue of higher
utilization.[22]

Four of the ten variables—the extent of discrimination against the
disabled, strength of antidiscrimination policies, level of labor demand,
and the rate of labor force ejection—are expected to influence in obvious
directions rehabilitants' satisfaction with life. Although these variables
must impinge on the sense of security of handicapped persons, any
predictions about causality amidst the entangled set of factors that
contributes to life satisfaction should be regarded as highly speculative.

Four of the fourteen policy and politico-economic variables thought to affect the social benefits of rehabilitation present a somewhat atypical pattern of expected effects. Community attitudes taking the form of a strong work ethic and the proper timing and sequencing of rehabilitation services are both expected always to have positive effects. When the composition of the workforce shows an increasingly large segment of older workers, this is expected to depress post-service earnings of rehabilitants, simultaneously increase unpaid work in the home and elsewhere, and also increase medical, nursing, and custodial costs. Age is seen both as reducing the worker's adaptability and as requiring more frequent service expenditures to cope with recurring disability. The stabilizing effects of rehabilitation on labor market turnover amidst an aging workforce are unpredictable as retirement becomes more and more possible for older workers. Displacement of more productive workers by hiring less productive handicapped individuals, if it occurs, is likely to increase labor market turnover among both the able bodied and handicapped workforce. After initial displacement, the firm eventually may be forced to fire or, more likely, retire the handicapped worker on disability pension in order to regain lost productivity and to remain competitive.

The factors influencing the social costs of rehabilitation can be dealt with in summary fashion. First, lower productivity resulting from possible displacement effects, as mentioned earlier, must be treated as a cost and weighed with other costs in the balance against the present value of the aggregate social benefits that flow from rehabilitation. Second, the high rates of inflation which prevail in the United States and in many of the northwestern European countries boost the immediate costs of providing rehabilitation services and, through the higher interest rates that must be paid in times of inflation, increase the opportunity costs of spending for rehabilitation. Inflation increases the risks attached to making all kinds of investments, including rehabilitation. The net effect of simultaneous increases in price levels and opportunity costs during times of inflation will be a reduction in the overall benefit/cost ratio for investments in rehabilitation.[23]

Concluding remarks

Do the "lessons" from the northwestern European countries support any predictions relating to the United States and how it will shape its disability and rehabilitation policies in the course of the next twenty years? I believe so and shall make some predictions, but in terms clear enough that, unlike the Oracle of Delphi, I shall not be able to avoid history's judgment of accuracy. The period with which we are concerned, it should be noted, will be marked by a decline in size of the economically active segment of the population while persons over 62 years of age increase by 24 percent and those over 75 years grow by 50 percent.[24]

Relentless pressure from myriad provider and client constituencies will prevent successive Administrations and the Congress from developing a coherent and mutually reinforcing set of disability and rehabilitation policies, responsive to changing politico-economic conditions. In consequence, lack of concern for how the different policy subsystems influence one another and the political infighting, which my West German correspondent mentioned in the opening paragraph of the paper, will promote continued fragmentation and waste of a dwindling resource base. Governments, from the municipal level on up, will successfully pursue strategies which shift the cost burden of dependency to the next level. Increasingly, work created by government in both the public and private sectors will provide outlets for rising expectations among the severely disabled. As pressure on the limited supply of jobs grows, antidiscrimination legislation will be found wanting as an instrument of public policy. "Earmarking" of created jobs will bring the United States to a form of quota system.

Despite valiant efforts to limit the scope of what is encompassed within the meaning of "disability," the disability rolls and associated expenditures will continue to grow. The failure of rehabilitation efforts on behalf of persons whose disability benefits exceed 60 percent of prior wages will provoke, first, efforts to limit the maximum payable benefit to less than 60 percent of prior wages and, that failing, probably cause adoption, for purposes of judging "rehabilitative" feasibility, of a definition of "severity" that takes into account both the type of impairment and the size of the wage replacement ratio. Cases defined as "severe" because of a high wage replacement ratio and assessment that no job paying more than the net value of the benefit is realistically attainable, will be considered infeasible for vocational rehabilitation. The effect of such a policy, of course, would be to limit opportunities for vocational rehabilitation to persons of higher socioeconomic status, whose wage replacement ratios under social security disability insurance are well below 60 percent compared to ratios sometimes exceeding 100 percent which prevail, by virtue of the minimum "social adequacy" benefit guarantee, among beneficiaries whose former earnings were low.

The disability pensions paid to upper echelon civil servants are a different matter. The wage replacement ratios, the maximum amounts payable, and apparent lack of work restrictions are getting bad press. But, despite the notoriety, the more generous fringe benefits of civil servants are likely to continue as they have in the northwestern European countries.

The United States will eventually permit general taxes to supplement payroll taxes as the source of revenue for the social security system. This will bring the U.S. policy closer to the progressivism of the northwestern European tax structures. I do not expect, however, that shifting to general revenues will make American attitudes toward welfare any more liberal. Americans will continue to evaluate welfare recipients negatively and will expand the means-test, ostensibly to contain costs and to allocate resources efficiently to persons having greatest need. Such a policy toward the disabled has the bad effect of adding the stigma of welfare to the burden of disability and the good effect of increasing the incentive for these persons to return to work—sometimes even at wages lower than the net value of the transfer payment.

As previously mentioned, rehabilitation services that do not carry the welfare connotation can be expected to receive higher value in countries which impose a means-test before granting cash benefits than in those which adhere to the principle of social insurance. For this reason, Americans will continue to support rehabilitation services for social assistance recipients, regardless of their chances of securing substantial gainful employment. Resort to government created jobs and sheltered work will be necessary to assure successful job placement. But, as in the Netherlands, this combination of rehabilitation services and sheltered work will yield a net social cost rather than a gain if calculated in measurable economic terms. "Make-work" is just not as good for anybody as work for which there is a demand in the economy.

Notes

1. Personal communication, 15 January 1978.
2. Personal communication, 12 February 1978.
3. J. E. Kolberg and A. Viken, "Om Trygdeforbrukets Samfunnsmessige Bakgrunn," in *Levekårsundersøkelsen: Uførepensjon og Samfunnstruktur, Norges Offentlige Utredninger* 2 (Oslo: Universitetsforlaget, 1977), pp. 7–48.
4. Personal communication, 12 February 1978.
5. R. H. Haveman, *A Benefit-Cost and Policy Analysis of the Netherlands Social Employment Program* (Leiden: University of Leiden, 1977).
6. B. G. Reubens, *The Hard-to-Employ: European Programs* (New York: Columbia University Press, 1970), p. 212.
7. Kolberg and Viken, para. 9.1.
8. Haveman, p. 8.
9. D. O. Sewell, "Discussion: Occupational Training Programs and Manpower Programs for the Disadvantaged," in *Cost-Benefit Analysis of Manpower Programs*, ed. G. G. Somers and W. D. Wood (Kingston, Ontario: Queen's University Industrial Relations Centre, 1969), pp. 160–169.
10. S. Courant, "The Influence of Sex and Government on Disability Experience," Paper delivered at Meeting of the Norwegian Society of Actuaries, Oslo, 10 March 1977.
11. The statistics undoubtedly overstate the relationship between benefit levels and disability claims. Lower paid persons tend to receive higher benefits relative to earnings and also experience higher illness and impairment rates. Thus, the relationship between benefit levels and disability claims is hopelessly confounded by social class related phenomena. An English official, commenting on the Courant statistics, noted that the overall income

replacement ratio is more favorable for the better paid in the United Kingdom due to better non-state benefits, while their corresponding sickness absence/incapacity rates are lower than those for lower income/socioeconomic groups (Personal correspondence, 19 June 1978). Despite the shortcomings of the statistics, many economists and insurance actuaries, government officials, legislators, and lay persons share Courant's interpretation of the statistics: high benefits relative to earnings encourage disability claims. More generally, the majority of Americans, including close to half (46 percent) of those having substantial experience with unemployment, subscribe to the theory that high welfare and unemployment benefits are the reason unemployment is so high in the United States. See A. H. Cantril and S. D. Cantril, *Unemployment, Government and the American People* (Washington, D.C.: Public Research, 1978).

12. Estimates provided during a personal interview with an official of the city-state of Hamburg, Federal Republic of Germany, February 1977.

13. M. Pflanz and U. Geissler, "Rapid Cost Expansion in the Health Care System of the Federal Republic of Germany," *Preventive Medicine* 6 (1977): 290.

14. B. R. Anderson, "Sociomedical Aspects of Disability and Rehabilitation," Section G Position Paper, Fourth International Conference on Social Science and Medicine, Elsinore, 12-16 August 1974.

15. E. J. Mishan, "Evaluation of Life and Limb: A Theoretical Approach," *Journal of Political Economy* 75 (April 1971): 687–705.

16. This can be expressed by the general formula:

$$PV = \sum_{i=1}^{n} \frac{EE_i p\ (S,\ Em,\ A,\ Sx,\ R,\ Ed,\ I,\ D,\ G)}{(1 + r)^i}$$

where

PV = present value of aggregate benefits,
n = retirement age minus age at completion of rehabilitation,
EE_i = expected earnings in i^{th} year,
S = survival,
Em = employment,
A = age,
Sx = sex,
R = race,
Ed = education,
I = type of impairment,
D = recurring disability, and
G = productivity growth of the economy.

17. J. H. Noble, Jr., "The Limits of Cost-Benefit Analysis as a Guide to Priority-Setting in Rehabilitation," *Evaluation Quarterly* 1 (August 1977): 347–380.

18. R. J. Lurito and E. W. Dinkelacker, "The Social Rate of Discount: Theory, Measurement and Implications," Paper delivered at the Allied Social Science Associations Meeting, New Orleans, 27 December 1971.

19. R. W. Conley, "Problems of Discounting Future Benefits from Investing in People," paper delivered at the Allied Social Science Associations Meeting, New Orleans, 27 December 1971.

20. M. S. Feldstein, "Opportunity Cost Calculation in Cost-Benefit Analysis," *Public Finance* 19 (1964): 117–139.

21. The positive and negative signs are those expected for the regression coefficients which express in a separate linear equation for each dependent variable the direction and magnitude of any direct relationships between the dependent variable and each variable in a set of independent variables, holding the rest constant. Only the direction and nothing about the magnitude of the expected relationships is asserted here. Nor is anything said about numerous possible interactions among the independent variables and their effects on the dependent variables. Within limits, cross-national and perhaps inter-regional investigations within individual countries could supply the quantitative data needed for testing via regression analysis the postulated relationships.

22. Psychological distress is a statistically significant correlate of perceived health status. Perceived health status, in turn, conditions relationships between patients and providers. See R. Tessler and D. Mechanic, "Psychological Distress and Perceived Health Status," *Journal of Health and Social Behavior* 19 (September 1978): 254–262. Work stress, job loss, and economic recession, it also should be noted, increase rates of psychiatric impairment and hospitalization for mental disorder. See R. Liem and J. Liem, "Social Class and Mental Illness Reconsidered: The Role of Economic Stress and Social Support," *Journal of Health and Social Behavior* 19 (June 1978): 139–156.

23. It is conceivable, however, that the rise in interest rates that usually occurs during an inflationary period will be less than the rise in prices and wages. Since future benefits are often calculated as: $B_o(1 + p)/(1 + r)$ where B_o equals current earnings, p equals the rate of price level change, and r equals the discount rate, then it follows that if p is greater than r, future benefits and the benefit/cost ratio will rise during inflation. Conversely, future benefits and the benefit/cost ratio will fall if the wage increases of rehabilitated workers are less than the rise in interest rates. Evidence in the United States suggests that the wages of rehabilitated workers are more likely to fall behind rising interest rates, since the vast majority obtain low paying jobs in which wages tend to decline or fail to keep up with inflation. See Noble, pp. 368–369.

24. Bureau of Census, *Projections of the Population of the U.S.: 1975–2050*, Series P-25, No. 601 (Washington, D.C.: U.S. Department of Commerce, 1975).

HEALTH AND WELFARE

The area of health and welfare illustrates the diametrical opposition between the moral rights of people to maximum health care and security at minimum levels of satisfaction and the inequities in health care based on the ability to pay for such specialized services. The finite character of health services assures differential levels of treatment. Policy has mediated much of the dispute, guaranteeing the very poor services and life supports almost equal to those of the very rich. Here, the problem is often with policies for a huge middle class which feels singularly deprived of legislative relief aimed at alleviating their payments for services to others and maximizing their own usages. Containing the costs of health care and minimizing the pain of a welfare system have led to evaluation of economic systems—socialism, welfarism, and mixed economies. Again, the issue is not simply support for the poor, but how to maintain quality service, a sense of professional worth, technological innovation, research facilities, and high status for the medical and nursing professions. At the other end of the stratification spectrum the questions are equally acute: How are finite technological innovations to be distributed? What will be the basis for determining who shall live or for what length of time? The emerging role of patients as independent political actors in this area of health and welfare has thrown into sharp relief the world of the past in which policies were made for the needy and poor. Policies now are insisted upon by their adversaries in the blue-collar and white-collar industries. Containing costs is one end of the problem; delivering services is the other end. Policy in this area involves the effort to find some median point that the citizenry finds tolerable if not reasonable.

The Kahn and Kamerman study is extremely important in noting the growth of a worldwide consensus on policies and options, even if results tend to be radically different. Increasingly, health and welfare policy, whether in free market, mixed, or planned societies, stresses the following: local delivery services, consumer participation, multipurpose outlets for social services, policy makers with an overview of needs as well as specialists in different areas, and free-standing personal service with its delivery network. The authors doubt that efforts to create a human service integration are useful and may actually defer settlement of basic issues of health and welfare in a service context. Measuring policies is an area of increasing concern to government agencies and to the political process generally. Rocheleau indicates that, in addition to spatial dimensions, policy has a time dimension, and that evaluating the policy results of a Great Society program or any program initiated in the recent past requires a much longer period of time before it can be judged a success or failure. This is especially true in health programs which are complex, serve a shifting clientele, and must operate under serious budgetary constraints. Weiner argues that health care policies have undergone considerable change over the past several decades. The system of service delivery has become competitive and fragmented, and the former respect accorded to professionals and institutions has deteriorated. Weiner suggests some major policy overhauls for the 1980s if health and welfare policies are to be maintained. He urges an enlarged role for consumers; demystification of the medical profession, institutional commitment to a patient's bill of rights, reassessing and reducing the role of hospitals, enlarging community-based facilities, and in general replacing national health approaches with local initiatives. The area of health policy must be reconsidered—from the bottom up instead of from the top down, as has occurred too often in the past. This is a *cri de coeur* of many policy analysts at this point.

34

THE PERSONAL SOCIAL SERVICES
Policy, Program, and Implementation

Alfred J. Kahn and Sheila B. Kamerman

A COMPARATIVE VOLUME on social security concludes that "there is no theoritical incompatibility between genuine social security and capitalism."[1] To which we might add "or between universal personal social services and either capitalism or socialism." Whatever the *general* validity of hypotheses about the convergence of social systems in their institutional responses, as they reach high levels of economic development and/or urbanization, it certainly applies here. These mixed-economy ("social market") capitalist countries and the two very different East European socialist nations clearly recognize their need for, and are investing resources and manpower in, what we have begun to call the personal social services. There is even some convergence in conceptualizations, despite differences in the vocabularies of the several social systems and of the specific national cultures in which they are implanted. The variance between countries East and West is in this regard apparently as significant as the variance among countries within each of the two systems in our small sample.

It is difficult to decide whether to characterize these elements of compelling national choice as "beyond ideology" or as ideology

---

1. Gaston V. Rimlinger, *Welfare Policy and Industrialization in Europe, America, and Russia* (New York: John Wiley & Sons, Inc., 1971), p. 303.

shared within these different social systems, which are in many basic senses similar. For these urbanized and urbanizing societies are all experiencing changed or changing family life and are seeking to cope in a fashion which protects their core values. If mothers work, children need satisfactory care and attention. If more old people live longer, yet cannot manage without some help or support, the help should be provided in a fashion which does not violoate the precious dicta of the culture. And if there is antisocial behavior, child neglect, intrafamilial difficulty, personal maladjustment—to offer a very incomplete list—there should be help which protects the community's sense of reasonable conduct and fundamental obligations. In intimate urban living one cannot quite ignore suffering and maladjustment because they spill over into everyone's daily life—in any social system.

Common societal needs seem to generate somewhat similar institutional response, in part, certainly, because of international communication and a "demonstration" effect. Each society rejects and adapts according to its own situation, and each initiates as it experiences special circumstances. The personal social services, if they are to become a recognized and basic system—paralleling health and education, for example—would appear to require both national initiatives and international sharing as they seek optimum forms and variations. Standardization obviously has not arrived. One cannot rank countries on the overall effectiveness of their personal social services, yet there are obvious high points in some which deserve attention by all—and the overview does delineate implications of some of the options.

In some sense, we might hypothesize, the investment in the personal social services and their growth comes only with national capacity, no matter how long-standing the need. The more prosperous countries are further along. The more urbanized, whose populations have greater access to service centers, offer more services. The most developed states, or provinces, or regions, respond most adequately to need and to "wants." Thus the personal social services are not unlike other societal institutions in claiming their share of resources and seeking to grow. Nor will they escape the long-range resources questions, no matter how modest their current claims and demands: as the dependency ratios continue to rise (more children and old people per labor force member), there will be expenditures pressure. As other competing demands expand, in other social services or for personal consumption goods, or for national security and defense, each country will need to come to terms with its priorities. As competing groups and problems bid for expansion of personal social services responsive to their circumstance, there will be a new balance between case services and public social utilities, between categorical and general approaches, between the requirements of different groups which are focused on their own service needs.

Convergences and Options

At the outset we expected sharply conceptualized and structured options, and we fully intended to compare their respective costs and benefits. We conclude, instead, that there are no pure and fully delineated general social service systems and that the various countries are more alike than different in essentials. While there are important distinctions, not to be ignored, there are in fact more basic convergences. Response to task and shared objectives lead to commonalities which cross national boundaries. Those who are concerned with the social services may find encouragement in this; indeed, there may evolve everywhere a personal-general social service system, manifested at the local level through an identifiable, coherent delivery system. Perhaps experience can be assembled on a comparative basis to yield eventual answers on difficult questions of policy and organizational strategy.

A Local Delivery System

There is, first, convergence on the notion of a delivery system based in the local governmental authority. Our countries differ in their degrees of centralization, which means that some have quite uniform local governmental structures and others show more variability. Within the three-tier government countries (U.S., Canada, F.R.G., Yugoslavia), some states-provinces allow greater local autonomy than others and may even themselves operate services through local outlets. (The population and geographic definition of "locality" varies with country traditions, demography, political history.) Nonetheless, the generalization remains: demographic, cultural, and political variations lead increasingly to recognition of the need for a delivery outlet based in, and responsive to, locality. In many instances there are special provisions for local participation and control, whether within the governmental system or parallel to this, to create local citizen involvement and influence. Social services are major activities for local government.

Some distinction should be made here between localization and decentralization, even though the line is as yet not sharp. Localization is the better term for situations in which the pattern is relatively standard and centrally directed (as in Israel), but it is felt that neighborhood locations are essential for sensitively rendered service delivery. Decentralization implies a degree of local power and discretion to adapt and change in accord with local purposes and needs. It may cover community control outside the statutory system or options and initiatives by local governmental authorities. In any case, whereas almost any of the other social sector programs seem to have a locus which reflects the predominant pattern of the country's governmental arrangements, for the personal social services all seek localization-decentralization. Elementary education is the only other comparable service, generally, although health sometimes is. Perhaps the reasons for personal social service decentralization or localization are historical; the services are often more comprehensive and bureaucratized substitutes for primary group effort and small charities based in the locality. By now, however, the phenomenon is supported by a professional and governmental rationale everywhere which is convincing and apparently buttressed by experience: the character and quality of personal social services should be attuned to the preferences and traditions of the neighborhood or subgroup. The balance in service components should vary by demographic, racial, and ethnic factors in an area and by the varied preferences of residents.

Programs are best if there is a user contribution to shaping them and local volunteer participation in their implementation. Programs are psychologically and physically most accessible if chosen by, and felt to "belong" to, the community. Case integration, moreover, is easiest on a small-area basis. The only observed departures—where there is opportunity for advice and planning—grow out of economy of scale (some neighborhoods are simply too small to sustain some services) and the wish to have access to specific expertise (some scarce expertise must be shared over large areas).

Thus the picture repeats in country after country. England locates a social service department as a mandated local authority activity, as are education, housing, and planning. Central government guides, requires planning, leads, pushes, inspects. The F.R.G. develops policy centrally; states supervise and guide localities, but the locality takes service delivery initiative. We have seen that France, too, for all its centralization implements personal social services with much local initiative and variation. Poland is more like Israel—a central pattern with selective local uniformity. But the large volunteer role in front-line access services makes each locality in some ways unique. The U.S. and Canada are structurally similar: sometimes there is state operation through a localized outlet; in the provinces/states the situation is more like the F.R.G.—state-province policy and decentralized developments in local government, with all three tiers sharing costs. Yugoslavia is the extreme case. At least in a formal sense, major initiatives are highly decentralized; but central policy and political cadres unify and lead.

Except for Yugoslavia most major policy-making and large initiatives even for the personal social services belong to central government; but this may mean only high policy—or it may involve specific program mandates or encouragement. This holds for the two-tier and three-tier countries. Yugoslavia has sharing by all tiers. In general, localities are weaker in governmental social service initiative in two-tier than in three-tier countries, where variations in approach by province/state/republic are visible in great locality variations and more local power. In all three-tier countries here reviewed, the basic formal responsibility for most personal social services is assigned the middle tier, which may decide to delegate it downward (Canada, U.S., F.R.G.).

The pattern generates its problems, which then engender restraints. That is why no role divisions are sharp, pure, or apparently permanent. Yugoslavia serves to illustrate: just as other countries have varied proportions of aged in different regions, Yugoslavia has variations among the republics. Since republics may affect the attention accorded to different groups through their policy initiatives, republics do show useful variations. The problem is that in republics where, for demographic reasons, the aged are not strong politically, there may be a lack of policy initiative.

Or in the F.R.G., Canada, and Yugoslavia differential, income-related fees for child care programs are a factor in a policy of "equalization." However, decentralized administration by local government means a lack of uniformity in implementation and an effect other than the equalization sought. In Canada, to carry the illustration further, locality implementation is not uniform because provinces have varied fiscal capacities to produce the matching funds required to generate financial assistance for the services from central government.

This, in effect, is the generalizable problem where central governments leave initiatives to middle tiers (states, provinces), or the latter cede all allocational and programatic decision to localities. Therefore, there is a constant search everywhere for a balance which meets national circumstance.

Consumer Participation

Social service programs strive for consumer participation, but the intensity of involvement varies substantially. The very rationales offered for personal social service decentralization also argue for active "consumer participation." The term is popular, in its several variations, among the countries but has differing meanings: elite advisory committees or agency boards; neighborhood advisory committees; local volunteers; official citizen participation in local governmental planning activity; a structure for consumer control of a program unit or of a planning operation outside the formal political governmental system; consumer cooperation in service operations as client, where one is not the primary client or patient, so as to buttress the service to one's child or parent or spouse.

In general, Yugoslavia has the structure in which citizen participation is most natural: a commune or enterprise creates a service by assembling consumers and providers; otherwise the service is not established. The assemblies at the various levels, beginning with communities of interest, are policy bodies at which consumer and provider and community representative meet.

The U.S. and Canada have large amounts of consumer participation in all the categories listed above, perhaps having undertaken more frequently than most over the past decade to create extragovernmental community controls outside of statutory authority. The lack of confidence in governmental representatives felt by deprived minority groups has provided the rationale. Hepworth asks whether strengthening local government would not be wiser in the long run than bypassing it. U.S. developments suggest that as minority groups enter the political mainstream more successfully, this type of community bid for control may be advocated less frequently. The success of personal social services as decentralized enterprises probably will continue to require all the other modes of participation, however.

Volunteering remains a major mode of community involvement, creating a community presence which is essential for programs dealing with the weak and dependent in the society, rendering valuable service, and assuring a pluralistic character for the service system, if that is sought. Poland, as noted, is unique in relying overwhelmingly on volunteers, but it too has decided to expand its professionally trained social work cadres. The volunteer totals are relatively very large, especially in the U.S. and the U.K., but they do not substitute for technically and professionally trained staffs—or at least for paid personnel whether or not they are highly trained.

Multipurpose Outlets

There is also convergence on the idea of locally based multipurpose outlets for social services. Once all was combined in mixed almshouses and local poor-law authority offices—to use U.K. and U.S. terms. Then more and more categorical and specialized, often universal, programs were developed. Now fragmentation is of concern, and there is commitment to case integration and program coordination. There is recognition of the need to improve information and facilitate access. These tendencies to locally based multiservice outlets take several forms and reflect different outlooks. Some unify their services around a conceptualization of the personal social services (U.K., Israel), but others use the nucleii of two different systems (social and youth or child welfare and social welfare) for parallel service models (F.R.G., Yugoslavia) within the personal social services. Transition countries (Canada, U.S.) have elements of completely comprehensive co-location in some places and remnants of two, three, or four separate categorically organized or social-class-related service systems. In Poland on a modest scale and in France on a substantial basis, major social institutions have their separate personal social services, but the coordination structure of the sector and circonscription (France) offers a place or places or persons to whom one can turn for access to all the personal social services elements.

These outlets may merely involve co-location and what that adds by way of better program coordination and case integration (and its achievements may be quite modest).[2] This is the situation under some of the U.S., Canada, and F.R.G. initiatives mentioned and was the picture under French sectorial coordination. Or the new multipurpose outlets may be part of a strategy involving real surrender of categorical independence and an effort to develop a unified, comprehensive service, as in the U.K. local authority, the Israeli local welfare office, and some Yugoslavian social work centers. Or there may be evidence that the unity of outlook may involve leadership by the host agency—the health service in Poland's centers.

In some places, we note below, there is interest in service delivery outlets that include all or many of the six social service systems. This development is discussed subsequently.

Generalist Practitioner or Team

There also may be evidence of convergence on the need for a "generalist" practitioner or team at the core of the local service system. The picture remains mixed, but some countries do not see the possibility of a comprehensive and universal program unless there is at the front line, offering the core service, a person or unit with scope and range, not too tied to one intervention strategy or one type of response to need.

The U.K. offers the purest model of a team of generalists, yet it does not preclude intrateam expertise, special liaison assignments, and experimentation with specialties. Recent experience has argued for children's services units to preserve accountability and expertise. The French polyvalent worker is such a generalist, too, but many people do not enter the system through her alone, and all have the right to begin with specialists. In many Yugoslav centers the client meets a generalist, but others assign him at once to a categorical specialist. In Canada and the U.S. the pattern varies by place. Israel is tending toward the U.S. approach, but there are distinctions by demographic group. The F.R.G. is organized in two systems, and the categorical personnel within each span broad ranges. Polish categorical separatisms are greater, but the volunteers in social

2. Alfred J. Kahn, "Service Delivery at the Neighborhood Level: Experience, Theory, and Fads," *Social Service Review*, L, No. 1 (1976), 23-56.

welfare specialize in social care for the aged, disabled, handicapped, retarded.

Practice is very mixed, yet our analysis of the internal tendencies in the several countries has shown that the need for a generalist at the entry point does follow from commitment to a comprehensive and universal service. To serve all population groups and to meet all of the commitments of a general social service requires capacity for the following minimal base-line personal social service functions:

1. Giving information and advice and making referrals about all of the social sector (human services, in the broadest sense)
2. Giving access to a range of social care services which enable handicapped, frail elderly, and disturbed people to remain in community living under some protection and with needed services and resources
3. Providing front-line counseling, if only on a simple level
4. Coping with emergency daytime, afterhour, weekend needs for housing, food, protection, institutionalization for the vulnerable aged, children, the mentally ill, and others —whether directly or by access to other community service personnel
5. Carrying out appropriate ongoing social treatment, including efforts in individualized, group and residential contexts to bring about changes in adjustment, functioning, view of self or others
6. Providing case integration, assuring that sequential service (institution to community aftercare, for example), or work with different family members within the personal-general social services or between programs in different systems (health and social assistance; probation, school, and child welfare), is mutually supportive and properly meshed.

Except for social treatment (which some see as specialization), these are the front-line generalist tasks on which there is convergence despite differences in detail. Some add administration of cash grants. The U.S. puts very little social care into local social services, unlike most of the countries. Some countries give more of the emergency task to police or special authoritative personnel or to the medical system. Categorically organized systems divide up emergencies involving children, the aged, the mentally ill, and homeless families. Some reports indicate more confidence about the current discharge of the case integration function (F.R.G.) than others (U.S.). Yet the convergence on generalist function is there: information and access, major social care services, emergency aid, basic counseling, and service integration. The generalist worker or team binds the system together, indeed makes it a system.

The service unit remains the team in the U.K. and the practitioner in France. There are mixes everywhere. Yet the straining for the generalist function also is everywhere, even in the categorical systems. However, it is also recognized that these services cover a wide range: different age groups; healthy average people needing developmental and preventive services as well as disabled or sick people and those needing protection; complexities of social-physical-psychological causalities; interventions ranging from giving cash, to counseling, to foster care and adoption, to institutionalization; short-term and long-term work; clients from different cultural, racial, and class groups. There is, therefore, a parallel searching for specialization, too, in some places within the generalist role and in others as a second-tier operation. If specialization of the second sort, does it belong in a categorical service? On the latter point there is as yet little consensus. There are many variations. It is an issue for social work education, for the social work profession, as it is for public administrators.

The differences among countries are not in the identification of service repertoires—the range of interventions and alternatives for a given type of case. The commonalities rise above political and ideological differences, and the variations reflect wealth and how long the system has had to mature. What is different among countries is the particular mix of elements in the generalist role, the conceptualization of specialty and its organizational base, and the work being done to resolve these critical questions of social service organization and professional development.

Whether, at the end, personal social service networks will remain general or (depending upon issues of geography and scale) will have some age-related service units (protective work with children, services to the aged, services to adolescents), it does appear that such structuring need not undermine the development of personal social services as system just as the specialization of hospital out-patient clinics or wards does not necessarily fragment medicine. The issue is whether, given specialties and categorical access systems, the cement that binds is also properly in place.

Personnel for the Personal Social Services

Interestingly, except for the U.S. and Canada, where special political and historical factors may be cited in explanation, the new patterns do not involve a decreasing credentialism. Whatever the training routes or the resolution of the boundary debate, there is concern with well-prepared personnel, the definition of strict standards, supervision, quality of service, continued certification, and improved enforcement of regulations.

Social work is the central profession for the personal social services as is medicine for health, the teaching profession for education. However, given the range of activities within the personal social services, social workers may not necessarily be a majority in many places: there will be need for teachers and child care counselors in institutions, for attendants, recreation workers, homemakers, clerical staff, and so forth. Many of the programs can and will utilize many volunteers.

Social work is a paraprofessional or subprofessional discipline in some of the countries and a graduate profession in others. In several countries there are levels of education and certification, ranging from secondary school to graduate education. Except for the U.S., the tendency has been to upgrade requirements in recent years, often to associate previously "unattached" social work schools to universities. In the U.S., a continued growth of graduate education, the universal social work professional education patterns from the early 1940's, has been accompanied over the past five to seven years by an enormous expansion of professional courses at the baccalaureate level as well and the admission to full status in the social worker professional association of graduates of undergraduate degree programs. There is much struggle to define just which tasks and assignments require the graduate degree (M.S.) and which should be assigned to the large—and perhaps less expensive—pool of undergraduate trainees.

Nowhere has social work education produced a well-qualified and accepted cadre of administrators-managers for the personal social services out of special social work training. In the past, social workers were prepared for direct-service tasks, and those with special abilities or predilections or considerable experience moved on to administration. At the same time, people trained and experienced in public administration, law, business, or other related disciplines were often recruited more directly for the task. In recent years a number of countries have developed special professional educational programs to prepare personnel for management and administration positions, whether in the social services generally, for the personal social services in particular, or for one or another subcategorical program (nursing homes for the aged, children's institutions, social insurance offices, and so on). These programs are generally located in special schools—not the ones which educate for direct social work practice—but the separation is not universal or always complete: at times, there is a separate department in the one faculty or school. In the U.S. currently graduate social work schools are tending to organize in two "streams": direct practice in one and administration, management, and program development in the other. However, the latter track has not yet become the major route to administration of the personal social services.

The issue goes beyond personal social services, of course. Should hospital administrators be prepared in schools of public health or might they come, as well, from schools of business or public administration? Should all college presidents or elementary school principals be prepared in graduate schools of education? There are differences among fields, but the issue is widely experienced.

We might hazard the view that if the personal social services continue to evolve as system they will want to recruit substantial numbers of their managers and administrators from special social work educational sequences. An integrated network will not emerge without considerable sharing of values and objectives. Wise staff deployment and imaginative shaping of interventive repertoires cannot be expected unless the leadership is in the hands of social-work-trained personnel. Others should obviously be brought in for their technology and special talents, but not in the majority role.

The premise is that social work educators concentrated on direct service will rise to the challenge of preparing the social work generalists for the base-line services as described, will create educational sequences for necessary specialties (which, as indicated, are not yet sorted out), will train supervisors, researchers, theoreticians. This is a large and important agenda not yet fully in focus.

The success of the personal social services requires range, innovation, imagination. Our international overview leads to the conviction that full identification with this challenge might rescue social work in several countries from a major identity crisis. Too often now its direct-service interests span all the human services, and its social action concerns cover the entire social sector. The resultant lack of a readily identifiable responsibility for a specific, coherent service system or recognized expertise in a policy domain leaves social workers unfocused, their activities diffuse, and their personnel not accepted as predominant where they should be. While the problem is not apparent everywhere, it is serious in several places. Identification with a personal social service system may be a solution for the social work profession—a solution which also serves the society well—because only qualified cadres for direct service and administration-management can assure the full development of the emerging personal social service network and the policy substructure on which it must be constructed.

A Freestanding System?

Another significant convergence emerges, one which is contrary to our expectations. Initially, we asked: Which countries have freestanding social services and which place the services as adjuncts to other systems? We see, if rather dimly, and thus describe, if tentatively, a convergence toward elements of a freestanding system everywhere, even if not formalized and even if sharing co-location of delivery outlets with income-maintenance or health programs. Of the countries studied, France has based large elements of general-personal social service as adjuncts to other institutions, but it has a freestanding polyvalent worker network and a coordination structure which implicitly recognizes the personal social services (if not in name) as an identifiable entity. Poland sees its social workers as adjuncts to the central functions of other institutions, but the logic of social work service development is moving the system forward toward what could become something else. Elsewhere, the U.K. has one system, a clear freestanding system, while Yugoslavia has one system in some places and two in others. The U.S., Canada, and Israel have elements of a freestanding system and other social services clearly adjunctive to other institutions. Each shows some signs of evolving towards a more integrated freestanding system or (as in Canada) one which is more interrelated with health but not necessarily secondary to it.

All of these generalizations require qualification, of course. For example, freestanding systems may not be completely comprehensive. They may leave out probation and correctional services (assigned to "justice" in some places) or work with the mentally ill (sometimes a function of health or a special program). School social work or various types of institutional care for the young (an option for educational authorities) may be omitted, as well as social services tied to employment services and training (a task of labor ministries), and medical social work (in health). This would seem to suggest that the concept of general-personal social services as a comprehensive, freestanding system, particularly as it moves toward universalism, is contradicted neither by specialist social work services (not yet defined) nor by either basic or specialist services in related institutions which provide a strategic operational base. The issue, as identified and debated by the British, is whether the social work in these various locations is to be done by using staff outposted from a local authority personal social service unit or by hiring and supervising from within the host institution. As the precedents from health and education suggest, there may be no worldwide or permanent answer.

Unresolved Issues

While there is some convergence on a freestanding system, with much left outside, there also in general recognition of boundary problems and of the need to provide for effective multidisciplinary work, especially teamwork crossing one or more social services, in certain types of case situations. The analysis of operational realities in the field of the aging in almost all the countries, consideration of the most effective case-finding and intervention strategies for abused and battered children, the reported initiatives in two Canadian provinces which are restructuring social service delivery in relation to health, all illustrate this unavoidable challenge in planning for social service delivery.

One possible response could be to question further advocacy of freestanding personal social services. To elaborate: Much of what we have reported implicitly makes a case for a freestanding personal social service system, with permeable boundaries and some well-integrated ties to specialist programs in (or also perhaps outposting generalist workers to) other social institutions, such as health agencies, schools, unions, income-security offices, and so on. However, other experiences also could be cited to argue for another principle of organization, the Polish and French tendencies to locate social work personnel in these other institutions.

As we pursue this, however, we are impressed with the superiority of outposting personnel from a personal social service center for such assignment rather than their employment by a host profession not equipped to strengthen their competences through assurance of an ongoing base in their own profession and supervision by qualified peers. There is much historical evidence that social work adjunctive services are seldom coequal.

The other alternative to the freestanding personal social service—based in its own delivery network and also outposted as needed to health, housing, social security, and related programs—is to call for organization on demographic principles: a multidisciplinary program for the aged not anchored in any one of the six social service systems. After all, it is noted, social care services to the aged involve an intertwining of medical and social programming. Why not have a service system for the aged, make it multidisciplinary and multisystem, and build the program units around needs, not professions or organizations? The argument is attractive, if possibly unique to services to the aged. The potential price, on the other hand, could be the segregation of the retirees who require community-based or residential care sooner than necessary, because of the age-categorical service system which would take over at retirement, whatever the service needed. The service theory calls for "normalization" and ongoing participation in all of community life. The research suggests that this is wise policy, reducing dependency and even prolonging life. Why not simplify and symbolize normalization by keeping services to the aged integrated into general systems, into all the social services? Furthermore, any service system for the aged which is cross-disciplinary is certain to be dominated by medicine, the strongest of the related professions. This, too, could be dysfunctional under a philosophy of "normalization."

None of this, of course, is an argument against either a neutral or a medical base for such social care specifics as home-health visitors, homemakers, home renovation specialists for the handicapped, and transportation services, as long as they serve the several social services systems which need to draw upon them.

While only in the field of the aged are there extensive efforts to ignore major system boundaries among the six social services and organize along demographic lines, there are many experts who question a preoccupation with conceptualizing and organizing the sixth system, the personal social services. Why not, they ask, focus on the obvious need for human service integration? The subject is of some importance.

Human Services or Personal Social Service

It is not that even the basic question of personal social service parameters is fully settled. We have described some convergence on an integrated system through a tendency to organize and interrelate these often semi-independent categorical services (aged, children, youth) and different intervention approaches (development-socialization, substitute care, community-based treatment, information-referral, residential care, social care in the community, amenities, in-kind benefits, and so forth). Yet we have seen that the degree of organization of these components and others as a personal social service system varies from the commitment and formal structural measures in the U.K., to the partial and incomplete steps—clearly in that direction—in several countries, to the somewhat ambiguous movements in France and Poland, which, as noted, could sustain a very different ultimate design.

One of the visible alternatives noted is a pattern under which personal social services are and remain as adjuncts to other systems (unions, schools, hospitals, social security) and do not develop their own integrated delivery base. However, even here, experience suggests, the various personal social service adjunctive components may tend to come together in one location to achieve case integration, program coordination, and accountability and thus could evolve into a more organized system.

Another tendency is to organize personal social services for delivery purposes into categorical subcomponents, particularly child welfare, the aged, and social welfare (which means everything else and which may include services to the aged). This approach may, overall, support the evolution of personal social services as system, part of one overall governmental structure, with categorical elements in need of coordination.

An even larger departure involves the decision to organize for service integration and more coherent delivery on a human services system basis; this means bringing together several of the social services, using the term in its broad sense. While the emphasis on human services systems does not necessarily contradict the notion of an integrated personal social service system conceptually, it perhaps does create a degree of confusion and competition for resources and attention.

The U.S. is the prime example of this tendency. Federal service integration initiatives have spanned many of the social services in the European sense of the term and have not coped with the fact that the personal social service components do not enter into the cooperative relationships with the same relatively clear base in system and with defined boundaries and mission as do education, health, income maintenance, housing, and employment—whatever the boundary problems even in these fields. The result is a condition in which, thus far, no apparent pattern emerges and there is no evidence of any significant progress in service delivery from the consumer's perspective—whatever the achievements of individual special experimental efforts in service delivery, management information systems, information and referral service, or program coordination. It would appear from the U.S. experience that efforts at human service integration before the personal social services gain their own coherence do not achieve much, may tend to defer basic issues, and are in fact probably frustrated by the poorly organized state of a personal social services system.

France is experiencing a similar phenomenon, but our analysis has not taken us far enough to assess its full implications. Or perhaps the process is too new. As we have seen, there have been forces in France seeking to achieve some coordination among the many categorical personal social service efforts. At the same time, numerous new occupations are evolving in both personal social services and in the related social service systems, which Americans often call human services. A new coordinations push, which at the level of service delivery is not unlike some service integration initiatives in the U.S., has evolved on an area basis in the circonscription.

It is not clear how these several tendencies will be resolved. From a national perspective, certainly, the evolution and systematization of the personal social services have a high priority. There is otherwise no way for personal social services to play their part in integrated human services. Or at least this is certainly true in the

U.S., where the acceptance of personal social services as having validity apart from income programs and as needed by all income groups is only emerging and where they lack a base as firm as that in France.

In the long run—and whether or not human services become a conceptual base for service delivery planning—boundaries within the social services will need to be viewed dynamically, so that no system can or should expect permanent stabilization and, therefore complete coincidence between its functions and administrative practices in a given country and what may be found in other countries. This should be no surprise as we recall at random a few of the phenomena already reported on a few of the issues introduced.

Several of the countries have perfected their child health care systems so as to assure careful screening and check-ups on a routine basis, especially in the first few years of life. Poland, France, and Israel may serve to illustrate such provision under different systems in countries of different degrees of wealth. One would not expect in countries such as these the same formula for child welfare protection-prevention as in the U.S., which lacks universal child health provision. And one would expect change in the U.S. as its health system evolves and its current large special case-finding investments become redundant.

With reference to the final years of childhood, we find: *(a)* some countries, in what is an early historical stage of this development, removing children from adult criminal procedures and sanctions and engaging them in educational or child welfare corrective measures; *(b)* other countries which have traveled this path and are now restoring some of "delinquency" to the justice system; and *(c)* others with firm conviction about their notions as to the respective ongoing roles of juvenile and adult justice and either child welfare or education. Then, too, on the one hand, one may contrast the U.S., with its social services and mental health emphasis, with, on the other hand, the relatively heavy reliance on educational intervention in the F.R.G. and the U.K., which have quite different administration patterns.

The boundaries problems are everywhere in the social services. The poor-law history of the U.K. and the U.S. is quite different from that of France; so the former have insisted on separating the fundamental service delivery structure from that which delivers means-tested social assistance grants, whereas this is not at all an organizational dictum of social aid in France. The U.S. and the U.K. have believed that only such separation eliminates arbitrary discretion in implementing the right to cash assistance and affirms the need for nonmonetary services by those who do not need means-tested cash aid. The several Canadian provinces offer a mixed picture, less because of ideology than because of financing arrangements, as described by Hepworth:

> . . . the present arrangements between the federal and provincial levels of government for sharing the costs of social services have tended to preserve the linkage as far as low-income people are concerned, and limit the provision of services for people outside the low-income category.

The F.R.G., by way of contrast, also offers means-tested cash assistance in the local social offices which also deliver other social services, but attempts to obviate the case for separation by offering and implementing rights in relation either to cash aid or to service.

The different attitudes toward separation of means-tested cash from services create different options for service delivery, at least in the short run. For any cash benefit system serving the needy requires social service personnel to administer discretionary grants, too, and any personal social service system offering help for those with problems and crises requires access to emergency cash.[3] Thus it is necessary to decide where the service-cash grant boundaries belong at a given moment in the light of overall administration logic, consequences for imagery, and assurance of effective access. Again, the historical moment is important: Israel, with a sophisticated approach to supplementary income, has not yet achieved full separation but favors it; Yugoslavia and Poland are illustrative of preseparation systems where some services are seen as essential components and inseparable from the social assistance; the U.S. has barely separated and needs to reorganize (because of new social service legislation) before the options have matured.

Sometimes, of course, key boundary questions are resolved as a direct consequence of the major conceptualization of problems and intervention. Where community mental health is essentially an extension of medically based outpatient psychiatry, concerned with community care and continuity of service as well as with emergency service, it is viewed as part of the medical system and its parameters

---

3. For an interesting account, see Olive Stevenson, *Claimant or Client?* (London: George Allen and Unwin, 1973).

are set accordingly. Where community mental health departs from a medical model of causation and intervention, many of its programs, even its staffing patterns, parallel and overlap those of the personal social services. If the U.S. represents the latter situation and still faces major unresolved program planning problems as a result, Poland and Yugoslavia appear to fit the former classification. Most of the Western countries show some of each, with the U.S. and Canada facing the greatest boundary ambiguities.

As employment-training programs become part of the social services, focused in various ways on the "hard-to-employ,"[4] they too experience boundary problems. Market-oriented employment services are relatively identifiable—training, unemployment insurance, placement, replacement, continuing education, special protections for groups facing discrimination. In this sense some countries do not think of employment programs as part of the social services or as a human service system. Social insurance, as we have seen, may be based in a labor ministry. However, when there are special rights and supportive measures for the physically handicapped, counseling for those with attitudinal problems or emotional difficulties in the work area or for those who face complex cultural transitions in moving into urban work environments from rural areas or from other countries, then the personal social service-employmemt boundaries become vague. In the U.S. these are today different departments and occupational groups carrying on activities which would at least appear quite similar.

Boundary ambiguity and change might appear to make the case for one comprehensive human service delivery system. Unfortunately, the division of labor in modern society has premises which cannot be ignored: sheer size and complexity; different needs which require specialized attention; occupational groups which must have unique training. The various human services may include interventive approaches which depend on unique equipment, space, or value bases. Such services thus justify their own arrangements to assure their needed nurture and protection. Programs delivering differing types of benefits may also require unique supervision and accountability procedures, as well as rules and atmosphere which encourage those approaches to knowledge development most appropriate to different interventive tasks.

4. Beatrice G. Reubens, *The Hard-to-Employ: European Programs* (New York: Columbia University Press, 1970).

The social processes which have created six major social services therefore deserve respect. There is little reason to think that one could or should wipe out overall distinctions among income-transfer programs, education, health, employment-training, housing, and personal social services. Each is in itself extremely broad and should be encouraged to achieve optimum development as system by its own logic—and each has its own dynamic processes which also require nurture. As much should be said for the personal social services in this regard, the most underdeveloped and nuclear of all the systems. And one should not be surprised in the course of the evolution by boundary confusion, competition, and change—especially change attributed to a shifting social scene which redefines problems and needs.

Nor should one question the wisdom of experimentation with service delivery approaches that join or coordinate elements from more than one system to deal with a group, a problem, or a task. We are, in this regard, more impressed with modest efforts covering elements of two or three systems, uniting for specific purposes, than with human services "department stores." Thus we have noted in various countries such joint activity as: personal social services and health working with the aged; pediatrics, psychiatry, and child welfare coping with child battering and abuse; education and social services creating special forms of child care for children with special problems—and so forth. Where housing, health, personal social services, employment, and all the rest attempt to come together in a very large comprehensive system serving all needs in a geographic area—and if it is a complex urban area with relatively high population density—there is achieved at most convenience of place; where possible this is worthwhile. But real case integration, of course, cannot cover many professions and systems, given the obvious interventive complexity and the legitimate needs of various institutions to protect their boundaries and ensure the maintenance of visibility and constituencies for ongoing support. It would be important progress—indeed, very satisfactory—to seek service integration within each of the large systems dealing with people under stress and facing major crises or inadequacy, particularly in health, psychiatry, personal social services. Wherever possible, in these as in other social services, clients would be encouraged to be their own program coordinators and case integrators, as most people must in any country.

35

HOW DO WE MEASURE THE IMPACT OF INTERGOVERNMENTAL PROGRAMS?
Some Problems and Examples from the Health Area

Bruce Rocheleau

Abstract. It is difficult to evaluate public programs of any kind but the task is particularly complex when the programs are intergovernmental in nature. Such programs often necessitate a long developmental period before they are likely to have measurable impact. The early stages are often devoted to developing support from local power structures. These programs have many unintended consequences—both positive and negative—that short-term evaluations will usually fail to note. An exploratory study of the Federal Health Planning and Community Mental Health programs is used to illustrate the importance of the "time dimension" in evaluation research.

Assessing the impact of a program is never an easy matter. If the evaluation is negative, the evaluators are likely to be criticized by program personnel and supporters. It is often difficult to identify adequate outcome measures or control groups to give unbiased measures of effectiveness. These difficulties are multiplied when the program involved is an intergovernmental one. This paper argues that in assessing the impact of intergovernmental programs:

(1) Evaluators need to have a much longer time perspective than is usually the case; intergovernmental programs may take years to develop the complex network of formal and informal relations necessary to make them effective.
(2) Expectations concerning the impact of intergovernmental programs are often too high; indeed, the overly high level of expectations

The author wishes to thank Mr. Daniel Zwick for his comments on an earlier draft of this paper.

The research was supported by Contract No. HRA 230-77-0079 of the Department of Health, Education, and Welfare. When this article was written, the author was a faculty fellow with the Office of Planning, Evaluation and Legislation of the Health Resources Administration of DHEW. The views expressed in this paper are solely those of the author and do not necessarily represent the position of the Health Resources Administration.

Journal of Health Politics, Policy and Law, Vol. 4, No. 4, Winter 1980. Copyright© 1980 by the Department of Health Administration, Duke University.

concerning program success will usually lead to later disappointment and premature abandonment of the program.

(3) An overly narrow focus on outcome measures is likely to miss subtle effects, negative as well as positive, of intergovernmental programs; these unexpected and often unintended consequences are frequently more important than more obvious results of the programs.

The arguments are supported by our study of the impact on local areas of two programs, health planning and community mental health. This study is admittedly exploratory; the generalizations made here should be regarded as hypotheses for testing in future, more extensive studies. Local areas in South Carolina and Michigan were chosen as sites for the study because they had been sites of similar studies at the state level the year before.[1] By returning to these states information collected earlier can be used to supplement that collected in this exploratory effort. A number of documents and background information, such as the plans of the Health Systems Agencies (HSAs) and grant applications submitted by the community mental health centers, were collected to support the generalizations made in this paper. However, most of the generalizations made here are based on results of informal discussions with a wide range of persons at each local area visited (70 in all), including the following:

(1) members of health systems agencies;
(2) members of federally funded community mental health centers;
(3) consumer groups interested in health planning (e.g., United Fund agencies);
(4) consumer groups interested in mental health (e.g., mental health association members);
(5) groups interested in health planning and mental health (e.g., representatives of local medical societies, unions, hospital associations).

The community mental health center program. The community mental health center program was enacted in 1963 and amended in 1965 to provide initial staffing assistance. Among further amendments has been an expansion of the number of services that a mental health center is expected to offer from 5 to 12 (P.L. 94-63). One of the key characteristics of a mental health center is that federal funds do not go through state agencies but are funnelled directly to the center and its board. This feature was included in the program at the outset because the National Institute of Mental Health perceived most state mental health agencies as being strongly tied to institutional concerns.

The literature on intergovernmental program evaluation. In recent years, there have been many judgments—most of them negative—about the success of Great Society and New Deal programs. Research on many of these programs has emphasized their difficulty in achieving intended goals. For example, Pressman and Wildavsky found that the necessity of acting jointly with other agencies and individuals made it unlikely that a program could be implemented as planned. Great delay and failures occur even when all persons involved agree as to the major purposes of the program.[2] Murphy has shown that lax enforcement on the part of federal officials may allow states to do virtually as they please with some federal funds.[3] Derthick's study of the New Towns program emphasized the extraordinary difficulty of implementing a program within an intergovernmental context.[4] She argues that in this case federal officials often were not able to offer sufficient incentives to local officials to achieve the intended purposes of the program. A study of another program, the Maternal and Child Health Care legislation, found that states often act to effectively contravene federal policy.[5]

Undoubtedly, these researchers are correct in pointing out that the programs they evaluated did not achieve the expectations and promises of many advocates. However, it is equally true that many of the previous studies of implementation have approached the study of impact with very high expectations. Any program, particularly one involving complex intergovernmental relations, may take many years to achieve an acceptable rate of effectiveness. Therefore, an adequate assessment of such a program requires a long-term perspective. This is not to argue that shorter-term evaluations should not be carried out, only that a longer term perspective is likely to reveal both positive and negative aspects of programs that might be ignored in shorter term studies.

An excellent and dramatic example of using a long term evaluation perspective is Lester Salamon's study, "Follow-ups, Letdowns, and Sleepers: The Time Dimension in Policy Evaluation."[6] Salamon reexamined the New Deal "resettlement program" which began in 1934 and ended in 1943. The program aimed to provide land to blacks in certain areas of the South. Like many current social programs, it encountered stiff opposition and criticism and, according to Salamon, was often cited as a failure. However, there was no systematic evaluation covering the course of the program.

Using an imaginative and varied series of effectiveness measures, Salamon reexamined the program based on data available 30 years after it had ended. He found that it had contributed to a long term increase in the number of black landowners that contrasted sharply with declines in areas not served by the program and that it had many effects perhaps not originally envisioned by even its most enthusiastic proponents. For example, the resettlement project participants were in better nutritional and mental health than comparable blacks who had not participated in the program. Moreover, there was evidence of much greater participation rates in the civil rights movement on the part of blacks who received land.

In *The Implementation Game,* Bardach suggests that it is important to design programs so that they are "implementable," but he also agrees that, in the longer run, it is essential to "become more modest in our demands on, and expectations of" governments and their programs.[7] This is especially true when the program is dealing with complex social factors—as health programs generally do—and intergovernmental relations.

Impact on local government. The more changes a program seeks and the more participation it mandates, the more likely it is to be affected by the local power structure. On the one hand, this tends to mesh national purposes with local values; on the other, it makes it likely that changes emanating from these programs will be small and slow in evolving, though their cumulative effect may be quite large.

Both the health planning and community mental health laws demand the active participation of local communities. Indeed, according to several discussants involved with both the health planning and community mental health programs, a major focus of regional level attention has been to assure that legislative mandates concerning community participation have been strictly enforced. For a typical example:

(HSA staff person) They (Regional Office) faulted us because we didn't have an allied health person. . . . There was also a question if an HMO (Health Maintenance Organization) representative could be designated as a consumer. . . . Six months ago, we got a note that the OGC (Office of General Counsel) had classified chiropractors as health professionals and they would have to be included in the provider category. I had classified them as consumers and went back to the OGC for another opinion. Maybe we don't have a banker on our board but bankers have a cordial relationship with (Name of auto company) which has a representative on the Board. . . . I know that right now the MDs are as mad as hell at me—they had two representatives last year but only one osteopathic physician this year. They weren't satisfied with it.

Similarly in mental health, Regional offices were emphasizing that the rules concerning board representation must be fulfilled. Several board members were forced to resign because they resided outside the catchment area served by the CMHC.

Because of the need to secure this participation, HSAs and CMHCs have to come to terms with the dominant groups in the community power structure. For example, the power structure of the Southeastern Michigan Area is clearly dominated by automobile interests including the major auto makers and the United Auto Workers (UAW) union. They played an important part not only on the Board but also on the Nominating and Membership Committee, the Executive Committee, and the Plan Implementation Committee (PIC). County Commissioners, members of the Medical Society, county public health officials, United Fund corporation members, nursing groups and many other influential groups were represented on the HSA Board. Indeed, a review of the membership of the Board and other committees reveals very few persons who are not affiliated with some key governmental or private interest group and, according to some discussants, these affiliates view the HSA as a means of achieving their group's ends:

> (Health Planner) I would guess that the unions view it (HSA) as a vehicle to gain the (name of union) aims, though they have their own problems with it (HSA). The reasons why they are somewhat dissatisfied is because the HSA can't always be mobilized to deal with their concerns. The major automakers have also discovered health planning... they also see it as a vehicle. For example, that (name of automaker) representative agreed to be Chairman of the Executive Committee reflects this point of view.

With key interest groups so well represented, it is unlikely that HSAs will take positions which consistently oppose the interests of the powerful in a direct way.

A good example of what happens when an HSA takes on the community power structure is provided by a South Carolina HSA which has just gone through an experience which they have termed "educational." The HSA rejected a proposal by a local hospital to carry out a very large expansion program. The reason for rejecting the application was that one part of the program, the creation of a 24-hour emergency service program at the Hospital, would duplicate the service being offered by a public, County Hospital across the street. The County Hospital serves mainly indigent patients while the private hospital was described as being the "Citadel" of the city, serving mainly well-to-do patients and not accepting Medicaid/Medicare patients. Since the private hospital did not have 24-hour emergency service, many of its clients had to use the public County Hospital. These paying clients furnished income to the County Hospital which served mainly indigents.

Actually, the creation of the new emergency services program at the private hospital was only a small part of the total expansion proposed.

Many persons at the HSA had planned to give approval to the expansion until they came across the small section concerning the emergency services program. In some negotiation between the HSA and the private hospital, the hospital insisted on acceptance of the entire package. Some HSA staff voiced regret that they did not have an "item" veto, since much of the expansion program was attractive. When the total HSA board argued the issue, the majority were against the proposed expansion with the emergency service program included.

The private hospital is a prestigious institution and the rejection became a very sharp issue. It apparently received great visibility in the local area. By their own account, HSA staff came out the worse because their decision became depicted as "representing the heavy hand of government" holding back needed services. The HSA decision was appealed by the Hospital to the state level, where it was overturned. According to several discussants, the key factor in overturning the decision was apparently the Governor who, in fact, is an oral surgeon on the staff of the hospital involved.

There were differing reactions to the entire case. Both HSA staff and others, county administrators, medical society officials, and community mental health persons, felt that they had been taught some important lessons. In particular, they had previously thought that the hospital would have to prove that the expansion was needed. However, the issue became redefined so that the HSA had to prove that it was not needed.

In short, the HSA's impact is much greater on procedural matters than on outcomes. The health planning program has made issues that were formerly decided privately more visible and publicly debated. Moreover, although the HSA is not likely to take positions (successfully) which oppose powerful interests, it is still quite possible that HSA decisions will have impacts. For example, even though the HSA "lost" in the above case, it is possible that prestigious hospitals are likely to be more careful about the nature of their future proposals for expansion.

HSAs and similar organizations are more likely to be influential in those situations where the balance of forces is less clear. Such a situation appears to be developing in another HSA area where a private hospital is planning an expansion, part of which is the addition of about fifteen inpatient beds. A planning document for the area has established eight additional beds as a necessary addition through 1982. Thus, this expansion, like the one above, is likely to create some conflict (though the HSA has not yet taken any position concerning this case). As in the other case, the hospital has proposed the additional beds as only one part of a larger expansion in which ancillary services attractive to the community are also offered. It would appear that even if HSAs do not act to control the number of excess hospital beds in an area, they may influence the nature of expansions. Hospitals are likely to include services needed by the community (that they might otherwise not have) in order to make proposed expansions more attractive to HSAs.

There would appear to be some important forces working against the expansion: the public health people, and the County Hospital Administrator. However, in this case, the County Hospital is much more potent than in the other: it serves the indigent but, in addition, serves a large percentage of patients supported by private insurance. Moreover, every physician in the area has an affiliation with this County Hospital.

There are also strong subregional planning bodies in this health service area which are very sensitive to the "representation" issue. The leadership of the subregional Council has instructed its members to go to their groups and find out their positions on the hospital expansion issue. Overall, it would appear that the balance of power is quite different than in the former case. The forces opposing expansion and particularly the County Hospital appear much stronger.

A major part of the task of federal programs like health planning and community mental health is to build political support through community participation and other mechanisms. However, there appear to be wide variations in the degree to which HSAs and CMHCs emphasize the importance of building local support. For example, the HSA which lost the battle in the first case cited above has been devoting a great deal of effort lately to these purposes. It has been concentrating on improving its visibility and attempting to communicate its philosophy and purposes to the media, and, apparently, it feels it has been successful. In its plan, the HSA has very much emphasized health education and primary prevention as its highest priorities. It has apparently gotten substantial amounts of volunteer help and has carried out some efforts in the preventive area. These volunteer activities seem to be a useful way of establishing visibility and acceptance in the community as well as accomplishing important substantive goals. Some respondents criticized HSAs for failure to develop visibility among key elements of the community. For example, we discovered that certain representatives of significant governmental bodies (e.g., Council of Government officials) in certain areas had never heard of their HSAs.

Some community mental health centers spent substantial time during their early years cultivating relationships with the local elite and county commissioners. However, after they had established themselves, they found it unnecessary to keep up such a high level of activities on this "front:"

(Director of CMHC) Early on, we built credibility from the ground up. The City Council didn't know what we were about. We kept them well informed. There is little direct interaction with them now that we are established.... Our interaction has been routinized. We don't even go down to meet with them. We need to identify power structures—cultivating them is important and essential. We are very aware of who is elected to the County Council. Changes can have very subtle effects. For example, the change in the black-white ratio of the Council—when several black members were elected in areas formerly represented by whites—had made us very sensitive to the affirmative action issues.

By way of contrast, the director of a mental health center at a much earlier stage of development, still receiving a high percentage of federal funds (federal contributions to mental health centers start at a very high percentage level and then decline each year until the grant runs out) stated just the opposite:

(Director of CMHC) We don't spend much time on the County Councils—maybe 10 minutes a year. In time we may spend more time with them.... The Mental Health Association is not very active. They give packages for people at the State hospitals.

According to more experienced directors of mental health centers, such a lack of attention to local elites and political officials can lead to great difficulties later when the CMHC needs to get increased local funds. Some CMHCs had gained thousands of dollars of support by inviting members of Councils and other influentials of the community to functions such as luncheons. In general, it appears that the best established HSAs and CMHCs are those that have effectively cultivated elite support at the local level. Thus, social change through intergovernmental programs takes place slowly. The degree and nature of the change that does take place is strongly conditioned by dominant local interests and values.

Federal programs, like all organized entities, have certain "organizational biases"—they do not favor all members or groups in the community equally. Some members of the community tend to benefit from federal programs more than others and some may even be threatened by the programs.

The last section argued that a federal program must come to terms with the power structure of a community. However, a community is composed of many forces, some of them in conflict with others. A program like health planning which has some regulatory power—however ill-defined and weak—is potentially threatening to a wide range of community groups. The HSAs were often perceived by some discussants as acting to the advantage of the larger and more powerful groups in the community. For example, some administrators of small hospitals in one HSA area argued that the health planning act and the HSA were taking positions consistently favorable to large hospitals and detrimental to small ones:

(Small Hospital Administrator) The big hospitals breeze through the HSA.... The HSA's position is that they weren't going to "mess with the Mayor" (who was building a large new general hospital) or (names of two large hospitals)—don't bother the big guys.

Furthermore, they argued that certain characteristics of the health planning law are structured to make the domination by the "big guys" inevitable. The powerful organizations are most likely to be able to afford to have members who devote full-time to HSA activities such as participating on committees (assuming that the smaller and weaker organizations are able to get elected or nominated to the committees in the first place). For example, members of the automakers and UAW were able to have representatives who worked virtually full-time on HSA activities. Thus, they were able to play key roles in the decision making aspects of the HSA. According to some observers, the more powerful interest groups focused their participation on the regulatory aspects of health planning—not on the "planning" parts. They concentrated their attention on the plan implementation committee—where "the action is" according to several observers.

Though the HSA is often reviewed as having not many formal powers, it does have control over one resource which looms especially large to the less powerful and wealthy organizations: time. Because of their authority to review proposed expansions in the health area, the HSA can, and according to a few observers, does delay actions concerning certain hospital expansions. Some persons argued that the HSA will delay decisions for a long period of time until a deadline nears and then suddenly raise a whole new set of questions to which the hospital must respond. One hospital administrator described how he thought that the HSA had manipulated the scheduled meeting for his hospital unfairly:

(Small Hospital Administrator) The agenda for our item was scheduled for noon. However, we were suddenly put first on the agenda. They knew that the person supposed to represent us would not be there until 10:00 a.m. We were given five minutes then to present a 4 million dollar expansion.

Such tactics are less likely to be attempted, much less be effective, with a powerful organization with a full-time staff working on HSA clearance.

Thus, intergovernmental programs tend to act to the benefit of certain local interests and to the detriment of others. The differential impact of the program on these interests may help or hinder efforts to achieve social change. Programs that are perceived as potentially threatening to powerful local interests will take much longer to develop and succeed. Often, an unspoken but essential task of persons implementing an intergovernmental program is to develop support among key local interests.

The impact of intergovernmental programs is often difficult if not impossible to measure in the short run. Many of the most important impacts are of the "non-decision," or unintended variety that require examination of how the program has influenced decision making processes.

The health planning program under 93-641 has only been in existence for a short period of time. Over the long run, there are some obvious measures of outcomes which might be used to assess the success of the program such as the rate of growth (changes in) of excess hospital beds or the improvement in access to primary care on the part of the disadvantaged or underserved. However, it is also true that the health planning program is likely to affect these key outcomes only in indirect ways.

Our limited study of HSAs showed that they have had a much more direct and important impact on the *process* by which hospitals and other health organizations go about developing plans for expansions in hospital beds, new equipment, and other services. In the above case studies, we noted that it is often difficult for the HSA to effectively oppose expansions of large and important hospitals. However, the types of expansions proposed may be quite different under the Health Planning Act than they would have been otherwise. For example, in one case, the proposed expansion of beds was accompanied by the provision of needed coronary care and outpatient units.

HSAs appear to have modified the decision making processes of hospitals and other institutions. In one HSA area, according to two hospital administrators, both of whom were critical of the HSAs overall performance, the HSA has helped them govern the hospitals more efficiently. The administration frequently gets requests from physicians heading programs in the hospital for new equipment, "exotic new services," and other expansions which seem unnecessary or too costly.

The administrators now feel that the existence of the HSA and its review has enabled them to reject expansion proposals which they might formerly have had to support.

Certain physicians and hospital administrators complained that 93-641 had increased their administrative costs substantially (e.g., by several hundred thousand dollars a year). However, it can be argued that these increased administrative costs for hospitals and physicians can be construed as an index of the success of the HSAs, and that, by increasing processing costs, the providers would be more likely to forward to the HSA only the better proposals. In short, an adequate evaluation of the impact of a program like health planning cannot rely on simple outcome measures. It needs to examine the nature and quality of expansions that have occurred.

The community mental health program has been in existence for a far longer period of time than health planning. In some respects, the program has been highly successful with a large number of community mental health centers flourishing across the country where previously few, if any, community services had been available. However, our visits to South Carolina and Michigan revealed a major limitation on the CMHC program in that it has been unintendedly structured to work best in those areas that need it least and to have the most difficulties in those areas that need federal CMHC support the most.

The CMHC program was flourishing in areas like Washtenaw County of Michigan, a fairly well-to-do area including the University of Michigan in its catchment area. This mental health center had a budget in excess of a million dollars *before* it received a federal staffing grant. In the Washtenaw area, there appears to be an abundance of qualified persons to serve on boards and act as volunteers.

By way of contrast, the mental health centers in some parts of South Carolina and Detroit appear to be struggling to stay afloat financially. Also, several of the Detroit centers are reported to have had difficulties in securing adequate participation on the part of community board members. According to several persons, there is a dearth of persons interested and qualified to serve on the boards. Many of these centers had little hope that they would be able to survive financially as the federal grant contribution declined, unless either the federal government continued to support them or the state took over to replace declining federal funds. There was no hope that increased local support or other funds (e.g., from third party payments) would be able to replace decreasing federal contributions. Other centers had had difficulty in developing all of the services eventually required by the mental health act (94-63). Comments of these mental health persons reflect some of their dissatisfaction with the feasibility of 94-63:

(Mental Health Center Director) The whole damn thing (94-63) is unreasonable. The legislation was needed but the expectations are impossible to meet—2 years to get 12 services in place. The great needs in this area are jobs, services for alcoholics, and physical health care. We also have problems with under-utilization.

(Mental Health Center Director) I think that the federal government will have to support us continually. The legislation is very unrealistic. I don't see how we will ever be self-supporting unless we refuse treatment to those who can't pay—which we can't do.

(State Mental Health Department Representative) The federal model acts as if communities actually exist. But this is not often the case. The community hospitals are not interested in providing psychiatric inpatient care which is needed very much here. . . . The idea of setting up so many services in such a short period of time is unrealistic—we haven't yet seen a center do what the federal model wanted. . . . If you want to be effective in this area, you would probably pick a small elite board—not a grass roots board.

In short, there appear to have been certain underlying assumptions made concerning the original CMHC legislation for the law to be successful which are able to be met in certain middle class areas like Washtenaw County but fail in other areas like Detroit and much of South Carolina:

(1) The legislation tends to assume that the area has capable and interested people who can form community boards and mobilize people for community mental health.
(2) It assumes that the local areas have the potential financial resources to support the CMHC as the federal contribution declines. It assumes that there are grantsmen who can pull in dollars from other levels of government to supplant declining federal support.
(3) It assumes that communities need and are able to establish within a short period of time a wide variety of services. (Note: According to several observers, the greatest mental health need in the Detroit area was for inpatient psychiatric beds—not community services.)

In certain respects, it is localities like Detroit and South Carolina which have the most serious mental health problems and thus need the federal program the most. But, according to several observers, it is these needy areas which are not able to use the program effectively because they fail to meet the assumptions outlined above. It is these CMHCs that have experienced great budgetary and administrative difficulties.

It should be noted that this paradox is far from being an uncommon one among intergovernmental federal programs. For example, programs that depend on the state to take the initiative to provide matching funds are almost always more highly used by progressive states where need for the services is often less. This phenomenon took place with the juvenile delinquency program in which the more progressive states with the capacity to engage in the program took advantage of the trade-off between state financial support and state control.[8] Similarly, within states, it is often the poor communities which make out more poorly than well-to-do areas. For example, in the Maternal and Child Health Care Program, poor communities were not able to put up the matching funds required by some states.[9] Consciously or unconsciously, legislators and administrators appear to structure legislation and regulations so that the middle-class well-to-do areas are likely to benefit the most.

Conclusions and implications. Intergovernmental programs are highly complex and take a long time to develop. When local participation is mandated for these programs as in the health planning and community mental health programs, they take all the more time to construct the web of formal and informal relations with local communities necessary to make them operational and effective. It is important that these programs be given sufficient time to develop before any summary judgments are made about their impact. Persons involved in administering the programs need to develop effective relationships with key members of the local community power structure. Failure to do so may lead to serious difficulties as it has with some HSAs and CMHCs. In their efforts to build support locally, it appears that programs inevitably tend to favor certain interests more than others. This "favoritism," however, may facilitate or frustrate desired changes.

One of the most important findings is the importance of giving intergovernmental programs time to develop sufficiently. Several respondents brought this issue up themselves, pointing out the fact that the federal government often appears to bring programs to an end just as they are beginning to work effectively:

(Health Planner) The "B" process (Comprehensive Health Planning legislation which preceded (P.L. 93–641)) is only getting to the point where it had credibility when it was ended. I predict that Congress will run out of patience with HSAs and go toward more centralized control. The PSRO program is another good comparison. Michigan was late in getting Federal dollars from this program. Our first PSRO just began last summer. You should have heard the furor when there was talk of not funding PSROs again. People give up before the programs have a chance to do anything at all.

Likewise, people in community mental health stated that they would like to see more continuity in regard to services required and other regulations. Clearly the time perspective of evaluators is an important determinant of the kind of results they are likely to find. For complex intergovernmental programs, evaluations carried out prematurely are likely to find limited or negative results.

A related point concerns the kind of effectiveness measures that should be employed in impact studies. This small study found that the health planning program, for example, is more likely to influence qualitative factors (e.g., the nature of proposed expansions) than gross quantitative measures (e.g., changes in the number of excess beds or health status of an area). A longer term perspective is also able to reveal limitations or negative aspects of programs which might not be obvious in shorter term studies. There was some indication that certain types of areas are unable to meet certain assumptions which appear to be inherent in the community mental health center legislation. Such unexpected consequences of intergovernmental programs are frequently more important than more obvious features that evaluators tend to focus on.

The argument here is that assessing program impact in an intergovernmental context is much more difficult than even the previous literature would suggest. In recent years, frequent statements have been made about the "bankruptcy" of Great Society and New Deal programs. Many of these programs may indeed have been failures. However, there is also evidence that the impact of many intergovernmental programs is never adequately assessed. It often appears that the time perspectives of both legislators and evaluators are too short to support the development of effective programs. However, the generalizations made in this study are based on a very small and exploratory study. More research emphasis would appear to be fruitful on what Salamon calls "the time dimension" in evaluation research.[10]

Notes

1. See Miller and Byrne, Inc., *The Impact of PHS Programs on State Goals and Activities* (Rockville, Md.: Health Resources Administration, 1977).
2. Jeffrey Pressman and Aaron Wildavsky, *Implementation* (Berkeley: University of California Press, 1973).
3. Jerome Murphy, *State Education Agencies and Discretionary Funds: Grease the Squeaky Wheel* (Lexington: Lexington Books, 1974).
4. Martha Derthick, *New Towns In-Town* (Washington, D.C.: The Urban Institute, 1972).
5. Christa Altenstetter, James Warner Bjorkman, Anne-Marie Foltz, and George A. Silver, *Politics and Social Policy: Failures in Child Health Services* (Rockville, Md.: National Center for Health Services Research, August, 1976).
6. Lester M. Salamon, "Follow-ups, Letdowns, and Sleepers: The Time Dimension in Policy Evaluation," *Public Policy Making in a Federal System,* eds.: C. O. Jones and Robert D. Thomas (Beverly Hills: Sage Publications, 1976).
7. Eugene Bardach, "The Skill Factor in Politics," *The Implementation Game: What Happens After a Bill Becomes a Law* (Cambridge: The MIT Press, 1977) p. 283.
8. Donald Haider, *When Governments Come to Washington* (New York, The Free Press, 1974).
9. Altenstetter, ibid., p. 32.
10. Salamon, ibid.

36

HEALTH CARE POLICY AND POLITICS
Does the Past Tell Us Anything about the Future?

Stephen M. Weiner

ABSTRACT

The American health care delivery system, and the attitude of the public toward that system, have undergone considerable change during the past two decades. According to the author, the belief during the 1960s that adequate funds were available to broaden access to health services, to enhance their quality and availability, and to support medical innovation, gave way during the 1970s to an awareness of limited resources, to a skepticism about the motives and competence of established institutions, and to a conviction that the system's problems were too complex to be solved easily, if at all. Moreover, the author states, the system has become fragmented and highly competitive; the respect formerly accorded both professionals and institutions has deteriorated; and the government's role in health care delivery is being challenged.

The result, the author says, may well be a paralysis of policymaking in health planning, as exemplified by the failure of both public and private institutions to achieve the cost-containment goals of the last decade, either through regulation or competition.

To gain perspective on these problems and to determine the direction of the health care delivery system for the 1980s, the author calls for a national health care debate. He suggests four concepts that should be included in such a debate, and recommends a new context of pragmatic idealism in which to conduct it.

I. OUR INHERITANCE FROM THE 1970s: GENERAL PROBLEMS OF THE HEALTH CARE DELIVERY SYSTEM

And we begin the 1980s, it is time to assess recent developments in the national health care delivery system in order to determine the direction in

---

* Associate Professor of Law and Director, Center for Law and Health Sciences, Boston University School of Law; Contributing Editor, *American Journal of Law & Medicine*.

This Comment was developed from a speech given by the author at Laventhol and Horwath's Twelfth Annual Symposium on Health Care, in Chicago, Illinois, on October 25, 1979.

Reprinted from the AMERICAN JOURNAL OF LAW & MEDICINE Vol. 5, No. 4, pp. 331-341, with permission of the AMERICAN SOCIETY OF LAW & MEDICINE, 520 Commonwealth Ave., Boston, MA 02215.

which we will be, or ought to be, headed during the next decade. In order to understand where the health care delivery system is going, however, we must first examine the current politics of that system. Any changes that might occur in its methods of organization or of delivery will require prior changes in public and in private policy; and policy of both kinds will be determined, as always, by the political relationships and attitudes of the people concerned with the health care delivery system—those who favor change and those who don't. Unfortunately, based on an assessment of the current political situation, predictions of the system's future direction will not proceed from any optimistic premises. In this respect, health care is no different from many other parts of the American economy and society in 1980.

What are the dominant features of the health care delivery system's political landscape that require us to be cautious, at best, in thinking ahead about the 1980s? Three factors emerge as particularly significant: (1) the reality of limited resources, a theme of health care policy discussions for the past decade, but now exacerbated by double-digit inflation and tight monetary policies; (2) skepticism about the motives and competence of established institutions, an attitude born in the radical movement of the 1960s and codified in popular beliefs of the 1970s; and (3) a widespread feeling that problems have become too complex, that easily identified or implemented solutions are unavailable, or that, perhaps, there are no solutions. These do not constitute a pretty landscape, but elaboration on these three characteristics gives one a better sense of how they affect health care politics and policy at the beginning of the 1980s.

Our present awareness of the limitations on our resources conflicts with the perhaps naively optimistic view of the mid-1960s that there were adequate funds to broaden access to health services, to enhance their quality and availability, and to continue to support medical innovation. In contrast with that view, the reality of our limited resources means that there are not even enough dollars to keep most people happy, especially those practitioners who entered the health care system imbued with the expansive psychology of the 1960s. In this changed climate, we are confronted with the problem of how to ensure both appropriate access to available resources and equitable sharing of them. The mechanisms for solving these problems, however, have yet to evolve.

As a result, there is a sense of anxiety and of increasing incivility among the competing grazers on the medical common. Providers and consumers alike worry about ways of improving access and of increasing entitlement to treatment. While these are still treasured objectives, attempts to realize them can make excessive demands on resources, as the Medicare program has shown us. Moreover, other deep-seated conflicts abound within the health care system. Hospitals and HMOs engage in the business of "marketing" their services, in effect promoting demand in order to maintain their financial stability, as institutional, physician, and nonphysician providers compete to retain or to expand their share of patients and of funding. Physicians argue with hospital administrators about the purchase of new equipment; increasingly militant nurses demand an increased share of the hospital dollar and greater responsibility for patient care; and unions grow ever more forceful, as workers learn that collective action may be the most effective way to maintain or to increase their "piece of the action."

Interprofessional hostility is rife. An oversupply of physicians limits the professional and financial options of other health care personnel; for example, psychologists and social workers struggle to attain equal footing with psychiatrists in terms of reimbursement from third party payors. Home health agencies and neighborhood health centers resent the competition of hospitals and sometimes of each other. The patient-care-team model seems to be disintegrating into rival constituencies as new professional specialties and sub-specialties develop and assert their "rights." It appears that the civility that once characterized professional relationships is unlikely to survive the constraints now placed upon health care resources.

What has emerged in the health care delivery system, as the President has observed in the society at large, is the growth of narcissism: the fragmentation of the body politic into competing self-interest groups, each out for itself, with little concern for understanding others' objectives or for developing broader perspectives on the system and its needs.

The division that exists within the health care delivery system is reflected outside of it as well: the system's component institutions no longer receive the respect society traditionally has accorded them. The ideologies of the 1960s and the economics of the 1970s have conspired to erode the status of institutions and professionals alike. Studies indicate, for example, that while people generally admire their own physicians, many of them no longer respect physicians as a class. The prevalence of malpractice litigation against physicians gives further evidence of the deterioration of the sanctity of the physician-patient relationship; together with the Federal Trade Commission's antitrust attacks on professions that ban advertising and the publishing of fee schedules, the increase in such litigation suggests that, in a society where elitism connotes snobbery, membership in a profession no longer guarantees either respectability or immunity from suit.

The government is perhaps even more affected by skepticism about traditional values and institutions than are the professionals and institutions themselves. A neocynicism, now ensconced in the public awareness as neoconservatism, represents in part an economic response to the government's need for tax revenue, and in part a psychological response to perceived failures of the activist government of the 1960s. Partisans of this cynicism are demanding a reexamination of government's role in the health care delivery system; specifically, their questions concern the propriety of regulation as a cost-containment policy. In their view, moreover, the government's responsibility for both financing and regulating the health care delivery system raises additional concerns: What demands or conditions will the government, in its role as a major purchaser, place on the health care delivery system? Does the government seek genuine improvements in the system, or are its actions motivated solely by its own budgetary aims? Such questions underlie much of the ambivalence surrounding the various national health insurance proposals. Indeed, the government itself seems to have doubts about its role, as numerous political battles between and within the Administration and Congress suggest.

With the government increasingly stymied, consumer groups seeking major changes in the accessibility and availability of services no longer can rely on it as the expediter of reform. Unfortunately, no alternative institutions have emerged to fulfill that role. Indeed, the combination of cynicism and narcissism described above discourages the growth of strong constituencies supporting positive change, just as the economics of health care tends to neutralize constituencies that support cost-containment objectives.

Provider groups, like consumer groups, are becoming better organized, greater in number, and increasingly willing to play by the rules of interest-group politics in the present environment, in which single-issue groups usually dominate. In contrast, both Congress and the Executive, long accustomed to a political process that involves a relatively small number of groups with relatively broad agendas—where the desirability of compromise is understood from the outset—are having difficulty adjusting to a proliferation of interested parties, to narrowly defined agendas, and to a spirit that views compromise as unavailable, or at least as a last resort. Moreover, the increasing use of litigation by both hospital associations and consumer advocacy groups suggests that the courts also are being brought into the health care delivery system's political process.

The outcome of all these developments may very well be a paralysis of policymaking in which the government, hamstrung by self-doubt, becomes incapable of addressing major issues, of examining and evaluating them rationally, or of committing itself to a clearly articulated policy that can produce any coherent result. Thus immobilized, the government, at best, can engage in relatively insignificant tinkerings on the margins of health care problems.

What has emerged from the late 1970s, therefore, is a political system that has great difficulty in resolving important issues. Policy discussion has become enveloped in new rhetoric, reminiscent of earlier decades, that polarizes rather than clarifies. What better example of this stalemate could we have than the current debate over regulation versus competition? It takes thoughtful, and perhaps optimistic, vision to see that an accommodation between the two policies actually can be reached, that both policies can co-exist, and that, indeed, each reinforces the other. In so complex a structure as the American health care delivery system, a diversity of approaches is both possible and desirable.

In the absence of such vision, and despite the incessant discussion during the 1970s of our ideals and objectives in health care, significant questions concerning cost, quality, availability, accessibility, and continuity of care remain unanswered. As the 1980s begin, there is a growing negativism, a feeling that perhaps these questions cannot be answered, that their resolution is beyond the capacity of our current institutions, or beyond the capacity of democratic institutions at all. Such extreme proposals as explicit rationing of health care services or mandatory life-style changes are a reflection of this reaction against the optimism of the 1960s. The question that confronts us now is whether the current situation is the best we can hope for?

II. THE PROBLEMS OF COST CONTAINMENT: AN EXAMPLE OF OUR PRESENT DILEMMA

The problems of cost containment, a leading theme of the health care debate of the 1970s, illustrate how cynicism, narcissism, and negativism work together to frustrate policymaking and policymakers. At the root of cost-containment problems are two realities that the political system has been unable to alter. First, the structure of third party insurance reimbursement creates financial incentives that induce unnecessarily costly behavior and that help to maintain current patterns of provider dominance, particularly by hospitals and by specialty physicians. Second, direct consumers of health care services (patients, that is, not physicians or insurers) are not equipped either intellectually (because they do not possess adequate medical information) or emotionally (because their need for treatment generates anxiety, which often prevents them from seeking information concerning alternative forms of treatment), to make rational decisions on the quantity and quality of services they purchase.

Thus far, we have failed, not only to meet the challenges of these realities, but even to agree on a comprehensive system that can tackle the tough questions of cost containment. Instead, we have piecemeal strategies that only loosely are tied together. As ad hoc responses to the complexity of the health care system, very few of these strategies can withstand either rigorous intellectual scrutiny or political attack. The fragility of some of these strategies becomes even more apparent upon closer examination.

Regulation still appears to be the dominant approach to cost containment, yet, increasingly, its credibility is challenged—ideologically, by neoconservatives, and politically, by the regulated providers. In addition, its credibility is threatened by the loss of esteem for government regulators, one side effect of the general erosion of respect for government.

Most cost-containment regulation, particularly rate setting and certificate-of-need programs, is fragmented. It concentrates on hospitals, despite the fact that a large proportion of hospital costs are generated by physicians who remain largely unregulated. Further, much regulation is tied to particular third party programs, which raises many important questions about the third parties' motivations toward cost containment, and about the fairness of regulation as a proper cost-containment strategy. Although some states' hospital budget control programs appear to be effective, the opposition of private-interest groups and of hospital associations has successfully prevented the development of a similar program on the national level. Court challenges and special legislative exemptions, moreover, wear down the intellectual and physical resources of the agencies administering promising regulatory schemes.

As an alternative to regulation, increasingly we are hearing proposals to achieve cost-containment ends by fostering competition. Here, too, however, analytic problems exist that dispel any illusion of easy solutions. To what extent, for example, can we rely on consumer choice in order to achieve cost containment? Do we really want competition among providers, particularly hospitals, when what this implies is competition to add more services and more technology to satisfy physicians' demands?

Among those who propose strategies to encourage competition, some stress enforcement of the antitrust laws as a means to this end. It appears, however, that antitrust remedies have had, at most, a very small impact on the health care delivery system, and in fact they may have been counterproductive, as, for instance, when fear of antitrust action has inhibited consolidation of hospitals, where such consolidation might have contributed to cost containment. The problem, moreover, is still more complex, because we don't really know whether hospital consolidation is conducive to efficiency and to cost containment. When one enters the hospital arena, the laws of economics sometimes appear to be suspended.

Another proposed cost-containment strategy has been to shift resources from hospital settings to nonhospital settings. The first problem to emerge with this strategy was the discovery by cost analysts of the unit-cost/total-cost phenomenon. To give an example of this phenomenon, an ambulatory center may have lower unit costs than a hospital, but establishing an ambulatory center may do more than simply shift demand away from the hospital. Instead, it may induce more demand, thus increasing the total cost of the health care delivery system.

Further, the resource-shifting strategy assumes the existence of a rational plan for financing the health care delivery system. At present, however, only spotty coverage is available for many ambulatory or community-based services. So, while it may be valuable to talk about expanding these services, implementing the strategy of resource shifting may require substantial reform of health care financing, reform that may be resisted and stymied by those who benefit from current arrangements.

Finally, any effort to shift resources away from hospitals raises their anxiety level. To reduce their anxiety, hospitals have attempted to dominate the developing system of ambulatory and home health care. It would be nice to think that hospitals are motivated by the desire to provide sophisticated management and back-up services for nonhospital modes of treatment, but their real interests are more closely associated with their need to spread overhead, to develop new patient sources to feed inpatient referrals, and to dampen or eliminate real competition.

As an alternative to the proposals discussed above, some proponents of cost containment have suggested that we tackle the cost problem by adopting healthier lifestyles, by improving the environment, by more vigorously enforcing the fifty-five mile per hour speed limit, by improving housing and nutrition, or by a number of other related approaches. Ultimately, however, any attempted solution inextricably intertwines us in complex social, economic, and political problems. The absence of easy, equitable solutions to these problems raises the frustration level within the system; that frustration, in turn, feeds the politics of narcissism, which leads to rejection of both the approach and the system.

III. PROPOSAL FOR THE 1980s: A NATIONAL HEALTH CARE DEBATE

Based on this gloomy assessment of our current situation, what can we look forward to in the 1980s? We know that change in American society rarely occurs in quantum leaps; significant change can occur, however, in incremental stages. The key to moving ahead is having a sense of where we want to go and then moving step by step to get there, a process that, to be effective, requires some capacity to control the direction, if not the rate, of change. Although it is naive to talk about a rational process of change unless we have authoritative institutions that are willing to promote it, the current state of affairs demands that we attempt, once again, to develop a serious public debate about the future of the health care delivery system.

A "serious" debate could not be, as many debates on this subject have been in the past, clouded in the rhetoric, but not the reality, of "competition," or "quality," or "concern only for the patients' well-being." The participants in this debate would have an obligation to evaluate their own objectives critically, to articulate them concretely, candidly, and explicitly, and to specify what steps are necessary in order to achieve them. Present initiatives, policies, and political positions must be evaluated in light of efforts to evolve common policy objectives.

Such a debate would not foreclose the possibility that our present situation best accommodates the various conflicting goals described above; if that conclusion is correct, however, it should emerge through open and self-critical discussion. The debate need not be initiated formally—with an announcement and an agenda—if the participants are aware of the need for the debate and take advantage of existing machinery to begin it. One possible approach would be to use the present health planning system for this purpose, with discussions occurring simultaneously at the national, state, and local levels. In a few geographical areas, such as Massachusetts, this already has begun to happen.

A. Four Suggested Concepts for a Health Care Debate

The initial goal of a new health care debate would be to conduct a principled reevaluation of our health policies. This Comment suggests four concepts that should be included in a debate on directions for the health care delivery system.

(1) First, the role of consumers—whether patients or other interested persons—in medical decision making should be enlarged significantly. This does not mean merely that we develop more consumer advisory councils, or that we rely exclusively on consumer/provider planning bodies. Rather, we need to pursue a conscious policy to ensure that consumers are well-enough informed about health care delivery issues to participate much more extensively in both personal and institutional decisions. In order to implement this concept:

(a) The medical profession should be demystified. Physicians should be trained in medical school to explain their procedures and to treat their patients as equals, not only to avoid potential liability by obtaining informed consent, but also to ensure that medical treatment decisions genuinely will be the patient's.

(b) Physicians should be trained to explain medical issues to patients in nontechnical language. At the same time, physicians should not assume either that they know what is best for the patient or that they are better suited than the patient to understand all the factors relevant to a medical decision. Recent court opinions—like the *Saikewicz* opinion in Massachusetts— support the view that physicians are not always the most appropriate parties to make treatment decisions.

(c) Patients' bills of rights should be made into more than pieces of paper; they should be made to represent an institutional commitment to providing patients with sufficient data so that they can be informed consumers. As a further means of involving the public in health care questions, hospitals should consider developing non-hospital-based patient advocacy services.

(d) Hospitals should overcome their predilection for confidentiality and should take steps to assure widespread distribution of financial and service information to the public. In pursuit of this goal, a restructuring of the role of hospital trustees may be necessary. Trustees, as consumers, should represent the community that receives the hospital's services (not simply an elite portion of that community) and should participate more actively and knowledgeably in institutional decision making than they do at present. To make such a representative role for trustees effective, they need to be educated, not only about specific institutional goals or hospital objectives, but also about the health care delivery system as a whole—where it is going or should be going—and about the role their institution should play in it. The trustees should feel a responsibility to the hospital, but not simply as an autonomous entity, rather as an integral part of the health care delivery system.

(2) Second, the role of hospitals should be reassessed. The technological base of modern medicine and the structure of health insurance have made the hospital the dominant institution in the health care delivery system. Now, however, it may be necessary to reduce this dominance. For one thing, hospitals are expensive, even for routine services. For another, their internal financial arrangements, particularly with physicians, encourage specialization and reliance on expensive technology. Finally, their approach to the organized practice of medicine perpetuates the physician-centered model of health care, which results in the withholding of status and respect from other health professionals and in the loss of potential savings from making broader use of such nonphysicians.

Reassessing the role of hospitals involves the following:

(a) Financial incentives should be changed, in order to discourage overutilization of hospital-based services and to limit the growth of specialization. Proposals along these lines have been much discussed, but little acted upon.

(b) Hospitals need to be restrained from dominating the development of nonhospital and community-based systems. In addition to encouraging economy and diversification, such a policy could increase consumer control by enlarging the role in health care delivery of new institutions whose boards of trustees include a majority of consumer representatives.

(c) The role of nonphysician health professionals within the hospital setting should be enhanced to afford them a key part in decision making. This approach would lessen the current emphasis on specialty physicians and would foster innovative approaches to care.

(d) Hospital administrators and trustees need to question whether it is necessary to maintain their hospital with its existing array of services. Hospitals should consider mergers and closures, and initiate them where warranted. If the hospital system has excess bed capacity, hospital administrators should take responsibility for identifying and eliminating it, instead of merely reacting to external regulatory or financial pressures. As service (and usually nonprofit) organizations, hospitals should not be perpetuating themselves if their services are no longer needed.

(3) Reassessment of the future of hospitals is closely tied to the third major concept: the role of regulation must be reexamined. So much political effort is devoted to opposing extension of regulatory programs or to cutting back on existing ones, so much intellectual effort is devoted to achieving cost-containment objectives without regulation, that any discussion of health

policy must examine the role that regulation should play in the future. A number of observations are pertinent to such a discussion:

(a) The current economic incentives of the health care delivery system suggest that regulation will sustain its status as a major policy tool. Before another approach can take its place, other cost-containment methods will have to be proven equally effective, which does not seem imminent.

(b) The objectives of regulation must be identified specifically. Too often, regulatory programs are created with broad mandates that fail to set discrete and explicit objectives. As a result, such schemes are overwhelmed by ambiguity and appear to fail, because they cannot meet goals that were never adequately defined to begin with. Regulation should be evaluated in terms of its objectives, and public discussions should determine whether the objectives are valid and whether regulation is the appropriate means to achieve them.

(c) Regulation should be used creatively as a framework for other policy approaches. Proponents of competition should consider how regulation can encourage free-market-type innovations in the health care delivery system. For example, both the recent National Health Planning Amendments and Utah's certificate-of-need law look to regulation to foster or to protect competitive alternatives. How this relationship between regulation and competition will work out in practice is unclear, but it could provide a unique example of cooperation between advocates of public and of private interests. While some may view this situation as anomalous, regulation seems to be a prerequisite to developing competitive approaches within the structure of the health care delivery system, just as the threat of regulation encouraged a voluntary cost-containment effort by the hospital industry.

(d) Regulation explicitly should encourage both the public and the private sectors to play a creative part in the health care delivery system. Regulators should be willing to take risks in carving out areas where private decision makers—carefully controlled and monitored—can devise their own techniques for achieving regulation's agreed-upon aims. Such an outcome-oriented approach is valid for rate setting as well as for licensure. The health care delivery system is too diverse to force all decisions into predetermined channels and processes, or to sustain the assumption that only governmental agencies can make decisions that achieve desired regulatory objectives.

(4) The final area of concern is that Great Debate item of both the 1960s and the 1970s, national health insurance—an idea, as one observer has noted, whose time may already have passed. The core concerns underlying the debate were: improving access, assuring that people are financially able to obtain needed health care, and avoiding the creation of a system so expensive that it jeopardizes its own political and administrative support.

Although these objectives are simply stated, they are by no means simply achieved. Since any national health insurance proposal will have a substantial effect on many aspects of the health care delivery system, every interest group has something at stake in whatever design is adopted. No one program has been able to satisfy enough people to obtain general support; consequently, no program has passed.

Indeed, all of the elements described earlier that have produced a paralysis of policymaking in American health care can be seen in the history of national health insurance. Perhaps, therefore, the subject of national health insurance is an appropriate one on which to begin the debate over the future of the national health care delivery system.

B. A New Context for Health Planning in the 1980s

Whatever the subject of a national health insurance debate, or any debate on health policy and objectives, the participants' ultimate guiding principle should be compassion for people who have no choices within the health care delivery system. Institutional and vested self-interest must yield to that principle.

Norman Cousins, in a recent edition of the *Saturday Review,* describes what he sees as a new consciousness emerging from the 1970s, one that will enable people to accept responsiblity for themselves and for one another. People, he writes, have a pervasive awareness of their interconnection in a fragile estate. This concept is particularly germane to any resolution of the urgent problems plaguing our health care delivery system.

Only by identifying such transcendent values as compassion for human needs, and by transforming these values into operating principles, can we move beyond the cynicism, narcissism, and negativism of the 1970s. In light of all our problems, it may be naive to make optimistic predictions, but if the 1960s belonged to the dreamers, and the 1970s to the cynics, then perhaps the 1980s should belong to a new breed of pragmatic idealists—people who keep their values and goals foremost in mind, but are willing to proceed step by step to satisfy them. Perhaps such a pragmatic idealism will help us to get real reform of the health care delivery system moving again in the 1980s.

EDUCATION

Education has been subjected to policy alteration as a consequence of society's inability to rationalize living space without regard to color or wealth, and also as education has come to mean not simply elementary forms of learning which young people are entitled to but the rights of an entire citizenry throughout life. Problems of education become subject to policy especially as the needs of society demand lifelong education: retooling and retraining to fit new job requirements, the use of pedagogic mechanisms to equalize opportunities for public and parochial education, and the use of testing and tracking to determine life chances at very young ages. The field of education is especially vulnerable to policy decisions because of the commonly accepted notions—perhaps not always accurate—that upward social mobility is profoundly affected by the length of years spent in an educational environment. As advanced postindustrial societies move toward a knowledge base and away from an industrial base, one can expect policy-regulating education output and opportunity to dramatically increase. Whether such policy activities can reduce racial, religious, and social divisions, or will simply compel countermoves by a private, unregulated sphere, remains a major acid test for educational systems and for the public policy style—for the interventionist approach in human affairs, as such.

Sowell's piece indicates the overlap of areas such as race and education, but also the autonomous development areas of education and how this can sometimes become subverted by special pleading and special interests. Sowell argues that the mindless pursuit of busing, banning educational tests because they tell people things they don't want to hear, and searching out role models rather than sound pedagogy are not policy solutions but policy problems. He argues instead for a policy encouraging upward mobility and class openness rather than college education as a prelude to mobility. Reversing characteristic American patterns, he claims, has enlarged black problems, not provided racially sound solutions. Lynch's paper on "Public Policy and Competency Testing" takes a middle road position, noting that such tests should be used to enhance and improve schooling and not, as is too often the case, employed as a tracking or an exclusionary device. He urges policies that would strike a balance between the liberation of the child and judgments concerning the adequacy of schooling. The essay by Rost notes that public policy-making will encourage educational myths only up to a certain point, as exemplified by California's Proposition 13. The assault on policy takes the form of an attack on what Rost refers to as "public sector imperialism." The return to market considerations changes the face of education in the present; and it must also begin to shape policy if the myths of the benefits of the educational system as a whole are to survive—even in fragmented form.

37

HERESIES ON RACE AND EDUCATION

Thomas Sowell

All public policies are based on assumptions or beliefs which in turn reflect a general vision of man and society. In the debate on public policy, even on policies affecting millions of people, most such assumptions are taken as given and are rarely challenged or even tested against either current or historical facts.

The problem is particularly evident in judicial educational policy on race and ethnicity—as much in the commitment to busing, as to equalizing educational expenditures per-pupil.

The best publicized assumptions guiding judicial educational policy today are that segregated schools are inherently inferior (*Brown v. Board of Education*), and that equalizing per-pupil expenditures is essential to equalize education (*Serrano v. Priest*). Two more general assumptions encompassing these and other policies and judgments are first, that large disparities in school performances among racial or ethnic groups are unusual and suspicious, and second, that they necessarily reflect differences in the way those groups are treated by the schools and/or the society.

Apparent reasonableness is no substitute for empirical verification.

These are not unreasonable assumptions—indeed they are so apparently reasonable as to have become well-nigh unshakable articles of faith. But apparent reasonableness is no substitute for empirical verification, especially when so much is at stake.

Other common educational doctrines of our times are that school perfor-

---

Published by permission of Transaction, Inc. from TAXING & SPENDING, Vol. 3, No. 4. Copyright © 1980 by the Institute for Contemporary Studies.

mance is greatly influenced by, variously: family socioeconomic status, class size, teacher-student differences in ethnicity, and—a favorite whipping boy of late—the cultural bias of tests. These doctrines have seldom been seriously tested. Statistical correlations are abundantly available in support of some of them, but the principle that "correlation is not causation" is fundamental to any sort of statistical research, including that of social science. It cannot be simply a pious disclaimer uttered in passing, while proceeding posthaste to equate the two in cognitive conclusion or policy application.

Astonishingly, the truth—and it can be proven with a wealth of data—is that all of these key policy presuppositions are dead wrong.

Segregation is not the villain

There is no serious question that the segregated black schools long traditional in the South had overall educational results far inferior to those in the white schools in the same communities. The Supreme Court in *Brown v. Board of Education* attributed causation, thereby declaring segregation the reason for educational and psychological problems in the black schools, and in turn deciding that this state-enforced educational inferiority constituted a denial of the equal-protection clause of the Fourteenth Amendment to the Constitution. But the mere contemporaneous existence of two striking social phenomena—rigid racial segregation and large differences in academic performance, in this case—does not automatically establish one as the cause of the other. There are other possibilities.

Among the best-known competing theories are that deficiencies in educational performance are the result of either (1) a unique black heredity, or (2) a unique black environment or history. Tempting as it is to plunge into the Jensen controversy (as I have done elsewhere[1]), we must recognize how irrelevant these hotly disputed theories are for the issue at hand. Before resorting to either hereditary or environmental theories which—even if true—would be applicable only to the special case of blacks, we must first determine whether the performance disparities between blacks and whites are themselves unique. In other words, we need to frame some *general* hypotheses, going beyond black-white differences, and at least *see* whether these larger patterns apply to racial as well as ethnic or other socioeconomic group differences. If such an attempt fails, then we may formulate theories applying solely to blacks and whites. But we should not begin by presuming such an attempt must fail, before even trying.

> *The mere contemporaneous existence of racial segregation and large differences between blacks and whites in academic performance does not automatically establish one as the cause of the other.*

So the question is, what would we expect to see if segregation did *not* cause significant educational differences? Setting aside the assumption of a genetic basis, we might expect to find at least three major phenomena. First, black intellectual or educational performance would not be unique in level or pattern, but would closely approximate the performance of some other group(s). Second, some groups who live in the same neighborhoods and attend the same schools together would exhibit intellectual or educational differences comparable to black-white differences in the segregated South. Third, performance differences *within* the set of segregated black schools would be comparable to those *between* black and white schools in the segregated South.

One might argue that blacks' unique historical background might substitute for a unique genetic background in preventing emergence of these phenomena. However, if these phenomena *do* emerge, despite some unique features of black history, then the argument about the importance of segregation is undermined all the more. That is, the uniqueness of racial segregation *plus* all the other unique features of black history together would have been unable to prevent the emergence of a pattern found among other American ethnic groups not subject to these unique influences. In fact, the phenomena not only exist and have long existed, but are easily uncovered and readily documented.

"Blackness" is not the point

The habit of comparing black IQs, reading scores, or other indices of aptitude or performance with "the national average" glosses over the question whether that "national average" is itself only an amalgam of results as disparate as the black-white differences under discussion. This is also true of comparison of economic or other indices of any given group with the so-called "national average."

However, this caveat aside, the fact is that the average IQs of blacks in the United States have been consistently around 85, compared to the national norm of 100. Despite a long and bitter controversy over how best to explain this supposedly unique black IQ level, neither the hereditary nor the environmental advocates have established said uniqueness in the first place. History presents an entirely different picture from that which most people assume. There has been nothing unique about the black IQ level. Group IQ averages at or below 85 have been common in history and are still common. Back in the 1920s, for example, numerous studies showed these IQ averages for such American ethnic groups as the Italians, Greeks, Poles, Hispanics, Slovaks, and Portuguese.[2] A more recent study shows Mexican-Americans with lower average IQs than blacks in the 1940s, 1950s, and 1960s, and Puerto Ricans with lower average IQs than blacks in the 1970s.[3] Similar group averages have been found in white mountaineer communities in the United States, among isolated people in the Hebrides Islands off Scotland, and among children raised in canal-boat communities in England.[4]

There has been nothing unique about the black IQ level.

Sometimes it is the performance pattern, not the performance level, that is considered unique to blacks. The so-called "Moynihan Report" in the 1960s demonstrated that black female performance on tests and grades significantly exceeded black male performance, explaining this by a supposedly "matriarchal" black culture going back to slavery. However, Moynihan ignored the possibility that this pattern extends well beyond blacks. Higher female performances have been common among low-IQ groups, now and in the past, in the United States and abroad.[5] There was, for example, a time when Jews scored below the national average on mental tests,[6] and in that era Jewish girls scored higher than Jewish boys.[7] Today, Mexican-American girls score higher than boys on IQ tests and are over represented among high-IQ Mexican-American students.[8] The record invariably shows that sex differences are especially pronounced among high-IQ members of low-IQ groups.[9] The most plausible speculation is that this is an example of a more general phenomenon of greater female insulation from either the positive or negative features of the environment.[10] But whatever the explanation, the facts speak for themselves, debunking the Moynihan Report, along with all other myths based on the assumption that black IQs are uniquely low.

Ethnic IQ disparities

There are serious practical difficulties in testing the proposition that without the segregation effect intergroup differences among non-segregated ethnics would be comparable to black-white differences. Inter-ethnic comparisons of educational performance among European-origin groups have become rare since the 1920s.

Earlier studies did, however, show IQ differences as great as (or greater than) those between blacks and whites. While Polish and Italian youngsters, for example, scored in the low to middle 80s in IQ, scores at or above 100 were common among youngsters who were German or Irish or from a number of other groups that had immigrated far enough in the past to be assimilated to American norms in general.[11] The sociologist Diane Ravitch has written a history of the New York City school system that shows German and Jewish schoolchildren in the early 20th century completing high school at a rate more than 100 times greater than that of Irish or Italian schoolchildren.[12]

A recent study by the present writer has attempted to trace the IQ records of a number of ethnic groups from that early period to the present. This research has involved the collection of more than 70,000 IQ records for students attending 58 schools in communities across the country. The general results of that survey have already been published,[13] but what is relevant here is the performance of different groups in the *same schools* at the same time.

The two European immigrant groups with the most pronounced cultural differences in their approach to education were the Jews and the Italians. The centuries-old tradition of reverence for learning in the Jewish culture is well known. Among the people of southern Italy—from whom most Italian-Americans are descended—an opposite tradition of hostility to formal schooling existed. For example, the introduction of compulsory school-attendance laws in Italy in 1877 provoked riots in southern Italy, in the course of which schoolhouses were burned to the ground.[14] Much of the literature on the Italian immigrants to the United States mentions various indicators of their low esteem for formal schooling.[15] Moreover, the peak of Italian and Jewish immigrations coincided in time (late 19th and early 20th centuries), so that they would have been present in the immigrant ghettoes at the same time and their assimilation processes would not have been out of phase, as would those of the Irish, for example. The Italians and the Jews would then clearly be among the candidates for testing whether non-segregated ethnics have had as substantial differences in their performances in the same school as segregated races have had in different schools. Another pair who would have been in the same schools at the same time and at a similar phase of their assimilation would be the Japanese-Americans and Mexican-Americans in the West. They also have many cultural contrasts, well-documented in the literature. For example, over half of all Mexican-American women get married in their teens, while only 10 percent of Japanese-American women get married that young.[16]

The nationwide sample of 58 schools was searched to find schools in which students from either of these pairs (Italian-Jewish or Japanese-Mexican) were present, with at least 10 students per year from each group for at least five years. Only two sets of data in the nationwide sample proved to meet these specifications—one for each ethnic pair. One was a school in a northeastern metropolis with a population of more than one million. An unexpected bonus was that the same school also turned out to contain a significant Puerto Rican population during the same years as the Italian and Jewish populations. The other was a unified school district in a western community with less than 20,000 inhabitants.

The results of this study demonstrate substantial and persistent IQ differences between non-segregated ethnic groups—differences comparable in magnitude to national black-white differences. As already noted, the national black-white IQ difference is 15 points. In the segregated southern schools black-white IQ differences have been slightly greater—almost 20 points.[17] Over a period of more than 20 years, Jewish youngsters averaged 13 points higher IQs than Italian youngsters attending the same school. Indeed the highest Italian IQ average for any of these years was lower than the lowest Jewish IQ average for any of these years. Puerto Rican IQs averaged 26 points lower than Jewish IQs. In short, the Jewish-Italian IQ difference was almost the same as the national black-white IQ difference, and the Jewish-Puerto Rican IQ difference was even greater than black-white IQ differences in segregated southern schools. These huge disparities existed among children living in the same neighborhoods and sitting side-by-side in the same classrooms.

A similar pattern of difference existed between Japanese-Americans and Mexican-Americans. Although these results were based on school-district

There are substantial and persistent IQ differences between non-segregated ethnic groups—differences comparable in magnitude to national black-white differences.

data, rather than individual-school data, children of Japanese and Mexican ancestry were not separated from each other in different schools, either *de jure* or *de facto*. Furthermore, it was determined that the large IQ differences between Japanese and Mexican children were not due to more "middle class" occupations or incomes among the Japanese parents, during the 1950s, when data were available for both groups. The parents of the high-IQ Japanese-Americans were generally "unskilled and semi-skilled" workers to an even greater extent than the parents of low-IQ Mexican-American youngsters. Only 2 percent of the parents of either group of children in this school were white collar workers, and another 2 percent had skilled or supervisory occupations. Nevertheless, the average IQ differences between these Japanese-American and Mexican-American schoolchildren ranged from 16 to 30 points for the six years for which data are available for both—averaging 20 points' difference for the whole period. Again, this is larger than national black-white IQ differences, and about the same as the IQ difference between southern blacks and whites in racially segregated schools.

IQ gaps among black schools

If racial segregation is not the crucial determinant of disparate educational performances which it has been assumed to be, we should expect to find performance disparities among all-black schools comparable in magnitude to black-white disparities. The same survey of 58 schools shows the two highest IQ and two lowest IQ all-black schools to differ by more than 20 points—that is, by more than the IQ differences found in racially segregated schools in the South. Nor were the two high-IQ black schools unique. Similar IQ levels have been found in other all-black schools surveyed elsewhere.[18] The low-IQ schools were likewise not unique. Just among the all-black schools in this study, there were five more with IQs at least 20 points below the average IQ at the top-ranked school.

The top-ranked school was a public high school in a northeastern city of between half a million and one million population. The lowest achieving scores were from a private elementary school in the South, in a city of between 100,000 and 500,000 population, and two public schools in a southern town of less than 20,000. These various schools are not alleged to be comparable in any way other than being all-black schools. No doubt there were many reasons for their large IQ differences. Segregation was not among them.

The non-black experience of segregated schools

Blacks have not been the only group segregated even *de jure*, much less *de facto*. Other groups have attended schools whose student bodies have consisted exclusively, or almost exclusively, of members of their own ethnic group. In our nationwide IQ sample, there were two schools that were more than 95 percent Chinese, one that was 95 percent Puerto Rican, one that was 100 percent American Indian, and one that was more than 99 percent Mexican-American. Did these segregated schoolchildren of various ethnicities have test performances inferior to their respective compatriots in non-segregated schools? Let us consider the groups one by one.

The above-average IQ of the more than 1,500 segregated Chinese schoolchildren in our sample directly contradicts the *Brown v. Board of Education* doctrine that separate schools are inherently inferior. The IQs of the segregated Chinese are certainly no lower than the IQs of Chinese-Americans in general nor Americans in general.

The segregated Chinese children in our sample came from four schools in the same city (population between half a million and one million) in the West—three public elementary schools and one private school. Like most other "private" schools in our sample, it is *not* located in an affluent area. Such schools in this study, at least, were much more likely to be Catholic parochial schools than the popular image of "private" schools as academically selective and socially exclusive. The median family income of the census tract in which the private school was located was about half the national average in the 1950 census, and just under a third of the national average in the 1960 and 1970 censuses. Such income disparities have been common in "Chinatown" neighborhoods, even after the Chinese rose above the national average in income, for the more affluent Chinese tend to live away from Chinatowns.

Our Puerto Rican school sample was only one school and for only one year (1952). The mean IQ there was 81—compared to 79 for Puerto Ricans nationally in the same sample for the decade of the 1950s.[19] Although the IQs were below the national average of 100, the all–Puerto Rican school did *not* have inferior results to those of Puerto Ricans scattered through other schools, which is the point at issue. As might be expected, this all–Puerto Rican public school was in a low-income urban neighborhood. The median family income in its census tract in 1950 was just under half the national average. The city was in the Northeast, and had a population of more than one million.

Our American Indian sample was also for only one school (and only one tribe), but included data for a number of years. For this tribe of Indians, at least, an all-Indian school did not mean an inferior peformance. Their IQs were consistently just above the national norms. They were also just above the national IQ level found among American Indians in this survey (106)—not significantly above, but *not below,* which is what is relevant to the *Brown v. Board of Education* doctrine. This sample, while too limited in scope to tell us much in itself, is one more piece of evidence at odds with the doctrine that separate is automatically inferior.

With Mexican-Americans as well, the evidence goes directly counter to the doctrine that segregation reduces the group's performance. The Mexican-

American mean IQ of 90 in one school of our sample was below the national average, but *above* the average of Mexican-Americans nationally. No income data were available for this school, a public school in the West, in a community of between 20,000 and 50,000 inhabitants. However, we do know that parental occupations were slightly higher than for Mexican-Americans nationally. While only 2 percent of the parents were professionals and 4 percent small businessmen, about 25 percent were skilled or supervisory workers. However, the mean IQ of the children whose parents fell into the "small business" or the "skilled or supervisory" category was the same as the school average, and the children of the "unskilled and semi-skilled" were only one point below. The children whose parents were professionals had mean IQs of 102, but because they were only 2 percent of the student body, this could hardly explain the school's IQ level. For this 99-percent Mexican-American school at least, economic status seems to have had as little overall effect as segregation.

The class system is not to blame

We are well familiar with the fact that parental social class and economic position affects the child's school performance, and that the quantity and quality of schooling affects the child's eventual socioeconomic position. Perhaps we are *too* well acquainted with these relationships, and therefore inclined to be overly deterministic in our thinking about education.

One of the problems in trying to disentangle the effects of family background on school performance is that so many of the relevant variables vary together. High-income parents tend to live in high-income neighborhoods with higher quality schools and have homes where books, magazines, conversation, and child-rearing patterns all enhance development of the child's intellectual potential. Sorting out which of these factors is most responsible is like trying to unscramble an egg.

Do children's school performances match their parents' socioeconomic realities—or their parents' aspirations and pressures?

A more manageable analysis may be possible when dealing with historical data. At particular times in history, there have been immigrant ethnic groups having the values and aspirations that go with good educational peformance, but still lacking the parental education, incomes, or occupations considered "middle class." Have their children's school performances matched their parents' socioeconomic realities—or their parents' aspirations and pressures?

Two of the classic cases of groups whose history in America began in poverty and ended in affluence are the Jews on the East Coast and the Japanese on the West Coast.[20] We have already seen, from the record of Japanese-American children in one school district, that parental occupations overwhelmingly in the unskilled and semi-skilled category did not prevent offspring from meeting or exceeding national test norms. For our nationwide sample as well, Japanese-American youngsters whose parents' occupations were low-skilled still had IQs of 103 and 102 for the two decades (1940s and 1950s) for which we have a national sample size of 50 or more. The national sample of Jewish schoolchildren likewise shows that those whose parents were unskilled and semi-skilled had mean IQs of 104 through 106 for the three decades for which sufficient data are available.

While our historical data for 10 ethnic groups generally show a higher IQ for the children of professionals than for the children of low-skilled workers, it is difficult to explain the substantial intergroup differences by parental occupations. For example, the children of Irish, German, or Chinese low-skilled workers scored consistently higher than the children of Mexican white-collar workers, small businessmen, or skilled and supervisory personnel. This is not to say that parental background meant nothing and the school everything. Clearly the school is not everything, for we have already pointed out that different ethnic groups may have very different test performances in the same schools. The point here is simply that the kinds of class backgrounds we traditionally measure—occupations or income—seem to explain little. No doubt the values and attitudes of the parents meant much. That, however, does not mean that good schooling requires parental "participation" in school decisions. Neither the immigrant Jewish parents nor the immigrant Japanese parents "participated" in school decisions—except to back up whatever the teacher said.[21] The same was true of parents in high-quality black schools.[22]

Parental occupational data from a number of high-performance black schools reinforce the point that socioeconomic background is no more of an insurmountable handicap to good school performance among blacks than among other groups. Data were gathered on children whose parents' occupations fall in the "unskilled and semi-skilled" category, and it was found that the childrens' IQs approximated the national norm. This finding is all the more significant because three of the schools were in the South as commonly understood, and all four were in the South as defined by the census. As noted earlier, the average IQ of southern blacks has usually been around 80. These four schools could all be considered "selective," in that the individual student had to choose to attend them. However, they were by no means selective in the sense in which Andover or Exeter are selective: none had cutoff scores which students had to meet to gain admission, all admitted substantial numbers of students with IQs in the 80s or below, and one enrolled at least one-third of all the black students in its city during most of the period covered by our study. "Selective," like "private," is a label that must be used cautiously.

Can the schools really help?

Many studies have suggested that schools alone cannot improve matters. Before determining the potential effectiveness of school differences, we must first have some idea of how different the schools are in the first place. For example, if most ghetto public schools differ little among themselves in the first place, we should expect little difference in their pupils' performances—but this in no way indicates that it is futile to expect the schools to make a real difference if they themselves improved. On the other hand, if there are significant differences among ghetto schools, we will be able to determine how important these differences prove to be. And, in fact, a growing literature has shown numerous ghetto schools with good to high academic performance,[23] often among children either wholly unselected, or differing in no demonstrable socioeconomic way from other ghetto children. One example which I studied was P.S. 91 in Brooklyn, where over half the children were eligible for the free-lunch program and many were on welfare. Yet whole grades were reading above the national norms, and the school's performance was far above the performances of the other schools in the same school district.

The point here is not to claim that schools can achieve success in spite of parents, or even to apportion the blame for low-performance ghetto schools between the parents and the schools. There is plenty of blame to go around. Instead, the point is to determine which of the many factors that differ among groups make no major demonstrable difference in results, so that we can concentrate attention on those that do. Clearly schools cannot do it alone, as shown by the historical examples of groups with vast performance differences in the same schools. But clearly, too, poverty or low parental status are not fatal either.

The false notion of educational ''prerequisites''

Nothing is easier than to put together a list of desired things and call them ''prerequisites'' for quality education, and to blame the absence of these things for all present shortcomings. But historically, many of these ''prerequisites'' have been missing in high-performance schools, as well as low-performance schools. Adequate physical plant, small class size, parental ''participation'' in the school, teacher ''role models'' of the student's own ethnic background, bilingual education—these are among the many ''prerequisites'' almost universally *lacking* in the schools from which the children of Jewish or Japanese immigrants emerged, or the high-quality black schools I have studied.

My study of high-performance black schools repeatedly took me into ancient school buildings—notably P.S. 91 in Brooklyn, where there were still gas jets in the halls, from the era before there was electric lighting. Other researchers have found good academic performances in ''store front'' ghetto schools. At least one of the schools in my study had lacked central heating for most of its history, and relied on pot-bellied stoves in each classroom. This was neither desirable nor morally right; but neither did it prevent good education from taking place.

Historically, the most outstanding of all black schools—whether measured by IQ or by the later achievements of its alumni—was Dunbar High School in Washington, in the period from 1870 to 1955. In the 19th century, the average class size at Dunbar was over 40, and it continued to have the largest class size of any high school in Washington on into the 20th century. In New York at the turn of the century, it was not unusual for Jewish schoolchildren to be in classes of 60 or more pupils.[24] And there were no teacher's aides.

Teacher "role models" of the student's own ethnic background have been equally rare. When the Irish-Catholic immigrant children went to public school in the middle of the 19th century, they were likely to be taught by Protestant Anglo-Saxon teachers. By the time the Jewish immigrant children were flooding into the public schools of New York at the turn of the century, they were far more likely to be taught by Irish-Catholic teachers than by Jewish teachers. By the time I went to school in Harlem in the early 1940s, Jewish teachers outnumbered black teachers many times over. Similar patterns of group succession existed in labor

> *Teacher "role models" of the student's own ethnic background have been rare in history.*

unions and other organizations. The only real difference in the situation today is our naive insistence that all statistical disparities are unusual and/or evidence of sinister designs. Among the high-performance black schools in my study, some had all-black teaching staffs, some all-white, some predominantly clerical, some exclusively layman. Some of the principals were warm and friendly, others tough and blunt. The notion that there is one formula that can be applied across the boards does not fit the facts, either as regards schools or homes. Much has been made of the home well-stocked with books and magazines, and enriched with a continuous stream of conversation between parents and children. This model fits the history of Jewish immigrants on the East Coast, but not the history of Japanese immigrants on the West Coast. Books were rare in their homes and conversation between the generations infrequent and usually unilateral.[25] But the Japanese children were the delight of their teachers,[26] even in an era of anti-Japanese sentiment in the society at large, and their educational performances demonstrated the payoff of diligent application—even in the absence of other "prerequisites" of good education.

Among the many fashionable "prerequisites" for good minority education (or excuses for its absence) is bilingual schooling. As in so many other areas of social policy discussion, this expression defines a process not by its own characteristics, but by its hopes. So-called "bilingual" education in practice means a certain portion of the schoolwork (sometimes a majority or virtually all) being taught in the student's native language, rather than in English. Whether or not that leads to bilingual students is a *question,* not a foregone conclusion. History does, however, show that preceding generations of students—from the Jews and Italians on the East Coast to the Chinese and Japanese on the West Coast—became bilingual through opposite policies: being taught exclusively in English in school and speaking their respective native tongues at home.

The argument here is not over whether decent buildings, smaller class sizes, and so forth are desirable, but over whether they are genuine "prerequisites''—or (more to the point) whether their absence provides blanket excuses for educational failure.

Do the schools determine our upward mobility?

The effect of schooling on socioeconomic mobility has become as deeply embedded in the folklore as the effect of socioeconomic variables on the schools. The strength of this belief is demonstrated not by the evidence marshalled to support it, but by the lack of any felt necessity to produce evidence. Most prosperous groups are of course well-educated—and usually well-housed, well-clothed, and well-entertained. Yet no one regards that as proof that housing, clothing, or entertainment produce economic advancement. History again permits us to see various ethnic groups *before* they became prosperous, to find out which came first, the chicken or the egg.

It is by now a familiar story how the immigrant Jews brought to New York a long tradition of reverence for learning, how they crowded into the public libraries, the lecture halls, and the free colleges and universities of the city.[27] What is not so familiar is that the occupations through which they rose out of poverty were *not* primarily occupations requiring or utilizing formal schooling. In 1880 and in 1905, over half the Russian Jews in New York worked in manual occupations—and that is not counting the great number who were pushcart peddlers, who were classified as "white collar" workers. Only 2 percent of the Russian Jews in 1880 were clerks or semi-professionals[28]—the kind of occupations normally thought of as "white collar." After a quarter of a century of upward mobility, there was a *smaller* proportion of Russian Jews in lower "white collar" jobs, because pushcart peddling had declined.[29] But although Jewish upward mobility was well under way by the early 20th century, Jewish children at the turn of the century seldom went far in school, because they were working—at home or outside. In 1908, 38 percent of all clothing workers in New York City were teenage Jews.[30]

The upward mobility occurred first, and sending the next generation to college was the consequence—not the cause—of that socioeconomic rise.

Even among Jewish children under 10 years of age, between 7 and 10 percent were out of school and working at home[31]—in the "sweatshops."

The upward mobility of Jews in the last two decades of the 19th century could hardly have been due to education, and certainly not to higher education. No Jewish youngster graduated from a New York City public high school in the 19th century, for the first graduating class for any New York City public high school was the class of 1902.[32] A 1951 survey of City College students (mostly Jewish) showed that only 17 percent of their fathers born before 1911 had completed the 8th grade.[33] The massive eastern European influx into the City College of New York (CCNY) and Hunter College occurred later, in the 1920s and 1930s.[34] By then their parents could afford to support them through high school.

It is clearly the case that the upward mobility occurred first, and sending the next generation to college was the consequence—not the cause—of that socioeconomic rise. The experience of Japanese immigrants on the West Coast demonstrates this pattern even more dramatically. As late as 1940, a majority of Japanese-American males were in farming—and they produced about a third of all the commercial truck crops grown in California.[35] They were also successful as small businessmen. As early as 1919, Japanese-Americans owned almost half the hotels and one fourth of the grocery stores in Seattle.[36] First-generation Japanese also owned hundreds of produce markets in Los Angeles,[37] and more than a thousand were contract gardeners in southern California.[38] None of this required education, and most of the first-generation Japanese immigrants spoke little English.[39] Education was one of the things the next generation acquired with its affluence—it was a result and not a cause of upward mobility.

When morality replaces thinking, people suffer

The dire state of American public education has been well documented, as is the fact that it has generally been getting worse, rather than better, over the past decade or more. As public trust—and public money—threaten to ebb away, many panicky "explanations" of failure or "prerequisites" for success have emerged. The quarter-of-a-century-old crusade for racial integration overlaps and complicates this educational picture, and generates its own "explanations" and "prerequisites."

It is not clear that there is any single solution to our educational crisis. The constant grasping for some one answer or magic formula or "innovation" may itself be part of the problem. What should be clear, however, is that blindly self-serving mythology is not the answer. We are never going to solve the problems unless we can first face them as they are—not with a long list of excuses, pious hopes, or open-ended demands for "more."

More generally and more fundamentally, how have we all managed for decades to repeat dogmas and mount crusades without first testing our facts? Much of the discussion of the educational effects of segregation, and of socioeconomic status, has proceeded as if fashionable assumptions and moralistic pronouncements were irrefutable facts. But our assumptions, however fervently we hold to them, have never been facts but only what the great sociologist Robert Merton has called "pseudo facts." The problem with pseudo facts, as Merton warns, is that they "have a way of inducing pseudo problems which cannot be solved because matters are not as they purport to be."[40] The problems of education—and particularly of minority education—are all too real. But what we are trying to solve are the pseudo problems —how to extract more government money for more projects, studies, and "innovative" gimmicks. And the extraction process is now in serious trouble. The taxpayers' revolt, symbolized by spending-limitations initiatives (beginning with California's

The discussion of the educational efforts of segregation, and of socioeconomic status, has proceeded as if fashionable assumptions and moralistic pronouncements were irrefutable facts.

celebrated Proposition 13) and by the defeat of school-bond issues that used to pass routinely, suggests that the pseudo problems may not be solved for many years, if at all. The real problem—teaching youngsters to read and think—has already been solved by many institutions in both rich and poor neighborhoods, by people with varying ethnicities, personalities, and approaches. The mindless pursuit of busing, the banning of tests that tell us things we don't like to hear, or the seeking of "role models" instead of the best teachers, only evade the issue. The real problem can be solved, but it must first be addressed. &

[1] Thomas Sowell, "Race and IQ Reconsidered," *Essays and Data on American Ethnic Groups,* ed. Thomas Sowell (Washington: The Urban Institute, 1978), pp. 203-238.

[2] See studies cited in *Ibid.,* pp. 207-208.

[3] *Ibid.,* pp. 214, 217.

[4] *Ibid.,* pp. 210-211.

[5] *Ibid.,* pp. 219-224.

[6] *Ibid.,* pp. 207-208.

[7] *Ibid.,* p. 222.

[8] *Ibid.,* p. 223.

[9] *Ibid.,* pp. 222-224.

[10] *Ibid.,* pp. 219-220.

[11] *Ibid.,* p. 210.

[12] Diane Ravitch, *The Great School Wars* (New York: Basic Books, 1974), p. 178.

[13] See note 1 above.

[14] Richard Gambino, *Blood of My Blood* (Garden City: Anchor Books, 1974), p. 249.

[15] *Ibid.,* pp. 246-257; Herbert J. Gans, *The Urban Villagers* (New York: Free Press, 1962), pp. 130-132, 134; Sr. Mary Fabian Matthew, C.S., "The Role of the Public Schools in the Assimilation of the Italian Immigrant Child in New York City, 1900-1914," *The Italian Experience in the United States,* ed. S.M. Tomasi and M.H. Engels (New York: Center for Migration Studies, 1970), pp. 139-140.

[16] Peter Uhlenberg, "Demographic Correlates of Group Achievement: Contrasting Patterns of Mexican-Americans and Japanese-Americans," *Race, Color, or National Origin,* ed. Robert K. Yin (Itasca, Illinois: F.E. Peacock Publishers, 1973), p. 91.

[17] Audrey M. Shuey, *The Testing of Negro Intelligence,* 2nd ed. (New York: Social Science Press, 1966), p. 500.

[18] Thomas Sowell, "Patterns of Black Excellence," *The Public Interest,* Spring 1976, pp. 26-58.

[19] Thomas Sowell, "Race and IQ Reconsidered," *op. cit.,* p. 214.

[20] See, for example, Harry H.L. Kitano, *Japanese Americans* (Englewood Cliffs: Prentice-Hall, 1969); Irving Howe, *World of Our Fathers* (New York: Harcourt Brace Jovanovich, 1976).

[21] Harry H.L. Kitano, *op. cit.,* pp. 23, 76n; Howe, *op. cit.,* p. 273.

[22] Thomas Sowell, "Patterns of Black Excellence," *op.cit.*

[23] *Loc. cit.* See also Derrick A. Bell, Book Review, *Harvard Law Review,* vol. 92 (1979), p. 1841n.

[24] Diane Ravitch, *op. cit.*

[25] Harry H.L. Kitano, *op. cit.,* pp. 23-24, 72-73.

[26] *Ibid.,* pp. 23, 72-73.

[27] Irving Howe, *op. cit.,* Chapter 7.

[28] Thomas Kessner, *The Golden Door* (New York: Oxford University Press, 1977), p. 61.

[29] *Ibid.,* pp. 60, 64.

[30] Selma, C. Berrol, "Education and Economic Mobility: The Jewish Experience in New York City, 1880-1920," *American Jewish Historical Quarterly,* March 1976, p. 262.

[31] *Loc. cit.*

[32] *Ibid.,* p. 261.

[33] *Loc. cit.*

[34] *Ibid.,* p. 262.

[35] Robert Higgs, "Landless by Law: Japanese Immigrants in California Agriculture to 1941," *Journal of Economic History,* March 1978, p. 207.

[36] Ivan H. Light, *Ethnic Enterprise in America* (Berkeley: University of California Press, 1972), p. 10.

[37] *Ibid.,* p. 17.

[38] Harry H.L. Kitano, *op. cit.,* p. 22.

[39] William Petersen, *Japanese Americans* (New York: Random House, 1971), p. 183.

[40] Quoted in Herbert Gutman, *The Black Family in Slavery and Freedom* (New York: Vintage Books, 1977), p. 63.

38

PUBLIC POLICY AND COMPETENCY TESTING

Patrick Lynch

The numerous rationales offered for the luxuriant growth in statewide mandates for achievement competency testing can be subsumed under the headings of concern for what students are getting out of their schooling, and making sure the public gets a return on its investment in education. Some states mention both purposes in their legislation. Like all movements, great and trivial, original purposes are displayed by others. The complexity of motivation and the difficulty and futility in ascribing motivation to groups of policy makers are great. This paper identifies different rationales for public policy concerning competency testing, and some consequences.

Oregon's law is an example of the first rationale. It was designed to allow early or delayed graduation (Oliver, 1974). Providing flexibility in the high school requirements was seen as a way to accommodate the students who were not served by the rigid, Carnegie-unit system. As a condition of flexibility, the state required school districts to identify their own competencies, criteria for showing mastery of them, ways of evaluating them and planning instruction to reach them. The Oregon law was the first mandate, and it gave the task to the district, with assistance from the State Department of Education (Hall, 1974).

An example of the second type of rationale is the Florida law passed in 1976 which required the Department of Education to establish a statewide assessment program. The law forbids social promotion and calls for a test constructed and administered by the state agency (Pipho, 1977). Standards are set by the state with the participation of local units. The contrasts with the Oregon approach are centralization versus dispersal of responsibility for planning and decision making about programs, and emphasis on a test as opposed to emphasis on a process. Accountability was the theme and the name of the act in Florida, whereas in Oregon the theme was alternative secondary education with measured goals.

California combines both approaches, in two separate "waves" of legislation. The earlier legislation—a California senate bill enacted in 1972—allows sixteen- or seventeen-year-old high school students to take the California High School Proficiency Examination or to attend a regional occupational center in order to graduate. Those who passed the CHSPE were to receive a proficiency certificate rather than a diploma. This act required the California State Department of Education to develop standards of competency in basic skills and to deliver the final product to the districts for use by 1975. In 1975 another California senate bill was passed permitting people with the proficiency certificate to be admitted to a public community college. The Reagan administration was reputed to have favored the Hart Bill because it was estimated to be a means of saving state money which would otherwise have to be paid to districts for their high school enrollees (Polgar, 1976). This early-out act, like Oregon's, was the result of legislative sentiment to create an alternative to high school education. The intention of allowing students to become employed before graduation was assisted by the concept that early high school leavers could earn money and pay taxes instead of having money spent on them.

A more comprehensive approach to competency testing in California was legislated in 1977. According to these statutes, the State Board of Education was required to provide each school district a framework for assessing pupil proficiency in reading comprehension, writing, and computation skills, with a range of assessment items in each skill area. The purpose was solely to assist each school district in the development of its own pupil assessment as required by Section 51216 of the California Education Code. The State Board of Education was not permitted to adopt statewide minimum proficiency standards for high school graduation. No pupil was to receive a diploma from a secondary high school unless the proficiency standards prescribed by the secondary school district governing board were met.

School districts were required to set standards of proficiency. in reading comprehension, writing, and computation, all in the English language, for its pupils (California Education Code, 1978, S 51215). Each district must assess its pupils once during grades 4 through 6, once between grades 7 and 9, and twice during grades 10 and 11. All must be ready for the graduation class of 1980. The district must describe an appropriate instructional program in a conference with the parent and the pupil (if not secondary school) so that students will have numerous opportunities to achieve mastery (California Education Code, 1978, S 51216). California moved from a concern for economy with flexibility to a combination of those concerns with guaranteeing help for students who were tagged long before graduation as problem students.

While California's Hart Act and the Florida Act carried the theme of protecting students, employers, and society against faulty credentials, the theme of getting the state's and taxpayer's money's worth is present in the same legislation. In the 1960s, the age of innovation was announced by the federal government agencies and foundations. Many old notions about standards for students were quietly abandoned. By the 1970s, the glory days of innovation were a memory; new procedures preached a return to standards and accountability. The alternative school movement which came at the very end of the innovation period provided an out for those who would call back to righteousness those who had strayed. The Oregon model allowed alternatives to substitute for the "real" high school. In California, the diploma would be once again a pristine document, but early school leavers could obtain a certificate which would allow entry to junior college.

The potential effects of the alternative high school credential were studied by Polgar (1976). She compared the results of the first applications of the CHSPE and the GED, and found the latter to be more rigorous. Fewer than half who took the CHSPE the first two times—in 1975 and 1976—passed it. Those who took the GED were older; by far the biggest reason for taking the CHSPE was the desire to leave early. In 1975-1976 a score of 75% was required to pass the exam, but the examinee was only sent a report of pass or fail, with no score. The test was constructed by contract with the Educational Testing Service of Princeton, New Jersey. The cutoff score of 75% was arbitrary, as are all such cutoffs. No attempt was made to establish criteria from observation of high school graduates relating to what a successful test passer would have to do in life. The test lacked any construct or predictive validity. According to Polgar, some of those who passed and left high school tended to be frustrated with high school. While the junior colleges must accept the proficiency certificate holder, Stanford will not. The University of California, Berkeley, in 1976, as well as the California state colleges, would accept a certificate holder only if the person met all other requirements, such as a certain grade-point average. A public employer listed in order of acceptability a GED, a regular high school diploma, and a certificate of proficiency.

Protecting employers and the public against diplomas certifying graduation from an approved high school program when in fact the recipient can scarcely read can be seen as a desirable public policy (Lott, 1979). If the policy is accompanied by an opportunity to the high school student who does not spend four years in an academic program to obtain a kind of certification based on passing some kind of equivalency or mastery test, then the policy would seem to be benevolent in two ways: eliminating debased high school diplomas and providing alternatives to those who cannot obtain the diploma which requires passing academic work.

The reform of the high school in America which came near the end of the nineteenth century saw the birth of the Carnegie unit as the building block of the curriculum. A diploma could be obtained if one satisfied state course requirements. The competency testing was done course by course. A certain number of failures prevented one from obtaining a diploma. This system accommodated a growth in high school attendance from hundreds of thousands to millions. Nevertheless, until World War II, the high school diploma was seen as a receipt for completing an academic program. The General Education Development (GED) test was begun to allow those who had not a chance to finish high school to take an examination on material equivalent to high school material. The proof of success of the GED program is that it is no longer challenged as an alternative to high school graduation. Those who fail to pass a competency test in order to receive a diploma—in New York, for example—or who must accept or choose a less highly valued proof of completion of program will eventually move into the labor market. They will seek employment, presenting whatever they have. If the employer in the Polgar article is representative of many, the certificate or non-diploma holder would be well advised to prepare for the GED examination and obtain the equivalency diploma.

A consideration of the effects of the competency examinations is certainly in order as we look at the chances the non-diploma holder has in the labor market. It is fair to ask what kind of differential effects the competency tests have on various ethnic or racial classes. In Florida, in 1977, about 77% of the black students who took the test failed compared with 24% of the whites who took it. The communications portion of the exam was failed the same year by 26% of the black juniors who took the examination but by only 3% of the white juniors (Report on Education Research, 1978). As of December 1978, the data on the 1978 administration of the test was not broken down by race or other factors.

The author of the California Pupil Proficiency Law defended the fact that testing of mastery of the basic skills required for graduation is to be in the language of the majority (Hart, 1978). The effects of the examination on the Spanish surnamed students may well be to fail a larger proportion of them than of the Anglo students taking the same examination. The California law permits school districts to set different standards and assessment procedures for students with diagnosed learning disabilities. The California law does not classify the speaking of another language than English as a learning disability.

FEDERAL POLICY ON TESTING

The use of examinations and diplomas as entry requirements for occupations is the subject of many suits. Following the passage of the Civil Rights Act of 1964, many tests of employers' requirements were brought, applying Title VII of that Act (United States Code, 1976, S 200e). That title forbids the use of classifications of race, color, religion, sex, or national origin in hiring practices, promotions, or distribution of benefits. Employers, employment agencies, or labor organizations shall not limit opportunities for application, membership, or training based on the above qualifications.

The guidelines published by the Equal Employment Opportunity Commission carry a list of practices which prohibit discrimination against the above classes (Code of Federal Regulations, 1978, S 1607.1-1607.14).

The use of any test which adversely affects hiring or any other employment opportunity of classes protected by Title VII constitutes discrimination—unless:

(1) the test has been validated and shows a high degree of utility.

(2) the person acting upon the test results can demonstrate that alternative suitable hiring practices are unavailable for his use [Code of Federal Regulations, 1978, S 1607.3].

The EEOC guidelines were tightly drawn, emphasizing validity and usability rather than reliability, because in order to be valid a test must be valid consistently. The guidelines include the following requirements to satisfy validity:

(1) The test must be validated for each minority and non-minority group with which it is used, with a requirement of showing that any differential rejection rates that may be based on the test be relevant to performance on the job in question.
(2) Evidence of validity should consist of empirical data demonstrating that the test is predictive of important elements of work behavior which comprise, or are relevant to, the job for which candidates are being evaluated [Code of Federal Regulations, 1978, S 1607.4].

Further refinements of validity stipulate:

(3) The sample for validation must represent a typical and normal candidate group for the job in question.
(4) Work behavior and other criteria which the test is intended to predict must be fully described [Code of Federal Regulations, 1978, S 1607.5].

Concerning utility of the test, guidelines specify:

(5) The relationship of the test and at least one relevant criterion must be statistically significant at the .05 level.
(6) The larger portion of applicants hired for the jobs, the higher the relationship needs to be practically useful. Low correlations may be useful for a smaller number of jobs available [Code of Federal Regulations, 1978, S 1607.5].

The guidelines make it impossible to accept the general reputation of the test, its author or publisher, or casual reports of its utility in lieu of the requirements above (Code of Federal Regulations, 1978, S 1607.8). No tests can be used only for the protected classes, and employers, unions, and employment agencies should provide opportunity for retesting failed candidates (Code of Federal Regulations, 1978, S 1607.11-1607.12).

The EEOC guidelines are so complete that they could constitute a much better textbook for a course in test construction than many now used in university courses. More important, these guidelines would be failed by every competency test being used by a state or local school system today. Henry Brickell (1978) identifies two uses of competency tests, one relating to content covered, the other for testing for skills which a graduate will have to use after graduation. A choice must be made for the competency test constructors, based on which use is to be made of the test—a mastery examination of key concepts and skills, or a predictive test for skills needed after leaving school.

The doctrine of business necessity, which is court created, is used by employers to defend their use of tests even though the tests discriminate against the protected classes (American Law Reports, 1978). Courts have consistently upheld the EEOC guidelines in the tests. In Boston Chapter, NAACP, Inc. v. Beecher (1974), the civil service test given to applicants for firefighters' positions which discriminated against blacks and Spanish-surnamed people was not job-related. Only concurrent validity had been established, not predictive. Further, it failed because no minorities had been included in the validation sample as separately validated subsamples.

In United States v. Georgia Power Co. (1973), the court declared it apparent that no relationship was established between successful job performance and the ability to achieve the company-established cutoff score on each test of the battery.

The League of Latin American Citizens v. City of Santa Ana case (1976) is interesting in that it is the first time a validation study was not fatal to an application test for policemen.

In that case, the test used to screen applicants for firefighters' positions was found to be defective, in that validation was shown only for experienced firefighters and not inexperienced firefighters. The court in considering the "diploma test" ruled that the requirement that an applicant have a valid diploma was not justified by business necessity, because non-diploma holders were already functioning effectively in the positions. The court held differently for the application process for policemen. Even though the selection process discriminated against protected classes under Title VII, holding a diploma was ruled a necessity, because a validation study showed that in 164 interviews in 30 jurisdictions, a high school education was needed to prepare a person for the increasingly complex tasks of a police officer in an urban environment. The validation study agreed with the recommendations of a Task Force Report of the Presidents' Commission on Law Enforcement and the Administration of Justice, which recommended that no person be hired in a sworn capacity unless that person held a high school diploma or demonstrated by performance on an achievement test the ability to perform college work successfully.

Glass (1977) details with terrifying exactness and completeness the technical failures of the competency tests now in use, including (with my comments added):

(1) The construction of items based on nothing more than a small group's interpretation of life needs and/or the curriculum, with no attempt to seek "field" validation of the type the EEOC guidelines call for, or even a disciplined approach to sample the content of some identifiable slice of curriculum.

(2) Use of arbitrary cutoffs, one method of which he calls "counting backward from 100." Selecting 70%, 80%, or some other cutoff for passing a competency test is simply done by fiat, based on a group compromise. (The guidelines require and subsequent court tests support the practice of establishing cutoff points based only on correlation with job performance.)

(3) Not recognizing the impact of items with high or low difficulty on those being tested, with subsequent claims being made that a sample tested did better or more poorly on the skill in question. For example, children do better adding the same figures vertically than horizontally.

(4) Using complex quantitative decision methods in arriving at cutoff scores which mask the lack of any psychological rationale in selecting the cutoff.

(5) Confusion between a criterion (an external norm of work to be performed or course to be passed) and a standard (how much of the criterion needs to be mastered by the person taking the test to function successfully).

States can be arbitrary in imposing or allowing districts to construct competency tests, whether for mastery or for predicting postschool behavior. After all, education is a state responsibility. Let us hope that a rumor of a federally imposed competency test remains that, until educators clean up their testing act.

The problem of poorly constructed tests is particularly serious when one considers that the science of test construction has been routinely ignored not only by the small districts and states in a hurry but also by those institutions which could construct decent tests. The test publisher, whose business in purveying and correcting standardized tests runs into the billions each year, still reports faithfully and completely reliability data, and concentrates on the cheapest form of reliability, which is internal consistency. Test-retest reliability data for long periods of time are unreported or are reported skimpily. No validity data of the kind the EEOC guidelines call for are presented concerning relationship of performance with external criteria such as job performance, completion of training or, postsecondary programs. Only those data which predict entrance or selection into programs are reported. Completely absent are reports of correlation between test performance and selection criteria by minority or nonminority group.

The validity test publishers present relate to concurrent validity—how the test in question correlates with another achievement test.

This chain of concurrent validity is interesting. The achievement tests which are widely used correlate highly with each other—take your pick; they're all the same really. The so-called achievement tests correlate highly with the so-called aptitude tests. If a sixth grader does well on a commercial aptitude test, that sixth grader will do well on any standardized achievement test. The scholastic aptitude tests all correlate highly with the Stanford-Binet; many, in fact, are deliberately constructed to correlate highly with it—in order to attain concurrent validity. The test constructors are simply redoing versions of one test over and over. Scratch a standardized achievement test and you have a scholastic aptitude test—and scratch one more layer and you've got the Stanford-Binet. One criterion measure dominates the field, and has since World War I.

It is more likely that one district's clumsy effort will be valid, at least for that district's content than that a standardized test will be. The content sampled by standardized test makers is perforce national rather than local. The state which calls in the commercial experts to set up "sample" items, a framework or an "exemplary test," is likely to be buying what has been in the drawer of the firm for many years. The commercial group simply covers up its sins with item analysis techniques which touch none of Glass's or EEOC's concerns.

The expressed concern of states for guaranteeing the student preparation for the jobs and training programs which are a requisite to support oneself can only be praised. Well-constructed tests could assist that end. Poorly constructed tests have unintended effects, many of which discriminate against those at the bottom end of the socioeconomic scale. Poor schooling for such people is then followed by testing which puts the job seeker from the lower classes in a double bind. Disadvantaged by bad schooling, the student from a poor family is then shown that he is indeed bad enough not to deserve a diploma.

The school is a referral agency for students to employers. Its referral activities have not been carefully studied, but every secondary and postsecondary school acts as an agency of recommendation or placement of student to employer.

The EEOC guidelines state that:

(1) An employment agency, private, state, or federal, shall not make applicant or employee appraisals or referrals based on results from any psychological test or any other selection device not validated in accordance with its guidelines.

(2) An employment agency requested to devise a testing program is not excused from its obligation because the test user (employer) didn't ask for such validation.

(3) Where an employment agency is required only to administer a testing program devised elsewhere, the agency shall request evidence of validation, as discussed in the guidelines, before it administers the testing program or makes referrals.

(4) The employment agency or service will be expected to refuse to administer a test where employer or union does not supply sufficient evidence of validation [Code of Federal Regulations, S 1607.10].

A suit in which a person is denied employment for a job based on failure in a competency test devised by a state and administered by a school district may determine whether a school is an employment agency. If it is found to be, it could be found in violation of the guidelines given present testing practices. In the case of administering a test devised elsewhere, the district would not be excused from obtaining the necessary validation data (see point 3, supra). The burden is not on the employer but on the agency administering the test (point 2, supra). Given a plethora of poorly constructed tests, the only way out is to refuse to administer such tests (point 4, supra).

THE EFFECTS OF COMPETENCY TESTS

Many states pronounce in their constitutions the provision of a thorough and efficient education for all children. The relationship of a constitutional requirement to competency testing mandated by the courts displays a version of protection for the student. In Robinson v. Cahill I (1973: 295) the court pointed out that the state had never spelled out the content of the educational opportunities the constitution required. "In some discernible way the scope of this obligation would be made apparent, if the tax burden could have been shifted to the local district."

In Robinson v. Cahill V (1976) the constitutionality of the 1975 Public Education Act of the New Jersey legislation was reviewed and approved. Justice Pashman noted in his dissent that in order to equip a child for his role as citizen and competitor in the labor market and to meet statutory and constitutional requirements, standards of pupil performance must be set. These must include a reasonable proficiency in such basic skills as reading, writing, and simple mathematics. While differences will exist among districts, a failure to assure constitutionally minimum education to children from disadvantaged districts cannot be tolerated on the basis of diversity.

The court approved the provisions of the 1975 act, which requires the Commissioner of Education who finds that a district has failed to show sufficient progress in reaching pertinent goals and standards must direct the local board of education to prepare and submit a remedial plan for the commissioner's approval.

The New Jersey statute which directs competency testing, with a standard somewhere below 100%, is designed to correct inequities in finance. The State Department of Education must identify what level of education is guaranteed under the constitution (New Jersey Statutes Annotated, 1975). The remedy for inequality is to set standards for all districts. This is not a law which started with the premise of debased diplomas, but it seeks to provide a kind of floor for performance for each district. The method used is not individual analysis but group analysis, district by district. What the state accomplishes in so doing is to promulgate standards of pupil performance in order to conform to constitutional and statutory requirements (Robinson v. Cahill V, 1976: 174). What has been done is to create a basis for statutory and constitutional duty of care flowing from the state through the district to the pupil. The implications for an educational malpractice suit in New Jersey are interesting. In Donohue v. Copiague Union Free School District (1978), the court did not find a duty of care flowing from state or district to the student, but found that the state provided a good not guaranteed in any specific amount.

One concern of the courts and of some legislatures has been that the person who fails an examination, whether applying for a job or trying to secure a diploma, be given another chance. This is sound psychologically. We know that emotions and physical state can affect a person's test taking. Reliability theory treats the margin of error of obtaining a person's true score.

The aim of schools and of states' constitutional and statutory provisions is to educate. It is not to deny, keep out, or punish. More recent legislation uses competency testing as a means of determining where the student is. Then remediation is indicated for the student who is not ready for the next step in the learning sequence. Many laws, happily, speak not of repeating a grade but of fashioning instruction appropriate to teaching a student those concepts and skills deemed necessary for graduation and entrance to the world of work.

The school is a vast institution which prepares students for occupations. Its role as a shaper of children to become docile, obedient, and ready for the routine of factory work has been well described by Bowles and Gintis (1976). It may well be that competency testing is one more way of shaping the child to the one best answer, the one and only way to behave. Somehow the school and the state must find a balance between the liberation of the child to become inquisitive, creative, or at least questioning and a way to monitor the success of the school. One state has guaranteed a level of education to each child, but it has not redirected that guarantee only to the basic skills (Robinson v. Cahill V., 1976: 174). A state need not concern itself only with a floor under the educational process, since the tendency is universally to treat the floor as a ceiling. Minimums become maximums, if the legislation does not force an "opening up" to widest possible kinds of education. The Oregon law seems to have been the earliest example of an "opening up" type of directive to high schools.

Legislated minimums, if we look at other nations with centralized educational systems and prescribed curricula, have the effect of narrowing, and prescribing, rather than of opening up.

In guaranteeing a basic amount of skill, the district may be vulnerable to two kinds of suits from those who fail competency tests; those by people of protected classes under Title VII of the Civil Rights Act of 1964 who have not attained employment because of their failure in tests, standardized or locally produced, which do not meet validation requirements of the EEOC guidelines, and those brought by graduates who charge malpractice by the schools which have not provided them with the level of mastery guaranteed by statute or constitution.

CASES

BOSTON CHAPTER, NAACP, INC. v. BEECHER (1974) 504 Federal Reporter 2d: 1017-1029.

DONOHUE v. COPIAGUE UNION FREE SCHOOL DISTRICT (1978) New York Supplement 2d: 874-885.

LEAGUE OF LATIN AMERICAN CITIZENS v. CITY OF SANTA ANA (1976) 410 Federal Supplement: 873-912.

ROBINSON v. CAHILL (1973) 303 Atlantic Reporter 2d: 273-298.

ROBINSON v. CAHILL (1976) 355 Atlantic Reporter 2d: 129-189.

UNITED STATES v. GEORGIA POWER CO. (1973) 474 Federal Reports 2d: 906-927.

REFERENCES

BRICKELL, H. (1978) "Seven key notes on minimum competency testing." Phi Delta Kappan 59 (May).

36 American Law Reports, Federal (1978): 23, n. 7.

BOWLES, S. and H. GINTIS (1976) Schooling in Capitalist America: Educational Reform and the Contradictions of Economic Life. New York: Basic Books.

California Education Code, Reorganized (1978) S 51215-S 51217, S 60614. St. Paul: West Publishing.

29 Code of Federal Regulations (1978) S 1607.1-S 1607.14.

FISHER, T. (1978) "Florida's approach to competency testing." Phi Delta Kappan 59 (May).

GLASS, G. (1977) Standards and Criteria. Kalamazoo: Western Michigan University College of Education Evaluation Center.

HALL, M. (1974) "Competency-based education in Oregon: an overview." ED 104026. American Educational Research Association Conference.

HART, G. (1978) "The California pupil proficiency law viewed by its author." Phi Delta Kappan 59 (May).

LOTT, W. (1979) "Stiff fourth year test." New York Times (January 21): 1.

New Jersey Statutes Annotated (1975) S 18A: 7A-14, 15.

OLIVER, G. (1974) "School graduation requirements in Oregon: a discussion of the events surrounding the change in requirements." ED 098663.

PIPHO, C. (1977) "Minimal competency testing." Educ. Leadership 34 (May).

POLGAR, E. (1976) "The California high school proficiency exams." ED 129859.

Report on Education Research (1978) December 27.

42 United States Code (1976) S 2000e-2000h-2.

39

EDUCATION MYTH
AND PUBLIC POLICYMAKING

Joseph Rost

According to a time-honored myth, the public schools and universities in the United States and the educators who people these organizations are sacred institutions in our society, and as a result they have been placed above the sweaty world of public policymaking. Never mind Proposition 13, desegregation mandates, and demands for accountability. Never mind that once every year or two educators condescend to do some politicking with state governmental officials to gain some fiscal advantages for the coming budget year or biennium. Education remains separated from the ordinary political processes that govery all the other services provided by the public's representatives. These examples only serve to remind us how difficult and different it is to make education and educators toe the political line. Beyond them, the world of education and the world of politics are planets apart and are, therefore, in different orbits.

Thus, according to the politics of education myth, education and politics should be kept separate. Education is too sacred and too important to the future of the citizens of the country—both collectively and individually—to allow it to be swallowed up in the murky political sea. Education is too important for it

From Joseph Rost, "Education Myth and Public Policymaking," 15(4) *Urban Education* 419-434 (January 1981). Copyright 1981 by Sage Publications, Inc.

to be controlled by politicans and for educational policy to be made in the political arena using the methods of public policymaking. Rather, educational policy should be made, the myth goes on to say, by the professionals who are trained to know what is best for the students, the people, and the state. Therefore, the professional educators must be free to make their decisions—free from political control, that is—so that they can decide policy using the rational decision-making method. Since these people are educators, it is only natural that they make policy on the basis of rational considerations and that educational decisions reflect the best rational thought available at the time.

In the end, the myth proclaims that education is inherently different from other governmental services and must therefore be treated differently. The different treatment, of course, is that the politicians will keep their hands off the schools and universities and leave educators free to make their own decisions.

Additional reasons given for keeping education separate from politics are: (1) learning is a fragile thing and can be bruised easily by the rough and tumble of politics; (2) academic freedom demands considerable liberty from political interference; and (3) the research and social reconstruction functions of the community of scholars cannot operate in a climate of governmental control. Background assumptions accompanying this myth include the beliefs that the academy is clean and wholesome, motivated by rational considerations, public spirited, knows what is best for the people, and is generally beyond reproach, whereas politics is dirty and corrupted, motivated by political (irrational) considerations, self interested, knows what is best for politicians and their friends, and is generally raffish beyond compare.

Like all myths, its statement in bald form is shocking, and the immediate reaction is one of disbelief. "How can that be?" we ask. "It hasn't happened that way, at least not in the last decade," we add. The fact is, however, that the myth remains, and it shows very few signs of dying, even in the last decade. The politics of education myth has been a persistent and pervasive force on the American scene, and it is deeply imbedded in our social consciousness. Part of its persistence can be explained by the very nature of a myth, which can be defined as "an unquestioned belief held in common by a large group of people that gives events and actions a particular meaning." (Edelman, 1971: 53) If the belief is unquestioned by the people, those who believe it are not going to change their minds about it without some kind of earth-shaking turn of events. The nature of myths is that we tend to disregard facts that are contrary to the unquestioned belief or we tend to revise them to fit the mythological beliefs.

It is not a matter of evidence to the contrary. There is plenty of evidence to suggest that public education has always been involved in politics. Ontologically, a very good rational case can be made for the proposition that public education must by its very nature be involved in politics. But, no matter, the myth persists, and if in educated circles we no longer talk about keeping "public education out of politics," we certainly do talk about "public accountability and institutional autonomy," (see Carnegie Commission on Higher Education, 1971: 99-109; Berdahl, 1971: 239-270) for instance, or "local control," or "delivery-level autonomy" and "user-driven system," (see Mann, 1978: 389-412). These are euphemisms at best, and one doesn't have to be very perceptive to recognize the same old myth in modern language.

The politics of education, as a field of inquiry, has been concerned with the relationship between politics and education. To that end, those academicians who have studied the politics of education have given some attention to the myth of the nonpolitical nature of education. Generally, their attention took the form of an attack on the myth as being irrational and untrue. Documentary evidence was produced, and research studies showed that education was, indeed, very deeply involved in politics; and it became commonplace for those of us who fancied ourselves enlightened educators to recognize that superintendents, for example, were political statesmen and that politics wasn't all that bad. The political nature of boards of education was unveiled, and the board-superintendency supremacy question became a hotly debated issue with important political considerations at stake. State and federal political processes for making policy in education were examined and analyzed by a number of scholars and then compared with the processes used to make policy in other areas of public services. The major purpose of much of this research was to expose educational policymaking for what it was, a political process.

While the attack was undoubtedly necessary, it did not slay the dragon, and the politics of education myth continues to live on. It seems pointless, therefore, to continue to attack the myth, as if bigger and better bombs will do the job that previous salvos have failed to accomplish. Nothing so insignificant as academic research intended to prove that the myth was false and unreal will make the myth any less pervasive. The fact is that, despite the knowledge that politics is intrinsically involved in educational policymaking, we Americans continue to believe that it isn't or that it shouldn't be and wish that it wouldn't be.

The preceding suggests that the time may now be ripe for a different tactic, a new approach. Perhaps what we need is an effort directed toward understanding the myth and its significance in the policymaking process. If the myth will not go away, it seems plain that more ought to be known about how it operates, what impact it has on the people who make policy in education, and what role it plays in the process of making educational policy. My own view is that the politics of education myth plays an important part in the formulation of education policy. An extensive study done in Wisconsin in 1972 suggested this conclusion, and the events of the past year in California tend to support the same explanation.

Murray Edelman (1964) has written extensively on the symbolic uses of politics, and the analysis which follows relies heavily on his framework. Myths, Edelman states, have three functions: (1) to create quiescence, (2) to create mass arousal, and (3) to be used as a tactic in the play for power. Supporters and detractors of a controversial policy (in the making or already implemented) use the myth as a means of obtaining peace and calm—quiescence, or unrest and agitation—mass arousal.

Quiescence may result because myths tend to quiet resentments, reassure the people, and reaffirm their belief in the fundamental rationality of the system. Myths induce a feeling of well-being, of reassurance. The politics of education myth has been used consistently throughout our history to convince people that educators know what they are doing, that they are the experts, that education has been the major reason for the country's success, that education is the only route to upward mobility, and that the schools have done an excellent job in the past and will continue to do so in the future if they are left alone. Generally, the public has accepted such leadership because it doesn't feel qualified to make decisions about educational matters and because it is willing to let educators take the responsibility of educating children. Time and people's job-related activities are important factors, of course, but it is reassuring to the public to believe that educators know what they are doing and that they have the ability to bring order into this confusing world.

Myths also have the ability to arouse the public, and so people on both sides of an issue may use the myth for this purpose. Myths help to produce collective actions and sometimes these may be violent and self-defeating. The public can be aroused to protect the myth from being violated by either politicians (who might want to establish more control over the schools) or by educators (who might not be fulfilling their traditional—mythological—role and as a result need to be encouraged to get back to the basics). Classic examples of the myth being used for mass arousal purposes are the battles over school district consolidation. More recent examples would be those over school desegregation.

Finally, myths serve the purpose of allowing various actors to engage in the play for power. Rational as we educators tend to be, we may think that policymaking has as its end some policy or decision that will serve some intended purpose (such as solving a problem). There is considerable research (and a good deal of common sense) which suggests that goals or objectives are not the stuff from which many policies emerge nor the satisfiers that motivate much of what policymakers do. Maneuver, strategy, tactics—whatever you want to call it—is often the end-point of the game, for in the process (rather than in the policy) leaders gain and lose followings, followers achieve a role and gain identity, and money and power are reallocated. All of this may have little to do with, and often may be contrary to, the objectives of the policy which gave rise to the play for power. In such cases, the politics of education myth becomes an instrument of influence, a way of fighting over policy—indeed, the very reason why the actors fight over the policy in the first place. In those situations, the myth becomes more important than the policy and thus becomes the end-point in the play for power.

"But," I hear you say, "how can that be? The politics of education myth is dead! Proposition 13 killed the myth and we are holding the wake right now." I would like to suggest that we ought not think about burying it just yet. With that idea in mind, let's examine the situation in Wisconsin using the conceptual framework borrowed from Edelman which was summarized above. Using the instructive elements of the Wisconsin example as our guide, we can then apply the framework to the present battle in California.

In 1972, Governor Patrick Lucey introduced a bill in the Wisconsin Legislature which attempted to merge the two state university systems, the University of Wisconsin system (UW) and the Wisconsin State University system (WSU), under one board of regents. The bill was hotly contested throughout the state by politicos and educators alike and became the most controversial piece of legislation that engaged the lawmakers that year. In the end, the governor emerged victorious, and Wisconsin now has one system of higher education called the University of Wisconsin under one board of regents. Without going into detail—the situation was extremely complex—I want to summarize some of the results of the (Rost, 1973) study as they relate to the politics of education myth.

Concerning the play for power function of the myth, these points about the ultimate reasons for the merger battle came out of the study.

(1) The governor staked so much of his political career on the merger bill that he needed a victory in order not to suffer a tremendous defeat.

(2) The Republicans in the Legislature fought the bill primarily as a political issue. They were not so much opposed to the merger as they were interested in defeating the governor on this important issue. In fact, many Republicans linked the objectives of the bill and privately were not unhappy that the bill passed.

(3) The Democrats in the Legislature supported the bill as a means of strengthening and unifying the Democratic Party (Wisconsin was previously known as a Republican stronghold) and as a means of expanding their support among the common man and in the northern sections of the state.

(4) The UW leaders fought the bill because it represented a political interference into the sanctuary of Academe and also because the UW had a reputation for defeating the state government when it was attacked and the UW wanted to preserve that reputation.

(5) The WSU people favored the bill as a good opportunity to flex their political muscles and as a means of obtaining equal status with the prestigious University of Wisconsin.

Objectively speaking, the bill didn't make a lot of sense, and the rational arguments both for and against the bill were even more meaningless, especially in the context of what was making the world go round in 1972. Symbolically, the bill had a big impact and therein lie reasons for the battle lines. The bill was an attempt to slap the wrists of the universities (particularly the Madison campus) for allowing the Vietnam riots to happen and to show the universities that what had happened on their campuses had weakened their support among the politicians and the people. The people of Wisconsin had put a lot of faith in their universities and particularly the University of Wisconsin—Madison (the "jewel in the crown," as Lucey called it). A higher education was symbolic of all the good things most parents wanted for their children. Merger was an attempt to reassure the people of Wisconsin that at least the governor had some sense and could control the universities and prevent further excesses so that their sons and daughters could go to these universities in peace.

Much of the governor's efforts in trying to get his bill passed was to assure the legislators, university officials, and the people that merger meant no harm to the prestigious Madison campus. Much of the opposition's effort to defeat the bill was an attempt to arouse fear in the same people that the internationally famous University of Wisconsin would decline and would deteriorate to just an ordinary university.

Both sides knew that the politics of education myth had within it the potential of arousing the public. Neither side was sure that it could win if the public were aroused, so both sides hesitated to use the myth for that purpose. The Republicans and UW leaders decided to play the game within the confines of the political system because they felt they had a better chance of winning in that arena. It was probably their most important tactical error.

Lucey also flirted with the idea of using the merger as a populist issue, but after a couple of unsuccessful attempts, he redirected his strategy to use the politics of education myth as a means of gaining quiescence. The issue was framed in the best rational context as if the merger of the university systems was the only rational way to organize and govern the higher education system in Wisconsin. The bill was very general so as to allow the university officials the opportunity to work out the details and thus put their own house in order after the politicians decided the broad policy. The bill was proclaimed as the solution to *the* university problem—which problem remained vague and ambiguous in the minds of the public who tended to confuse it with the campus unrest problem.

If the people believed that the universities were at fault for not doing something about the student riots, or if they thought that the universities were receiving too much of the tax dollar or causing their taxes to rise inordinately, the merger policy was a means of quieting their resentments, since it symbolically attacked the university systems and because it was widely heralded as a means of not only redistributing the resources of the state but of saving tax money and therefore lessening the amount of the tax levy increase for the 1971-1973 biennium. If the public was resentful that the WSU system was not getting its fair share of the higher education tax dollar, the merger bill quieted their anxieties by promising equity through a merged system. If they distrusted the government's interfering with the higher education establishment, the proponents of merger assured them that this policy was a necessary, but temporary, intrusion into the ivory tower to (a) modernize the structure of higher education so it could govern itself more efficiently or (b) redirect the goals of the academy to the needs of the common man (rather than to the interests of research-minded professors, the wild ideas of student activities, or the exaggerated notions of the elitist, ivy league set).

In the end, merger was ultimately not understandable by the public. It was too confusing, too complicated to reduce to a single issue, and the rhetoric of both sides was more or less meaningless. That allowed them to take comfort in the belief that the politicians and university officials knew what they were fighting over and would figure out the best way to handle what to them appeared to be a complex problem. So, the public trusted their political leaders and remained quiescent, and the bill passed the Legislature using the rules of the political game.

The key, then, to understanding the merger policymaking process is to understand that the politics of education myth was adroitly handled or skillfully sidestepped and, as a result, the people and the politicians did not display any violent opposition to the bill and defeat it because it violated the myth. The merger bill passed because the belief was widespread that merger was not an unwarranted interference by the state government in the area of higher education, and therefore the public officials and the public were not aroused to defend education from governmental control since they did not believe that the myth was being violated.

In point of fact, the merger bill badly hurt the university system, and it has not been the same since. The reason merger was not looked upon as a violation of the politics of education myth was that the University's image was tarnished in 1972. Higher education was suffering from a credibility gap, and the result was a breakdown in the hold that the politics of education myth had over the politicians and the people.

If these views are fairly accurate and if they are generalized, several conclusions follow quite naturally.

(1) When the public image of education is tarnished, the public's perception of the politics of education myth is such that some interference by the government in the sacred preserve of educational policymaking is acceptable and even praiseworthy.

(2) When the public image of education is good, the public's perception of the politics of education myth is such that no unnecessary interference with the system of education on the part of governmental officials is acceptable.

(3) Thus, major public policy changes in the field of education will take place only during those times when education's image is tarnished.

(4) Minor (but still somewhat significant) policy changes may take place when education's image is good if the politicos maintain a low profile, use tactics that are clothed in rationality and pay obeiscance to the politics of education myth, and

obtain the cooperation of the education establishment or at least obtain acquiescence through some form of co-optation. These, of course, will give the public symbolic reassurance and tend to maintain quiescence.

What does all this have to say about the situation in California in 1978-1979? It seems to me that the analysis helps us to understand why Proposition 13 passed in June 1978.

The fact is that the image of K-12 public education in California (and the nation) is badly tarnished, and so the time is ripe for political interference in educational policymaking. Such interference is not only tolerated by a public which a few years ago would have been crying wolf, it is welcomed as a means of showing the public's displeasure and disaffection with our system of education.

Proposition 13 had all the earmarks of that kind of revolt. What was interesting about this particular revolt remains relatively unnoticed. The people did not say, "We want the state politicans to cut the taxes," which was the basic meaning behind Proposition 8. "We the People are cutting the taxes" was the message of Proposition 13. That seems to be one step further than the usual kind of directive given by the public, and the credibility gap implied is monumental. The credibility gap applied to all public policymakers at the state and local level, not only eductors. By implication, federal policymakers were not off the hook, and they might want to take another hard look at operation of the federal government in education.

Proposition 13 was heralded as a message for local governments, including education, to trim the fat, to get back to the basics. It is a message that has not been well received by the local public policymakers and so it is little wonder that much of the intended effect of Proposition 13 was lost as local public agencies, including public schools, went about their business as usual, aided and abetted by the bail-out money from the state. It is not too surprising that Paul Gann had little difficulty obtaining signatures on his spending limit initiative. The message obviously did not get through, and so many people feel they must try again to penetrate the system and somehow pound the message in.

An analysis of the campaign prior to the passage of Proposition 13 would suggest that several elements of the framework fit perfectly.

(1) Educators tried to use rational, persuasive arguments against the initiative. They tried to show how essential a vital system of education was to the progress of our nation and the state, how important education was to their sons and daughters, how much education did for the communities and the many services it provided to them, ad infinitum. These were intended to produce a sort of quiescence, a calm deliberation concerning the detrimental impact the initiative would have on the sacred institution of the public school. Proponents of the initiative, of course, countered with the argument that Proposition 13 would not harm the public school or its ability to provide those essential services traditionally associated with schooling in the United States. There was, Jarvis and Gann said, plenty of fat to cut. In the main, quiescence was not achieved, and the public became aroused.

(2) Jarvis knew how to arouse the public. He went up and down the state committing unpardonable errors of human relations, getting outrageous press coverage as the state's number one madman, making ridiculous tactical mistakes according to the conventional wisdom of almost all the professional politicans. He set the people to stewing in righteous indignation over the absurd property tax increases and made them justifiably angry at the public policymakers (including educators) for not limiting their spending and for not setting their own houses in order. Education, for example, came under attack as being all frills and no substance, and Proposition 13 proponents told the people in very clear terms that they were not getting a solid return on their investment in the public schools. For their part, educators throughout the state attempted to convince people that Proposition 13 would destroy the public school system. Meetings were held in

schools and service clubs; anywhere an audience could be gathered people were buttonholed and given the message. The PTA, teacher unions, and administrator associations, among others, got on the bandwagon, printing literature, and financing advertisements and so on in an effort to counter-arouse the people and protect the public schools from everlasting damage.

Faced with the alternative of destroying the public schools or obtaining tax relief by cutting the fat, the public chose the scalpel, and they may have perhaps been willing to use an axe. Jarvis had aroused the people to such an extent that they were willing to risk the possibility of destroying the public schools in order to obtain some tax relief. An alternative analysis would be that the public simply didn't believe the educators when they said that the schools would be destroyed. Either way, the conclusion that seems overwhelmingly obvious is that an aroused public wanted to send a message that the public school system was out of control and educators needed to take some drastic steps to get back to the basics. "Put your house back in order, and we will go back to our comfortable mores of the politics of education myth," the public seemed to say. The corollary of this is: "And we won't go back to our comfortable myth until we see some action."

Finally, the play for power and the tactics used in a power struggle suggest a similar analysis. As with the Wisconsin merger struggle, the Proposition 13 movement gives additional confirmation to the conclusion that the stated objectives of a policy initiative are often not the heart of the matter. It was (and is) naive to think of Proposition 13 as a property tax revolt. The bottom line is that Proposition 13 is a revolt against big government and a movement to make government smaller. In the language of education, it means get back to basics. Many local and state government people (including educators) still don't understanding that. The cat, however, is now out of the bag.

An essay needs to be written about the tactics used during the battle over the initiative. In the meantime, it seems safe to say that the Legislature's failure to pass significant tax relief legislation and then passing Proposition 8 as a means of combating Proposition 13, Governor Brown's dramatic shift from the leadership position of the anti-Proposition 13 forces to the pro side at the midnight hour, the presence of a huge state surplus, the successful appeal of Jarvis-Gann to the renters, the emotionality of the issue and the willingness of the public to accept the angry outbursts of Jarvis and other Proposition 13 supporters, the inexplicable indifference shown by the higher education establishment, and the difficulty educators and other local government types had in adjusting to and working effectively within the political process all suggest that the forces opposed to the Proposition 13 movement did not have their act together individually and collectively. It is probably the understatement of the year to conclude that they didn't play the power game with consummate skill.

If the above is reasonably accurate, educators have their work cut out for them. It is perhaps not too strong to suggest that the public has not been impressed with our post-Proposition 13 behavior. The situation may be ripe to pay attention to an editorial in the San Francisco *Chronicle* (January 15, 1979) which in turn quoted some parts of several editorial essays writen by Norman Macrae in *The Economist*. "Public sector imperialism in democratic countries," Macrae wrote, "is not going to be rolled back by electing some monk to dissolve his own monasteries nor . . . by the 1789 or the 1871 types of bloody revolution. But over the next few decades it is now probably going to be rolled back by a worldwide series of broad but changing equivalents of California's Proposition 13."

What Macrae appears to mean is that people are going to turn on their "imperialist" public-sector masters and interrupt, interfere with, even in some cases abolish, the concentration of spending power that has been held in the hands of bureaucrats. This has long been sanctified on the supposition that lots of services are more efficiently produced by state monopoly than by the market. "In the past few years it has become probable that none of these [more efficient services] now exists."

Hear his dismissal of the old order in the schools: "Education ministers must be living in either Toytown or Prussia if they think that they can continue to give monopolies to whatever sorts of teacher-dominated institutions fit their political party's social prejudices best." This is heady stuff but not unlike what the people are actually saying on the streets, in their offices and homes, and at strategy meetings preparing for the next onslaught.

This essay began with the thought that despite some apparent evidence to the contrary, the politics of education myth was alive, and although perhaps not completely well, was still living in California and the rest of the nation. It may be appropriate to end with the thought that a myth is not some permanently fixed commandment etched in stone. It is a living, growing, vibrant, existential belief, and it can also die. It is possible that Proposition 13 was the beginning of the end. We probably won't know until another decade passes and we see where the whole movement has taken us. Myths die hard. It takes more than one hard blow to cause a fatal stroke. In the meantime, we can assume that the politics of education myth has some life left in it and, depending upon our outlook, we may want to work toward its reconstruction in what might be called a revitalized set of beliefs.

Now *that* is an extremely challenging agenda.

REFERENCES

BERDAHL, R. O. (1971) Statewide Coordination of Higher Education. Washington, DC: American Council on Education.

Carnegie Commission on Higher Education (1971) The Capitol and the Campus. New York: McGraw-Hill.

EDELMAN, M. (1971) Politics as Symbolic Action. Chicago: Markham.

——— (1964) The Symbolic Uses of Politics. Urbana: Univ. of Illinois Press.

MANN, D. (1978) "The use-driven system and a modest proposal." Teachers College
    Record 79 (February).
ROST, J. (1973) "The merger of the University of Wisconsin and the Wisconsin State
    University systems: a case study in the politics of education." Ph.D. dissertation,
    University of Wisconsin—Madison.
San Francisco Chronicle (1979) "The economist looks at 13." January 15.

STATE POWER AND PUBLIC POLICY

It is fitting that the final section of the book deal with state power and its linkages to public policy. Increasingly, as the state becomes a giant allocative mechanism, it assumes the multiple roles formerly performed by voluntary agencies in the social sector. Moving entire societies out of the past, from traditionalism to modernization, is the most obvious way in which the state intervenes in developing nations to affect outcomes. More conventionally, in developed areas the state serves as mediator for interest groups, social classes, racial blocs, and the like. It sets the legal tone and the authoritative model for problem-solving. But as this increased role of the state grows, so do the burdens of managing an ever-larger bureaucracy, creating a higher degree of centralization and greater reliance upon mandated programs rather than individual initiatives. The state, which initially invokes its sovereign duties to maintain decent levels of equity among a recalcitrant citizenry, increasingly invokes its authorities to establish guidelines and frameworks within which groups must accept restrictions upon their actions. Limiting acceptance of the very role of the state—as law enforcer or as social benefactor—becomes the object of both specific policies and general social systems.

The study of state power and public policy takes us full circle, bringing us back to the nature of federal government/individual relationships. And yet there is a difference, for, as Grob amply notes, the study of policy in a historical context allows us to see that what starts as a mechanism for alleviating ailments in society can become a sickness in itself. Involved are notions of internal dependency, public policy as fixed instead of variable, policies that grew out of politics and organizations, preferences rather than basic human needs, the place of economic costs no less than benefits in the policy spectrum, and professionalization and bureaucratization as the essence of policy-making rather than delivery of services and goods. In recent years, many of the concerns Grob expressed are being addressed, but the need for doing so in a historical context is carefully pointed up. Hicks' statement on policy issues for the 1980s does a great deal to verify Grob's approach; arguing for policies that reflect physical movement and social mobility rather than force decisions and practices upon an unwanting and unsuspecting populace. Hicks is essentially arguing for a great shift from an urban to a national policy; for a policy based on top-down consideration of special interest pleas and a bottom-up regard for general interests. The difficulty is in locating that general interest and responding to it, rather than forcing citizens to support with their tax dollars policies they find repugnant. Beginning with history, the section properly ends with futurology, with a near-future scenario designed by Labedz of a populace unprepared and unwilling to respond to imminent threats from abroad. The image of a third world war having been lost without a shot being fired, like the image of an America drowning in an inflationary spiral through never-ending federal increments, is after all the kind of fear and concern which has resulted in a significant transformation of American and world society in the 1980s—and unquestionably in the deepest transformation of domestic and foreign policy apparatuses—since the New Deal some half-century ago.

40

PUBLIC POLICY-MAKING AND SOCIAL POLICY

Gerald N. Grob

I

Since World War II historians and social scientists have become increasingly interested in the concept of "social policy." A vague term, social policy generally refers to actions taken by government to deal with social and economic distress and other problems of an urban-industrial society. More specifically, social policy has a variety of different but related goals: (1) to mitigate or to abolish poverty; (2) to provide for groups unable to survive without some form of assistance; (3) to improve and to humanize conditions of work; (4) to grapple with the sanitary and hygienic problems resulting from modern technology and urbanization; (5) to control and punish crime; (6) to establish surrogate structures for functions once performed by family, church, or the immediate community.

The reasons for the contemporary fascination with social policy are not difficult to understand. Intrinsic issues aside, many human beings hold values that imply the possibility of a better or an ideal society, as contrasted with an imperfect reality. It is not surprising, therefore, that interest in social policy issues should be on the rise; scholarly detachment and moral commitment have rarely been viewed as inherently antagonistic. Long-standing reformist and melioristic traditions within history and other social science disciplines have merely stimulated a kind of scholarship that is intended as much to change the world as to understand its ways.

Historians have long been concerned with the manner in which American society dealt with dependent groups. For the most part, however, they did not produce policy-oriented studies, nor were they concerned with the formulation, implementation, or administration of social policy. Generally, historians during the first half of the twentieth century were primarily interested in politics and elections, and they tended to study social problems within a conceptual framework that emphasized alternating chronological periods of liberal reform and conservative consolidation. Such an approach was not conducive to differentiating between dependent and distressed groups on one hand and the general population on the other. The history of social policy, to the degree that it was studied, remained an adjunct to political history.

From Gerald N. Grob, "Public Policy-Making and Social Policy," original manuscript. Copyright © 1981 by Sage Publications, Inc.

Other barriers also inhibited the systematic study of social policy issues. Overlapping and fragmented political jurisdictions made it difficult to treat social policy in a coherent manner. Leaving aside the role of the federal government, the care of dependent groups was subject to a multiplicity of state and local governments. The resulting variety of political jurisdictions complicated the task of defining public policy as an entity. The important role played by private philanthropy only compounded the problem. Moreover, a lack of economic sophistication led historians to ignore fiscal issues or to treat them in a manner that obscured rather than clarified the problem. There is not a single analysis of nineteenth-century aggregate welfare expenditures and the relationship of such expenditures to the GNP or prevailing price and wage levels.

Recently, however, social historians have begun to study the lives and experiences of dependent groups and the inarticulate masses of Americans. In doing so they implicitly define the contours of public policy dealing with dependency. Books and articles dealing with almshouses, prisons, mental and general hospitals, schools, and houses of refuge (to cite only a few examples) have revealed how nineteenth-century Americans turned to institutional solutions to deal with various types of distress.

Nevertheless, contemporary scholarship has not yet resolved a series of logical, conceptual, and empirical questions pertaining to social policy issues. Those studies that emphasized the nineteenth-century thrust toward institutional solutions to alleviate distress and resolve other social problems were largely internal in nature. Most of them assumed rather than demonstrated a relationship between social policy on one hand and politics and the political system on the other; they did not deal with the origins of the very concept of dependency and its change over time or how dependency became a social policy question. Nor did these studies describe with any degree of precision the goals of social policy. Was dependency to be abolished, alleviated, or simply explained? Moreover, much of recent scholarship deals only implicitly with the replacement of individual solutions by bureaucratic ones. The establishment of institutions, after all, was not synonymous with bureaucracy; the process of bureaucratization remains unexplored for the most part. Finally, there are aspects of social policy that have been virtually ignored. Our knowledge of governmental activities dealing with welfare and dependency is superficial; economic analysis is all but absent; the intellectual climate partly responsible for the creation of the concept of public policy has not been adequately studied; the nineteenth-century proclivity to explain social phenomena in statistical terms (which proved important in the debate over social policy issues) has yet to be accounted for; and knowledge about the composition of dependent populations is still lacking.

Because the history of social policy is both a new and complex subject, it is difficult—if not impossible—to deal with it as a whole in a brief presentation. I should like, therefore, to present first a brief critique of some of the literature, drawing a disproportionate number of examples from my own work on the history of the care and treatment of the mentally ill. Then I should like to consider some alternative approaches, problems, and conceptual frameworks that might serve to guide future work.

II

Much of the historical literature that touches upon social policy implicitly takes its lead from contemporary issues and concerns. The history of the care and treatment of the mentally ill is a case in point. For the last thirty years Americans have engaged in an animated debate over the best means of fulfilling responsibility toward this particular group. There are those who argue that confinement in hospitals is the worst possible policy; others urge greater public expenditures to upgrade institutional care and treatment; still others deny that there is any such thing as mental disease; and, finally, there are those who insist that only a totally new approach involving the entire community can resolve painful dilemmas.

Interestingly enough, the contemporary differences over social policy issues are startlingly similar to the differences among historians concerned with dependency and its alleviation. On one side stand those traditionalists who celebrate such institutions as schools, hospitals, and prisons as evidence of human progress, humanitarianism, and increasing liberal sentiment. Although these scholars concede that there are serious flaws and imperfections in such institutions, they operate on the assumption that with additional effort and funding most defects could have been eliminated. On the other side are revisionist scholars who denigrate these very same institutions. They view them as agencies by which dominant elites restrained deviant groups or largely lower-class elements, thereby ensuring some measure of social control (if not hegemony). Although I have deliberately set forth these two general approaches in dichotomous and perhaps extreme terms, I believe that such a framework is not far from the truth—even though some individual studies do not fall within either category.[1]

Curiously enough, there were some striking similarities between the traditional and revisionist approaches. Both began at precisely the same starting point: the failure of institutions. However, whereas the former saw this failure as only transitory, the latter saw it as an inevitable consequence of institutional solutions. Influenced by the critics of orthodox psychiatry and the sociological concept of the total institution, the revisionists came up with a quite different interpretation. Mental illness, some of them argued, was not an objective category; it was a concept designed to penalize disruptive and abberant behavior rather than to describe physiological malfunctions. Similarly, mental hospitals grew out of the fear of social disorder; consequently, they served custodial and penal functions rather than therapeutic roles. Although there are significant differences in the outlooks and historical methods of such commentators as Michel Foucault, Thomas S. Szasz, and David J. Rothman, they have in common a point of view—a critical stance toward psychiatry and mental hospitals—which largely accounts for their popularity and widespread influence.[2]

The historiography of mental hospitals and psychiatry is by no means unique. Comparable examples can be found in the historiography of American education and social welfare. In the former, the older or traditional view—best symbolized by the writings of Elwood P. Cubberly—depicted public schooling in terms of the triumph of democracy and progress over the forces of reaction. Revisionist scholars, on the other hand, emphasized the undemocratic nature of public education. Schools, they contended, were never intended to provide quality education for all; their basic function was to act as instruments of manipulation and social control in order to safeguard the hegemonic position of dominant elites.[3]

Historians of social welfare have also divided along similar lines. Traditionalists interpreted welfare in terms of the fulfillment of the nation's liberal democratic heritage, even while conceding that at times too few resources were allocated for the alleviation of distress. Revisionists, by way of contrast, maintained that welfare in America was never intended to relieve or to eliminate economic distress or to aid social unfortunates in a compassionate or sympathetic manner. On the contrary, welfare—irrespective of the form it took or the manner in which it was administered—was based on the harsh premise that poverty, crime, and disease derived from individual character defects. Public policy, therefore, had as its goal the control of those immoral and undesirable results that flowed from the behavior of various groups in order to minimize potential dangers to dominant groups.[4]

Although yielding some rich insights and opening certain kinds of primary source materials hitherto ignored, the traditionalist/revisionist debate had several undesirable side effects. By adopting a presentist framework and social science models or paradigms, historians often fell into the trap of assuming that past problems and policies were not fundamentally dissimilar from present ones. The result was a kind of historical scholarship that lacked elements of change. If mental hospitals were places of incarceration and schools were instruments of social control from their inceptions, why was it necessary to trace their development, given their static qualities? The pronounced commitment to presentism in historical scholarship has sometimes inhibited the development of alternative conceptual frameworks and new avenues of research.

The debate over "social control" versus "meliorism" also precluded consideration of other kinds of issues. Did social policy, to cite one illustration, exist as a conceptual reality? Or did society face a series of dissimilar problems ranging from illness to unemployment to old age that gave rise to individual responses, the sum total of which are aggregated under the rubric of "social policy"? In a sense this question is merely a rephrasing of the classic dispute in philosophy between the nominalists and the realists. This kind of issue is troubling, if only because of the difficulty in providing relevant data. In recent years the tendency has been to deal with institutions in terms of their common characteristics and then to infer generalizations about the nature of the society that created them. While yielding important insights, such an approach is vulnerable to several criticisms. Is it appropriate to classify within a single category the varied kinds of populations confined in different institutions as though there were few significant differences between them? Were the experiences of institutionalized populations similar or comparable? Did levels and sources of support, geographical location, varied legal and administrative environments, and other phenomena give rise to institutions that were not as monolithic as is commonly assumed?

III

In order to make my point in a less abstract manner, I would like to discuss the relationship between social policy and the political system. Clearly, the theme of growing governmental authority, particularly at the state level, is a major element in nineteenth-century American history. Since the publication of Oscar and Mary Handlin's and Louis Hartz's pioneering studies of Massachusetts and Pennsylvania, respectively, some thirty years ago, historians have done much to shed light on the relationship between governmental activities and economic growth.[5] Yet, for reasons that are not altogether clear, historians of social policy have generally avoided any substantive analysis of the role of the state in social policy problems.[6]

Although it is clear that many nineteenth-century Americans demonstrated an affinity for institutional solutions, the linkages between preference and policy have yet to be demonstrated. One explanation commonly offered is that middle-class citizens by the early nineteenth century had become obsessed with deviant behavior of all kinds, especially that associated with the poor and with immigrants. Fear of disorder inevitably led to the adoption of institutional solutions to impose social controls or to demarcate lines between "productive" and "nonproductive" groups, according to various revisionist scholars.

Implicit in this general approach was the assumption that there was a direct relationship between public demands and expectations on one hand and policies on the other. Certain citizens and groups expressed their views by participating in the political arena. The result was the election of representatives who translated the views of their constituents into laws and policies. Paraphrased simply, fear of social disorder led people to vote for legislators sympathetic to the incarceration of deviant groups; the result was the establishment of different kinds of custodial institutions.[7]

There are, however, both theoretical and empirical problems with such an approach. John C. Wahlke, a political scientist, recently criticized the facile acceptance of a model that postulates a linkage between the policy preferences of citizens and the public policy decisions of representative bodies.

Wahlke noted that all models of representation should (but rarely do) take account of certain demonstrable facts. It is doubtful, for example, that substantial numbers of people entertain interests that represent policy demands or policy expectations, or that they know enough about political structures and processes to communicate such demands or expectations. Moreover, relatively few citizens either communicate with their representatives or express any interest in policy-making matters. Finally, voters do not appear to have any clear notion that they are making policy demands or policy choices when they cast their ballots. How, then, asked Wahlke, can it be assumed that government "is essentially a process for discovering policies which will maximally meet the policy expectations of citizens"?[8]

The validity of Wahlke's position is supported when one looks at American historiography dealing with political concerns in the nineteenth century. Political historians have yet to demonstrate empirically that the policy expectations and demands by citizens in the decades before the Civil War were first identified by legislators who proceeded to process them into policies that conformed to popular expectations. Indeed, most studies of antebellum voting behavior are stronger in categorizing the characteristics of the electorate and weaker in demonstrating any linkages between voting behavior and policy results.

If a direct result between demands/expectations and policy cannot be clearly established, how is it possible to explain the formulation of social policy during the nineteenth century? One approach to this problem is to attempt to reconceptualize the structure and role of government during this period in ways that deviate from the more traditional representational model. Structure, after all, can exert a pronounced influence on function, just as function can influence structure. Scholars have yet to study the structure of nineteenth-century state governments and the degree to which a particular political structure contributed to the shaping of public policy. Indeed, so strong has been the hold of both a rational model of politics and a rational model of human behavior (based on self-interest) that alternative approaches to the history of public policy have not been adequately considered. This fact is all the more surprising in light of current concern with administrative, legal, and bureaucratic history.

Most state governments shortly after 1800, for example, were engaged in anything but systematic policy formulation. On the contrary, state legislatures seemed to view their primary function as processing individual and group demands that involved the distribution of the country's vast land resources, monetary surpluses, patronage, and the benefits accruing from tariff policies.[9] This emphasis on distributive functions was in most respects consistent with the Madisonian view of government. Given the local, decentralized, and preindustrial nature of early nineteenth-century American society, the pluralistic model of government was by no means illogical or irrational.

Beginning in the nineteenth century, however, the United States underwent profound economic and social changes that at present are associated with the term "modernization." In addition to demographic, economic, and social changes, modernization, to use Samuel P. Huntington's typology, was also accompanied by changes in the structure and functions of political systems. Political modernization involved three developments. First, there was a rationalization and centralization of authority. Second, there was a sharp differentiation of new political functions and the development of specialized structures to perform these functions. Finally, political modernization meant increased political participation by social groups throughout society.

Except for increased political participation, the American political system failed to modernize during the first two-thirds of the nineteenth century, according to this typology. The absence of foreign threats to national security, rising standard of living, and modest degree of social mobility may have retarded political modernization or rendered it a less pressing problem. Whatever the reasons, the American political system continued to follow the Madisonian model. It did not—as compared with some European nations—centralize and rationalize authority, nor did its political institutions become differentiated in structural terms.[10]

While the political system retained its traditional form, society was transformed by economic and demographic forces that created new tensions and social problems. The spontaneous and informal way in which rural areas, small villages, and towns during the colonial period met the problems of disease and dependency failed to function as well or as efficiently in growing urban areas. In the cities an extraordinarily high rate of geographical mobility tended to limit social cohesion, and the informal and traditional means of dealing with dependent groups proved less effective. Once the informal mechanisms were undermined, more systematic and institutionalized patterns for dealing with dependency-related problems came into favor.

The structure of the American political system, however, by its nature hampered the development of clear policy-formulation and social planning. Most state legislatures, for example, were not yet institutionalized in their operations. The tenure of their members was often brief, and a high proportion of legislators served only a single term.[11] Moreover, no internal division of labor existed within legislatures; the complex legislative structures that developed in the twentieth century were absent throughout much of the nineteenth. Precedents and rules were vague, and there was often little continuity either in personnel or deliberations from session to session. Bills were frequently introduced by petitions or memorials from private individuals or organizations; rarely did the enactment of specific pieces of legislation reflect broad currents of public opinion.[12] Investigating committees were sometimes made up of the very individuals who petitioned the legislature for some particular cause. In other cases they were composed of individuals who were not even members of the legislature. Standing committees were not especially effective, and the inexperience of their membership and lack of any permanent staff limited their autonomy and importance. There were also few supporting services; most legislatures had neither a legal staff nor a reference or research division. Consequently, the legislative process inhibited rather than promoted the formulation of comprehensive and rational policies toward dependent groups. The relative lack of institutionalization within legislatures gave rise to laws that reflected only individual and immediate concerns.[13]

In the early nineteenth century the legislative process did not rely heavily upon professional expertise and bureaucratic personnel. Although legislatures were aware of the need for data that would serve as the basis for rational policy-making, the personnel, procedures, and even theories of social planning simply were not available. To cite one example, the censuses—both federal and state—were relatively simple and rudimentary compilations (as compared with those of some Western European nations) and they often did not provide the kind of information needed for the legislative process. The relatively unsophisticated nature of the information-gathering process was not simply a matter of being unable to amass the necessary data. The absence of broad theoretical models relating to public policy made it difficult to gather or to use empirical data in a meaningful way. Legislative decisions, as a result, often reflected external factors or assumptions that were never questioned. This is not to imply that nineteenth-century legislators and administrators were deficient or malevolent. Rather, the lack of theory and methodology often led to policies whose results in the long run were at variance with the goals envisaged when the original legislation was passed.

Admittedly, most nineteenth-century legislators *were* responsive to demands by constituents for such things as land grants, charters, and special acts of incorporation. But these demands were usually formulated not by broad social or political coalitions but by individuals or small and transient interest groups. Too often historians have identified individuals as symbols of social movements when no such movements existed. The success of a Dorothea L. Dix in persuading state legislatures to establish mental hospitals may have been due to the fact that although a particular group benefited from government action, the costs were so widely distributed that those who paid had little or no incentive to oppose such projects and therefore remained indifferent or ignorant. The result was often a series of individual legislative acts, each having little or no connection with what preceded or followed their enactment. The broad framework of public policy, therefore, for the most part was not the conscious choice of legislators and officials, but rather the sum total of a series of unrelated decisions. Consequently, the incremental nature of policy formulation often gave rise to laws that generally bore little or no relationship to expectations of either legislators or the public.

One concrete illustration of these broad generalizations may help to clarify the nature of the political system and the policies it produced. In dealing with dependency and welfare-related problems in the three decades following 1830, many legislatures authorized the establishment of public mental hospitals. By 1860 most states had at least one of these institutions. The establishment of mental hospitals was part of the thrust toward modernization, in the sense that the responsibilities of the state were enlarged at the expense of traditional structures such as the family or local community. The increase in the number of state mental institutions between 1830 and 1860, however, was not a product of careful analysis and evaluation of existing and future needs. On the contrary, most states acted only after being prodded by individual activists. Discussions in the legislature about hospitals were generally perfunctory; there was virtually no effort to place the specific problems of the mentally ill within a larger perspective. Nor was any consideration given to the impact of the general legal, administrative, and economic environment upon any individual hospital. The absence of a cohesive and clearly defined system of policy formulation also meant that each succeeding legislature discussed the problem in a virtual vacuum. There was little realization that past actions had created an institutional framework that would have a marked influence on current decisions. Although this type of decision-making partly reflected technical institutional inadequacies, it was often the result of the lack of authority within the political system that made the legislature receptive to pressure from individuals or small interest groups.

Consider, for example, the objectives of the laws that provided for the establishment of mental hospitals and what actually happened to these institutions over a period of time. These laws reflected the belief that a single therapeutic hospital could meet the needs of the state, since the continuous discharge of supposedly recovered patients would make room for new ones. Moreover, the central geographical location of most state hospitals was based upon the conviction that all citizens would thus have equal access to the facility.

Theory, of course, bore little relation to practice. Within a short time the gap between the ideal and social reality widened sharply. Mental institutions were intended to house a transitory patient population; yet from the beginning they were forced to accept and to retain large numbers of chronic cases, thereby curtailing sharply their therapeutic capabilities. Hospitals were also supposed to remain small in order to promote the type of relationship deemed conducive to therapy. Instead, they grew in size because most laws made admission of certain cases mandatory and at the same time failed to place a ceiling on total resident population or to provide for the construction of new or expanded facilities. In theory, all patients were to receive the same quality of care. In practice, class, ethnicity, and race played a significant part in creating differential patterns of care. The functions of hospital superintendents were defined theoretically in medical terms; in actuality superintendents became administrators concerned with managerial problems. Central location of hospitals was intended to ensure equal access; in practice, the use of facilities was greatest among those living in adjacent areas. The result was inadvertent discrimination against those who lived at a distance from the geographical center of a state. Indeed, urban populations were especially hard hit, since location of many cities had been determined by access to transportation facilities.[14]

By the 1850s many states had become aware that public welfare was beset by significant tensions and contradictions. The early promises of activists who had promoted institutional solutions to social problems had not been fulfilled. Despite the proliferation of almshouses, penitentiaries, hospitals, schools, and houses of refuge, neither illness, dependency, nor even crime seemed to be on the wane; if anything, they were all on the rise. The massive increases in the activities and expenditures of state governments, some charged, had not produced commensurate benefits. Why was this so? More important, how could this dismal state of affairs be reversed? Above all, upon what basis could a sound and economical public policy rest?

At the same time that legislatures were becoming more concerned with welfare-related issues, the political system was beginning to change in character. State legislatures in particular underwent a peculiar transformation. Specific acts of incorporation, for example, gave way to general acts of incorporation, indicating that governments were not necessarily becoming more democratic, but rather were surrendering some of their policy-making authority. During this same period constitutional conventions began to limit the powers of state legislatures by curbing their distributive activities. Such developments did little to enhance the power of state governments in formulating general policies. On the contrary, legislative authority was diminished in scope. The most curious aspect about this development was that it occurred precisely at the time when other advanced nations were developing functionally differentiated and complex governmental structures to deal with the changing social order. In the United States, on the other hand, the reverse process seemed to occur; modernization was accompanied by a political system that appeared to be growing less authoritative and less active.[15]

The initial response to welfare-related problems, however, seems to contradict this generalization, for the role of state governments—at least on the surface—seemed to be expanding. In the 1850s both the Massachusetts and New York legislatures began to discuss the possibility of establishing a regulatory agency to be responsible for public welfare. During the succeeding two decades interest in regulation broadened, and a number of states founded boards of charity and health, railroad and banking commissions, and bureaus of labor statistics. Upon closer analysis, it would appear that the thrust in the direction of establishing regulatory agencies did not necessarily imply a strengthening of the powers of the state. Indeed, under certain circumstances, a delegation of power by a legislature to an agency resulted in a sharp diminution in political authority (particularly if clear policy guidelines were absent) and enhanced bargaining between the regulatory agency and private groups.[16]

The establishment of state boards of charity offers a dramatic illustration of the compatibility of regulation and the diminution of state authority. In the decade following 1863, nine states created public boards of charity.

Although most of them subsequently evolved into elaborate bureaucratic structures, at the time of their founding they were given a mandate to introduce greater efficiency and rationality into public welfare and ultimately to dismantle the public welfare apparatus. In other words, the reaction of many states to welfare and dependency-related problems was simply to establish a structure that would terminate public responsibility. Since the political system had always existed on a base of distrust of power and authority, the negative response of many states was neither unpredictable nor surprising.

It is clear, in retrospect, that few regulatory agencies came close to fulfilling their mandate. This fact was partly due to the vagueness of the mandate given them. But another consideration was that many of the early boards were staffed by strong-willed and organizationally minded individuals who laid the foundations for a complex bureaucratic structure. Ultimately, these agencies seemed to reflect the feeling that any right-minded, intelligent, educated individual, when placed in a responsible managerial position, would be able to deal effectively with social problems and thereby help to ensure the preservation of a fundamentally moral and healthy society. The absence of any clear legislative policy guidelines and the tendency to deal with problems through an incremental decision-making process permitted board members wide latitude in exercising judgment and authority.

In suggesting that the structure of the political system played a role in the emergence of certain kinds of policies, I do not wish to denigrate the importance of social class differences or ideology. Social class and ideology *were* significant, but not necessarily in a simple or direct manner. In his sensitive portrayal of the rise and fall of the nineteenth-century dispensary, for example, Charles Rosenberg has shown how one institution served as a focal point for a variety of pressures. The urban dispensary offered opportunities for young physicians that subsequently facilitated their entrance into the community's medical elite. Internally, the dispensary provided a structured setting for the interaction of individuals from various social classes, an interaction marked by "customary relations of deference and stewardship." And, as Rosenberg emphasizes, the dispensaries grew and prospered precisely because they catered to the working-class poor (as contrasted with prostitutes, alcoholics, lunatics, and cripples, many of whom were assigned to the public almshouse or city physician). By the end of the century the dispensary was fast declining, not because it did not play an important medical and social role, but because the absence of government authority permitted internal medical needs and perceptions (which changed sharply after 1880) to determine the specific institutional structures that provided medical care for Americans.[17]

The work of Rosenberg and others has made it abundantly clear that the tradition of voluntarism, at least in its nineteenth-century form, permitted social class and ideological factors to play an important part in an environment where political solutions were regarded with skepticism and suspicion by a substantial percentage of the population. As a matter of fact, the relationship between voluntarism and social policy was a shifting and ambivalent one. At times both were partners in the effort to deal with dependency; at other times voluntarism was perceived as a means of rescuing Americans from the dangers of social policy. Unfortunately, contemporary scholarship has portrayèd voluntarism and institutional heterogeneity in a hostile light, thereby confusing rather than clarifying basic issues. The ideology and practice of voluntarism did not rest only on a foundation of self-interest or class hegemony, and a full study of its importance in the nineteenth century remains to be written.

Finally, any comprehensive discussion of the relationship between the political system and social policy must deal with basic economic issues. Indeed, one way of illuminating policy is to look at the relative allocation of resources. Surprisingly, little is known about nineteenth-century aggregate welfare expenditures related to living standards. Too often historians and other scholars have stipulated that social expenditures were "inadequate" without specifying the precise meaning of this term. Economic allocations, after all, are relative; the luxury of one decade becomes the necessity of a future decade. Even if we hypothesize that social welfare expenditures and wage levels for particular groups were inadequate, we must be careful to specify the results of income transfers. It is entirely possible, to cite a hypothetical example, that a shift in the distribution of income to lower-class groups in the 1880s might have resulted in a lower level of economic activity and standard of living in the 1920s, given the possibility that the transfer might have diminished resources for investment. In arguing for a greater sophistication in dealing with economic issues, I am not defending what existed or exists; I am merely calling for a more knowledgeable and informed analysis of the economics of policy issues.

IV

The treatment/incarceration dichotomy has also inhibited careful study of institutionalized populations and other dependent groups. The result has been a history that implicitly viewed dependent persons as passive victims caught up in situations where they had little autonomy and still less power to influence their condition. More important, generalizations about the results of social policy have not had a sound factual foundation. What groups required assistance, and for what reasons? What kinds of assistance were offered, and what were the results? How did levels of support compare with prevailing living standards? These are only a few of the questions that must be answered if we are to understand formal public policies and the ways in which they actually functioned.

The task of delineating the contours and development of social policy must take into account the nature of dependent populations. This is not always a simple task, partly because dependent populations changed over time and partly because of the complexities in defining with precision the nature of such populations. To focus on the theme of dependency, for example, tends to blur sharp differences between dependent groups. The aged, the sick, the crippled, and the unemployed were all dependent, but the sources of their condition were quite different. When a group fell into two or more categories (for example, sick and old), the problems facing public policy were compounded, particularly as the composition of dependent groups changed over time.

In a recent microanalysis of public poor relief in a single Wisconsin county between 1846 and 1866, Elizabeth Gaspar Brown provided some data that does not support many of the familiar generalizations concerning the nineteenth-century response to dependency. She found that between 1857 and 1866 more than half of all welfare recipients were given outdoor relief. Of these, most went to the county poor farm. Two groups provided the bulk of admissions to the farm: those who were sick and disabled and hence unable to work and those families without a male head, whether headed by the mother or composed of an orphan or group of siblings, and therefore without any means of support. Surprisingly, those persons sent to the county poor farm remained for only short periods of time; the poor farm "was not a dumping bin but a way station," and the rate of recidivism was less than five percent of the total admitted. If the goals of any effective relief program were "the support of those absolutely unable to support themselves and the assistance of those who can be brought to care for themselves so that, in fact, they can and will," Brown concluded, then the superintendents of the poor "achieved these goals."[18]

Similarly, a close analysis of institutionalized mentally ill persons renders at least part of the traditionalist/revisionist debate irrelevant. For example, if the function of such hospitals was the control of deviant populations, it should be possible to demonstrate that individuals involuntarily committed to mental hospitals were perceived as threats to the community and accordingly were incarcerated through the use of judicial procedures. Unfortunately, there are relatively few historical data to support such an interpretation.

Even a cursory analysis of individuals institutionalized in the nineteenth and twentieth centuries provide data that alters the current view that fear of social disorder and perceived threats to the safety of the community led to the establishment and proliferation of mental hospitals. If fear was the sole or most important element in judicial proceedings, we might expect public authorities or social elites to take the lead in initiating involuntary commitment. Such, however, was hardly the case; the majority of commitment proceedings originated within the family. In a recent analysis of commitment proceedings in San Francisco during the first three decades of the twentieth century, Richard W. Fox found that 57 percent of commitment proceedings were begun by relatives, 21 percent by physicians, and only 8 percent by the police.[19] The clientele did come from lower-class or lower-middle-class backgrounds, but these were precisely the families that lacked the financial resources to pay for private home or institutional care when one of their members became mentally ill.

Historical studies about conditions within the family that led to the commitment of members to mental hospitals are still lacking. But it is clear that in many instances families, particularly when confronted with either behavior that threatened its internal integrity or situations with which it could not cope, decided on institutionalization as the lesser of two evils. "I reluctantly enclose application filled out for admission of my mother," a bank employee wrote to the superintendent of the Wisconsin Hospital for the Insane in 1875.

> Of late she had grown materially worse, so that we deem it unsafe for the female portion of the family to be left alone with her during the day and especially unsafe for the little 2 year old that is obliged to remain continually there as she has stated several times of late that she or the children must be sacrificed. Should she destroy another us [sic] could never forgive ourselves if the state has a place provided for their comfort and possible need.

Indeed, many families were reluctant to have members discharged from hospitals for fear that interpersonal relationships might again be disrupted or that an intolerable burden would be placed on household finances.[20]

The characteristics of institutional populations in the late nineteenth and early twentieth centuries shed considerable light upon the function of mental hospitals; they do not sustain the allegation that hospitals were intended as instruments of control or, for that matter, served primarily therapeutic functions. For example, nearly 18 percent of all first admissions to New York State mental hospitals in 1920 were diagnosed as psychotic either because of senility or arteriosclerosis. By 1940 this category accounted for nearly 31 percent of all first admissions. During this same period the average age at first admission rose from 42.69 years to 48.47. Indeed, the trend toward an older population continued even after World War II (Table 1).[21] New York was not unique in this respect. Between 1916 and 1925 16.3 percent of all first admissions to Warren State Hospital in Pennsylvania were 65 and older; the comparable figure for 1936-1945 was 23 percent. The statistics for Illinois and Massachusetts reveal a comparable pattern.[22]

These figures indicate that mental hospitals were to some extent serving as homes for older persons suffering from some sort of physical and mental impairment. A breakdown of the 800 patients over 65 in Massachusetts in 1900 (13 percent of the total institutionalized population) demonstrates that 127 (14.4 percent) were confined to bed; 211 (24 percent) were unable to maintain minimum personal hygiene; 215 (24.4 percent) were helpless and had to be cared for like young children; and 272 (27.5 percent) had no friends.[23]

The number of aged persons in state hospitals varied by period and geographical locale. Within a given state wide variations among institutions were not uncommon. In 1932, the average age of first admissions committed by the courts in Massachusetts was 48.6 years. Individual hospitals, on the other hand, had widely diverging patterns: the highest average age was 54.4 years (Boston State Hospital); the figures for Taunton State Hospital, Grafton State Hospital, and Boston Psychopathic Hospital were 50.1, 41.7, and 39.1, respectively.[24] Despite institutional variations (which were directly related to varying death, discharge, and retention rates), it is clear that the aged constituted a substantial proportion of the total institutionalized population. By the late nineteenth century age-specific admission rates of older persons began to rise markedly as compared with admission rates for younger persons. In their classic study of rates of institutionalization covering more than a century, Herbert Goldhamer and Andrew W. Marshall found that the greatest increase occurred in the 60-year and older category. In 1885, age-specific first admission rates in Massachusetts for males 60 years and over was 70.4 and for females 65.5 (per 100,000); by the beginning of World War II the corresponding figures were 279.5 and 223.0. A study of Warren State Hospital in Pennsylvania covering 1916-1950 showed much the same pattern.[25]

Why were aged persons committed to mental hospitals? Communities hardly perceived them as a threat. Nor can it be said that the function of institutionalization was to alter the behavior of such persons or to provide restorative therapy. "The question of the care of the aged is one that will confront us always," noted one superintendent, who conceded that no effective treatment was available.[26] Mental hospitals were in fact assuming the function of old-age homes, partly for lack of alternatives. The decline in mortality rates among younger elements in the population, in addition, led to a relative and absolute increase in the numbers of the aged, thereby giving rise to the social problems relating to an aging population. Between 1900 and 1940, the number of persons 65 and over increased from about three to nine million (as compared with a population rise from 76 to slightly more than 131 million).[27]

Older persons ended up in mental hospitals for numerous reasons. Some had no family to provide them with care. Families in many instances lacked the means to care for aged members. Other patients were institutionalized because of the inability or unwillingness of relatives to assume responsibility for them. Certain senile patients exhibited forms of behavior which was difficult for families to cope with. And for some indigent aged persons, a mental hospital provided the only means of survival.

The growing proportion of aged persons in mental hospitals undoubtedly reflected a transfer of population from almshouses—an institution that had been declining in significance and would eventually become extinct. Between 1904 and 1922 admissions to almshouses fell from 81,412 to 63,807 (a decline from 99.5 to 58.4 persons per 100,000). Although admissions were declining, the almshouse was simultaneously becoming a refuge for the indigent aged. In 1880 33.2 percent of its population was 60 and over; in 1904 and 1923 this group accounted for 53.1 and 66.6 percent of the total, respectively. For reasons that are not clear, the number of aged mentally ill in these institutions declined precipitously (Table 2). The decline, however,

TABLE 1
First Admissions to New York State Hospitals, 1919-1921 and 1949-1951
Classified According to Age

AGE (YEARS)	1919-1921		1920	1949-1951		1950
	NUMBER	PERCENT	PERCENT AGE DISTRIBUTION OF POPULATION FOR NEW YORK STATE	NUMBER	PERCENT	PERCENT AGE DISTRIBUTION OF POPULATION FOR NEW YORK STATE
UNDER 15	72	0.4	29.7	689	1.4	22.6
15-19	963	4.7	7.9	1871	4.0	6.1
20-24	1812	8.9	8.9	3187	6.8	7.3
25-29	2386	11.8	9.4	3612	7.7	8.1
30-34	2336	11.5	8.6	3314	7.1	7.9
35-39	2388	11.8	8.1	3367	7.2	8.0
40-44	2003	9.9	6.7	3158	6.7	7.6
45-49	1771	8.7	5.9	2998	6.4	7.0
50-54	1513	7.4	5.1	2989	6.4	6.6
55-59	1190	5.9	3.7	2935	6.3	5.6
60-64	1085	5.3	3.0	3155	6.7	4.6
65-69	907	4.4		3350	7.1	3.6
70 OR OVER	1877	9.2	4.7	12277	26.2	5.0

was more apparent than real, given the steadily rising number of aged mentally ill persons committed to asylums. In effect, the mental hospital assumed the functions once performed by the almshouse. In 1904, 16.3 percent of the patients in mental hospitals were 60 and over; by 1923 20.8 percent fell into this category.[28]

Psychiatrists and some public officials were well aware of the practice of committing older persons to mental hospitals. Although they were unhappy about this practice, they went along with the custom of confining such persons because there seemed to be no other alternative. Homes for the aged, which we now see about us, did not become common until after World War II. Dr. Charles C. Wagner, superintendent of the Binghampton State Hospital in New York, defined the issue in simple, yet moving terms. In 1900 he wrote:

> We are receiving every year a large number of old people, some of them very old, who are simply suffering from the mental decay incident to extreme old age. A little mental confusion, forgetfulness and garrulity are sometimes the only symptoms exhibited, but the patient is duly certified to us as insane and has no one at home capable or possessed of means to care for him. We are unable to refuse these patients without creating ill-feeling in the community where they reside, nor are we able to assert that they are not insane within the meaning of the statute, for many of them, judged by the ordinary standards of sanity, cannot be regarded as entirely sane.[29]

The secretary of the Pennsylvania Board of Public Charities expressed similar sentiments a few years later. The practice of institutionalizing aged senile persons, he noted, was related to the refusal by children to accept responsibility for their ailing parents.

> Selfishly neglected by those who owe to them every thing they are thrust into seclusion in order that they may not be burdens, and too frequently forgotten and neglected by those through whose veins flows the same blood, they must helplessly and hopelessly wait, receiving kindness and care from those who are neither kith nor kin, until the coming of the Great Messenger shall mercifully relieve and release them. A crime has been committed and yet a legalized crime and this will be repeated again and again until medical examiners shall more wisely discriminate in their certification of insanity.[30]

Such sentiments were not confined to the early part of the twentieth century. A study of the Illinois state hospitals in the early 1930s emphasized the degree to which these institutions were serving as homes for the aged. A major problem, the report emphasized,

> is the presence of increasingly large numbers of old people—primarily not mental patients—but described in medical parlance as 'senile'. Social revolutions, radical changes in housing and living problems, the growth of urban life, and countless other factors have tended to force the old man and or men from their homes. . . . The state mental hospital, organized for quite other purposes, has become their only haven. . . . An illustration of the enormity of this difficulty is found in the Chicago State Hospital which today is being converted into a huge infirmary, with nearly seventy percent of its 4,000 patients aged or

TABLE 2

Mentally Ill Paupers in Almshouses, 1880-1923

Year	Total Population	Total Almshouse Population	MENTALLY ILL PAUPERS Admitted During Year	Enumerated on a Given Date	Percentage of Mentally Ill Persons in Almshouse Population
1880	50,155,783	66,203	—	16,078	24.3
1890	62,222,250	73,044	—	16,440	22.5
1904	81,792,387	81,764	3,375	8,432	10.3
1910	91,972,266	84,198	1,847	3,518	4.2
1923	109,248,393	78,090	2,091*	2,052	5.6

*During 1922. Unfortunately, the census provided no data on the age distribution of mentally ill paupers in almshouses.

infirm, suffering from no psychoses which would be beyond the capacity of the old-fashioned detached city cottage or rural home or of a well-managed county home.[31]

Syphilis as well as senility was another major cause for admitting patients whose behavioral peculiarities were related to underlying physiological processes. Before the widespread use of penicillin and other antibiotics limited the course of venereal disease, insanity resulting from syphilis accounted for substantial numbers of admissions to asylums. Between 1911 and 1920 about 20 percent of all male first admissions to mental hospitals in New York State were cases of general paresis (the comparable rate for women during this same period was about one-third that of men). New York State, once again, was not unique in this respect; other states had comparable rates.[32] Statistics on syphilis became more reliable as the Wasserman test began being routinely administered in all mental hospitals after 1906. This test provided a fairly reliable (although not infallible) serological technique for determining whether the *trepenema pallidum* (the organism responsible for syphilis) was present in the blood.

To most Americans in the prepenicillin era, syphilis was more than a physical disease; it symbolized, in part, the penalty for moral corruption. We should not conclude, however, that syphilitic patients committed to mental hospitals were being punished for their transgressions. In the tertiary stage of this disease, massive damage to the central nervous system or brain resulted not only in bizarre behavior but in dramatic neurological symptoms, paralysis, and eventually death. For such cases, institutional care was a natural necessity; few households were prepared to cope with such problems. Since general hospitals did not have separate facilities to care for patients in the tertiary stage (who could live from one to five years), responsibility devolved upon the mental hospital.

Overall, at least one-third (and probably more) of all first admissions to state mental hospitals represented cases where behavioral symptoms were probably of somatic origin. In 1922, for example, 52,472 persons were admitted for the first time into state asylums. Of this number, 15,916 were sent there either because of senility, cerebral arteriosclerosis, general paresis, cerebral syphilis, Huntington's chorea, pellagra, brain tumor or other brain disease, or other somatic illnesses. The statistics a decade later showed much the same pattern. Indeed, between 1933 and 1942 the combined first admissions to state hospitals for paresis, cerebral arteriosclerosis, and senility increased from 31.3 percent to 35.8 percent.[33] There were, of course, significant regional differences. Pellagra (a disease caused by a dietary deficiency often accompanied by behavioral symptoms), was generally confined to the South. Between 1930 and 1932, the State Hospital at Goldsboro, North Carolina (which was limited to blacks) reported that no less than 19 percent of its admissions were due to pellagra. In northern hospitals, the disease was virtually unknown.[34]

Mental hospitals, in other words, cared for a variety of patients. Some individuals were institutionalized because of physical disability. In other cases, hospitals served as asylums for persons who, for one reason or another, seemed to require a structured environment. Noting that it was often alleged that public mental hospitals cared for persons who could just as easily have been sent home, the Pennsylvania Commission on Lunacy warned of the dangers of generalizing about such issues. The commission concluded that many patients no doubt could be sent home, "provided that the home existed, or that conditions at home were suitable for the patient's return"; unfortunately, such conditions did not always exist. Frederick H. Wines, one of the most influential figures in late nineteenth-century public welfare, observed that many mental hospitals were imposed upon in "that patients are sent to them who should not be so sent, because their friends wish to avoid the responsibility of keeping and caring for them at home."[35]

In dealing with such data, we must be careful not to read the past in terms of the present. To argue that aged and senile groups, as well as persons suffering from physical impairments with accompanying behavioral symptoms, did not belong in mental hospitals, or to insist that individual rights were being ignored, is to misunderstand the nature of social change in the nineteenth and twentieth centuries. In point of fact, high rates of geographical mobility, a rapid increase in the size of urban areas, and the inability of traditional means of alleviating distress and dependency by reliance on familial and community traditions and practices led Americans increasingly to turn to quasi-public or public institutions for the care of many dependent groups. Under these circumstances mental hospitals assumed the responsibility, often unwillingly, for providing care for groups, many of whose members were unable to care for themselves.[36]

The internal character of mental hospitals, furthermore, was in large measure dictated by the nature of their patient populations as well as by their medical staffs and attendant corps. The absence of a therapeutic environment, for example, may have simply reflected the age or physical condition of individuals for whom no known treatment existed. For such persons hospitals could provide but a form of custodial care at best. Nor were better or more effective alternatives necessarily available at that time. It is debatable whether the chronic nursing homes for the aged that came into existence after World War II provided better care than had their predecessors.[37]

Viewed in light of the past and the application of logical analysis, therefore, a good part of the debate dealing with mental illness becomes irrelevant. Mental hospitals were not intended to function *only* as therapeutic institutions, nor were they established primarily because fear of abnormal behavior threatened public safety or the social order. And to discuss the issue of involuntary commitment solely in terms of abstract individual rights is to avoid the far more difficult task of evaluating theory in light of concrete situations that rarely offered clear-cut moral choices. In many instances the application of a single general principle has the inadvertent consequence of invalidating another general principle that may be equally compelling. An absolutist definition of freedom, for example, may very well negate other humanitarian or ethical principles and rights. It is entirely possible to honor the absolute rights of persons in an advanced state of senility to liberty by not hospitalizing them while denying their right to care from society when they are helpless by not hospitalizing them and permitting them to die from exposure, starvation, and lack of care.

The significant role played by patient populations in determining the character of mental hospitals was not unique; the functions of other institutions partly reflected their inmate populations. In their study of the Temporary Home for the Destitute and of the Massachusetts School for the Feeble-Minded, (both established in Boston in 1847), Peter L. Tyor and Jamil S. Zainaldin have demonstrated the importance not only of institutional leadership and perceived social needs but also the significance of those who patronize institutions. In addition, their data render it virtually impossible to view institutions in static terms or to neglect the influence of client populations upon their internal development.[38]

There is considerable evidence, then, to indicate that the familiar therapy/ incarceration theme is misleading as a framework for understanding the development of institutions for dependent persons. Even a superficial analysis of the composition of inmate populations renders this dichotomy untenable. We need to know more about the characteristics of institutional populations, the reasons for admission, the ways in which clients influenced the character of institutions, and the relationships between demographic changes in admission rates and institutional functions.[39] In addition, we must also be aware that statistics dealing with institutional populations can easily be misinterpreted. Many prominent native-born Americans in the late nineteenth and early twentieth centuries emphasized the overrepresentation of foreign-born in mental hospitals and other institutions as compared with their percentage in the general population. Such data were then used to justify racial interpretations of culture or the passage of legislation designed to curtail unrestricted immigration to the United States of certain undesirable groups. Yet, when the data dealing with institutionalized foreign-born patients in mental hospitals are corrected by taking into account the dissimilar age distributions of native and immigrant, the differential between them narrows sharply. Moreover, the introduction of other variables (such as sex, income, urban-rural) alters the results still further and discredits the allegation that immigrants and their children, for genetic reasons, were liable to become mentally ill (or dependent) at a rate significantly higher than native-born persons.[40]

Although advocates may debate the wisdom or desirability of the shift in social policy toward institutional solutions, historians would be better advised to illuminate the sources of change, policy formulation, and administration and the dynamics of institutional growth and elaboration. It is also essential that they separate intentions from subsequent developments; the two were often not linked. And to argue that there had to be a better way is only to repeat a truism.

V

Although the history of social policy presents formidable challenges, it also offers opportunities to illuminate the structure and development of American society. In an exploratory essay of this nature, it is, of course, difficult to summarize with any degree of precision the specific kinds of problems that merit extended study. Instead, I should like to offer in a somewhat arbitrary and perhaps oversimplified manner some general problems that in my opinion deserve consideration in future research.

(1) The Nature of Dependency. At present, knowledge about dependent populations leaves much to be desired. We need studies that analyze the composition and demographic characteristics of dependent populations and how these characteristics changed over time. The structure and distribution of dependent populations played a crucial role in both the public response and the internal development of institutions established to provide care for those requiring some form of assistance and support.

(2) Social Policy as Process. Frequently, public policy has been presented as fixed and unchanging. Nothing could be further from the truth. The ways in which American society dealt with dependency changed sharply over time; it is as necessary to understand the process as the outcome. In addition, we need to know whether the results of policy were studied and evaluated and endeavors at revision or change attempted, under what circumstances, and out of what contending principles and arguments.

(3) Social Policy and the Political System. Too little attention has been given to the relationship between the origins and development of policy, the structure of the political system, and public perceptions of social issues. What were the origins of policy? How did a complex political system influence the determination and implementation of policy? How did various groups interpret the origins and nature of dependency, and in what way were broad social perceptions translated into public policy? Equally important, what were the linkages between public authorities and a kind of voluntarism that resulted in the creation of numerous quasi-public structures to resolve social problems?

(4) The Economics of Social Policy. The economics of social policy has been by far one of the most neglected subjects (particularly in the decades that preceded the New Deal). Yet, in many respects the manner in which a society perceives of dependency is reflected in its economic allocations. In this respect our knowledge is grossly deficient. What levels of support existed for various categories of dependency? How and when did these levels change, and how did they compare with prevailing living standards? Approximately what proportion of the GNP was devoted to social welfare?

(5) The Role of Administrative and Bureaucratic Structures. Too much is known about formal statutes relating to dependency and too little about how these laws were administered and how modes of administration altered policy. Indeed, historians concerned with social policy could benefit from the example of work in legal history. Moreover, our knowledge of organizational

growth, as compared with studies in business history, is rudimentary; there are few sophisticated analyses of the development of state welfare agencies, their personnel, and the conditions that promoted or retarded growth. In addition, the phenomenon of professionalization is still not adequately integrated into the history of public policy.

(6) Social Policy as Concept. The decline in interest in intellectual history has also had a detrimental effect on the study of social policy. Yet, the history of ideas has much to offer. When did individuals begin to think in policy terms? Why did statistical analysis become a characteristic mode of thought, and what was its influence on policy formulation and implementation? It is more than coincidental that the census became a key tool in policy issues during the nineteenth century; we need to know more about the origins of what might loosely be described as the "statistical mind" and its influence on behavior.

In undertaking further research into the history of social policy, we must not simplify and generalize when to do so may distort the past beyond recognition. Indeed, it is entirely possible that the very concept of social policy is misleading, particularly when the varied nature of dependent populations, geography, and political and cultural traditions are taken into account. We might also want to rethink the implicit assumption (accepted by historians and social researchers) that all phenomena are linked together within a single system; perhaps significant discontinuities exist in our world that preclude linking individual and social facts within some grand design. As a group, American historians have valued case studies only insofar as they illuminated national developments. The time may have come, however, when we should begin to value limited case studies as valid in their own right and recognize that the concept of social policy may have led us in an inappropriate direction. Whatever the outcome, a perceptive reconstruction of the past is worthwhile, apart from any policy implications.

NOTES

The author wishes to acknowledge that the research for this paper was supported by a grant from the United States Public Health Service, National Library of Medicine, No. 2306. A slightly different version was delivered at the First Conference on the History of Public Policy in the United States, Harvard Business School, Boston, Massachusetts, November 3-4, 1978.

1. For examples of works that do *not* fit a dichotomous conceptual framework see Norman Dain, *Concepts of Insanity in the United States 1789-1865* (New Brunswick: Rutgers University Press, 1964); Charles E. Rosenberg, *The Trial of the Assassin Guiteau: Psychiatry and Law in the Gilded Age* (Chicago: University of Chicago Press, 1968); Nathan G. Hale, *Freud and the Americans: The Beginnings of Psychoanalysis in the United States, 1876-1917* (New York: Oxford University Press, 1971); and John C. Burnham, *Psychoanalysis and American Medicine: 1894-1918: Medicine, Science, and Culture* (New York: International Universities Press, 1967).

2. The traditionalist point of view can best be followed in Albert Deutsch's *The Mentally Ill in America: A History of Their Care and Treatment from Colonial Times* (2nd ed., New

York: Columbia University Press, 1949) and *The Shame of the States* (New York: Harcourt, Brace and Co., 1948). The revisionist viewpoint appears in the following: Michel Foucault, *Madness and Civilization: A History of Insanity in the Age of Reason* (New York: Pantheon Books, 1965); Thomas S. Szasz, *The Myth of Mental Illness: Foundations of a Theory of Personal Conduct* (New York: Hoeber-Harper, 1961), *Law, Liberty, and Psychiatry: An Inquiry into the Social Uses of Mental Health Practices* (New York: The Macmillan Co., 1963), *The Manufacture of Madness: A Comparative Study of the Inquisition and the Mental Health Movement* (New York: Harper & Row, 1970), and *The Age of Madness: The History of Involuntary Mental Hospitalization, Presented in Selected Texts* (Garden City: Anchor Books, 1973); David J. Rothman, *The Discovery of the Asylum: Social Order and Disorder in the New Republic* (Boston: Little, Brown and Co., 1971) and *Conscience and Convenience: The Asylum and its Alternatives in Progressive America* (Boston: Little, Brown and Co., 1980); Robert Perrucci, *Circle of Madness: On Being Insane and Institutionalized in America* (Englewood Cliffs: Prentice-Hall, 1974).

3. The traditionalist approach has been described by Lawrence Cremin in *The Wonderful World of Ellwood Patterson Cubberley* (New York: Teachers College Press, 1965) and can be followed in Cubberley's *Public Education in the United States* (rev. ed., Cambridge: Houghton Mifflin Co., 1934). The revisionist view appears to one degree or another in the following: Michael B. Katz, *The Irony of Early School Reform: Educational Innovation in Mid-Nineteenth Century Massachusetts* (Cambridge: Harvard University Press, 1968) and *Class, Bureaucracy and Schools: The Illusion of Educational Change in America* (New York: Praeger, 1971): Carl F. Kaestle, *The Evolution of an Urban School System: New York City, 1750-1850* (Cambridge: Harvard University Press, 1973); Colin Greer, *The Great School Legend: A Revisionist Interpretation of American Public Education* (New York: Viking Press, 1973); Joel Spring, *Education and the Rise of the Corporate State* (Boston: Beacon Press, 1972); and Raymond E. Callahan, *Education and the Cult of Efficiency: A Study of the Social Forces that Have Shaped the Administration of the Public Schools* (Chicago: University of Chicago Press, 1962). For an analysis of the revisionist approach by a historian who does not fit the traditionalist/revisionist dichotomy, see Diane Ravitch, *The Revisionists Revised: A Critique of the Radical Attack on Schools* (New York: Basic Books, 1978).

4. See Clifford S. Griffin, *Their Brothers' Keepers: Moral Stewardship in the United States, 1800-1865* (New Brunswick: Rutgers University Press, 1960); Raymond A. Mohl, *Poverty in New York 1783-1825* (New York: Oxford University Press, 1971); and Rothman, *Discovery of the Asylum.*

5. Oscar and Mary F. Handlin, *Commonwealth: A Study of the Role of Government in the American Economy: Massachusetts, 1774-1861* (rev. ed., Cambridge: Harvard University Press, 1969) and Louis Hartz, *Economic Policy and Democratic Thought: Pennsylvania, 1776-1860* (Cambridge: Harvard University Press, 1948).

6. Two decades ago Oliver MacDonagh, an English historian, observed that most of his colleagues agreed that profound changes in the structure and functions of government took place during the nineteenth century. But if asked why they believed these changes to be important, MacDonagh noted, they would in all likelihood think of terminal conditions—the *ancien régime* of the eighteenth century and the collectivist state of the twentieth—and then posit the existence of a revolution. Moreover, their explanations of these changes would in all likelihood be somewhat indiscriminate. Such an approach does not provide a satisfactory answer. As MacDonagh shrewdly observed, the mere listing of "factors," no matter how elaborate, is not equal to explanation. Factors are different in kind and in actual operation; the absence of both analysis and a time-scale makes it impossible to distinguish between the relative weight and importance of each factor; and "without a clear recognition that a genuine historical process was at work, moulding men and ideas as it was moulded by them, the causal function of the factors is bound to be misunderstood." See Oliver MacDonagh, "The Nineteenth-Century Revolution in Government: A Reappraisal," *Historical Journal,* 1 (No. 1, 1958), 52-67.

7. Such an explanation is not unique. Nearly seventy-five years ago A. V. Dicey published his famous and influential *Lectures on the Relation Between Law and Public Opinion in*

England During the Nineteenth Century (London: Macmillan and Co., 1905). Dicey's underlying thesis was that the history of legislation was related to changes in public opinion, and that the concepts that eventually transformed public opinion and ultimately were incorporated into law originated with a small number of activists and intellectuals. Many American scholars have implicitly followed Dicey's lead in assuming that economic and intellectual elites were responsible for the adoption of a particular kind of social policy. Although they differed from Dicey, in that the latter did not disapprove of the governmental changes that transformed English society in the nineteenth century, the explanation of American scholars was not dissimilar in kind.

8. John C. Wahlke, "Policy Demands and System Support: The Role of the Represented," *British Journal of Political Science,* 1 (1971): 271-290. For a perceptive analysis of American political historiography see Richard L. McCormick, "Ethno-Cultural Interpretations of Nineteenth-Century American Voting Behavior," *Political Science Quarterly,* 89 (1974): 351-377.

9. I have been influenced by Theodore J. Lowi's threefold policy typology, in which he seeks to define policies in terms of their impact on society. Lowi defines three general policy categories: distributive, regulatory, and redistributive. Distributive policies are characterized by the ease with which they can be disaggregated; they are policies in which the indulged and deprived, the loser and the recipient, need never come into direct confrontation. Such an approach also creates what Lowi defines as an arena of power. In the distributive arena, a large number of small, intensely organized interests operate, and self-interest is paramount. Distributive issues individualize conflict and provide the basis for coalitions that are virtually irrelevant to the larger policy outcome. Lowi's analysis of distributive policies and their unique arena of power seems partially applicable (but not fully) to the political system existing in the United States before 1860. Lowi, "American Business, Public Policy, Case-Studies, and Political Theory," *World Politics,* 16 (1964): 677-715. See also Richard L. McCormick, "The Party Period and Public Policy: An Exploratory Hypothesis," *Journal of American History,* 66 (1979): 279-298.

10. Samuel P. Huntington, *Political Order in Changing Societies* (New Haven: Yale University Press, 1968), Chapters 1 and 2; Richard D. Brown, *Modernization: The Trans-formation of American of American Life* (New York: Hill & Wang, 1976).

11. The turnover rate in the New York State Assembly offers a dramatic illustration of this point. The following is the percentage of first-termers by decade:

1820-1829	64.2
1830-1839	69.1
1840-1849	78.6
1850-1858	82.7

The absence of institutionalization is further confirmed by the fact that between 1820 and 1860 the average speaker of the New York State Assembly had only 2.53 years of prior legislative experience (and in the period from 1850 to 1858 the average was only one year). These figures have been supplied by L. Ray Gunn of the University of Utah, who is currently working on a study of public policy and modernization in New York State. See also Gunn, "The Crisis of Authority in the Antebellum States: New York, 1820-1860," *Review of Politics,* 41 (1979): 273-297. Comparable statistics for the United States House of Representatives can be found in Nelson W. Polsby, "The Institutionalization of the U.S. House of Representatives," *American Political Science Review,* 62 (1968): 144-168.

12. Some historians have maintained that nineteenth-century welfare policies reflected the disdain, fear, and hostility of middle- and upper-class Americans toward impoverished and lower-class persons. To my knowledge, there has not been a single effort to *demonstrate* that such attitudes were taken over directly by legislatures and processed into clear and distinct policies; the connection is usually assumed rather than proven. Moreover, a cursory examination of sources demonstrates the existence of a broad range of attitudes. The relationship between attitudes and policies, therefore, has yet to be empirically established.

13. See Polsby, "The Institutionalization of the U.S. House of Representatives," 144-153.

14. For an extended discussion of these points see Gerald N. Grob, *Mental Institutions in America: Social Policy to 1875* (New York: Free Press, 1973), 174-220.

15. See Wallace D. Farnham, " 'The Weakened Spring of Government'; A Study in Nineteenth-Century American History," *American Historical Review,* 68 (1963): 662-680; and Gunn, "The Crisis of Authority in the Antebellum States: New York, 1820-1860," 273-297.

16. Theodore J. Lowi, *The End of Liberalism: Ideology, Policy, and the Crisis of Public Authority* (New York: Norton and Co., 1969), discusses the role and function of regulatory agencies in the absence of firm legislative policy guidelines.

17. Charles E. Rosenberg, "Social Class and Medical Care in Nineteenth-Century America: The Rise and Fall of the Dispensary," *Journal of the History of Medicine and Allied Sciences,* 29 (1974): 32-54. See also Rosenberg's "And Heal the Sick: The Hospital and Patient in 19th Century America," *Journal of Social History,* 10 (1977): 428-447, and Morris J. Vogel, *The Invention of the Modern Hospital: Boston, 1870-1930* (Chicago: University of Chicago Press, 1980).

18. Elizabeth Gaspar Brown, "Poor Relief in a Wisconsin County, 1846-1866: Administration and Recipients," *American Journal of Legal History,* 20 (1976): 79-117.

19. Richard W. Fox, *So Far Disordered in Mind: Insanity in California, 1870-1930* (Berkeley: University of California Press, 1978), 84 *and* passim.

20. Dale W. Robison, "Wisconsin and the Mentally Ill: A History of the 'Wisconsin' Plan of State and County Care 1860-1915," unpublished Ph.D. dissertation, Marquette University, 1976, pp. 7ff. Robison's comments about the role of the family in commitment are based upon an examination of the incoming correspondence of the Wisconsin State Hospital for the Insane, which are in the State Historical Society of Wisconsin, Madison, Wisconsin.

21. Statistics from Benjamin Malzberg, "A Comparison of First Admissions to the New York State Civil Hospitals During 1919-1921 and 1949-1951," *Psychiatric Quarterly,* 28 (1954): 314; United States Bureau of the Census, *Fourteenth Census of the United States,* vol. II, *Population 1920* (Washington, D.C.: Government Printing Office, 1922), 248; *idem., Census of Population: 1950,* vol. II, *Characteristics of the Population,* Part 32 (Washington, D.C.: Government Printing Office, 1952), 58.

22. New York State Department of Mental Hygiene, *Annual Report,* 52 (1939-1940): 174-175; Benjamin Malzberg, "A Statistical Analysis of the Ages of First Admissions to Hospitals for Mental Disease in New York State," *Psychiatric Quarterly,* 23 (1949): 346; Morton Kramer, Hyman Goldstein, Robert H. Israel, Nelson A. Johnson, *A Historical Study of the Disposition of First Admissions to a State Mental Hospital: Experiences of the Warren State Hospital During the Period 1916-50* (Public Health Service Publication No. 445: Washington, D.C.: Government Printing Office, 1955), 10; Carney Landis and Jane E. Farwell, "A Trend Analysis of Age at First-Admission, Age at Death, and Years of Residence for State Mental Hospitals: 1913-1941," *Journal of Abnormal and Social Psychology,* 39 (1944): 3-23.

By the 1930s and 1940s there was a growing appreciation of the age distribution of the mentally ill and some of its implications for psychiatry. For selected examples see the following: Benjamin Malzberg, *Social and Biological Aspects of Mental Disease* (Utica: State Hospitals Press, 1940), chap. 2; Neil A. Dayton, *New Facts on Mental Disorders: Study of 89, 190 Cases* (Springfield, Ill.: Charles C Thomas, 1940), chap. 8; Harold F. Dorn, "The Incidence and Future Expectancy of Mental Disease," *Public Health Reports,* 53 (1938): 1991-2004; William F. Ogburn and Ellen Winston, "The Frequency and Probability of Insanity," *American Journal of Sociology,* 34 (1929), 822-831; Nelson A. Johnson, "The Growing Problem of Old-Age Psychoses: An Analysis of the Trend in One State Hospital from 1910 to 1944," *Mental Hygiene,* 30 (1946): 431-450. See also Aubrey Lewis's "Ageing and Senility: A Major Problem of Psychiatry," *Journal of Mental Science,* 92 (1946): 150-170.

23. Massachusetts State Board of Insanity, *Annual Report,* 2 (1900): 32.

24. Neil A. Dayton, "A New Statistical System for the Study of Mental Disease and Some of the Attained Results," *Bulletin of the Massachusetts Department of Mental Diseases,* 18 (1934): 179-180.

25. Herbert Goldhamer and Andrew W. Marshall, *Psychosis and Civilization: Two Studies in the Frequency of Mental Disease* (Glencoe, Illinois: Free Press, 1953), 54, 91; Kramer et al., *A Historical Study,* 10.

26. Ohio Department of Public Welfare, *Annual Report,* 15 (1936): 303-304.

27. United States Bureau of the Census, *Historical Statistics of the United States: Colonial Times to 1970* (Washington, D.C.: Government Printing Office, 1975), part 1, p. 15.

28. United States Bureau of the Census, *Paupers in Almshouses 1904* (Washington, D.C.: Government Printing Office, 1906), 182, 184; *idem., Paupers in Almshouses 1910* (Washington, D.C.: Government Printing Office, 1915), 42-43; *idem., Paupers in Almshouses 1923* (Washington, D.C.: Government Printing Office, 1925), 5, 8, 33; *idem., Insane and Feebleminded in Hospitals and Institutions 1904* (Washington, D.C.: Government Printing Office, 1906), 29; *idem., Patients in Hospitals for Mental Disease 1923* (Washington, D.C.: Government Printing Office, 1926), 27.

29. New York State Commission in Lunacy, *Annual Report,* 12 (1900): 29-30.

30. Pennsylvania Committee on Lunacy, *Annual Report,* 22 (1904): 8-9, in Pennsylvania Board of Commissioners of Public Charities, *Annual Report,* 35 (1904).

31. "The Care of the Mentally Disordered in Illinois: The State Hospitals," pp. 7-8, typed manuscript, c. 1931, in American Foundation for Mental Hygiene Papers, Box 4, Library of the New York Hospital, New York, N.Y.

32. New York State Department of Mental Hygiene, *Annual Report,* 52 (1939-1940): 176. For other examples see the following: Washington (State) Department of Business Control, *Biennial Report,* 7 (1933-1934): 27; Ohio Department of Public Welfare, *Annual Report,* 11-12 (1932-1933): 349, 358-360, and 15 (1936): 304; Oregon State Board of Control, *Biennial Report,* 4 (1919-1920): 47; Illinois Department of Public Welfare, *Annual Report,* 12 (1928-1929): 310; North Carolina Charitable, Penal, and Correctional Institutions, *Biennial Report* (1930-1932): 48.

33. United States Bureau of the Census, *Mental Patients in State Hospitals: 1926 and 1927* (Washington, D.C.: Government Printing Office, 1930), 9, and *Mental Patients in State Hospitals: 1931 and 1932* (Washington, D.C.: Government Printing Office, 1934), 6; American Psychopathological Association, *Trends of Mental Disease* (New York: King's Crown Press, 1945), 31.

34. North Carolina Charitable, Penal, and Correctional Institutions, *Biennial Report* (1930-1932): 48.

35. Pennsylvania Committee on Lunacy, *Annual Report,* 16 (1898): 44-45, in Pennsylvania Board of Commissioners of Public Charities, *Annual Report,* 29 (1898); *Proceedings of the National Conference of Charities and Corrections,* 17 (1890): 431.

36. This situation was by no means misunderstood by those involved in caring for the mentally ill. Winfred Overholser, who headed the Massachusetts Commission of Mental Diseases and then succeeded William A. White as superintendent of Saint Elizabeth's Hospital in Washington, D.C., noted in 1941 that many aged persons ended up in mental hospitals because "the change in living conditions . . . where many families live in apartments rather than in separate houses, much greater disorganization of the home takes place by the presence of a [n aged] patient." Winfred Overholser, "Some Mental Problems of Aging and Their Management," *Medical Annals of the District of Columbia,* 10 (1941): 216. See also Manfred S. Guttmacher to Dr. Solomon Lowenstein, October 15, 1934, Guttmacher Papers, Countway Library of Medicine, Harvard Medical School, Boston, Massachusetts.

Some scholars have argued that economic and technological changes associated with industrialization introduced a distinction between home and work, thereby undermining the integrated nature of the preindustrial family. In the new industrial society public and quasi-public institutions took over functions once performed by families (e.g., education of the young, care of the dependent). This thesis, however attractive, is based on the questionable assumption that the structure and functions of families were simply the result of external forces. The preindustrial family, for example, may have cared for mentally ill members because no alternative was readily available and in spite of the human costs incurred. When presented with an institutional alternative, many families opted for its use. Few families, on the other hand, evinced any eagerness to institutionalize members; the general practice was to retain them at home as long as possible. In offering this analysis, I am suggesting not that changes in social structure did not influence family life, but that the behavior of families involved some autonomy on the part of their members. Nor should the strains of retaining mentally ill relatives in a home setting be idealized or minimized.

37. It should be noted that part of the decline in the population of mental hospitals during the past two decades has been more apparent than real. The number of elderly persons in such institutions declined sharply, but the number of aged mentally ill persons in nursing and personal care homes rose sharply. Richard W. Reddick, "Patterns in Use of Nursing Homes by the Aged Mentally Ill," National Institute of Mental Health, *Statistical Note 107* (1974). Between 1962 and 1975 the number of first admissions to state and county mental hospitals fell from 163.7 per 100,000 to 36.7. Laura Milazzo-Sayre, "Changes in the Age and Sex Composition of First Admissions to State and County Mental Hospitals, United States 1962-1975," National Institute of Mental Health, *Statistical Note 145* (1978): 9.

38. Peter L. Tyor and Jamil S. Zainaldin, "Asylum and Society: An Approach to Institutional Change," *Journal of Social History,* 13 (1979): 23-48.

39. For an interesting study of the ways in which prison inmates influence their institutional environment see Gresham M. Sykes, *The Society of Captives: A Study of a Maximum Security Prison* (Princeton: Princeton University Press, 1958). There is no retrospective study of the ways in which patients influenced the development of mental hospitals.

40. Malzberg, *Social and Biological Aspects of Mental Disease,* 143-176; Malzberg, "Are Immigrants Psychologically Disturbed?," in *Changing Perspectives in Mental Illness,* ed. by Stanley C. Plog and Robert B. Edgerton (New York: Holt, Rinehart and Winston, 1969), 395-421; Neil A. Dayton, *New Facts on Mental Disorders: Study of 89, 190 Cases* (Springfield, Illinois: Charles C Thomas, 1940), chap. 8; United States Bureau of the Census, *Insane and Feebleminded in Institutions 1910* (Washington, D.C.: Government Printing Office, 1914), 25ff.

Richard W. Fox appropriately points out the fallacies in some of the data relating to immigrants in Grob's *Mental Institutions in America,* and Rothman's *Discovery of the Asylum* (Fox, *So Far Disordered in Mind,* 107-108). It must be kept in mind, however, that many individuals believed that there was a clear relationship between certain immigrant groups and the incidence of mental disease, and acted accordingly; data to the contrary were simply ignored.

41

PERSPECTIVES ON URBAN AMERICA AND KEY POLICY ISSUES FOR THE EIGHTIES

Donald A. Hicks

Until 50 years ago, the proper federal role vis-a-vis the nation's cities was easily summarized. Because the Constitution had not explicitly specified otherwise, the responsibility for cities devolved to state governments. With the onslaught of the Depression, the federal government began for the first time to consider cities as national, rather than merely state, assets. Accordingly, New Deal recovery policies included federal assistance for both distressed people and beleaguered local governments. The rationale behind this action was that "the American economy was dependent upon the health of the many urban industrial economies within it and that it was in the best interests of the federal government to aid those [local] economies."[1] This national economic calamity henceforth legitimized the appropriateness of a general federal urban policy presence, even though a commitment to continuing federal involvement in the functioning of local economies was never intended.

In the past 20 years, the time-honored logic of a federal commitment to assisting people in cities has been extended to assisting the cities as well. Welfare and income maintenance programs have been supplemented by programs that emphasize physical redevelopment, local economic development, and direct fiscal aid to local governments. The transition from the War on Poverty and Great Society era of the 1960s to the New Federalism of the 1970s did much to legitimize an increasing federal emphasis on places in the country. This emergent spatial sensitivity in public policy has become particularly apparent during the past 4 years, as illustrated by the dominant thrusts of the national urban policy and executive orders devoted to urban impact analysis, federal facility siting, and targeted procurement. The New Deal emphasis on helping distressed people in cities directly has evolved into an emphasis on helping distressed places (local business and government) directly for the purpose of helping people indirectly. Today most federal funds directed to urban problems go to "place" recipients rather than distressed people. In the late 1970s, a spatial sensitivity

From Donald A. Hicks, "Perspectives on Urban America and Key Policy Issues for the Eighties," 97-109 in *Urban America in the Eighties: Perspectives and Prospects,* Washington, D.C.

appears to have overtaken in large part a social sensitivity developed during the previous decade. Politically, this shift is justified by the assertion that aiding places with problems is easier than aiding people with problems. Economically, this shift is justified by the assertion that direct aid to local economies multiplies its impact so that benefits reverberate throughout the economy in ways that direct aid to people does not.

The 1980s may well require a new perspective on aiding distressed people in urban America. To import the 1930s rationale for a federal urban policy role across the decades may not be wise. Although the economy in the 1930s was indeed dependent on the health of local urban industrial economies in ways not fully appreciated, and it undoubtedly was in the best interest of the federal government to aid those local economies, circumstances have conspired to weaken that rationale.

Unlike a half-century ago, contemporary urban economies are no longer confined within the political jurisdictions of cities. Modern urban economies have an expanded scope that integrates central city, suburban, and nonmetropolitan economies. The deconcentration trends accompanying the arrival of a postindustrial era highlight the fact that the nation's economic vitality no longer arises from or is tied to specific types of places. It increasingly derives its strength from all kinds of places, both local political jurisdictions and beyond. Today it may be in the best interest of the nation to commit itself to the promotion of locationally neutral economic and social policies rather than spatially sensitive urban policies that either explicitly or inadvertently seek to preserve cities in their historical roles. A federal policy presence that allows places to transform and assists them in adjusting to difficult circumstances can justify shifting greater explicit emphasis to helping directly those people who are suffering from the transformation process.

Our cities are truly national assets. Hence, the federal policy presence should recognize that the health of a city, or any other settlement, is determined not by population or employment levels, but by its ability to perform vital functions for the larger society. As national assets, cities and their residents are the resources and responsibilities of us all during their adjustment to the postindustrial era. With this perspective in mind, a redefined federal policy role in urban America for the coming decade is presented.

The economic health of our nation's communities ultimately depends on the health of our nation's economy. Federal efforts to revitalize urban areas through a national urban policy concerned principally with the health of

**A National
Urban Policy
Reconsidered**

specific places will inevitably conflict with efforts to revitalize the larger economy. Federal efforts to nurture economic growth through increased productivity, expanded markets, job creation, and controlled inflation will require that settlements, their residents, and local governments adjust to changing economic realities. Accordingly, **the purpose and orientation of a "national urban policy" should be reconsidered. There are no "national urban problems," only an endless variety of local ones. Consequently, a centrally administered national urban policy that legitimizes activities inconsistent with the revitalization of the larger national economy may be ill advised.**

Priority should not be assigned to the implementation of a spatially sensitive policy effort designed to retard or reverse the emergence of new economic patterns and relationships within and among the nation's settlements. The federal government should assign greater priority to meeting the needs of the residents of the nation's communities rather than to reconciling or resolving the array of constituent intrametropolitan and interregional conflicts. The federal government should exercise its policy presence carefully so as not to exacerbate unnecessarily the circumstances facing certain localities and regions that cause them to lose population and economic vitality. **Where federal policies and programs are used to assist the transformation of local communities to achieve health and vitality at new population levels and with restructured economic bases, such national policies should endeavor to ameliorate the undesirable impacts of these transitions on people, primarily, and on places, secondarily.**

Although no national urban problems exist, myriad problems do exist within all localities and regions of the nation. Our nation's settlements, and the households, firms, and local governments within them, exhibit a bewildering diversity of conditions that reflect the confluence of long-term demographic, economic, and governance trends and that link them to emerging patterns of metropolitan and regional change. The forces underlying these transformations are relatively persistent and immutable. However, the local and regional problems left in their wake are not uniform in cause; therefore, the urban policies proposed as remedies cannot be expected to be uniform in consequence.

It is unlikely that the federal government can act wisely on behalf of the nation as a whole if economically healthy metropolitan areas are not appreciated because their vitality is discounted or obscured by a preoccupation with transforming core areas of central cities. Neither will the nation benefit if the newly prospering regions that historically have been economically depressed are defined as inimical to historically prosperous regions that are now experiencing relative economic decline. A national urban policy cannot be enunciated and implemented when the very national focus it should assume and the national well-being it should foster are sacrificed to a concern for the diverse fates and fortunes among cities, among metropolitan areas, among states, and among regions.

Certainly, there is merit in anticipating the locational consequences of federal government actions, but many federal policies aimed at promoting the efficiency and productivity of the nation have unavoidable negative consequences for certain localities and regions. Knowing that spatial tilts are embedded in federal policies provides no necessary justification for weeding them out. They often may be entirely justified. Indeed, anti-industry biases in federal policies may be more pernicious than anti-urban biases, given that the health of all places is directly or indirectly dependent on the strength of the larger economy. These tradeoffs should be clearly recognized, and choices should be made consistent with the functioning of the national system of settlements and the national economy, which benefits the entire country at the risk of abiding a series of smaller scale, and often painful, subnational adjustments. A national urban policy designed to place the swirl of local and regional concerns ahead of an overall concern for the nation is both inappropriate and ill advised.

Federal urban policy can be used to channel and target the enormous, if seldom adequate, resources of the federal government and to guide or influence the flows of private sector resources. Nonetheless, despite the importance of the government resources, and the far greater weight of the private resources that at times may be influenced, problems do not yield to massive infusions of resources alone. Rather, a great proportion of urban ills stems from inevitable competition for advantage among groups within localities and between regions. The litany of urban problems is a reflection of this underlying competition in a pluralistic urban society. The very competition that dictates our urban strengths may determine the nature of our urban ills, although not the character of the solutions to those ills. An explicit national urban policy can do little more than make that irony more salient.

The limits to what a federal urban policy effort can achieve are defined by several factors. First, **recognition should be made of the near immutability of the technological, economic, social, and demographic trends that herald the emergence of a postindustrial society and that are responsible for the transformation of our nation's settlements and life within them.** These major formative trends are likely to continue not only through the coming decade, but also well into the next century. Major deflection or reversal of these broad-gauge trends is not likely to result from purposive government action. **Clearly, on the basis of these trends, a federal policy of active anticipation, accommodation, and adjustment makes more sense than efforts to retard or reverse them.** The efforts to revitalize those communities whose fortunes are adversely affected principally by the inadvertent consequences of past public policies are entirely justified, but these instances are judged to be rare. **It is far more judicious to recognize that the major circumstances that characterize our nation's settlements have not been and will not be significantly dependent on what the federal government does or does not do.**

What should constitute a reasonable federal urban policy role in the light of domestic trends that are transforming this nation and transnational trends that are drawing us into closer community with the world? Policy responses to such complex and changing circumstances are inevitably difficult to conceive and develop. Not only do limits to what can be accomplished with policies and programs exist, but also in many substantive areas, the local readjustments may not require vigorous federal intervention. Accordingly, a proper federal presence in urban affairs should reflect a blend of actions to be avoided as well as actions to be taken. That powerful forces are creating multiple forms of distress in local communities and regions, and that they are not likely to be deflected or defused by public policy, do not inherently justify more or less federal urban policy. Rather, this situation serves as an argument for a different concept of what the federal urban policy role should be.

Redefining the Federal Role in Urban Policy

The federal government can best assure the well-being of the nation's people and the vitality of the communities in which they live by striving to create and maintain a vibrant national economy characterized by an attractive investment climate that is conducive to high rates of economic productivity and growth and defined by low rates of inflation, unemployment, and dependency. Where disadvantage and inequality are selective and cumulative, federal efforts should be expended to ameliorate these consequences in ways that are consistent with developmental trends within the society and the economy as a whole.

The federal government, in partnership with the business community and state and local governments, should carefully consider developing a policy perspective on industry in order to maintain a dynamic national economy and secure a strong role in the transforming international economy. The industrial bases of our nation's economic strength must be allowed to transform, and localities and regions should be assisted in anticipating and adjusting to national and international trends. A positive industry policy should include national economic planning, a coherent science policy, and invigorated research and development efforts to nurture and enhance our existing comparative advantages within and between industrial sectors vis-a-vis other nations. Such efforts should acknowledge that much can be learned from certain individual firms that may be in the most challenged industrial sectors but are able to compete successfully in international and domestic markets. Increased productivity and employment growth, together with diminished inflation, will do more to benefit people in this nation, regardless of where they may live, than efforts to resist the local and regional impacts of a changing international economic order.

People-oriented national social policies that aim to aid people directly wherever they may live should be accorded priority over place-oriented national urban policies that attempt to aid people indirectly by aiding places directly. If the ultimate goal of federal policies and programs is to aid people in their adjustment to or migration from transforming local circumstances, the most direct and effective ways to do that should be chosen. **A national social policy should be based on key cornerstones, including a guaranteed job program for those who can work and a guaranteed cash assistance plan for both the "working poor" and those who cannot work.** Federal job creation, subsidies to private employers, and manpower training and retraining programs can significantly reduce minority, youth, and displaced worker unemployment. Where public employment programs are used, they should be considered a temporary supplement for and provide a transition into private sector employment. A federal guaranteed-income plan, implemented through either a negative income tax or a direct cash transfer program, would effectively and properly shift the welfare burden to the federal government, which can administer it more efficiently and with a greater capacity for responding to equity considerations than subnational governments.

Where the problems faced by people exist in such concentrations that the impacts of people-oriented social policies and programs are negated, or where communities bear the brunt of special circumstances (such as massive foreign immigration), federal funds should be carefully targeted to local governments and to the private sector to assist them in meeting collective needs. Nonetheless, the federal government should develop the will and capability to assist local governments in identifying both places that are unlikely to realize any significant improvement through targeted urban aid and appropriate strategies to disinvest public resources and to channel public and private resources to locations that retain the capacity to absorb and benefit from federal assistance.

These major social policy initiatives and realignments should largely substitute for, rather than add to, existing federal policies. Prime candidates among the federal urban (and rural) development assistance program efforts that should be scrutinized for eventual reduction or elimination are in the place-oriented policy domains, including economic development, community development and public facilities investment, housing, transportation, and development planning. Instrumentalities such as community development block grants, urban development action grants, general and countercyclical revenue sharing, CETA grants, and water and sewer construction grants can be useful tools for an adjustment process. However, their use can be justified only during localities' major transitions in size and function. In addition, such mechanisms should be tilted toward the goal of assisting localities to adjust to changing circumstances and should be used to supplement marginally, but not substitute for, efforts that aid people directly. Because guidelines for establishing timeframes for ending interim transitional efforts in view of a more spatially neutral federal presence will be exceedingly difficult to adopt, efforts should begin now.

It is important to realize that identifying tradeoffs among policies and programs with explicit urban foci is not sufficient. Tradeoffs among nominally nonurban federal policies and programs also should be considered, because they often have major, if inadvertent, urban impacts. Among the explicitly nonurban policies and programs that should be scrutinized for major restructuring or elimination are the panoply of in-kind benefits for the poor (such as legal aid services and Medicaid), the growing inventory of subsidies that indiscriminately aid the nonpoor as well as the poor (for example, veteran's benefits), protectionist measures for industry (trade barriers for manufacturers and price supports for farmers), and minimum wage legislation.

Although the original goals of each policy and program may be laudable in isolation, once set into place alongside all others, their aggregate result has been policy incoherence, inconsistency, internal contradictions, and inertia. Solutions regarded as permanent or sacrosanct tend to outlive and become poorly articulated with the characteristics of the problems that they were intended to address. The thrust of this extended proposal is that the problems of people and the places where they live can be handled in better ways than by continuing to tinker with hundreds of different programs that assist individuals, households, neighborhoods, businesses, and subnational governments. Although a "people-place" distinction may often be more apparent than real, the aim should be a reorientation of emphasis, which involves avoiding the temptation to use place-oriented assistance to prop up localities rather than allowing them to transform. People are best assisted directly, and policies that best insulate people from or compensate them for painful transitional consequences should be emphasized.

Federal urban policy efforts should not necessarily be used to discourage the deconcentration and dispersal of industry and households from central urban locations. Interregional and intrametropolitan shifts of households and industry are essential to the efficient functioning of the national economic system on a scale that supercedes local and regional economies. Each emerging deconcentration trend is nothing more than an aggregate of countless choices by and actions of individuals, families, and firms influenced by social, cultural, and economic considerations; our public policy tools are least useful when attempting to alter in a predictable way what the individual household or firm will do. Yet, an inability to alter these developments should be appreciated apart from the fact that their net impact is probably positive and beneficial. The ongoing deconcentration processes that leave very undesirable local consequences in their wake justify a federal policy role that principally attends to these consequences, rather than flails against the change processes that generate them.

The relocation of population and economic vitality to nonmetropolitan and previously rural areas also should not be discouraged. The current revitalization of traditionally rural areas should neither obscure the fact that much of the traditional basis for urban-rural distinctions no longer exists, nor veil the fact that much of formerly rural America remains unaffected by expanding and diversified economic bases. Although the poor of this nation are largely city-bound, the incidence of poverty in rural areas still exceeds that in urban areas.

The energy and environmental implications of the continuing trends toward relatively low-density development in new growth areas and the thinning out of existing high-density areas do not unequivocally justify the need for a national effort to encourage reconcentration in historically central locations. The emergence of decentralized social and economic systems, which encompass increasing scope and territory and dictate that new, more specialized functions be performed by cities, should generally be encouraged. Although energy and environmental considerations will and should assert themselves in important policy debates in the coming decade and beyond, as yet little compelling and unambiguous empirical evidence exists to justify explicit public policy designed to alter the way in which our nation's communities grow and contract. Conservation of existing energy and environmental resources is not necessarily inconsistent with, and may even be enhanced by, the shift to lower density development, small-scale reconcentration in new growth areas, and the thinning out of large-scale, centrally located concentrations of people and activities. Nonetheless, the federal government should not abdicate its responsibility to assist localities and states in anticipating and countering the negative consequences that low-density development may have in some locations, including those instances where prime agricultural land is invaded indiscriminately by urban uses.

Federal policies should not be revamped, without careful consideration given to their primary functions and net effects, simply because unintended or inadvertent "anti-urban" consequences are discovered. Bending federal policies that do not have an explicit urban focus to serve locational or spatial outcomes may be undesirable. Although countless federal policies initiate a barrage of unintended anti-urban effects, these policy thrusts most often have simply reinforced larger demographic and economic trends or marginally increased the pace with which they have unfolded.

In the end, the federal government does not have that much control over what happens to localities and regions. There is little justification for using explicit urban policies to do more than assist people primarily and places secondarily to anticipate and adjust to the emergence of a continually transforming national economy and society. Federal policies, including investment tax credits and environmental regulations, have important narrow sectoral goals that may be unwisely sacrificed if they are manipulated to secure specific urban outcomes.

In close partnership with the private sector, the federal government should develop strategies to assist localities in adjusting to economic-base transformation and population change. In a federal policy lexicon, "development policy" should be expanded to imply policy-guided local contraction and not simply local revitalization and expansion. Policy-guided contraction and disinvestment can help to ease the impact of decline on individuals and local institutions and to position communities for regaining their health at new lower levels of population and industrial activity.

The federal government should acknowledge that the problems of population and economic growth can be as troublesome and painful as those of shrinkage. Shifts in population and economic activity, which current policy instrumentalities probably cannot reverse, pose specific adjustment problems for metropolitan and nonmetropolitan communities in all regions. Both growth and decline present opportunities to local governments to become better articulated with their populations and economic bases through carefully planned expansion or contraction. **The federal government should assist communities during**

**their transition and adjustment to new levels of population
and economic activity.**

Federal policies aimed at achieving beneficial urban
outcomes should be consistent with efforts to ensure a
strong national economy and to implement national programs in health, welfare, housing, transportation, energy,
environmental protection, and local governmental assistance that are consistent with dominant trends. These
policy domains should not use allocational strategies for
federal efforts that attempt to counter larger social and
economic transformations or to maintain specific local or
regional advantages that are slowly being eroded in the
course of metropolitan and regional development. Nonetheless, the federal government should be fully sensitive to
the fact that even though certain large-scale transformations bode well for the nation, they do imply serious transitional distress for some localities.

Accordingly, **the federal government should continue
to assist localities in providing basic services to local
residents.** Meeting the collective needs of citizens wherever
they live will continue to require close federal-local
cooperation. **The federal government should refrain
wherever possible from assigning new responsibilities to
localities unless they also provide the resources that
localities need to meet those obligations.** This intergovernmental relationship recognizes both the well developed
capacity of the federal tax system to collect and disperse
revenues efficiently and the developing capacity of localities to provide the necessary services in the most efficient
manner. Although much place-oriented federal assistance
to localities is ill advised to the extent that it is expended to
reverse the largely inevitable shrinkage of larger and older
communities, some short-term federal transitional assistance to localities is justified to assist them in meeting the
expanding range of their responsibilities. As localities experience difficulty in funding basic services or in meeting
the financial obligations incurred through federal orders
and mandates, the principle of federal adjustment assistance to localities should be inviolate.

Improved access to jobs involves helping people relocate to take advantage of economic opportunities in other
places, as well as retraining them to take advantage of
economic opportunity in their own communities. Enhancing the mobility of Americans to enable them to relocate to
areas where economic opportunity exists should receive
greater attention. Accordingly, **a people-to-jobs strategy
should be crafted with priority over, but in concert with,
the jobs-to-people strategy that serves as a major theme in
current federal urban policy.** Greater emphasis on developing a policy of assisted migration would help underemployed and displaced workers who wish to migrate to

locations of long-term economic growth. This option is especially necessary for residents of severely distressed, older industrial cities facing relatively permanent contraction of their economic and population bases.

States should be encouraged and aided in their efforts to assist local governments, as well as their individual and corporate residents, to adjust to changing social and economic circumstances. The nation's cities are national assets that will continue to perform vital, although changing, functions for the United States. Although transforming socially and economically, cities remain the legal creations of the states. In past decades, many subnational governments have improved substantially their capacities to implement economic, community, and manpower development policies. Intergovernmental relationships in the coming decade should preserve the spirit of the federal-local government ties without undermining the emergence of state governments as key urban policy partners.

The State Government Role

Localities should be encouraged to reexamine their municipal service packages and their funding and delivery arrangements. Much local fiscal distress can be traced to an inability to adjust public service infrastructures to changing population size and composition. Municipal service arrangements should either expand in growing communities or contract in shrinking communities in ways that give localities the flexibility to adjust to future changes. Growing localities should be encouraged to consider carefully the breadth of functions and depth of responsibilities that they wish to assume, thereby avoiding a ritualistic imitation of those local governments that assumed their responsibilities in an earlier historical era. Greater reliance on private sector delivery of public services and the transfer of fiscal/administrative responsibility for selected functions to other levels of government should be carefully considered.

The Local Government Role

The patterns of relationships between localities, counties, states, and the federal government have grown increasingly complex. Responsibilities for funding and administration have become hopelessly intergovernmentalized. The unfortunate and inescapable consequence of our broader, bigger, and deeper federal aid system is intergovernmental overload. This report endorses the general recommendations made by the Advisory Commission on Intergovernmental Relations aimed at the decongestion of the federal system.[2]

Implementing Federal Urban Policy: Partners and Partnerships

The federal role in urban policy should allow for the sorting out of roles and responsibilities among levels of government and between the public and private sectors. Once those reassignments are made, policy and program activity should seek to abide by and to maintain those assignments. In addition to seeking to reintroduce distinctions between federal and subnational responsibilities, efforts should proceed to decide under what conditions and to what extent state and local budgets should become dependent on federal revenues.

Any policies targeted at the nation's communities should engage the federal government as a policy partner with other levels of government and with the private sector to assist people (primarily), places, business, and political jurisdictions (secondarily) to cope with changing circumstances. The resulting policy division of labor should continue to emphasize the decentralization of federal power and the assignment to each partner of the tasks that it can best undertake.

The federal level of government is relatively efficient at enunciating broad policy goals and raising revenues for distribution to subnational levels of government which, in turn, can best define specific program features. Over time many subnational governments have expanded their capacities to initiate and to implement localized community and economic development efforts without complex federal controls. Local general purpose governments should continue to be the principal policy implementers at the local level, and policy instruments that encourage local initiative consistent with national purpose should be emphasized. **Despite problems associated with granting wider discretion to local governments, on balance accepting local judgments is wiser than implementing federal policies that are relatively unable to be articulated with local circumstances.**

The federal government should retain responsibility for ensuring that local initiatives, while reflecting local circumstances, are consistent with national goals—particularly in the area of civil rights. The nation needs to develop ways of accomplishing this valid purpose without requiring duplication of the federal government's organizational complexity at the local level. The public sector should endeavor to enhance and encourage private sector vitality and, where necessary, to alleviate its undesirable consequences without hampering that vitality.

Although place-oriented federal urban and rural development policies and programs eventually should be reduced in significance in favor of more people-oriented national economic and social policies, during the transition between emphases, the former should become more coordinated and coherent, with greater emphasis on policy consistency than on level of program funding. While housing, transportation, and urban economic, community, and manpower development programs marshal relatively meager resources in efforts to ameliorate the impacts of unfolding demographic and economic trends, their potency can be enhanced through better organization and consolidation. General fiscal and monetary policies, transfer payments to individuals, and development assistance to the public and private sectors have their collective impact diluted by indefinite lines of responsibility, divergent delivery systems, and program procedures (including idiosyncratic funding cycles, planning requirements, and eligibility criteria) that often differ and even conflict. Consequently, the efforts of subnational governments and the decisions of private sector actors are unnecessarily hampered by gaps, overlaps, and shifting goals at the federal level.

Notes

1. R. B. Miller, "The Federal Role in Cities: The New Deal Years," *Commentary,* Washington, D.C.: National Council for Urban Economic Development (July 1979):110.
2. Advisory Commission on Intergovernmental Relations, *An Agenda for American Federalism: Restoring Confidence and Competence.* (Washington, D.C.: U.S. Government Printing Office, forthcoming).

42

1983
How Europe Fell

Leopold Labedz

Writing from the vantage point of 1984, we can see with the benefit of hindsight that, in the delicate balance of power between NATO and the Warsaw Pact, Norway had always occupied a special position. In spite of its membership in the Alliance, it had never permitted the stationing of allied troops or of nuclear weapons on its soil. Norwegian political and military attitudes have always been torn between fear of its powerful Soviet neighbor and fear that outside support would serve only to provoke Soviet hostility, between the traditional Scandinavian impulse towards neutrality and the lingering trauma over the German invasion of April 1940. The resulting compromise involved the concept of defense based on the "tripwire" idea whereby Norway expected to be rescued by allied reinforcements arriving within three weeks of a Soviet invasion. Leaning over backwards to avoid Soviet wrath, Norway produced a strategic and logistical conundrum which disregarded the lesson of the 1940 Allied Narvik expedition. As long as the overall balance between the two superpowers was maintained, the Norwegian tripwire was relatively safe and Norway could have its cake and eat it too. It was only when SALT I recognized the Soviet claim to nuclear parity with America that new anxieties about Norwegian (and European) security began to creep in. They were intensified with the continuing Soviet military build-up in the 1970s and particularly after SALT II consecrated the Soviet drive towards strategic superiority.

The Spitzbergen trouble of 1983 can be traced back to what happened both before and after SALT II, but the immediate cause of the crisis was the Soviet attempt to establish a military base on the island.

Although Norway possessed sovereignty over the archipelago, the Soviet Union chose to exercise the right to exploit Spitzbergen's mineral resources granted to it (and to 39 other nations) in the international treaty of 1920. Using its coal-mining operations as a cover, the Soviet Union began to introduce military personnel on to the island. In the 1970s there were only a few of them, but in the early 1980s the number of Russians in Spitzbergen increased dramatically, and they even began to drop the pretense that they were there to extract coal. As before, the Norwegian government turned a blind eye and NATO was reluctant to precipitate a confrontation with its mighty adversary, in spite of the strategic importance of Spitzbergen as a gatepost between the Barents Sea and the northern Atlantic.

However, the Soviet decision to issue an open challenge was not dictated only by strategic considerations. Rather, it was a deliberate attempt to create and exploit a political imbroglio in the Atlantic Alliance, leading to a demonstration of its disunity and impotence. As good chess players, the Russians knew that moving a humble pawn when the situation is favorable may have far-reaching consequences for the game. And they were not mistaken.

By 1983 the global strategic situation was indeed favorable for the Soviets. Two decades of unremitting effort to expand its military capabilities — both conventional and nuclear — on land, sea, and in the air, put the Soviet Union at the peak of its power *vis-a-vis* the United States which, having neglected its defenses in the '60s and '70s, could not repair them before the end of the '80s. In the meantime NATO was getting increasingly jittery, American foreign policy was in disarray, and when President Carter avoided additional defense spending after the Soviet invasion of Afghanistan, Europe felt particularly vulnerable because of the growing discrepancy between Western and Soviet forces. This discrepancy rendered the doctrine of "flexible response" (on which NATO strategy has been formally based since 1967 and which asserts that its forces should be able to respond appropriately at every level of threat) a surrealistic joke. In tanks alone the Warsaw Pact already had a 3 to 1 superiority in the '70s, and this had not diminished in the '80s. The Mutual and Balanced Force Reduction talks in Vienna proved to be as illusory about the Western goal of cutting the Soviet edge in conventional weapons as the SALT negotiations had been about achieving the goal of nuclear arms control between the two superpowers. They only brought nearer the possibility of the "decoupling" of European and American strategic interests, of European defense and American deterrence, and contributed to the undermining of the reliability of the latter. In view of the fact that the entire land-based part of the American deterrent "triad," the Minuteman missiles, could now be wiped out by a fraction of the Soviet giant SS-18 missiles, while any attempt at an American counterstrike would only invite a devastating Soviet retaliation against American cities, President Carter was not inclined, as President Kennedy had been, "to pay any price for the defense of liberty." It was the architect of "detente" and of the "SALT process," the over-inflated Henry Kissinger himself, who admitted in 1979 that the means of deterrence were currently wanting.

Today, four years later, such means are even less impressive. The idea of a Eurodeterrent, essentially based on Anglo-French or Franco-German cooperation, has not materialized, for national political reasons. In the meantime the Soviet Union has increased the number of its SS-20 nuclear missiles and of its Backfire bombers, which were excluded from the SALT II agreement as "non-strategic," but which can, with their respective ranges, easily hit the obsolete French and British nuclear arsenals and the European airports on which the strategic air-forces are based.

It is not surprising therefore that what looked to the Europeans like a "window of danger" appeared to the Soviet Union as a "window of opportunity." More and more, Europeans began asking themselves: If deterrence was indeed dead, how long could NATO survive? The Russians were of course no less aware of it and therefore decided gently to test NATO's will to resist, and possibly bring about its dissolution by strategic "salami tactics." So as to minimize the risk, they chose as a testing ground an area which was evidently far less sensitive from the point of view of vital Western interests than, for instance, the southern flank of NATO (in an area dubbed in the '70s as "an arc of crisis" with its oil deposits) or the "central front" in Europe. Either of these two strategic directions might have united the NATO countries. But an action in the remote northern waste might perhaps contribute to the divisions in NATO and produce a political chain reaction catastrophic for the alliance. In the circumstances there was no need to obfuscate too much the character of the Soviet action in Spitzbergen and deny that they had combat troops there, as the late Leonid Brezhnev had done in 1979 when replying to the American protest at Soviet military activities in Cuba.

The Russians wanted to challenge Norwegian sovereignty in such a way as to probe the political will of the West in the early '80s.

The thinly disguised Soviet action in Spitzbergen produced the greatest commotion in the West since the 1962 Cuban missile crisis, but this time the outcome was quite different.

Remember that at the beginning of the trouble the Norwegian Prime Minister, the Social Democrat Odvar Nordli (who was re-elected in 1981 by a hair's breadth against his Conservative opponent, Kaare Willoch), issued a strongly worded protest and demanded Soviet withdrawal from Spitzbergen. The Foreign Minister, Rolf Hanson, consulted his NATO allies and requested from them an expression of solidarity and support. An official NATO declaration regretted the Soviet action and announced that it was a violation of "the code of detente."

Rolf Hanson promptly departed to Washington to discuss the matter with the new American Secretary of State, Andrew Young. It is interesting to remember that it was Mr. Hanson who in 1979, reluctantly supported by the Minister of Defense, Johan Holst, had been instrumental in arranging for the construction on Norwegian territory of a new monitoring station which had made it possible for the Americans to achieve better observation of the Soviet compliance with the provisions of SALT II, which were still observed by the U.S. government although not formally ratified by the Senate. This Norwegian decision, taken very much against the grain of neutralist tendencies and in the teeth of bitter internal opposition, particularly impressed those who, like Senator John Glenn (the former astronaut) were worried about the effectiveness of the American "national means of verification" through electronic sensors after the monitoring stations in Iran were lost in the 1978/9 upheaval. Remember also that when the Americans asked Turkey to allow U-2 flights over its territory, the Turkish Prime Minister, Bulent Ecevit, made permission conditional on Moscow's agreement, thus in effect putting the decision in Soviet hands.

In contrast, the Norwegian government granted the Americans new facilities, in spite of internal protests, Soviet pressures, and pleas by the Finnish President. Referring to the Turkish refusal, the Oslo *Aftenposten* explained:

Norway cannot follow such a pattern when we make our

decision. On the Norwegian side a determining factor must be that we see our interests served by the ratification of the SALT II agreement and its subsequent verification in a satisfactory manner. Obviously, the ratification debate ·in the United States will be greatly influenced by the U.S. potential to monitor Russian compliance with the treaty, and this should make Norway accommodating to the American request.

When SALT II was finally ratified, after the delay due to the Cuban and Afghanistan episodes, the NATO allies of the United States did not realize that European security had been thrown to the winds. Even the sensational *volte face* of Henry Kissinger, who admitted at a Brussels conference in September 1979 that the basic premises of his SALT policy had been wrong and warned the Europeans not to rely on the American nuclear deterrent, failed to shake European complacency and negligence. The SALT problem did not become the subject of a Grand Debate in Europe, as it did in the United States, although it was of vital importance to Europe's survival.

All NATO members (including the U.S.A.) pursued the shortsighted policies of national rather than collective defense, although in principle they were all agreed on the need for the latter (with the exception of France). The inability of NATO even to achieve standardization of weapons was just one manifestation of the fundamental difficulties involved in reconciling the general military needs of the Alliance with the separate interests of its members. These interests were often so narrowly conceived that they were undermining the basic purpose of the coalition.

It should have been obvious that once the point had been reached when the American deterrent could no longer be taken for granted, European security and the unity of NATO were now in jeopardy. Yet all proposals to rectify the situation and to compensate for the emergent weaknesses by new arrangements failed because of the political myopia of individual European countries pursuing their *sacro egoismo*, through the inertia of the French *defense de tous les azimuts*, because of the German *Ostpolitik*, and the British indifference towards Europe. Because of these attitudes to the question of common defense, no program has been agreed upon which would redress the enfeebled balance on this side of the Atlantic. Europeans provided 75% of NATO's conventional forces at the end of the '70s, but those forces were no match for the Warsaw Pact armies, in spite of increasing military expenditures. They reached the yearly sum of 150 billion dollars, of which Americans contributed most, both per head of the population and as a percentage of the total, yet which in spite of its size was not used rationally enough to provide, as it should have, an effective common defense.

President Carter's career as a "born-again hawk" following the Afghanistan invasion was short-lived. In his second term, he reverted to his earlier inordinate fear of seeming anti-communist, and made it clear that he was determined to achieve a lasting accommodation with the Soviet Union. He immediately put on the agenda of the SALT negotiations a proposal for symmetrical "deep cuts" in the American and Soviet nuclear arsenals. He declared his readiness to stop the development of the MX missile system immediately, if the Soviet Union agreed to the phasing out of its own SS-18 heavy missiles. *The Washington Post* published an editorial about this proposal entitled "An Opportunity for Mankind." *The New York Times* hailed it as "an imaginative and constructive initiative to remove the nuclear cloud from the horizon." The Manchester *Guardian, Le Monde* and *Die Zeit* all welcomed warmly "the American decision to end the cold war." Senator Jackson pointed out that the symmetry was spurious, that it required the abandonment of the weapons system (the implementation of which had been the asking price for the SALT II ratification by the Senate), and that it was matched only by unverifiable Soviet putative actions in the future. But this was not well received by the media in the "honeymoon period" that followed Governor Reagan's narrow defeat.

By a curious coincidence, President Carter's second inauguration coincided with the death of Leonid Ilich Brezhnev. His successor, Ilya Vissarionovich Leonidov, popularly known as "Muromets," emerged as leader only in the second phase of the struggle for succession. At the beginning of it he was still unknown, being an obscure member of the Central Committee of the CPSU. He was nominated to the Party Secretariat when Suslov, Kirilenko, and Kosygin, the elderly "Troika," blocked an attempt by Chernenko and his "Dnepropetrovsk mafia" to take over the vacant leadership. They decided to abolish the post of the Party General Secretary, knowing well the threat it had posed to the Politburo oligarchy on past occasions. They packed the Secretariat with their own proteges, establishing a balance between them similar to the one between themselves in the Politburo. To minimize the risk of challenges to their own authority, they picked up relatively young and unknown *apparatchiki* for these positions. *Pravda* praised it as an example of Soviet democracy in action, and declared that the recently departed great Leonid Ilich was always upholding the principle of "collective leadership."

The new American administration was pleased with the prospect of the divided authority in the Soviet Union because it hoped that it would be less inclined to indulge in foreign adventures. It was ready to help it overcome one of the permanent features of the Soviet economy: its "temporary difficulties" in agriculture, hoping thereby to improve the position of the mythical Soviet "doves" against the less mythical Soviet "hawks" in the struggle for succession. For that purpose, it borrowed the idea first put forward by the economist John Kenneth Galbraith and by the chairman of Pepsi Cola, Donald M. Kendall, (both members of George Kennan's Committee on East-West Accord) who proposed, in the interest of Soviet-American understanding and for the sake of human rights, to exchange 50 million tons of grain for the Kirov and Bolshoi Ballets. It was all the more acceptable to the Soviet government as the two companies were already severely depleted by the defections of their most prominent dancers: Nureyev, Makarova, Baryshnikov, Godunov, the Panovs, and the Kozlovs, and it was difficult to send the two ballets on their tours abroad without risking further defections. It was therefore not altogether disagreeable to the Russians to make the best of it and get the grain to fill in the deficiencies created by the repeated harvest failures.

The deal was at first negotiated by the then American ambassador in Moscow, the former head of IBM, Thomas Watson, and successfully concluded by Sargent Shriver, who was appointed to replace him in a Presidential gesture aiming at unity in the Democratic party. Like Mr. Watson, who believed that "What is good for IBM is good for the United States," Ambassador Shriver was on excellent terms with the Russians, having also done a good deal of business with them (after his defeat as Senator McGovern's vice-presidential candidate in the 1972 election). As a former head of the Peace Corps under President Kennedy and previously a founding member of the isolationist America First Committee in 1940, he had not only the necessary connections for his new job, but also the right attitudes and experience to perform it with distinction in the second Carter administration.

The arrangement was applauded by the press as a step towards the revival of detente and an example of cultural exchange and economic cooperation in the spirit of the Helsinki agreement. The first performance of the newly born Bolshoi Kirov Washington Ballet Company at the Kennedy Center was a glittering affair attended by "everybody who was somebody" in the new administration in Washington.

Two former Presidents, Nixon and Ford, graced the occasion. The Red Army choir sang the old Soviet song: "*Ya drugoi takoi strany nye znayu gdye tak volno dyshet chelovyek*" ("I know no other country where man can breathe so freely!"), which was already a favorite in Stalin's Gulag time. In an interview published in *Time* magazine, Ambassador Dobrynin extolled the agreement as a modest but important step satisfying mutual interests of the two countries.

When soon after, Ilya Vissarionovich Leonidov became a member of the Politburo, the Western press interpreted it as an indication that the post-Stalinist generation was taking over in the Soviet Union, that the days of gerontocracy were numbered (the average age of the members of the Politburo was then above 70), and that the new, peaceful and rational, bourgeois-ified and reformist, Soviet Union was finally in sight. *La Repubblica* and *l'Espresso* criticized Signor Berlinguer for not seeing that the changes in the Soviet Union were likely to be more rapid than those in the Italian Communist Party. The *International Herald Tribune* published an editorial entitled "The Changing of the Guard" in which it ventured the opinion that new blood in the Soviet leadership was long overdue. And when Mr. Leonidov officially became the First Secretary of the Party, the Manchester *Guardian*'s imaginative Soviet specialist, Victor Zorza, wrote that he had predicted it long ago and that anyway there was a profound Kremlinological difference between the title of the First Secretary and that of the General Secretary.

However, the new leader and his rejuvenated Politburo have

shown few signs that their foreign policy will be different from the one pursued by their predecessors. Neither the Troika of gerontocrats nor the elderly Young Turks who succeeded them have been willing to accept President Carter's "deep cuts" proposals. As readers will recall, after the short Soviet "offensive of smiles" the situation in the Middle East and Yugoslavia created new tensions between the superpowers.

In the Middle East, in spite — or perhaps paradoxically because — of the continuing turmoil, the Soviet Union could not consolidate the political gains and strategic opportunities offered by the Iranian revolution and the final mopping-up operation in Afghanistan. Although it continued with its efforts to penetrate the area and to exploit the religious, ethnic, and political antagonisms there for its own purposes, the traditional Russian thrust to the south could not be finally consummated without a direct military drive, which the Soviet leaders were still reluctant to undertake. Still, even without direct Soviet military intervention there were enough fires stoked in the Middle East to make the situation potentially explosive and the West with its oil preoccupations constantly on edge.

In Yugoslavia, since Tito's death, the situation has ostensibly not changed, but everybody realizes that it is fundamentally new. This is not simply because of the disappearance of the leader whose authority cannot be replaced. In spite of his efforts to ensure a smooth succession and continuity of his policies in the institutional framework he had been elaborating with this purpose in mind over many years before his death, the plain fact is that it didn't work. Nobody can rule, even indirectly, from six feet under, as even Stalin must have discovered. Nor is it because the only Yugoslav who could unite Serbs, Croats, Slovenes, Bosnians, Montenegrins, and Macedonians is no longer there. It is because the premises of Tito's policy already began crumbling before his death. He succeeded in keeping Yusgoslavia communist and non-aligned. It was a balancing act which assured both the independence of Yugoslavia and the dominant position of Tito's regime in it. But when Fidel Castro, as the new chairman of the non-aligned movement, succeeded during the 3 years after the 1979 Havana conference in tilting it towards alignment with the Soviet Union, some of the non-aligned countries, headed by Yugoslavia, left the organization in protest against the subversion of its fundamental platform. This has not changed the fact that Yugoslavia can no longer afford to pursue effectively the old Titoist policy. The undermining of its external leg — the support of the non-aligned — made the balancing between the two blocks more difficult, and in the long run, because of Yugoslavia's geopolitical situation, impossible. Besides, even the remaining rump of the former more or less genuinely non-aligned states, through the inevitable polarization, began to lean more towards the West, even though, as the then Foreign Minister of Singapore, R.S. Rajaratnam, made perfectly clear, they had their doubts about its reliability. But, like Egypt under President Sadat, they had little choice. Faced with the growing Soviet threat of subversion and renewed Soviet political pressures after Tito's death, Yugoslavia could either succumb to them or move closer to the West. There was no more room for the old balancing act; a new game was afoot in the Balkans. The external polarization of the non-aligned had been paralleled by the internal polarization in Yugoslavia, thus undermining the other leg of the Titoist position. Two distinctly opposite orientations began to emerge, the one advocating a move from non-alignment to the Westernized, Austrian type of neutrality and the other which was for a *rapprochement* with the Soviet Union and consisted of the remnants of "Kominformists," some traditionally pro-Russian Serbians, and those Party and UDBA elements who were worried about the future of the communist regime in Yugoslavia. Although Soviet support for the latter was not matched by Western support for the former, new tensions between East and West have inevitably arisen in the area as the loss of the non-aligned Yugoslavia would have had far-reaching political and strategic implications for NATO. As the official newspaper *Borba* put it: "The Balkans are now a powder keg between the hegemonist arsonists and the imperialist firemen on strike." China supported Yugoslavia's independence, but as the late Chou En-lai once said in this connection: "Distant waters do not extinguish fires."

Here also, the new Soviet leaders were reluctant to engage in a military confrontation, the threat of which might have reconsolidated the NATO alliance. But although there were continuous disagreements among the new Soviet leaders about the strategy of expansion, with some advocating a southern and others a western direction, Ilya Vissarionovich Leonidov prevailed with his proposed salami tactics in the north.

That 65 years after the revolution the expansionist urge was not dead in the Soviet Union should not have come as a surprise. As it happened, two factors coincided in 1983: one was that the Soviet Union was more powerful than ever before in relation to its adversaries, a state of affairs unlikely to persist forever, and the other was that its internal difficulties were growing.

The first factor was a result of two decades of Soviet military effort and two decades of Western military neglect. Already at the end of the '70s there was a general agreement among military specialists, both pro- and anti-SALT, that strategically the West would reach the point of maximum danger in 1983 and it should have been clear even to non-experts that this danger would persist unless and until urgent measures were taken to reverse the trend and rectify the balance.

The second factor was not unconnected with the first. Soviet obsession with considerations of ideology and power dictated its political priorities and produced the highest peace-time military budget of a great power over the longest period in history. This contributed to the neglect of other preoccupations and thus to the aggravation of some internal as well as external difficulties. As a result, the Soviet Union finds itself in the '80s with a host of problems which sharpened still further its dilemma of internal reform or external expansion. Its economic growth has slowed down to an unimpressive rate. Its technology would have become obsolete without Western transfers. Its agriculture cannot feed its population. Its oil production has become insufficient. It has had troubles with its East European satellites and some of its minorities have become restless. Its ideological appeal has worn thin. And it has itself helped cement politically its diverse antagonists: the U.S.A, China, Japan, and Western Europe. Its only remaining historical asset is its growing power, its ability to intimidate and to compel, to instill and to exploit fear.

By 1983 the ascending line of Soviet external potency had crossed the descending line of Soviet internal potential weaknesses. The dilemma presented itself to the Soviet leaders more sharply than ever before: either to achieve external successes (for which so much had been sacrificed and to which political and economic investments had been geared all the time in the past) or turn to internal reform (which had been rejected in the past when it clashed with the vested interests of the groups and institutions dominating the Soviet regime — even though reform had been somewhat less threatening to the regime's legitimacy and survival than it would be now). There were of course many analysts in the West who were always arguing that because of the perceived Soviet difficulties, the new generation of leaders would turn inwards. That was the Shulman-Vance school of thought under President Carter, but all experience, previous and subsequent, has shown that these were the voices expressing wishful thinking and complacency. The internal weaknesses were there for all to see in the '80s, but they only acted as an additional spur to foreign policy action. For the new leaders it was a question of moving forwards or sliding backwards, of compensating for internal failures by successes in the international arena or facing the music at home without the benefit of patriotic euphoria.

Once again the hoped-for change in the character of Soviet foreign policy proved to be a chimera. Its essential continuity was as much in evidence in the '80s as in the previous period. The new leaders were not only pursuing the same goals as their predecessors, they were also circumspect in taking risks. The Young Turks might have been bolder than the old gerontocrats, but it was only because they were more powerful and could afford it. But although they were in no less of a hurry, they were no more disposed to take undue risks. They were not adventurers, they wanted to win without a nuclear holocaust.

For all these reasons, Ilya Vissarionovich Leonidov decided that the test of Western will over Spitzbergen involved the lowest risk, while offering a chance of political gains in Europe. Potential general Soviet benefits were out of all proportion to the intrinsic strategic value of the island and the perils of escalation involved. A demonstration of American and European impotence might have far-reaching political consequences for NATO, for the prospects of European "self-Finlandization," and for the power balance in the world. As all good strategists do, Mr. Leonidov concentrated on the main goal: a strategic breakthrough. Europe has remained the supreme prize ever since 1945. As the Spitzbergen crisis has demonstrated, he was not mistaken.

Readers will recall how at the beginning a Swedish journalist reported in Stockholm's *Dagens Nyheter* that the Russians were beginning to build a naval base in Spitzbergen. Although it was a fact with obvious military implications, the official reaction in Europe and America was at first subdued. The Americans, under the Carter administration, were not inclined to be alarmed about an island in the frozen wilderness across the Atlantic, when not so long ago they had consented to the Soviet presence in Cuba, only 90 miles from their own Key West. The Europeans were also reluctant to make a fuss about the story. There was perfunctory disapproval in the Western press of the Soviet action, but it seemed too insignificant to get very agitated about. It was not quite clear what its nature was, how serious a danger it constituted, or indeed whether it was pregnant with any important consequences. The fact that it was reported by a "neutralist" Swedish newspaper made it more difficult to doubt its authenticity, but did not stop many Western politicians and journalists from doing precisely that, or at least from minimizing its significance. Confusion was added to ambiguity, when Mr. Gromyko issued a strongly-worded denial, accusing Western cold-warriors of stirring up anti-Soviet feelings about a non-existent Soviet threat. The TASS communique published in *Pravda* referred to the "routine Western falsification" (*"ocherednaya zapadnaya falshivka"*) and called it "a lie and a provocation" (*"Vse eto yavlaetsya sploshnoi lozhyu i provokatsyey"*). It declared that naval facilities in Spitzbergen were built for peaceful purposes: namely to facilitate the transportation of coal. With its usual heavy irony, *Pravda* added: "The bourgeois gentlemen find it difficult to recognize an expansion of coal production at a time when monopoly capitalism is closing the coal-pits and creating unemployment among the miners." It did not mention of course the presence of the submarine repair workshop or of the dry dock among the new peaceful facilities at Spitzbergen. The German liberal *Die Zeit* was somewhat uneasy about it, but it pointed out that in Hamburg, where it is published, similar facilities exist to help move the coal: it is normal for repair workshops and dry docks to be used for merchant shipping.

Yet the story did not die down, perhaps because the Soviets would not let it. An article by the Moscow correspondent of *Stern* magazine, quoting "reliable sources" mentioned a forthcoming visit to Spitzbergen of the retired Soviet Naval chief, Admiral Gorshkov. That naturally created a flurry of puzzled comment in the Western press. It could not feed any more on the information provided at governmental briefings, which were based on official (as opposed to innate) intelligence: the CIA and other Western spying agencies had by now been rendered impotent. In their frantic search for a "news story," Western journalists were ready to swallow any bit of information, including Soviet disinformation. The Moscow correspondent of the London *Evening News*, the KGB-sponsored "journalist," Victor Louis, wrote that there were no Soviet submarines in Spitzbergen, but also dropped a hint that there was more to the story than met the eye, that there were indications of forthcoming new Soviet diplomatic initiatives. Being in the dark, but having to meet their deadlines, *Newsweek* and *Time* printed (as usual by coincidence) the picture of "the father of the Soviet Navy," Admiral Gorshkov, on their covers, while *The Sunday Times* of London (resuscitated in 1980) published a profile of the peace-loving Soviet First Secretary, Ilya Vissarionovich Leonidov, by its Moscow correspondent, Edmund Stevens.

Yet gradually the serious character of the problem began to be grasped. The Swiss liberal-conservative *Neue Zurcher Zeitung* and the German liberal-conservative *Frankfurter Allgemeine Zeitung* both pointed out that the Soviet action challenged NATO by violating the sovereignty and territorial integrity of one of its members. *The Wall Street Journal,* the London *Daily Telegraph,* and *Die Welt* elaborated on the theme, reminded their readers of Soviet expansionist actions in the past, and warned against appeasement. What become known as "the Spitzbergen crisis" began to develop.

Soon enough, the Norwegian government (or one of its Ministers) leaked to the press the *aide memoire* it had sent to the member countries of NATO containing the story of the creeping Soviet occupation of Spitzbergen. It also disclosed the repeated protests which it had lodged with the Soviet government, as it happened, to no avail: they were all ignored. The disclosure created a sensation, particularly because it revealed that the Nordli government called upon its NATO allies to provide diplomatic, political, and, if necessary, military aid to help Norway deal with the situation.

The cat was now out of the bag. Western governments and the Western public now began to display their attitudes to the crisis. Few were ready to stand up and be counted. The Europeans knew in their bones that this time they had to face the challenge without relying on the ultimate deterrent of American nuclear superiority. Indeed, this was a reversal of the 1962 confrontation over Cuba: we now had to face the consequences of the erosion of Western strength which had occurred during the 21 years between the two dates. It was obvious that if things were to come to the crunch, the United States would not be ready this time to take an "eyeball to eyeball" stand on the issue of Spitzbergen, and such knowledge was enough to paralyze politically the European members of NATO, even though they were now directly involved. They continued to procrastinate, but apart from some obscure diplomatic inquiries, they did nothing. As is still fresh in our memory, the prevailing attitude in governmental circles has been that "it is imperative to avoid producing a crisis."

While governments were doing their best not to call a spade a spade, the world media were displaying a jittery fear reminding one of Europe in 1938 and 1962. The former editor of *Le Monde*, Jacques Fauvet, published a signed article under a suggestive title, "Mourir pour Spitzbergen?" (reminiscent of the celebrated article by the future collaborationist, Marcel Deat, "Mourir pour Dantzig?" published by *l'Oeuvre* in 1939). M. Fauvet argued that it would be folly to risk a nuclear war over such a miserable piece of territory. *The Washington Post* commented in an editorial entitled, "What Price Spitzbergen?" that "although the principle of national integrity of the NATO states must be preserved, the Spitzbergen affair is far from a clear-cut case on which it can be tested, fraught as it is with unimaginable dangers for mankind." The liberal Manchester *Guardian* said that Norwegian democracy would be better preserved without a direct confrontation with its powerful neighbor and pointed out that this had been the case with Finland. In Japan, the three establishment newspapers, *Asahi Shimbun, Yomiuri Shimbun,* and *Mainichi Shimbun*, explained to their readers that Spitzbergen, like Kuriles, is an archipelago, that like the southern Kurile islands, Etorofu, Kunashiri, Shikotan and Habomai — known in Japan as the Northern Territories — it was now occupied illegally by the Soviet Union, but that unlike them it was not worth the candle. The more "progressive" Western journals were inclined to see the Spitzbergen affair as a CIA invention. They attacked their governments, as they had done during the 1962 Cuban missile crisis, for "playing the American game."

Faced with the indifference and inactivity of his allies, the Norwegian Prime Minister, under strong pressure from the neutralist elements of the government and opposition, decided to initiate direct separate talks with the Soviet government. The previously pro-NATO *Berlingske Tidende* provided a sympathetic comment in Copenhagen:

> Norway is deeply involved in difficult negotiations with the Soviet Union. So far as Denmark is concerned it can be expected that it will also actively strive to achieve a modus vivendi. Denmark has always refused to have any nuclear weapons on Danish soil, and now it is clearer than ever before that, as the Minister of Foreign Affairs, Henning Christophersen said yesterday, we must not provoke the Warsaw Pact countries into a new and costly armament race. We are now faced with the problem of bridling the underlying tension in the Nordic balance and we hope that Scandinavian solidarity can achieve it. The Danish government must lend credence to this idea.

When the negotiations with the Soviet Union produced a deadlock, with the Russians installed in Spitzbergen, the Norwegian Prime Minister resigned. A new all-party government was formed. It decided to leave NATO in the hope that as a neutral power its relations with the USSR would improve. It also proposed a merger with Sweden (from which Norway had separated in 1906). But Olaf Palme, who was now the Swedish Prime Minister again, rejected this proposal, the implementation of which, he felt, might be considered provocative by the Soviet Union.

The Norwegian decision had further repercussions inside and outside NATO. Turkey, where the "right-winger," Suleyman Demirel, had replaced the "left-winger," Bulent Ecevit, as Prime Minister, had for years been toying with the idea of neutrality. In Greece the influence of the "left-winger," Andreas Papandreou, had dramatically increased since the retirement of the "right-wing" President Karamanlis. Both countries had been competing for Soviet favors ever since the '70s. After the example of Norway demonstrated how little support a country can expect from its allies in times of national emergency, Mr. Papandreou, who was always fervently anti-NATO, pressed for the final termination of the on-and-off negotiations about the return of Greece to NATO's military wing and for giving up membership of the alliance for good. The mood in the country was increasingly sympathetic to these proposals. The pro-Karamanlis, though somewhat "progressive" publisher, Helen Vlachos, wrote in the daily, *I Kathimerini* (which she resumed publishing when she returned to Greece from her exile in London after the fall of the Colonels' regime):

Surely the discussions about the return of Greece to the military wing or the full membership of NATO have been overtaken by events. In the light of the Spitzbergen sequel there is hardly any point in reviving the old Haig plan or negotiating any other arrangements with NATO. It is not just a question of their being contrary to our national sovereignty, but of the simple fact that it is the existence of NATO which is now in question. In view of its present prospects it is certainly necessary to put a new Greek foreign policy on the agenda.

The pro-Papandreou paper, *Rizopastis*, put it more bluntly:

We have been advocating the ending of Atlantism for a very long time. Today we ask: Is it not clear that we were right in insisting on the anti-national character of Karamanlis's Atlantic policy; Is it not obvious at this moment that it was never in Greece's interest? Has not the Spitzbergen affair shown the total error of the line that 'we belong to the West'? The withdrawal from NATO will not undermine the country's security, as the followers of Karamanlis, so discredited at present, always maintained. On the contrary: it can only be of national benefit by enhancing the position of Greece vis-a-vis the socialist countries at a time when the cold warriors call for another crusade against them, a crusade which, as recent events have made manifestly plain, is doomed to failure.

Shortly thereafter Greece formally left NATO. Not to be outdone, Turkey also decided to move out of the Atlantic alliance. Although the decision was undoubtedly precipitated by the Spitzbergen "demonstration effect," it was the outcome of a long process. Already in 1979, when, after the Iranian debacle, the United States asked Turkey for new observation facilities, the then Turkish Foreign Minister, Gunduz Okcun, said: "We have told the United States not to consider us a spearhead of NATO." Now the Istanbul paper, *Cumhuriyet*, declared:

The long history of Western neglect of Turkish interests, of the lack of understanding of our position, and the growing distrust between Turkey and other NATO countries have made the continuing cooperation between us and them inconceivable. We welcome therefore the statement by our Foreign Minister, the honorable Ihsan Sabri Caglayangil, that Turkey has decided to quit NATO and return to our traditional policy of neutrality.

Neither Greece nor Turkey was inclined to join what remained of the non-aligned grouping of countries which had earlier been moving closer to the West, but at the moment were in growing disarray.

Thus the fat was in the fire, or to change the metaphor, dominoes were falling. The incompatibility of the "SALT process" with NATO strategy and with the preservation of the morale of NATO countries has been made obvious by history itself. At this late hour Her Majesty's Government proposed that the remaining NATO members should pool their technological and economic resources to create a genuine common defense which would include a European nuclear deterrent based on the integrated and modernized Anglo-French nuclear forces.

Unfortunately, like Churchill's offer to merge the British and French empires, made in 1940 just before the fall of France, the proposal came too late. It could not be implemented because it was politically impractical. It was an attempt to close the stable door after the horse had bolted. The smaller West European countries supported the idea, but the most important states, France and Germany, refused to accept it.

The French President, Francois Mitterand, elected in 1981 by a small majority, had no majority in Parliament and had to face shifting coalitions there to produce a government. He was personally inclined to go along with the British initiative, but was persuaded against it by his political ally in the Socialist Party, the leader of the left-wing faction, Jean-Pierre Chevenement, who argued that this would result in another governmental crisis.

The Communist leader, George Marchais, and the Gaullist leader, Jacques Chirac, organized powerful demonstrations in

Paris to defeat the proposal. One consisting of the Communists and their allies from the CGT (*Confederation Generale du Travail*) completely filled the traditional route of such demonstrations from the Place de la Republique to the Place de la Bastille. Its participants carried all-purpose placards against multinational corporations, as well as the ones more fitting for the occasion, placards depicting Mrs. Thatcher as an "Iron Lady" sitting on a mangy British lion. To express the solidarity of the British working class, a delegation from the other side of the Channel participated in the demonstration, with Vanessa Redgrave marching between Tony Benn (nee Lord Stansgate) on her left and Michael Foot on her right. The other demonstration consisted of the right-wing elements. Young Gaullists and old Petainists marched in it as usual towards the Place de la Concorde. They carried placards with such slogans as: "*A bas le gouvernement de trahison nationale!*" ("Down with the government of national treason!"), "*Mitterand au poteau!*" (Mitterand to the gallows!"), and similar ideas inspired by the occasion.

George Marchais gave an interview on the popular TV program, Antenne II, in which he fulminated against "the surrender of French sovereignty and independence," while Michel Debre, one of the surviving Gaullist "barons," denounced the British proposal as a crime against *La France libre et eternelle*. Giscard d'Estaing remained somewhat ambiguous. In the circumstances, the French government rejected the British initiative. Shortly after, a formal invitation was issued from Palais .Mattignon asking the Soviet leader Leonidov to come on an official visit to France.

In Germany the reaction was similar, even if the reasons given were different. Also, unlike in France, there were fewer voices (such as those of Raymond Aron and Jean Francois Revel in *l'Express*) advocating the acceptance of the British conception. Fundamentally, the German rejection was based on the same arguments which were already thoroughly rehearsed when the Germans refused to entertain the idea of the two French Gaullists, Alexandre Sanguinetti and Georges Buis, who proposed in 1979 the creation of a nuclear Eurodeterrent based on Franco-German cooperation which was to have laid the foundations of a new "European Defense Community." Also at that time, the "grand old man" of Gaullism, Michel Debre, had been strongly critical and stressed that defense could only be "national." The Communists said that it would undermine detente with the Soviet Union and it was of course also strongly disapproved of by Moscow. The German government, which had contemptuously dismissed it then, was even more peremptory now. The present situation intensified German fears, increased their tendency towards neutralism and "self-Finlandization," and made the alternatives starker in the light of the post-Spitzbergen experience. Although Herbert Wehner, the Social Democratic advocate of Soviet-German *rapprochement*, was dead, the Wehner-Bahr tendency was now more tempting than ever. It was embraced with particular fervor by the former *Jusos*, the quondam Marxist leaders of the socialist youth organization, who were at present strongly entrenched in the apparatus of the Social Democratic Party and many of whom had already reached positions in its leadership. They were agitating strongly for the rejection of the British plan which, according to them, "could only reinforce the hold of state capitalism over Western Europe and increase the danger of war." It was also strongly criticized by the ex-minister of defense, Hans Apel, and no less strongly opposed by the majority of Christian Democrats, who were afraid that it might spell the end of their dream of a reunited Germany. West German Chancellor, Helmut Schmidt, re-elected in 1980, in spite of a spirited electoral performance by the leader of the opposition, Franz Josef Strauss, had little doubt about what he was going to do, and had little difficulty in ditching the British scheme. It found few adherents in Germany. Not even Franz Josef Strauss could be found openly advocating it.

Indeed, there was only lukewarm support for it in Great Britain itself. The Shadow Foreign Secretary, Tony Benn, again condemned it in the House of Commons as "a cynical move, lightheartedly playing with fire and risking the lives of all our nearest and dearest, all British men, women and children." Barbara Castle, who was still active as an anti-European in a European Parliament in Strasbourg, denounced it there as "a betrayal of the European idea" which, she hastened to add, was not a good idea in the first place. Enoch Powell castigated it as a plot against the national sovereignty of Great Britain and Northern Ireland and pointed out that Russia was after Portugal, Britain's oldest ally. James Callaghan, "the sunny Jim" now retired on his not-so-sunny farm, gave persuasive reasons for being both for and against it. Margaret Thatcher, who had recently emerged bloody but unbowed from another winter of Trade Union discontent, and was soon to be facing a general election, had to admit the failure of her initiative.

It was the swan song of Europe, the last attempt to preserve what remained of its independence. It had been successfully undermined by the patient efforts of the Soviets over four decades. In 1945 they swallowed Eastern Europe. In 1984 Western Europe lies prostrate and in mortal fear of the *Russian bear*. From now on it is *sauve qui peut* for the nations of the West, a predicament long feared and predicted by some, a quandary in which it is every country for itself and the devil take the hindmost. In such circumstances it was evident that NATO had no chance of survival even in a truncated form. A small pebble from Spitzbergen produced a European avalanche. Mr. Leonidov had good reason to feel pleased. Deterrence of the Soviet Union has been replaced by a deference towards it.

It is curious how many of those who were worried about the growing threat to Europe failed to understand the nature of the danger. In particular, the NATO generals always thought of it simply as a question of warfare, not realizing the complex relationship between the military potential and political strategy, as well as their interdependence with the morale and resolution of societies and nations. They visualized the perils as uniquely martial in nature and wrote about them within this restricted perspective. In 1976, the Belgian general Robert Close published a book, *Europe Without Defense*, in which he warned that the Warsaw Pact forces in a surprise attack could reach the Rhine in 48 hours and inflict an irremediable defeat on NATO. In 1978, General Sir John Hackett published a futurological scenario, *The Third World War, August 1985*, which became a best-seller in Europe and America, and was even read by President Carter. (You are of course aware that in the fall of 1977 President Carter said: "There are only two alternatives as to what the Soviet leaders are up to. One is that they are out to destroy the world. The other is that they are out to improve the standard of living of their people. I have to assume the latter.") General Sir John Hackett considered in his book the other alternative — war — and described with a wealth of realistic detail the way it would be fought. He changed his original scenario for the outcome of the 1985 war in Europe and provided the book with a happy ending, in the form of a NATO victory after a short military action during which one city on each side was destroyed by nuclear bombs. A "cautionary tale" intended to highlight the weaknesses of NATO and the need to eliminate them, it was in effect a Panglossian gloss on a horror story (which somehow turns out all right in the end). But the basic flaw of all these assumptions, of President Carter and of the Generals, was that, whether they were optimistic or pessimistic, they lacked the understanding of the political dimension of the problem. We now know from experience that President Carter was wrong in assuming Soviet domestic benevolence. And we also know that the Generals were wrong because NATO has disintegrated without Soviet military action. The Third World War, if it is to be so called, was lost by the West without a shot having been fired. The Soviet Union intended all along to win a *cold* war. It is ironical that the issue which finally defeats the Russians in General Hackett's fantasy — the restlessness of Eastern Europe — was the one issue the importance of which the West was always ready to disregard. While the East Europeans had been written off — from Yalta to the Sonnenfeldt doctrine — it was the West Europeans who were preparing their own demise through their lack of political courage and the consequent lack of political foresight.

The disintegration of NATO, coming as the outcome of the Spitzbergen crisis, has made a great impact on the American scene. It could no longer help Europe, but it had the effect of a Pearl Harbor on the United States. The national debate concentrated not only on the question of who was to blame for the "loss of Europe," but also on what could be done in the circumstances. The "doves," such as Earl C. Ravenal, argued that "NATO's unremarked demise" had already occurred in the '70s and was due to the defective nature of the alliance itself. The "hawks," such as Senator Jackson, could only say, "I told you so," but this left a bitter taste. The popularity of President Carter has fallen disastrously and there has been talk in Washington about the inevitability of the Sino-American alliance and the Republican president whom everybody expects to be elected in 1984.

But all this is too late for the Europeans. They have to face the prospect that the first concentration camps may be under construction in the same year of 1984...

ABOUT THE EDITOR

Irving Louis Horowitz is Distinguished Professor of Sociology and Political Science at Rutgers University, Hannah Arendt Chair, and founding director of Studies in Comparative International Development. He is also editor-in-chief of *Transaction/SOCIETY,* the leading multidisciplinary periodical in American social science. Before coming to Rutgers in 1969, Horowitz was Professor of Sociology at Washington University. He has held visiting professorships at the Universities of Stanford, Wisconsin, and California; and overseas at the London School of Economics, the University of Buenos Aires, the National University of Mexico, Queen's University in Canada, Hebrew University in Jerusalem, and Tokyo University in Japan.

Professor Horowitz has edited and/or written a trilogy of volumes on policy: *Social Science and Public Policy in the United States* (1975); *Equity, Income, and Policy* (1977); and *Constructing Policy* (1979). Other works on the interaction between social science and policy making include *The Rise and Fall of Project Camelot: Studies in the Relationship Between Social Science and Practical Politics* (1967, rev. ed. 1975) and *The Use and Abuse of Social Science: Behavioral Science and National Policy Making* (1971, rev. ed. 1975). His most recent books include *Ideology and Utopia in the United States* (1976), *Dialogues on American Politics* (1978), and *Science, Sin and Scholarship: The Politics of Reverend Moon and The Unification Church* (1978).